HISTORICAL DICTIONARY OF FASCIST ITALY

HISTORICAL DICTIONARY OF FASCIST ITALY

Philip V. Cannistraro

EDITOR-IN CHIEF

Greenwood Press
WESTPORT, CONNECTICUT · LONDON, ENGLAND

Library of Congress Cataloging in Publication Data
Main entry under title:

Historical dictionary of Fascist Italy.

    Bibliography: p.
    Includes index.
    1. Fascism—Italy—Dictionaries. 2. Italy—Politics
and government—1922-1945—Dictionaries. I. Cannistraro, Philip V., 1942-
DG571.A1H57   945.091'0321   81-4493
ISBN 0-313-21317-8 (lib. bdg.)   AACR2

Library of Congress Catalog Card Number: 81-4493
ISBN: 0-313-21317-8

First published in 1982

Greenwood Press
A division of Congressional Information Service, Inc.
88 Post Road West
Westport, Connecticut 06881

Printed in the United States of America

10 9 8 7 6 5 4 3 2 1

FOR MY PARENTS

CONTENTS _____

LIST OF MAPS ⸺⸺⸺⸺⸺⸺⸺

EDITORIAL ADVISORY BOARD ———

CONTRIBUTORS _____

Baer, George W. (GWB), University of California, Santa Cruz
Beck, Earl R. (ERB), Florida State University
Bernardini, Gene (GB), San Jose State University
Bertrand, Charles L. (CLB), Concordia University
Butler, David (DB), University of Missouri
Cannistraro, Philip V. (PVC), Florida State University
Cardoza, Anthony L. (ALC), Loyola University of Chicago
Carrillo, Elisa (ECa), Marymount College
Cassels, Alan (AC), McMaster University
Cortada, James W. (JWC), West Orange, New Jersey
Craver, Earlene (ECr), University of California, Los Angeles
Collin, Richard O. (ROC), Oxford University
Cunsolo, Ronald S. (RSC), Nassau Community College
De Felice, Renzo (RDF), University of Rome
De Grand, Alexander J. (AJD), Roosevelt University
De Grazia, Victoria (VDG), Rutgers University
Delzell, Charles F. (CFD), Vanderbilt University
Devendittis, Paul J. (PJD), Nassau Community College
DiScala, Spencer (SD), University of Massachusetts, Boston
Eshelman, Nancy G. (NGE), Philadelphia
Finkelstein, Monte S. (MSF), Florida State University
Flynn, Michael J. (MJF), Tallahassee
Fornari, Harry D. (HDF), New York City
Gregor, A. James (AJG), University of California, Berkeley
Gressang, Jean C. (JCG), Tallahassee
Gristina, Mary Campbell (MCG), Jacksonville, Florida
Halpern, Paul G. (PGH), Florida State University
Hembree, Michael (MH), Florida State University

The initials following each name have been used in the text to indicate authorship of the entries.

Henry, Jean (JH), University of New Haven

Hess, Robert L. (RLH), Brooklyn College (CUNY)

Johnson, William A. (WAJ), Chattahooche

Killinger, Charles L. III (CLK), Valencia Community College

Knox, Bernard M. (BMK), University of Rochester

Kogan, Norman (NK), University of Connecticut, Storrs

Lavine, Marsha F. (MFL), Nashville

Leparulo, William E. (WEL), Florida State University

Miller, James E. (JEM), National Archives, Washington, D.C.

Missori, Mario (MM), Rome

Morgan, Philip (PM), University of Hull

Moyer, Roy A. (RAM), Atlanta

Nello, Paolo (PN), University of Pisa

Neuman, Robert M. (RN), Florida State University

Noether, Emiliana P. (EPN), University of Connecticut, Storrs

O'Brien, Albert C. (ACO), San Diego State University

Oldson, William O. (WOO), Florida State University

Panish, Jeffrey M. (JMP), New York City

Pernicone, Nunzio (NP), Brooklyn, New York

Roberts, David D. (DDR), University of Rochester

Robertson, Esmonde M. (EMR), London School of Economics

Rogari, Sandro (SR), University of Florence

Saladino, Salvatore (SS), Queens College (CUNY)

Segrè, Claudio G. (CGS), University of Texas, Austin

Sullivan, Brian R. (BRS), New York City

Turner, Ralph V. (RVT), Florida State University

Vance, Maurice M. (MMV), Florida State University

Zagarrio, Vito (VZ), Florence, Italy

PREFACE ———————————————————————————

No aspect of contemporary history has been more vigorously debated or subject to more radically exclusive interpretations than fascism. Whether viewed in the theoretical context of a "universal" phenomenon that transcends place and time, or in its more limited form as a phase in the experience of a given country, the historical reality of fascism engenders visceral ethico-political reaction and deeply divides scholarly opinion.*

Italian Fascism has not escaped from this storm of controversy but instead has been at its very center. In the generation following the first appearance of Fascism in Italy in 1919, a remarkably large literature was produced on the subject. Much of that material was the product of Fascist publicists, who sought to explain the movement and the regime they had helped to create, and it is therefore difficult to separate history from propaganda. At the same time, Italian anti-Fascist writers, working mostly in exile and determined to expose the hollowness and corruption of Fascism to the outside world, also published widely on Mussolini's regime. And while the anti-Fascists contributed some extremely incisive and valuable analyses, their work naturally reflected the deadly partisan struggle in which they were engaged. Similarly, most contemporary foreign observers who wrote on Fascism found it difficult to remain above the fray, although they sometimes offered new methodological approaches (particularly from philosophy, psychology, and the social sciences). This "external" literature placed Fascism in the more general theoretical framework of an international phenomenon and simultaneously reflected the mounting ideological debate that was taking shape in a world increasingly divided between fascist and non-fascist powers.

Since the collapse of fascism at the end of World War II—and especially during the last two decades—scholarly work on Italian Fascism has been multiplying at what seems to be a geometrical rate of progression. The opening of the Italian archives in the 1960s and the resulting availability of a vast quantity of unpublished material have had a healthy and profound impact on research methodology. Consequently, a spate of broad, interpretive surveys is taking its place alongside highly specialized monographs on every conceivable facet of the Fascist experience. The subject has therefore become a mature and sophisticated field of scholarly research. The trend has not been accompanied by a decline in the interpretive debate, but by its intensification: historians in postwar Italy work in a highly politicized atmosphere, one in which the Fascist/anti-Fascist struggle that climaxed in the armed resistance of 1943–45 is continually played out in

*Following what is now accepted procedure, in this work the generic phenomenon of fascism has been referred to with a lower-case "f," while an upper-case "F" has been used for the Italian variety of fascism.

historiographical battles, which assume new but equally intense ideological con-
figurations. There is no indication that the controversy will disappear in the near
future.

The Greenwood *Historical Dictionary of Fascist Italy* is both a result of and a
response to this ever-growing scholarly interest in the Italian variety of fascism. Its
purpose is twofold: (1) to provide students with basic information, definitions, and
descriptions, and (2) to provide scholars with a fundamental research tool containing detailed factual data not easily obtained elsewhere. Every effort has been made
to incorporate the findings of recent scholarship while keeping the interpretive
controversies to a minimum.

Although the *Dictionary* undoubtedly represents the most comprehensive reference source on Italian Fascism published to date, obviously no such work can
claim to be complete. Limitations of space made decisions as to what to include
difficult, but several general considerations determined the final choices. The title
Fascist Italy was deliberately chosen in order to indicate a coverage not only of
Fascism, but also of those major sectors of Italian life affected by it. Hence, while
the traditional areas of political, military, diplomatic, and economic history are
included, the *Dictionary* also encompasses topics and people important to the
cultural, intellectual, and social history of Italy during the Fascist period. Similarly,
the editor and his consultants agreed at the outset that a work of this nature would
be scientifically and ethically indefensible without a considerable body of information on anti-Fascism. Particular emphasis has been placed on the biographical
entries, both because of the conviction that to produce a genuinely useful research
tool coverage could not be limited to only well-known figures of first rank
importance, and because accurate biographical information on Italians of the
period is frequently difficult to obtain without recourse to archival research.

Whenever possible, birth and death dates of individuals have been provided. It
should be noted, however, that in view of the lack of an index system for Italian
newspapers, death dates are often impossible to determine for figures of secondary
importance. The bibliographical citations at the end of the entries contain contemporary sources of information and up-to-date scholarly works when both are
available for a given topic, as well as important published primary sources. All
translations of entries from the Italian are by the editor.

One final observation: given the controversial nature of scholarly opinion on
many aspects of Italian Fascism, the editor sought the collaboration of a wide
variety of experts from different disciplines and from diverse historiographical
schools. This conscious decision was made because of the belief that as a
reference work rather than a work of synthesis, the *Historical Dictionary of
Fascist Italy* should not be the product of a predetermined historiographical
system.

ACKNOWLEDGMENTS ⸻

This volume has been the product of an extraordinary degree of scholarly and technical collaboration, and a large number of individuals and institutions was involved in its planning, writing, and completion.

The distinguished scholars who agreed to serve on the editorial advisory board for this project provided invaluable counsel and assistance during each phase of the work, in addition to writing some of the entries. More than fifty experts, whose names are to be found on the contributors' list, wrote original essays that now appear in print for the first time. Alexander J. De Grand, Spencer DiScala, Jean Henry, James E. Miller, and David D. Roberts went beyond their earlier commitments and generously authored a number of entries at the eleventh hour. Regretfully, Ferdinando Cordova, long-time friend and colleague, was forced to withdraw from active participation in the project because of circumstances beyond his control.

Four individuals made contributions of major proportions to this book. Monte S. Finkelstein worked closely with me on every aspect of its production, giving unstintingly of his time and ability. Charles L. Killinger, Bernard M. Knox, and Brian R. Sullivan each wrote innumerable entries and devoted many hours to researching information, offering perceptive advice, and meeting my often unreasonable requests for assistance. It is no exaggeration to say that this volume would not have been possible without them.

At The Florida State University I am indebted to the Department of History and to the College of Arts and Sciences for their support, and to the staff of the Strozier Library—especially to the Interlibrary Loan and Reference departments—for its prompt and expert help in tracking down and securing obscure material.

Sharon Cook, Betty Davis, Gerry Frost, and Mary Kirlin shared the grueling task of typing the manuscript. Michael J. Flynn carefully proofread the typescript with stoic determination. William A. Johnson executed the maps for this volume with great patience and skill. A very special thanks goes to Terry M. Simpson for his research assistance in the last stages of this project.

The editors and staff of Greenwood Press conceived, encouraged, and sustained this project. I am particularly grateful to: James T. Sabin, vice president of Greenwood; Arthur H. Stickney, under whose care the work began; Cynthia Harris, who handled countless queries, requests, and delays with expertise; and Lynn Taylor, Marie Smith, and Mildred Vasan, who skillfully guided the volume to its conclusion.

It would be comforting to be able to share the shortcomings of the finished work with all of these people; instead, as editor of the volume I assume that responsibility and offer them my deep but inadequate appreciation.

And, for someone who shared the dream, these lines—*Nothing moves on the lawn but the quick lilac shade. Far up gleams the house, and beneath flows the river. Here lean, my head, on this cool balustrade.*

Philip V. Cannistraro

ABBREVIATIONS _____

The following abbreviations have been used throughout the present volume, either in the text or in the bibliographical references* at the end of each entry:

REFERENCES

Chi è? (1936):   *Chi è?*. *Dizionario degli italiani d'oggi*, 3rd edition (Rome: Formiggini, 1936)

Chi è? (1948):   Chi è?. *Dizionario biografico degli italiani d'oggi*, 5th edition (Rome: Scarano, 1948)

DBI: *Dizionario biografico degli italiani*, 23 volumes to date (Rome: Enciclopedia Italiana, 1960-1979)

DSPI: *Dizionario storico politico italiano*, ed. Ernesto Sestan (Florence: Sansoni, 1971)

EAR: *Enciclopedia dell'antifascismo e della resistenza*, ed. Pietro Secchia, 3 volumes to date (Milan: La Pietra, 1968)

MOI: *Il movimento operaio italiano: Dizionario biografico*, ed. Franco Andreucci and Tommaso Detti, 5 volumes (Rome: Riuniti, 1975-78)

NO (1928):   Edoardo Savino, *La nazione operante. Profili e figure di ricostruttori* (Milan: Esercito Stampa Periodica, 1928)

NO (1937):   Edoardo Savino, *La nazione operante. Albo d'oro del fascismo. Profili e figure*, 3rd edition (Novara: Istituto Geografico De Agostini, 1937)

ORGANIZATIONS, AGENCIES, AND PARTIES

ACC	Allied Control Commission
ACI	Azione Cattolica Italiana (Italian Catholic Action)
ACLI	Associazioni Cristiane Lavoratori Italiani (Christian Associations of Italian Workers)
AGIP	Azienda Generale Italiana Petroli (Italian General Petroleum Company)
AMG	Allied Military Government
AMGOT	Allied Military Government of Occupied Territory
AOI	Africa Orientale Italiana (Italian East Africa)
ARMIR	Armata Italiana in Russia (Italian Armed Forces in Russia)

*The definitive reference work for the titles and dates of ministers, prefects, and other high officials of the Italian government is Mario Missori, *Governi, alte cariche dello stato e prefetti del regno d'Italia* (Rome: Ministry of the Interior, 1973). Missori's book has been indispensable for the writing and researching of hundreds of entries in this volume, but has not been cited in the bibliographical information because of the frequency that would have been required.

ARS	Azione Repubblicana Socialista (Socialist Republican Action)
CAUR	Comitato d'Azione per l'Universalità di Roma (Action Committee for the Universality of Rome
CCLN	Comitato Centrale di Liberazione Nazionale (Central Committee of National Liberation)
CGII	Confindustria, or Confederazione Generale dell'Industria Italiana (General Confederation of Italian Industry)
CGIL	Confederazione Generale Italiana del Lavoro (Italian General Confederation of Labor)
CGL	Confederazione Generale del Lavoro (General Confederation of Labor)
CIL	Confederazione Italiana dei Lavoratori (Italian Confederation of Workers)
CIL	Corpo Italiano di Liberazione (Italian Corps of Liberation)
CISE	Confederazione Italiana dei Sindacati Economici (Italian Confederation of Economic Syndicates)
CISL	Confederazione Italiana Sindacati dei Lavoratori (Italian Confederation of Worker Syndicates)
CLN	Comitato di Liberazione Nazionale (Committee of National Liberation)
CLNAI	Comitato di Liberazione Nazionale per l'Alta Italia (Committee of National Liberation for Northern Italy)
COGEFAG	Commissariato Generale per Fabbricazione di Guerra (General Commission for War Production)
CONI	Comitato Olimpico Nazionale Italiano (Italian National Olympic Committee)
CREDIOP	Consorzio di Credito per le Opere Pubbliche (Credit Consortium for Public Works)
CSI	Comitato Sindacale Italiano (Italian Syndical Committee)
CSIR	Corpo di Spedizione in Russia (Expeditionary Corps in Russia)
CTLN	Comitato Toscano di Liberazione Nazionale (Tuscan Committee of National Liberation)
CTV	Corpo Truppe Volontarie (Corps of Voluntary Troops)
CVL	Corpo Volontario della Libertà (Voluntary Corps of Liberty)
X^{ma}MAS	Decima Flottiglia Motoscafi Anti-Sommergibili (Tenth Torpedo Boat Flotilla)
DC	Democrazia Cristiana (Christian Democracy)
EIAR	Ente Italiano per le Audizioni Radiofoniche (Italian Agency for Radio Broadcasting)
ENAC	Ente Nazionale per la Cinematografia (National Agency for Cinematography)
ENAL	Ente Nazionale Assistenza Lavoratori (National Agency for Worker Assistance)

ENEF	Ente Nazionale per l'Educazione Fisica (National Agency for Physical Education)
ENIC	Ente Nazionale Industrie Cinematografiche (National Agency for Cinematographic Industries)
EUR	Esposizione Universale di Roma (World Exposition of Rome)
FIAT	Fabbrica Italiana Automobili Torino (Italian Automobile Factory of Turin)
FIGS	Federazione Italiana Giovanile Socialista (Italian Socialist Youth Federation)
FIL	Federazione Italiana del Lavoro (Italian Federation of Labor)
FIOM	Federazione Italiana Operai Metallurgici (Italian Federation of Metal Workers)
FUCI	Federazione Universitaria Cattolica Italiana (Italian Catholic University Federation)
GAP	Gruppi di Azione Patriottica (Groups of Patriotic Action)
GIL	Gioventù Italiana del Littorio (Italian Youth of the Lictor)
GL	Giustizia e Libertà (Justice and Liberty)
GNR	Guardia Nazionale Repubblicana (Republican National Guard)
GUF	Gruppi Universitari Fascisti (Fascist University Groups)
ICIPU	Istituto Nazionale di Credito per le Imprese di Pubblica Utilità (National Credit Institute for Public Utilities)
IMI	Istituto Mobiliare Italiano (Italian Personal Property Institute)
INA	Istituto Nazionale d'Assicurazione (National Insurance Institute)
IRI	Istituto per la Ricostruzione Industriale (Institute for Industrial Reconstruction)
IWW	Industrial Workers of the World
LCGIL	Libera Confederazione Generale Italiana dei Lavoratori (Free Italian General Confederation of Workers)
LIDU	Lega Italiana dei Diritti dell'Uomo (Italian League for the Rights of Man)
LUCE	L'Unione Cinematografica Educativa (Union for Educational Cinematography)
MSI	Movimento Sociale Italiano (Italian Social Movement)
MVSN	Milizia Volontaria per la Sicurezza Nazionale (Voluntary Militia for National Security)
NGI	Navigazione Generale Italiana (Italian Navigation Line)
ONB	Opera Nazionale Balilla (National Balilla Organization)
ONC	Opera Nazionale Combattenti (National Veterans Organization)
OND	Opera Nazionale Dopolavoro (National Afterwork Organization)
ONMI	Opera Nazionale Maternità ed Infanzia (National Organization for Maternity and Infancy)
OSS	Office of Strategic Services

OVRA	The acronym, either meaningless or unknown, for the regime's secret police. The most widespread speculation is that it stood for Opera Volontaria Repressione Antifascista (Voluntary Organization for Anti-Fascist Repression)
Pd'A	Partito d'Azione (Party of Action)
PCI	Partito Comunista Italiano (Italian Communist Party)
PFR	Partito Fascista Repubblicano (Republican Fascist Party)
PLI	Partito Liberale Italiano (Italian Liberal Party)
PNF	Partito Nazionale Fascista (Fascist National Party)
POI	Partito Operaio Italiano (Italian Worker Party)
PPI	Partito Popolare Italiano (Italian Popular Party)
PRI	Partito Repubblicano Italiano (Italian Republican Party)
PSDI	Partito Socialista Democratico Italiano (Italian Social Democratic Party
PSI	Partito Socialista Italiano (Italian Socialist Party)
PSIUP	Partito Socialista Italiano di Unità Proletaria (Italian Socialist Party of Proletarian Unity)
PSLI	Partito Socialista dei Lavoratori Italiani (Socialist Party of Italian Workers)
PSU	Partito Socialista Unitaro (Unitary Socialist Party)
RSI	Repubblica Sociale Italiana (Italian Social Republic)
RSS	Reparto di Servizi Speciali (Department of Special Services)
SD	Sicherheitsdienst (SS Security Service)
SIM	Servizio Informazioni Militari (Military Information Service)
SIPE	Società Italiana Prodotti Esplosivi (Explosive Products Company of Italy)
SITA	Società Italiana Trasporti Automobilistici (Italian Auto Transport Company)
SOE	Special Operations Executive
SS	Schutzstaffel (Nazi Storm Troopers)
STAMAGE	Stato Maggiore Generale (Supreme General Staff)
UIL	Ufficio Internazionale del Lavoro (International Labor Office)
UIL	Unione Italiana del Lavoro (Italian Labor Union)
URI	Unione Radiofonica Italiana (Italian Radio Union)
USI	Unione Sindacale Italiana (Italian Syndical Union)
USM	Unione Sindacale Milanese (Milanese Syndical Union)

MAPS

The first four maps provide a visual account of the growth of Fascism in Italy during the crucial period from March 31, 1921 to May 31, 1922. Both numerically and geographically Fascism expanded enormously during this period, due in part to Mussolini's success in making the movement an important component of the national political scene, but largely because of the rapid development of rural-based Fascism in the agrarian zones of northern and central Italy. The final transformation of Fascism into a reactionary-conservative movement, allied with the agrarian, commerical, and industrial bourgeoisie, assumed an official character through the adoption of the agrarian and the new party programs of 1921. Fascism also benefitted from the mounting tide of anti-Socialist violence that swept through the country in that year. By the middle of 1921 the Fascist squads effectively controlled almost the entire Po Valley, Venezia Giulia, the provinces of Alessandria and Novara, and large areas of Tuscany, Umbria, and Puglie.

The numerical-geographical spread of Fascism as revealed in this sequence of four maps requires some explanation. They are based on official figures from the files of the Public Security division of the Italian Ministry of Interior, which correspond in general but not specifically with figures for the same period issued by the secretariat of the Fascist party.* Moreover, the maps indicate the expansion of Fascism not in terms of actual membership, but rather from the viewpoint of the number of Fascist organizations (Fasci di Combattimento) located in each of the provinces.

The PNF (Partito Nazionale Fascista) secretariat reported that by the end of 1920 there were 88 *fasci* in Italy with a total membership of 20,615; by December 1921, the PNF claimed 834 *fasci* and 249,036 members, whereas the Interior Ministry lists noted 1,333 *fasci* and 218,453 members in that same month (the differences are explained by the fact that the government counted the individual, local subsections of *fasci* and their squads, while the PNF listed only the official *fasci* that controlled or dominated particular cities and towns).

The geographical distribution of these *fasci* organizations and their membership in 1921, clearly shows that Fascism had achieved a national base, although its strength continued to be heavily concentrated in the northern section of the country.

---

*For the statistical details see Renzo De Felice, *Mussolini il fascista, 1921-25* (Turin: Einaudi, 1966), 6-11.

Region	Fasci	Membership
Northern Italy	817	135,349
Central Italy	266	26,846
Southern Italy	183	42,576
Sicily and Sardinia	67	13,682

NOTE: The Public Security reports on which the maps are based contained specific figures for seventy-one provinces during the months from March through December 1921, as well as for April and May 1922. Limitations of space dictated that maps be provided for four key sample months only, and they were selected largely because they revealed substantive increments in the growth of the *fasci*.

In most instances areas on the maps revealing the presence of a particular numerical range of *fasci* (that is, 1-4, 5-11, 12-24, 26-41, 42-60) actually contain more than one province. Blank areas or provinces are present either because there were no *fasci* in them at a particular date or because the official records do not record their presence, but it has been impossible to determine which circumstance prevailed.

The five numerical ranges used here were selected in order to obtain some degree of statistical accuracy in the context of relatively small maps that were easily readable. In the chronological span covered by the first four maps, only 13 instances occurred in which particular provinces contained more than 60 *fasci*: in May 1921 Ferrara had 89; in April 1922 Ferrara still had 89 and Trieste had 62; in May 1922 Ferrara had 95, Alessandria 65, Bologna 72, Cremona 107, Florence 133, Mantua 93, Naples 77, Pavia 108, Perugia 64, and Rovigo 71.

The last two maps give a view of the Italian Colonial Empire and of Italy in 1939.

FASCISM IN ITALY

(MARCH 31, 1921)

Fasci Per
Province

1- 4
5- 11
12- 24
26- 41
42- 60

0   200
          miles

FASCISM IN ITALY

(APRIL 30, 1921)

Fasci Per
Province

1-4

5-11

12-24

26-41

42-60

0   200
miles

FASCISM IN ITALY

(APRIL 30, 1922)

Fasci Per
Province

1-4
5-11
12-24
26-41
42-60

0   200
          miles

FASCISM IN ITALY

(MAY 31, 1922)

Fasci Per Province

- 1 - 4
- 5 - 11
- 12 - 24
- 26 - 41
- 42 - 60

0   200
miles

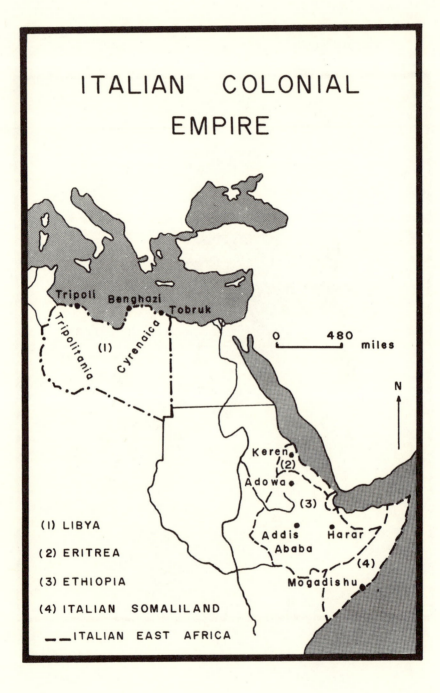

ITALIAN COLONIAL
EMPIRE

Tripoli Benghazi Tobruk

Tripolitania Cyrenaica

(1)

0   480 miles

N

Keren
(2)
Adowa
(3)
Addis
Ababa   Harar
(4)
Mogadishu

(1) LIBYA

(2) ERITREA

(3) ETHIOPIA

(4) ITALIAN SOMALILAND

▬▬▬ ITALIAN EAST AFRICA

SWITZERLAND   AUSTRIA

Brenner
Pass

L.
Garda

Milan   Salò   Venice   Trieste

Turin   Fiume

FR.   Cremona

Parma   Ferrara   YUGOSLAVIA

Genoa   Bologna

Forlì

Florence

N

ROME   ALB.

Anzio   Monte
Cassino   Bari

Naples   Brindisi

Salerno   Taranto

SAR.   Corfu   GRC.

Cagliari

Palermo

SICILY

Gela   Syracuse

Pantelleria   Cassibile

TUNISIA   Malta

ITALY
(1939)

0   40   80   miles

HISTORICAL
DICTIONARY
OF FASCIST
ITALY

A

ACERBO, GIACOMO (b. Loreto Aprutino, Pescara, July 25, 1888; d. Rome, January 9, 1969). An important political figure in Mussolini's regime, Acerbo graduated with a degree in agriculture and was a volunteer in the First World War. He joined the Fascist party in August 1920 and founded the Fasci di Combattimento (q.v.) in the province of Abruzzi. Elected to the Chamber of Deputies (*see* PARLIAMENT) the next year, he served as secretary of both the Parliamentary Commission on the Economy and the Fascist Parliamentary group. In 1921 he and Giovanni Giuriati (q.v.) conducted talks with the reformist Socialists that led to the Pacification Pact (q.v.).

Acerbo served as undersecretary of state in Mussolini's first cabinet. In June 1923 he drafted the famous majority electoral bill (known as the Acerbo Law) that enabled the Fascists to obtain control of parliament the following year: the electoral list that received the largest number of votes, provided this was more than 25 percent of the total cast, would win two-thirds of the 535 seats in the Chamber of Deputies. The remaining seats would be divided proportionally among the other parties. The bill was bitterly denounced by the Socialists, many of the *Popolari* (members of the Partito Popolare Italiano [q.v.]), and by Giovanni Amendola (q.v.) of the Constitutional Democrats, but most of the Liberals (including former premiers Giovanni Giolitti [q.v.], Vittorio Emanuele Orlando [q.v.], and Antonio Salandra [q.v.]) supported the reform which they believed would stabilize the political system. The bill passed the Chamber of Deputies on July 15 with 235 votes against 139 (mostly Socialists and Communists), and 77 abstentions (mainly Popolari). Mussolini dissolved parliament in January 1924, and the general election took place on April 6. Using widespread violence against the opposition, Mussolini secured the election of 374 supporters from his national ticket (the so-called *listone*, or 'big list'), of which 275 were Fascists. The opposition divided the remaining 161 seats, with the Popolari winning 39, the Socialists 46, the democratic groups 30, and the Communists 19. The elections spelled the end of parliamentary government as it had operated since the unification of Italy.

Acerbo was made Baron of Aterno in 1924, but in July he resigned from the cabinet after having been accused of complicity in the Matteotti murder (*see* MATTEOTTI CRISIS). In September 1929 Mussolini appointed him minister of agriculture, where he remained until 1935, and in February 1943 he was made minister of finance.

During the July 1943 Fascist Grand Council (q.v.) meeting, Acerbo voted for the Dino Grandi (q.v.) motion against Mussolini and was subsequently condemned to death at the Verona Trials (q.v.). He was sentenced to 30 years in prison by the Italian High Court of Justice but served only two.

For further information see: NO (1928); Giacomo Acerbo, *Fra due plotoni di esecuzione* (Bologna: Cappelli, 1968).

PVC

ACQUARONE, PIETRO, DUCA D' (b. Genoa, April 9, 1890; d. San Remo, February 13, 1948). Acquarone was King Victor Emmanuel III's closest adviser during the last years of his reign. Embarking upon a career in the cavalry, he was in Libya in 1913, served in the Great War, and rose to the rank of general before retiring from the Army in 1924. Having married Maddalena Trezza, he took over direction of the Trezza firm in Verona.

Because of Acquarone's business reputation, the king appointed him senator in 1934. In 1938 he was named minister of the royal household and in 1942 created duke. An excellent administrator, Acquarone became the king's closest confidant and played an important role between 1940 and 1943 as an intermediary between the court and certain Fascist hierarchs, Army generals, businessmen, and anti-Fascist politicians who were conspiring against Mussolini. He was aware of the plot of the Fascist Grand Council (q.v.) to unseat Mussolini, and he helped the king arrange for the Duce's arrest at the royal villa on July 25, 1943. Acquarone made sure that Marshal Badoglio's (q.v.) new government was composed only of technicians.

After announcement of the armistice on September 8, 1943, Acquarone followed the king and Badoglio to Brindisi. With the future of the House of Savoy now at stake, he continued his work as intermediary between the Crown and the opposition. He opposed Premier Badoglio's efforts to get the king to declare war against Germany in October 1943. Acquarone ceased to play a major role after May 1944, when the king appointed Prince Humbert to be lieutenant general of the realm. But he remained close to Victor Emmanuel III (q.v.) until the latter's abdication on May 9, 1946, at which time Acquarone also retired from public life. In the postwar purge, Acquarone's name was not included in the list of senators who lost their seats because of previous actions favorable to Fascism.

For further information see: EAR (1); F. W. Deakin, *The Brutal Friendship* (New York: Harper & Row, 1962).

CFD

ACTION PARTY. See **PARTITO D'AZIONE**.

AFRICA, ITALIAN EAST (AOI, AFRICA ORIENTALE ITALIANA). Africa Orientale Italiana was the official governmental designation for the reconstituted colonial possessions of Italy in northeast Africa after the conquest and annexation of Ethiopia. Established by decree on June 1, 1936, the territory contained an area of approximately 666,000 square miles and had a population officially estimated in 1939 to number about 12 million. AOI consisted of the Red Sea colony of Eritrea, the Indian Ocean colony of Somalia, and the former Empire of Ethiopia (occasionally called Abyssinia). The new colony was a federation of six administrative units: Eritrea, which was a union of the older colony and the former Ethiopian province of Tigre; Somalia, which was a union of that older colony and the Ethiopian Ogaden region; Shoa, the central heartland of Ethiopia;

Amhara, the historical Christian areas of northwest Ethiopia; Harar, an eastern Muslim region annexed to Ethiopia a half century earlier; and Galla Sidama, the southern provinces conquered by the Ethiopians between 1890 and 1910. The principle underlying this organization was the partition of the Ethiopian empire into more or less homogeneous religious, political, and/or ethnic blocs that would transfer their loyalty from Haile Selassie I (q.v.) to Victor Emmanuel III (q.v.), who now bore the title "King of Italy and Emperor of Ethiopia." In the process, Tigrinya-speaking populations of Eritrea and Tigre province were "reunited," as were the Somali of the Ogaden and their ethnic cousins in Somalia. The policy of reconstitution was intended to favor Muslims like the Galla, Somali, and Afar (or Danakil) over the former ruling elites of Ethiopia, who were, for the most part, Christian Amhara.

Despite the federal constitution of AOI, real power lay on the one hand in the metropolitan government and in the six regional states (*governorati*). The viceroy (*vice re*) in Addis Ababa was advised by a general council; each of the six governors-general was advised by a similar local body (*consulta*). The governors-general had a wide degree of autonomy in budgetary, judicial, and administrative matters, as well as the right of direct communication to the colonial ministry (Ministero dell'Africa Italiana, or MAI). The first viceroy of AOI, Marshal Pietro Badoglio (q.v.), had been commander of the Italian Army invading from the north; six weeks after the fall of Addis Ababa Badoglio, whose military responsibilities had been discharged, was replaced by General Rodolfo Graziani (q.v.) who had commanded the Italian Army invading from the south. Known for his brutality in Libya during the early 1930s (he was popularly called the "hyena of Libya"), the ruthless Graziani acquired among the Ethiopians the reputation of being "the butcher of Addis Ababa" following an assassination attempt on his life in February 1937. In retaliation he ordered the execution of the monks and nuns of the famous monastery of Debra Libanos, north of Addis Ababa, where his would-be assassins had briefly taken refuge, and a reign of death among educated Ethiopians in Addis Ababa. These events were symptomatic of the failure of the Italian Army to gain effective control over the countryside. Large sections of AOI never came under direct Italian rule during the five years of the Italian occupation. Graziani was replaced in November 1937 by the duke of Aosta, Amedeo di Savoia (q.v.), who governed the colony until its demise in 1941 and attempted a policy of reconciliation.

Despite the fact that the countryside was never fully pacified and that occasionally Ethiopian guerrilla patriots came perilously close to disrupting the new public order, the Ministry of Italian Africa was determined to develop the new colony as rapidly as possible. It proved to be a Herculean task, for mountainous Ethiopia lacked a basic telecommunications and transportation infrastructure. The costs of the military campaign and the costs of development were enormous. For the first year of colonial administration (1936-1937), the government of AOI put together a budget request of 19.136 billion lire (MAI had estimated a budget of five billion lire), while the revenue for all Italy that year amounted to 18.581 billion lire! On the road system alone the Italians eventually spent more than two billion lire. Clearly, the empire was to be a very costly proposition for autarchic Italy.

Although plans for the conquest of Ethiopia had been drafted in great detail, virtually no plans had been formulated for the development of the colonial territory after the projected victory. Indeed, initially there were no clear ideas and no established programs, although Mussolini preferred colonization based on agriculture. Because of the paucity of knowledge of the climate, soil fertility, and the system of land tenure, a number of investigatory expeditions were undertaken. Initially, it was decided to encourage the settlement of Italian peasants first in Shoa (near secure Addis Ababa) and in Harar Province along the Addis Ababa-Djibouti railway, and then in Amhara and Galla-Sidama provinces after the construction of feeder roads. A number of colonizing agencies (*enti di colonizzazione*) were recognized, but by the end of 1940, only about 3,200 farmers had settled in Ethiopia, or less than 10 percent of the agencies' goals. Nonfarming colonists were numbered variously between 2,000 and 4,255—far fewer than the millions of peasant farmers Mussolini aspired to settle in Ethiopia. The seven *enti di colonizzazione* earmarked 578 million lire for investment capital in agriculture, but only 121 million lire were actually invested in AOI.

In sum, Italy's policies in AOI were neither realistic nor coherent. Sullen colonials, occasional guerrilla incursions, problems of terrain and resources as well as lack of capital, and the uncertainty of political and military conditions hampered the development of AOI and discouraged prospective immigrants. Behind the facade of the dramatic military triumph of 1936 was the failure to achieve a sustained colonial development in the few short years remaining before the spread of World War II to Africa and the end of Mussolini's dream of an East African empire. On January 20, 1941, Ethiopian patriots and British forces crossed into Ethiopia from the Sudan, while other Allied forces overran Eritrea and Somalia. On May 5, 1941, five years to the day after the Italian capture of Addis Ababa, the Ethiopian capital was reentered by Haile Selassie as the Fascist colonial empire crumbled.

For further information see: Cesare Marinucci and Tomaso Columbano, *L'Italia in Africa, serie giuridico-amministrativa, I: Il Governo dei Territori Oltremare* (Rome: Istituto Poligrafico di Stato per Ministero degli Affari Esteri, Comitato per la Documentazione dell'Opera dell'Italia in Africa, 1963); Royal Institute of International Affairs, *The Italian Colonial Empire* (London: RIAA, 1940); Alberto Sbacchi, "Italian Colonialism in Ethiopia, 1936-1940" (Ph.D. diss., University of Illinois at Chicago Circle, 1975).

RLH

AGENZIA STEFANI. A news agency founded in 1853 by Guglielmo Stefani in Turin on the Reuter model, it was moved to Rome in 1870 and became a quasi-official agency of the government. Stefani was fascisticized under the direction of Manlio Morgagni (q.v.), who was its chief from 1924 to 1943 under the auspices of the Ministry of Popular Culture (q.v.). Its foreign division distributed all authorized news releases to foreign correspondents, while a special World Wide Service (Servizio Mondiale) provided news stories, bulletins, and collected foreign news items for Italian papers. Internally, the government used Stefani to provide papers and stations with all official communiques, and produced its own radio news programs. After July 1943 Stefani was reinstated in the Italian Social Republic (q.v.), where it was directed by Ernesto Daquanno.

For further information see: Philip V. Cannistraro, *La fabbrica del consenso: Fascismo e mass media* (Bari-Rome: Laterza, 1975).

PVC

AGNELLI, GIOVANNI (b. Villar Perosa, Turin, August 13, 1866; d. Turin, December 16, 1945). One of the most important Italian industrialists, Agnelli received a military education and a commission as a cavalry lieutenant in 1886. Four years later he left the military and went to work for a motor-tricycle factory in Turin and subsequently took over the small Ceirano carriage company. In July 1899 Agnelli, together with a group of investors, founded the automobile company known as Fabbrica Italiana Automobili Torino, or FIAT, of which he became director. Over the next few years he greatly enlarged FIAT, adding a ball-bearing factory and a bus company (SITA) in 1906-1907, and branching into the making of airplane, naval, and industrial diesel engines in 1908. During the Italo-Libyan War (1911-12) FIAT built the first military trucks, and in the First World War the company made enormous profits from military contracts that enabled Agnelli to expand even further. By 1920 FIAT had become a major vertical monopoly, which controlled natural resources, transport facilities, and the manufacturing of finished products.

In the postwar period, Agnelli organized the industrial and business opposition against the Socialist and trade union movements. He spearheaded a major lockout of workers in the 1920 "occupation of the factories" (q.v.) and began to move closer to Fascism, particularly by subsidizing newspapers (he had already been one of the financial supporters of *Il Popolo d' Italia* [q.v.] in 1915). Mussolini appointed Agnelli to the Senate in March 1923, and that December he was one of the signers for the Confindustra (*see* INDUSTRY) of the Palazzo Chigi Pact (q.v.).

Agnelli wielded great economic and political power in the Fascist period and moved increasingly toward government protection for private industry. During the late 1920s he established a huge holding company that controlled investments in numerous financial and industrial enterprises.

For further information see: DBI (1); Valerio Castronuovo, *Giovanni Agnelli* (Turin: UTET, 1971).

PVC

AGRICULTURAL POLICY. See **BATTLE FOR GRAIN; BONIFICA INTEGRALE; SERPIERI, ARRIGO; TASSINARI, GIUSEPPE.**

AIMONE CAT, MARIO (b. Salerno, November 5, 1894). A leading light of the Regia Aeronautica (Air Force) (q.v.), General Aimone Cat served both as chief of staff and as commander of the air forces supporting the conquest of East Africa. In this capacity he supervised the systematic bombardment of Ethiopian livestock, civilians, and troops with mustard gas. In World War II he took over the almost defunct Fifth Air Force (V^a Squadra Aerea) in North Africa after Rodolfo Graziani's (q.v.) defeat; after World War II he served as chief of staff of the Air Force.

MK

AIR FORCE. The Regia Aeronautica, most Fascist of the armed forces, was created by combining the small air arms of the Army and Navy on January 24, 1923, with Mussolini as high commissioner for aviation, Aldo Finzi (q.v.) as vice commissioner (and actual director), and the World War I ace, Pier Ruggero Piccio (q.v.) as commandant general. Finzi attempted to create a thoroughly Fascist service. This goal, combined with Mussolini's interest in flying and Fascist espousal of daring and modernity, resulted in large Air Force budgets and interservice jealousy. Finzi's replacement during the Matteotti Crisis (q.v.) by the conservative Army General, Alberto Bonzani (q.v.) created political divisions within the service. Despite Mussolini's creation of an Air Ministry in 1925, with himself as minister, Bonzani as undersecretary, and Piccio as chief of staff, these problems continued.

In November 1926 Mussolini replaced Bonzani with Italo Balbo (q.v.), and the Regia Aeronautica attained true independence. Balbo's strong personality and Party position shaped the Air Force for the next seven years. The influence of Giulio Douhet (q.v.), Balbo's close friend and adviser, meant emphasis on bombers, while Balbo's political ambitions required spectacular successes and a service wed to Fascism. Piccio fought these trends, then departed in February 1927. In March the Fascio Littorio (q.v) became the Regia Aeronautica wing symbol. In May 1928 Balbo led the first of a series of mass long-distance flights across Europe, capped with an expedition to Brazil in January 1931. Balbo reinforced his hold on the service after appointment as Air Minister in September 1929.

The practical needs of the Air Force, in contrast with these propaganda exercises benefiting Balbo and the regime, created conflicts leading to frequent changes in chiefs of staff. In August 1933 after his final mass flight (to Chicago), Balbo sought vast Air Force expansion and command of the armed forces. In November, however, Mussolini dismissed Balbo, assumed his post, and appointed Giuseppe Valle (q.v.) undersecretary. The following March Valle also became chief of staff and began preparing enthusiastically for the Ethiopian War (q.v.).

Valle attempted to prove Douhet's theories in Ethiopia. He applied terror bombing, perfected against the Libyan Bedouins, on a large scale. But although the Regia Aeronautica gassed and bombed the Ethiopians with impunity, it failed to gain the independent role Douhet had advocated. Valle jumped at the chance to try again in Spain, with unfortunate consequences. The achievements of the Aviazione Legionaria (Italian air personnel in Spain) there blinded the Air Force to its deficiencies. The combat successes of the FIAT biplane delayed development of modern fighters, as did an earlier decision to abandon liquid-cooled in-line engines in favor of radials; the resulting lack of adequate power plants meant that no Italian fighter comparable tc Spitfire or Messerschmidt 109 saw action until 1942, when it was too late. The apparent effectiveness of Italian medium bombers distracted the Regia Aeronautica from developing strategic bombers, dive bombers, and adequate ground attack aircraft. (In conflict with the Navy, Valle blocked the formation of torpedo squadrons despite the availability of the excellent Whitehead aerial torpedo). The Air Force's primary method of attacking warships remained high altitude bombardment with ineffectual small-caliber bombs.

Valle departed in the October 1939 "change of the guard," after he was unable to deny the service's unpreparedness and the inaccuracy of earlier aircraft readiness reports. Valle's successor, Francesco Pricolo (q.v.), formed aerial torpedo units (not fully effective until 1941) and raised the number of modern line combat aircraft from about eight hundred to about fifteen hundred by June 1940. However, Pricolo followed his predecessor in avoiding close cooperation with the Army or Navy. Until after the Battle of Matapan (q.v.) in March 1941, fleet requests for air support passed to the Navy staff, across Rome to the Air Force staff, and down through the Air Force chain of command to airfields in southern Italy and the islands, with predictable garbling and delays; nor did the fleet have any way to communicate with the aircraft when they finally arrived on station.

In North Africa and Greece the Air Force failed to exploit initial superiority, largely because of a lack of modern ground attack aircraft and fighters. Subsequently, strategic necessity compelled the Air Force staff to give priority to North African convoy protection. Crushing Allied superiority after the battle of El Alamein (October-November 1942) and the Allied landings in Morocco and Algeria rendered the Regia Aeronautica powerless. Reduced to fewer than two hundred operational aircraft by August 1943, it ceased to exist as an effective fighting force.

For further information see: Roberto Gentili, *L'aviazione da caccia italiana, 1918-1939* (Florence: n.p., 1977); Jonathan W. Thompson, *Italian Civil and Military Aircraft, 1930-1945* (Fallbrook, Cal.: Aero Publishers, 1963); and the relevant bibliography in Giorgio Rochat and Giulio Massobrio, *Breve storia dell'esercito italiano dal 1861 al 1943* (Turin: Einaudi, 1978).

MK/BRS

ALBANIA, INVASION OF. Twenty-two thousand troops under Alfredo Guzzoni (q.v.) and Giovanni Messe (q.v.) landed at four Albanian ports on April 7, 1939. Impeded by Mussolini's instructions, poor organization, and Albanian resistance at Durazzo, the main column only reached Tirana on April 8, after King Zog's flight to Greece. After twice visiting Albania, Galeazzo Ciano (q.v.)

persuaded Mussolini to preserve the appearance of separate Albanian government under King Victor Emmanuel (q.v.), who accepted the crown on April 16. Francesco Jacomoni (q.v.), previously Italian ambassador to Albania, would actually rule as lieutenant general, supervised by Ciano and Zenone Benini, undersecretary for Albania.

Ciano had contemplated occupying Albania since August 1937 and gained Mussolini's approval in April 1938. While Albania was already an Italian protectorate, King Zog was ineffectually attempting to escape Italian influence, which controlled Albania through investments, subsidies, and military advisers. Mussolini and Ciano dreamed of acquiring huge mineral deposits and dominating the Balkans and Adriatic. Ciano and Yugoslav Premier Stoyadinovich agreed to partition Albania in January 1939.

Stoyadinovich's dismissal in February and Hitler's seizure of Czechoslovakia in March gave Mussolini pause. In late March Mussolini decided to occupy Albania, with or without Zog's acceptance, despite Victor Emmanuel and Badoglio's opposition. The end of the Spanish Civil War (q.v.) had freed slender Italian military resources and lessened Anglo-Italian friction. Mussolini hoped to restore the balance with Hitler (whom he did not inform of his plans) without alienating England's Neville Chamberlain. While Jacomoni negotiated with Zog, Alberto Pariani (q.v.) hastily organized an expedition and Ettore Muti (q.v.), on Ciano's orders, prepared "incidents" to justify intervention. His patience exhausted by Zog's procrastination, Mussolini ordered the invasion on April 2.

Mussolini's contradictory orders to his ramshackle invasion force could have created disaster, had the Albanians fought effectively, but Guzzoni's able improvisations and the effects of bribes prevented military humiliation. By April 18 Italian forces controlled Albania. Official Western reaction was muted, but England and France issued guarantees to protect Greek independence.

For further information see: Carlo Baudino, *Una guerra assurda* (Milan: Cisalpino, 1965); Denis Mack Smith, *Mussolini's Roman Empire* (New York: Viking, 1976).

BRS

ALBERTINI, LUIGI (b. Ancona, October 19, 1871; d. Rome, December 29, 1941). Director and co-owner of Italy's leading liberal daily, the *Corriere della Sera*, and historian of the Great War, Luigi Albertini was one of the great Italian notables during the rise and triumph of Fascism. He was the son of a prominent banker and businessman who died in 1892, thrusting responsibility on Albertini at a very early age. After receiving a law degree from the University of Turin in 1893, he joined the Laboratorio di Economia Politica, the business firm of Salvatore Cognetti di Martiis, and formed a lasting friendship and partnership with Luigi Einaudi (q.v.). Soon thereafter he met the economist Luigi Luzzatti, who introduced him to Ernesto DeAngeli, wealthy industrialist and co-owner of Milan's *Corriere della Sera*. He was named secretary to the editor of this newspaper in

1896 and began a meteoric rise to power, becoming administrative director in 1898, and director and co-owner in 1900. Under the early guidance of C. F. Moberly Bell, director of the *Times* of London, Albertini was convinced that control of a newspaper provided the best means to promote the ideals he cherished. These ideals, formed in the crucible of the days of 1898, reflected his adherence to the principles of the liberal constitutional state created by the unification of Italy.

He reconstructed the *Corriere della Sera* into a political organ voicing his conservative liberal faith and fought tenaciously to save the liberal state from what he saw as an onslaught from the forces of clericalism and socialism. As the leading anti-Giolittian spokesman in pre-Fascist Italy, Albertini symbolized a conservative liberalism fighting against the betrayal of genuine liberalism by "subversive" forces personified by the democratic liberalism of Giovanni Giolitti (q.v.) and Benedetto Croce (q.v.). The Libyan War and the Great War led him to even more conservative and patriotic rhetoric. He concluded that Giolitti's rule represented a dictatorship, the death of liberal Italy. As authoritarian alternatives appeared more necessary to him, he became Italy's leading interventionist and initially—and cautiously—welcomed Fascism as an antidote to Giolittism and socialism.

In 1923-24, however, he concluded that Mussolini was the direct heir to Giolitti, and he became a courageous leader of anti-Fascist opposition. Mussolini was infuriated at Albertini's intransigence and had the Albertini brothers removed from the *Corriere della Sera*, which became a Fascist publication in 1925. Albertini, who had been named a senator in 1915, continued to speak forcefully against Fascist excesses from the Senate floor. Even former opponents, such as Gaetano Salvemini (q.v.) and Pietro Nenni (q.v.), came to respect him as one of the few outstanding liberal enemies of Mussolini's regime.

Under constant harassment and threats, he retired to an estate outside of Rome, and from 1929 to 1941 he wrote his masterful *Origins of the War of 1914* and his monumental memoirs, *Venti Anni di Vita Politica*.

For further information see: Paolo Alatri, *Le origini del fascismo* (Rome: Riuniti, 1961); Alberto Albertini, *Vita di Luigi Albertini* (Milan: Mondadori, 1945); Ottavio Bariè, *Luigi Albertini* (Turin: UTET, 1972); Paul J. Devendittis, "Luigi Albertini: Conservative Liberalism in Thought and Practice," *European Studies Review* 6 (January 1976).

PJD

ALBINI, UMBERTO (b. Portomaggiore, Ferrara, August 26, 1895). Fascist prefect and bureaucrat, Albini had a degree in social science. An early Fascist, he fought in World War I, participated in the March on Rome (q.v.), and was an officer in the Militia (q.v.). In 1923 he was police chief for the province of Spezia, after which Mussolini moved him into the prefectural system. From 1925 to 1943 Albini was prefect of numerous important provinces: Teramo (1925-26), Taranto (1926-28), Bari (1928-29), Palermo (1929-33), Genoa (1933-41), and Naples (1941-43).

During the last "changing of the guard" in 1943, Mussolini appointed Albini undersecretary for the interior in the place of Guido Buffarini-Guidi (q.v.). Together with Chief of Staff Vittorio Ambrosio (q.v.), Police Chief Renzo Chierici (q.v.), and Chierici's successor Carmine Senise (q.v.), Albini took part in the conspiracy to oust Mussolini from office. He attended the last meeting of the Fascist Grand Council (q.v.) on July 25, 1943 on Mussolini's invitation, but voted for the Grandi (q.v.) motion against the dictator. At the Verona Trials (q.v.) in January 1944, Albini was tried in absentia and condemned to death for his "treason" against Mussolini.

For further information see: *Chi è?* (1936); F. W. Deakin, *The Brutal Friendship* (New York: Harper & Row, 1962).

PVC

ALESSANDRINI, GOFFREDO (b. Cairo, November 19, 1904; d. Rome, 1978). A noted film director, Alessandrini created a wide variety of motion pictures that responded to both the public taste for escapist-sentimental films and the regime's propaganda demands. He began his career as an assistant director collaborating with Alessandro Blasetti (q.v.) on *Sole* (1928), and then worked for MGM in Hollywood in 1930. His first major film was the commercially successful *La segretaria privata* (1931). In 1936 he directed romantic *Cavalleria*, which starred Amedeo Nazzari, one of the most popular actors of the period. Alessandrini's most important film, however, was *Luciano Serra pilota* (1938). This film, which also starred Nazzari and was supervised by Mussolini's son Vittorio, portrayed the patriotic "redemption" of a selfish air pilot who discovered the Italian cause during the Ethiopian War.

For further information see: Philip V. Cannistraro, *La fabbrica del consenso* (Rome-Bari: Laterza, 1975); Edward R. Tannenbaum, *The Fascist Experience* (New York: Basic Books, 1972).

PVC

ALESSI, RINO (b. Cervia, Ravenna, April 30, 1885). A Fascist writer and journalist, Alessi was a childhood friend and schoolmate of Mussolini. He began his career with Leonida Bissolati (q.v.) on the staff of the Socialist *Avanti!* and then with *Il Resto del Carlino* (Bologna). Between 1911 and 1914 he directed *Il Mattino* (Bologna), and during World War I was a correspondent for *Il Messaggero* (Rome) and *Il Secolo* (Milan). In 1919 Alessi assumed the directorship of *Il Piccolo* (Trieste). During the 1920s and 1930s he wrote plays and theater criticism, and in World War II gained public prominence for his radio broadcasts on the *"Commenti ai fatti del giorno"* ("Comments on Today's Events") program. He died in the late 1960s.

For further information see: *Chi è?* (1948); Rino Alessi, *Calda era la terra* (Bologna: Cappelli, 1958); Alessi and Sante Bedeschi, *Anni giovanili di Mussolini* (Milan: Mondadori, 1939).

PVC

ALFIERI, DINO (b. Bologna, July 8, 1886; d. Milan, January 2, 1966). One of Galeazzo Ciano's (q.v.) leading associates in the propaganda apparatus and diplomatic service, Alfieri was founder (1910) and leader of the Nationalist group in Milan, and an interventionist and volunteer in World War I. Decidedly opposed to fusion with the PNF (Partito Nazionale Fascista) (q.v.) in 1923, he adapted swiftly and secured election as a Fascist deputy in 1924. Undersecretary for corporations (1929-32) and responsible for the "Exhibit of the Fascist Revolution" (*see* MOSTRA DELLA RIVOLUZIONE FASCISTA) in 1932, he served as head of a number of the regime's cultural organizations. When Ciano departed in August 1935 for Ethiopia, Alfieri, as undersecretary for press and propaganda, replaced him and orchestrated the regime's unprecedentedly massive wartime propaganda campaign. Upon Ciano's elevation to the Foreign Ministry in June 1936, Alfieri became minister for press and propaganda (rebaptized Ministry of Popular Culture [q.v.] in 1937), and remained until the October 31, 1939 "change of the guard." Briefly ambassador to the Holy See, he succeeded Bernardo Attolico (q.v.) in Berlin in May 1940 at Hitler's request (Alfieri's pro-German sentiments were long-standing).

Alfieri was unable to influence or forecast German policy, and tended (as Ciano put it) to "know nothing and say nothing, but with many words." After the visible turning point of the war, Alfieri tried at the inconclusive Klessheim and Feltre Führer-Duce conferences (April and July 1943) to induce Mussolini to find a way out of the war. Alfieri supported Dino Grandi's (q.v.) resolution at the Fascist Grand Council (q.v.) of July 24-25 and urged that Mussolini tell Hitler that Italy must leave the war. Alfieri escaped to Switzerland, but sought to regain Mussolini's favor. The Verona tribunal (*see* VERONA TRIALS) condemned him to death in absentia (January 1944); after the war the Ministry of Foreign Affairs conceded him an ambassador's pension.

For further information see: Dino Alfieri, *Due dittatori di fronte* (Milan: Rizzoli, 1946); Michele Lanza (pseud. Leonardo Simoni), *Berlino, Ambasciata d'Italia 1939-1943* (Rome: Migliaresi, 1946).

MK

ALICATA, MARIO (b. Reggio Calabria, May 9, 1918; d. Rome, December 6, 1966). Anti-Fascist activist and literary critic, Alicata joined the Communist party in 1940 after having participated in the underground in Rome and Milan. He was arrested and condemned by the Special Tribunal for the Defense of the State (q.v.) in 1942 but was released in August 1943. He then rejoined the underground, coediting *Il Lavoro Italiano*, editing *Unità* during the Nazi occupation of Rome, and then directing *La Voce* of Naples. In the postwar period he was a deputy in Parliament and a member of the Communist party directorate. In 1952 he founded, with Giorgio Amendola, *Cronache Meridionali*.

For further information see: DBI (1).

PVC

ALLEANZA DEL LAVORO. An anti-Fascist alliance formed in February 1922 by a number of trade unions, the Alleanza obtained the support of the Socialist, Republican, and eventually of the Communist parties, as well as of the anarchists, but the Catholics refused to adhere. The purpose was to combine strike action with parliamentary negotiations in order to form a new government and undermine the Fascists. The Alleanza declared its intention to restore political and trade union liberty, and following an intensification of Fascist violence in the summer, the Alleanza proclaimed a "legalitarian" general strike. Poorly organized, the strike proved a failure, and the Fascists retaliated as defenders of "order," burning the Milan headquarters of the Socialist newspaper *Avanti!* and unseating the Socialist administration of the city. With the end of the Alleanza, the last concerted effort at a united front against the Fascists collapsed, and Mussolini became convinced that his seizure of power would not be seriously resisted by organized labor.

For further information see: Renzo De Felice, *Mussolini il fascista*, I (Turin: Einaudi, 1966); Paolo Spriano, *Storia del Partito Comunista Italiano*, I (Turin: Einaudi, 1967).

PVC

ALLIED CONTROL COMMISSION (ACC). The Allied Control Commission (ACC) was established on November 10, 1943, to supervise the activities of the Italian government and ensure that Italy observed the terms of the armistice agreements it signed in September 1943. In addition, until October 1944, the ACC served as the channel through which the Allied and Italian governments communicated.

The ACC was an "indirect" military government. The Commission transmitted the instructions of the Allied commander in chief in the Mediterranean to the Italian government for implementation. In order to assure compliance with these instructions, administrative elements of the Commission were established at the headquarters of the Italian government and at regional and provincial levels. These ACC representatives aided in the reconstruction of Italian civil administration and also strictly limited the political and administrative autonomy available to the Italians.

At the time of the signature of the "Long Armistice" (September 29, 1943), the Allied governments pledged themselves to the removal of their controls and restrictions in return for Italian cooperation in the prosecution of the war. The degree and speed of the removal of armistice controls became a point of increasingly heated dispute between the United States and United Kingdom during 1944. By the fall of 1944, Italy's worsening economic situation gave major impetus to a reform of the structure, functions, and objectives of the ACC. In September 1944, President Roosevelt and Prime Minister Churchill met at Quebec, Canada, and Hyde Park, New York, for discussions of the Italian situation and issued a broad directive calling for increased Italian responsibility for its own affairs. Soon thereafter the ACC was symbolically redesignated the Allied Commission (AC).

Detailed and prolonged interallied negotiations followed before the Allied Commission's acting president, Harold Macmillan, conveyed the new joint policy to the Italian government on February 24, 1945. The Allied Commission gave up its oversight of Italy's diplomatic affairs and reduced or completely phased out its supervisory functions at the regional and provincial levels.

These policy changes had barely been initiated when German forces in Italy surrendered (May 2, 1945). The surrender and the cooperation of Italian partisans with the initial stages of the Allied occupation of northern Italy sped up the pace by which the Allied Commission turned over responsibilities to the Italian government. In March 1946, the AC turned over the majority of its responsibilites for economic aid programs for Italy to the United Nations Relief and Rehabilitation Administration. During the second half of 1946, most of the Commission's remaining functions were handed back to the Italian government, while the United States and United Kingdom attempted to secure the agreement of the Soviet Union to the abolition of the armistice and its enforcement bodies. Following the conclusion of peace negotiations, the Soviet government withdrew its representatives from all armistice control bodies. The Allied Commission was abolished on January 31, 1947.

For further information see: Harry Coles and Albert Weinburg (eds.), *Civil Affairs: Soldiers Become Governors* (Washington, D.C.: U.S. Government Printing Office, 1964); David W. Ellwood, *L'alleato nemico* (Milan: Feltrinelli, 1977); Nicola Gallerano, "L'influenza dell'amministrazione militare alleata sulla reorganizzazione dello stato italiano," *Italia Contemporanea* 115 (April 1974); C.R.S. Harris, *Allied Military Administration in Italy* (London: Her Majesty's Stationery Office, 1957).

JEM

ALLIED MILITARY GOVERNMENT (AMG). Allied Military Government was the initial phase of joint American and British political and military control in Italy in 1943. Operating with army combat units and in areas immediately behind the combat zone, AMG insured the security of the Allied armies' lines of communication by providing minimal necessary subsistence for the liberated civilian population and reestablishing law and order, local administration, sanitation, and public health services. When Allied forces occupied an area, the existing civil administration was suspended. AMG officers, operating at the communal, provincial, and regional levels, assumed responsibility for all civil administrative functions. Italian officials judged to lack competence or to be compromised by Fascist activities were dismissed and replaced by AMG appointees. The reconstructed Italian civil administration was responsible through AMG to the Allied commander in chief. Liberated areas remained under the "direct" control of AMG until the Allied governments authorized transfer of administrative responsibility to the Italian government under the supervision of the Allied Control Commission (q.v.).

AMG was initially employed during the Allied campaign in Sicily under the designation Allied Military Government of Occupied Territory (AMGOT). Following the Italian surrender and the Allied invasion of the mainland (September 1943), AMG was imposed on all liberated areas except the provinces of Bari, Brindisi, Taranto, Lecce, and the island of Sardinia, which remained under the administration of the Italian government. This area, which was initially referred to as the "King's Italy," would be increased by subsequent transfers of administrative control of liberated territory from AMG to the Italian government under the supervision of the Allied Control Commission. This pattern remained essentially unchanged between the first transfer of territory in February 1944 and the German surrender in Italy (May 2, 1945). The process of transfer was then accelerated. On December 31, 1945, AMG was abolished in all of metropolitan Italy except the provinces of Udine and Venezia Giulia.

During 1944 representatives of the French and Yugoslav provisional governments and spokesmen for an independent postwar Austria all laid claims to portions of territory under Italian rule. Allied policymakers were determined that the relative merits of all territorial claims would be determined at a postwar peace conference and decided that AMG would be established in certain disputed areas to prevent a settlement based on force. In May 1945, as German military resistance in northern Italy crumbled, both France and Yugoslavia seized portions of Italian territory. The French were quickly ejected by firm diplomacy. However, the Yugoslavs were not so easily moved, and eventually a compromise was struck, which provided for a partial Yugoslav withdrawal from the western portion of the disputed area of Venezia Giulia. AMG Thirteenth Corps was established in this area and in the strategically vital province of Udine, pending a final settlement of the issue. The Italian peace treaty (1947) resolved a majority of the outstanding territorial issues, but the victorious powers were unable to settle the issue of which nation should have the port of Trieste and its hinterland. Allied Military Government remained in this area until 1954, when Yugoslavia and Italy finally agreed to a division of the remaining disputed land.

For further information see: Harry Coles and Albert K. Weinburg (eds.), *Civil Affairs: Soldiers Become Governors* (Washington, D.C.: U.S. Government Printing Office, 1964); C.R.S. Harris, *Allied Military Administration in Italy* (London: Her Majesty's Stationery Office, 1957).

JEM

ALMIRANTE, GIORGIO (b. Salsomaggiore, Parma, June 27, 1914). Fascist journalist and postwar neo-Fascist leader, Almirante began his career as a war correspondent in North Africa, was editor of *Il Tevere* (Rome) and editorial secretary of the journal *La Difesa della Razza*. He covered World War II until the July 1943 coup against Mussolini. He joined the Salò Republic (*see* ITALIAN SOCIAL REPUBLIC), where he served as Cabinet Chief for the Ministry of Popular Culture (q.v.) and head of the special propaganda unit. In the postwar period he was among the founders and the secretary general of the neo-Fascist Movimento Sociale Italiano (MSI) (q.v.), and director of its newspaper, *Il Secolo d' Italia*.

For further information see: Philip V. Cannistraro, *La fabbrica del consenso: Fascismo e mass media* (Bari-Rome: Laterza, 1975); Angelo Del Boca and Mario Giovana, *Fascism Today* (New York: Pantheon, 1969); *Panorama biografico degli italiani d'oggi* 1 (Rome: Curcio, 1956).

PVC

ALOISI, POMPEO (b. Rome, November 6, 1875; d. Rome, January 15, 1949). After extensive service as a naval officer and a diplomat, Aloisi became league commissioner at Memel in 1923, and then Italian ambassador to Romania between 1923-25. He helped reestablish Italian influence over Albania in 1926-28, before representing Italy in Tokyo and Ankara. In July 1932 Aloisi became Foreign Ministry head of cabinet, leading the delegations to the Geneva Disarmament Conference and the League of Nations. With Fulvio Suvich (q.v.) Aloisi pursued Mussolini's policies of dismembering Yugoslavia and Ethiopia, diverting German expansion from Austria and the Balkans, and selling Italian support to the West in return for concessions. He brilliantly defended Italy's position at Geneva in 1935-36, limiting the breach with Britain. Mussolini dismissed Aloisi in July 1936, after Galeazzo Ciano's (q.v.) appointment signalled accommodation with Germany. He became a senator in 1939 and returned to naval service in World War II.

For further information see: DBI (2); Fulvio D'Amoja, *Declino e prima crisi dell'Europa di Versailles* (Milan: Multa Paucis, 1967).

BRS

ALVARO, CORRADO (b. San Luca, Reggio Calabria, April 15, 1895; d. Rome, June 11, 1956). An anti-Fascist writer, Alvaro fought in World War I and was wounded at Carso. He was editor of *Il Resto del Carlino, Corriere della sera,* and *Il Mondo*, and was on the editorial staff of *La Stampa* and of many other Italian and foreign newspapers. During the forty-five days of the Pietro Badoglio (q.v.) government, he directed *Il Popolo di Roma*. He founded the National Writer's Syndicate and the National Writers' Fund.

The basic themes of his stories are descriptions of the archaic world of the peasants in Calabria and their hopes for improvement, for rising above the land, and emigrating to the more civilized cities. His best stories are *Gente in Aspromonte* (1930) and *L'età breve* (1946). The social and political problems of poverty and the exploitation of southern Italy are felt intensely, but Alvaro exposes the problems without offering real solutions. The political and social impact of Alvaro's stories and novels has neither severity nor urgency. Instead it conveys either an intense pity for the weak, or the discovery of poetic motives in the lives of Calabrian farmers.

Alvaro's characters do not aspire to radical changes in the social and political structures of the time, but they examine the situation from all sides, convinced that there are always other possible hypotheses and therefore other truths. Alvaro is first and foremost a lyrical narrator. The social problems of southern Italy and the political issue of Fascism, even though intense, are resolved in poetry, in dreams, and in a continuous escape from the world of reality described by the author.

For further information see: Carlo Bo, *Realtà e poesia di Corrado Alvaro* (Rome: Cultura, 1958); *Omaggio a Corrado Alvaro*, edited by C. Bernari (Rome: Sindacato, 1957); E. Vittorini, *Diario in pubblico* (Milan: Bompiani, 1957).

WEL

AMBROSIO, VITTORIO (b. Turin, July 28, 1879; d. Alessio, November 20, 1958). Chief representative of the military establishment in the July 25, 1943 coup, Ambrosio had enjoyed a steady but unspectacular career. A cavalryman in the Libyan War, divisional chief of staff in World War I, and peacetime divisional and corps commander, he had risen by 1939 to command the Second Army on the Yugoslav border. In April 1941 he hesitantly moved into Yugoslavia after the Germans broke Serb resistance, and he remained as commander of the Italian occupation forces. On January 20, 1942, he exchanged posts with Mario Roatta (q.v.), replacing the latter as chief of staff of the Army. On February 1, 1943, Mussolini appointed Ambrosio to succeed Ugo Cavallero (q.v.) at the Comando Supremo (q.v.). With Mussolini's approval Ambrosio attempted to bring back to Italy forces dispersed in the Ukraine and the Balkans, and "dig in his feet" with Germans. After the Axis military collapse in Tunisia (May 1943) he attempted in vain to persuade Mussolini to leave the war. Following the July 19, 1943 Feltre conference, at which Ambrosio, Giuseppe Bastianini (q.v.), and Dino Alfieri (q.v.) made a final attempt to induce Mussolini to tell Hitler that Italy could not continue, Ambrosio, with the king's approval, set in motion already laid plans to arrest Mussolini. Afterwards Ambrosio assisted Pietro Badoglio (q.v.) in the inept negotiations with the Allies, while the Germans prepared countermeasures. On September 9, Ambrosio, Badoglio, and the king fled Rome after the Allied armistice announcement, leaving the Italian armed forces leaderless. Ambrosio retired as chief of the Comando Supremo in November 1944.

For further information see: DBI (2).

MK

AMENDOLA, GIOVANNI (b. Naples, April 15, 1882; d. Cannes, April 7, 1926). A major figure in the anti-Fascist movement, Amendola studied philosphy and wrote for many important journals at the beginning of the century, including *La Voce, Il Rinnovamento*, and *L'Anima*. He taught at the University of Pisa and directed the journal *Biblioteca filosofica*. An antipositivist, he abhorred the policies of Giovanni Giolitti (q.v.), the Freemasons, and socialism. He also opposed, however, the liberal traditions of the historic right in Italy and belonged to the conservative wing of the Liberal party. Although a nationalist, he disdained the extremists and Gabriele D'Annunzio (q.v.). In 1913 he collaborated with *L'Azione* in Milan, the journal of the liberal nationalists.

Although he had reservations about the Libyan War of 1911, he supported it as a means of building the moral character of the Italians. In 1914 he joined the staff of *Il Corriere della Sera* in Rome but was drafted into the Army and fought at the front. By the end of the conflict, however, he had completely reversed many of his positions, and was now antinationalist and against the liberal right. He became a follower of Francesco Nitti (q.v.) and was elected to Parliament in 1919. In 1920 he was undersecretary for finance in the second Nitti government, and began to attack Fascist excesses and the revolutionary policies of the Socialists. He opposed efforts to bring the Fascists into the government and in January 1922 founded *Il Mondo* as an anti-Fascist review. He then served as minister of colonies in the Luigi Facta (q.v.) cabinet. His anti-Fascism grew more intense, and he urged action to prevent the March on Rome (q.v.). After Mussolini came to power he became an intransigent opponent of the Fascists and recognized that the movement was not to be a temporary one. He was severely beaten by *squadristi* (q.v.) on a number of occasions.

After Giacomo Matteotti's death (*see* MATTEOTTI CRISIS) in 1924, Amendola joined the Aventine Secession (q.v.) and became one of its most important leaders. *Il Mondo* emerged as the unofficial organ for the opposition, and in December 1924 he published Cesare Rossi's (q.v.) "Memoriale" implicating Mussolini in the Matteotti crime. He also organized the so-called Unione Democratica Nazionale, which included a wide variety of anti-Fascist political leaders and intellectuals, and opposed the reentry of the Aventine deputies into Parliament. *Il Mondo* also published Benedetto Croce's (q.v.) "Manifesto of Anti-Fascist Intellectuals" (q.v.) in May 1925.

Amendola died in France in 1926, where he had gone to recover from the beatings he had received from the Fascists.

For further information see: Giampiero Carocci, *Giovanni Amendola* (Milan: Feltrinelli, 1956).

                                                                                     MSF

AMICUCCI, ERMANNO (b. Tagliacozzo, January 5, 1890; d. Argentina, 1955). A noted Fascist journalist and deputy, Amicucci was instrumental in bringing the Italian press under Mussolini's control. Shortly after the March on Rome (q.v.) he helped to found the Rome section of Fascist journalists, and in the early 1920s he edited *La Nazione* (Florence), *Il Piccolo* (Trieste), and *Il Corriere d'America* (New York). In 1927 he established the Fascist Federation of Italian Journalists and then became the secretary of the Fascist Journalist Union. For more than ten years he was editor of *Gazzetta del Popolo* (Turin) and in 1938 served as a member of the Commissione per la Bonifica Libraria (commission for the improvement of books) that established the regime's book censorship policies. In

November 1939 Mussolini appointed Amicucci undersecretary in the Ministry of Corporations, a post he held until February 1942. Between October 1943 and April 1945 he edited the important *Il Corriere della Sera* (Milan) in the Salò Republic (*see* ITALIAN SOCIAL REPUBLIC), and his activities during this period resulted in a death sentence. He was given amnesty and fled to Argentina.

For further information see: Ermanno Amicucci, *I 600 giorni di Mussolini* (Rome: Faro, 1948); Ermanno Amicucci, *La stampa della rivoluzione e del regime* (Milan: Mondadori, 1938).

PVC

ANFUSO, FILIPPO (b. Catania, January 1, 1901; d. Rome, December 13, 1963). Italian diplomat and politician, Anfuso took a degree in law, worked as a journalist, and entered the Foreign Ministry in 1925. He was in the consular service in Munich, Budapest, and Berlin in the 1920s. He was transferred as chargé d'affaires to Peking in 1933, and then to Athens the next year. In January 1936 Anfuso returned to Rome, where he ultimately rose to be cabinet chief at the Foreign Ministry and became a close confidant of Galeazzo Ciano (q.v.).

In 1941 Anfuso was made ambassador in Budapest, where he remained until September 1943. Having expressed loyalty to Mussolini after the July coup, he served in various capacities at Salò and then went to Berlin as ambassador. In March 1945 he was made undersecretary for Foreign Affairs.

After the liberation Anfuso was condemned to death in absentia but was absolved in 1949. In 1953 he was elected to Parliament for the neo-Fascist MSI (*see* MOVIEMENTO SOCIALE ITALIANO), and acted as director of its newspaper *Il Secolo d'Italia*.

For further information see: Filippo Anfuso, *Roma Berlino Salò* (Milan: Garzanti, 1950); *Annuario diplomatico del Regno d'Italia* (Rome: Ministry of Foreign Affairs, 1937).

PVC

ANSALDO, GIOVANNI (b. Genoa, November 28, 1895; d. Naples, September 1, 1969). A Fascist journalist, Ansaldo was descended from the noted steel manufacturing family. He was an interventionist in World War I and in 1919 was editor for the Socialist *Il Lavoro* (Genoa), and then for *La Stampa* (Turin). From 1922 to 1924 he collaborated with Piero Gobetti (q.v.) on the anti-Fascist *Rivoluzione Liberale* (Turin) but then switched to the Fascists and fought as a volunteer in the Spanish Civil War. In the late 1930s and during World War II Ansaldo worked on the Ciano newspaper *Il Telegrafo* (Livorno) and was a well-known radio commentator. As a result of the coup against Mussolini, the Nazis imprisoned him in Germany, and after the liberation he served a prison term in Italy. In 1950 he became editor of *Il Mattino* (Naples).

For further information see: DSPI; EAR (1).

PVC

ANSCHLUSS. The German term *Anschluss* stands for the annexation of Austria by Hitler on March 13, 1938. Austria had maintained a special relationship with Italy since the establishment of the semi-Fascist dictatorship of Engelbert Dollfuss in March 1933. Like Mussolini's regime, that of Dollfuss was a one-party government, recognizing Catholicism as a state religion. Dollfuss made frequent visits to Italy, and Prince Ernst Rudiger von Starhemberg, Commander of the reactionary Heimwehr (Home Guard), organized it on the model of the Italian *squadristi* (q.v.). In February 1934 the government launched military action against its potential opponents, the Social Democrats. Their paramilitary units were destroyed and the party outlawed. On July 25, 1934, Austrian Nazis sought to take over the Austrian government. They occupied the government headquarters building and the main radio station in Vienna and awaited support from Nazi units inside Germany. But the massing of Italian troops on the Brenner Pass deterred Hitler from aiding the abortive coup. Not until the *Anschluss* did Hitler pay tribute to the Austrian Nazis who died in this effort.

Although the Austrian government established better relations with Nazi Germany in 1936 while Italy was engaged in Abyssinia and Spain, the state remained independent. On November 5, 1937, Hitler revealed to a small group of associates his plans to take over Austria. When two of his army leaders expressed criticism at this conference, they were pushed out of their posts early in 1938. On February 12, 1938, Hitler met with Austrian Chancellor Kurt von Schuschnigg at Berchtesgaden. Although Hitler had promised before the conference to maintain Austrian independence, he placed the Austrian chancellor under extreme pressure, threatening armed invasion, and forced him to make the Austrian Nazi, Arthur Seyss-Inquart, the minister of the interior.

During the period of crisis which followed Schuschnigg vainly sought aid from Italy as well as from England and France. When Schuschnigg tried to hold a plebiscite to demonstrate Austria's determination to remain independent, Hitler demanded the cancellation of the plebiscite and the resignation of Schuschnigg. Under German pressure Schuschnigg yielded and the new chancellor, Seyss-Inquart, "invited" the entry of German troops "to restore order." Prior to the entry of those troops, Hitler obtained from Prince Philip of Hessen, his ambassador in Rome, the promise that Mussolini would not oppose his action. In return Hitler made the effusively stated promise that he would stick with Mussolini "through thick and thin," a promise he honored when he rescued Mussolini from imprisonment after his fall from power.

The occupation of Austria was effected without resistance. Although this state became the first national victim of Hitler's aggression, the German troops were met with joyful demonstrations. Recent scholarship suggests that Hitler had not fully determined upon the full annexation of Austria until he encountered the cheering crowds greeting him in his triumphal entry into the state.

For further information see: Gordon Brook-Shepherd, *The Anschluss* (Philadelphia: Lippincott, 1963); Hans A. Schmitt, "The End of the First Republic of Austria," *The Southwestern Social Science Quarterly* (March 1959), 291-306.

ERB

ANTI-COMINTERN PACT. On November 25, 1936, Nazi Germany and Japan signed this treaty, which had the openly ideological aim of a "common defense against the communist international." Nevertheless, the pact also contained a secret protocol directed explicitly against the Soviet Union.

Italy's involvement developed from the increasingly closer ideological cooperation with Germany that began in December 1935, when the two countries concluded a propaganda accord (between the Berlin Antikomintern and the Rome CAUR, or Comitato d'Azione per l'Universalità di Roma [*see* COSELSCHI, EUGENIO]). In October 1936 Galeazzo Ciano (q.v.) signed the "October Protocols" in Berlin that established the Rome-Berlin Axis (*see* AXIS, ROME-BERLIN). Italy did not, however, formally adhere to the Anti-Comintern Pact until November 6, 1937, because Mussolini was concerned with the secret protocol against Russia and also feared that Hitler intended to use the alliance against England and France. The Anti-Comintern Pact formed the ideological-diplomatic basis for the Pact of Steel (q.v.) and the future Berlin-Rome-Tokyo Tripartite Pact of September 27, 1940 that bound each power to support the others militarily if attacked.

For further information see: Philip V. Cannistraro and Edward D. Wynot, Jr., "On the Dynamics of Anti-Communism as a Function of Fascist Foreign Policy," *Il Politico* 38, 4 (1973); Leonid Kutakov, *The Diplomacy of Aggression: The Berlin-Rome-Tokyo Axis* (Moscow: 1970); Gerhard L. Weinberg, "Die Geheimen Abkommen zum Antikominternpakt," *Vierteljarhshefte für Zeitgeschichte*, 2, 1 (January 1954).

PVC

ANTI-FASCISM. Anti-Fascism in Italy covers the broad phenomenon of political opposition and eventually Armed Resistance to the Fascist movement and regime of Benito Mussolini between 1919 and 1945. Anti-Fascism embraced a wide spectrum of opinion, ranging from anarchism and communism to Catholicism and liberal-conservatism. It varied from a mere state of mind to organized movements that might logically include any non-Fascist political current. The term has also come to be employed in a generic sense, first by Marxists and later by non-Marxists as well, to describe opposition to other more or less fascistic movements that emerged in Germany, Austria, Portugal, Spain, and elsewhere.

In Italy the history of anti-Fascism was closely intertwined with that of its foe, Fascism. From its inception in March 1919, the Fascist movement had emphasized bitter hostility toward the Socialists and Bolsheviks. In its early phase anti-Fascism was identified mostly with the working class and leftist parties (Socialists, Communists, and the left wing of the Catholic Popolari). But their opposition to Fascism, chiefly in the form of strikes, was sporadic and inadequate, partly because of friction between the Communists and Socialists, as well as rivalry between the latter's reformist and maximalist wings. Moreover, there was still widespread misunderstanding of the real nature of Fascism. Most of the non-Marxist political forces were under the illusion that Fascism could be "normalized" and brought into the political system. A majority of non-Fascists entered Mussolini's first ministry in October 1922 with this notion in mind.

By the spring of 1923 a clearer picture was emerging. In April, Luigi Sturzo (q.v.), secretary of the Popolare Party (PPI) (*see* PARTITO POPOLARE ITALIANO), led a fight against the clerico-fascistic wing of his party at its congress in Turin. This led to the withdrawal of Popolare ministers from Mussolini's government and a resumption of Fascist violence against the "white" (Catholic) labor organizations. Sturzo had to resign the secretaryship of his party because of Vatican pressure. By 1923 Giovanni Amendola (q.v.), a Liberal Democrat, was becoming the leader of the parliamentary opposition. Anti-Fascist editorials were appearing in Turin's *La Stampa*, Milan's *Corriere della Sera*, and Rome's *Il Mondo*. Outside the framework of organized parties, Piero Gobetti's (q.v.) Turin's *Rivoluzione Liberale* (1922-25) also engaged in sharp opposition to Fascism.

In the parliamentary elections of April 1924, most of the conservative Liberals, including V. E. Orlando (q.v.) and Antonio Salandra (q.v.) chose to join the Fascist party's "big list" (*listone*) of candidates while Giovanni Giolitti (q.v.) and such Liberal Democrats as Amendola remained apart. Though these elections were conducted in a climate of Fascist intimidation, the opposition polled 34 percent of the vote, and in the north the opposition votes were greater than the government ones.

Following sharp denunciation in parliament of the Fascist irregularities in that election, Giacomo Matteotti (*see* MATTEOTTI CRISIS), secretary of the reformist Partito Socialista Unitario (PSU), was assassinated by Fascists on June 10, 1924. Investigations revealed that the murderers had been very close to Mussolini. In the ensuing political crisis, most of the parliamentary opposition, from the Popolari to the Communists, decided on June 27 to boycott Parliament and organize the Aventine Secession (q.v.). (The Salandra and Giolitti Liberals did not join.) Amendola led the Aventine bloc. Giuseppe Donati (q.v.), editor of the PPI newspaper, *Il Popolo*, played a prominent role. The Aventine carried out a vigorous press campaign and tried, unsuccessfully, to persuade King Victor Emmanuel III (q.v.) to dismiss his compromised prime minister. Fairly soon the Communist party criticized the nonviolent strategy of the Aventine. The Communists were also very hostile toward the Socialists, whom they accused of being "counterrevolutionary." When the Communists failed to convert the Aventine into an "Anti-Parliament," they decided to return to the Chamber (October 20, 1924). Efforts by the Communists and some others to incite uprisings among the working class failed.

The weakness and uncertainty of the Aventine opposition, combined with prodding from Fascist party leaders and the disinterest of the king, made it possible for Mussolini to launch a counteroffensive. In a speech in parliament on January 3, 1925, the premier took full responsibility for the Matteotti affair and the Fascist violence. Thereafter he gradually imposed the dictatorship—a series of attempted assassinations of him providing him with further pretexts. Mussolini's "Exceptional Decrees" (q.v.) of November 1926 marked the culmination of this move toward the "totalitarian state." Henceforth all remaining opposition parties, labor unions, and newspapers were banned. The Fascist Special Tribunal for the Defense of the State (q.v.) and the secret police (OVRA) (*see* POLICE AND INTERNAL SECURITY) were inaugurated.

After the Aventine debacle, anti-Fascism operated on two fronts—at home and abroad. Among the anti-Fascists who emigrated were certain democratic Liberals, some of the Popolari, leaders of the Socialist and Republican parties, and a number of labor organizers, for example, F. S. Nitti (q.v.), L. Sturzo, G. Donati, G. Salvemini (q.v.), P. Gobetti, G. Amendola, C. Sforza (q.v.), F. Turati (q.v.), C. Treves (q.v.), G. Saragat (q.v.), P. Nenni (q.v.), Bruno Buozzi (q.v.), and others. Amendola and Gobetti, who had suffered physical beatings by the Fascists, died soon after their arrival in France. Many of the emigres were to regroup and resume an active campaign against Fascism. Those anti-Fascists who chose to stay in Italy tended to engage in a more passive kind of resistance, with the noteworthy exception of the anarchists and Communists. The anarchists, though numerically small, continued their violent struggle against the centralized state and carried out some abortive attempts against the life of Mussolini in the early 1930s (for example, Michele Schirru in 1931 and Angelo Sbardellotto in 1932). There was also sporadic anti-Fascist violence among the ethnic minorities in Venezia Giulia and the Alto Adige.

Senator Benedetto Croce (q.v.) of Naples provided much moral inspiration for liberal-minded anti-Fascists. He favored a cautious but uncompromising intellectual opposition. On May 1, 1925, he published a blistering "Manifesto of the Anti-Fascist Intellectuals" in reply to Giovanni Gentile's (q.v.) "Fascist Manifesto." He also set himself the task of writing books that praised the liberal eras in European and Italian history, in rebuttal to the Fascist denigration of those periods. Many of Croce's followers wound up in positions considerably to the left of his own. It is to be noted, too, that in the late 1920s a handful of older Liberals, for example, G. Giolitti, M. Soleri (q.v.), and F. Ruffini (q.v.), occasionally voiced on the floor of parliament their distaste for Fascist policies.

The Catholic political forces found themselves in an awkward position, since the Vatican was clearly turning its back on the Popolare party. That party's founder and secretary, L. Sturzo, felt constrained to emigrate in 1924. The Fascists arrested his successor, Alcide De Gasperi (q.v.) in 1927 but two years later agreed to let him take employment in the Vatican Libraries. There he prepared for the day when the dictatorship would weaken, and he could reorganize the forces of Christian Democracy. Though Pius XI (q.v.) was happy to sign the Lateran Pacts (q.v.) of February 11, 1929 with Mussolini ("the man whom Providence has caused Us to meet"), his authoritarian Church soon found itself engaged in a bitter dispute with the would-be totalitarian Fascist regime over the competition of Catholic Action and youth organizations with the new Fascist youth and mass organizations. Fascism was largely the victor in this clash, but a resolute minority of Catholic university students in Igino Righetti's University Federation of Italian Catholics (FUCI—Federazione Universitaria Cattolica Italiana) and the Movimento Laureati continued to engage in clandestine opposition. Piero Malvestiti's Neo-Guelf Movement in Lombardy was also of importance in the early 1930s.

In October 1931 Mario Vinciguerra's anti-Fascist National Alliance sought to use both the Church and the House of Savoy in an effort to bring down the regime. It arranged for a daring flight over Rome by the poet Lauro De Bosis (q.v.), who flew from France over the city center, dropping leaflets urging the king to take action. De Bosis died on the return in a crash at sea.

Meanwhile, by 1927 anti-Fascist emigres were regrouping. While the Popolari and Liberals made no attempt to reorganize formal party structures, others did—notably the two Socialist parties and the Republicans. The Communists chose to maintain both a foreign center in Paris and an internal center in Milan.

At a conference held in Nerac, France, in April 1927 the Anti-Fascist Concentration came into existence. This coalition opened its headquarters in Paris, with the maximalist Socialist Pietro Nenni serving as secretary-general. The Concentration was composed of the two Socialist parties (which were to merge in July 1930), the Republican party, Bruno Buozzi's skeletal emigre General Confederation of Labor (CGL—Confederazione Generale del Lavoro) and the anticlerical International League for the Rights of Man (LIDU—Lega internazionale dei diritti dell'uomo). At first, the Concentration's program was similar to that of the Aventine, but by 1929 it adopted a clearly republican and anticlerical stance. The reformist Socialist, Filippo Turati, was the respected elder statesman of the Concentration until his death in 1932. A weekly newspaper, *La Libertà*, was published in Paris (May 1927-May 1934) under the editorship of another reformist Socialist, Claudio Treves, who died in 1933. The bloc was sometimes infiltrated by Fascist agents, and the Communists openly scoffed at it. But its newspaper propaganda was important, and its leadership encouraged sober action rather than foolhardy deeds.

Meanwhile in 1929 a rival movement, Giustizia e Libertà, was founded in Paris by Carlo Rosselli (q.v.) after his sensational escape from the Fascist prison isle of Lipari. (Earlier Rosselli and Gaetano Salvemini had published in Florence the first clandestine anti-Fascist paper, *Non Mollare!*). Rosselli was assisted by Salvemini, Alberto Tarchiani (q.v.), and others in organizing GL. They were unhappy with the programs of the existing parties and wanted to create a movement that would appeal to moderate Socialists, democratic-Liberals, and libertarians. Thoroughly antimonarchical and anticlerical, GL also rejected any partnership with the Communists. Otherwise its outlook was pragmatic. Above all, it sought to galvanize the opposition into action. In 1930 it promoted a flight over Italy by the liberal-socialist exile Giovanni Bassanesi. Inside Italy GL organized a network in Lombardy that included Ferruccio Parri (q.v.) and others until this was largely smashed in 1930.

Thereafter a new network was established in Turin. When it, too, was crushed (1932), Aldo Garosci (q.v.), the historian Franco Venturi, and others escaped to Paris. Later a new Turin group was formed by Leone Ginzburg (q.v.), Carlo Levi (q.v.), and others until it, too, was discovered in 1934. Meanwhile, in Paris GL decided to join the Anti-Fascist Concentration in November 1931, with the understanding that the former would have primary responsibility for anti-Fascist activity within Italy, and the latter in France. But this relationship was uneasy, especially after Rosselli decided to publish the *Quaderni di Giustizia e Libertà* in Paris. By 1933 GL had to pull out of the Concentration.

A new chapter in anti-Fascism began in 1933-34. Hitler had come to power in Germany, causing the Soviet Union to fear for its own national security. The Communists began to perceive the Comintern's previous error in castigating Social Democrats as "social-Fascists." Seeking a rapprochement now with the Communists, Nenni presided over the dissolution of the Concentration on May 5, 1934. When its newspaper ceased publication, Rosselli launched his own Paris weekly, *Giustizia e Libertà*. On August 17, 1934, the Italian Communists, headed by Palmiro Togliatti (q.v.) and the Socialists (P. Nenni and G. Saragat) signed their first "unity of action" pact, which was to be renewed periodically until the German-Soviet agreement of August 23, 1939. This rapprochement was further strengthened in the summer of 1935 when the Comintern VII Congress proclaimed the Popular Front line, a strategy that was to enable the Communists to gain predominance in the anti-Fascist struggle, especially at the expense of *Giustizia e Libertà*.

Hitherto, the Italian Communist party (PCI—Partito Comunista Italiano) (q.v.) had remained quite separate from the Socialists and others. In the Aventine era the PCI had been split in two factions. The Turin Ordine Nuovo group of Antonio Gramsci (q.v.) and Togliatti enjoyed the support of Moscow, while the Neapolitan Amadeo Bordiga (q.v.) headed an extremist faction that advocated abstention from all parliamentary activity. In January 1926 a clandestine PCI congress in Lyon expelled the Bordiga faction and adopted the "theses of Lyon," which called on the party to work among the southern peasants as well as the northern industrial workers. In November 1926 the PCI had to go under deep cover. One calamity followed another. The police arrested Gramsci and other parliamentary deputies despite their legal immunities. Only a handful of leaders, including Togliatti, escaped the Fascist dragnet. (He had gone to Moscow, where he was to become an official in the Comintern.) In May 1928 the Fascists held a "super-trial" in which they condemned the arrested PCI leaders to a total of 238 years of imprisonment. (There is no doubt that the Communists were the principal victims of Fascist police repression.) During Gramsci's imprisonment he managed to jot down thoughts on a wide range of topics before he died of tuberculosis in Rome in

1937. The party faithful eventually retrieved these notebooks, publishing them after the liberation.

The PCI's foreign center in Paris was led by such men as Togliatti, Angelo Tasca (q.v.), and Ruggiero Grieco, while its internal center in Milan was headed at first by Pietro Tresso, Alfonso Leonetti, and Paolo Ravazzoli. In 1930 the party expelled the latter three. New internal centers had to be formed repeatedly after police crackdowns. Clandestine PCI publications included *L'Unità* and *Battaglie sindacali*, while the more theoretical *Stato operaio* was published in France and later in New York. The Communists reorganized an underground CGL in 1927 in opposition to the emigre CGL that had been set up in Paris by the Socialist, Bruno Buozzi. From time to time during the depression, the Communists incited strikes among Italian rice workers and others. Meanwhile the party carried out a series of purges that included Tasca in 1929 and Ignazio Silone (q.v.) in 1931. The party held its fourth congress in Germany in April 1931, at which time it claimed seven thousand members.

Mussolini's successful war against Ethiopia (1935-36) in the face of the League of Nations' sanctions policy brought his regime to the pinnacle of its popularity at home. But the ensuing Spanish Civil War (q.v.) (1936-39) brought at least some satisfaction to the Italian anti-Fascists. Rosselli's Giustizia e Libertà volunteers were among the first to reach Spain, where they fought alongside the Catalan anarcho-syndicalists. Rosselli beamed a radio speech to Italy in which he proclaimed the slogan, "Today in Spain, tomorrow in Italy!" This so angered Mussolini that Foreign Minister Galeazzo Ciano (q.v.) arranged for the assassination of Rosselli (and his brother Nello) in France on June 10, 1937. After that, GL rapidly ebbed.

Meanwhile Italian Socialists and Communists helped organize the international brigades that fought in behalf of the Spanish Republic. The victory of the Garibaldi Battalion, commanded by the Italian Republican, Randolfo Pacciardi (q.v.), against Italian Fascist troops at Guadalajara (March 1937) was particularly humiliating for Mussolini. All told, some three thousand Italian anti-Fascists participated in the Civil War and some six hundred died. Veterans like the Communist, Luigi Longo, gained valuable military experience that was to serve them well in Italy's Armed Resistance of 1943-45 (*see* RESISTANCE, ARMED).

Within Italy the late 1930s saw the Communists embark on a new tactic of infiltrating various Fascist mass organizations such as GIL and GUF (*see* YOUTH ORGANIZATIONS), often with effective results. Meanwhile Guido Calogero organized the Liberalsocialismo movement in 1936 at the University of Pisa, while Ferruccio Parri (q.v.) was busy with analogous activities in Milan. The Calogero and Parri groups would eventually merge with remnants of GL to form the Partito d'Azione (q.v.) in 1942.

The Nazi-Soviet neutrality and nonaggression pact of August 23, 1939, broke up the Social-Communist partnership until June 1941 when Germany attacked Russia. Hitler's invasion of France in 1940 forced many Italian emigres to flee to the United States and elsewhere. In New York much friction occurred between

Italian Communists and the anti-Communist Mazzini Society (q.v.). The emigre Carlo Sforza, a liberal who had been foreign minister in 1920-21, came to be regarded by the U.S. State Department as the most prestigious spokesman of Italian anti-Fascism. In 1942 Sforza went to Montevideo in an unsuccessful attempt to organize a Free Italy combat unit that would fight alongside the forces of the United Nations.

The Italian military setbacks in World War II hastened the clandestine reorganization in Italy (1942-43) of political parties (Communists, Socialists, Actionists, Christian Democrats, Labor Democrats, and Liberals). By 1943 several of their leaders looked to the elderly former premier in Rome, Ivanoe Bonomi (q.v.) (a Labor Democrat), as a spokesman who might persuade the king to overthrow Mussolini. Meanwhile in March of that year, a strike in the northern industrial cities revealed deep popular unrest with the war and the dictatorship. Within the Fascist party conspiracies against the Duce were being hatched by Dino Grandi (q.v.) and Galeazzo Ciano (q.v.). The Allied invasion of Sicily and aerial bombardment of Rome in July 1943 hastened the meeting of the Fascist Grand Council (q.v.), which voted against Mussolini. A few hours later (July 25, 1943) the king arrested him and named Marshal Pietro Badoglio (q.v.) head of the government. The ensuing armistice with the Allies and the German seizure of northern Italy (September 8, 1943) marked the beginning of anti-Fascism's final phase, the Armed Resistance.

For further information see: Aldo Garosci, *Storia dei fuorusciti* (Bari: Laterza, 1953); Charles F. Delzell, *Mussolini's Enemies: The Italian Anti-Fascist Resistance*, rev. ed. (New York: Howard Fertig, 1974); Luigi Salvatorelli and Giovanni Mira, *Storia d'Italia nel periodo fascista* (Turin: Einaudi, 1964); Paolo Spriano, *Storia del Partito comunista italiano*, 5 vols. (Turin: Einaudi, 1967-75); Richard A. Webster, *The Cross and the Fasces: Christian Democracy in Italy* (Stanford, Cal.: Stanford University Press, 1960).

CFD

ANTI-SEMITISM. Anti-Semitism became official Fascist policy shortly after the publication of the *Manifesto of Fascist Racism* in July 1938, which announced that Italians were Aryan in origin and biologically different from Jews and Africans, who belonged to "extra-European" races. There followed a series of decrees specifically forbidding intermarriage between Italians and Jews, removing Jews from positions of influence in government, banking, and education, and restricting their property holdings. Foreign Jews who had immigrated into Italy since 1919 were ordered to leave the country. This policy took almost everyone by surprise. Italy was one European country which had been historically free from anti-Semitic persecutions, a fact explained partly by Italy's humanistic traditions, and partly by the fact that there were simply very few Jews in Italy. (During the Fascist period they constituted little more than one-tenth of 1 percent of the total population.) More important, the ideology of Italian Fascism, unlike Nazism, had never been grounded on racial doctrines, and Mussolini himself had gone on record over the years denouncing racism as "unscientific," "ridiculous," and "absurd." *The Manifesto* therefore signalled an abrupt about face and seemed obviously designed to establish closer ideological ties with the Nazis and to solidify the alliance with Germany.

Although the turn toward racism and anti-Semitism appeared sudden, there had been signs of its coming at least two years earlier, and the potential for anti-Semitism in Italy existed even before that. There had long been an anti-Semitic minority within the Fascist movement and in the Catholic Church as well, which viewed Jews as inherent enemies of both Fascism and Catholicism. These anti-Semites based their opposition to Jews on ideology, not race, arguing that since the French Revolution, Jews had been dedicated exponents of the materialist doctrines of utilitarianism, rationalism, liberalism and socialism. They viewed Jews as either exploitative capitalists or revolutionary socialists whose international and religious ties to "world Jewry" preceded their allegiance to any single nation, and whose divided loyalties made them unassimilable in a totalitarian and Catholic society. The growth of Zionism only further encouraged this view of Jews as representatives of a potentially subversive "state within a state." And Mussolini himself, though maintaining personal friendships with Jews and opening Italian borders to Jewish refugees from Germany in the early thirties, often voiced anger and concern over the malignant power of international Jewry and its traditional opposition to Fascism.

This undercurrent of anti-Semitism remained little more than an ideological tendency within Fascist Italy until 1935 when the embarkation on imperial conquest in Ethiopia rapidly transformed the situation. International hostility to the Italian invasion of Ethiopia and the sanctions imposed by the League of Nations drove Mussolini in spiteful retaliation toward an alliance with a resurgent Nazi Germany. Hitler's successes, coupled with Mussolini's own triumph, convinced Il Duce that Fascism was indeed the prevailing force of the future and increased his contempt for the "decadent" western democracies and their principles. Becoming ever more belligerent and doctrinaire after the Ethiopian War (q.v.), he struck back at those Jewish organizations abroad that had vigorously protested against Fascist aggression by unleashing an anti-Semitic press campaign against the Jews in 1936. This anti-Semitism was still primarily ideological and not racial. But at the same time the Italians had begun to introduce anti-miscegenation laws in Ethiopia to enforce separation of the races, and increasingly they adopted a racial vocabulary to justify the domination of one race over another. By 1938, the confluence of these factors, the racism engendered by a new imperialist consciousness, the anti-Semitism inherent in Fascist ideology, and Mussolini's desire to keep abreast of Hitler for the leadership of international fascism, culminated in the *Manifesto*.

Mussolini's adoption of biological racism proved to be a mistake, as he himself later admitted. He had made the decision voluntarily, with no direct pressure from the Nazis, simply for political reasons. By adopting the myth of Aryan superiority, Il Duce had hoped to infuse Italians with the same prideful arrogance that the Germans had and to recapture the early Fascist spirit of *menefreghismo* ("Don't-give-a-damn") in preparation for the conflicts which lay ahead: "the fight against these powerful forces [the Jews], as many consider them to be, serves to give the Italians a backbone...and to show that certain mountains are no more than blisters." But the new racial theories conflicted with the idealist principles of the Fascist ethical state, and they were poorly received by most Italians who saw the new policy as an embarrassing emulation of crude Nazi doctrines. Anti-Semitic Catholics writing in the Jesuit journal, *La Civiltà Cattolica*, also rejected the Nazi racist and materialist theories, and Pius XI was one of the first to ask "Why, unfortunately, did Italy have to go and imitate Germany?" Though angered by these accusations, Mussolini betrayed his own lack of commitment to racism by granting legal exemptions to Jewish families whose members had been war veterans, early members of the Fascist party, or had earned "exceptional recognition." Moreover, the Italians never went beyond the initial policy of discrimination against the Jews, and during the war, Jews in Italian-occupied zones of Europe felt relatively secure. By 1943, when the Italians became aware of the full extent of Nazi fanaticism, they began to protect Jews under their jurisdiction, and Mussolini himself secretly encouraged his military commanders to stall, ignore, and otherwise frustrate Nazi efforts to have Jews shipped to Germany. Although he could not carry out the Nazi racial policies, neither could he openly confront and oppose the Nazis on this issue for fear of personally betraying Hitler and revealing to the Germans once again, as in World War I, Italian weakness of will. Mussolini's ambivalent stance, which he feared would be viewed as a failure of nerve, in fact represented the reassertion of a deep Italian virtue: the triumph of old humanitarian values over new Fascist principles.

For further information see: Renzo De Felice, *Storia degli ebrei sotto il fascismo* (Turin: Einaudi, 1961); Meir Michaelis, *Mussolini and the Jews* (Oxford: Clarendon Press, 1978); Luigi Preti, *Impero fascista, africani ed ebrei* (Milan: Mursia, 1968).

GB

ANZIO, JANUARY 22, 1944. On January 22, 1944, an Allied invasion took place on the Italian peninsula composed of the U.S. Sixth Corps under the command of Major General John P. Lucas. The purpose of the landing was to outflank the right side of the Gustav Line (q.v.), to make a quick breakout toward the Alban Hills south of Rome, and finally to liberate Rome. The landing failed to achieve the desired objectives when the Allied Commander opted to consolidate his beachhead position instead of thrusting inland. This decision allowed the German forces under the command of Field Marshal Albert Kesselring (q.v.) time to pull troops from quiet sectors of the Gustav Line and send them to the Anzio sector along with reinforcements from the Luftwaffe. The German counterattack prevented the Allies from achieving their objectives and for a time it appeared that the entire Allied position was in jeopardy. The situation confronting the Allies did not improve until the first week of May 1944.

Lucas was accused of being overly cautious and failing to exploit his initial advantage and was replaced on February 23, 1944 by the commander of the U.S. Third Division at the Anzio landing, Lieutenant General Lucian Truscott. From strong defensive positions surrounding Anzio, the German forces were able to keep the Allies pinned down and prevent the breakout that was essential to the Allied plans. The Allied force was finally able to achieve its breakout in early May 1944 for two reasons: the spring rains slackened, which allowed heavy equipment to once again travel the roads, and the U.S. Fifth and British Eighth armies launched a massive assault upon the Gustav Line, which relieved most of the pressure confronting the Allies at Anzio. Instead of a quick move inland, the Allies encountered stiff opposition and Rome was not liberated until June 4, 1944.

For further information see: Martin Blumenson, *Anzio: the Gamble that Failed* (New York: J. B. Lippincott and Co., Inc., 1963); W. G. F. Jackson, *The Battle for Italy* (New York: Harper & Row, Inc., 1967); Gordon A. Shepperd, *The Italian Campaign, 1943-1945* (New York: Frederick A. Praeger, Inc., 1968).

WAJ

APPELIUS, MARIO (b. Arezzo, July 29, 1892; d. Rome, December 27, 1946). Popular journalist and radio announcer, Appelius was one of the best known Fascist propagandists. He traveled widely as a young man, studied law at the University of Rome, and joined the Italian Navy in World War I. In 1922 Arnaldo Mussolini (q.v.) persuaded him to become a journalist for *Il Popolo d'Italia* and for Agenzia Stefani (q.v.). Appelius covered both the Ethiopian campaign (*see* ETHIOPIAN WAR) and the Spanish Civil War (q.v.). A brilliant writer, he won wide acclaim during World War II for his forceful articles and in 1941 was made a radio commentator for the *"Commenti ai fatti del giorno"* ("Comments on Events of the Day") program. His broadcasts provoked highly emotional responses and became so harsh and uncompromising that Mussolini dismissed him in February 1943.

For further information see: DBI (3); Mario Appelius, *Parole dure e chiare* (Milan: Mondadori, 1942); Philip V. Cannistraro, *La fabbrica del consenso: Fascismo e mass media* (Rome-Bari: Laterza, 1975).

PVC

A PRATO, CARLO (b. Trento, April 7, 1895; d. Geneva, September 1968). An anti-Fascist militant, a Prato began his career first in the military and then in the diplomatic corps under Carlo Sforza (q.v.). From an aristocratic family, he joined the Socialist party in 1924 and fled to France the following year. In Paris, where he gravitated to the Republican party, he co-edited the *Corriere degli Italiani* and was European correspondent for the *New York Times*; in Geneva he edited the *Journal* *des Nations*. Until 1940 a Prato was a close associate of Sforza, but the two broke because of personal differences. A Prato reached New York in 1941, joined the staff of *Free World*, and collaborated with Giuseppe Lupis's *Il Mondo*. A member of the Mazzini Society (q.v.), in 1942 he was hired by the Office of War Information to direct Italian-language broadcasts for the Voice of America.

For further information see: Nanda Torcellan, "Per una biografia di Carlo a Prato," *Italia Contemporanea* 28, 124 (July-September, 1976).

PVC

ARCHITECTURE. Architecture in Italy from 1919 to 1945 exhibited two major but contradictory streams—traditional and modern—which under Fascism were often combined and received alternating support. Milan, nearer the northern cities in Europe, fostered both the Futurist and the International style (so-called "modern" architecture). Turin, also aligned more closely with the general European cultural climate, served as a center for architectural criticism, led by Edoardo Persico (q.v.). Rome, repository for Roman antiquity, served as an historical prod aiming toward the Imperial revival and other historical styles such as the Baroque and Neoclassical.

Among the major architectural styles of the period was Futurism (q.v.), which advocated the modern industrial revolution in Italy. But its chief architects, Antonio Sant' Elia and Mario Chiattone, committed more works to paper than were ever erected due to adverse economic conditions. Filippo Tomaso Marinetti (q.v.), the founder of Futurism, insisted Italy must bury its past and open its future to technological change. By 1912 the movement permeated painting, sculpture, architecture, theater, music, literature, and philosophy. Among the prominent members of the Futurists were Umberto Boccioni, Giacomo Balla (q.v.), Gino Severini, Carlo Carrà (q.v.), Luigi Russolo, Anton G. Bragaglia (q.v.), and Emilio Settemelli.

The Novecento (or Milanese 1900) Movement (q.v.) was a twentieth-century art and literary trend based in Milan, but which emphasized the Roman tradition as a source to renew Italian culture. The group sought a synthesis of the old and new cultures. Begun in the early 1920s, the artists hoped to represent the Fascist state, but by the 1930s their modernized classical style caused strong debate among party members. Novecento supporters included Margherita Sarfatti (q.v.), Mario Sironi (q.v.), Arturo Martini (q.v.), Mario Mafai (q.v.), Ottone Rosai (q.v.), and former Futurist supporters Giorgio Morandi (q.v.), Carlo Carrà, and Felice Casorati.

The "Group of Six," established in Turin in 1928 and influenced by critic Edoardo Persico, favored rational (International style) architecture. Its members included Edoardo Persico, Enrico Paulucci, Carlo Levi (q.v.), Francesco Mesuno, Giorgio Chessa, Nicola Galante, and Jessie Boswell. Similarly, the "Group of Seven" brought together young architects in 1926 who also supported rational architecture but insisted on emphasizing the Mediterranean past and employing arches and curves. An anti-Futurist group led by Adalberto Libera (who organized the first Italian Movement of Rationalist Architecture—MIAR [Movimento italiano d'architettura razionalista]), exhibited in a Fascist Union of Architects show in 1928. It included Luigi Figini, Guido Frette, Sebastiano Larco, Libera, Gino Pollini, Carlo Rava, and Giuseppe Terragni (q.v.).

Rationalism brought to Italy the International style (so-called "modern" architecture), which swept the rest of Europe. This style was opposed to traditional architecture, and responded to the Futurist cry for the incorporation of the new industrial view.

Many of the threads, however, were strongly connected to the Italian historical past, and rationalism became imbued with Roman characteristics. By the late 1930s rationalism took final form in the Monumental Style, an Imperial Roman revival officially sponsored by the regime, which was best exhibited in the Esposizione Universale di Roma (EUR) project. The stark, monumental, classical revival buildings in what was to be Mussolini's new capital—the "third Rome" —located between Ostia and Rome, came under the general direction of Marcello Piacentini (q.v.), the son of a traditional academic architect. During most of the Fascist period Mussolini was unwilling to commit the regime to one definite architectural style exclusively, so that it was not unusual to see a traditionally styled building—such as the Biblioteca Nazionale in Florence—erected in the same city and at the same time as an internationally styled structure—the Florence train station; both buildings were sanctioned by the Fascist government. After Germany's influence gained strength in Italy, Mussolini increasingly rejected the International style and favored the return to architecture symbolizing Rome's glorious past, much as Hitler saw himself connected to the Greek civilization.

The complexities of architecture and its connection to politics during the 1930s may best be understood through the polemics recorded in the major architecture journals of the period: *Casabella*, published in Milan and edited by Giuseppe Pagano (q.v.) and Edoardo Persico (in 1930 it changed its name to *Casabella-Costruzioni*, and in 1940 reversed the title to *Costruzioni-Casabella*); *Architettura*, published in Milan and Rome and successor to *Architettura e Arti decorativi* (organ of the national union of architects), became the official journal of the National Fascist Union of Architects in January 1932 and was edited by Marcello Piacentini until the last issue in 1942. In 1943 the journal was succeeded by the review *Architettura, Rassegna di Architettura*, published in Milan. Other major architecture journals of this era include: *L'Arte*, a bi-monthly journal published in Rome and Milan from 1898-1962; *Casa d'Oggi*, a monthly publication under the auspices of *La Casa* and sponsored by the Civil Engineering Section of the Fascist Union of Engineers between January 1934 and December 1944; and *Il Vetro*, published in 1938 in Milan as the official journal of the Fascist Association of Glass Manufacturers.

For further information see: Carlo Cresti, *Appunti storici e critici sull'architettura italiana dal 1900 ad oggi* (Florence: G. & G. Editrice, 1971); Vittorio Gregotti, *New Directions in Italian Architecture* (New York: George Braziller,

1968); Luciano Patetta, *L'architettura in Italia, 1919-1943. Le polemiche* (Milan: Cooperativa libraria universitaria del politecnico, 1972); Pietro Secchia, ed., *Enciclopedia dell'antifascismo e della resistenza*, 1 (Milan: LaPietra, 1968), 113-117; Bruno Zevi, *Storia dell'architettura moderna* (Turin: Giulio Einaudi, 1955).

JH

ARDEATINE CAVES MASSACRE. On March 24, 1944, Nazi commanders perpetrated one of the most savage and brutal German terrorist acts in Italy, killing 335 Italians in a cave outside of Rome on the Via Ardeatine.

The slaughter was in reprisal for a partisan attack against SS troops. On the previous day, a small group of young anti-Fascists belonging to GAP (Gruppi di Azione Patriottica, the Communist underground military command in Rome), ambushed a column of 150 SS security troops on the Via Rasella, killing 33 and wounding 70.

German and Fascist authorities reacted fiercely, spraying the neighborhood with gunfire and rounding up local inhabitants. Field Marshal Albert von Kesselring (q.v.) telephoned Hitler and then announced that ten Italians would be killed for every one German. The process of selecting the victims was decided by German Ambassador Hans Von Mackensen (q.v.), General Kurt Maelzer, the Commandant of Rome, and Lieutenant Colonel Herbert Kappler (q.v.) of the SS security service. Kappler took charge of rounding up the victims, who included Jews, men already awaiting death sentences, those arrested at the Via Rasella, and a group selected by Roman police chief Pietro Caruso (q.v.). That night Kappler transported the prisoners in closed trucks to the caves. There the victims, hands tied behind their backs and kneeling on the floor, were systematically shot in the neck in groups of five, after which the bodies were sealed up by exploding mines in the cave entrance.

Following the liberation of Rome, the cave was reopened, the bodies identified (with the exception of thirteen), and a large but simple monument built on the site to commemorate the massacre.

A series of postwar trials sentenced those responsible for the reprisal, but none were executed.

For further information see: Attilio Ascarelli, *Le fosse ardeatine* (Rome: Palombi, 1945); Robert Katz, *Death in Rome* (New York: Macmillan, 1967); Enzo Piscitelli, *Storia della resistenza romana* (Bari: Laterza, 1965).

PVC

ARDITI. The Arditi ("Daring Ones") were Italy's World War I assault troops. Many Arditi veterans later followed Gabriele D'Annunzio (q.v.) and Mussolini.

Informally organized in October 1915, developed afterwards by Luigi Capello (q.v.), and officially established as the *riparti d'assalto* (assault units) in January 1917, the Arditi provided forces for offensive spearheads, trench raids, and reconnaisance. Between actions the Arditi withdrew from the trenches for intensive physical and combat training. Excessive Comando Supremo (q.v.) propaganda plus Arditi prowess, privileges, swagger, and distinctive black-faced uniforms marked them as an elite.

Originally formed in company- and battalion-sized units, the Arditi eventually formed two assault divisions in mid-1918. The 1st Assault Division, commanded by Ottavio Zoppi (q.v.), later served in Libya in 1919, while its 3rd *Gruppo* (regiment) also fought in Albania in 1920.

Discharged Arditi often found civilian life boring and liberal politics sordid. The Arditi Association, founded January 1919, channeled these discontents in radical but anti-Marxist directions. Mussolini subsidized the Association, hoping to use it, as he plotted a coup with the Nationalists and some Army commanders. While some Arditi formed the first Fasci di Combattimento (q.v.), others distrusted Mussolini. Many flocked to D'Annunzio's Fiume (q.v.), attracted by Syndicalist (*see* SYNDICALISM) notions, where their braggadocio, black uniforms, and slogans ("*me ne frego*" ["I don't give a damn"], "*vivere pericolosamente*" ["live dangerously"], and so forth) gave the city its special flavor. The collapse of the Regency of Carnaro (*see* CARNARO, CHARTER OF) in December 1920, coupled with Mussolini's swing to the right and betrayal of D'Annunzio, left many ex-Arditi politically isolated. The Arditi Association leadership broke with Fascism in July 1921, expelling Giuseppe Bottai (q.v.) and Cesare De Vecchi (q.v.) among others. But many members joined the Blackshirt ranks (*see* SQUADRISTI) anyway, viewing Mussolini as their only hope.

Mussolini used them to militarize his squads, then launched these Blackshirts against the Socialists, Communists, and Slavs in 1921-22. After the March on Rome (q.v.), the new Fascist Militia (q.v.) adopted the Arditi's external trappings, but failed to emulate their exploits in Mussolini's wars.

For further information see: Ferdinando Cordova, *Arditi e legionari dannunziani* (Padua: Marsilio, 1969); *Enciclopedia Italiana* 4 (Milan: Rizzoli, 1929); Adrian Lyttelton, *The Seizure of Power* (New York: Scribner's, 1973).

BRS

ARDITI DEL POPOLO. An anti-Fascist military group created in Rome in 1921 by former Arditi (q.v.) officers of republican persuasion to combat Fascist violence. The group gained thousands of adherents, including Socialists, Communists, and anarchists, throughout northern and central Italy, but the Socialist and Communist parties officially disassociated themselves from it. Guido Picelli, a young Socialist militant (who later joined the Communist Party) assumed a particularly energetic leadership in Parma. The Italian police severely repressed the Arditi del Popolo, and it declined rapidly, but autonomous branches continued to fight the Fascists defiantly in several local areas. Picelli led a valiant resistance against Italo Balbo's (q.v.) Blackshirt (*see* SQUADRISTI) assaults in Parma, but the Pacification Pact (q.v.) between Socialists and Fascists signalled its demise. The Arditi del Popolo may well have represented the "lost opportunity" of militant anti-Fascism before Mussolini's seizure of power.

For further information see: Ferdinando Cordova, *Arditi e legionari dannunziani* (Padua: Marsilio, 1969); MOI 4, "Picelli, Guido;" Paolo Spriano, *Storia del partito comunista italiano*, 1 (Turin: Einaudi, 1967).

PVC

ARMELLINI, QUIRINO (b. Legnaro Padova, January 31, 1889). One of Pietro Badoglio's (q.v.) most faithful associates, General Armellini served as Badoglio's operations chief in Ethiopia and as commander in Amara during the subsequent pacification until a major guerrilla outbreak led to his relief in May 1940. He returned to Rome to join the high command under Badoglio and remained until January 1941, keeping a diary that is a valuable source on Italian strategy and politics in 1940. Subsequently he commanded an occupation corps in Dalmatia and in 1943 took over and dissolved the Militia (q.v.); then he served as Badoglio's emissary in German-occupied Rome.

For further information see: Quirino Armellini, *Con Badoglio in Etiopia* (Milan: Mondadori, 1937); Quirino Armellini, *La crisi dell'Esercito* (Rome: Edizioni Priscilla, 1945); Quirino Armellini, *Diario di guerra. Nove mesi al Comando Supremo* (Milan: Garzanti, 1946).

MK

ARMISTICE (September, 1943). The Fascist dictator, Benito Mussolini, was overthrown on July 25, 1943, and a government led by Marshal Pietro Badoglio (q.v.) was constituted with the objective of gaining a separate peace for Italy. Diplomatic contacts were initiated by Italy at Tangiers and subsequently at Madrid and Lisbon.

While Italian peace feelers and Allied preparations for an invasion of the mainland continued, President Roosevelt and Prime Minister Winston Churchill met at Quebec, Canada, with their commander in chief in the Mediterranean, General Dwight D. Eisenhower, to receive Italian representatives for the purpose of arranging a surrender. They also began drafting comprehensive surrender terms. On August 31 the Italian representative, General Giuseppe Castellano (q.v.), arrived in Sicily for final discussions.

In September 1943 Badoglio's government signed two armistice agreements with the Allied powers led by the United States and the United Kingdom. The first agreement, the so-called "short terms," was signed by Italian and Allied officers at Cassibile, Sicily on September 3, 1943. This document provided for a military surrender, repatriation of Allied prisoners of war, the use of Italy as a base for Allied military operations, and the cooperation of Italian military and naval units with the Allies. The final clause of the "short terms" provided that Italy would observe additional political, economic, and financial terms, which would be imposed at a later date.

These additional conditions (the "long terms") were signed on September 29, 1943 by Badoglio and Eisenhower. The terms gave the Allies total control over the diplomatic, administrative, economic, and financial activities of the Italian state. An Allied Control Commission (q.v.) was established to oversee Italian compliance with the other terms.

The Allies somewhat softened the rigors of the terms in supplementary documents. Nevertheless, the armistice terms were considered to be so harsh that the United States refused to permit their publication until the end of the war. From October 1944 until the end of 1946, the U.S. government pursued a series of approaches intended to release Italy from the armistice terms. After prolonged negotiations an Italian peace treaty was ratified by all involved parties on September 15, 1947. The armistice conditions were superseded.

For further information see: Albert N. Garland and Howard McGraw Smyth, *Sicily and the Surrender of Italy* (Washington, D.C.: U.S. Government Printing Office, 1965); *Foreign Relations of the United States. The Conferences at Washington and Quebec, 1943* (Washington, D.C.: U.S. Government Printing Office, 1970); Robert J. Quinlan, "The Italian Armistice," in Harold Stein (ed.), *American Civil Military Decisions* (Birmingham, Alabama: University of Alabama Press, 1963).

JEM

ARMY, ITALIAN. The generals brought Mussolini to power. Twenty years later they overthrew him. In between, Army and regime gradually merged, at the expense of military autonomy and Party interests. Only total defeat, for which each blamed the other, prompted the generals to place their interests before Mussolini's.

Little doubt remains that leading generals—Armando Diaz (q.v.), Gaetano Giardino (q.v.), the duke of Aosta (*see* SAVOIA, AMEDEO DI), Pecori Geraldi—saw Mussolini as their savior. Since 1920 Army elements had aided Fascist attacks on the Left with sympathy, training, and arms. But radical Fascist demands for a people's army threatened Army Council (high command) power more than the increased civilian control imposed by postwar Liberal governments. Mussolini offered Army autonomy in return for passive cooperation with the March on Rome (q.v.). Diaz agreed, forcing the king's surrender.

When he was in power, Mussolini disappointed followers like Cesare De Vecchi (q.v.), Italo Balbo (q.v.), and Emilio De Bono (q.v.), who expected Fascist domination of the Army. Many Fascists considered the Army part of the system their revolution would supplant. But Mussolini, influenced by the nationalists, preferred state power to party dictatorship. Rebuffing the radicals, Mussolini gave Diaz free rein as war minister (within fiscal limits), placed the Blackshirts (*see* SQUADRISTI) under generals in the state Militia (q.v.), and forbade Fascist interference with the Army.

The coincidence of the Mattcotti Crisis (q.v.) with the proposed reforms of Antonino Di Giorgio (q.v.), Diaz's successor as war minister, brought Mussolini and the high command to a confrontation. Privy to Mussolini's imperialist dreams, Di Giorgio proposed a smaller Army, stressing equipment over manpower. The war minister, controlling Italy's limited military resources, would direct the Army, not the Army Council. The high command, particularly Giardino, expecting Mussolini's imminent replacement by military dictatorship, refused approval.

Even after becoming dictator in January 1925, Mussolini accepted temporary defeat. He forced Di Giorgio's resignation and asked Ugo Cavallero (q.v.) and Pietro Badoglio (q.v.) to design a financially realistic compromise that still stressed Army primacy over Navy (q.v.) and Air Force (q.v.). The resultant Army had many conservative generals and little modern equipment. But Mussolini, becoming war minister himself, castrated the Army Council, dividing its responsibilities between the obsequious Cavallero and opportunistic Badoglio.

Neither general won their ensuing three-year power struggle, but it allowed Mussolini increased control over military affairs and the opportunity to reduce Army influence over foreign policy. By early 1929 Cavallero was dismissed and Badoglio, holding the empty title *capo di stato maggiore generale* (Chief of the Supreme General Staff), governed Libya. But their conservative successors, Pietro Gazzera (q.v.) (war undersecretary) and Alberto Bonzani (q.v.) (Army chief of staff), were Badoglio protégés and his influence permeated the Army, particularly after Gazzera became war minister in July 1929.

Gazzera and Bonzani disdained mechanization, interservice cooperation, or colonial operations. Planning concentrated on further Alpine wars of attrition (though Gazzera's request for new artillery was rejected for financial reasons). They stifled intellectual dissent, insisting on strict apoliticality in an expanding totalitarian regime. Rigid rank and class distinctions, symbolized by fervent monarchism, continued.

Despite his pretensions, Mussolini lacked deep military understanding, but came to equate Army conservatism with resistance to Fascism. Progressive military thinkers, like Federico Baistrocchi (q.v.), Emilio Canevari (q.v.), Francesco Grazioli (q.v.), or Ottavio Zoppi (q.v.), were often Fascists. When Gazzera and Bonzani opposed Mussolini's Ethopian plans, after resisting Fascist propaganda in the barracks and military innovation, Mussolini heeded their critics.

But Hitler's rise to power, Balbo's bid to obtain command of the armed forces, and Mussolini's admiration for Bonzani all complicated the situation. Mussolini proceeded cautiously. He replaced Gazzera himself (with Baistrocchi as war undersecretary) and in July 1933 he exiled Balbo to Libya, and entrusted the Colonial Ministry with Ethiopian preparations. Baistrocchi encouraged Fascism in the Army, pushed mechanization, and anticipated war for Mediterranean supremacy. Reducing the German threat by a military buildup at the Brenner Pass and rapprochement with France, Mussolini gained Baistrocchi's agreement to the African war by giving him Bonzani's post as well and promising funds for Army modernization after victory. Badoglio, whose conservative influence balanced Baistrocchi's authority, opposed these policies and feared confrontation with

Britain over Ethiopia. While Baistrocchi captured Army control over the Ethiopian campaign, Badoglio urged delay of operations there, possibly plotting an anti-Mussolini coup during the Mediterranean Crisis, August 1935.

Mussolini, confident of British military weaknesses, persevered. Once war began Badolglio maneuvered successfully to gain command, overwhelmed the Ethiopians (thanks to Mussolini's prodigal preparations and Rodolfo Graziani's [q.v.] advance from Somalia) and returned to Italy with unprecedented prestige. He and Mussolini, who now considered himself a military genius, shared the glory, though Baistrocchi's planning had brought victory. The Colonial Ministry attempted to exclude Army influence from the Empire. But constant rebellions required continuous infusions of Army officers and equipment.

Success welded Army and regime, and Mussolini's control over both. Brooking no military rival, Mussolini maintained Badoglio as a figurehead. When Baistrocchi opposed diversion of arms to Spain and demanded promised modernization funds, Mussolini replaced him with the pliant Alberto Pariani (q.v.). After the Militia collapsed at Guadalajara, the Army appeared thoroughly Fascist. In 1938 Mussolini assumed equal military rank with the king (first marshal of the Empire), introducing the goose step (*passo romano*) and Roman salute.

Pariani continued many of Basitrocchi's policies but lacked his ability. Pariani's doctrines parodied blitzkrieg. Spain and Africa devoured scarce resources, preventing adequate rearmament and retraining. Mediterranean primacy required Navy and Air Force expansion at Army expense. Despite bellicose propaganda, the Army remained largely antiquated in philosophy and materiel. Pariani supported the German alliance, expecting lengthy preparation, Wehrmacht assistance, and adequate funding before war.

An August 1939 mobilization revealed chaos. Poorly trained reservists swamped an Army organized into too many divisions, lacking everything. Mussolini replaced Pariani with a triumviate (Graziani, Mario Roatta [q.v.], Ubaldo Soddu [q.v.]) under Badoglio as armed forces coordinator. But no coherent operational planning emerged, because of a lack of consensus and Mussolini's refusal to explain his political strategy or create a combined services staff. The high command struggled everywhere, but succeeded nowhere. France's collapse prompted Mussolini to drag the generals into war, assuring certain victory after little fighting.

Mussolini assumed supreme command but proved unable to correlate political goals with military means. Disaster in Greece and Africa followed, forcing him to accept a true armed forces high command under Cavallero. Regaining some confidence after German-led victories in the Balkans and Libya, Mussolini again placed political goals before military realities. He forced the subservient Cavallero to disperse Italy's limited forces to Yugoslavia and, especially, Russia, starving the decisive North African theater. While Army performance improved markedly from combat lessons and German example, raw material shortages crippled armaments production. After the battle of El Alamein, monarchist sentiments stirred, and the high command urged a separate peace. When Mussolini refused, it removed him.

The subsequent debacle so discredited army leadership that Mussolini could rally some soldiers under Graziani for the Salò Republic (*see* ITALIAN SOCIAL REPUBLIC). But German and Fascist opposition prevented recreating more than four small divisions for antipartisan operations. Mussolini lost control over these forces, which surrendered independently in April 1945.

For further information see: Giovanni De Luna, *Badoglio* (Milan: Bompiani, 1975); Antonio Giachi, *Truppe coloniali italiane* (Florence: n.p., 1977); *Handbook on the Italian Military Forces* (Washington, D.C.: U.S. War Department, 1943); Massimo Mazzetti, *La politica militare italiana fra le due guerre mondiali* (Salerno: Beta, 1974); Fortunato Minniti, "Il problema degli armamenti nella preparazione militare italiana dal 1935 al 1945," *Storia contemporanea* 9 (February 1978), and "Aspetti territoriali e politici del controllo sulla produzione bellica in Italia (1936-1943)," *Clio* 15 (January-March 1979); Giampaolo Pansa, *L'esercito di Salò* (Verona: Mondadori, 1970); Giorgio Rochat and Giulio Massobrio, *Breve storia dell'esercito italiano dal 1861 al 1943* (Turin: Einaudi, 1978); John Sweet, *Iron Arm* (Westport, Conn: Greenwood, 1980); Massimo Adolfo Vitale, *L'opera dell'esercito*, 5 vols. (Rome: Istituto Poligrafico, 1960-64).

BRS

ARPINATI, LEANDRO (b. Civitella di Romagna, February 29, 1892; d. Malacappa, Bologna, April 22, 1945). Leandro Arpinati, *ras* (q.v.) of Bologna and undersecretary at the Interior Ministry between 1929-33, was the son of an anticlerical Socialist innkeeper. Of genuine proletarian origins and background, he was a mechanic in various places including Turin, where he became an anarchist of sorts, and from 1913 worked as a railways electrician at Bologna. Among a small group of anarchists campaigning for intervention in the Great War, he was exempted by his profession from military service.

He was one of the founders of the Bologna Fasci di Combattimento (q.v.) in April 1919 and became its leader in the spring of 1920. Under Arpinati's guidance, the *fascio* became, from October 1920 on, the organized center of the city's middle-class offensive against socialism. In the notorious Palazzo d'Accursio (the Bologna town hall) incident of November 21, Fascist violence resulted in the death of ten people and effectively prevented the newly-elected Socialist municipal council from taking office. Financed by the Po Valley agrarians, Arpinati's city squadristi (*see* SQUADRISTI) extended their violence into rural areas, establishing a pattern for much of north and central Italy. Like other exponents of squadrist agrarian Fascism, he opposed the Pacification Pact (q.v.) and the transformation of the movement into a party.

After the March on Rome (q.v.), Arpinati dominated affairs in Bologna, simultaneously as provincial Party secretary, deputy, and Podestà (q.v.), enhancing his own and the city's reputation with the construction of a vast modern sports stadium, opened by Mussolini himself in October 1926. He was suspected of complicity in the 1926 Tito Zaniboni (q.v.) attempt on Mussolini's life, because

Zaniboni's father was among the old anarchist acquaintances he continued to meet, but Mussolini quickly rejected such insinuations.

Arpinati's considerable standing with Mussolini was confirmed by his appointment in September 1929 as undersecretary to the Interior Ministry, whose titular head was Mussolini. In this influential and powerful post, Arpinati accumulated enemies with uncompromising individual and unorthodox views. Apparently personally incorruptible, he was openly and scathingly contemptuous of other "hierarchs" and investigated graft with crusading zeal.

He won the respect of his Ministry officials by his determined resistance to party encroachment on State functions, insisting that competence rather than Fascist pedigree should be the condition for state employment. Reflecting his own belief in the primacy of individual liberty, perhaps the one consistent strand that made some sense of a contradictory career, and the influence of his friend and mentor, Mario Missiroli (q.v.), he was critical in particular of the State's interventionist economic policies and of State powers over the citizen marking the consolidation of Mussolini's dictatorship.

By 1932 Arpinati was almost a dissident element within the regime, perhaps now more a Liberal than a Fascist, protected only by Mussolini's respect and friendship. Even this weakened in face of Party secretary Achille Starace's (q.v.) detailed accusations against him, and in May 1933 he was asked to resign.

Returning to Bologna, Arpinati occupied a small holding at Malacappa, but subject to increasing harassment in July 1934 he was expelled from the party, arrested for "seditious" activity and sentenced to five year's banishment on Lipari. He was allowed to return in 1936 because of his wife's illness, but was still kept under surveillance.

Arpinati saw brief military service in 1940-41, and when he was discharged and returned to his farm, by now totally disillusioned with the regime and its disastrous Nazi alliance, he made contact with Ivanoe Bonomi (q.v.) and members of the royal family, though these meetings had little bearing on the July 1943 coup.

In a final meeting with Mussolini in October 1943, he rejected a political comeback under the Salò Republic (see ITALIAN SOCIAL REPUBLIC) and continued at Malacappa to aid escaped Allied POW's and friends in the Resistance (see RESISTANCE, ARMED). Under threat from both Fascists and Communists, he was killed by a partisan group on April 22, 1945, the day after Bologna's liberation.

For further information see: DBI (7); Y. De Begnac, *Palazzo Venezia: Storia di un regime* (Rome: La Rocca, 1950); A. Iraci, *Arpinati l' oppositore di Mussolini* (Rome: Bulzoni, 1970).

PM

ART. See PAINTING AND SCULPTURE

ASCOLI, MAX (b. Ferrara, June 25, 1898; d. New York, January 1, 1978). Anti-Fascist leader and intellectual, Ascoli came from a wealthy Jewish business family and took a degree in law at the University of Rome. In 1929 he was arrested by the Fascist police for collaboration in the underground movement Italia Libera (q.v.) and in 1931 came to the United States on a Rockefeller grant. In America he established close and important friendships with liberal circles and in the Roosevelt government, and from 1933 to 1958 he was on the faculty of the New School for Social Research. Ascoli became a U.S. citizen in 1939 and the next year married Marion Rosenwald, a wealthy heiress who generously financed aspects of the anti-Fascist cause.

A firm antitotalitarian, in 1940 Ascoli became president of the Mazzini Society (q.v.) and attempted to steer it toward a liberal-democratic, anti-Communist coalition of exiles and Italian-Americans in support of American policy. He resigned from the Mazzini Society in 1942 to serve on the staff of Nelson Rockefeller's Coordinator of Inter-American Affairs office, but continued to have a great influence on the government's Italian policy, especially through his friendship with Assistant Secretary of State Adolf A. Berle, Jr.

After World War II he founded and directed *The Reporter* (1949-1968) and was a member of the Council on Foreign Relations.

For further information see: Max Ascoli and Arthur Feiler, *Fascism for Whom?* (New York: Norton, 1938); *New York Times*, January 2, 1978.

PVC

ATTOLICO, BERNARDO (b. Canneto di Bari, January 17, 1880; d. Rome, February 9, 1942). Italian diplomat, Attolico played a vital role in political-military relations with Nazi Germany during the 1930s. From a wealthy landowning family, he took a degree in jurisprudence and began an extensive career abroad. Attolico served in London during World War I, at the Paris Peace Conference in 1919, as high commissioner for Danzig from 1920-21, and with the League of Nations, where he was vice-secretary from 1922 to 1927. In 1927 he became ambassador, first at Rio de Janeiro, then at Moscow from 1930 to 1935 (where he negotiated the Italo-Soviet Pact of Friendship in September 1933). In July 1935, after Hitler had induced Mussolini to recall Ambassador Vittorio Cerutti (q.v.), Attolico was sent to Berlin. A nonideological diplomat, he opposed the Anti-Comintern Pact (q.v.) and when Joachim von Ribbentrop became Nazi foreign minister in February 1938, he began to grow apprehensive of German ambitions, warning Foreign Minister Galeazzo Ciano (q.v.) and Mussolini of Hitler's intentions. Attolico provoked disapproval from Nazi officials for his growing anti-German stance, but he encouraged the signing of the Pact of Steel (q.v.) because he believed Mussolini could thereby keep Hitler in check. When Hitler attacked Poland, Attolico tried desperately to keep Italy out of the war, and in April 1940 he was recalled as a result of pressures from Hitler, serving thenceforth as ambassador to the Holy See.

For further information see: DBI (4).

PVC

AUDISIO, WALTER (b. Alessandria, June 28, 1909). A partisan fighter, Audisio joined the underground Communist movement in 1931. Arrested by the Fascist police in 1934, he was condemned to five years confinement on the island of Ponza. In September 1943 he organized the first partisan group in Monferrato (Piedmont), using the pseudonym "Colonel Valerio," and later commanded the Communist "Garibaldi" forces in Mantua and the lower Po Valley.

In January 1945 Audisio was assigned as an officer to the headquarters of the Corpo Volontari della Libertà in Milan. On April 28 he was sent with a group of partisans to Dongo, where Mussolini and Claretta Petacci (q.v.) were being held. Audisio convened a partisan military tribunal that ordered the death penalty for Mussolini, Petacci, and fifteen other captured Fascists. On the late afternoon he moved Mussolini and Petacci to the Villa Belmonte at Giulino di Mezzegra, where he carried out the execution of the dictator and his mistress (some sources attribute the actual execution to Michele Moretti). Later that day he also supervised the execution at Dongo of Alessandro Pavolini (q.v.), Paolo Zerbino, Fernando Mezzasoma (q.v.), Ruggero Romano, Augusto Liverani, Paolo Porta, Luigi Gatti, Goffredo Coppola, Ernesto Daquanno, Mario Nudi, Vito Casalinuovo, Pietro Calistri (Salustri?), Niccolò Bombacci (q.v.), Francesco Barracu (q.v.), and an obscure journalist named Utimberger (Hintermayer?).

Audisio was elected a deputy in 1948, and in 1963 went to the Senate.

For further information see: EAR (1); Attilio Tamaro, *Due anni di storia, 1943-45* 3 (Rome: Tosi, 1950).

PVC

AUTARCHY. The policy of achieving Italian economic independence, autarchy became a major element in Fascist planning during the 1930s. Mussolini believed that a forceful foreign policy hinged on Italy's ability to be self-sufficient in the economic sphere. Agriculture was the first sector to be affected by the goal, primarily through the "Battle for Grain" (q.v.). In January 1929 all government agencies were required by decree to purchase only nationally produced goods, and in September 1931 the regime increased tariff duties on all foreign products.

In the face of the League of Nations economic sanctions in 1935 (due to the Ethiopian War [q.v.]) autarchy was given a major impetus, and high tariffs, import quotas, and embargos on industrial goods were increased significantly. In 1937 a High Commission for Autarchy was created to supervise these policies. The state-owned petroleum monopoly, AGIP (Azienda Generale Italiana Petroli), developed refineries to handle imported oil and undertook oil and natural gas explorations, coal mining was stepped up and allocations imposed, concerted efforts were made to discover minerals and other raw materials (bauxite was found in the Gargano region), and research programs were set up to create synthetic fibers.

Autarchy was an unrealistic goal for a country with such limited resources, and it imposed severe hardships on many Italians. Higher prices, a production decline in some industries, and job layoffs occurred, and some plant and work techniques had to be changed. Textiles and construction were particularly hard hit. Nevertheless, a group of about thirty large firms (Ansaldo, Terni, Fiat, and others) were given fixed quotas of iron and coal that enabled them to survive the government's policies.

For further information see: Shepard B. Clough, *Economic History of Modern Italy* (New York: Columbia University, 1964); Felice Guarneri, *Battaglie economiche tra le due guerre*, 2 vols. (Milan: Garzanti, 1953); S. La Francesca, *La politica economica del fascismo* (Bari: Laterza, 1973).

                                                                                                                              PVC

AVENTINE SECESSION. One of the most important phases of the Italian anti-Fascist opposition (*see* ANTI-FASCISM), the Aventine Secession occurred as a result of the murder of Matteotti (*see* MATTEOTTI CRISIS) and the resultant crisis. Within days after Matteotti's kidnapping by Fascists, about 150 deputies from the Socialist, Popular, Republican, Constitutional Democratic, and Communist parties vacated the Chamber of Deputies (*see* PARLIAMENT) in protest. Taking their name from the protest of Gaius Gracchus and his followers during the ancient Roman Republic (the Aventine is one of the hills of Rome), the leaders of the anti-Fascist Aventine declared themselves the only true representatives of the Italian people and announced their dedication to the overthrow of Mussolini and the Fascist government. The foremost leaders of the movement were F. Turati (q.v.) of the Socialist party, Antonio Gramsci (q.v.) of the Communist party, and Giovanni Amendola (q.v.). Along with Mario Ferrara and Meuccio Ruini, Amendola carried on a constant campaign against Mussolini in the columns of *Il Mondo*, trying to persuade King Victor Emmanuel III (q.v.) to dismiss Mussolini and call for new elections.

The king, fearing both a leftwing revolution and the possibility that he would be replaced by the duke of Aosta (*see* SAVOIA, AMEDEO DI, DUKE OF AOSTA), refused to take action, even though he was confronted with the most overwhelming evidence of Fascist complicity. The reliance and hope the Aventine leaders placed in the king was, in fact, their greatest weakness. With the exception of the Communists, all of the participants in the movement were dedicated to the legal overthrow of the Fascist government through constitutional methods. By withdrawing from the Chamber, they had committed a symbolic revolutionary act, but they refused to adopt revolutionary tactics, assuming instead a "moral" position. Gramsci, who realized that a different strategy was necessary, called for a united front of political parties and revolutionary action among the workers and peasants. But the other political forces were tied to traditional, legalitarian methods and rejected the call for violence.

Between June and November 1924 the Aventines tried to keep anti-Fascist sentiment alive, but Mussolini acted after initial uncertainty. Parliament had been recessed after the Aventine withdrawal, rendering their protest less conspicuous;

on June 30 Mussolini appointed a new cabinet that included some leaders from the Aventine parties, thus demonstrating his "moderate" policies. The Aventine was further weakened by refusal of Pope Pius XI to sanction a political alliance between the Socialists and the Popolari. In November Amendola assembled the National Union of Liberals and Democrats, but it, too, continued to be tied to legalistic tactics. At the same time the Communist deputies deserted the Aventine and returned to Parliament, where they constantly attacked Mussolini and the Fascist government. Finally, on January 3, 1925 Mussolini, pushed on by the intransigent Fascists, confronted the nation with the assumption of total responsibility and in effect declared his dictatorship. The Aventine, which issued a "Manifesto of Protest," remained powerless. In the first six months of 1925, they prepared for new elections and in July they publicly accused Emilio De Bono (q.v.) of crimes against the anti-Fascist opposition. In September the revolutionary, or Maximalist, Socialists abandoned the Aventine, followed a month later by the Republicans. In 1926 Mussolini's "Exceptional Decrees" (q.v.) declared the seats of all Aventine deputies forfeit, along with those of the Communists.

For further information see: Alberto Giovannini, *Il rifiuto dell'Aventino* (Bologna: Mulino, 1966); Ariane Landuyt, *Le sinistre e l'Aventino* (Milan: Feltrinelli, 1973); Adrian Lyttelton, *The Seizure of Power* (London: Weidenfeld & Nicolson, 1973); Giuseppe Rossini, *Il delitto Matteotti* (Bologna: Mulino, 1966).

MSF

AXIS, ROME-BERLIN. The Axis was the Fascist regime's dominant international relationship from 1936 to 1945. Mussolini first publicly used the phrase in his November 1, 1936 Milan speech: Rome-Berlin was "an axis around which may cooperate all European states animated by a will to collaboration and peace." Collaboration had little to do with it, and peace still less, but the Axis did operate on a variety of levels: ideological, personal, political, and ultimately military. Ideological ties came first, and dated from the 1920s; Mussolini's hostility to Weimar and support of the German extreme right was a constant in his early diplomacy. On the German side, Hitler wooed Mussolini from afar with requests for meetings, but only the National Socialist election victory of 1930 induced the Duce to take his German "pupil" seriously and begin offering advice on political tactics through Giuseppe Renzetti (q.v.).

Mussolini's patronage of Hitler did not survive the first year of National Socialist power. The Führer moved more rapidly than Mussolini thought politic to persecute the Jews, pressure the Church, and defy the Western powers by rapid rearmament. The dictators' first meeting at Venice on June 14-15, 1934 was fraught with misunderstandings, particularly over Austria, where the local Nazis rose six weeks later against the government of Mussolini's protege Dollfuss and messily assassinated the latter. The putsch failed, and Mussolini moved temporarily closer to the West to counter German expansionism. But that same expansionism was indispensable to the Duce's own imperial aspirations. French Foreign

Minister Pierre Laval's offers of a free hand in Ethiopia, which led to the January 1935 Rome Agreements (q.v.), were a direct consequence of fear of Germany.

Italian estrangement from Hitler did not survive British opposition to the conquest of Ethiopia, despite covert German arms shipments to Haile Selassie I (q.v.). By January 1936 Mussolini insisted to an emissary of the Führer's that Fascist Italy and National Socialist Germany shared a "common destiny." That the Duce never said anything of the sort to other powers attests to his relative sincerity; as prophecy, the mark was accurate indeed. In the summer joint intervention in Spain led to further rapprochement and to Galeazzo Ciano's (q.v.) visit to Berlin and Berchtesgaden in October to conclude agreements on cooperation in Spain, in the Balkans, and in opposing multilateral international agreements. Mussolini set his seal on the bargain with his November 1 speech. The Axis would paralyze Western opposition to Italy's self-assertion in Spain and to its drive for Mediterranean hegemony. The implicit price of German support was the eventual surrender of Austria. By late 1936 Ciano was already preparing a rapprochement and possible alliance with Yugoslavia as a fall-back defense line for Italy's Balkan sphere.

Western mockery of the Guadalajara (*see* GUADALAJARA, BATTLE OF) fiasco, and Mussolini's summer 1937 "unknown submarine" campaign against the Spanish Republic further estranged Italy from Britain and France. Mussolini's September 1937 visit to Germany was a public display of solidarity between Fascist and National Socialist revolutions and a further step in the reinforcement of the Axis. Mussolini returned dazzled with the display of German power and unity. By the end of 1937 he had left the League of Nations and joined the German-Japanese Anti-Comintern Pact (q.v.), a connection which ultimately led to the Tripartite Pact of September 27, 1940 and, after Pearl Harbor, to the Rome-Berlin-Tokyo wartime alliance.

Paradoxically, Hitler's surprise absorption of Austria in March 1938 further strengthened the Axis, not because of his protestations of gratitude for Italian acquiescence but because the German army was now at the Brenner Pass. Fear of Germany henceforth reinforced anti-Western expansionism, although Hitler did his best in his May 1938 visit to Italy to reassure Italian opinion with pledges of eternal respect for the Italo-German border. Privately, Hitler also pressed for a military alliance. Ciano persuaded Mussolini to refuse at this point, despite the dictator's conviction that a military dimension to the Axis would overwhelm the West. To reassure Hitler of Italian loyalty and show his contempt of the "Jew-ridden" democracies, Mussolini did move that summer and fall to draft German-style anti-Jewish laws (*see* ANTI-SEMITISM). The legislation made no distinction between practicing and converted Jews, and thus estranged the Vatican; the apparent imitation of Germany alienated important Party figures and an influential segment of public opinion.

Even more alarming was Hitler's handling of the Czech crisis that he had created without consulting his Italian partners. Despite German secretiveness and the absence of Italo-German military agreements, Mussolini did not shrink in September 1938 from promising Hitler Italy's intervention if Britain went to war; Mussolini's bellicosity as recorded in Ciano's diary suggests the Duce meant it. But a last-minute British offer of surrender if Mussolini saved the West's face was too good to resist. He therefore fleetingly played at Munich his old role of senior dictator and patron of Hitler. The explosion of joy that greeted the peacemaker's return to Rome was highly embarrassing; the Italian people were clearly not ready to "die for Prague" or for an empire stretching from Gibraltar to the Persian Gulf to which Mussolini aspired.

In the unquiet fall and winter which followed, Mussolini attempted to exploit the Axis for Italian gain. First came the apparently pusillanimous French, from whom demonstrators in the Fascist Chamber demanded "Tunisi, Nizza, Corsica, Gibuti!" The French were unimpressed. Then came Albania, which Mussolini had long considered "an Italian province without a prefect," and of which Ciano had urged annexation since April 1938 by alleging that the Germans too coveted that small and uninviting country. But before Mussolini could act, on March 15, 1939, Hitler seized rump Czechoslovakia in violation of the Munich agreements and without consultation with Rome. The shock to the Axis and to Mussolini's self-esteem was severe, and German appetite presaged encroachment on Yugoslavia and the rest of Italy's Balkan hunting preserve. Mussolini consoled himself with German reassurances and the thought that Italy could not "play the whore" with the democracies, and went on to occupy Albania on April 7. Berlin received official notice only the night before.

With the West convinced that the two dictators were acting in unison, further delay in concluding the Italo-German alliance seemed neither necessary nor desirable. In early May, during Ciano's talks with Joachim von Ribbentrop, German Foreign Minister, in Milan, Mussolini suddenly ordered immediate agreement to the automatic defensive-offensive pact the Germans proposed; French press reports of Milanese popular hostility to Ribbentrop appear to have piqued him. But he agreed only on the verbal understanding, which the Germans immediately ignored, that the state of Italian and German armaments made postponement of the inevitable war against the West advisable until 1943.

The day after the signing of the Pact of Steel (q.v.) on May 22, Hitler informed his generals he intended to crush Poland "at the first favorable opportunity"; Wehrmacht preparations already assumed September 1, 1939 as the target date. Rome had news of German-Polish friction, but until early August assumed that Hitler would consult, as the alliance required, if action impended. Realization of German duplicity led to Ciano's abortive mission to Salzburg (August 11-13); the correct judgment of Mussolini and Ciano that the West would belatedly fight failed to move Hitler. Fear of ridicule and of the ideological enmity of the democracies, and lust for "our part of the booty in Croatia and Dalmatia" (Ciano) vied in Mussolini's mind with a new-found awareness of Italy's serious military weaknesses. Western assurances of goodwill, pressure from Ciano, the king, and the military, and the public's obvious dismay at war finally won out. While the Germans struck at Poland, Mussolini embarrassedly secured Hitler's release from the obligation to fight. Italy remained Germany's ally, but a "nonbelligerent" one.

The German military, to whom the task of shoring Italy up in war would have fallen, breathed easier, even while they muttered about Italian "betrayal." Hitler still hoped for Italian intervention to confuse the French. Mussolini carefully avoided committing himself to genuine neutrality, and Italo-German friction over control of the Alto Adige and Berlin's too-close ties with Moscow failed to produce a breach. The most Mussolini did was urge Hitler in a January 1940 letter to seek a compromise peace. The Duce's real purpose, as his contemporaneous military preparations made clear, was to postpone the expected German offensive in the West until Italy could participate.

But Hitler refused to wait, and Mussolini's military subordinates and the monarchy refused to fight. Not until the great German victories of May 1940 freed him could the Duce belatedly enter the war on June 10 (*see* FRANCE, INVASION OF). Despite propaganda about "*Due popoli, una guerra*" ("Two peoples, one war"), this was no coalition war with joint objectives and coordinated military action. Neither nation had much use for its ally; German opinion still regarded the Italians as traitors, cowards, and shameless freeloaders, while Italians viewed the Germans as rigid, overbearing, brutish, and insatiable. Mussolini himself refused to tolerate German units in the Mediterranean. He evaded German offers in April to incorporate an Italian Army in the attack on the Maginot line in Alsace, and in September-October 1940 refused German armored divisions for North Africa. But Mussolini's own military refused to do the job; as he complained, the generals waited for everything to resolve itself "on the political plane." Only a barrage of threats from Rome drove Rodolfo Graziani (q.v.) hesitantly forward into Egypt in September and overcame the foot-dragging of Pietro Badoglio (q.v.) over the October 1940 attack on Greece (an operation Hitler had vetoed in August, along with a joint Italo-German attack on Yugoslavia Mussolini had also urged). In October, Hitler's occupation of Romania, as usual without adequate consultation, impelled Mussolini to act in Greece behind his ally's back. Hitler swallowed the affront, but the Greeks routed Visconti Prasca's (q.v.) legions and threatened to conquer Albania. The British also struck, sinking three Italian battleships at Taranto on November 11-12 and destroying Graziani's numerically superior but ill-armed and worse-trained and worse-led troops in North Africa in December 1940-February 1941.

The collapse of Italy's independent war effort and claim to great power status aroused a certain *Schadenfreude* in Hitler. He had lost much of his earlier reverence for the Duce, whom he came to compare unfavorably with Romania's Marshal Antonescu. But further damage to Mussolini's prestige, or the collapse of the regime, which demoralization and internal ferment in Italy presaged, was unacceptable. It would hand the British their first strategic success of the war and would give Hitler's own military subordinates dangerous ideas. Hitler therefore moved to salvage Italy while saving Mussolini's face and preserving "the strongest binding link of the Axis, the mutual trust of the respective chiefs of state." The Luftwaffe, Field Marshal Erwin Rommel, and massive German concentrations in Romania took over the Mediterranean, North African, and Balkan war, while preserving a facade of Italian independence. Italy had nevertheless passed irrevocably from theoretically equal Axis partner to being the first of Greater Germany's satellites.

What little independence Mussolini still preserved derived from Hitler's judgment that the Mediterranean was a strategic backwater. Germany would outdistance all rivals in the race for world mastery by crushing the Soviet Union in a "Weltblitzkrieg" before the United States could intervene. Characteristically, Hitler gave Mussolini no official word of the final decision to attack until the Wehrmacht had begun to roll on June 22, 1941. Shortly before, Mussolini had attempted to raise his stock within the Axis by offering Hitler troops for the impending campaign; the consequence was the dispatch of many of Italy's best units to the Ukraine. Mussolini also followed Hitler lightheartedly after Pearl Harbor in the latter's imprudent declaration of war on the United States.

Nineteen forty-two did not bring the expected Axis victories. By early 1943 Allied landings in French North Africa and the uninspired but implacable British pursuit after El Alamein had confined Rommel to Tunisia. The Soviets, in encircling Stalingrad, virtually destroyed the Italian Army in Russia. Defeat dictated a reassessment of Italy's ties with Germany. As spring 1943 drew on and the Axis bridgehead in Tunisia collapsed, Mussolini's diplomats and high command advised Italy's exit from the conflict with increasing urgency. In the background a variety of establishment plots against the regime flourished under the silent and ambiguous patronage of the monarch.

The Allied landing in Sicily on July 10, 1943 was decisive. Mussolini met Hitler near Venice and, despite the insistence of Vittorio Ambrosio (q.v.) and others, evaded telling Hitler face to face that Italy could not continue. Ambrosio, the King, and the Carabinieri (*see* POLICE AND INTERNAL SECURITY) thereupon exploited the Fascist Grand Council's (q.v.) quasi-repudiation of Mussolini to dismiss and arrest the dictator on July 25 and replace him with the resurrected Badoglio. The Germans were at first too preoccupied in Russia to do more than strengthen their forces in Italy, and Badoglio's profuse assurances that Italy would live up to its Axis obligations confused the issue. But the Allied armistice announcement on September 8 swept away all remaining ambiguity. Hitler swiftly and ruthlessly executed FALL ACHSE, his contingency plan against Italian defection. All over the peninsula German units closed the Italian armed forces down with a minimum of fighting. One of Hitler's closest advisers later remarked that Italy's main contribution to the joint war effort was the huge arms and supply dumps it surrendered in September 1943; the remark was not entirely just, but it was typical of the German view of the other end of the Axis.

In the aftermath, Hitler set up Mussolini, whom German paratroops and SS commandos had rescued from Badoglio's Carabinieri, as titular leader of northern Italy. Mussolini was now at Hitler's mercy. The latter had lost what remained of his respect for the Duce, and a residual sentimental attachment did not prevent him from annexing Trentino, Alto Adige, Venezia Giulia, and part of Venetia in violation of his 1938 pledge. Nor did the Salò Republic's (*see* ITALIAN SOCIAL REPUBLIC) variegated and ferocious private armies and police forces conceal Wehrmacht and SS rule of northern Italy. At the end, in April 1945, the German commanders and Mussolini both broke their Axis pledges and raced to secure separate agreements with the Allies. The Germans won, and absentmindedly turned Mussolini over to the partisans who shot him on April 28, two days before Hitler committed suicide. Only Mussolini's removal finally separated the two regimes—for had the Allies caught him, they could scarcely have evaded the duty of reuniting Fascists and National Socialists in the dock at Nuremberg.

Interpretation of the Axis relationship inevitably involves a judgment on the nature of the Fascist regime. The majority view, which Jens Petersen has restated forcefully, is that the alliance between the two regimes was a consequence of common ideological and, in Petersen's version, social roots; the latter claim is doubtful in view of the enormous disparities between the two societies. Renzo De Felice has countered with an analysis of the pre-1933 relationship, which emphasizes differences between the two leaders and movements, and he suggested that the Axis was primarily a tactical political alignment comparable to the allegedly nonideological Russo-German Pakt. But De Felice has undermined his own case by conceding elsewhere that by the late 1930s the character of the regime, especially "subjectively," was decisive: ". . . Fascist Italy could not avoid allying itself with Hitler."

For further information see: F. W. Deakin, *The Brutal Friendship* (New York: Harper & Row, 1962); Renzo De Felice, *Mussolini e Hitler. I rapporti segreti 1922-1933* (Florence: Le Monnier, 1975); Giordano Bruno Guerri, *Galezzo Ciano: una vita 1903-1944* (Milan: Bompiani, 1979); Meir Michaelis, *Mussolini and the Jews* (Oxford: Clarendon, 1978); Jens Petersen, *Hitler—Mussolini. Die Entstehung der Achse Berlin-Rom, 1933-1936* (Tübingen: Niemayer, 1973); Ferdinand Siebert, *Italiens Weg in den Zweiten Weltkrieg* (Frankfurt A. M., Bonn: Athenzum, 1962); Mario Toscano, *The Origins of the Pact of Steel* (Baltimore: Johns Hopkins, 1967); D. C. Watt, "The Rome-Berlin Axis, 1936-1940. Myth and Reality," *Review of Politics* 22 (1960); Elizabeth Wiskemann, *The Rome-Berlin Axis* (London: Collins, 2nd. rev. ed., 1966).

MK

AZIONE CATTOLICA ITALIANA. According to its official statute, Azione Cattolica Italiana (Italian Catholic Action) is the name of the "organization of Catholic laity for a special and direct collaboration with the apostolic hierarchy of the Church."

Italian Catholic laymen began to organize themselves in 1867-68 in order to defend the Church within the context of the newly recreated Kingdom of Italy. For this purpose Pope Pius IX endorsed the creation of the Società della Gioventù Cattolica Italiana (Society of Italian Catholic Youth). Various other organizations were established over the years, and in 1905 Pius X reorganized them all into four groups: Unione Popolare per la Propaganda (Popular Union for Propaganda), Unione Economico-Sociale (Economic-Social Union), Unione Elettorale (Electoral Union), and the Società della gioventù (Youth Society). In order to coordinate them—and to link them together with two additional groups, the Federazione Universitaria Cattolica Italiana (Italian Catholic University Federation) (1892) and the Unione fra le Donne Cattoliche Italiane (Union of Italian Catholic Women) (1908)—Pope Benedict XV set up an executive council in 1915 for what was to be the umbrella organization known as Azione Cattolica Italiana.

With the birth of the Partito Popolare Italiano (q.v.) after World War I and the creation of three Catholic syndical confederations (Lavoratori, Cooperative, and Mutualità e Previdenza), the activities of Catholic Action were greatly reduced. In 1919 the Unione Economico-Sociale and the Unione Elettorale were both abolished, and a sharp distinction was made between the political-economic activity of the Popolari and the unions on the one hand, and the religious-spiritual functions of Catholic Action on the other. With the encyclical *Ubi Arcano Dei* (December 23, 1923), Pius XI (q.v.) specifically defined the role of the laity as subordinate to and integrated into that of the Church and gave to Catholic Action a primary role as mediator between civil society and the ecclesiastical hierarchy. In October 1923 new statutes had already given Catholic Action a better-defined national structure by creating three coordinating organs—a central committee, a diocesan committee, and a council of parishes—each directed by laymen with the assistance of priests; in each of these organs participated representatives from the various men's, women's, youth, and university groups.

This overall strengthening and unification of Catholic Action was largely a response to the rise and triumph of Fascism. The Vatican abandonment of the Popolari in 1923-24, and of the Catholic trade unions in 1926, meant that Catholic Action remained the only organization in Italy to represent the socio-economic interests of the Church and to assume responsibility for "politics as it affected the altar."

Although Catholic Action was an openly declared apolitical organization, the Fascist regime resented and opposed its activity in some areas of Italian life. Especially crucial was the education of youth, and the crisis of 1931 broke out over that issue, despite the fact that article 43 of the Concordat (*see* LATERAN PACTS) of 1929 had recognized the existence of Catholic Action and sanctioned its functions. Attacks in the Fascist press and physical assaults against local Catholic Action groups (coordinated by G. Giuriati [q.v.]) led to protests from the Pope, culminating in the blistering anti-Fascist encyclical *Non abbiamo bisogno*. An agreement was finally reached on September 3, 1931, stipulating that Catholic

Action would pursue only recreational and educational goals of a strictly religious nature (but no sports activity), that its clerical and lay leaders were responsible to the bishops, and that former members of the Partito Popolare Italiano were to be removed from its leadership.

The 1931 crisis caused a temporary decline in the membership of Catholic Action, but by the mid-1930s its enrollment began to rise even higher than it had been. Further Fascist hostility against Catholic Action was unleashed in 1938 over the regime's racial policies, but in 1939 Pius XII (q.v.) replaced the lay leadership with clerics in order to protect its directors from Fascist attacks.

In the long run, the Church's careful policy and constant organizing efforts meant that when Fascism collapsed in 1945, the new postwar Catholic political leadership was to emerge out of the ranks of Catholic Action.

For further information see: Sandro Rogari, *Santa Sede e fascismo. Dall'Aventino ai Patti Lateranensi* (Bologna: Forni, 1977); Sandro Rogari, "Azione cattolica e fascismo," *Nuova Antologia* (January-June, July-September, 1978); Pietro Scoppola and Francesco Traniello, eds., *I cattolici tra fascismo e democrazia* (Bologna: Mulino, 1975); Giovanni Spadolini, *Le due Rome. Chiesa e stato fra '800 e '900* (Florence: Le Monnier, 1973).

SR

B

BADOGLIO, PIETRO (b. Grazzano Monferrato, September 28, 1871; d. Grazzano Monferrato, November 1, 1956). Mussolini's preeminent Marshal and successor as head of government rose meteorically from Lieutenant Colonel in 1915 to Lieutenant General in 1917. His Twenty-seventh Corps broke under the Austro-German onslaught at Caporetto (q.v.), but he survived through political connections and became Armando Diaz's (q.v.) Deputy Chief of Staff; although Badoglio had been at fault, his enemies later exaggerated his responsibility for the disaster. Diaz, Badoglio, and Ugo Cavallero (q.v.) reorganized the Army and led it to final victory. Badoglio succeeded Diaz in November 1919 but resigned in February 1921, after Ivanoe Bonomi (q.v.) curtailed his authority.

Badoglio did not share his fellow general's partiality to the Fascist movement and was willing forcefully to oppose the March on Rome (q.v.) (the Monarchy was not interested). Afterwards Badoglio improved his relations with Mussolini, and became ambassador to Brazil in December 1923. Following Antonino Di Giorgio's (q.v.) failure to modernize the Army, Cavallero (now undersecretary of war) invited Badoglio to become Army Chief of Staff in April 1925. In June this post was combined with the newly created position of Chief of the Supreme General Staff (Capo di Stato Maggiore Generale). Theoretically Badoglio was now responsible for coordination of the war planning and preparations for all other service divisions, as well as for the Army. In practice Mussolini reserved the higher direction of the armed forces to himself, and forced the Fascist Francesco Grazioli (q.v.) on Badoglio as deputy. With Cavallero and Grazioli, Badoglio planned a limited reorganization in March 1926, which imprinted Badoglio's conservative thinking on the Army. Differences developed between Badoglio and Cavallero, and although Badoglio became a Marshal in June 1926, Cavallero increasingly undermined him. Rumors of a Fascist antimonarchical coup apparently led Badoglio to reinforce the Rome garrison; Cavallero then persuaded Mussolini to reduce Badoglio's power. In February 1927 Mussolini separated the position of Army Chief of Staff from that of Capo di Stato Maggiore Generale. Badoglio continued in this grand position, but was ineffectual.

In September 1928 Badoglio readily accepted Mussolini's offer of the governorship of Tripolitania and Cyrenaica and the task of completing their pacification, but retained his previous post. After unsuccessful negotiations in June 1929 with the Senussi guerrilla leader Omar el Muktar, Badoglio employed Rodolfo Graziani (q.v.) in a vain attempt to defeat the Libyans with traditional methods. In June 1930 Badoglio decided on drastic measures and ordered the native population confined in camps (sixty thousand died), then he barricaded the Egyptian frontier with wire. Graziani's force hanged Omar el Muktar in September 1931, and eliminated the last guerrillas by December; Badoglio left Libya in December 1933.

Through 1934 Badoglio opposed Mussolini's Ethiopian plans, stressing the uncertainty of reaction in Europe. After the January 1935 Rome Agreements (q.v.) with French Foreign Minister Pierre Laval, Badoglio urged delay, while maneuvering for command. In June he concluded with General Maurice Gamelin, Inspector of the French army, an agreement for Franco-Italian military collaboration against Germany. As tension with Britain mounted in August and September, Badoglio begged Mussolini to avoid a Mediterranean war, which he insisted would reduce Italy "to a Balkan level."

Mussolini held firm, however, and when Emilio De Bono (q.v.) invaded Ethiopia Badoglio intrigued to replace him. After De Bono bogged down, Mussolini appointed Badoglio commander in late November. An Ethiopian offensive surprised Badoglio in mid-December, and his counterattacks met limited success. But in later operations he routed the Ethiopians with lavish employment of artillery and mustard gas, and destroyed Haile Selassie's (q.v.) army at Mai Chew on March 31, 1936. On May 5 Badoglio entered Addis Ababa, and Mussolini appointed him viceroy of Ethiopia. Realizing the difficulties ahead, Badoglio relinquished his post after two weeks and returned home to enjoy honors and perquisites; the king named him duke of Addis Ababa in July. In the ensuing years Badoglio failed to press for the modernization of the armed forces with sufficient vehemence and did not appreciate the importance of armor; the Nazi tank units he saw in action during Mussolini's 1937 visit to Germany left Badoglio ostensibly unimpressed. Politically Badoglio was privately critical of Italian intervention in Spain until Mussolini ordered a public display of solidarity.

In 1939-40 Badoglio initially opposed war, but in April and May of 1940, once Mussolini's aim was clear, the Marshal acquiesced and seized for himself as much authority as possible. As chief of the Comando Supremo (q.v.), Badoglio was Mussolini's principal military adviser, but his prerogatives were vague and subject to circumvention through the Duce's direct relationship with the service undersecretaries. Badoglio exercised retarding influence on plans against Yugoslavia and Greece throughout the summer of 1940 (although a German veto was decisive). In October Badoglio grudgingly approved the Greek enterprise once Mussolini had decided upon it (the Marshal believed Greek resistance would be ineffectual although he considered the operation strategically inopportune). Once the attack proved a fiasco, Badoglio hastened to assemble proof that he had opposed it, and insisted to Mussolini and to the Germans that the dictator alone bore responsibility. After Badoglio's claims spread in informed circles, Roberto Farinacci (q.v.) accused Badoglio in *Il Regime Fascista* of incompetence (November 23, 1940). The Marshal demanded a retraction, and when Mussolini did not order one, ultimately resigned on December 4. News that Cavallero was to succeed him prompted a last-minute attempt to hang on, but the king supported Mussolini.

In vengeful retirement Badoglio began to stir in mid-1942, and attempted to mend his relations with monarchy, Church, and even the Allies. By early July 1943 he had emerged as the only suitable candidate to succeed Mussolini. Enrico

Caviglia (q.v.) lacked support in the armed forces, and Vittorio Ambrosio (q.v.) was essential at his military post. Upon Mussolini's arrest on July 25, 1943, the king appointed Badoglio chief of government. The Marshal attempted to reassure the Germans ("the war continues") while belatedly and ineptly negotiating with the Allies. The Allied armistice announcement of September 8 caused him, Ambrosio, and the king to flee Rome for the Allied lines, leaving the Italian armed forces leaderless under German guns. Badoglio subsequently led the rump Italian government into "cobelligerence" alongside the Allies. He returned to private life after the Allies reached Rome in June 1944.

For further information see: Pietro Badoglio's unreliable *L'Italia nella seconda guerra mondiale* (Milan: Mondadori, 1946); Lucio Ceva, "Appunti per una storia dello Stato Maggiore generale fino alla vigilia della 'non belligeranza,'" *Storia Contemporanea* 10, 2 (April 1979); Giovanni De Luna, *Badoglio. Un militare al potere* (Milan: Bompiani, 1974); Piero Pieri and Giorgio Rochat, *Badoglio* (Turin: UTET, 1974).

MK/BRS

BAISTROCCHI, FEDERICO (b. Naples, June 9, 1871; d. Rome, June 1, 1947). Army Chief of Staff, Baistrocchi aided Fascist activities throughout 1922 when he was Naples Corps artillery commander. A Naples municipal councillor from 1922 to 1924 and then appointed a Fascist deputy, Baistrocchi remained in Parliament until 1939. He commanded the Naples Division from 1926 to 1931 and the Verona Corps from 1931 to 1933 before his appointment as war undersecretary in July 1933. Baistrocchi sought Army modernization and politicization, infuriating Pietro Badoglio's (q.v.) clique. While Baistrocchi supported Italo Balbo's (q.v.) attempt to replace Badoglio and opposed Emilio De Bono's (q.v.) Ethiopian War (q.v.) plans, his Fascism, modernization plans, and military response to Engelbert Dollfuss's murder (*see* ANSCHLUSS) impressed Mussolini. He appointed Baistrocchi Chief of Staff in October 1934. Baistrocchi, remaining war undersecretary, effectively organized the Ethiopian campaign. In turn, Mussolini promised ample modernization funds after an Ethiopian victory. Struggling against Alessandro Lessona (q.v.), Badoglio, De Bono, and Rodolfo Graziani (q.v.), Baistrocchi created a coherent campaign strategy. As difficulties mounted in December 1935, Baistrocchi gained ascendancy. He proposed replacing Badoglio in January 1936, cementing their enmity. Thereafter Baistrocchi's efforts were crucial in achieving victory. Baistrocchi then resumed creating a mobile Army with increased firepower, oriented toward Mediterranean-African warfare. But disputes with Lessona over Ethiopian military organization, with Galeazzo Ciano (q.v.) over aid to Francisco Franco, with Thaon di Revel (q.v.) over finances, and with Badoglio over policy, brought Baistrocchi down. Mussolini dismissed him in October 1936 with a count's title. Baistrocchi refused commands in Spain and Ethiopia in 1937, while failing to replace Alfredo Dallolio (q.v.) in 1938. He became a senator in March 1939. From retirement Baistrocchi attacked Alberto Pariani's (q.v.) policies. Arrested in April 1945 for pro-Fascism, Baistrocchi was acquitted in September 1946.

For further information see: DBI (5); Giorgio Rochat, *Militari e politici nella preparazione della campagna d'Etiopia* (Milan: Angeli, 1971); John Sweet, *Iron Arm: The Mechanization of Mussolini's Army, 1920-40* (Westport, Conn.: Greenwood, 1980).

BRS

BALABANOFF, ANGELICA (b. Chernigov, Russia, 1869; d. Rome, November 25, 1965). Despite her Russian birth, Angelica Balabanoff was closely identified for much of her life with Italian socialism and anti-Fascist exiles. She broke decisively with her privileged family background by enrolling at the controversial Université Nouvelle of Brussels in 1897. A few years later, after being converted to Marxism by Antonio Labriola (q.v.) at the University of Rome, she joined the Italian Socialist party (*see* PARTITO SOCIALISTA ITALIANO—PSI). Between 1903 and 1907 Balabanoff worked as a propagandist among Italian emigrants in Switzerland, where she and Maria Giudice created *Su, Compagne*, a special woman's journal.

In 1911 Balabanoff joined the intransigent faction of the PSI, despite her reservations about its ideological coherence. At the Socialist party congress of Reggio Emilia in 1912, she supported Mussolini's motion for expulsion of the right reformists. After the intransigent victory, Balabanoff became a member of the PSI executive and assisted Mussolini as coeditor of *Avanti!* With the outbreak of World War I, Balabanoff assumed a radical internationalist stance. Forced to flee to Switzerland in 1915, she became a vital link between the PSI and the Zimmerwald movement, which brought the leftist factions of European Socialist parties together in an effort to bring about the end of the war. As a member of the international Socialist Commission, she gradually drifted further left; at the Kienthal Conference of Socialists (April 1916), she voted for the Leninist resolution that urged conversion of the pacifist struggle into a proletarian revolution. It was not until she returned to Russia in May 1917, however, that Balabanoff became a Bolshevik. Her "Letters from Russia" encouraged the pro-Leninist stance *Avanti!* eventually assumed.

After her disillusionment with Comintern policies in 1921, Balabanoff emigrated to Stockholm and Vienna. In 1926 she went to Paris to become director of the *Avanti!* in exile. Bitterly anti-Fascist, Balabanoff represented the PSI in the Anti-Fascist Concentration (*see* ANTI-FASCISM). She nonetheless opposed Pietro Nenni's (q.v.) attempt to unify the Maximalist PSI with Filippo Turati's (q.v.) PSU (Partito Socialista Unitario). Following the Socialist split at the Congress of Grenoble in 1930, Balabanoff continued to defend Maximalism (*see* PARTITO SOCIALISTA ITALIANO) as editor of *Avanti!* In 1936 she emigrated to the United States where she often spoke out against Fascism. Balabanoff returned to Italy in 1948. Pehaps her most enduring contributions to anti-Fascist propaganda are the mocking sketches of Mussolini in her numerous memoirs.

For further information see: Gaetano Arfé, *Storia dell'Avanti!*, 2 vols. (Milan: Edizioni Avanti!, 1956-58); Angelica Balabanoff, *Memorie* (Milan: Società Editrice Avanti!, 1931); Angelica Balabanoff, *Wesen und Werdegang des italienischen Fascismus* (Leipzig: Hess, 1931); Luigi Cortesi, *Le origini del Partito comunista italiano. Il PSI dalla guerra di Libia alla scissione di Livorno* (Rome-Bari: Laterza, 1973).

NGE

BALBO, ITALO (b. Quartesana, June 6, 1896; d. Tobruk, June 28, 1940). Politician and pioneering aviator, organizer and *ras* (q.v.) of Fascism in Ferrara, *quadrumvir* (q.v.) of the March on Rome (q.v.), minister of aviation, and governor of Libya, Balbo was one of the most powerful and most popular of the Fascist *gerarchi* (leaders). Courageous, enthusiastic, an excellent organizer and a born leader, he was one of the few genuine heroes that Italian Fascism—which boasted of transforming an entire nation into heroes—ever produced. Often mentioned as a rival and heir to Mussolini, Balbo ranked second only to Costanzo Ciano (q.v.) on the list of succession.

Balbo's boyish charm and his stylish manners sometimes misled foreigners to assume that he came from an aristocratic background. In fact he came from a family of schoolteachers. His formal education was fitful. As a youth he preferred to frequent political cafes in Ferrara and Milan, where he met the major radical and revolutionary figures of the day, including Mussolini. Unlike many of his fellow *gerarchi* (including the Duce), who came to Fascism from socialism or syndicalism, Balbo was a republican. An ardent interventionist in 1914-15, then during World War I a decorated lieutenant in the Alpini, in the immediate postwar period Balbo edited a military newspaper *L'Alpino* (to which he gave a strongly anti-socialist slant) and earned a degree in political science from the Istituto Cesare Alfieri (University of Florence) with a thesis on Giuseppe Mazzini.

Balbo was not a Fascist of the "first hour." Until the winter of 1920-21, he was still actively campaigning for the republicans. On February 13, 1921, however, he accepted an appointment as political secretary of the Fasci di Combattimento (q.v.) in Ferrara. Behind this "conversion" lay a heavy dose of careerism. The great landowners around Ferrara, frustrated and frightened at the power of the Socialist agricultural labor unions, saw in the local *fascio* the nucleus of an organization that could break the socialists. In Balbo they saw a leader who could transform the Fascists into a fighting unit. Balbo's contribution was to organize the Fascists along military lines. In a campaign that lasted about a year and a half, his Blackshirt squads (*see* SQUADRISTI) destroyed the socialists around Ferrara and then joined forces with other Blackshirt groups from neighboring cities until the entire Po Valley was in Fascist hands. In preparation for an eventual march on Rome, in early 1922 Balbo (together with General Asclepia Gandolfo [q.v.], Ulisse Igliori, and the Marchese Dino Perrone Compagni [q.v.]) laid the basis for the Fascist Militia (q.v.). During the March on Rome (q.v.) in October 1922, Balbo, together with Emilio De Bono (q.v.), Cesare Maria De Vecchi (q.v.), and Michele Bianchi (q.v.), was appointed *quadrumvir*, responsible for the party and the Militia. His main activity was to make whirlwind tours between Rome, Perugia, Florence, and Foligno to inspect and encourage the Fascist columns.

Once Mussolini was in power, Balbo remained head of the Militia until his moral implication in the murder of the anti-Fascist priest, Don Giovanni Minzoni (q.v.), fatally beaten August 23, 1923, by two Fascist thugs, forced Balbo to resign. During his temporary political eclipse, Balbo founded *Il Corriere Padano*, which developed into one of the best provincial newspapers of the era. In 1924 he married Countess Emanuella Florio, whose family ranked among the minor nobility. The Balbos eventually had two daughters and a son.

Following a brief period as Undersecretary to the Minister of National Economy, in 1926 Balbo was appointed undersecretary (1926-29) and then minister (1929-33) of aviation. Between 1928 and 1933 Balbo participated in or personally led four mass training flights (*crociere*). The most famous was the "Crociera del Decennale" (1933) from Orbetello to Chicago and back, a double crossing of the North Atlantic at the head of twenty-four seaplanes. The *crociere* lifted Balbo from the status of provincial politician to an international celebrity who ranked with Lindbergh, Amelia Earhart, St. Exupéry, Francesco De Pinedo (q.v.) and other heroes of aviation's "Golden Age" of record flights.

Although these expeditions were an enormous propaganda success both for the Fascist regime and for its fledgling Air Force in its struggle to gain recognition as a service equal to the Army and the Navy, critics argued that the *crociere* were like Italy's participation in international racing competitions (such as the Schneider Cup) and world record attempts: they were only sporting successes. Meanwhile military aviation, the aircraft industry, and commercial aviation languished. Balbo himself admitted that the *crociere* were an attempt to compensate "with will power and with enthusiasm" for Italy's lack of material means. Moreover, his ideas, especially for building military aviation, often suffered from lack of funds, inter-service rivalry, and the Duce's own questionable political judgments. For political reasons Mussolini rejected Balbo's plan to reorganize the armed forces in 1933, a program that would have greatly strengthened the Navy and the Air Force at the expense of the Army. On Balbo's return from the expedition to Chicago, Mussolini informed him of his appointment as governor of Libya.

Stunned and bitter at this sudden "exile," Balbo left for Tripoli in January 1934. Flattered by comparisons of his work with that of Lyautey in Morocco and by the authority and prestige inherent in the governor's office, Balbo plunged into building Libya into a "quarta sponda," a fourth shore integral to the mother country, an old dream of Italian colonists. Through government-financed and directed colonization programs, Balbo rooted hundreds of peasant families on small farms along the bleak coastal plain of Tripolitania and in the more hospitable highlands of Cyrenaica. In preparation for the mass colonization (a first migration of twenty thousand in 1938 was followed a year later by a group of ten thousand colonists), Balbo transformed the colony socially, economically, and culturally. He completed the 1,800 kilometers of coastal highway (inaugurated in 1937), rebuilt Tripoli, promoted tourism, and hosted scientific and religious congresses. In January 1939 the four coastal provinces were proclaimed an integral part of Italy. For the eight hundred thousand indigenous Libyans, who outnumbered the Italians in 1940 by about eight to one, Balbo favored full citizenship and integration into Fascist social and economic organizations. His proposal, however, conflicted with the Fascist regime's anti-Semitic legislation and was rejected by the Fascist Grand Council (q.v.).

Throughout his career, Balbo had a reputation as a dissident and a frondeur. In fact, Balbo cared little for Fascist achievements such as the Lateran Pacts (q.v.) or for the corporative state (*see* CORPORATIVISM AND THE CORPORATIVE STATE). However, he generally supported Mussolini's policies until they took a markedly pro-German turn at the time of the Axis (*see* AXIS, ROME-BERLIN). Balbo joined Luigi Federzoni (q.v.), Giuseppe Bottai (q.v.), Dino Grandi (q.v.) and others in a "loyal opposition" within the Grand Council. On the issues of the anti-Semitic legislation, the Axis, and Italy's intervention in World War II, Balbo was virtually the only one of the *gerarchi* to make his opposition unequivocal and vociferous. Significantly, however, he never broke with Mussolini. When war came in June 1940, even though he was pessimistic about its outcome, Balbo accepted the command of Italian forces in North Africa. While on an inspection mission, trying to rally his badly trained, demoralized, and poorly equipped troops, Balbo was shot down over Tobruk by Italian batteries which mistook his aircraft for an enemy incursion.

For further information see: DBI (5); Italo Balbo, *Diario 1922* (Milan: Mondadori, 1932); Italo Balbo, *Sette anni di politica aeronautica* (Milan: Mondadori, 1936); Paul Corner, *Fascism in Ferrara* (London: Oxford University Press, 1975).

CGS

BALDESI, GINO (b. Florence, September 22, 1879; d. Rome, February 12, 1934). Syndicalist leader and an early member of the Socialist party (*see* PARTITO SOCIALISTA ITALIANO), Baldesi became editor of *La Difesa* (Florence) and advocated intervention in World War I. In 1918 he was made assistant secretary of the Confederazione Generale del Lavoro (q.v.). Elected a deputy in 1921, Baldesi attended the Livorno Congress of the Socialist Party that same year and took a reformist position, arguing in favor of syndical autonomy. After the congress he adhered to the Partito Socialista Unitario and edited its organ, *La Giustizia* (Rome). He attempted unsuccessfully to join with the Fascists in creating an apolitical syndical movement, and in August 1922 he was among the signers of the Pacification Pact (q.v.). By 1924 he had turned completely against Fascism, participated in the Aventine Secession (q.v.), and was ousted from Parliament in 1926. He collaborated from time to time with *Il Lavoro* (Genoa) but essentially retired to private life thereafter.

For further information see: DBI (5); MOI (1).

PVC

BALLA, GIACOMO (b. Turin, July 14, 1871; d. Rome, March 5, 1958). A painter who joined the Futurist movement in its early stages, Balla merged "Divisionist" (or Neo-Impressionist) painting techniques with social themes and helped set the style of early Futurist painting. Although Carlo Carrà (q.v.), Luigi Russolo, and Umberto Boccioni wrote the document, Balla signed the original *Manifesto on Futurist Painting* on February 11, 1910, and he later participated in the *Technical Manifesto of Futurist Painters* in April 1910. Balla also worked on sculpture and theater presentations and devised "words-in-freedom" art. Somewhat older than the other members of the group, and teacher of two of them (Gino Severini and Boccioni), Balla executed some intriguing paintings incorporating vigorous motion such as *Dynamism of a Dog on a Leash* (1912). This painting clearly shows the simultaneity of image characteristic of Futurist painting. By the 1920s he had fully entered the period of so-called "second futurism," and his work became increasingly suited to commercial and political publicity.

For further information see: Ettore Colla, "Pittura e scultura astratta di G. Balla,"*Arte Visive* 2 (September-October 1952); Fernando Tempesti, *Arte dell'Italia fascista* (Milan: Feltrinelli, 1976).

JH

BARRACU, FRANCESCO MARIA (b. Santu Lussurgiu, Cagliari, November 1, 1895; d. Dongo, April 28, 1945). Barracu was undersecretary to the president of the Council of Ministers in the Salò Republic (*see* ITALIAN SOCIAL REPUBLIC). After a military career in Libya during and after World War I, Barracu returned to Italy in 1928. Ordered to Somalia for the Ethiopian War (q.v.), he commanded counterguerrila operations for seventeen months. On March 3, 1937, Barracu led his Third Arab-Somali Battalion in fierce battle at Uara Combo, losing an eye but winning a gold medal. Pensioned off, he became a journalist and minor Fascist official. Barracu was *federale* (provincial party secretary) of Bengasi in 1941-42, and of Catanzaro in 1943. He rallied to Mussolini in September 1943, helping persuade Rodolfo Graziani (q.v.) to become his defense minister. Appointed ministerial undersecretary, Barracu established Mussolini's Cabinet Office at Bogliasco near Salò. His extreme Fascism led him to accuse even Alessandro Pavolini (q.v.) and Guido Buffarini-Guidi (q.v.) of moderation. In 1945 he proposed a last-ditch defense of Milan but followed Mussolini in flight. Captured by partisans, Barracu was executed at Dongo.

For further information see: DBI (6).

BRS

BARZINI, LUIGI SR. (b. Orvieto, February 7, 1874; d. Milan, September 6, 1947). A prominent journalist, Barzini was one of the most celebrated and effective Italian correspondents. He began his career in 1899 working for a small newspaper in Rome, and then Luigi Albertini (q.v.) sent him to London as a correspondent for *Il Corriere della sera*. He covered the Boxer Rebellion in China in 1900, and during the next few years he traveled widely in Argentina, the United States, Russia, Japan, and Morocco; he gained fame for his participation in a Peking-to-Paris automobile trek, and reported many of the most important international events of the time. In 1921 he went to the United States with Albertini to attend the Washington Naval Conference and in January 1923 founded the Italian language daily *Il Corriere d'America* (New York), which became a Fascist propaganda organ. Barzini returned to Italy in 1931 after selling his paper to Generoso Pope, but his reputation had long since declined. He directed *Il Mattino* (Naples) for a year with the backing of Arnaldo Mussolini (q.v.) but resigned after arousing some criticism. Mussolini made him a senator in 1934, and thereafter he was a correspondent for *Il Popolo d'Italia*, in which capacity he covered the Spanish Civil War (q.v.) and the Russian campaign in World War II. During the Salò Republic (*see* ITALIAN SOCIAL REPUBLIC) he was appointed president of the Agenzia Stefani (q.v.).

For further information see: DBI (7).

PVC

BASILE, CARLO EMANUELE (b. Milan, 1885; d. Pavia, 1946). Fascist bureaucrat and deputy, Basile took a degree in law from the University of Turin (with a thesis on Georges Sorel), was elected mayor of Stresa in 1914, and then volunteered in World War I. He became Fascist federal secretary of Novara in 1925, president of the Associazione Combattenti (Veterans Association) in 1927 and entered Parliament in 1929. During the 1930s he held a number of important posts, including membership in the party directorate and on the Consiglio Nazionale (National Council) for the Camera dei Fasci e delle Corporazioni. In October 1943 he was appointed prefect of Genoa, a position he held until June 26, 1944 when he was made undersecretary for the army in the Salò Republic (*see* ITALIAN SOCIAL REPUBLIC). Captured by partisans in April 1945 while attempting to escape with a large amount of money, Basile was accused of war crimes and the deportation of Italian workers to Germany and was condemned to thirty years' imprisonment.

For further information see: EAR (1); NO (1928).

PVC

BASSO, LELIO (b. Varazze, Savona, December 25, 1903). Socialist leader and journalist, Basso was educated by his father with the purpose of entering politics. By 1919, when he went to Milan for schooling, he became a Socialist and in 1921 was a member of the Socialist youth organization at the University of Pavia. While still a student he became a committed anti-Fascist, collaborating in 1924 with Piero Gobetti's (q.v.) *Rivoluzione Liberale* and founding in 1925 the journal *Pietre*. He was active in the Maximalist or revolutionary wing of the Socialist party (*see* PARTITO SOCIALISTA ITALIANO) and in 1928 was arrested for anti-Fascist activity and imprisoned on the island of Ponza. Returning to Milan in 1931, he worked as a lawyer and wrote extensively on Fascism and Socialism. In March 1940 he was arrested again and accused of trying to reconstruct the Socialist party and imprisoned in Perugia for several months. Between 1940 and 1943 he worked diligently to reorganize militant Socialist opposition to Fascism. In January 1943 Basso and others formed the Movimento di Unità Proletaria, which in August was renamed the Partito Socialista Italiano di Unità Proletaria (PSIUP, *see* PARTITO SOCIALISTA ITALIANO). He helped organize the April 1945 strikes against the regime in Milan.

In July 1945 Basso was made vice secretary of the party and then served in the Constituent Assembly (*see* COSTITUENTE) and in the first postwar Chamber of Deputies. In 1947 he founded the journal *Quarto Stato* and became secretary general of the Socialist party. His position in the Socialist party was never on solid ground, however, and in 1963 he opposed the formation of the center-leftist government. As a result, he reestablished the unitary party, from which he resigned in 1970.

For further information see: DSPI; MOI (1); Lelio Basso, *Neocapitalismo e sinistra europea* (Bari: Laterza, 1969).

MSF

BASTIANINI, GIUSEPPE (b. Perugia, March 8, 1899; d. Milan, December 19, 1961). Diplomat and bureaucrat, Bastianini was a Fascist "of the first hour" and a squad leader who later gained prominence in the field of foreign policy.

His first international activity was among Italian emigrant communities as secretary of the Fasci all'Estero (q.v.) (Fasci Abroad) in 1923-26. Moving into a more conventional diplomatic environment, Bastianini held a series of posts, notably ambassador to Poland (1932-36), undersecretary at the Foreign Ministry under Galeazzo Ciano (q.v.) (1936-39), and ambassador in London (1939-40). In the context of prevailing Italian policy, he was a moderate who counseled avoidance of too close an entanglement with Nazi Germany and war with Britain.

Ironically, Bastianini's career reached its apogee during World War II. He was governor of Dalmatia (1941-43), thereby incurring after the war the unproved accusation of war criminal. Summoned back to Rome in February 1943 as undersecretary to Mussolini, now foreign minister, Bastianini struggled to free Italy from German domination. With Hungary and Romania he advocated greater autonomy for small states within Hitler's New Order and, through the Vatican, approached the Western Allies for a separate peace. His efforts were overtaken by the fall of the Fascist government, which he helped to precipitate by voting against Mussolini in the fateful Fascist Grand Council (q.v.) session of July 24 and 25, 1943. For this he was condemned to death by the Salò Republic (*see* ITALIAN SOCIAL REPUBLIC), but found refuge in Switzerland.

During the Fascist era Bastianini had published widely on nationalist themes, and his memoirs appeared shortly before his death.

For further information see: DBI (7); G. Bastianini, *Uomini, cose, fatti* (Milan: Vitigliano, 1959).

AC

BASTICO, ETTORE (b. Bologna, April 9, 1876; d. Rome, December 1, 1972). Commander in Libya in 1941-43, Bastico led a division, then the Third Corps in Ethiopia, and returned to head the Alessandria Corps. In April 1937 he replaced Mario Roatta (q.v.) in Spain, capturing Santander in August, but was relieved in October after clashes with Francisco Franco. Bastico received command of the Second Army facing Yugoslavia in May 1938 and in November was given the newly motorized Sixth (Po) Army. He became a senator in March 1939. Despite his poor showing in the August 1939 maneuvers, Mussolini named Bastico Governor of the Dodecanese in December 1940. The following July he became Governor of Libya and Erwin Rommel's nominal superior. Bastico clashed repeatedly with Rommel over his refusal to accept subordination. While Rommel's tactics were brilliant, he foolishly ignored Bastico's strategic and logistical directives. Promoted to marshal in August 1942, Bastico was relieved in February 1943 after Tripoli's fall.

For further information see: E. Bastico, *Il ferreo terzo corpo* (Milan: Mondadori, 1937); Ruggero Fainizza, *De Vecchi—Bastico—Campioni* (Forlì: Valbonesi, 1947).

BRS

"BATTLE FOR GRAIN." The main objectives of Fascist agricultural policy were placating the rural classes, preserving the nature of rural life, and increasing Italy's food supply. In July 1923 Arrigo Serpieri (q.v.) organized the first efforts to examine the country's agricultural problems since Mussolini came to power. He was particularly concerned with protecting the small landowners, tenant farmers, and sharecroppers, although other Fascists desired to sacrifice these interests to those of the larger landowners. As part of this overall program, Serpieri announced the idea of Bonifica Integrale (q.v.) in order to improve the arable land available. In 1925, however, Mussolini altered the emphasis by proclaiming the "Battaglia del Grano," which became an integral part of his broader policy of autarchy (q.v.). The essential purpose of the policy was to increase Italy's production of wheat and other cereals and therefore make Italy independent in food production. A "*comitato permanente del grano*" (Permanent Grain Commission) was created, and the program was accompanied by an enormous propaganda campaign that presented the "battle" as a phase of Italy's struggle for national prestige.

The "Battle for Grain" was also in part an aspect of Mussolini's rural policies, in which the values of the clean, sober life of the peasantry were extolled over the decadent life of the cities. Restrictions against moving from the countryside reinforced this point (*see* DEMOGRAPHIC POLICY), and the peasants were in effect tied to the soil.

By the use of marginal lands, land reclamation, and persuading farmers to grow wheat instead of other crops, an increase in production was in fact attained, but the program's overall impact on the Italian agricultural economy was negative. The price of grains remained artificially high despite increased production, largely because of protectionist tariffs, and the government was forced to buy neglected crops whose production was declining. In the south it encouraged the preservation of the *latifondi* (large estates) and extensive agricultural methods. (Although in 1938 a program to break up the large landed estates of the south was begun, its results were insignificant.) The soil was drained of needed minerals, grazing land and crop diversification were limited, and by World War II the impact of the program was evident.

For further information see: Shepard B. Clough, *Economic History of Modern Italy* (New York: Columbia University Press, 1964); Renzo De Felice, *Mussolini il duce* (Turin: Einaudi, 1974); Felice Guarneri, *Battaglie economiche tra le due guerre* (Milan: Garzanti, 1953); Adrian Lyttelton, *The Seizure of Power* (London: Weidenfeld & Nicolson, 1973).

MSF

BAUER, RICCARDO (b. Milan, January 6, 1896). Anti-Fascist journalist, Bauer received a degree in economics and fought as a volunteer in World War I. In 1924 he was editor of *Il Caffè* (Milan), a weekly journal which he founded with Ferruccio Parri (q.v.), an outspoken anti-Fascist, and others. He also collaborated with Piero Gobetti's (q.v.) *Rivoluzione liberale* (Turin). After the passage of the "Exceptional Decrees" (q.v.) Bauer helped some of the leading anti-Fascist figures leave Italy and was arrested in 1927 and imprisoned on Lipari Island. Released a year later, he helped Carlo Rosselli (q.v.) and Ernesto Rossi (q.v.) establish Giustizia e Libertà (*see* ANTI-FASCISM). Arrested again in October 1930, he was sentenced to twenty years' imprisonment and sent to Ponza and Ventotene. Bauer was freed after the fall of Mussolini, and took part in the first meeting of the Party of Action (*see* PARTITO d'AZIONE). Between 1943 and 1945 he was a leading organizer for the resistance, both as head of the Action Party's military junta and a member of the general staff. After the liberation of Rome, he was director of the partisan groups for the party. He resumed his career as a writer after the war.

For further information see: DSPI; EAR (1); Riccardo Bauer, *Alla ricerca della libertà* (Florence: Parenti, 1957); Charles F. Delzell, *Mussolini's Enemies* (Princeton: Princeton University Press, 1961).

MSF

BELLONI, ERNESTO (b. Pavia, August 23, 1885). Italian chemical industrialist and Fascist bureaucrat, Belloni was a professor of pharmaceutical chemistry at the University of Pavia. During World War I he directed the chemical division of a large laboratory and lost his right hand in an accidental explosion. In

1919 he was attached to the Italian delegation at the Paris Peace Conference and to the reparations committee.

Belloni's business interests and political career were closely linked, and he frequently used his influence to enhance his own financial position. He joined the Fascists in 1920, first as a Blackshirt (*see* SQUADRISTI), and in 1921 became part of the directorate of the Milan *fascio*. He presided over the Rome Congress of Fascists in 1921 and was special commissar for Naples in October 1922. In 1921 he also founded a chemical company that later became a large combine (SIPE— Società Italiana Prodotti Esplosivi) of which he was president. Belloni was elected to Parliament in 1924 and again in 1929, and served as the president of a commission that drafted the corporate laws.

Belloni was Podestà (q.v.) of Milan in the 1920s, where he was embroiled in a scandal that ended his political career. In 1928 Roberto Farinacci (q.v.) charged Belloni with bribery in negotiating a large loan with Dillon Read Bank of the United States (also implicating Mussolini's brother Arnaldo). Belloni resigned as Podestà in September and sued Farinacci, but evidence of financial irregularities resulted in the former's suspension and subsequent expulsion from the party, and his exclusion from the Chamber of Deputies.

For further information see: NO (1928); Harry Fornari, *Mussolini's Gadfly: Roberto Farinacci* (Nashville: Vanderbilt University Press, 1971).

PVC

BELLUZZO, GIUSEPPE (b. Verona, November 25, 1876; d. Milan, May 21, 1952). A well-known engineer and minister, Belluzzo came from a poor working-class family. He studied at the Milan Polytechnical Institute on a scholarship and became a professor and the author of numerous treatises on engine construction.

An interventionist, during World War I he served on the war resources and industrial mobilization boards. In the early 1920s he supported the Fascist party and was elected to Parliament on the *listone* or coalition list of candidates of 1924. On July 10, 1925, Mussolini appointed him minister of national economy, directing many of the regime's important economic policies such as the stabilization of the lira and the "Battle for Grain" (q.v.). A true technocrat who distrusted capital when it was divorced from management, he believed the state should intervene directly in firms that it subsidized and should plan industry for defense purposes. Belluzzo's concern for developing Italy's raw materials made him a precursor of autarchy (q.v.).

In July 1928 Belluzzo was transferred to the Ministry of Public Instruction, where he instituted secondary technical education programs. In October 1929 he became a state minister, and in 1934 a senator. In addition to his political posts, Belluzzo also held numerous offices in industrial corporations.

For further information see: DBI (8); Adrian Lyttelton, *The Seizure of Power* (London: Weidenfeld & Nicolson, 1973).

PVC

BENCIVENGA, ROBERTO (b. Rome, October 2, 1872; d. Rome, October 23, 1949). One of the few conspicuous opponents of Fascism the military produced, General Bencivenga served in World War I as a close assistant of Luigi Cadorna (q.v.) and as a highly successful brigade commander. In 1919 he left the Army to become a commentator on military affairs. Elected deputy in 1924, he joined the Aventine Secession (q.v.) and challenged Mussolini's brother Arnaldo Mussolini (q.v.) to a duel in 1926. When the latter refused, Bencivenga publicly accused the Mussolini family of cowardice. The result was a sojourn at Ponza (1926-30). Like many opponents of the regime, Bencivenga wrote Mussolini in 1935 expressing solidarity with the Ethiopian enterprise. He resumed political activity in 1943, served as Pietro Badoglio's (q.v.) representative in occupied Rome, and secured election to the Constituent Assembly (*see* COSTITUENTE) in 1946, as a monarchist first and then as a member of the neo-Fascist Uomo Qualunque movement.

For further information see: *Chi è?* (1948); DSPI.

MK

BENEDUCE, ALBERTO (b. Caserta, March 29, 1877; d. Rome, April 26, 1944). A noted financier and industrialist, Beneduce took a degree in mathematics and in 1904 was employed by the Ministry of Agriculture as a demographic expert. He published widely and held several university posts. In the years before and during World War I he developed close ties with the democratic left, and worked with Leonida Bissolati (q.v.) and Francesco Nitti (q.v.). In 1912 he was responsible for the creation of INA (Istituto Nazionale d'Assicurazione), the national insurance agency.

An interventionist, he volunteered for combat in 1915, then helped launch the government loan drive, and in 1917 established the national veterans' organization known as Opera Nazionale Combattenti. In 1919 he was elected to Parliament, and in 1921 became minister of labor under Ivanoe Bonomi (q.v.). During this brief period in office he developed his idea that the government had to intervene directly in private sectors of the economy.

Beneduce joined the democratic opposition to Fascism after 1922, but continued to believe in the possibility of "legalizing" the movement and after 1925 grew increasingly closer to the regime. Because of his friendship with Giuseppe Volpi (q.v.) and connections in industrial and banking circles, he worked in various capacities for the government in the 1920s, and was instrumental in the "Stabilization of the Lira" (*see* QUOTA NOVANTA) in 1927. In 1926 he was made president of Bastogi, a major electrical company.

During the 1930s Beneduce developed a plan whereby the government raised money for industry by selling secure shares through public agencies (Consorzio di Credito per le Opere Pubbliche [CREDIOP] and Istituto Nazionale di Credito per le Imprese di Pubblica Utilità [ICIPU]) for utilities and public works projects and was instrumental in the growth of the Institute for Industrial Reconstruction or IRI

(Istituto per la Riscostruzione Industriale) (*see* INDUSTRY), of which he was president.

In April 1939 Mussolini made him a senator, and he received membership in the Fascist party. In 1940 he resigned, because of declining health, from all public positions, but he maintained numerous and powerful posts in the private sector. During the last years of his life he was active in promoting the electrification of Italy's southern regions.

For further information see: DBI (8).

PVC

BENELLI, SEM (b. Filettole, Prato, August 10, 1877; d. Zoagli, Genoa, December 18, 1949). A celebrated playwright, between 1898 and 1905 Benelli wrote a number of unsuccessful plays, worked for newspapers, and collaborated briefly with F. T. Marinetti (q.v.). His first theatrical success was *Trignola* (1908), followed by *La Maschera di Bruto* (1908) and *La Cena delle Beffe* (1909). He fought as a volunteer in World War I, joining the Nationalist furor over the peace treaties, and actively campaigned for the seizure of Fiume (q.v.). Elected a deputy in 1919, he adhered to Fascism in 1922. Although Benelli was again elected to Parliament in the *listone* (Fascist list of candidates) of 1924, he broke with Mussolini after the Matteotti murder (*see* MATTEOTTI CRISIS) and signed Benedetto Croce's (q.v.) "Manifesto of Anti-Fascist Intellectuals" (q.v.). In the mid-1930s he drew closer to Fascism again, volunteering in the Ethiopian War (q.v.) but then broke definitively with the regime and fled to Switzerland during World War II.

For further information see: DBI (8); S. Benelli, *Schiavitù* (Milan: Mondadori, 1945).

PVC

BENNI, ANTONIO STEFANO (b. Cuneo, April 18, 1880; d. Lausanne, December 27, 1945). One of the most influential industrialists in the Fascist period, Benni began his career working for the small electrical parts company owned by Ercole Marelli. As the firm grew, Benni rose to executive positions. In 1920 he, Marelli, and Giovanni Agnelli (q.v.) created FIMM (Fabbrica Italiana Magneti Marelli), the largest magnet producer in the country, and on Marelli's death in 1922 he took over the entire enterprise.

Benni collaborated with Mussolini as early as 1917, and in 1919 was one of the founders of Confindustria (*see* INDUSTRY). He was also a member of the industrial delegation that attempted to negotiate with the metal workers union shortly before the Occupation of the Factories (q.v.) in September 1920. Benni was elected a deputy in May 1921 on an electoral list supported by the Fascists.

On the eve of the March on Rome (q.v.), Benni believed that Mussolini would tame the intransigent Fascists if he were given a cabinet post, and was instrumental in paving the way for Mussolini's appointment as prime minister. At the end of

1922 Benni was elected president of the Confindustria, in which position he negotiated both the Palazzo Chigi Pact (q.v.) and the Palazzo Vidoni Pact (q.v.). Although he tried to convince Mussolini to normalize the political situation during the Matteotti Crisis (q.v.), he joined the PNF (Partito Nazionale Fascista) (q.v.) in 1925 and became a member of the Fascist Grand Council (q.v.).

Benni aroused the enmity of many Fascist elements by his vigorous opposition to the Corporate State (*see* CORPORATIVISM AND THE CORPORATIVE STATE) and was criticized for simultaneously holding government and private posts. He was removed as Confindustria president in 1933, but two years later Mussolini appointed him minister of communications. Over the next four years he succeeded in electrifying the Italian railway system, reorganizing the merchant marine, and greatly improving the telephone and postal systems.

Benni returned to private business in November 1939 and withdrew from active politics during the Second World War. He was arrested by Fascist police in August 1944 after his refusal to adhere to the Salò Republic (*see* ITALIAN SOCIAL REPUBLIC), but he fled to Switzerland.

For further information see: DBI (8).

PVC

BERGAMINI, ALBERTO (b. San Giovanni in Persiceto, Bologna, June 1, 1871; d. Rome, December 22, 1962). Newspaper editor and liberal politician, in 1899 Bergamini joined the Rome office of *Il Corriere della Sera*. In 1901 Sidney Sonnino (q.v.) invited him to become director of the newly established *Il Giornale d'Italia* (Rome), the chief organ for the liberal right wing. He successfully turned the paper into one of the most authoritative and influential newspapers in Italy (inaugurating the famous "third page" of cultural commentary soon adopted by most other papers in the country) and developed close contacts with the liberal leadership. Under his direction the paper supported the Libyan War, intervention in World War I, and the postwar movement for territorial aggrandizement. Giovanni Giolitti (q.v.) made him a senator in 1920.

Bergamini initially gave cautious support to Fascism—especially in view of its anti-Bolshevik stance—and backed Mussolini's appointment as prime minister, but by late 1923 he joined the opposition and resigned from *Il Giornale*. After a Fascist attack against him in February 1924, Bergamini also resigned as president of the National Press Association and was expelled from the journalists' trade union. *Il Giornale* then came under the control of Fascist journalist Virginio Gayda (q.v.).

In 1942 Bergamini became the center of the liberal anti-Fascist opposition in Rome and established contacts with political leaders like Ivanoe Bonomi (q.v.), Alcide De Gasperi (q.v.), and Giovanni Gronchi (q.v.), forming the nucleus of what became the Committee of National Liberation (q.v.). In July 1943 he held secret talks with Pietro Badoglio (q.v.) and the royal household in an effort to divest Mussolini of power. Following the July 25 coup, Bergamini resumed direction of *Il Giornale* but was arrested during the Nazi occupation. Escaping from prison, he took refuge in the Vatican until the liberation of the city.

In the postwar period, he founded the Concentrazione Nazionale Democratico-Liberale (National Democratic-Liberal Concentration) and headed the promonarchist movement. In 1946 he was elected to the Consulta Nazionale (q.v.) and the Constituent Assembly (*see* COSTITUENTE), and was in the Senate from 1948 to 1953.

For further information see: DBI (9); Biblioteca Comunale G. C. Croce, *In memoria de Alberto Bergamini* (San Giovanni in Persiceto, 1964).

PVC

BERGAMO, GUIDO (b. Montebelluna, Treviso, December 26, 1893; d. Rome, June 26, 1953). A Republican anti-Fascist, Bergamo took a degree in medicine and was highly decorated in World War I. His left-wing interventionism led him to found, together with his brother Mario Bergamo (q.v.) and Pietro Nenni (q.v.), the *fascio* of Bologna in April 1919. By the end of the year, however, he broke with the Fascists and became a dedicated anti-Fascist. Elected a deputy in 1921 and again in 1924, he opposed the legalistic tactics of the Aventine Secession (q.v.) and was forced to retire from politics in 1926. In September 1943, however, he organized partisan formations in the north and fought in the Resistance.

For further information see: DBI (9).

PVC

BERGAMO, MARIO (b. Montebelluna, Treviso, February 8, 1892; d. Paris, May 24, 1963). A leading Republican and anti-Fascist, Bergamo received a law degree from the University of Bologna in 1914, where he cofounded the Alleanza Universitaria Repubblicana. Bergamo was an interventionist and World War I volunteer, who after the war led the Republican wing that advocated major social and political reform for Italy. In April 1919 he founded, along with his brother Guido Bergamo (q.v.), Pietro Nenni (q.v.), and Leandro Arpinati (q.v.), the *fascio* of Bologna, but he joined the anti-Fascists in 1920. His law office was repeatedly destroyed and he himself beaten by Fascist squads.

In 1924 he was elected to Parliament and was made political secretary of the Republican party. Like his brother, Bergamo opposed the purely "moral" opposition of the Aventine Secession (q.v.). In November 1926 he was accused of having participated in a plot to kill Mussolini and, together with Nenni, fled to Switzerland and then to France.

In Paris Bergamo reorganized the Republicans in exile and adhered to the Concentrazione Antifascista (*see* ANTI-FASCISM). Although he resigned as political secretary in 1928 after serious disagreements with his colleagues, he remained a tireless anti-Fascist. He wrote and published widely, frequently in conjunction with fellow anti-Fascists and Republicans, and in 1933 launched a periodical called *I novissimi annunci*. After the Nazi invasion of France, he worked under great personal danger to help Jews and anti-Fascists sought by the Nazis.

Bergamo remained in France after the war, refusing to return to an Italy that he believed had learned nothing from its history.

For further information see: DBI (9).

PVC

BERGONZOLI, ANNIBALE (b. Cannobio, Novara, November 1, 1884). General "Electric Beard" Bergonzoli distinguished himself in Ethiopia under Rodolfo Graziani (q.v.). He commanded the Army's "Littorio" division in Spain, emerged with credit from the Guadalajara disaster (*see* GUADALAJARA, BATTLE OF), and won the gold medal at Santander. In World War II he commanded the forward units in the September 1940 drive on Sidi el Barrani during the Italian invasion of Egypt; without his insistence (unusual among Italian generals of his generation) on leading from the front, the advance might have been even slower than it was. During the ensuing British counteroffensive, Bergonzoli commanded the rear guard until capture in the final encirclement of Italian forces at Beda Fomm on February 7, 1941.

For further information see: Comando delle Forze Armate della Somalia, *La guerra italo-etiopica* (Addis Ababa: Ufficio Topocartografico, 1937); Olao Conforti, *Guadalajara* (Milan: Mursia, 1967); Ufficio Storico dell'esercito, *La prima offensiva britannica in Africa settentrionale* (Rome: Istituto Poligrafico, 1964).

MK

BERNASCONI, MARIO (b. July 7, 1892). Air Force general Bernasconi directed Rodolfo Graziani's (q.v.) warplanes during the Ethiopian campaign (*see* ETHIOPIAN WAR) (November 1935-February 1936), contributing greatly to victory at Ganale Doria in January 1936. Appointed commander of Aviazione Legionaria (Italian air personnel in Spain) in May 1937, Bernasconi began systematic assaults on Republican communications, while supporting Franco's operations. In early 1938 his bombers pounded Republican coastal cities, switching to antishipping strikes after western European and Nationalist protests. Lacking resources for both a strategic bombing campaign and tactical intervention, Bernasconi questioned Gastone Gambara's (q.v.) demands for air support and was relieved in December 1938. Named director of studies and experiments in December 1939, Bernasconi strove for Air Force modernization against tremendous obstacles, a struggle he continued as deputy chief of staff for air armaments in 1942. Receiving command of the Fifth Air Corps in North Africa, he performed wonders despite quantitative and qualitative enemy superiority but collaborated poorly with the Luftwaffe, Ettore Bastico (q.v.), and Giovanni Messe (q.v.). In mid-April 1943, with his command virtually annihilated, Bernasconi was repatriated.

For further information see: Jose Luis Alcofar Nassaes, *La Aviacion Legionaria en la guerra española* (Barcelona: Euros, 1975).

BRS

BERNERI, CAMILLO (b. Lodi, May 20, 1897; d. Barcelona, May 5, 1937). A militant anarchist and anti-Fascist, Berneri was politically active in the Socialist party from his youth. By 1916, however, he left the Socialists and joined the anarchist movement. In 1917 he was drafted but was condemned by a military tribunal and imprisoned on the island of Pianosa. Toward the end of the war he worked on anarchist journals, including *Guerra di classe* (Bologna) and *Il grido* (Naples). Berneri received a degree in philosophy from Florence after the war and wrote for anarchist newspapers. His writings were highly influential and he frequently collaborated with Gaetano Salvemini's (q.v.) *L'Unità* (Florence) and Piero Gobetti's (q.v.) *La rivoluzione liberale* (Turin).

Between 1923 and 1926 Berneri taught school and was in contact with the Florentine anti-Fascist group "Non Mollare." He fled to France shortly thereafter and became highly active in the exiled anti-Fascist movement (*see* ANTI-FASCISM). In Belgium he organized a kind of counterespionage group that sought to expose Fascist agents and spies and continued to publish widely. He was arrested in 1930 and for the next six years spent much time in and out of prison and moving from one country to another. Expelled from France in 1934, he finally settled in Spain two years later. Maintaining contact with Giustizia e Libertà (*see* ANTI-FASCISM), Berneri evolved an independent theory of a future "federalist" revolution in Italy.

In Spain his activities centered on Barcelona, where he edited *Guerra di classe* and helped to promote an Italian volunteer corps to fight against the Fascists. He bitterly criticized the Stalinists, but in 1937 he sought to halt the divisive struggle among Communists, Socialists, and anarchists. On May 5, 1937, Berneri was arrested during a Communist-anarchist fight and two days later was found dead.

For further information see: DBI (9): *Scritti scelti di Camillo Berneri*, ed. P. Masini and A. Sorti (Milan: Feltrinelli, 1964).

MSF

BERTI, GIUSEPPE (b. Naples, July 22, 1901). A radical Socialist, founding member of the Italian Communist Party (*see* PARTITO COMUNISTA ITALIANO), and anti-Fascist, Berti took a law degree from the University of Palermo. In 1918 he was a member of the Federazione Giovanile Socialista (Socialist Youth Federation) and the next year secretary of that group in Palermo. He took part in peasant land seizures in Sicily in 1920, organized student groups, and founded the review *Clarte*. In 1921 he participated in the Congress of Livorno and went over to the Communist party. He was national secretary of the Communist youth federation. Although he originally followed the leadership of Amadeo Bordiga (q.v.), by 1922 he had shifted over to the right wing led by Angelo Tasca (q.v.). He was arrested in 1923 but was released shortly thereafter and helped found the review

Cultura, which took a Gramscian (*See* GRAMSCI, ANTONIO) approach. Arrested again in November 1926 following the "Exceptional Decrees" (q.v.), Berti was imprisoned for three years and then fled to France. He participated in the Comintern as a representative of the Italian party in 1930-31, worked on *Lo Stato Operaio*, and collaborated on a number of other newspapers. He helped negotiate the Pact of Unity with the Socialists in 1934. After the fall of France in 1940, he went to the United States, where he continued to publish *Lo Stato Operaio*. Returning to Italy in 1945, he was elected to Parliament and in 1958 to the Senate.

For further information see: DSPI; MOI (1); Giuseppe Berti, *Russia e stati italiani nel risorgimento* (Turin: Einaudi, 1957).

MSF

BERTI, MARIO (b. La Spezia, February 3, 1881; d. 1960). Reputedly one of the Army's most promising staff officers, Berti helped reorganize Italian forces in Spain after Guadalajara. He served as deputy under Ettore Bastico (q.v.), then as commander from October 1937 to October 1938, when Gastone Gambara (q.v.) displaced him after a lengthy rivalry. In September 1940 Berti commanded the advance on Sidi el Barrani during the Italian invasion of Egypt. His lack of drive led Rodolfo Graziani (q.v.) to take control personally, but the British made good their withdrawal. In December Berti returned from leave in Italy five days after the British counteroffensive had begun, but then proved unable to cope. Graziani dismissed him.

MK

BEVIONE, GIUSEPPE (b. Turin, December 27, 1879). Fascist newspaper editor and bureaucrat, Bevione received a law degree but became a professional journalist. In 1904 he was made editor of *La Stampa* (Turin) and later was that paper's special correspondent in England, Argentina, Tripolitania, and Turkey. A Nationalist and vigorous proponent of the Libyan War, he was elected to Parliament in 1913, 1919, and 1921. In May 1915 Bevione resigned from *La Stampa* in disagreement with its neutralist stance and fought in World War I. Between 1919 and 1923 he was political correspondent for the *Gazzetta del Popolo* (Turin). In July 1921 prime minister Ivanoe Bonomi (q.v.) appointed him undersecretary in the Council of Ministers, and from 1923 to 1926 he was director of *Il Secolo* (Milan), a post he secured with Roberto Farinacci's (q.v.) help after that paper was purchased by Senatore Borletti (q.v.). Mussolini made Bevione a senator in September 1924 and he subsequently was president of the National Insurance Institute. After the liberation of Rome, he was arrested and tried but eventually freed for lack of evidence.

For further information see: *Chi è?* (1948); NO (1928); Giuseppe Bevione, *Due settimane di passione* (Milan: Poligrafia degli operai, 1930).

PVC

BIANCHI, MICHELE (b. Belmonte Calabro, July 22, 1883; d. Rome, February 3, 1930). A leading revolutionary syndicalist labor organizer before World War I, Bianchi was one of Mussolini's closest collaborators during the early years of Fascism. He became an active Socialist while a student in Rome, promptly gravitating to the revolutionary syndicalist wing of the party. Bianchi was active in Socialist journalism, first with *Avanti!*, then with *Gioventù socialista*, and soon became a labor organizer as well, working in Genoa, Savona, Ferrara, and Naples between 1905 and 1910. In 1910 he returned to Ferrara to lead the Chamber of Labor and to edit its newspaper, *La scintilla*. Ferrara had been a major center of revolutionary syndicalism, but the local movement was in some disarray when Bianchi took over. Tactically flexible and politically effective, he managed to restore the strength of the Chamber of Labor, which grew from nine thousand members at the beginning of 1910 to thirty-four thousand by 1912. However, his vehement opposition to the Libyan War of 1911-12 produced friction with the authorities, and Bianchi left Ferrara in August 1912.

With syndicalism on the national level still relatively unsuccessful, Bianchi was one of a number of syndicalists favoring supplementary political action. He went further than most when he stood unsuccessfully for election to the Chamber of Deputies in 1913, but he soon reconverged with his colleagues in the struggle for Italian intervention in World War I. He had a major hand in drafting the manifesto which a committee of syndicalist interventionists issued on October 5, 1914, and he served as political secretary of the Fascio Rivoluzionario d'Azione Internazionalista (*see* FASCI DI AZIONE RIVOLUZIONARIA) that was organized in the aftermath. It was especially through this group that Bianchi came into close contact with Mussolini.

After the war, in which he served as a volunteer, Bianchi participated in the founding meeting of the Fasci di Combattimento (q.v.) and was named to the first central committee of the new organization. At this point he was still much concerned with the working class and with trade union matters, and he was among those Fascists seeking an accommodation with the existing labor movement, especially the Confederazione Generale del Lavoro (q.v.). Certainly he did not view Fascism as an instrument of antilabor reaction. Despite these concerns, however, and despite his syndicalist background, Bianchi was not a significant source of syndicalist ideas within Fascism. He had not been influential in the development of Italian syndicalist theory, nor was he important in the doctrinal transformation that led from syndicalism to corporativism. Though generally sympathetic to the kind of change which former syndicalists like Sergio Panunzio (q.v.) and A. O. Olivetti (q.v.) sought through Fascism, Bianchi was more a day-to-day tactician, politician, and administrator than an ideologue and publicist.

Bianchi was an important proponent of the change of Fascism from a movement to a party during the dispute with dissident provincial Fascists in 1921, and when the party was established in November he became its first general secretary. He promptly helped to engineer a dominant role for the party vis-à-vis the new Fascist labor movement. Mussolini generally left organizational matters to Bianchi and his collaborators in the party oligarchy, and Bianchi proved an effective mediator between intransigent and parliamentary Fascists.

Still, Bianchi himself strongly favored an insurrectionary seizure of power—to avoid alliance with the old political class—and he played a central role in preparing the March on Rome as one of its Quadrumvirs (q.v.). Its ambiguous outcome disappointed him, however; he feared that the continued compromise with non-Fascist politicians would impede a full Fascist transformation of the state. His protest resignation was not accepted, but his influence quickly began to diminish. Appointed general secretary of the Ministry of Interior in November 1922, Bianchi became less active in party affairs and devoted much of his energy to developing a personal clientele through the appointment of prefects in Calabria. Finally, with the internal squabbles of 1923-24, in which he opposed Massimo Rocca (q.v.) and the revisionists, he was forced out of the party.

As a member of the Fascist Grand Council (q.v.), Bianchi was active in the electoral law reform of 1923 (*see* ACERBO, GIACOMO), and when he himself was elected to the Chamber of Deputies in 1924, he resigned his post in the Ministry of Interior. In October 1925 he was appointed undersecretary in the Ministry of Public Works and sought from this position to foster the economic development of his native Calabria. He became undersecretary in the Ministry of the Interior in March 1928, then was made minister of public works in September 1929.

For further information see: Giuseppe Bardellini, *Dall'officina a Palazzo Madama* (Bologna: Brunelli, 1964); Michele Bianchi, *I discorsi, gli scritti* (Rome: Libreria del Littorio, 1931); Renzo De Felice, *Mussolini il fascista* (Turin: Einaudi, 1966); Alessandro Roveri, *Dal sindacalismo rivoluzionario al fascismo* (Florence: Nuova Italia, 1972).

DDR

BIANCO, DANTE LIVIO (b. Cannes, France, May 19, 1909; d. Punta Saint-Robert, Cuneo, July 12, 1953). Italian political leader and partisan, Bianco attended the University of Turin and became a follower of Piero Gobetti (q.v.). An anti-Fascist, in July 1942 he helped found the Partito d'Azione (q.v.). On September 9, 1943 he and a few friends formed a partisan band known as "Italia Libera" which later became incorporated into the Giustizia e Libertà partisan formation. In 1944-45 Bianco was a leading figure in the Piedmontese Committee of National Liberation (q.v.). After the war he resumed his law practice and was among the directors of the Action party in Piedmont.

For further information see: DBI (10); Dante L. Bianco, *Venti mesi di guerra partigiana nel cunese* (Cuneo: Panfilo, 1946).

MSF

BIANCO, VINCENZO (b. Turin, February 11, 1898). An early organizer of the Communist party, Bianco was an industrial worker and a member of the Turin section of the Socialist party in his youth. He was a close friend and collaborator of Antonio Gramsci (q.v.) and participated in the Occupation of the Factories (q.v.) in 1920. After the March on Rome (q.v.) he fled to the Soviet Union, where he trained as a "professional revolutionary." He returned to Italy to organize the Communist anti-Fascist movement and was arrested in 1931. Freed in 1934, Bianco went back to Russia and during the Spanish Civil War (q.v.) he fought with the International Brigades. After Franco's victory, he worked for the Comintern in Russia and the Italian Communist Party. Bianco participated in the armed resistance (*see* RESISTANCE, ARMED) after 1943 and in the postwar period was editor of *Unità* (Milan).

For further information see: MOI (1).

MSF

BIGGINI, CARLO ALBERTO (b. Sarzana, December 9, 1902; d. Padua, November 19, 1945). Fascist intellectual and minister, at the age of eighteen he joined the Fascist youth movement in Genoa. He interrupted his studies to serve in the Army from 1920 to 1924. Biggini adhered to the "Manifesto of Fascist Intellectuals" (*see* "MANIFESTO OF ANTI-FASCIST INTELLECTUALS"), and wrote for the journal *Pietre* (Genoa). Until 1927 Biggini followed the philosophical tradition of Giovanni Gentile (q.v.) and insisted on an open dialogue between Fascism and Italian intellectuals. In 1928 he took a law degree and in 1929 a political science degree, devoting himself thereafter to the study of the corporative system and to Gentile's philosophy of the state.

Biggini joined the PNF (Partito Nazionale Fascista) (q.v.) in 1928, was a professor of constitutional law at the University of Sassari (1932-38), and president of the University of Pisa (1938-41). He was elected a deputy in 1934, and was a member of numerous parliamentary commissions and of the Mistica Fascista (q.v.) commission for the Littorial Games (*See* YOUTH ORGANIZATIONS). Despite the fact that he maintained a good rapport with Mussolini and all currents within Fascism, he often polemicized with intransigents who questioned his political orthodoxy.

Biggini fought as a volunteer in both the Ethiopian War (q.v.) and the Greek campaign, and in 1942 Mussolini made him inspector general of the PNF. In February 1943 he was appointed minister of national education and made a member of the Fascist Grand Council (q.v.) and the party directorate. As minister, he stressed a classical, elitist educational system.

During the July 24-25, 1943 Grand Council meeting that unseated Mussolini, Biggini supported the dictator and drafted a memoir on the unconstitutionality of the vote for King Victor Emmanuel (q.v.). In the Salò Republic (*see* ITALIAN SOCIAL REPUBLIC) Biggini reluctantly became minister of national education again (September 23, 1943) and was responsible for removing university professors who held purely political appointments, prevented schoolteachers from taking an oath to the new government, and fought to save Italian art treasures from the Germans. As a member of the "conciliatory" wing of the Salò regime, he established contact with Resistance elements and non-Fascists in 1944. After the liberation of northern Italy Biggini, who was terminally ill, was protected by anti-Fascists and died in a hospital in Padua.

For further information see: DBI (10).

PVC

BISI, TOMMASO (b. Milan, November 11, 1888). Fascist journalist and bureaucrat, Bisi fought in World War I, later directed the Fascist newspaper *Il Popolo* (Pavia), and with Italo Balbo (q.v.) founded *Alpino*. He held numerous posts in local government and private industry, was secretary for the province of Pavia and was a deputy from 1924 to 1939. Bisi served as undersecretary for the national economy from November 6, 1926, to July 9, 1928. A confidant of Gabriele D'Annunzio (q.v.), he had an intense interest in motion pictures and in 1929 became director of the Ente Nazionale per la Cinematografia (ENAC) (National Cinematography Agency), a semipublic agency that regulated agreements between Italian and foreign film companies.

For further information see: *Chi è?* (1936); NO (1928).

PVC

BISSOLATI, LEONIDA (b. Cremona, February 20, 1857; d. Rome, May 6, 1920). Bissolati was a pioneer of Italian socialism and among the founders of the Italian Socialist party. He began his political activity as a Mazzinian and later as a land organizer, and was a boyhood friend of Filippo Turati (q.v.). In 1896 Bissolati became the first editor of the party newspaper *Avanti!*, a post he held until 1903 and again after 1908.

Bissolati strongly supported Turati's moderate policies, but eventually wished to collaborate much more actively with the government than Turati was willing to sanction. From about 1906 Bissolati became head of an ultra-reformist faction which predicted the disappearance of the Socialist party and its replacement by a "labor party" based upon the Confederazione Generale del Lavoro (q.v.). As the party's foreign policy expert, Bissolati became convinced of the inevitability of a war between Italy and Austria, which led him to sympathize with increasing government requests for arms appropriations. This attitude conflicted both with the party's left wing and Turati. In 1911, Giovanni Giolitti (q.v.) offered Bissolati a cabinet post, promising universal suffrage and nationalization of the life insurance companies. Turati dissuaded him from accepting the position, but Bissolati strongly endorsed Giolitti and set off a crisis in the party by consulting with the king. Bissolati also supported the Libyan War, for which he was expelled at the Congress of Reggio Emilia (1912). He then founded the Partito Socialista Riformista, which never achieved a large following.

In 1914 Bissolati advocated Italian intervention against the Central Powers for the purpose of defending European democracy. In 1915 he volunteered in the Alpini mountain force of the army and was seriously wounded. He joined the government of Prime Minister Paolo Boselli as a minister without portfolio with responsibility for liaison between the government and the Army. In November 1917 he became minister of military aid and war pensions. He resigned in December 1918 because he favored conciliation with Yugoslavia and thus came into conflict with Sidney Sonnino (q.v.).

For further information see: Leonida Bissolati, *La politica estera dell' Italia dal 1897 al 1920* (Milan: Treves, 1923); Ivanoe Bonomi, *Leonida Bissolati* (Milan: Martinelli, 1929); Raffaele Colapietra, *Leonida Bissolati* (Milan: Feltrinelli, 1958).

SD

BLACKSHIRTS. See **SQUADRISTI.**

BLASETTI, ALESSANDRO (b. Rome, July, 1900). A well-known film director of the Fascist period, Blasetti received a degree in law. In 1926 he founded the film journal *Cinematografo* and the production company Augustus. His first major film was *Sole* (1928), an openly Fascist-inspired work dealing with the Pontine Marshes reclamation program. This was followed by the equally Fascist but realist-inspired *Vecchia Guardia* (1934), which had a great impact on the public and portrayed the Blackshirt-Communist (*see* SQUADRISTI) struggles before the March on Rome (q.v.). In 1942 he directed *Quattro passi fra le nuvole*, a poignant film about middle-class lives during World War II.

For further information see: Philip V. Cannistraro, *La fabbrica del consenso* (Rome-Bari: Laterza, 1975); Edward R. Tannenbaum, *The Fascist Experience* (New York: Basic Books, 1972).

PVC

BOCCHINI, ARTURO (b. San Giorgio del Sannio, Benevento, February 12, 1880; d. Rome, November 20, 1940). Police chief for most of the Fascist period and the major architect of the police state, Bocchini took a degree in law from the University of Naples and entered the civil service in 1903, working for the Ministry of Interior in various capacities and cities. Intelligent and energetic, Bocchini rose quickly to positions of responsibility. In 1922 he became prefect of Brescia, in 1923 was transferred to Bologna, and then in 1925 to Genoa, having accomplished in all three provinces extremely difficult work in maintaining public order.

On September 23, 1926, Mussolini appointed Bocchini chief of police, a position he held until his death in November 1940. His appointment had been carefully arrived at and was supported by Interior Minister Luigi Federzoni (q.v.). Bocchini was a career civil servant with no defined political position and no record of Fascist activism. He carried out his duties as a "technocrat" without ideological fervor. Moreover, he recognized that his work in reorganizing the police structure of the country was bound intimately to the personal dictatorship of Mussolini, so that he immediately established an almost daily rapport with the Duce.

Bocchini completely revamped the organization of the Italian police (*see* POLICE AND INTERNAL SECURITY) in order to insure efficiency, maintain public order, eliminate or repress anti-Fascist activity, and establish an effective information network. He is credited with the creation of OVRA, the secret Fascist police system, and yet by the late 1930s he sought to temper the impact of the anti-Semitic laws and other examples of Fascist extremism. He was made a member of the important advisory body the Consiglio di Stato (Council of State) in 1927 and a senator in 1933.

For further information see: Paola Carucci, "Arturo Bocchini," in F. Cordova, ed., *Uomini e volti del fascismo* (Rome: Bulzoni, 1980).

PVC

BODRERO, EMILIO (b. Rome, April 3, 1874; d. Rome, November 29, 1949). Fascist intellectual and minister, Bodrero came from a wealthy family and while still a university student he obtained a post in the Italian financial court system (Corte di Conti). He graduated with degrees in law, philosophy, and letters and was a professor of ancient philosophy at the University of Messina (1914-15) and later at Padua.

Bodrero joined the Nationalist movement, collaborated with *Il Regno* (Florence), and was a vigorous interventionist. He fought with the Arditi (q.v.) during World War I. In 1923 he joined the PNF (Partito Nazionale Fascista) (q.v.) after advocating its fusion with the Italian Nationalist Association (q.v.), and became a federal secretary at Padua. He was in Parliament from 1924 to 1934.

In 1925 Bodrero attended the Bologna Congress of Fascist Intellectuals and was one of the proponents of the "Manifesto of Fascist Intellectuals" (*see* "MANIFESTO OF ANTI-FASCIST INTELLECTUALS"). He was strongly opposed, however, to the philosophical idealism of Giovanni Gentile (q.v.) and disagreed with a number of aspects of the latter's school reform. In November 1926 Mussolini made him undersecretary for public instruction, and from his resignation in 1929 until 1934 he was vice-president of the Chamber of Deputies. He was also head of the National Confederation of Professionals and Artists from November 1930 to December 1933. Bodrero was appointed to the Senate in 1934, and in 1940 was made a professor of Fascist doctrine at the University of Rome. He served briefly as undersecretary for national education from February to May 1941.

For further information see: DBI (11); NO (1928); Emilio Bodrero, *Auspici d'impero* (Milan: Alpes, 1925).

PVC

BOLZON, PIERO (b. Genoa, November 24, 1883; d. Genoa, November 5, 1945). A Fascist bureaucrat, Bolzon came from a wealthy family. He was a member of the Socialist party in his youth, studied at the University of Rome under Enrico Ferri, and then took up painting. In the years before World War I he traveled widely in Europe and Latin America, but returned to Italy to fight in the war, rising to the rank of captain. A member of the Arditi (q.v.), he was editor of *Roma futurista* in 1918 and of *L'Ardito* in 1921.

Bolzon represented the right wing of the Arditi, and joined the Fascist movement in March 1919. In November he stood for election to Parliament on a joint list with the Fascists and was a member of the National Council of the Arditi. Closely allied to Mussolini, in 1921 Bolzon pushed for the fusion of the Arditi with the PNF (Partito Nazionale Fascista) (q.v.) and ultimately resigned from the former.

A hard line Fascist, Bolzon opposed the Pacification Pact (q.v.) with the Socialists. He was secretary of the *fascio* of Milan and of Genoa and held a number of important party posts, including head of the propaganda office and membership in both the directory and the Fascist Grand Council (q.v.). A deputy from 1924 to 1939, in November 1926 Mussolini appointed him undersecretary of the colonies. He resigned in 1929 and was then made a member of the National Council. Bolzon also served as an administrator for the Istituto Nazionale Infortuni sul Lavoro (National Institute for Work Accidents).

For further information see: NO (1928); P. Bolzon, *Le verghe e la scure*, 2 vols. (Florence: La Voce, 1923); Ferdinando Cordova, *Arditi e legionari dannunziani* (Padua: Marsilio, 1969).

PVC

BOMBACCI, NICOLÒ (b. Civitella di Romagna, Forlì, October 24, 1879; d. Dongo, April 28, 1945). Socialist turned Fascist, Bombacci was originally a schoolteacher but soon became involved in worker and Socialist politics. In 1911 he was elected to the National Council of the Confederazione Generale del Lavoro (CGL) (q.v.) and between 1917 and 1918 rose to the highest ranks of the Socialist party. He was acknowledged as one of the leading revolutionary Socialists and his political activities during World War I led to his arrest and imprisonment. Bombacci's position as a leader of the revolutionary Socialists was confirmed at the party's congress at Bologna in 1919 when he, as vice-secretary, enunciated their beliefs. Elected as a parliamentary deputy from Bologna in 1919, Bombacci was also a member of the Italian delegation to the Comintern.

In January 1921, on the basis of the rising tide of radicalism in the worker's movements and a need for personal glorification, Bombacci joined the newly born Italian Communist Party (PCI) (*see* PARTITO COMUNISTA ITALIANO). He became a member of the party's central committee and directed two Communist newspapers, *Il Comunista* in Bologna-Imola and *Avanti Comunista* in Rome. A man of constantly shifting ideological position, Bombacci was eventually caught up in the PCI's leadership struggles and in 1927 was expelled from the party for "opportunism."

Isolated from the Communists, Bombacci began to give his tacit support to the regime. In 1936, with financial help from the Fascist regime, Bombacci founded *La Verità*. Within the columns of his journal, Bombacci sought to demonstrate the existence of an Italian proletariat state which was in conflict with an imperialist-capitalist world. Given its small readership and its compromising position toward the anti-Fascist movement, the periodical accomplished little.

Bombacci fled to the Salò Republic (*see* ITALIAN SOCIAL REPUBLIC) along with many other loyal Fascists and helped inspire the Charter of Verona, which served as the basis for the new government. As one of Mussolini's advisors, he sought to negotiate an accord with the Committee of National Liberation (q.v.). Bombacci accompanied Mussolini on his flight from Milan in April 1945 and after being captured by Italian partisans he was executed.

For further information see: DBI (2); Nicolò Bombacci, *Questo è comunismo* (Venice: n.p., 1944).

MSF

BONGIOVANNI, LUIGI (b. Reggio Emilia, December 8, 1866; d. Rome, April 4, 1941). Governor of Cyrenaica, Bongiovanni retired as a general in 1920 but was recalled as governor in January 1923. On orders he attacked the Senussi tribes of Libya without warning in March, starting an eight-year war. A flying accident forced him to retire in May 1924. He remained active in colonial affairs, however, becoming a senator in 1929.

For further information see: DBI (12).

BRS

BONIFICA INTEGRALE. The Fascist program of land reclamation and improvement, Bonifica Integrale became one of the central domestic policies of the regime. The program aimed at increasing agricultural production (*see* "BATTLE FOR GRAIN") by draining marshes along the sea to reduce malaria and bring more land under cultivation, reforesting mountain areas to stop soil erosion and conserve water, and constructing irrigation systems.

The *bonifica* plan was largely the work of Arrigo Serpieri (q.v.), a first-rate technician and undersecretary for integral land improvement from 1919 to 1935. A December 24, 1928 law (n. 3134) established the operations of the program (later revised by the February 13, 1935 law n.215), which were based on large government subsidies and the participation—sometimes forced—of private landowners.

The program achieved some success until 1932, when the depression forced the regime to reduce its efforts in favor of other public works (q.v.) projects. (Serpieri resigned in January 1935 because of the decreased government commitment.) But between 1922 and 1938 Mussolini had spent more than seven billion lire on Bonifica Integrale. Although the amount of land actually affected is still disputed, estimates range from 2.6 million to 5.7 million hectares, of which perhaps 250,000 to 350,000 hectares were significantly improved. The greatest success was achieved in the Pontine Marshes near Rome where the regime built new towns like Latina (1932) and Sabaudia (1933) and resettled farm workers.

The *bonifica* program was the focus of one of the regime's most important propaganda campaigns and was used to reinforce Mussolini's ruralization and agricultural programs.

For further information see: Mario Bandini, "Sulla bonifica," *Rivista di politica agraria*, 1, 10 (March 1954); Renzo De Felice, *Mussolini il duce* (Turin: Einaudi, 1974); Arrigo Serpieri, *La legge sulla bonifica integrale nel quinto anno di applicazione* (Rome: Istituto Poligrafico, 1935); Giuseppe Tassinari, *La bonifica integrale nel decennale della legge Mussolini* (Rome: Arti Grafiche, 1939).

PVC

BONOMI, IVANOE (b. Mantua, October 18, 1873; d. Rome, April 20, 1951). Ivanoe Bonomi, a moderate conservative who represented Italy's pre-Fascist tradition, occupied positions of critical importance during the transition from Fascism to democratic rule. He used his position to block a thorough political transformation and to insure the continuity of institutions inherited from both the liberal state and Fascism.

After receiving his *laurea* in jurisprudence in 1898, Bonomi joined the Italian Socialist Party (PSI—Partito Socialista Italiano [q.v.], where he quickly associated himself with the leaders of the "reformist" (gradualist) wing of the party. Bonomi's *Le vie nuove del socialismo* (1906) was one of the most important theoretical justifications of reformism. In 1912 Bonomi, by this time a deputy in Parliament, was expelled from the PSI for his support of the Italian invasion of Libya. He then founded the Reformist Socialist party together with other defecting Socialist deputies. Bonomi supported Italian entry into World War I, and in 1916 he joined the war cabinet of Prime Minister Paolo Boselli as minister of labor. After the war Bonomi was the minister of public works in the successive V. E. Orlando (q.v.) and Francesco Nitti (q.v.) governments (1919-20) and minister of war and then of finance in the Giolitti government (1920-21). He succeeded Giovanni Giolitti (q.v.) as prime minister in June 1921 and served until February 1922. As prime minister Bonomi's attitude toward Fascist violence was ambivalent, leading to charges that he secretly favored the movement. After Mussolini took power in October 1922, Bonomi increasinly withdrew from public life and played no effective part in the political opposition to Fascism prior to the outbreak of World War II. In 1942, as it became apparent that the military defeat of Italy and collapse of Fascism were imminent, Bonomi resumed political activity, putting himself in contact with representatives of both the monarchy and the anti-Fascist parties. After a royal *coup de main* overthrew Mussolini in July 1943, Bonomi served as spokesman for the anti-Fascist parties in their dealings with the Pietro Badoglio (q.v.) government.

Badoglio and King Victor Emmanuel (q.v.) fled Rome on September 9, 1943, shortly after Italy's surrender to the Allies was announced. Bonomi, together with with major leaders of the anti-Fascist parties, remained in the city and after its occupation by the Germans went underground. Bonomi was elected chairman of the Rome Committee of National Liberation (q.v.) (CLN—Comitato di Liberazione Nazionale), the executive committee of the parties. Using this position, Bonomi intervened to block the efforts of southern anti-Fascists to force the king's abdication in November 1943 and to insure the liberation of Rome was not accompanied by a radically inspired insurrection.

Rome was liberated on June 4, 1944. On June 9 Badoglio and the leaders of the anti-Fascist parties in the south flew into the city for negotiations with Roman leaders on the formation of a new government. After Allied officials in the city made it clear that they would accept any government the parties agreed upon, the Rome CLN forced Badoglio out of power and replaced him with Bonomi. On June 10, 1944, Bonomi formed a six-party government which led Italy until November 26, 1944 when he handed his resignation to the lieutenant general of the realm, Prince Umberto. After a major crisis caused by Bonomi's actions, a second government was formed on December 12, 1944, consisting of four of the CLN parties. This government resigned on June 12, 1945, after the liberation of all of Italy had been completed.

Bonomi's governments were marked by conflict between the left- and right-wing parties of the CLN over the extent and thoroughness of the purge of Fascists. Bonomi sided with the conservatives on this and other issues. In November 1944 he provoked the crisis that led to the fall of his first government in order to weaken the hand of the left. By offering his resignation to the lieutenant general, Bonomi strengthened the position of the monarchy. In addition, Bonomi actively sought to curb the powers of a postwar constituent assembly and intrigued to force a postwar national referendum on the fate of the monarchy. As a result, Bonomi became anathema to the parties of the left and especially to the leaders of the northern resistance movement. After the liberation Bonomi held on to his office for a month, maneuvering to form a third government. When it became apparent that the left would have no further dealings with him, he resigned. Thereafter he played a fairly active political role as a senior statesman. He served as a member of the Italian delegation to the Paris Peace Conference in 1946. He was elected president of the Italian Senate in 1949 and served in that position until his death.

For further information see: Ivanoe Bonomi, *Diario di un anno: 2 giugno 1943-10 giugno 1944* (Milan: Garzanti, 1947); Elena Aga Rossi Sitzia, "La situazione politica ed economica dell'Italia nel periodo 1944-45: I governi Bonomi," *Quaderni dell'Istituto Romano per la storia d'Italia dal fascismo alla resistenza* 2 (1971).

JEM

BONTEMPELLI, MASSIMO (b. Como, May 12, 1878; d. Rome, July 21, 1960). A noted writer, Bontempelli began his artistic evolution at the turn of the century with poetry inspired by classical literature and the works of G. Carducci. During the next phase he turned to Futurism and surrealism, and shortly after World War I he began to introduce grotesque and fantastic elements into his work.

He was editor of *Cronache Letterarie* (Florence), and director of *Il Secolo* (Milan) and *Il Mondo* (Rome). During World War I he served at the front, joined the Fascist party in 1924, and in 1927-28 was secretary of the Fascist Union of Authors and Writers. He was made a member of the Royal Academy of Italy (q.v.) in 1930.

In the mid-1920s he developed the idea of "magical realism," which he used to describe his new poetry. In 1926 he and Curzio Malaparte (q.v.) started a new journal, *Novecento,* and Bontempelli became the major exponent of the cultural movement bearing that name. Related to the Stracittà movement (*see* STRACITTÀ/ STRAPAESE) which advocated a modern, antiprovincial culture, the *novecentisti* argued that twentieth-century literature and art were more objective than the romanticism, sentimentalism, and aestheticism of the previous century. His new "realism" viewed individuals as separate from space and time. Reality is transitory, indeterminable, and accidental, and truth is attained by gathering through myth or fable what happens from moment to moment. Stylistically, the Novecento Movement (q.v.) was an effort to reconcile the conflict between past and future and to give Fascist Italy a cultural base that was a compromise between the ancient and the modern. Bontempelli fought hard but unsuccessfully to have Mussolini adopt the Novecento Movement as the cultural basis of his regime.

Bontempelli began to break from the regime in the late 1930s. In 1937 he established contact with anti-Fascists and Communists, and the following year he participated in a protest against the regime's censorship policies. Moreover, when a Jewish professor at the University of Florence was fired by Mussolini, Bontempelli refused to accept that same post. As a result, he was expelled from both the Fascist party and the Royal Academy of Italy.

In 1948 Bontempelli was elected to the Senate as a Communist, but he was not permitted to take his seat because of his compromising activities during the Fascist period.

For further information see: EAR (1); Luigi Baldacci, *Massimo Bontempelli* (Turin: Borla, 1967); Massimo Bontempelli, *L'avventura novecentista* (Florence: Vallecchi, 1938).

WEL

BONZANI, ALBERTO (b. Rimini, February 1, 1872; d. Bologna, April 26, 1935). Air undersecretary and Army Chief of Staff, Bonzani was appointed aviation vice commissioner in June 1924, then undersecretary in May 1925. He administered his posts efficiently and apolitically, but Mussolini removed him in November 1926 to create a Fascist service. After commanding the Cuneo Division (until March 1928) and the Alessandria Corps (until February 1929), Bonzani became Army Chief of Staff. He collaborated closely with Pietro Gazzera (q.v.).

Both Pietro Badoglio's (q.v.) conservative protégés, they unsuccessfully proposed artillery renovation, opposed doctrinal innovation and Fascist interference,
orienting the Army against France and Yugoslovia.

Friction with Gazzera's Fascist successor, Federico Baistrocchi (q.v.), and
opposition to the Ethiopian War (q.v.) brought Bonzani's dismissal in September
1934. Appreciating Bonzani's abilities, Mussolini appointed him Bologna Army
Commander, but he died shortly thereafter.

For further information see: Emilio Canevari, *La guerra italiana* (Rome: Tosi,
1948); Giorgio Rochat, *Militari e politici nella preparazione della campagna
d'Ethiopia* (Milan: Angeli, 1971).

                                                                                          BRS

BORDIGA, AMADEO (b. Resina, June 13, 1889; d. Formia, July 24, 1970). A
Socialist and later a Communist leader, Bordiga's family moved to the south
where his father taught agricultural economics at the *scuola superiore* in Portici
near Naples. Although Bordiga had declared himself a Marxist while a student at
the *liceo*, he did not officially join the Italian Socialist party (PSI-Partito Socialista
Italiano) (q.v.) until 1910 during his last university years in the Faculty of
Engineering. He quickly became a leader in both the Socialist Youth Federation
(FIGS—Federazione Italiana Giovanile Socialista) and local Socialist movement.
As were most Socialist youths, he was an anticleric opposed to masonic anticlericalism, an antimilitarist outraged by the Libyan War and an antireformist critical
of the moderate Socialists' reliance on electoral methods and tactical approval of
blocs. Incensed by the participation of Neapolitan Socialists in a bloc encompass-
ing freemasons and syndicalists, he organized a campaign against the "morbid
degeneration" of Neapolitan socialism, demonstrating even at this early age the
tenacity and indefatigable energy that later led Antonio Gramsci (q.v.) to comment
that Bordiga's efforts were worth that of two to three men. In 1912 he led a tiny
band of ultraintransigents out of the local party and in 1914 won their recognition
by the national party as the official local representative of socialism.

With the outbreak of World War I Bordiga arrived on the national scene of
Socialist politics as the extreme left spokesman. An admirer of Mussolini during
the latter's tenure at *Avanti!*, he nonetheless condemned Mussolini's first move in
favor of intervention. Rejecting the popular view that Austro-German militarism
was the cause of the war, he instead held the "bourgeoisie" of all warring nations
"equally responsible." The independent development of Bordiga's views in 1914-15
brought him close to Lenin's view that the war could be turned into a civil war.
With Italy's 1915 intervention Bordiga's political voice was silenced but by May
1917 he had resurfaced as a member of a revolutionary intransigent faction urging
a policy of sabotage.

At the war's end he founded the paper *Il Soviet*. Believing that mass unrest in
1919-20 meant that Italy had entered a revolutionary period, he opposed PSI
participation in the 1919 national elections, thereby earning the label "abstentionist,"
and called for a purge of the party's reformist wing. In July 1919 he organized a

Communist abstentionist faction but, failing to obtain his objectives at the PSI congress in October, he decided for schism. Bordiga appealed for support to the Comintern which, though rejecting abstentionism, gave him partial support in the Twenty-One Points (July 1920) that imposed upon the PSI the choice of either expelling the reformists or being expelled. A November 1920 agreement between Bordiga's faction and Gramsci's Turin-based Ordine Nuovo movement paved the way for the anticipated Communist schism. When the PSI failed to accede to the Comintern's demand, the Communists left to form the Partito Comunista Italiano (PCI) (q.v.) in January 1921.

Bordiga became the party's leader but he soon came into conflict with the Comintern which, in viewing the international situation pessimistically after 1921, shifted toward a policy of securing the Russian Revolution. Comintern proposals for a united front and a "fusion" (merger into the PCI of Socialists belatedly willing to accept the Twenty-One Points) were opposed by Bordiga and the party majority as compromising the Revolution's future in Italy. The Rome Thesis (March 1922), drafted largely by Bordiga and approved by the party's majority, gave the following reason that Bordiga brought before the Fourth Comintern Congress in November: that "variations in the situation should not change the fundamental program, organization and tactics of the Party." Unable to win Bordiga's cooperation, the Comintern used the occasion of his arrest in Italy (February 1923) to appoint a new executive committee. This direct intervention in the Italian party's internal affairs began the process of "Bolshevization" of which Gramsci became the protagonist.

Unlike Gramsci, whose reassessment of Fascism made him accept the Comintern's line, Bordiga maintained the stance of the Rome Thesis (as did a majority of party activists at Como in May 1924). Bordiga tried to appeal to party regulars against "Bolshevization" in a "manifesto" smuggled from prison but not distributed in 1923, and, after his acquittal, before the Fifth Comintern Congress in July 1924. Having refused to stand as a Communist candidate in the 1924 elections and to lend his prestige to policies he repudiated, Bordiga was completely silenced in 1925, and the party was reorganized. In 1926 at Lyons Gramsci's leadership and the new Communist party charter were ratified by party members. In that same year Bordiga was arrested by the Fascists and sentenced to island exile. Upon release in 1930 he was formally expelled from the PCI. For over thirty years he was treated as an historical "non-person," but he lived to see a revival of interest in his ideas by left-wing dissidents in the late 1960s.

For further information see: Earlene Craver, "The Rediscovery of Amadeo Bordiga," *Survey* 91-2 (spring-summer 1974); Andreina De Clementi, *Amadeo Bordiga* (Turin: Einaudi, 1971).

ECr

BORELLI, ALDO (b. Vibo Valentia, Catanzaro, February 2, 1890; d. Rome, August 2, 1965). A Fascist journalist, Borelli began his career as an editor of *L'Alfiere* (Rome). In 1911-12, he was a reporter for *Il Mattino* (Naples) and editor of *La Nazione* (Florence). He supported Italy's entrance into World War I and spoke for the conservative liberals led by Antonio Salandra (q.v.) and Sidney Sonnino (q.v.). Under his leadership *La Nazione* flourished, and in the postwar period it became closely identified with the extreme nationalists. Anti-democratic and anti-Socialist, Borelli attacked the Italian parliamentary system and supported Fascism as a movement of order. Between 1924 and 1929 he was closely tied to the Fascists personally and politically. In 1929 he was president of the Tuscan Union of Journalists and a member of the Militia (q.v.). On September 1, 1929, Borelli became editor of *Il Corriere della Sera* (Milan), a post he held until July 25, 1943. Under his direction the paper became a faithful and enthusiastic propaganda organ for the regime. He attracted the disdain of some high Fascist officials for his support of Augusto Turati (q.v.), but in 1935 he went to Ethiopia as a volunteer. After the fall of Mussolini, Borelli was charged with acts favorable to Fascism but was subsequently freed. After the war he continued his journalistic career and worked for *Il Tempo* and *Epoca*.

For further information see: DBI(2).

MSF

BORGESE, GIUSEPPE ANTONIO (b. Palermo, November 12, 1882; d. Fiesole, December 4, 1952). A prolific writer and distinguished professor of literature and aesthetics, Borgese in 1931 joined a number of Italian intellectuals in the United States who actively opposed the Fascist dictatorship.

Borgese had been influenced strongly by the liberal philosophy of Benedetto Croce (q.v.), who published Borgese's first major work, *Storia della critica romantica in Italia* (1905). He wrote lyrical poetry and criticism and from 1910 to 1917 was professor of German literature at the University of Rome. During World War I Borgese headed the Press and Propaganda Bureau in the Orlando government (1917-18) and then moved to the University of Milan where he taught German literature, aesthetics, and literary criticism until his departure for the United States.

Borgese joined a handful of Italian university professors in refusing to sign a Fascist loyalty oath and accepted a position as visiting professor at the University of California in 1931-32. In 1932 he lectured at the New School for Social Research and then taught comparative literature at Smith College until 1936. He moved to the University of Chicago as professor of Italian literature until 1948, publishing in a broad range of subjects that reflected his deepening concern with the political plight of mankind.

While in the United States Borgese participated with other *fuorusciti* (q.v.) in the Mazzini Society (q.v.) and contributed generally as a liberal democrat to the various campaigns against Mussolini. He worked with the International Committee for Political Prisoners to focus world attention on political repression in Italy. In 1937 Borgese made his most significant contribution to anti-Fascism by publishing *Goliath: The March of Fascism*, his first book in English. In spirited and bold style, Borgese traced the intellectual origins of Fascism, Mussolini's pre-Fascist career, and the development of the Fascist state, which he condemned as a barbarian state of "hollowness and nil." *Goliath* remains—along with the works of Gaetano Salvemini (q.v.)—one of the major critiques of Italian Fascism written in the 1930s.

With the advent of war in Europe, Borgese began to anticipate the construction of postwar civilization. After the Allied invasion of Italy, he joined other anti-Fascists in America in publishing (in *Life Magazine*) an "Italian Manifesto" in which they opposed the continuation of Fascism without Mussolini. And in 1948 he contributed to the publication of a proposed world constitution which he considered his most significant effort.

For further information see: DBI (12); Giuseppe A. Borgese, *Goliath: The March of Fascism* (New York: The Viking Press, 1937).

CLK

BORGHESE, JUNIO VALERIO (b. Rome, June 1906; d. Cadiz, August 27, 1974). Scion of a Roman noble family, naval hero, counterinsurgency specialist, and neo-Fascist politician, Prince Borghese took a commission in the Navy in 1928. During the clandestine submarine campaign against the Spanish Republic's supply lines, his skillful night attack on the destroyer HMS *Havock* (August 31-September 1, 1937) brought him to Mussolini's attention. He subsequently took part in development of the Navy's frogman-guided torpedoes (*maiali*), and took command in March 1941 of the underwater section of the X MAS (Decima Flottiglia Motoscafi Antisommergibili) (Tenth Motor Torpedo Boat Squadron), the unit responsible for Italy's unconventional naval weapons. Borghese commanded the carrier submarine *Scirè* with great skill and dash; the *maiali* he and his frogmen delivered sank 30,000 tons of merchant shipping at Gibraltar (September 20, 1941) and the battleships *Valiant* and *Queen Elizabeth* at Alexandria (December 18-19, 1941). Commander of the entire X MAS from May 1943, Borghese refused to accept the armistice and took his unit over to the Germans, then reported to Mussolini and became undersecretary of the new-born Fascist republic's (*see* ITALIAN SOCIAL REPUBLIC) navy. In the manner of a Renaissance *condottiere* he raised a private army, and devoted himself to savage reprisals against the rapidly spreading partisan movement. The X MAS also operated the republic's small force of submarines and motor torpedo boats. Borghese was too successful, however, and Renato Ricci (q.v.) had him arrested in the Duce's antechamber to curb his independence. Freed after his officers threatened reprisals, Borghese led X MAS ground forces (now a division)in brutal sweep operations in Piedmont and Friuli. In 1945 Borghese received a twelve-year imprisonment term, but time already served, amnesties, and extenuating circumstances (his naval exploits) resulted in immediate release. Prominent in the MSI (Movimento Sociale Italiano) (q.v.), he fled to Spain in March 1971 after involvement in a coup attempt. His Roman funeral was the occasion for a major neo-Fascist ceremony.

For further information see: Junio Valerio Borghese, *Decima Flottiglia MAS* (Milan: Garzanti, 1950).

MK

BORGHI, ARMANDO (b. Castelbolognese, Ravenna, April 7, 1882; d. Rome, April 21, 1968). A major syndicalist and anarchist leader, Borghi grew up in a family tradition of anarchism. He engaged in anarchist propaganda as a young man and was arrested for the first time in 1902. He took part in the 1904 general strike, edited the periodical *Aurora* (Ravenna) in 1906, and the next year became local secretary of and a provincial representative for the Confederazione Generale del Lavoro (q.v.). During the Libyan War he agitated vigorously for peace and was forced to flee to France.

After returning to Italy in 1912, Borghi became secretary general of the Unione Sindacale Italiana (USI) of the revolutionary syndicalists. He was arrested for pacifist agitation during World War I. In 1920 he wrote for the *Umanità Nova* (Milan) and helped to establish the Unione Anarchica Italiana in Florence. After attending the international syndical congress in Russia (during which he advised Lenin of the urgent necessity for immediate revolution in Italy), he was again arrested. In 1922 he was one of the organizers of the Alleanza del Lavoro (q.v.).

Between 1923 and 1926 Borghi traveled between Berlin and Paris, and then went to the United States, where he remained until 1945. In America he worked with anarchists among the Italian immigrants, writing for *L'Adunata dei refrattari* (New York) and publishing a number of books. In Rome after the war he edited *Umanità Nova*.

For further information see: DBI (12); Armando Borghi, *Mezzo secolo di anarchia* (Naples: Edizioni Scientifiche, 1954).

PVC

BORLETTI, SENATORE (b. Milan, November 20, 1880; d. Milan, December 13, 1939). A wealthy Milanese industrialist, Borletti controlled holdings in textiles, machine making, and—during World War I—munitions. A friend of Gabriele D'Annunzio (q.v.), he gave strong financial backing to the Fiume (q.v.) expedition in 1919 and in the 1921 elections backed Mussolini's candidacy. In 1923 he and a group of industrialists brought the Milan newspaper *Il Secolo* into the Fascist camp by buying controlling interest and—through the intervention of Roberto Farinacci (q.v.)—making Giuseppe Bevione (q.v.) editor. Borletti was an executive in the Banca Italiana di Sconto, founded in 1917 the Rinascente department store firm, and in the 1930s held numerous industrial executive positions. He joined the Fascist party in 1924 and was made a senator in February 1929 and Count d'Arosio in 1937.

For further information see: DBI (12); *Il Corriere della sera* (Milan), December 14, 1939.

PVC

BOTTAI, GIUSEPPE (b. Rome, September 3, 1895; d. Rome, January 9, 1959). Fascist journalist and minister, after service as an officer in the Arditi (q.v.) during World War I, Bottai was drawn first to Futurism (q.v.) and the veterans' movement and then to Fascism. Although he was elected to Parliament in 1921, his rise to prominence began after the March on Rome (q.v.) in 1922. The next year he founded the periodical, *Critica fascista*, which became a sounding board for the managerial and technocratic currents within Fascism. Bottai also became associated with revisionist Fascism, a politically sophisticated offshoot of the movement that sought to avoid a total rupture with the old liberal parliamentary system and to advance the position of the Fascist party by making it into the nucleus of a technocratic political elite.

From 1926 to 1943 Bottai was almost always at the center of political life. On November 6, 1926, he was appointed undersecretary at the Ministry of Corporations and on October 12, 1929, became minister of corporations. He held this position until July 1932. From mid-1932 to November 22, 1936, Bottai was out of the cabinet. He served as president of the Istituto Nazionale della Previdenza Sociale and in 1935 and 1936 as governor of Rome. Finally in November 1936 he rejoined the government as minister of national education, a position which he held until February 1943.

Bottai was also a member of the Fascist Grand Council (q.v.) from the time of his service at the Ministry of Corporations. As such, he played a major role in the last act of historic Fascism. Along with Dino Grandi (q.v.) and Luigi Federzoni (q.v.), Bottai engineered the revolt against Mussolini at the July 25, 1943, meeting of the Grand Council and voted for Grandi's motion. In 1944 he escaped to North Africa, where he joined the French Foreign Legion. He served in France and Germany during the last year of the war and again in North Africa from 1945 to 1947. In 1948, after a general amnesty, Bottai returned to Rome where he resumed his journalistic activities, founding in 1953 the periodical *abc*.

Bottai attempted through Fascism to change the structure of the Italian political elite. Throughout the Fascist period his *Critica fascista* argued for a small, selective party, which would become the nucleus of the new political class. Like many of the wartime generation, Bottai lost faith in the capacity of parliamentary democracy to bring about the necessary changes in society. At the same time he feared that unless debate were allowed the Fascist party would rapidly become merely a bureaucratic, ossified structure. Unable to conciliate his own liberal and authoritarian inclinations, Bottai found his revisionism increasingly irrelevant during the repression of the opposition after the murder of the Socialist deputy Giacomo Matteotti (*see* MATTEOTTI CRISIS) in June 1924. Thwarted in his efforts to reform the Fascist party and unable throughout the twenty-one years of Fascist rule to become secretary of the party, Bottai turned his energies to the corporative system (*see* CORPORATIVISM AND THE CORPORATIVE STATE) through which he sought by other means to pursue his vision of Fascism. Although he had a role in drafting the early stages of the Charter of Labor (q.v.) of 1927,

Bottai's major contribution at the Ministry of Corporations came in March 1930 with the reform of the National Council of Corporations. He rejected an elaborate organizational structure for the Italian corporative system. His reform stressed the technical and overseeing role of the Ministry of Corporations, which would mediate between capital and labor, a sort of state directed, planned economy. In fact, he found that neither Mussolini nor the industrialists viewed his ideas with favor. His reforms were inadequate for the propaganda requirements of the regime, which demanded a more impressive (but nonfunctioning) organizational facade on the model of that created in 1934. Bottai's plans were also too ambitious for the industrialists who feared his technocratic aspirations. Moreover his position was undermined by the bureaucratic inadequacies of the Ministry of Corporations, which lacked the necessary regulatory power over industry or agriculture. Nor were Bottai's managerial and technocratic views appealing to the workers, who were offered no opportunities to participate freely within the system through leaders of their choice. He did, however, attract a group of young middle-class intellectuals who saw in corporativism an alternative to both capitalism and communism and who envisaged for themselves an arbitral role in the corporative bureaucracy. Two of Bottai's reviews, *Critica fascista* and the *Archivio di Studi corporativi*, leave a record of the aspirations and failures of these Fascist planners as they found themselves shut out from any meaningful role in setting economic and social policy during the 1930s.

As minister of national education, Bottai, who had always been associated with an urban, modernizing Fascism, conformed to the rural and racial orientation of the regime during the late thirties. Not only did Bottai apply the anti-Semitic legislation to the schools, but his 1939 Carta della Scuola (*see* SCHOOL CHARTER) combined a basically conservative approach with some populist and even totalitarian elements. The introduction of manual labor and the establishment of rural and craft schools were attempts to reinforce the rural basis of Fascist Italy and to freeze the social structure. The reform also sought to direct lower-middle-class students away from the overcrowded professions and toward more practical careers by establishing a variety of technical schools that did not lead to the university. Both the onset of World War II and the resistance of the middle class to any impediment to upward social mobility in the classic manner sabotaged much of the reform.

More important were Bottai's cultural initiatives. He maintained close ties to both Catholic and lay, non-Fascist culture. In 1938 Bottai established the Bergamo Prize to reward currents of modern art, not always well received by the regime. His literary review, *Primato*, published between 1940 and 1943, became a link to those intellectuals whose alienation from the regime would soon carry them out of Fascism's orbit. Although it was too late to recapture the intellectual avant-garde for the regime, many of Italy's finest writers and artists collaborated on Bottai's periodicals.

As a conservative modernizer, Bottai failed to achieve any substantial changes through Fascism. Yet he rendered a major service to the regime by creating an illusion of dynamism and creativity where nothing existed. The internal criticism of Fascism that was expressed in the *Critica fascista* and the *Primato* became part of the process of intellectual clarification for a generation as it measured the achievements of Fascism with its rhetoric.

For further information see: Alexander De Grand, *Bottai e la cultura fascista* (Bari: Laterza, 1978); Giordano Bruno Guerri, *Giuseppe Bottai: un fascista critico* (Milan: Feltrinelli, 1976); Luisa Mangoni, *Primato: 1940-1943* (Bari: De Donato, 1977).

AJD

BRACCO, ROBERTO (b. Naples, September 21, 1862; d. Sorrento, April 20, 1943). An anti-Fascist playwright and critic, Bracco signed Benedetto Croce's (q.v.) "Manifesto of anti-Fascist Intellectuals" (q.v.) in 1925 and collaborated with Giovanni Amendola (q.v.) and the Aventine Secession (q.v.). In November 1926, after an attempt on Mussolini's life, Bracco's house was attacked by Fascist squads and his vast library destroyed. He refused all compromises with the regime and turned down appointment to the Royal Academy of Italy (q.v.). His collected works number twenty-five volumes.

For further information see: DBI (13); EAR (1).

PVC

BRAGAGLIA, ANTON G. (b. Frosinone, February 11, 1890; d. Rome, July 15, 1960). A well-known Futurist playwright, Bragaglia came from a family with a long artistic tradition. As a young man he worked in theater and for various newspapers and traveled widely. He also had experience in photography and film. After World War I he and his brother Carlo were in the vanguard of the modern arts movement in Italy, opening an experimental theater in Rome and in Milan.

In the late 1920s Bragaglia became attached to the regime's cultural policies and although he worked within the official orbit, he maintained considerable independence. He was an advisor for the Corporazione dello Spettacolo (Corporation for Entertainment) and was secretary of the Comitato Nazionale Scenotecnici in the National Confederation of Professionals and Artists. In his book *Il teatro della rivoluzione* (1929) he theorized about building a state theater. He then established the Teatro degli Indipendenti (later called the Teatro delle Arti) in 1937 in order to expose young avant-garde actors and playwrights to the public. Despite official policies to the contrary, Bragaglia put on numerous productions by foreign writers such as Eugene O'Neill, Maxwell Anderson and George B. Shaw. In March 1943 the Teatro delle Arti was attacked by *squadristi* (q.v.) in protest over his "unorthodox" work. He continued to write and produce plays after the war.

For further information see: DBI (13); Philip V. Cannistraro, *La fabbrica del consenso* (Rome-Bari: Laterza, 1975).

PVC

BRASINI, ARMANDO (b. Rome, September 21, 1879; d. Rome, February 18, 1965). A noted architect, Brasini represented the academic stream of architects and concentrated on monumental public projects. He reduced the classical traditional motif to its simplest expression and was responsible for government buildings in many Italian cities. Brasini served in a military construction unit during World War I and afterwards held a position on the Commission of Restoration of the Palazzo Venezia in Rome. He contributed to the continued work on the Monument to Vittorio Emanuele in Rome and drafted the plans on which Mussolini had much of the ancient sectors of Rome restored. Brasini was appointed to the Royal Academy in March 1929.

For further information see: DBI (14); *Annuario della reale accademia d'Italia* (Rome: Reale Accademia, 1938).

                                                                                                    JH

BRESCIANI, ITALO (b. Maenza di Priverno, Latina, October 28, 1890; d. Rome, June 2, 1964). Fascist squad leader and local bureaucrat, Bresciani was at first a revolutionary syndicalist who headed the interventionist movement in Verona and fought in World War I. He wrote for *Il Popolo d'Italia* from 1915 to 1923, was at Piazza San Sepolcro (*see* SANSEPOLCRISTI) for the founding of the first Fascist movement, and then launched the *fascio* in Verona. He led *squadristi* (q.v.) attacks against local Socialist and syndicalist organizations and became a member of the Central Committee of the party in 1920. At the Naples congress in October 1922 he helped plan the March on Rome (q.v.) and was a general inspector for one of the twelve military zones (the Trentino and Venezia) organized for the march.

In January 1923 Bresciani was appointed a political commissar for the party and later a provincial inspector. In these capacities he attempted to bring local prefects under his control and protected many personal friends against rival political factions. In May 1926 he was transferred to the Istituto LUCE (*see* LUCE, ISTITUTO NAZIONALE) and in 1930 was made a party inspector and then a deputy. He joined the Salò Republic (*see* ITALIAN SOCIAL REPUBLIC) in September 1943. Although arrested and tried in June 1946, he received amnesty and in the postwar period supported the neo-Fascist Movimento Sociale Italiano (q.v.).

For further information see: DBI (14).

                                                                                                   PVC

BUFFARINI-GUIDI, GUIDO (b. Pisa, August 17, 1895; d. Milan, July 10, 1945). An intransigent Fascist and minister, Buffarini-Guidi was a World War I volunteer and took a law degree in 1920. One of the founders of the *fascio* of Pisa and a squad leader in Tuscany, he was elected mayor of Pisa in 1923 and a deputy the following year. Mussolini later made him a Fascist federal secretary and a Podestà (q.v.).

His administrative talents led him to be named undersecretary of the interior in May 1933. In this post he was particularly effective in extending government authority (through the prefects) over local party officials. He directly controlled much of the state apparatus and reported to Mussolini daily on public opinion in the country. A close associate of Galeazzo Ciano (q.v.), he opposed the expansion of Fascist party bureaucracy in the late 1930s and attempted to limit the impact of the anti-Semitic laws.

Buffarini-Guidi was removed from office in February 1943 as a result of pressures from rivals, but he remained a member of the Fascist Grand Council (q.v.) and voted in favor of Mussolini at the July 1943 meeting that unseated the dictator. Arrested together with Mussolini on July 26, he was liberated by the Germans in September and flown to Munich. In the Salò Republic (*see* ITALIAN SOCIAL REPUBLIC) he was made minister of interior and organized the police in repression of anti-Fascists and partisans, but was dismissed on February 12, 1945. Captured by partisans on April 26 while attempting to escape to Switzerland, he was executed in July after having been condemned to death by a special court.

For further information see: DBI (14).

PVC

BUOZZI, BRUNO (b. Pontelagoscuro, Ferrara, January 31, 1881; d. Storta, June 4, 1944). A Socialist and labor leader, as a young man Buozzi worked as a mechanic in Milan where he joined the Socialist party. In 1911 he was elected secretary general of the Federazione Italiana Operai Metallurgici (FIOM) (Italian Federation of Metal Workers), and the next year became a member of the executive council of the Confederazione Generale del Lavoro, or CGL (q.v.). When World War I began, Buozzi declared himself and FIOM in favor of absolute neutrality. But while he accepted the Socialist party position on the war, he also collaborated with the government on civil defense and was FIOM's representative on the Committee for Industrial Mobilization in Piedmont and Lombardy.

In the postwar period Buozzi initiated many labor reforms, including the eight-hour day and minimum wage agreements. During the factory occupations of September 1920 he favored enlarging the work stoppage but refused to assign revolutionary goals to the strike. Once it was over, he served on the committee to prepare the bill on worker controls. The Socialist split of 1921 once again placed him in the middle of a dispute among Socialists, Communists, and the CGL, maintaining that the CGL should continue its allegiance to the Socialist party.

After the Fascist seizure of power, talks to allow members of the CGL into the government began, and although Buozzi made contacts with the Fascists nothing came of the efforts. He denounced Fascism as a reactionary force, but he did help to negotiate an agreement with the regime in return for certain guarantees. Besides his union activities, Buozzi also served in Parliament. He was elected in 1919, 1921, and again in 1924. He joined the Aventine Secession (q.v.) movement against Mussolini following the Matteotti Crisis (q.v.). Buozzi became secretary general of the CGL in 1925 and tried to keep the labor movement intact despite Fascist antilabor laws.

Buozzi fled to Switzerland and then to Paris in 1926, where he announced that the CGL would continue to operate in exile. He worked with Claudio Treves's (q.v.) *La Libertà* and became an active member and officer in the anti-Fascist Lega Italiana dei Diritti dell'Uomo (Italian League for the Rights of Man). In July 1937 Buozzi was elected a member of the Socialist party's directorate, but in March 1941 he was arrested by the Gestapo. Even while in prison he maintained contacts with the anti-Fascists in Italy and after the formation of Pietro Badoglio's (q.v.) government in 1943 he was freed and became commissioner of the Confederazione Sindacale dei Lavoratori dell'Industria (Syndical Confederation of Industrial Workers). He helped negotiate an end to the Turin general strike of August 1943 and then went to Rome to establish labor agreements between Communists and Catholics. He was arrested on April 13, 1944, by the Germans and was executed two months later.

For further information see: DBI (15); MOI (1); Gino Castagno, *Bruno Buozzi* (Milan-Rome: Avanti!, 1955).

MSF

C

CABRINI, ANGIOLO (b. Codogno, Milan, March 9, 1869; d. Rome, May 6, 1937). An early Socialist leader, Cabrini was a member of the Partito Operaio in the 1880s and established in Piacenza in 1889 the first Italian Camera del Lavoro (Chamber of Labor). In 1892 he was among the founders of the Italian Socialist party.

After a period in exile in Switzerland, Cabrini was elected a deputy and was instrumental in cooperating with Giovanni Giolitti (q.v.) in the passage of important social legislation. In 1902 he helped to form the Segreteria Nazionale della Resistenza (National Secretariat of Resistance) in Milan, a syndicalist organization that led to the creation of the Confederazione Generale del Lavoro (CGL) (q.v.) in 1906. He was expelled from the Socialist party in 1912 together with other reformists.

He volunteered for combat in World War I and was made a member of the government's Commission for Industrial Mobilization. In 1917 he started and directed the Italian branch of the Ufficio Internazionale del Lavoro (UIL) (International Labor Office). Cabrini remained in that position after the Fascist seizure of power and collaborated actively with Mussolini's regime.

For further information see: DBI (15); EAR (2); MOI (1).

PVC

CADORNA, LUIGI (b. Pallanza, September 4, 1850; d. Bordighera, December 21, 1928). Army Chief of Staff despite his disgrace after Caporetto (*see* CAPORETTO, BATTLE OF), Cadorna remained a hero to the Nationalists and some Army officers. For many Fascists, however, he represented the old military order they despised. Seeking to consolidate Army support during the Matteotti Crisis (q.v.), Mussolini engineered Cadorna's promotion to marshal in November 1924. In March 1925 Cadorna reentered public life, attacking Antonino Di Giorgio's (q.v.) reforms in the Senate. Thereafter, Cadorna exercised some influence in military affairs.

For further information see: DBI (16).

BRS

CADORNA, RAFFAELE (b. Pallanza, Novara, September 12, 1889). An anti-Fascist resistance leader, Cadorna was schooled in Modena and served in World War I. A stringent anti-Fascist, Cadorna fought the Germans around Rome after September 1943, and when the Germans occupied the city he fled to northern Italy. He served as a military advisor to the resistance groups in Milan, and in November 1944 he became the supreme commander of the Corpo Volontari della Libertà, the military arm of the resistance. Cadorna attempted to mold the anti-Fascist groups after the regular Army, but this was impossible given the composition of the bands and popular participation in the struggle. Cadorna resigned his post in February 1945 in opposition to a project to unify all Communist-oriented resistance organizations, a move Cadorna believed would give the party preeminence on the military level. In May 1945 Cadorna became head of the Army's General Staff, a post he held until January 1947. He served in the Senate in 1948 and was reelected to the second republican legislature.

For further information see: DSPI; EAR (2); Raffaele Cadorna, *La riscossa* (Milan: Rizzoli, 1948); Enzo Piscitelli, *Storia della resistenza romana* (Bari: Laterza, 1965).

MSF

CAETANI, GELASIO (b. Rome, March 7, 1877; d. Rome, October 23, 1934). An Italian diplomat, Caetani was descended from an old Roman noble family (the ancestral home was the Castello di Sermoneta). He graduated in engineering from the University of Rome in 1901 and then studied metallurgy at Columbia University in New York, after which he worked in the United States until the outbreak of World War I. He fought in the war and was promoted to colonel.

An ardent Nationalist, Caetani was an early supporter of Fascism and took part in the March on Rome (q.v.). He dedicated himself to improving his family estates after 1919, draining part of the Pontine Marshes (*see* BONIFICA INTEGRALE).

In November 1922 Mussolini appointed him ambassador to the United States, a post he held until 1925. Caetani successfully cultivated good relations in Washington, negotiating the end of Italy's war debts and attempting to establish closer ties with Italian-Americans. He strongly opposed the formation of *fasci* in America, however, and this led to conflicts with party officials in Rome.

After his return to Italy, Caetani held numerous public positions, including membership in the National Research Council and the vice-presidency of the petroleum monopoly, AGIP (Azienda Generale Italiana Petroli).

For further information see: DBI (16); Alan Cassels, *Mussolini's Early Diplomacy* (Princeton: Princeton University Press, 1970).

PVC

CALAMANDREI, PIERO (b. Florence, April 21, 1889; d. Florence, September 27, 1956). Eminent jurist and anti-Fascist, Calamandrei received a law degree from Pisa in 1912 and became a professor at various universities, teaching at Florence from 1924 until his death. A democratic interventionist, he volunteered for combat in 1915.

In 1919 he collaborated with Gaetano Salvemini (q.v.) on *Unità*. In 1922 he cofounded (with Carlo and Nello Rosselli [q.v.] and Ernesto Rossi [q.v.]) the Circolo di Cultura in Florence, one of the earliest anti-Fascist organizations in Italy, and helped to publish *Non Mollare*, one of the first underground newspapers. He was also a member of Italia Libera (q.v.), an anti-Fascist group that inspired the later Giustizia e Libertà (*see* ANTI-FASCISM) and the Party of Action (Partito d'Azione) (q.v.). In 1924 Calamandrei joined Giovanni Amendola's (q.v.) Unione Nazionale Antifascista and the next year signed Benedetto Croce's (q.v.) "Manifesto of Anti-Fascist Intellectuals" (q.v.).

In 1941 he joined Giustizia e Libertà and the next year was among the founders of the Party of Action. He returned to teaching but maintained contact with anti-Fascist forces, while contributing as one of the principal authors to the 1940 civil law code. After the fall of Mussolini in July 1943, he became president of the University of Florence. He founded the journal *Il Ponte* in 1944, was elected to the Consulta Nazionale (q.v.) and the Constituent Assembly (*see* COSTITUENTE), and helped to draft the 1948 Constitution of the Italian Republic (q.v.). He also served in the Chamber of Deputies from 1948 to 1953.

For further information see: DBI (16); DSPI; EAR (2); Piero Calamandrei, *Opere politiche e letterarie*, ed. Norberto Bobbio (Florence: Nuova Italia, 1966-).

PVC

CALOSSO, UMBERTO (b. Belvagio d'Asti, September 23, 1895; d. Rome, August 10, 1959). A journalist and anti-Fascist, Calosso taught at the University of Turin and in 1918 joined the Socialist party. In 1921 he worked on *L'Ordine Nuovo* with Antonio Gramsci (q.v.). After the seizure of power by Mussolini, he wrote anti-Fascist articles in clandestine journals and in 1931 was forced to flee into exile. He spent time in France, England, Malta, and Spain, making contact with the leaders of Giustizia e Libertà (*see* ANTI-FASCISM) in Paris and fighting in the Spanish Civil War (q.v.) against Franco. He made anti-Fascist broadcasts to Italy for the BBC in London, and in October 1944 returned to Italy and worked on the Rome edition of *Avanti!* In 1946 he was elected to the Constituent Assembly (*see* COSTITUENTE), later founded *Il nuovo mondo*, the organ of the PSDI (Partito Socialista Democratico Italiano) (Turin) and then *L'Umanità* (Rome). In 1948 he was elected a deputy for the Social Democratic party.

For further information see: DBI (16); DSPI; EAR (2); Maura Piccialuti-Caprioli, *Radio Londra* (Rome: Ministero Beni Culturali, 1976).

MSF

CAMERA DEL LAVORO. An Italian labor organization, the Camera del Lavoro (Chamber of Labor) was modelled after the Borse du Travaille (Labor Exchange) established in France during the late 1880s. Osvaldo Gnocchi-Viani, a Milan lawyer and Socialist, formally introduced Italians to the idea of a "chamber of labor" in his 1889 publication, *Le Borse del lavoro*. Labor leaders from the Milan Printers' Union and the Partito Operaio Italiano (Italian Worker Party) (*see* PARTITO SOCIALISTA ITALIANO) founded the first Camera del Lavoro in Milan in 1891. This *Camera* served as an organizational model for similar institutions throughout Italy. By 1904 ninety *Camere* representing almost 300,000 workers had been established.

The structure of each *Camera* varied but most consisted of a general assembly of representatives from participating labor organizations. These representatives in turn elected a directive body, usually an executive commission or committee, to oversee the operations of their *Camera*. In theory the Camera del Lavoro was an employment and labor information bureau, but in practice it assumed a variety of economic, cultural, and political functions on the local level. The *Camera* provided a meeting place for workers, reading and conference rooms, recreational facilities, and educational instruction. It played an important role in local labor-business disputes by organizing boycotts and demonstrations as well as directing, subsidizing, and mediating strike activity. The *Camera* also represented labor groups in their relations with the local government, though at the same time many *Camere* depended on municipal government subsidies to sustain their activities. Unlike the nationally federated trade unions (Federazioni di Mestiere), each Camera del Lavoro functioned as an autonomous institution which brought together diverse urban and rural labor organizations in a specific area. For those semi-skilled and unskilled labor groups excluded from the skilled trade union federations, the *Camera* provided the opportunity to participate more actively in the national labor movement.

Although established as purely economic organizations, the *Camere* were susceptible to the various political currents present in the labor movement—Socialist, Republican (*see* PARTITO REPUBBLICANO ITALIANO), revolutionary syndicalist (*see* SYNDICALISM), and anarchist. Each *Camera* tended to reflect the political inclinations of the labor groups in the area it represented, but in general the *Camere* were organized and directed by Socialist labor leaders and had close political ties with the Italian Socialist party. On the local level the *Camere* often took the lead in political protests, directing local general strikes and organizing popular demonstrations against the government's domestic and foreign policies.

The Camere del Lavoro joined with the federated trade unions in a national organization, the Confederazione Generale del Lavoro (q.v.) (General Confederation of Labor), in 1906. Those *Camere* controlled by revolutionary syndicalists remained independent, and united with other syndicalist groups in the Unione Sindacale Italiana in 1912. Immediately following World War I the *Camere* experienced a dramatic surge in membership, but during the early 1920s their numbers declined rapidly in the face of intimidation and frequent attacks by Fascist *squadristi* (q.v.). As a powerful local labor institution the *Camere* were special targets of Fascist "punitive expeditions." Fascist groups sacked and burned the offices and facilities of the *Camere* and assaulted local labor leaders. Along with other political and labor organizations not sanctioned by the Fascist regime, the *Camere* were suppressed by the government in the 1926 "Exceptional Decrees" (q.v.).

For further information see: Marinia Bonaccini and Renza Casero, *La Camera del Lavoro di Milano dalle origini al 1904* (Milan: Sugar Co, 1975); Maurice Neufield, *Italy: School for Awakening Countries* (Ithaca, N.Y.: Cayuga Press,

1961); Giuliano Procacci, *La lotta di classe agli inizi del secolo xx* (Rome: Riuniti, 1970).

MH

CAMERINI, MARIO (b. Rome, February 6, 1895). An important film director of the 1930s, Camerini took a degree in law and began working in motion pictures in 1920. His films were known for their poignant portrayal of the strivings of humble people in the urban environment. Among his best known works are *Gli uomini che mascalzoni* (1932) and *Il signor Max* (1937), both starring Vittorio De Sica and Assia Noris; *Darò un milione* (1935), *Il grande appello* (1936), *Grandi magazzini* (1939), and *Centomila dollari* (1939-40). Most of his films were especially effective in the context of the Great Depression, for he concentrated on the theme of finding happiness in love and personal relationships and the sentimental dreams of the petty bourgeoisie.

For further information see: Philip V. Cannistraro, *La fabbrica del consenso* (Rome-Bari: Laterza, 1975); Edward R. Tannenbaum, *The Fascist Experience* (New York: Basic Books, 1972).

PVC

CAMPIONI, INIGO (b. Viareggio, November 14, 1878; d. Parma, May 24, 1944). Commander of the battle fleet at Punta Stilo and Capo Teulada (July 9 and November 27, 1940), Admiral Campioni failed to press home a considerable advantage in strength. Replaced on December 8, 1940, along with Domenico Cavagnari (q.v.) whose restrictive orders were at least partly responsible for Campioni's caution, Campioni served for some months as deputy chief of the naval staff. In July 1941 he became governor of the Dodecanese, which he surrendered to the Germans three days after the 1943 armistice; the Salò Republic (*see* ITALIAN SOCIAL REPUBLIC) shot him for not surrendering immediately.

MK

CANEVARI, EMILIO (b. December 19, 1888). Polemicist, military commentator, and Fascist army officer, Canevari served as liaison between party and Army in 1922, and thereafter assisted Francesco Grazioli (q.v.) and Italo Balbo (q.v.) in their attempts to modernize the armed forces. Canevari's expertise on Libyan military affairs brought his appointment as Pietro Badoglio's (q.v.) adviser from 1922 to 1923 and from 1928 to 1930. But Badoglio encouraged his dismissal for embezzlement in June 1930, provoking Canevari's lasting enmity. Roberto Farinacci (q.v.) quickly hired him as military expert for *Il Regime Fascista*; Canevari attacked the Army leadership's closeminded conservatism and drafted Balbo's unsuccessful proposal for a unified defense ministry in 1933. After 1936 Canevari criticized Army overconfidence and in March 1937 predicted failure at Guadalajara. Later that year to Alberto Pariani's (q.v.) indignation, Canevari described Italian tanks and the proposed "binary" (two-regiment) division as worthless (although

Canevari did not fully understand mechanized warfare until May 1940). He apparently took part in Farinacci's campaign against Badoglio in November 1940, and while serving as Ugo Cavallero's (q.v.) press aide in Albania boasted that he had written the editorial which opened the crisis. After the 1943 armistice, Canevari help Rodolfo Graziani (q.v.) organize the Fascist republican armed forces, but fell foul of Renato Ricci (q.v.), Alessandro Pavolini (q.v.), and Heinrich Himmler, who were attempting to assert the primacy of the MVSN/Guardia Nazionale Repubblicana (see MILITIA). Mussolini and Graziani dismissed him in December 1943.

For further information see: Emilio Canevari, L'Italia 1861-1943. Restroscena della disfatta (Rome: Rivista Romana, 1965); Emilio Canevari, Graziani mi ha detto (Rome: Magi-Spinetti, 1947).

MK/BRS

CANTALUPO, ROBERTO (b. Naples, January 17, 1891). A diplomat and journalist, at the age of eighteen Cantalupo was editor of Il Pungolo (Naples) and then foreign correspondent for La Tribuna (Rome), Corriere d'Italia (Rome), and Corriere della sera (Milan). A Nationalist, he fought in World War I and in 1917 accepted an offer from Enrico Corradini (q.v.) to work for Idea Nazionale, for which he covered the Paris Peace Conference and other international events. Intensely interested in foreign and colonial affairs, in 1922 he returned to Italy and wrote for various newspapers, including Mussolini's Gerarchia. From 1922 to 1924 he was editor in chief of Idea Nazionale, and was then elected a deputy.

In July 1924 Cantalupo was appointed undersecretary for colonies, and was alternately envoy in Cairo (1926-32), ambassador in Rio de Janeiro (1932-36), a functionary of the Foreign Ministry in Rome, and then ambassador in Spain (1937). After two months in Madrid, Cantalupo's nonideological, moderate views brought about his recall (principally through Roberto Farinacci's [q.v.] criticisms), and his diplomatic career came to an end.

For further information see: Chi è? (1948); NO (1928); Annuario diplomatico (Rome: Ministry for Foreign Affairs, 1937); Roberto Cantalupo, Fu la Spagna: Ambasciata presso Franco (Milan: Mondadori, 1948).

PVC

CAPASSO TORRE DI CAPRARA, GIOVANNI (b. Rome, April 8, 1883). A diplomat and Fascist bureaucrat, Capasso Torre came from a noble family (he was Conte delle Pastene) and received a degree in law. He practiced journalism before World War I as foreign correspondent for Il Giornale d'Italia (Rome), traveling extensively. He fought in World War I and in 1918 was foreign news editor for Il Tempo (Rome). He served as private secretary to Foreign Minister Vittorio Scialoja from December 1919 to June 1920, and then returned to journalism as director first of Il Corriere Mercantile (Genoa) and then of Il Corriere Italiano.

For his support of Mussolini during the Matteotti crisis (q.v.) he was appointed head of the prime minister's Press Office in April 1925; in May 1926 he was also made head of the same office in the Ministry of Foreign Affairs and the two positions were unified into the Ufficio Stampa del Capo del Governo (Press Office of the Head of Government). Until his resignation in September 1928, Capasso Torre directed the regime's first propaganda office and established many of the latest techniques for controlling the press (*see* MINISTRY OF POPULAR CULTURE).

In 1929 he was appointed counsul general in Munich, then transferred to Tangiers in January 1932 and to Copenhagen in August. In February 1937 he became secretary general to the Italian Administration of the Dodecanese Islands and subsequently was attached to the Foreign Ministry. In June 1943, he became director of *Italia di Oltremare* (Italy Beyond the Seas).

For further information see: *Chi è?* (1948); NO (1927); *Annuario Diplomatico* (Rome: Ministero Affari Esteri, 1937); Philip V. Cannistraro, *La fabbrica del consenso* (Rome-Bari: Laterza, 1975).

PVC

CAPELLO, LUIGI (b. Intra, Novara, April 14, 1859; d. Rome, June 25, 1941). The defeated commander at Caporetto (*see* CAPORETTO, BATTLE OF), the disgraced Capello joined the PNF (Partito Nazionale Fascista) (q.v.) in 1920. While his reputation precluded a major role in the Fascist regime, Capello visited Germany in 1923-24 to secure secret collaboration with the Reichswehr (German Army). Upon return, Mussolini offered to clear Capello's name if he would end his Masonic activities. Capello refused. Shocked by Matteotti's murder (*see* MATTEOTTI CRISIS), Capello plotted with Tito Zaniboni (q.v.) to overthrow Mussolini but was arrested in November 1925. The Special Tribunal for the Defense of the State (q.v.) sentenced him to thirty years' imprisonment, but he gained parole for poor health in early 1936.

For further information see: DBI (18).

BRS

CAPORETTO, BATTLE OF. The worst defeat in modern Italian history, the Battle of Caporetto took place in October and November of 1917 After Italy entered World War I, twenty-nine months of slaughter exhausted the country and its Army. Luigi Cadorna (q.v.), Army Chief of Staff, drove his forces, under ferocious discipline, into repeated frontal assaults without adequate firepower or imaginative leadership. Behind the front the peasants suffered economic hardship while Cadorna destroyed their sons. National weariness prompted a response to Papal and Socialist peace calls. Cadorna failed to provide counterpropaganda. The Austro-Hungarians, equally sapped, persuaded the Germans to aid them. Seven German divisions, trained in new infiltration tactics and artillery techniques, arrived to spearhead an offensive. Although forewarned, Cadorna and the threatened sector commander, Luigi Capello (q.v.), did not prepare adequate defenses. When the Germans struck at Caporetto, (now Kobarid, Slovenia) on October 24, 1917, the local commander, Pietro Badoglio (q.v.), was absent. Italian defenses collapsed and the Germans broke through. Confusion, then panic, followed, and Capello's Second Army was routed. Cadorna ordered retreat to the Tagliamento River, failed to hold, and fell back further to the Piave River. By then, one-third of Cadorna's troops and half of his guns were gone. But Cadorna rallied his shattered forces and, before being replaced by Armando Diaz (q.v.), prepared successful defenses. Seven weeks of struggle followed, but the Italians held. Italy rallied and united behind new national leadership. After rebuilding, Diaz repulsed another Austrian attack in June 1918, then ended the war with the Vittorio Veneto offensive in October-November 1918. Postwar disillusionment followed painfully won victory, contributing to Fascism's triumph. Many Italians, viewing Caporetto as symbolic of national failings, hoped to perpetuate through Fascism the state of social mobilization that preceded Vittorio Veneto. Mussolini skillfully manipulated these hopes but eventually led Italy into a second war of multiple Caporettos.

For further information see: Piero Melograni, *Storia politica della grande guerra* (Bari: Laterza, 1969); Piero Pieri, *L'Italia nella prima guerra mondiale* (Turin: Einaudi, 1968).

BRS

CAPRONI, GIOVANNI BATTISTA (b. Massone, Trento, July 3, 1886; d. Rome, October 29, 1957). Aircraft designer and industrialist, Caproni's designs, influenced by his friend Giulio Douhet (q.v.), gave the Regìa Aeronautica (Air Force) (q.v.) excellent bombers until the late 1930s. But Caproni's concentration on winning records, rather than solving the problems of mass production, had dire consequences. While his companies expanded to produce equipment for all three services during World War II, lack of raw materials prevented their reaching full potential.

For further information see: DBI (19).

BRS

CARBONI, GIACOMO (b. Reggio Emilia, 1889; d. Rome, December 1, 1974). Best known for his ambiguous part in the events of September 8-9, 1943, General Carboni served the Fascist regime most conspicuously as chief of SIM (*see* SERVIZIO INFORMAZIONI MILITARI), the military intelligence, from November 1939 to September 1940. Despite a tendency to ingratiate himself with Mussolini and Galeazzo Ciano (q.v.), Carboni was consistently anti-German. In May 1940 he cautiously attempted to dissuade Ciano and Mussolini from entering the war, forecasting immediate United States intervention, but once committed he gleefully predicted Italian success in Egypt. Before that prognostication proved false, Carboni lost his post in a clash with Ubaldo Soddu (q.v.), who apparently disposed of a potential rival by denouncing to Mussolini Carboni's hostility to the Germans.

Carboni subsequently served as chief of military schools at Modena and Parma, as commander of an assault division for the planned Malta landing in 1942, and as Pietro Badoglio's (q.v.) head of intelligence and commander of the motorized corps which failed to guard Rome in 1943.

For further information see: Giacomo Carboni's far from reliable *Memorie segrete 1935-1948* (Florence: Parenti, 1955).

MK

CARITÀ, MARIO (b. Milan, 1904; d. Alpe di Siusi, Alto Adige, 1945). The leader of an infamous group organized to uncover and destroy the anti-Fascist underground (the so-called "Banda Carità"), little is known about Carità's background. At an early age he participated in the punitive expeditions led by Luigi Freddi's (q.v.) *squadristi* (q.v.) in and around Lodi, and in 1940 he commanded a company of Blackshirts during the Greek campaign.

In September 1943—after the Nazi occupation of northern Italy—a special police unit known as the Reparto di Servizi Speciali (RSS) (Special Service Department) was established in Florence, nominally attached to the Fascist Militia (q.v.), and Carità was made its commander. Its purpose was to discover the names of and arrest resistance leaders and anti-Fascist militants, and to develop a network of spies for that purpose. He worked closely with the German SS and SD security police and with other branches of the Italian police. Carità had about two hundred agents working under him, and his "general staff" included Roberto Lawley, Ferdinando Manzella, Guido Simini, Armando Tela, Eugenio Varano, and Pietro Koch (q.v.). After moving about Florence for a time, his headquarters was finally located in a villa on the Via Bolognese (the so-called "Villa Triste"), where captured partisans and suspects were brutally tortured and frequently killed. Carità was himself shot by American troops in northern Italy a few days after the end of the war, and in a famous trial in June 1951 (in which Piero Calamandrei [q.v.] served as the state's attorney), 178 of Carità's agents were prosecuted.

For further information see: EAR (2); Carlo Francovich, *La resistenza a Firenze* (Florence: Nuova Italia, 1961).

PVC

CARLI, MARIO (b. San Severo, Foggia, December 31, 1889; d. Rome, September 9, 1935). A noted Futurist (*see* FUTURISM) writer, in 1909 Carli joined with a group of young intellectuals in Florence (including Emilio Settimelli and Bruno Corra) to advance a new, avant-garde literature. Shortly before World War I he and many of his friends adhered to the Futurist movement and joined the board of the journal *L'Italia futurista* (Florence).

He campaigned with Filippo Marinetti (q.v.) for Italy's entrance into the war and fought as a captain in the Arditi (q.v.). In 1917 he cofounded the paper *Roma futurista*, and the next year became a political activist with the creation of the political group known as the Fasci politici Futuristi, later transformed into the

Partito Politico Futurista. In January 1919 he founded the first Arditi organization in Rome and its organ, *L'Ardito* (Milan). Carli was among the Sansepolcristi (q.v.) present at the founding of Mussolini's Fascist movement in March 1919, and later that year he established with Giuseppe Bottai (q.v.) the Roman *fascio*. In September 1919 he joined with Gabriele D'Annunzio (q.v.) in the Fiume (q.v.) expedition, and then took part in the March on Rome (q.v.). Carli's ideas combined a generic belief in activism with the cult of force and an intense nationalism. He was an ardent admirer of Mussolini and a friend and follower of the intransigent Roberto Farinacci (q.v.).

Carli held a number of minor government posts, including membership on the High Commission for the Press, in the executive committee of the Fascist Writer's Union, and as an officer in the Militia (q.v.). In 1925 he signed Giovanni Gentile's (q.v.) "Manifesto of Fascist Intellectuals" (*see* "MANIFESTO OF ANTI-FASCIST INTELLECTUALS). Between 1923 and 1929 Carli directed *L'Impero* (Rome), a "dissident" but faithful newspaper that was permitted some degree of criticism. During his last years, Carli was in declining health, and after a brief stay in Brazil and Greece as Italian consul, he returned to Italy.

For further information see: DBI (20).

PVC

CARNARO, CHARTER OF. The constitution for Gabriele D'Annunzio's (q.v.) government of Fiume (q.v.)—the so-called Regency of Carnaro—was drafted by Alceste De Ambris (q.v.) between January and March 1920, revised by D'Annunzio, and promulgated in September.

The charter was an unusual document, the product of the syndico-socialist and poetic-historical ideas of its authors. It provided for a decentralized parliamentary republic based on the organization of citizens into corporations (*see* CORPORATIVISM AND THE CORPORATIVE STATE). The executive branch consisted of seven "rectors" chosen by three legislative bodies; the latter included two elected institutions (Consiglio dei Provvisori [Council of Provisionals] and Consiglio degli Ottimi [Council of the Best]) and the Arengo del Carnaro (Assembly of Carnaro), composed of the two elected bodies meeting jointly. All citizens over the age of twenty could vote, with representation based on nine syndical corporations; local governments ("communes") had wide autonomy; a series of five courts formed the judiciary; and basic freedoms and social services were guaranteed. At the top of the entire structure stood the office of the Comandante (which D'Annunzio occupied), to be filled only in emergencies.

Although the charter combined neoreligious, spiritual, and mystical ideas stemming from D'Annunzio's poetic vision of life, it also corresponded to a rationalist tradition based on a belief in progress and the perfectability of the human condition.

For further information see: Renzo De Felice, ed., *La Carta di Carnaro*

(Bologna: Mulino, 1973); Michael A. Ledeen, *The First Duce* (Baltimore: Johns Hopkins, 1977).

PVC

CARNAZZA, GABRIELLO (b. Catania, April 26, 1871, d. Catania, April 17, 1931). A deputy and Fascist minister, Carnazza was a successful business attorney in Sicily before entering politics at the turn of the century. He and his younger brother Carlo (owner of *Il Giornale del' isola* and himself a deputy) represented an old Sicilian political tradition based on clientele relations, government influence, and local wealth, and they were both closely aligned with Giovanni Giolitti (q.v.). Locally they were opposed by G. De Felice Giuffrida, who enjoyed vast personal popularity and a political tradition that could be traced back to the *fasci* of 1892. Carnazza was elected to Parliament in 1906 as a radical, but lost to the De Felice proponents in subsequent elections.

In 1919 the two factions united on a common electoral list against the Socialists and Popolari and Carnazza was again sent to Parliament, where he gained a reputation for expertise in economic matters. In April 1921 Giolitti made him undersecretary of the treasury. In that same year he and other radical deputies formed the Social Democratic party.

Carnazza joined the PNF (Partito Nazionale Fascista) (q.v.) in December 1923 after he had secured Mussolini's support in his struggle against the De Felice faction. In July 1923 Mussolini made him minister of public works, but he was forced to resign the following year as a result of financial irregularities and the fact that he was implicated in the Matteotti murder (*see* MATTEOTTI CRISIS). A subsequent purge of the local Fascist movement in Catania further reduced his personal position, and in April 1928 he and his brother were both expelled from the PNF.

For further information see: DBI (20); NO (1928).

PVC

CARRÀ, CARLO DALMAZZO (b. Quargnento, Piedmont, February 11, 1881; d. Milan, 1966). One of the early and leading Futurist painters, Carrà was one of the original writers of the *Futurist Manifesto on Painting* (February 11, 1910) and the later *Technical Manifesto of Futurist Painters* (April 1910).

Before 1900 Carrà studied in the Brera art school in Milan and then traveled to Paris where he spent time learning from the Impressionist and post-Impressionist painters. He helped to bridge the gap between these two French painting styles and to form the basis of the early Futurist painting style. In 1909 Carrà met Filippo Tommaso Marinetti (q.v.) and Umberto Boccioni for the first time and in 1910 participated with them in the Futurist manifestoes. By 1911 Carrà had also been influenced by Picasso and the Cubist fragmentation of subject matter. In 1915, along with Giorgio De Chirico, he began to develop a style based on more traditional and classical origins, which emerged by 1917 as Pittura Metafisica

(Metaphysical Painting). During this same year Carrà wrote *Guerrapittura, futurismo politico, dinamismo plastico* in Milan responding to Boccioni's attack on him in *Futurist Painting and Sculpture* (1914). Carrà wrote for the Futurist journal *Lacerba* as well as for *Valori Plastici, Popolo d'Italia*, and *La Voce*. In 1917 he was judged mentally unfit to serve in the Italian Army. After the development of the Pittura Metafisica style, Carrà diverged from Futurism and along with others searched for a more historically based Italian style in painting. He taught in the academy in Milan for many years and influenced generations of young Italian painters until the 1940s. In 1943 Carrà wrote his autobiography. In it he explained his patriotic views. During the Fascist regime Carrà showed his work extensively and found support from the government.

For further information see: Carlo Carrà, *La Mia Vita* (Rome: Longanesi, 1943); Roberto Longhi, *Carlo Carrà* (Milan: Hoepli, 1945); Fernando Tempesti, *Arte dell'Italia Fascista* (Milan: Feltrinelli, 1976).

JH

CARTA DEL LAVORO. See **CHARTER OF LABOR.**

CARTA DELLA SCUOLA. See **SCHOOL CHARTER.**

CARUSO, PIETRO (b. Naples, 1900; d. Rome, September 21, 1944). A Fascist police chief in Rome during the Nazi occupation, Caruso was a Blackshirt (*see* SQUADRISTI) in the famous "Serenissima" squad of Naples. He participated in the March on Rome (q.v.), but information regarding his subsequent activities is lacking.

Caruso went north to the Salò Republic (*see* ITALIAN SOCIAL REPUBLIC) in 1943 and was in charge of the police at the Verona Trials (q.v.). In February 1944 he returned to Rome as police chief, where he worked closely with Nazi officials in the deportation of Italians to German labor camps and in the capture of anti-Fascists. Caruso become one of the most hated Fascist figures for his participation in the roundup of Romans who were executed in the Ardeatine Caves Massacre (q.v.).

Caruso fled Rome in June 1944 just ahead of Allied troops and hid in a hospital in Viterbo, but he was captured and returned to Rome for trial. In September he was condemned to death and executed.

For further information see: Zara Algardi, *Il processo Caruso* (Rome: Darsena, 1945); Robert Katz, *Death in Rome* (New York: Macmillan, 1967).

PVC

CASABLANCA CONFERENCE. The first major strategic decisions of World War II relating to Italy were made by the United States and Great Britain at the Casablanca Conference, which took place between January 14 and 24, 1943. The most pressing strategic question facing Allied leaders was what military operation would be mounted following the liberation of the remaining portions of North Africa. The British, led by Prime Minister Winston S. Churchill, stressed the availability of a veteran and victorious army and pressed for a continuation of operations in the Mediterranean. The British underlined the military and political advantages that would result from a successful Allied attack on Italy. American military leaders, however, were wedded to the notion of a cross-channel invasion of France at the earliest possible date. They realized that a military campaign in Italy would prohibit the necessary build up of men and materials needed for a cross channel invasion and resisted British strategy. On January 18 the Americans agreed to a compromise. Allied armies in the Mediterranean would be employed during the summer of 1943 in an invasion of Sicily. Control of Sicily would provide a number of immediate military advantages, and it was hoped that the loss of Sicily would lead to the overthrow of the Fascist regime in Italy. General Dwight D. Eisenhower was appointed Allied Commander in Chief in the Mediterranean and was instructed to lay plans for the invasion of Sicily.

At the conference's end President Roosevelt used a news conference to announce that the Allied powers would demand the unconditional surrender of all the Axis states. Roosevelt's statement was made on the spur of the moment, and its timing came as a surprise to Churchill. However, it represented a growing consensus within both governments that the Allies could not allow themselves to become involved in negotiations with Fascist regimes and that insistence on unconditional surrender would reassure the Soviet Union that its western allies would not make a separate peace. Italy would be the first nation whose unconditional surrender would be demanded.

For further information see: Ann Armstrong, *Unconditional Surrender* (New Brunswick, N.J.: Rutgers University Press, 1961); *Foreign Relations of the United States. The Conferences at Washington, 1941-1942 and Casablanca, 1943* (Washington, D.C.: U.S. Government Printing Office, 1968).

JEM

CASATI, COUNT ALESSANDRO (b. Milan, March 5, 1881; d. Arcore, Milan, June 4, 1955). A historian and political figure, during his youth Casati was active in the modernist Catholic movement and later was a disciple of Benedetto Croce (q.v.). He volunteered in World War I and was an early supporter of Fascism. In 1923 he was made a senator, and in July 1924 Mussolini appointed him minister of public instruction, but he resigned in January of the next year and was among those who sought to create a new Liberal party. Casati devoted the next eighteen years to historical scholarship, but in June 1943 he made contact with anti-Fascist groups and helped to establish the Central Committee of National Liberation (*see* COMMITTEE OF NATIONAL LIBERATION) in Nazi occupied Rome. He served as minister of war under Ivanoe Bonomi (q.v.) from June 1944 to June 1945, was a member of the Constituent Assembly (*see* COSTITUENTE), and a senator from 1948 to 1953.

For further information see: *Chi è?* (1948); DBI (21); EAR (2); Charles F. Delzell, *Mussolini's Enemies* (Princeton: Princeton University Press, 1961).

PVC

CASATI, ETTORE (b. Chiavenna, Sondrio, March 24, 1873; d. Rome, August 18, 1945). An Italian jurist and minister, Casati was appointed president of the high appeals Court of Cassation in November 1941 and remained in office until 1944. After the July 1943 coup against Mussolini, Casati refused to adhere to the Salò Republic (*See* ITALIAN SOCIAL REPUBLIC) and instead made his way south behind Allied lines. Pietro Badoglio (q.v.) appointed him minister of grace and justice in February 1944.

For further information see: DBI (21); EAR (2).

PVC

CASERTANO, ANTONIO (b. Capua, December 20, 1863; d. Naples, December 13, 1938). A deputy and minister, Casertano practiced law for many years in Naples before entering politics. An interventionist, he was elected to Parliament in 1919 as a radical, and was responsible for the vote of no confidence that produced the fall of Ivanoe Bonomi's (q.v.) government in February 1922. He was appointed undersecretary for the interior by Luigi Facta (q.v.) immediately thereafter. His rigid opposition to the Socialists and the Popular party and his growing support for Mussolini brought about his exclusion from the second Facta cabinet formed in August 1922. At the same time, however, he was elected to preside over the Parliamentary Commission on Internal Affairs, and together with Giovanni Giolitti (q.v.) and other Liberals, he recommended approval of the Giacomo Acerbo (q.v.) electoral law of 1923 that gave Fascists a majority. He also attempted to create a conservative block of southern deputies designed to increase Mussolini's power base in Parliament. Casertano was elected to the Chamber of Deputies again on the *listone* (Fascist list of candidates) of 1924 and engaged in a number of crucial debates with Matteotti (*see* MATTEOTTI CRISIS) over the outcome of the elections. In January 1925 he became president of the Chamber of Deputies (in which capacity he pushed for limiting debate) and in January 1929 became a senator.

For further information see: *Chi è?* (1936); DBI (21); NO (1928).

PVC

CASINI, GHERARDO (b. Pisa, November 8, 1903). A journalist and bureaucrat, Casini received a law degree and began to identify himself with the left wing, corporativist (*see* CORPORATIVISM AND THE CORPORATIVE STATE) current of Fascism. He wrote for *L'Assalto* in the early 1920s and became a friend and associate of Giuseppe Bottai (q.v.). Casini was one of a group of young Fascist intellectuals who wanted to give the trade unions real power in the economic and political life of the regime (he advocated syndical participation in the management of private firms) and make the corporations a reality. He was also tied closely to Bottai's belief that Fascism had to maintain a free and open dialog and attract intellectuals to it. He was often in dispute with Roberto Farinacci (q.v.) and other intransigents.

Casini founded and directed *Rivoluzione fascista* (Florence) in 1924, a paper that coordinated its editorial policy with Bottai's *Critica fascista*. He was editor of *Il Resto del Carlino* (Bologna) in 1925, and was director of *Battaglie fasciste* (Florence) in 1926. In 1929 Casini became codirector of *Critica fascista* and two years later was also director and editor of the Fascist syndicalist newspaper *Lavoro fascista* (Rome). He wrote widely in the 1920s for these and other papers, including *Il Popolo d'Italia*.

In 1927-28 Casini worked in the Ministry of Corporations. In 1935 he resigned from *Critica fascista* to head the Italian press division of the newly created Ministry of Press and Propaganda. He established a special section in the ministry for book censorship and in 1938 was a member of the Commissione per la Bonifica Libraria (Commission for the Improvement of Books) that determined book censorship policy.

For further information see: *Chi è?* (1936); Philip V. Cannistraro, *La fabbrica del consenso* (Rome-Bari: Laterza, 1975); Alexander J. De Grand, *Bottai e la cultura fascista* (Rome-Bari: Laterza, 1978); Giordano Guerri, *Giuseppe Bottai* (Milan: Feltrinelli, 1976).

PVC

CASTELLANO, GIUSEPPE (b. Prato, September 12, 1893; d. Porretta, Terme, August 2, 1977). Army general and a key figure in Italy's 1943 surrender, Castellano was commissioned in the artillery shortly before World War I and served during the hostilities. From 1935 to 1937 he was deputy chief of staff of the Sicilian army corps under General Ambrosio (q.v.), and the two men developed a close and long association. When Ambrosio became army chief of staff, Castellano served as his immediate subordinate.

Both Castellano and Ambrosio disliked and mistrusted the Germans, and during World War II they sought every opportunity to disengage Italy from the Axis. In the days preceding the July 1943 meeting of the Fascist Grand Council (q.v.) that unseated Mussolini, Castellano was in contact with Dino Grandi (q.v.), the Duke d'Acquarone (q.v.) and others involved in the conspiracy. After the creation of the Badoglio (q.v.) government he was sent to Lisbon in August to explore an armistice (q.v.) with Allied representatives and urged his military and political superiors in Rome to accept the so-called "short terms." On September 3, he signed the Cassibile armistice for the Italian government.

For further information see: Giuseppe Castellano, *Come firmai l'armistizio di Cassibile* (Milan: Mondadori, 1945), reprinted as *La guerra continua* (Milan: Rizzoli, 1963); DSPI; Albert N. Garland and Howard McGraw Smith, *Sicily and the Surrender of Italy* (Washington, D.C.: U.S. Government Printing Office, 1965).

PVC

CAVAGNARI, DOMENICO (b. Genoa, July 20, 1876; d. Rome, 1966). Chief of Staff from 1933 and Undersecretary of the Navy from 1934, Admiral Cavagnari prepared the Italian Navy for war and led it in the first six months of Italy's participation in World War II. His early career included service in the first Ethiopian War, the Libyan War, and World War I (in which he received several decorations as commander of a destroyer escort). As head of the Navy, he was active in preparing the second Ethiopian War (q.v.), and supervised the Navy's transition to an anti-British posture from 1935 on. In August 1939 his fleet was the only one of the Italian services even partially ready for action. However, in April 1940 Cavagnari advised against entering the war and expressed the fear that Italy might arrive at the peace table "without a fleet." He acquiesced in May after a French collapse but was unwilling to engage in a decisive battle with the British, despite Italian superiority in the Mediterranean waters around the peninsula. When Pietro Badoglio (q.v.) suggested an increase in Navy activity, Cavagnari refused to bow to the Marshal's authority; in the end, Badoglio accepted Cavagnari's views, which amounted to turning over to the Air Force and Army the task of asserting Italian supremacy in the Mediterranean. The consequence of this attempt to fight the war from the harbor was the Taranto disaster (q.v.) of November 11-12, 1940, which induced Mussolini to dismiss Cavagnari with the approval of the king and of Grand Admiral Paolo Thaon di Revel (q.v.).

For further information see: DBI (22).

MK

CAVALLERO, UGO (b. Casale Monferrato, September 20, 1880; d. Frascati, September 13, 1943). Cavallero, the most talented of Mussolini's marshals, received his commission in 1900, graduated in first place from the War College in 1911, and served in Libya in 1912-13. In May 1915 Luigi Cadorna (q.v.) chose Cavallero for his operations office; Cavallero helped plan the repulse of the *"Strafexpedition"* (the Austrian offensive in May-June 1916), the capture of Gorizia (1916), and the retreat after the Battle of Caporetto (q.v.). In November 1917, Cavallero became chief of operations under Armando Diaz (q.v.). With Pietro Badoglio (q.v.), Cavallero planned the Piave defense and the Vittorio Veneto offensive.

At Diaz's urging, Cavallero received accelerated promotion to brigadier general (at the unprecedented age of thirty-eight) and was appointed to the Italian Versailles delegation. With further rapid promotion unlikely, Cavallero left the Army in 1920 and soon became director of the Pirelli Company. Diaz proposed him for minister of war in 1924, but Mussolini refused Cavallero's conditions: increased appropriations and Badoglio as chief of staff. Following Antonino Di Giorgio's (q.v.) resignation, however, Cavallero became undersecretary of war (under Mussolini). After recalling Badoglio to assume the posts of Army Chief of Staff and then Capo di Stato Maggiore Generale (Chief of the Supreme General Staff), Cavallero fell out with him, and in early 1927 deprived Badoglio of most powers, only to find himself dismissed after a public altercation with the Marshal in November 1928.

Turning again to industry, Cavallero secured the presidency of the Ansaldo works, and attempted to modernize the armament industry. He resigned in 1933 after the Navy complained that the firm was supplying ordinary steel in place of armor plate; Cavallero was probably personally blameless, but his reputation suffered permanent damage. He subsequently served as delegate to the Geneva Disarmament Conference, but Badoglio blocked him from participating in the Ethiopian War (q.v.). Nevertheless, Cavallero secured command of Italian forces in East Africa in November 1937; he failed to suppress the widespread rebellion Rodolfo Graziani (q.v.) and Mussolini had conjured up. Cavallero's excessively optimistic reports and his plan to attack the Sudan and Egypt in the event of European war produced a confrontation with his superior, the duke of Aosta (*see* SAVOIA, AMEDEO DI, DUKE OF AOSTA).

Cavallero resigned in May 1939, and Mussolini quickly named him president of the Pact of Steel (q.v.) coordinating committee. In this capacity Cavallero conveyed to Berlin Mussolini's memorandum attempting to add to the Pact an understanding postponing war until 1942-43, when Italian armaments would be ready. After a period as military consultant to the Foreign Ministry, Cavallero emerged in late November 1940 as the leading candidate to succeed Badoglio at the Comando Supremo (q.v.). Appointed on December 4, Cavallero also took over the collapsing Albanian front from Ubaldo Soddu (q.v.). Cavallero's logistical and organizational talents saved the situation, but the March offensive Mussolini inevitably demanded failed. Cavallero returned to Rome in May 1941, purged the War Ministry and Comando Supremo, and secured considerable reinforcement of his own powers. Although a salutary shock to the military traditionalists, he was too aware that he held office at Mussolini's pleasure and too optimistic and pliable in the face of the Duce's insistence on a vast but ill-equipped army (rather than a small, efficient one) and on dispersing Italian forces in Russia and the Balkans, far from the theatre decisive for Italy—North Africa. Less justly Cavallero acquired the reputation of a German lackey. Unlike many of his fellow generals, he recognized that the Italian war effort depended on Germany, and he was therefore willing to pay the price Italy's allies implicitly demanded: control of Italian strategy.

Mussolini dismissed him on February 6, 1943, after the Axis collapse in North Africa. Badoglio had him arrested immediately after Mussolini's fall on July 25, and while in prison Cavallero (in an attempt to curry favor) dictated a memorandum relating his largely imaginary part in the plotting preceding Mussolini's overthrow; the document later figured in the Verona Trials (q.v.). Released after the 1943 armistice with the Allies, Cavallero apparently shot himself while a guest of the German commander in Italy, Field Marshal Albert Kesselring (q.v.), after refusing to lead Italian forces and to continue the fight alongside the Germans.

For further information see: DBI (22); Ugo Cavallero, *Comando Supremo. Diario 1940-1943 del Capo di S.M.G.* (Bologna: Cappelli, 1948); Lucio Ceva, *La condotta italiana della guerra. Cavallero e il Comando Supremo 1941-1942* (Milan: Feltrinelli, 1975).

MK/BRS

CAVAZZONI, STEFANO (b. Guastalla, Reggio Emilia, August 1, 1881; d. 1951). A Catholic deputy and minister, Cavazzoni was active in Milan in the Christian-democratic movement and had connections in high banking circles. In 1904 he was a member of the city council, and in 1919 and 1921 was elected to Parliament as a member of the Popular party. As a deputy he served as secretary of his party's parliamentary group and was on its executive committee. In 1920-21 Cavazzoni was a proponent, along with Luigi Sturzo (q.v.), of the Catholic trade union movement.

After 1922 he grew increasingly closer to the Fascists. He provided a link between the Fascists and conservative Catholics and supported Mussolini's parliamentary maneuvers, including efforts to suppress freedom of the press and to pass the Acerbo (*see* ACERBO, GIACOMO) bill. Cavazzoni was minister of labor in Mussolini's first cabinet (until April 1923) and in 1924 was reelected to Parliament on the Fascist list. He became a senator in 1929. From 1933 to 1943 he was the regime's representative on the administrative council of the Catholic University of Milan. Cavazzoni, never a genuine Fascist, accepted membership in the PNF (Partito Nazionale Fascista) (q.v.) only in 1940.

For further information see: DSPI; NO (1928); Richard A. Webster, *Christian Democracy in Italy* (London: Hollis & Carter, 1961).

PVC

CAVIGLIA, ENRICO (b. Finalmarina, Savona, May 4, 1862; d. Finalmarina, March 22, 1945). A leading general of World War I and the defender of Rome in September 1943, Caviglia ejected Gabriele D'Annunzio (q.v.) from Fiume (q.v.) in December 1920 but then blamed Giovanni Giolitti (q.v.) for manipulating him. While originally supporting Mussolini, Caviglia worked ineffectively against him during the Matteotti crisis (q.v.). He supported Gaetano Giardino (q.v.) in opposing Antonino Di Giorgio's (q.v.) army reorganization but failed to prevent his enemy, Pietro Badoglio (q.v.), from becoming Chief of Staff. Though promoted to Marshal in June 1926, Caviglia lost all his power and devoted himself to military history. He maintained an ambiguous attitude toward Mussolini. He urged the king to avoid war in August-September 1935, but applauded the conquest of Ethiopia. He also opposed the Axis (*see* AXIS, ROME-BERLIN) and war against France in 1940. Caviglia sought Italy's neutralization in 1942-43, then he became a candidate to succeed Mussolini. After Badoglio and the king's flight,

Caviglia directed Rome's defense, surrendering to the Germans on September 10, 1943.

For further information see: DBI (23); Enrico Caviglia, *Diario* (Rome: Cassini, 1952).

BRS

CECCHERINI, SANTE (b. Incisa Valdarno, Florence, November 15, 1863; d. Marina di Pisa, August 9, 1932). A Fascist general, Ceccherini was without a command after World War I and joined Gabriele D'Annunzio (q.v.) at Fiume (q.v.), which he left disillusioned in November 1920. Placed in reserve in March 1922, Ceccherini served Mussolini as military advisor. He urged postponement of the March on Rome (q.v.) but helped direct the northern column. Made Militia (q.v.) commander in Tuscany in July 1924, he became Tullio Tamburini's (q.v.) tool. Dismissed after Tamburini's downfall in December 1925, he was rehabilitated and became Militia inspector general in January 1927. Ceccherini retired after a stroke in 1928.

For further information see: DBI (23).

BRS

CERRUTI, VITTORIO (b. Novara, May 25, 1881; d. Novara, 1961). Ambassador in Berlin from October 1932 until Hitler demanded his removal in July 1935, Cerruti had joined the diplomatic service in 1904, served at the 1919 peace conference, as minister in Peking (1921-27) and as ambassador to the Soviet Union (1927-30) and Brazil (1930-32). In Germany he initially enjoyed (in the words of the French ambassador) the status of "Lord Protector" of the new National Socialist regime. However, as early as March 1933 Cerruti began to warn of the dangers Hitler's Austrian policy offered to Italian interests. On Mussolini's orders the ambassador also advised Hitler to moderate the new regime's anti-Jewish measures. In October 1933 Cerruti clashed with Hitler on disarmament policy shortly before Germany left the League of Nations Disarmament conference and the League of Nations. In November, Hermann Göring urged his recall, and Mussolini contemplated it, but Cerruti remained, probably because of increasing Italo-German tension over Austria. The ambassador continued to annoy the Germans (who read his dispatches and tapped his frequent and imprudent telephone calls). In June 1935, with Mussolini committed to the Ethiopian adventure, Hitler felt strong enough to summon Mussolini's agent Giuseppe Renzetti (q.v.) and demand Cerruti's recall. Immediately transferred to Paris, Cerruti aroused Galeazzo Ciano's (q.v.) and Mussolini's ire by failing to take a tough stand with the French. The ambassador's recall in November 1937 ended his diplomatic career.

MK

CHABOD, FEDERICO (b. Aosta, February 23, 1901; d. Rome, July 14, 1960). A historian of the Renaissance best known outside Italy for his work on Machiavelli, Chabod later turned his attention to postunification Italy. His works include an edition of Machiavelli's *Prince* (1924); several essays on Machiavelli and on Renaissance historiography; two studies on Milan under Charles V, *Lo Stato di Milano nell' impero di Carlo V* (1934) and *Per la storia religiosa dello stato di Milano durante il dominio di Carlo V* (1938); and two significant works on modern Italy: *Politica estera italiana dal 1870 al 1896* (1951) and *L'Italia contemporanea (1918-1948)*.

Chabod, a student of Benedetto Croce (q.v.), began his career as a history professor at the University of Perugia (1934-38), then at Milan (1938-46). After World War II he was professor of modern history at Rome, and Croce chose his former pupil to head his Italian Institute for Historical Studies at Naples. Chabod's fame extended outside of Italy, evidenced by invitations to deliver the Chichele Lectures at Oxford in 1951 and to lecture at the Sorbonne in 1958. He was elected president of the International Committee of the Historical Sciences in 1955.

Chabod was democratic and anti-Fascist politically. His first anti-Fascist activity began as early as 1925, when he guided Gaetano Salvemini (q.v.) to safety in France across the mountains of his native Val d'Aosta. Later he participated in the wartime Resistance in his native region, showing special concern for its future autonomy and hoping to forestall French attempts at annexation. After the liberation he became the first president of the autonomous Valdostano region in October 1946.

For further information see: EAR (2); the introduction by A. P. D'Entreves to F. Chabod, *Machiavelli and the Renaissance*, translator David Moore (London: Bowes & Bowes, 1958); Gennaro Sasso, *Profilo di Federico Chabod* (Bari: Laterza, 1961); Hans A. Schmitt, ed., *Historians of Modern Europe*, essay by A. William Salomone, "Federico Chabod" (Baton Rouge: Louisiana State University, 1971).

RVT

CHAMBER OF FASCES AND CORPORATIONS. See **PARLIAMENT**.

CHARTER OF LABOR. A document issued on April 21, 1927, embodying the general principles by which the Fascist state was supposed to regulate and protect labor, the charter came after a long series of agreements and laws that had effectively emasculated the Italian labor movement and the Fascist trade unions, including the December 1923 Pact of Palazzo Chigi (*see* PALAZZO CHIGI, PACT OF), the October 1925 Pact of Palazzo Vidoni (*see* PALAZZO VIDONI, PACT OF), the *legge sindacale* (syndical law) of 1926, and the establishment of the corporations (*see* CORPORATIVISM AND THE CORPORATIVE STATE) that same year.

The law of April 3, 1926 had empowered the corporations to establish the basic principles governing labor and labor contracts. But the Fascist syndical leader Edmondo Rossoni (q.v.) drafted his own specific and detailed norms in January 1927 that would have given labor and the unions considerable legal protection. After a discussion by the Fascist Grand Council (q.v.), Giuseppe Bottai (q.v.) produced a number of further drafts of the charter which, however, described only broad principles that would guide labor legislation and collective contracts and which removed many of the specific safeguards demanded by Rossoni. Mussolini ultimately selected a compromise plan that was the work of Alfredo Rocco (q.v.).

The completed charter contained thirty articles grouped under four categories: the corporate state and its organization; collective labor contracts and labor guarantees; employment offices; and insurance, aid, and education. In the place of minimum wage regulations, the charter established only that salaries would be regulated by fluctuations in the cost of living and that the consequences of economic crises had to be borne by both labor and capital. Collective contracts were made obligatory and disputes were resolved by labor tribunals. In the final analysis, the Charter of Labor largely recognized the government—and specifically the Ministry of Corporations—as the arbiter of the interests of the workers, and the government had already made its compromises with industry.

For further information see: Renzo De Felice, *Mussolini il fascista* (Turin: Einaudi, 1968); Herbert W. Schneider, *Making the Fascist State* (New York: Fertig, 1966).

                                                                                                        PVC

CHIAVOLINI, ALESSANDRO (b. Milan, July 29, 1889). Mussolini's private secretary, Chiavolini was trained in law and practiced journalism before World War I. He was editor of *Lombardia* (Milan) and in 1914 was an editor for Mussolini's *Il Popolo d'Italia* (Milan). He volunteered for combat in World War I.

When Mussolini was first elected to Parliament, Chiavolini became his personal secretary, and remained at this post from the time Mussolini became prime minister in 1922 until 1934. In this position he exercised a significant albeit unofficial influence: he maintained an extensive correspondence with most of the important figures in the regime, kept a detailed file of personal dossiers on government and party officials, and attended meetings of the cabinet, the Fascist Grand Council (q.v.), and other important bodies. Devoted to Mussolini and widely respected for his honesty and unassuming personality, Chiavolini retired in 1934 for personal reasons.

For further information see: *Chi è?* (1936); NO (1928).

                                                                                                        PVC

CHIERICI, RENZO (b. Reggio Emilia, January 11, 1895; d. Verona, December 1943). A Fascist prefect and police chief, Chierici was a volunteer and an Ardito (q.v.) in World War I and vice-president of the Associazione dei

Combattenti. He was a D'Annunzian (*see* GABRIELE D'ANNUNZIO) legionnaire in Fiume (q.v.) and became a close associate of Italo Balbo (q.v.) in the Fascist stronghold of Ferrara after 1919, emerging as a prominent local squad leader. He was Fascist political secretary and secretary of the Fascist syndical organization in Ferrara, took part in the March on Rome (q.v.), and became an officer in the Militia (q.v.). From 1929 to 1933 Chierici was federal secretary in Ferrara, and then a commissar in Tripolitania until 1935. In July 1935 he was made prefect of Pescara, and from August 1939 to December 1941 was prefect of Pola. Chierici was commander of the Forest Militia from 1941 to 1943.

On April 14, 1943—three months before the Fascist Grand Council (q.v.) coup—Mussolini summarily dismissed Carmine Senise (q.v.) as police chief and replaced him with Chierici. In the weeks that followed, Chierici was in contact with those who plotted the coup, warned Mussolini about them on July 23, and was present in Palazzo Venezia during the Grand Council meeting on July 25. He did not, however, take police action against the conspirators.

Chierici went north after the fall of Mussolini and was arrested by the Salò Republic (*see* ITALIAN SOCIAL REPUBLIC). At the Scalzi prison in Verona he was killed by a bomb under mysterious circumstances.

For further information see: *Chi è?* (1936); NO (1937); F. W. Deakin, *The Brutal Friendship* (New York: Harper & Row, 1962); Carmine Senise, *Quando ero capo della polizia* (Rome: Ruffolo, 1946).

PVC

CHIESA, EUGENIO (b. Milan, November 18, 1863; d. Giverny, France, June 22, 1930). A Republican leader and anti-Fascist, Chiesa was active in the democratic movement at the turn of the century, writing for such journals as *Italia del popolo* and *Il Ribelle*. He fled to Switzerland and France in 1898 after the Milan uprising but returned to Italy in 1904 to be elected a deputy (he was reelected until 1926). He was a severe critic of the monarchy, of government corruption, and of the Army.

In 1914-15 Chiesa pushed for Italian intervention in support of the Triple Entente (England, France, and Russia), and in 1917 he was appointed commissioner for aviation. In 1919 he was head of the war reparations commission for the Italian delegation at the Paris Peace Conference.

After the war Chiesa supported Gabriele D'Annunzio's (q.v.) Fiume (q.v.) expedition and in Parliament argued in favor of administrative decentralization. He gradually became more and more anti-Fascist, and after the Matteotti Crisis (q.v.) in June 1924 accused Mussolini of complicity in the crime. He opposed the Aventine Secession (q.v.), preferring more concrete action, and in 1925 was the victim of a Fascist assault. After having been expelled from Parliament by Mussolini, he fled to Switzerland and then to France. In Paris he was a major force in the Concentrazione Antifascista (*see* ANTI-FASCISM).

For further information see: DSPI; EAR (2); MOI (2); Mary and Luciani Chiesa, *La vita di Eugenio Chiesa nel centenario della nascita* (Milan: Giuffrè 1964).

PVC

CHIODELLI, RAOUL (b. Rome, March 29, 1896). A leading figure in the administration of the regime's radio (q.v.) policies, Chiodelli was an engineer by training and worked in the Ministry of Communications under Costanzo Ciano (q.v.). In January 1926 he was appointed director of the Unione Radiofonica Italiana (URI), the first agency permitted to broadcast in Italy, and was editor of its journal, *Radiorario*. In 1928, when the regime created the Ente Italiano per le Audizioni Radiofoniche (EIAR) (Italian Agency for Radio Broadcasting), Chiodelli became its general director, a position he held until December 1943. During these years he played an important role in establishing and implementing Fascist radio programming and propaganda.

For further information see: *Chi è?* (1948); Philip V. Cannistraro, "The Radio in Fascist Italy," *Journal of European Studies* 2 (1972): 127-54; Franco Monteleone, *La radio italiana nel periodo fascista* (Venice: Marsilio, 1976).

PVC

CHRISTIAN DEMOCRACY. Christian Democracy is the name of the movement and ideology that inspired the formation of the Popular Party (Partito Popolare Italiano—PPI) (q.v.) in 1918 and the Christian Democratic party (Democrazia Christiana) in 1943. The ideology stresses personalism, pluralism, and reformism.

Christian Democracy had its origins in the unification of Italy, which was accomplished at the expense of the Papal States. To protect the Church against further encroachments, Italian Catholics formed in 1875 the Opera dei congressi. The papal defenders saw Italian Liberals both as the enemies of Catholics and as exploiters of the poor. Inspired by Pope Leo XII's *Rerum Novarum* and the writings of Professor Giuseppe Toniolo, Catholics established trade unions, rural cooperatives, credit unions, and cultural societies.

The more militant of these Catholics, the so-called Christian Democrats of Don Romolo Murri, advocated a new party, composed of the Catholic masses. Their program of 1899 called for the organization of the various occupations and professions into "corporations"; the democratization of political life through proportional representation, initiative, and referendum; social legislation; religious education; and the protection of small landowners and agricultural laborers. These Christian Democrats were viewed as extremists by other Catholics, such as the followers of Filippo Meda (q.v.), who judged cooperation with the Italian state both licit and desirable. Factionalism within the congress movement became so pervasive that Pope Pius X dissolved the Opera dei Congressi, placing Catholic social and economic organizations under a new national union, the Unione Economico-Sociale. At the same time the pope modified the ban on Catholic participation in national politics, permitting Catholics to vote when anti-clerical candidates might be elected in the absence of Catholic electoral intervention.

In 1918 Pope Benedict XV completely rescinded the electoral ban, thereby making possible the formation of an interclass party of Christian Democratic inspiration, the Popular party. The time was opportune: World War I had greatly enhanced the prestige of Italian Catholicism, and the growth of Christian national federations ("White" unions) ensured the party the votes of workers. Led by Don Luigi Sturzo (q.v.), the party demanded decentralization, women's suffrage, proportional representation, an elective Senate, agrarian reform, social legislation, and universal disarmament. The Roman Question (as the entire series of problems regarding Church-State relations was called) was not mentioned because Sturzo was opposed to the party's involvement in ecclesiastical affairs. He was also opposed to any confessional designation for the party, even though it was of Christian inspiration.

In the elections of 1919 the Popularists won one-fifth of the seats in the Chamber of Deputies. The party was not united, however, having developed almost from the beginning right and left wings. The right wing stressed administrative and economic reforms, while the left favored drastic socioeconomic reforms in the name of "Christian proletarianism." Ideological differences and lack of political expertise prevented the Popularists from cooperating with other anti-Fascist parties to stem the advance of Fascism.

Although the Popular party participated in the first Mussolini ministry (a coalition), it went over to the opposition by the summer of 1923. Many members of the party's right wing joined the Fascist party. Pope Pius XI was hostile to the Popularists; he was suspicious of their socioeconomic program and fearful that they might impede a settlement of the Roman Question. Vatican pressure forced Sturzo to resign the secretaryship of the party and go into exile. With Alcide De Gasperi (q.v.) as party secretary, Popularists participated in the Aventine Secession (q.v.). A Socialist-Popularist combination, considered by De Gasperi and the reformist Socialist Filippo Turati (q.v.) as a means of weakening Mussolini, was effectively vetoed by the pope. In June 1925 the Popular party convened in Rome for its fifth and last national congress. In 1926 Parliament declared that the electoral mandate of the Aventine deputies had lapsed, and the prefect of Rome decreed the dissolution of the Popular party.

Despite the conclusion of the Lateran Pacts (q.v.), Catholicism and Fascism proved incompatible, and after Italy entered World War II, Catholic individuals and groups came together to revive Christian Democracy. The members of Italian Catholic Action, the Guelf movement of Lombardy, the FUCI (University Federation of Italian Catholics)—Movimento Laureati (Catholic university graduates) organizations combined with former members of the Popular party to form on July 25, 1943, the party called Democrazia Cristiana. De Gasperi was elected president of the party's central committee. The platform drew its inspiration from popularism but was also reflective of the new political, social, and economic realities.

For further information see: Elisa Carrillo, "Christian Democracy," in Edward Tannenbaum and Emiliana Noether, eds., *Modern Italy* (New York: New York University Press, 1973); Gabriele De Rosa, *Storia del Partito Popolare* (Bari: Laterza, 1958); Richard A. Webster, *The Cross and the Fasces* (Stanford: Stanford University Press, 1960).

ECa

CHURCH, CATHOLIC. See **AZIONE CATTOLICA ITALIANA; CHRISTIAN DEMOCRACY; PIUS XI; PIUS XII; LATERAN PACTS; PARTITO POPOLARE ITALIANO.**

CIANCA, ALBERTO (b. Rome, January 1, 1884; d. Rome, January 8, 1966). A prominent anti-Fascist leader, Cianca received a degree in law and worked for a series of newspapers (including *La Tribuna, Il Secolo, Il Messaggero,* and *L'Ora*) before Mussolini's seizure of power. Following the Matteotti (*see* MATTEOTTI CRISIS) murder, he became director of Giovanni Amendola's (q.v.) *Il Mondo* (Rome) and of the satirical *Il becco giallo.* His uncompromising anti-Fascist position resulted in numerous assaults against him and his home and finally his arrest. He escaped and fled to Paris in 1926, where he worked with Claudio Treves (q.v.) on *La Libertà.*

Cianca was among the founders of Giustizia e Libertà (*see* ANTI-FASCISM), and worked closely with Carlo Rosselli (q.v.). He traveled frequently to Spain during the Spanish Civil War (q.v.) on propaganda missions and to the United States in 1938. After the Nazi invasion of France in 1940, Cianca moved to New York, where he was an active leader in the Mazzini Society (q.v.) and the Party of Action (*see* PARTITO D'AZIONE).

In September 1943 he returned to Italy with the Allied armies, and organized the first national congress of the CLN (Comitato di Liberazione Nazionale) (*see* COMMITTEE OF NATIONAL LIBERATION) at Bari. He was minister without portfolio in the first Ivanoe Bonomi (q.v.) cabinet (June-December 1944) and minister for the Consulta Nazionale (q.v.) under Alcide De Gasperi (q.v.) (from February 1946). A member of the Consulta and the Constituent Assembly (*see* COSTITUENTE), he joined the Socialist party after the dissolution of the Party of Action and was elected a senator in 1953 and 1958.

For further information see: EAR (2): 542-43; Charles F. Delzell, *Mussolini's Enemies* (Princeton: Princeton University, 1961); Aldo Garosci, *Storia dei fuorusciti* (Bari: Laterza, 1953); *Giustizia e Libertà nella lotta antifascista e nella storia d'Italia* (Florence: Nuova Italia: 1978).

PVC

CIANETTI, TULLIO (b. Assisi, July 20, 1899). A Fascist syndical organizer and minister, Cianetti was a volunteer in World War I. One of the founders of the *fascio* of Assisi, he joined the Fascist Party in April 1921, and the next year was political secretary in Assisi.

Cianetti's career during the regime unfolded largely in the syndical sphere, and he held numerous posts on a local and national level. In the pre-Fascist period he had been involved in the "red" trade union movement and only in the mid-1920s did he fully abandon his connections with it. In 1922 he was secretary of the Fascist unions in Terni and a member of the Militia (q.v.).

During the Matteotti Crisis (q.v.) Cianetti seems to have had second thoughts about Mussolini and Fascism and was in contact with anti-Fascist syndicalists. As a result, he was forced to leave the Militia and expelled from the Fascist syndicalist organization. In 1925, however, he was reinstated and sent first to Syracuse as syndical leader, and then to Carra and Messina.

In the 1930s Cianetti rose quickly in the bureaucracy of the corporate state (*see* CORPORATIVISM AND THE CORPORATIVE STATE); a member of the National Council of Corporations and president of the Fascist Confederation of Industrial Workers, he was also elected to Parliament in 1934. In July 1939 Mussolini made him undersecretary of corporations, and during the April 1943 cabinet reshuffle Cianetti became minister of corporations. During the Fascist Grand Council (q.v.) meeting of July 25, 1943, Cianetti voted against Mussolini. He was later arrested and taken to Verona, where he was condemned to thirty years imprisonment.

For further information see: *Chi è?* (1936); NO (1928); Ferdinando Cordova, *Le origini dei sindacati fascisti* (Rome-Bari: Laterza, 1972); F.W. Deakin, *The Brutal Friendship* (New York: Harper & Row, 1962); Renzo De Felice, *Mussolini il fascista* (Turin: Einaudi, 1966).

PVC

CIANO, COSTANZO (b. Livorno, August 30, 1876; d. Ponte a Moriano, June 27, 1939). Admiral Ciano was a naval hero of World War I, an early adherent to Fascism, and a party hierarch.

Graduating from the naval academy of Livorno in 1896, Ciano rose easily through naval ranks before commanding a torpedo boat during the Libyan War. World War I helped Ciano forward his career through a series of *beffe* (operations designed to annoy the enemy), notably off Cortellazzo (for which he was given the title of Conte di Cortellazzo) and Buccari (with Gabriele D'Annunzio [q.v.] with whom he became close friends).

Leaving active service, Ciano joined the Fascist party, participated in the March on Rome (q.v.), and entered Mussolini's cabinet as undersecretary of the merchant marine. Ciano served as minister of posts and communications from 1924 to 1934. He then was elected president of the Chamber of Fasces and Corporations (*see* PARLIAMENT), a post he held until his death.

An ardent nationalist, Ciano won Mussolini's esteem and friendship. In 1926 Mussolini designated Ciano his successor as prime minister. His son, Galeazzo Ciano (q.v.), later became Mussolini's son-in-law and foreign minister.

For further information see: Duilio Susmel, *Vita sbagliata di Galeazzo Ciano* (Milan: Aldo Palazzi Editore, 1962).

MFL

CIANO, GALEAZZO (b. Livorno, March 18, 1903; d. Verona, January 11, 1944). Galeazzo Ciano, Mussolini's son-in-law, served for seven years as foreign minister and became a major power in the Fascist regime. His diary of the foreign ministry years has become one of the most important sources on Fascist politics and foreign policy.

Ciano was the son of Costanzo Ciano (q.v.). Following secondary education in Livorno, he moved to Rome where his father was a minister in Mussolini's government and where he completed his legal training in 1925.

Ciano's youth was devoted to journalism (in later life he controlled *Il Telegrafo*, a Livorno newspaper), literature and criticism, and a fast-paced social life that continued throughout his career. Entering the foreign service in 1925, Ciano's early diplomatic career took him from the ministry's codes office to consulates in South America and the Orient. In 1930 he joined the Italian legation to the Holy See.

On April 24, 1930, Ciano married Edda Mussolini, the Duce's eldest child. Thereafter his career moved rapidly. He was named consul general in Shangai and later chargé d'affaires and minister-plenipotentiary in Peking. In 1933 he became chief of the Duce's Press Office and subsequently undersecretary (September 1934) and minister (June 1935) for press and propaganda. Ciano left the ministry only at the outbreak of the Ethiopian War (q.v.) to become a bomber pilot with the "Disperata" squadron and won two medals of valor.

In Mussolini's "changing of the guard" of June 9, 1936, Ciano, then only thirty-three, was named minister for foreign affairs. His appointment shocked Italian and foreign observers, who felt his egomania, indiscretion, and strong ambition ill-suited him for such a sensitive position. Ciano's late entry into the Fascist party and his rapid ascendancy also disturbed veteran hierarchs who disliked the upstart intimate of the Duce.

Ciano's tenure at the Foreign Ministry was marked by a dramatic centralization of ministerial powers, a resultant breakdown of communications with Italian representatives abroad, a sweeping turnover of ministry personnel, and a highly personal style of diplomacy based larged on Ciano's friendships and antipathies among foreign diplomats. The centralization of power and Ciano's longevity as minister were the key to his power with the Fascist regime.

In policy terms Ciano's early years at the ministry did not evidence any marked divergence from Fascist (Mussolini) foreign policy up to that time. Ciano followed Mussolini's policies of Italian penetration in the Balkans, intervention in the Spanish Civil War (q.v.), and the rapprochement with Nazi Germany.

It was on the last point that Ciano's policies eventually diverged from Mussolini's. Fearful of Germany's leaders and power, Ciano did his weak-willed best to forestall the Pact of Steel (q.v.) with Germany and began to pursue the Balkan policies with the end of creating a barrier to German power. His first step in this direction was the Good Friday 1939 invasion of Albania, made in direct response to the German absorption of the rump state of Czechoslovakia and undertaken at Ciano's insistence and under his direction. He was awarded the Collar of the Annunciation for his role in the occupation.

Ciano's fear of German power and knowledge of Italian military unpreparedness caused him to insist in August 1939 that Italy remain outside the impending conflagration. In meetings with Joachim von Ribbentrop and Hitler in Berchtesgaden on August 11-13 Ciano was strongly opposed to action against Poland and later warned Mussolini of the danger to Italy from involvement in what Ciano considered to be a generalized war. Aided by Ambassador Bernardo Attolico (q.v.) Ciano forged the policy of nonbelligerency followed by Italy from September 1, 1939 to June 1940. During that period Ciano's influence reached its zenith, culminating in the "changing of the guard" of October-November 1939 that produced "Ciano's cabinet."

By early 1940 Ciano's power began to wane as a result of increasing distrust on the part of the Germans and the growing belief Germany would win a complete victory in which the Fascist regime would have had no part. Ciano's hitherto close relationship with Mussolini began to deteriorate, and members of "Ciano's cabinet" began to desert him. Easy German victories in the Low Countries changed even Ciano's attitude about intervention.

With Italian entry into the war, Ciano returned briefly to service as a bomber pilot. His new bellicosity also was directed toward action in the Balkans, this time against Greece. "Ciano's war" was a dismal military failure that further lowered Ciano's stock with Mussolini and the Germans and was in part responsible for Mussolini's exile of hierarchs from Rome. Ciano spent three months in Bari with a bomber squadron.

Returning to the ministry in April 1941, Ciano's role was sharply reduced to that of observer and messenger for Mussolini. He remained foreign minister until sweeping cabinet changes on February 5, 1943 forced him out of office. He then became ambassador of the Holy See.

Ciano was aware of the conspiracies to overthrow Mussolini and at the July 25, 1943 Fascist Grand Council (q.v.) meeting voted for Dino Grandi's (q.v.) order of the day. Without a means to leave the country, he was quickly placed under house arrest and singled out for investigation by a special commission on "illicit enrichment." With incredible naiveté, Ciano, through Edda, arranged escape via Germany where he was held until the establishment of the Italian Social Republic (q.v.). He was then removed to the Scalzi Prison in Verona.

Ciano was tried on January 8-10, 1944 and, along with other hierarchs who voted with Grandi, was sentenced to be shot as a traitor. Edda attempted unsuccessfully to save Ciano's life through her father and by threatening the Germans with publication of the diaries abroad.

For further information see: Galeazzo Ciano, *Ciano's Hidden Diaries 1937-1938* (New York: E. P. Dutton and Co., 1953); *Diario 1939-1943* (Milan: Rizzoli, 1946); *Ciano's Diplomatic Papers* (London: Odhams Press, 1948); Giordano B. Guerri, *Galeazzo Ciano* (Milan: Bompiani, 1979); Duilio Susmel, *Vita sbagliata di Galeazzo Ciano* (Milan: Aldo Palazzi Editore, 1962).

MFL

CIARLANTINI, FRANCO (b. Sanginesio, Macerata, September 28, 1885). A publicist and Fascist bureaucrat, Ciarlantini studied philosophy and law and taught for many years in elementary schools. As a young man Ciarlantini was a Sorelian syndicalist and worked with Mussolini on *Il Popolo d'Italia* (q.v.). During the Fascist period Ciarlantini held many positions in the Fascist hierarchy and was involved in many cultural activities. In 1923 he sat on the committee to reform schools and in 1924 became a member of the Fascist party's National Directorate and the Fascist Grand Council (q.v.). He was also elected as a deputy from the Venice area and was made director of the party's propaganda office. In this latter capacity Ciarlantini organized the first Congress of Fascist Culture which met in Bologna in March 1925. In the thirties, Ciarlantini served on the National Council of Corporations and the Corporation for Paper and Press. In 1938 Ciarlantini became one of the ten original members of the famous Commissione per la Bonifica Libraria (Commission for the Improvement of Books), which was responsible for establishing censorship policies.

For further information see: *Chi è?* (1936); NO (1928; 1937); Philip V. Cannistraro, *La fabbrica del consenso* (Rome-Bari: Laterza, 1975); Adrian Lyttelton, *The Seizure of Power* (London: Weidenfeld & Nicolson, 1973); Emilio R. Papa, *Fascismo e cultura* (Venice: Marsilio, 1974).

MSF

CINEMA. In the earliest days of Fascism Mussolini coined the slogan, "The cinema is the strongest weapon" (a takeoff of a maxim by Lenin), a phrase that demonstrated the ambiguous nature of Fascist cultural policy (*see* CULTURE). The cinema was, in fact, one of the most contradictory areas of Fascist culture, especially given the fact that as the newest of the mass media it was given a central role in the new mass society taking shape in Italy during the 1930s.

During the first decade of the regime, the Italian cinema was in search of a new identity. The glories of the earlier films (such as the colossal *Cabiria* of 1911) were over, and motion pictures had entered a period of crisis in which new ideas and talent were lacking. At first the regime began to be concerned only casually with motion pictures, above all in terms of censorship (with a law of 1923) and propaganda (the famous Istituto LUCE [*see* LUCE, ISTITUTO NAZIONALE] had its origins in 1925). At the same time businessmen like Stefano Pittaluga began to reinvest in the motion picture industry as sound films developed, while intellectuals began increasingly to regard film as a legitimate art form (for example, a special issue of the literary journal *Solaria* in 1927 was devoted to films). In this context a number of young men began to speak of the rebirth of the Italian cinema and gathered around Alessandro Blasetti (q.v.), founder of the review *Cinematografo*.

But it is above all, the period of the 1930s that is today the subject of intense dispute. Is it, for example, more accurate to speak of the cinema *under* Fascism, hence emphasizing its dependence on the dictatorship, or of the cinema *during* the Fascist period, thereby disassociating film from the history of Fascism? Those who argue for the former approach believe that the cinema of the 1930s was largely ideologically reactionary and a function of Fascism (either directly, with propaganda and rhetorical films, or indirectly, with escapist films of the so-called "white telephone genre" and petty bourgeois comedies). Those who argue the latter thesis observe that the film "text" is independent of historical "context," so that the cinema of the period must be reevaluated and reanalyzed with no preconceptions.

In order to clarify the issues, three different points of view may be adopted: (1) an historiographical viewpoint, which analyzes the use of the cinema for the creation of consensus; (2) the critical approach, which stresses the authors and the collective fantasy they produce and which may exist independently of Fascism; (3) the ideological point of view, which allows us to see a kind of long voyage through Fascism even in the cinema.

(1) The beginning of the systematic intervention of the Fascist state in the cinema may be dated from September 2, 1934 when the Direzione Generale per la Cinematografia (Office for Cinematography) was created in the Ministry of Popular Culture (q.v.). Then in 1935 a mechanism of preventive control through film credits was established, whereby producers received advances of up to one-third of the expected cost of a film. Also in 1935 ENIC (Ente Nazionale Industrie Cinematografiche—National Agency for Motion Picture Industries) was set up, and the famous Venice Film Festival (Mostra di Venezia) became an annual event. The following year the Centro Sperimentale di Cinematografia was opened as a school under the direction of Luigi Chiarini, a regime bureaucrat who was even willing to work with Marxists like Umberto Barbaro. Finally, on April 21, 1937, *Cinecittà*—the Italian Hollywood—was inaugurated. In fact, it was to Hollywood that the regime's new technicians looked: Luigi Freddi (q.v.), director of cinematography for the propaganda ministry, visited the American film capital in 1932 and was destined to have a major impact on government initiatives in the cinema.

The regime's overall film policy favored private industry. Between 1938 and 1939 a new system of financing was established whereby subsidies went to producers according to the box office receipts they earned, so that commercial films were at a great advantage over those made by the government. Hence when Mussolini ordered in 1937 that one hundred films a year be made in Italy, the industry could move from the modest figure of thirty-two to the famous "quota 120" in 1942.

In 1937 the regime made its best known "colossal" film, Carmine Gallone's *Scipione l'Africano*, which told the story of the Roman hero just at the time when Mussolini had completed his own imperial conquests. Other films typical of Fascist rhetoric—but, it must be noted, films that were in a minority compared to comedies and costume films—were Augusto Genina's *Squadrone bianco*, Mario Camerini's (q.v.) *Il grande appello*, Genina's *L'assedio dell'Alcazar*, and Luis Trenker's *Condottieri*. From 1937 on the regime's emphasis was increasingly on racial and military themes, but private industry maintained its own social values and collective fantasy unchanged.

(2) Among the producers who were prominent in the development of film aesthetic (culture) three names stand out: Blasetti, Camerini, and Renato Poggioli. Blasetti's films frequently celebrated the achievements of Fascism—*Sole* applauded the *Bonifica* (*see* BONIFICA INTEGRALE) programs, *Terra madre* the corporative ideal of peasant-landowner cooperation, and *Vecchia guardia* the March on Rome (q.v.)—but his craft and interests were of wider importance. On the other hand, Camerini's films are aimed at the petty bourgeoisie and offered, through the smiling adventures of the young Vittorio De Sica (*Gli uomini che mascalzoni*, *Il signor Max*, and others), a delicate escape from the problems of daily life. Poggioli represented a formalist approach, or a search for the beautiful form, in response to Fascism's call for rhetoric and created praiseworthy films such as *Sissignora*.

(3) Along with the formalists, another group also ultimately rejected the regime's demands—the group that worked in the Centro Sperimentale and collaborated with the review *Cinema*. The latter, although directed by Mussolini's son Vittorio, became a gathering place for young intellectuals like Michelangelo Antonioni, Giuseppe De Santis, and Luchino Visconti, who were interested in the literary realism of the Sicilian writer Verga and in the French and American cinema, but who eventually was drawn into the political struggle. Mussolini's strongest weapon, therefore, wound up being taken up by the young generation as a means of understanding and changing reality and was turned against Fascism itself.

For further information see: G. P. Brunetta, *Cinema italiano tra le due guerra* (Milan: Mursia, 1975); Philip V. Cannistraro, *La fabbrica del consenso* (Rome-Bari: Laterza, 1975); C. Carabba, *Il cinema del ventennio nero* (Florence: Vallecchi, 1974).

VZ

CINI, VITTORIO (b. Ferrara, February 20, 1885). An Italian industrialist and Fascist supporter, Cini (Count of Monselice) studied business and commerce in Switzerland. He possessed extensive holdings in agriculture, industry, and finance, and although little is known about his background, he was a key figure in securing the support of the landowner-industrialists for Mussolini. After having fought in World War I, he joined the PNF—Partito Nazionale Fascista (q.v.). In the 1920s he frequently spoke for the agrarian interests in and around Ferrara and was active in land improvement in the province. Cini was a major proponent of developing the industrial and port facilities of Venice, of which he was president, and he was head of both the Società di Navigazione (Society for Internal Navigation) and the Credito Industriale. His services to the regime led to his appointment as a senator in January 1934. In the late 1930s Cini also supervised the plans for the projected 1942 world's fair to be held in Rome (the Esposizione Universale di Roma).

In February 1943 Mussolini appointed him minister of communications, a very sensitive position in which Cini had to deal with the difficult problem of wartime transportation and supplies and the delivery of war materials from Germany. Cini grew increasingly more critical of Mussolini's leadership of the war effort and was involved in the efforts to secure the dictator's dismissal. Cini was himself dismissed after a number of months in office as a result of accusations by some Fascists that he was profiting from the war. He fled to Switzerland after the July 1943 coup that ousted Mussolini, but was captured by the Germans in September and taken to Dachau. He returned to Italy after the war, established the Cini Foundation in Venice, and was decorated by the government in 1959.

For further information see: *Chi è?* (1936); *Chi è?* (1948); NO (1937); Frederick W. Deakin, *The Brutal Friendship* (New York: Harper & Row, 1962).

PVC

CODIGNOLA, ERNESTO (b. Genoa, June 23, 1885). A Fascist educational reformer, in 1919 Codignola founded the Fascio di Educazione Nazionale (Fascio of National Education), which later became a *gruppo di competenza* (Group of Competency) of the PNF—Partito Nazionale Fascista (q.v.). Codignola was closely identified with the educational theories of Giovanni Gentile (q.v.) and attacked the Italian school system for maintaining democratic, anticlerical, and antinationalist ideas. He supported Gentile's school reform program in 1923-24, but by the late 1920s had become disillusioned with the Fascist educational system because of the PNF's interference. He was a professor of pedagogy at the University of Florence, president of the Ente Nazionale di Cultura (National Agency of Culture) of Florence, and a member of the Consiglio Superiore di Pubblica Istruzione (High Council for Public Instruction).

For further information see: *Chi è?* (1936; 1948); Adrian Lyttelton, *The Seizure of Power* (London: Weidenfeld & Nicolson, 1973); Edward R. Tannenbaum, *The Fascist Experience* (New York: Basic Books, 1972).

MSF

CODIGNOLA, TRISTANO (b. Assisi, October 23, 1913). Cofounder of the Party of Action (*see* PARTITO D'AZIONE), Codignola was an early anti-Fascist and served as director and editor of *Non Mollare*, the first clandestine anti-Fascist publication. He helped to found the liberal-socialist anti-Fascist opposition in Tuscany in 1937 and was arrested by the Fascist police in 1942. He was among the founding figures in the Party of Action in 1943 and organized its section in

Florence. He participated in the Resistance as an organizer for the Actionists. In 1946 he was elected to the Constituent Assembly (*see* COSTITUENTE) and later founded the Movimento di Autonomia Socialista (Movement of Socialist Autonomy). In 1958 he was elected to Parliament and directed the paper *La nuova repubblica*.

For further information see: *Chi è?* (1948); Charles F. Delzell, *Mussolini's Enemies* (Princeton: Princeton University Press, 1961); *I deputati e senatori del terzo parlamento repubblicano* (Rome: La Navicella, 1958).

MSF

COMANDO SUPREMO, 1940-43. The term for the Italian high command, the Comando Supremo (also known as STAMAGE, short for Stato Maggiore Generale) was originally the June 1940 incarnation of Pietro Badoglio's (q.v.) position of Capo di Stato Maggiore Generale (Chief of the Supreme General Staff). Despite the name it was little more than Badoglio's personal secretariat, equipped with vague powers of interservice coordination and strategic direction, powers Badoglio successfully sought to transform into control, under Mussolini, of Italian strategy. In practice, Mussolini (as minister of each of the services) frequently acted through his undersecretaries, two of whom, Domenico Cavagnari (q.v.) and Francesco Pricolo (q.v.), were also service chiefs of staff; the third, Ubaldo Soddu (q.v.), was Badoglio's nominal deputy. After Badoglio's dismissal in December, Alfredo Guzzoni (q.v.), who succeeded Soddu as deputy, in effect directed the war effort; Badoglio's successor Ugo Cavallero (q.v.) was defending Albania, and Mussolini's military self-confidence was at low ebb. After returning to Rome in May 1941, Cavallero proposed and secured the suppression of the post of deputy chief (eliminating his rival Guzzoni), and the reinforcement of the authority of the Comando Supremo over the service chiefs of staff. Even under the new dispensation the Navy and Air Force chiefs, in their capacity as undersecretaries, enjoyed direct access to Mussolini. But Cavallero did secure full control of the Army, and he and his successor, Vittorio Ambrosio (q.v.), enjoyed primacy under Mussolini in operational and strategic questions; the Comando Supremo organization, expanded to fulfill its increased functions, at last deserved its name.

For further information see: Lucio Ceva, *La condotta italiana della guerra. Cavallero e il Comando Supremo 1941/1942* (Milan: Feltrinelli, 1975).

MK

COMMITTEE OF NATIONAL LIBERATION (CLN). The Committees of National Liberation (Comitato di Liberazione Nazionale) were the political arm of the Italian resistance (*see* RESISTANCE, ARMED) movement. The CLNs began to take shape in the confused days after the ouster of Mussolini in July 1943, as representatives of the better organized and larger anti-Fascist parties began to meet to coordinate policy. These informal contacts led to a formal alliance in September 1943, when the announcement of the Italian surrender was followed by the flight of the royal government to southern Italy and German occupation of two-thirds of the nation. By late 1943 organized political committees directing the resistance to the Germans and their Fascist auxiliaries had been established in all major Italian cities. These committees comprised the representatives of five parties: Liberals, Christian Democrats, Socialists, Communists, and Actionists. In addition, in Rome and some of the cities further south, the CLNs included representatives of Democrazia del Lavoro (Labor Democracy). The Italian Republican party officially refused to join the CLNs but was represented on some northern CLNs.

The CLNs quickly asserted control over the various forms of armed resistance and developed ties among themselves. By early 1944 three major autonomous CLN groupings emerged. The largest and most active was the CLNAI (Comitato di Liberzione Nazionale per Alta Italia)—Committee of National Liberation of Northern Italy, which had its headquarters in Milan and extended its authority over all of Italy north of Tuscany. The Tuscan Committee of National Liberation (CTLN—Comitato Toscano di Liberazione Nazionale), based in Florence, directed a fiercely independent resistance movement. At Rome a Central Committee (CCLN— Comitato Centrale di Liberazione Nazionale) claimed leadership of the entire national resistance movement and was accorded nominal recognition by other CLNs. The presence of figures like Alcide De Gasperi (q.v.) and Pietro Nenni (q.v.) on the Rome CLN invested it with great prestige.

An additional development was the establishment of CLNs in liberated southern Italy. These organizations, which had no military forces and no formal ties with the Italian government, carried little weight in political affairs, but did indicate a growing political radicalization among parts of the southern population.

Under CLN's direction, Italians carried out a highly effective political, economic, and military resistance to the German invader and undermined the authority and institutions of both the German occupation and the "republican" Fascist government. Military resistance included terror and sabotage actions by small groups and increasingly well-organized and large scale military operations directed against the German Army's lines of communication. Plans were also laid for insurrections to coincide with the advance of Allied armies. Political resistance included the publication of a clandestine press, the reestablishment of anti-Fascist political organizations in occupied Italy, and the administration of newly liberated areas. The economic side of the resistance included strikes and slowdowns to hinder war production and the protection of factories and power stations from destruction by retreating German and Fascist forces.

By mid-1944 the power and influence of the CLNs of north Italy had become a matter of concern to Allied military and political leaders who viewed them as potentially revolutionary organizations. Clashes occurred between the representatives of AMG—Allied Military Government (q.v.)—and the representatives of the CLN. Nenni and other leftists enthusiastically backed the CLNs as an alternative form of government. The committees were not content to play the restricted role that AMG and the Italian government had laid out for them. The CLNs claimed the dominant role in the administration of liberated areas and in the creation of new structures of government. The Allies were committed to support the authority of the central government and attempted to contain the political influence of the CLNs, disarm the partisan bands, and postpone any final decision on Italy's constitution to the postwar period.

The Allied policy was aided by the coalition nature of the CLNs. The left parties blunted their more radical objectives in order to achieve cooperation with the conservative parties. In addition the CLNs relied on the Allies and the Italian government for both military supplies and financial support. Finally, the leaders of the CLNs genuinely sought to cooperate with the Allies. In November-December 1944 a CLNAI mission to Rome negotiated a political and military pact with the representatives of the Allied high command and the Italian government. The military resistance was placed under the overall command of the Supreme Allied Commander, Mediterranean, General Harold Alexander, and a representative of the Italian government, General Raffaele Cadorna (q.v.), was appointed to serve as titular chief of the Armed Resistance. In a separate agreement the CLNAI recognized the Italian government's authority over their activities in return for designation as the national government's representative in occupied Italy.

In April 1945 the CLNAI planned and executed the insurrections which liberated the cities of the North prior to the arrival of advancing Allied armies. Loyally abiding by its agreements, it then accepted imposition of an Allied Military Government over all the newly liberated areas and cooperated with that government.

During May and June 1945 the CLNAI stood at the apogee of its influence. It demanded and achieved a government representating the resistance when Ferruccio Parri (q.v.) was called upon to form Italy's first postwar government. The Parri ministry, however, proved ineffective. The unity of the CLNs disintegrated as each party sought electoral advantage. Parri was forced to resign in November 1945 and his successor, Alcide De Gasperi (q.v.), whittled away the remaining prerogatives of the CLNs. By mid-1946 when the CLNAI dissolved, the actions of the government in Rome had ended any hope of a radical reconstruction of Italy based on the committees of national liberation.

For further information see: Roberto Battaglia, *Storia della resistenza italiana* (Turin: Einaudi, 1953); Franco Catalano, *Storia del comitato di liberazione nazionale alta italia* (Milan: Bompiani, 1956); Gaetano Grassi (ed.), *Verso il governo del popolo* (Milan: Feltrinelli, 1977).

JEM

COMMUNIST PARTY. See **PARTITO COMUNISTA ITALIANO**.

CONCENTRAZIONE ANTIFASCISTA (ANTI-FASCIST CONCENTRATION). See **ANTI-FASCISM**.

CONCORDAT. See **LATERAN PACTS**.

CONFEDERAZIONE GENERALE DEL LAVORO (CGL). At the initiative of FIOM—Federazione Italiana Operai Metallurgici—(the metal workers association), the Constitutional Congress of the CGL met in Milan from September 29 to October 1, 1906. The delegates, after the revolutionary syndicalists had walked out, approved a constitution and elected Rinaldo Rigola, the blind reformist Socialist, as secretary-general. They established headquarters in Turin, where they remained until transferred to Milan in 1911.

The delegates in Milan, although concerned with the revolutionary syndicalist minority within the organization, made no attempt to expel them. Two years later, however, when the syndicalists led an unsuccessful general strike in the agricultural areas around Parma, the reformist leadership moved to strengthen the power of the executive committee of the CGL. The revolutionary syndicalists, threatened with tight reformist controls, left the CGL and within four years established the Unione Sindacale Italiana (USI).

Meanwhile, the CGL continued to repudiate revolutionary syndicalism and to support the reformist policies of its leadership at its Third and Fourth Congresses (Padua, 1911 and Mantua, 1914). The issue of reform versus revolution reached a climax in 1913. When several leaders were arrested during a strike against the automobile manufacturers in Milan, the revolutionary syndicalists, supported by the Italian Socialist Party (*see* PARTITO SOCIALISTA ITALIANO [PSI]) and the local Chamber of Labor (*see* CAMERA DEL LAVORO), demanded a general strike in Milan to protest the arrests. Rigola refused to support the general strike and resigned rather than, as he said, block the unification of the labor movement in Milan. The other CGL leaders also resigned, but the National Council, at a meeting on September 22, refused to accept the resignations. Thus, the CGL firmly rejected syndicalist tactics and, at the same time, repulsed the attempts of the PSI to interfere directly in trade union affairs.

Although the events in Milan made it clear that the Chambers of Labor throughout the country were a threat to reformist control of the labor movement, the leadership of the CGL could not subordinate them to the national unions. Over the years the policies of the leaders tended to strengthen the unions, but the CGL never successfully established the union's authority over the Chambers of Labor nor could it eliminate the strong tradition of localism within the working class movement.

During the war the CGL followed the political line of the PSI, but at the same time it collaborated with the government through the grievance committees and the regional committees for industrial mobilization. Just before the end of the war, however, the PSI adopted a more revolutionary posture and attempted to impose its new line on the CGL. Rigola, rather than accept party discipline, resigned as secretary-general. An equally ardent reformist, Ludovico D'Aragona (q.v.), replaced him and presided over the CGL until January 1926. During the "bienno rosso" (Red years) the CGL succeeded in winning important, although limited, concessions from the employers who, fearful of the revolutionaries and pleased by the

CGL's moderate tactics, agreed to shorter hours, higher wages, paid vacations, and the establishment of grievance committees.

In 1919 PSI failed in its attempt to unite the CGL and the USI. The USI refused to be absorbed into the CGL, and the latter rejected the syndicalists' proposal that the two groups establish a new organization. Following the "Occupation of the Factories" (q.v.), however, as employer intransigence and Fascist violence increased, labor unity became vital. The CGL joined the ill-fated Alliance of Labor (*see* ALLEANZA DEL LAVORO) in February 1922 in a vain attempt to prevent the destruction of the labor movement. After the March on Rome (q.v.), the CGL struggled to retain some freedom for labor. It was, however, too late. In 1925 the Pact of Palazzo Vidoni (*see* PALAZZO VIDONI, PACT OF) stripped the CGL of its right to negotiate and in April 1926 the government prohibited strikes. On January 4, 1927, the National Council declared that the CGL had ceased to exist.

For further information see: Daniel Horowitz, *The Italian Labor Movement* (Cambridge, Mass.: Harvard University Press, 1963); Adolfo Pepe, *Storia della CGdL dalla fondazione alla guerra di Libia, 1905-1911* (Bari: Laterza, 1972); Adolfo Pepe, *Storia della CGdl dalla guerra di Libia all'intervento, 1911-1915* (Bari: Laterza, 1971); Rinaldo Rigola, *Storia del movimento operaio italiano* (Milan: Domus, 1946).

CLB

CONFEDERAZIONE GENERALE ITALIANA DEL LAVORO (CGIL). A confederation of Italian trade unions, the CGIL was formed during the closing months of World War II. The revival of the major pre-Fascist trade unions, the socialist General Confederation of Labor or CGL (*see* CONFEDERAZIONE GENERALE DEL LAVORO) and the Catholic Italian Confederation of Workers or CIL (Confederazione Italiana dei Lavoratori) contributed to the fall of Mussolini and the disintegration of the Fascist regime. In accordance with the wartime policy of the collaboration of all anti-Fascist forces, including those of labor, the Christian Democrat Achille Grandi, the Communist Giuseppe Di Vittorio, and the Socialist Bruno Buozzi (q.v.) came together in the spring of 1944 to negotiate the formation of a single labor organization. On June 3, 1944 the Pact of Rome was signed, providing for the Confederazione Generale Italiana del Lavoro, headed by three secretaries-general, a Communist, a Socialist, and a Christian Democrat. The operations of the CGIL were to be based on democracy with the free election of officials. The general purposes of the CGIL were to assist in the economic reconstuction of Italy and to strengthen organized labor. The more specific objectives were to restore the pre-Fascist national federations of workers by trades and regions and to bargain collectively with employers.

Trade union recruitment by the CGIL was very successful, with more than three million in the organization by the summer of 1945. However, despite the assertion of the Pact of Rome that the CGIL would be independent of the political parties, the national federations were subordinate to the major political parties. With the onset of the cold war and increasing political polarization, the CGIL was beset by factionalism and dissension. The establishment of factory councils, supported by the leftists in the CGIL, was viewed with distaste by the Christian Democrats. Italy's acceptance of the Marshall Plan was opposed by the leftists and supported by the Christian Democrats. There was also disagreement over the use of the general strike for political reasons.

The outcome of the parliamentary elections of 1948—a victory for the Christian Democrats and their allies—accelerated the breakup of the CGIL as a national confederation. In October 1948 the Associazioni Cristiane Lavoratori Italiani (ACLI, Christian Associations of Italian Workers) decided to establish a Catholic confederation, the Libera Confederazione Generale Italiana dei Lavoratori (LCGIL). In June 1949 the Social Democrats and the Republicans founded the Federazione Italiana del Lavoro (FIL). In 1950 the LCGIL and the FIL combined to form the Confederazione Italiana Sindacati Lavoratori (CISL). Those in FIL who refused to join CISL formed the Unione Italiana del Lavoro (UIL), which was Social Democratic in orientation. Despite the secessions of the Catholics and Social Democrats (right-wing Socialists), the CGIL remained the largest of the unions and was under the domination of the Communist party.

For further information see: D. Horowitz, *The Italian Labor Movement* (Cambridge, Mass.: Harvard University Press, 1963); Nunzio Pernicone, "The Italian Labor Movement," in Edward Tannenbaum and Emiliana Noether, eds., *Modern Italy* (New York: New York University Press, 1973); Giuseppe Di Vittorio, Giulio Pastore, Italo Viglianese et al., *I Sindacati in Italia* (Bari: Laterza, 1955).

ECa

CONSTITUTION OF THE ITALIAN REPUBLIC. The Constitution of the Italian Republic came into force on January 1, 1948. Drafted by the Constituent Assembly (*see* COSTITUENTE) elected on June 2, 1946, it was completed on December 22, 1947. Given the political makeup of the assembly, it is an uneasy mixture of Catholic, liberal, and Marxist doctrines. It is lengthy and verbose, totaling 139 regular articles and 18 transitional arrangements to handle the conversion from the old monarchical to the new republican order.

Like any constitution, it looks both backwards and forwards, as its framers tried to prevent (on paper) the mistakes of the past which had produced the Fascist regime, and as they tried to produce a vision of an ambiguous and controversial future. Like other twentieth-century constitutions, it is packed full of policy prescriptions that do not belong in a constitution at all but should be properly left to subsequent legislative and executive policymaking. Eighteenth and nineteenth century constitutions were wisely restricted to outlining the fundamental structures of the state and the government, the basic legal and political procedures, and the bedrock rights of citizens. The Italian Constitution of 1948 reflects its own times in laying down utopian prescriptions and detailed regulations that almost impose upon future generations the necessity to ignore it or go through a complicated amending procedure to make ordinary policy changes. An example of the first is Article 4, which recognizes the right of all citizens to work, in a country that has had severe unemployment throughout its history and still has it. An example of the second is Article 34, which establishes free, compulsory education for every child for eight years. Since elementary school begins at the age of six this means that the only way to raise the minimum school leaving age from fourteen years to sixteen years is to amend the constitution. It cannot be done by ordinary legislation or through administrative action.

The predecessor to the Constitution was the 1848 *Statuto albertino*, which was an "open" constitution. Any act of Parliament was legal. Since the *Statuto* did not bind or restrict Parliament once the Fascists consolidated their domination (*see* PARLIAMENT), they were able to enact what they wanted "constitutionally." The fathers of the 1948 Constitution therefore drafted a "closed" constitution by creating checks on parliamentary supremacy. They thereby hoped to prevent a repetition of the Fascist consolidation of power. The innovations are:

1. An independent Constitutional Court empowered to declare legislation and executive acts unconstitutional, including legislation and decree laws carried over from previous years.

2. A special amending process. The Constitution cannot be changed by the ordinary legislative process.

3. Popular referenda, enabling the citizens to override Parliament or initiate laws Parliament refuses to pass.

4. A limited veto power is granted to the president of the Republic. A special majority is required for Parliament to override a presidential veto. In addition, the president has certain choices he can make in appointments and policies independent of his prime minister and cabinet.

5. The institution of regional governments to provide limited decentralization of the centralized Italian state, which had been further centralized by the Fascist regime.

A number of the above checks on Parliament also serve to check the prime minister and cabinet. The reaction to the Fascist experience is clear.

The Constitution provides for a parliamentary system with the prime minister and cabinet required to obtain and hold the confidence of a bicameral Parliament. The judiciary is organized on traditional lines with two exceptions; the Constitutional Court and a separate Superior Council of the Judiciary, created to reduce the control of the Ministry of Justice over the judges. The state bureaucracy is also organized on traditional lines.

The classic civil, legal, and political rights of citizens found in the liberal tradition of western bourgeois democracy are all present. The election system is based on the method of proportional representation. The voters are defined by the standard of universal adult suffrage. Women were granted the vote in 1946, and Article 3 of the Constitution outlaws all the standard forms of discrimination.

Catholic influences are found in those sections dealing with the family, with Church-State relations (particularly Article 7 which incorporates the Lateran Accords of 1929 [see LATERAN PACTS] into the Constitution), and in certain corporatist elements in the section dealing with economic issues. Marxist influences are found in the language glorifying labor (Article 1), in Title III dealing with the organization and functions of trade unions, in the welfare provisions (also Catholic influence), and the acceptance of the existing mixed economy. The system of state-owned and state-controlled public and semi-public enterprises inherited from the Fascist period (for example, the Institute for Industrial Reconstruction) receives endorsement. The Constitution neither imposes nor prevents a socialized economy.

There was and still is little sense of constitutionalism in Italy. Many of the new organs of the state were not actually established and functioning until years after the Constitution went into effect. The Constitutional Court was not created until 1955, the Superior Council of the Judiciary was not established until 1958, the regular regional governments were activated only in 1970, and the first popular referendum was held in 1974. Civil and criminal codes dating back to the Fascist era were not replaced for decades. But gradually more and more of the Constitution's provisions became implemented, although the civil and legal protections of citizens have become strained as Italian governments develop security measures to protect society from increasing violence and terrorism.

For further information see: Giuseppe Mammarella, *Italy After Fascism* (Notre Dame: University of Notre Dame, 1966).

NK

CONSULTA NAZIONALE. This consultative assembly was constituted by a decree of Umberto II (q.v.), lieutenant of the realm and son of King Victor Emmanuel III (q.v.), on April 5, 1945. It was formally organized on September 22, 1945 and held its first plenary session on September 25, 1945. Four hundred and forty members were appointed. They were nominated by Umberto's cabinet, who appointed them from the following categories: political parties forming the Committees of National Liberation (q.v.), former anti-Fascist parliamentarians, trade union groups, veterans and partisans, the free professions (lawyers, doctors, teachers, and others), high culture, public and private agencies. They had the rights of parliamentarians as established under the 1848 *Statuto albertino*, and received an honorarium for every day the Consulta was in session.

The Consulta created subject matter committees covering traditional divisions of political activity. It tried to function as a legislative assembly, the first free one after the fall of Fascism. It had no legal right to pass binding laws or to make or unmake a government, but through its debates and activities it could affect the political atmosphere. The cabinet was obligated to request its opinion on fiscal matters, taxes, and electoral laws and had the option of requesting an opinion on other issues. In no case was an opinion of the Consulta binding on the government. Members could propose legislation and question cabinet ministers.

In fact government budgets were never presented to the Consulta, although financial problems were discussed by appropriate cabinet ministers. In plenary session it debated the law on the Referendum of 1946 (q.v.) and on the election of Constituent Assembly (*see* COSTITUENTE). The Consulta held its last plenary session on March 9, 1946, although the committees continued to function into April. One hundred and twenty-eight of its members were elected to the Constituent Assembly.

For further information see: Giuseppe Mammarella, *Italy After Fascism* (Notre Dame: University of Notre Dame, 1966).

NK

CONTARINI, SALVATORE (b. Palermo, August 6, 1867; d. Rome, September 17, 1945). An archetypal diplomat of the old school, Contarini entered Italy's foreign service in 1891 and, serving mostly in Rome, rose by 1920 to the position of secretary-general of the Foreign Ministry.

Despite his eccentricity and irascibility, he commanded vast respect throughout the diplomatic community. By continuing at his post in October 1922 he helped to persuade almost all Italy's career diplomats, and foreign chancelleries too, to accept Mussolini. Conversely, his resignation in March 1926 flashed a warning signal that Fascist militancy was on the rise. Contarini's resignation followed a Mussolinian threat to cross the Brenner Pass in defense of the Alto Adige region. The secretary-general was further upset by Mussolini's combative policy toward Yugoslavia. But perhaps he left mainly out of personal chagrin at the Duce's increasing disparagement of the Foreign Ministry.

Although withdrawing from public life, Contarini bequeathed a powerful legacy. Above all, the esprit de corps with which the Foreign Ministry withstood Fascistization owed much to him.

For further information see: Alan Cassels, *Mussolini's Early Diplomacy* (Princeton: Princeton University Press, 1970); Legatus (pseud.), *Vita diplomatica di Salvatore Contarini* (Rome: Sestante, 1947).

AC

CONTI, ETTORE (b. Milan, April 24, 1871; d. Livorno, April 19, 1957). An important industrial leader, after a brief period teaching at the Polytechnic Institute of Milan Conti turned his attention to the electrical industry. He founded and directed the Imprese Elettriche Conti before World War I, which applied electrical power to mining and transportation. He was also a director of the important Banca Commerciale Italiana (Milan) and on the boards of numerous business firms. Toward the end of World War I he was head of the government's Arms and Munitions Commission and then directed the demobilization policies. He was made a senator in 1919.

A leading exponent of the Confindustria (*see* INDUSTRY), he refused Mussolini's offer to head the Ministry of Interior in 1922. However, although during the Matteotti Crisis (q.v.) he favored a return of former prime minister Giovanni Giolitti (q.v.), once Mussolini was firmly entrenched in power he accommodated himself to the regime. In 1926 Conti became president of the Azienda Generale Italiana Petroli (AGIP), a para-state petroleum company. Conti headed a number of diplomatic-commercial missions for the regime in the 1930s and was ambassador to Japan and Manchukuo in 1938, in which capacity he signed treaties of friendship and trade. In March 1939 he became Count of Verampio.

For further information see: *Chi è?* (1936); *Chi è?* (1948); E. Conti, *Dal taccuino di un borghese* (Milan: Garzanti, 1946).

PVC

COPPOLA, FRANCESCO (b. Naples, September 27, 1878; d. Anacapri, 1957). A Nationalist intellectual and Fascist political writer, Coppola took a law degree at Naples and worked as a journalist for *Il Giornale d'Italia* (Rome, 1904-1908), assuming an anti-democratic, anti-Socialist stance. In 1908 he moved to the Nationalist *La Tribuna* (Rome), emerging as a fervent imperialist. He was among the founders in 1910 of the Italian Nationalist Association (q.v.) and in 1911 launched, with Enrico Corradini (q.v.), Luigi Federzoni (q.v.) and others *L'Idea Nazionale* (Rome).

Coppola was a proponent of the Italo-Libyan War (1911-12) and a fierce interventionist in 1914-15. In 1916 he fought at the front, and between 1917 and 1918 undertook numerous propaganda and diplomatic missions abroad and attended the Paris Peace Conference. He became one of the most outspoken champions of territorial aggrandisement, bitterly attacking those he claimed were responsible for the "multilated victory." Together with Alfredo Rocco (q.v.), he founded *Politica* in 1918.

Associated with Mussolini and Fascism since 1919, Coppola represented a doctrinaire, conservative nationalism that included an expansionist, racist philosophy; he was one of the major advocates of the Nationalist fusion with Fascism in 1923.

In 1923 and 1925 Coppola was an Italian delegate to the League of Nations and a member of the Commission of Eighteen (*see* PARLIAMENT) in 1925. In 1929, when he became professor of international relations at the University of Perugia, Mussolini made him a member of the Royal Academy; in 1932 he transferred to Rome.

For further information see: *Chi è?* (1936); *Annuario della Reale Accademia d'Italia* (Rome: Reale Accademia, 1938); Renzo De Felice, *Mussolini il rivoluzionario* (Turin: Einaudi, 1965); Alexander J. De Grand, *The Italian Nationalist Association and the Rise of Fascism in Italy* (Lincoln: University of Nebraska, 1978).

PVC

CORBINO, MARIO (b. Augusta, April 30, 1876). A well-known scientist and government minister, Corbino taught experimental physics at the University of

Messina and then at the University of Rome. An independent conservative in politics, he was made a senator in October 1920 and minister of public instruction (July 1921-February 1922) under Ivanoe Bonomi (q.v.).

Corbino was never a Fascist, and in November 1922 had voted against Mussolini's government in the Senate, but he was willing to serve in the dictator's cabinet. In August 1923 Mussolini, over the objections of intransigent Fascists like Roberto Farinacci (q.v.), appointed Corbino minister of national economy—a position he held until July of the next year when, in the face of mounting pressure from the intransigents over the Matteotti Crisis (q.v.), Corbino was dismissed. Thereafter he returned to teaching and held a number of honorary posts such as president of the Italian Society of Sciences.

For further information see: *Chi è?* (1936); NO (1928); Renzo De Felice, *Mussolini il fascista* (Turin: Einaudi, 1966).

PVC

CORFU CRISIS. The Greek island of Corfu, situated at the entrance of the Adriatic Sea and facing the Gulf of Taranto, possessed considerable naval-strategic importance.

On August 27, 1923, four Italian nationals serving on an international commission to delimit Albania's frontiers (including the Italian chairman of the commission) were murdered near Janina on the Greek side of the border. Relations between Rome and Athens being already strained, Mussolini resolved to hold Greece responsible and dispatched an ultimatum demanding satisfaction. When the Greek government rejected the ultimatum, Mussolini ordered the occupation of Corfu as a pledge of reparation. Almost certainly he hoped to annex the island.

Fascist Italy's occupation of Corfu was accomplished on August 31 by means of a naval bombardment of the island's fortress. However, the fortress was being used to shelter civilian refugees from Armenia, sixteen of whom were killed and over fifty wounded. The atrocity provoked worldwide indignation, and on September 1 Greece invited the League of Nations to take cognizance of the matter.

As a nationalist Mussolini scorned the League of Nations; he denied its jurisdiction in affairs of national honor and threatened to cancel Italian membership if it intervened in the Corfu dispute. Confrontation was avoided largely through the diplomacy of the French who were anxious to avoid a precedent for League interference in their own Ruhr occupation. The League was persuaded to allow the Conference of Ambassadors (the erstwhile Allied Supreme War Council), under whose aegis the Albanian frontier commission had been operating, to find a solution. This politically conscious body arrived at a political compromise: it assumed Greek responsibility for the Janina incident and required Greece to pay Italy an indemnity of fifty million lire; in return, Corfu was to be evacuated. Mussolini was reluctant to accept such a settlement, and it was only under the veiled threat of British naval action that he did so, finally authorizing an Italian withdrawal from Corfu on September 29.

The Corfu Crisis was the first instance of Fascist Italy's bellicose nationalism in action and a foretaste of things to come. In particular, the barely averted clash with the League of Nations presaged the Ethiopian conflict of 1935 (see ETHIOPIAN WAR).

For further information see: Ettore Anchiere, "L'affare di Corfu alla luce dei documenti diplomatici italiani," *Il Politico* 20 (December 1955): 374-95; James Barros, *The Corfu Incident of 1923* (Princeton: Princeton University Press, 1965); Alan Cassels, *Mussolini's Early Diplomacy* (Princeton: Princeton University Press, 1970).

                                                                                    AC

CORPORATIVISM AND THE CORPORATIVE STATE. Corporativism can be defined as a system of institutional arrangements by which capital and labor are integrated into obligatory, hierarchical, and functional units (corporations) recognized by the state, which become organs of self-government for issues relating to the specific category as well as the basis for participation with other corporatively organized interests in policy decisions affecting the whole society (Corporative parliament). The corporations may be the controlling power in the state, or they may, as in Italy, be controlled by a political authority that exists independently of and outside the corporative system.

The two chief sources for Italian Fascist corporativism were syndicalism (q.v.) and authoritarian nationalism. Revolutionary syndicalism proposed autonomous worker organizations as the basis for the proletarian revolution. The theory rejected political action within the framework of traditional parliamentary parties in favor of action through functional economic organizations (syndicates). A number of syndicalists like Sergio Panunzio (q.v.), Agostino Lanzillo (q.v.), and A. O. Olivetti (q.v.) went even further by shifting their perspective from international proletarian solidarity to "national syndicalism" of all "productive classes" from the workers to the managers and entrepreneurs. Even more important were a group of authoritarian nationalists, led by Enrico Corradini (q.v.) and Alfredo Rocco (q.v.), who sought to strengthen the state by giving it control over the growing labor movement through a system of state regulated, national syndicates for each branch of industry.

Practical experience of large-scale industrialization contributed in yet another way to the development of a corporative mentality in Italy after the turn of the century. Not only workers, but industrialists, landowners, and professionals began to organize by sector to protect their interests.

During World War I the various theories of national syndicalism or precorporativism converged. The war itself offered a corporative model of hierarchical organization. Young middle-class officers discovered in the military an outline of a managerial or technocratic society in which their status would be protected. In the crisis of post-World War I the widespread conviction that the liberal parliamentary system of representation was inadequate for modern society led many to seek in these nascent economic, professional, and social solidarities a substitute for traditional political organization. These aspirations carried over into early Fascism, which organized "competence" or technical study groups in 1921 and 1922 for various sectors of society.

The development of the corporative system under Fascism began only after 1925, when the dictatorship was consolidated. Between 1922 and 1925 the Fascist government worked within the traditional parliamentary framework and followed a generally liberal economic policy. Under the circumstances little could be done to organize corporative structures. The rupture with the liberal constitution in 1925 led the Fascists to experiment with new ways of organizing political and economic society. Between 1926 and 1929 the key decisions that determined the nature of the corporative system were made. The cornerstone of the Fascist corporative state was the so-called *legge sindacale* (syndical law), officially known as the "Law for the Judicial Regulation of Labor Disputes," drawn up by Alfredo Rocco and passed by Parliament on April 3, 1926. The Rocco Law allowed only one officially recognized association of workers and employers for each branch of production. It abolished strikes and lockouts and created compulsory arbitration, which culminated in a system of labor courts. This act was followed on July 2, 1926 by the creation of a Ministry of Corporations to oversee the legally recognized associations. The third preparatory step was the decision in 1928 to destroy the power of the Fascist labor confederation by breaking it into several weak federations, which lacked the political and economic muscle of the employers' associations. Finally, in 1929 parliamentary elections were held under a new law that eliminated the old system of geographical representation in favor of nomination of candidates by various professional, social, and economic organizations (*see* PARLIAMENT).

The high point of corporative experimentation came between 1929 and 1934. In March 1930 the National Council of Corporations was established as an economic corporative parliament. It was made up of the seven large employer and worker organizations for industry, agriculture, banking, internal navigation, commerce, sea and air transport, and various professions and arts, which gathered in a corporative assembly and a central corporative council. The powers of the National Council of Corporations were mainly consultative and did not impinge on those of the national Parliament, but it could issue binding regulations in matters covered by collective contracts. The corporative structure grew further in February 1934 when no less than twenty-two corporations were created.

The beginning of the war in Ethiopia in 1935 (*see* ETHIOPIAN WAR) put an end to the major period of innovation, although in 1939 the old Chamber of Deputies was formally replaced by a Chamber of Fasci and Corporations. The corporative system as it existed before the outbreak of World War II was an artificial, bureaucratic creation of the state. It had no independent initiative and even lacked controls over the employer associations nominally under its jurisdiction. The decision to cripple the labor component of corporativism in 1928 deprived the system of any popular support. Moreover, the Fascist government excluded the corporative institutions from any meaningful role in economic policy. The Istituto per la Ricostruzione Industriale (Institute for Industrial Reconstruction), created in 1933 as the holding company for the large state-run sector of basic industry, operated without reference to the corporative system. The war policies of economic autarchy were also largely carried out with minimal reference to the corporative institutions.

Although Italian corporativism was a subordinate creation, it had a major role in Fascist ideology. Many Fascists saw in corporativism a "third way" between capitalism and socialism. The most advanced point of such radical thinking came in 1932 when Ugo Spirito (q.v.), a leading theorist of Italian corporativism, argued that the logical conclusion of corporativism was ownership of the means of production by the corporations. There was a brief revival of corporative theorizing in 1944 under the Italian Social Republic (q.v.), when projects for worker control of industry were advanced, but all such endeavors were blocked by the German occupying forces.

For further information see: Alexander De Grand, *Bottai e la cultura fascista* (Bari: Laterza, 1978); A. James Gregor, *The Ideology of Fascism* (New York: Macmillan, 1969); Charles S. Maier, *Recasting Bourgeois Europe* (Princeton: Princeton University Press, 1975); David Roberts, *The Syndicalist Tradition and Italian Fascism* (Chapel Hill: The University of North Carolina Press, 1979).

                                                                                              AJD

CORRADINI, ENRICO (b. San Miniatello, Florence, July 20, 1865; d. Rome, December 11, 1931). Enrico Corradini was the theoretician, principal founder, and leader of the Nationalist movement, which joined with Fascism in March 1923. A graduate of L'Istituto di Studi Superiori of Florence, Corradini pursued the career of a high school teacher of Italian literature and playwright with modest success. Cofounder and director of *Germinal* and director of *Marzocco*, Florentine periodicals of art and literature respectively, Corradini strove for a reconstruction of culture on a purely aesthetic and eclectic basis.

Italy's defeat at Adowa, Ethiopia on March 1, 1896 aroused Corradini to the cause of nationalism. *Il Regno* (1903-1906), Corradini's Florentine review of politics, was a milestone in his achievement of self-identification and patriotic dedication.

Through a variety of means Corradini developed an ideology of proletarian nationalism having radical and reactionary elements, which he eventually bequeathed to Fascism. It featured state sovereignty, executive leadership, national will, social cohesion, the disciplinary function of hierarchy (*gerarchia*), reconciliation between Church and State, irredentism, militarism, corporate replacement of the parliamentary system, and a colonial empire. Corradini utilized Marxian terminology to clarify and advertise his creed.

Austria's seizure of Bosnia on October 6, 1908 and the concern provoked over Italian security in the Adriatic offered Corradini the incentive and incident to activate his ideas. Combined efforts with his followers bore fruit in the Italian Nationalist Association (q.v.) which was formed on December 5, 1910.

Corradini led the Nationalists in mobilizing public opinion for the invasion of Libya in 1911-12. The Treaty of Ouchy that ended the Italo-Turkish War was denounced as humiliating, since Italy was confirmed in Libya without gaining from Turkey all the territories Corradini had envisioned. The democratic and masonic mentality of the Giolittian (*see* GIOLITTI, GIOVANNI) ministry had impaired the prosecution of the war and the securing of a satisfactory peace.

Campaigning outspokenly for Italy's entrance into World War I on the Allied side, Corradini balanced irredentist hopes against imperialist expectations. The war was hailed as "a revolution," encouraging the emergence of a society of producers. During the "Radiant Days" of May 1915, when massive demonstrations in favor of Italian intervention blanketed the country, Corradini threatened the monarchy and government with extinction unless Italy immediately entered the war. After the war Corradini joined those who demanded the annexation of all Istria and Dalmatia. He had an important part in the volunteers, money, and moral support Nationalists provided for Gabriele D'Annunzio's (q.v.) coup at Fiume (q.v.), on September 12, 1919, and was also involved in the initial stages of a plot aimed at a D'Annunzio takeover of the Italian state.

Once Mussolini obtained control, Corradini viewed Mussolini and Fascism as the strong man and mass movement through which the Nationalist elite would realize its program. He pressed for merger, assisted in negotiating the Pact of Union between Fascism and Nationalism (1923), and used his immense prestige among rank-and-file Nationalists to have it ratified. After fusion, he went into the Fascist Grand Council (q.v.), was appointed senator, and a member of the Committee of Eighteen (*see* PARLIAMENT), which formulated plans for the corporate state.

Notes discovered on his death revealed Corradini's disenchantment. He felt that one figure was being idolized and not the Italian people; focus of attention was one party and not Italy. Nevertheless, Mussolini, in his eulogy in the Senate, extolled Corradini as "a Fascist of the...very first hour." Newspapers spoke of the departure of "an apostle." Corradini was entombed in Santa Croce, Florence, Italy's Pantheon.

For further information see: Ronald S. Cunsolo, "Enrico Corradini e la teoria del nazionalismo proletario," *Rassegna Storica del Risorgimento* 65 (July-September 1978); Taeye Henen, *Le nationalisme d'Enrico Corradini et les origines du fascisme dans la revue florentine "Il Regno" 1903-1906* (Paris: Didier, 1973); Francesco Leoni, *Origini del nazionalismo italiano* (Naples: A. Morano, 1970); Pier L. Occhini, *Enrico Corradini e la nuova coscienza nazionale* (Florence: Vallecchi, 1925).

RSC

CORRIDONI, FILIPPO (b. Pausula, Marche, August 19, 1887; d. battle of the "Frasche," October 23, 1915). Like many revolutionary syndicalists in Italy, Corridoni began his political career as a Mazzinian. Early in his youth he flirted with Marxism but, impetuous by nature and disdainful of theory, he soon accepted the Sorelian doctrines of violence and direct action. In 1906 he founded, along with Maria Rygier, a fiercely antimilitarist newspaper, *Rompete le file!*, in which he elaborated the heroic and spiritual value of violence and direct action.

From 1906 to 1913 he waged a constant battle against the reformists in the CGL (*see* CONFEDERAZIONE GENERALE DEL LAVORO), until finally he abandoned his efforts to subvert the CGL and broke with the Chamber of Labor in Milan. On March 31, 1913, he established the Unione Sindacale Milanese and used it to engage in a struggle with Rinaldo Rigola and Mussolini for control of the working-class movement in Milan. He was a popular and superb speaker, who could sway crowds with his passionate rhetoric. In late 1913 only an alliance of convenience between Mussolini and the Milan Chamber of Labor prevented Corridoni from gaining control over the city's labor movement.

Frustrated by the failure of Red Week (June 7-14, 1914), during which insurrectional strikes failed to produce revolution, Corridoni recognized in August that the war could become the revolution and he, like Alceste De Ambris (q.v.), argued strongly for Italy's intervention in World War I. He enlisted in the infantry on May 23, 1915 and showed the courage of his convictions when he requested front-line duty. He fell five months later while shouting, according to legend, "Viva Italia!"

For further information see: Ivon de Begnac, *L'arcangelo sindacalista* (Verona: Mondadori, 1943); Tullio Masotti, *Corridoni* (Milan: Cornaro, 1932).

CLB

COSELSCHI, EUGENIO (b. Bagno a Ripoli, Florence, September 13, 1889). A poet and Fascist propagandist, Coselschi held degrees in law and French literature. In 1909 he and Gabriele D'Annunzio (q.v.) met, and the latter attempted to sponsor his poetic works. In 1914-15 together the two men worked vigorously for Italian intervention in World War I, and Coselschi fought as a volunteer until 1918, rising to captain. In 1919 he founded a veterans organization called the Associazione Nazionale Volontari di Guerra and then joined the expedition for Fiume (q.v.) where he served as personal secretary to D'Annunzio and as head of the Foreign Affairs Office.

After Mussolini's seizure of power, Coselschi held numerous posts in cultural and propaganda agencies and remained one of D'Annunzio's closest confidants. He was in Parliament from 1929 to 1939, was a radio commentator in the 1930s, and an officer in the Istituto Nazionale Fascista di Cultura (*see* ISTITUTO NAZIONALE DI CULTURA FASCISTA) and the Dante Alighieri Society. In 1933 he became head of the Comitato d'Azione per l'Universalità di Roma (CAUR), a propaganda office designed to spread the myth of *Romanità* (q.v.) and create a "universal" fascist movement.

For further information see: *Chi è?* (1936); *Chi è?* (1948); DSPI; Michael A. Ledeen, *Universal Fascism* (New York: Fertig, 1972).

PVC

COSTAMAGNA, CARLO (b. Quiliano, Savona, September 21, 1881). Corporativist theorist and Fascist bureaucrat, Costamagna received a law degree and then served as a judge. He joined the Fascist movement in 1920 and became a member of the party's national council and secretary-general for technical councils. In 1925 Costamagna served as secretary for the Council of Eighteen (*see* PARLIAMENT) for constitutional revision and worked closely with Giuseppe Bottai (q.v.) and Alfredo Rocco (q.v.) in drafting corporate laws and the Charter of Labor (q.v.). Costamagna served as a deputy from 1929-39 and in 1927 became a professor of corporative law at the University of Ferrara. For a time Costamagna directed *Lo stato* and contributed to Bottai's *Critica fascista* and other journals. Costamagna carried on a long-term debate with other Fascists over the nature of Fascist trade unions and corporations, which he believed were primarily instruments of state control and were not to assume major roles in reorganizing society.

For further information see: *Chi è?* (1936); Ferdinando Cordova, *Le origini dei sindacati fascisti* (Bari: Laterza, 1974); David D. Roberts, *The Syndicalist Tradition and Italian Fascism* (Chapel Hill: University of North Carolina, 1979).

MSF

COSTITUENTE. On June 2, 1946, the Italian people elected a Constituent Assembly to draft a constitution for the republic, which had been chosen by referendum on the same day. The election to the Assembly (Costituente) was conducted on the principle of proportional representation, with the voters' choice made from the lists of candidates presented by the political parties in large, multi-member, constituencies. The former constitution, the *Statuto albertino*, had been so corrupted by the Fascist regime that it had to be replaced, whether the results of the referendum produced a monarchy or a republic.

The election results produced the following distribution of political strength:

Parties	Percentage of Popular Vote	Assembly Seats
Christian Democrat	35.2	207
Socialist	20.7	115
Communist	19.0	104
Liberal	6.8	41
Republican	4.4	23
Neo-Fascist*	5.3	30
Monarchist	2.8	16
Various	5.8	20
Totals	100.0	556

*There was no party by this label. It is used to cover a number of political forces such as *L'uomo qualunque* (Everyman) and others which coalesced later into the Italian Social Movement (MSI—Movimento Sociale Italiano).

Elected to the Constituent Assembly were the major party leaders, outstanding anti-Fascists who had led the resistance struggle before and during the years of World War II, distinguished scholars and cultural leaders such as Benedetto Croce (q.v.) and Piero Calamandrei (q.v.), and pre-Fascist politicians such as Francesco Saverio Nitti (q.v.). The presiding officer was the Communist, Umberto Terracini (q.v.).

It had been the earlier intention of the government to endow the Constituent Assembly with full legislative powers as well as constitution-making powers. The intention had been to create an assembly with all powers for all purposes; to legislate, to appropriate, to make and unmake cabinets; to function in the general tradition of parliamentary supremacy. By June 2, 1946, however, these intentions had been aborted. The Assembly would be restricted to constitution-making, with the exception that it was authorized to ratify treaties. This exception was made in anticipation of the completion of a treaty of peace between Italy and the victorious Allied powers. In the meantime Italy was governed by a cabinet under the provisional president of the Republic, with the cabinet exercising the normal legislative functions.

It took one and one-half years for the Constituent Assembly to produce a constitution (*see* CONSTITUTION OF THE ITALIAN REPUBLIC). It was approved by a resolution of the Assembly of December 22, 1947 and promulgated by the provisional president to be effective January 1, 1948.

The Assembly of 556 delegates was divided into working committees constructed on the basis of proportionality, with each committee assigned to produce draft articles in its appropriate area: political relations, economic relations, governmental structures and powers, elections, subnational governments, and so on. A steering committee of seventy-five organized the work, negotiated the final bargains and compromises, pulled all the drafts together, and made the final decisions. The political parties dominated the drafting process through their ability, for the most part, to exercise party discipline. With some exceptions the Costituente was not an assemblage of independent notables.

For further information see: Giuseppe Mammarella, *Italy After Fascism* (Notre Dame: University of Notre Dame, 1966).

NK

CRESPI BROTHERS. Important participants in the Fascistization of the Italian press, the Crespi brothers were part of a large Milanese family of industrialists whose wealth was concentrated in the textile and hydroelectric industries. The family also gained partial control of the important *Corriere della Sera* (Milan) in 1882. Two of the brothers, Silvio (b. Milan, September 24, 1868; d. Como, 1944) and Mario (b. Bergamo, September 3, 1879; d. Milan, 1962), retained ownership of the paper. Both were active supporters of the Fascist regime. Silvio extended the family's influence into the financial sector while he was president of Banca commerciale from 1919 to 1930 and was a deputy from 1897 to 1919; Mario became a senator in 1934.

The directors of *Corriere* during the early years of Fascism were Luigi Albertini (q.v.) and Alberto Albertini, but when the latter adhered to the anti-Fascist opposition in 1925 Mussolini forced the Crespi brothers to fire him. During the Salò Republic (see ITALIAN SOCIAL REPUBLIC), the *Corriere* was "socialized," and both Silvio and Mario Crespi were briefly imprisoned.

For further information see: DSPI; Valerio Castronuovo, *La stampa italiana dall' unità al fascismo* (Bari: Laterza, 1970); Piero Melograni, ed., *Corriere della sera, 1919-1943* (Rocca San Casciano: Cappelli, 1965).

MSF

CRISPO-MONCADA, FRANCESCO (b. Palermo, May 9, 1867). A prefect and police chief, Crispo-Moncada was a career bureaucrat and gravitated to the Italian Nationalist Association (q.v.) before World War I. From 1919 to 1921 he served as civilian vice commissioner for Venezia Giulia, and then became a prefect: first at Treviso (July-September 1921), then at Trieste (November 1922-June 1924).

In June 1924, in the midst of the Matteotti Crisis (q.v.), Mussolini dismissed Emilio De Bono (q.v.) as police chief and replaced him with Crispo-Moncada. The appointment was a political one, for Mussolini was under mounting pressure from the opposition and wished to demonstrate his innocence in the Matteotti kipnapping and his desire to uncover the facts in the case. Crispo-Moncada came under increasing fire, however, from the intransigent Fascists, and in September 1926 he was fired, ostensibly as a result of an assassination attempt against Mussolini. In 1928 he was made a senator.

For further information see: *Chi è?* (1936); Renzo De Felice, *Mussolini il fascista* (Turin: Einaudi, 1966).

PVC

CROCE, BENEDETTO (b. Pescasseroli, L'Aquila, February 25, 1866; d. Naples, November 20, 1952). A major twentieth-century philosopher and one of the most important intellectuals during the Fascist period, Croce's thought had a profound impact on modern Italian culture. During his long and productive life he wrote prodigiously on philosophy, historiography, history, and literary criticism, greatly influenced generations of Italian intellectuals, and was an essential point of reference for many of the most vital cultural-ideological issues of his age.

Croce came from a wealthy landowning southern family, and his financial independence gave him the means to devote his life to scholarship. After his parents were killed in an earthquake in 1883, he lived for three years in Rome under the tutelage of philosopher and politician Silvio Spaventa, and then established permanent residency in the Palazzo Filomarino in Naples, a city to which he remained deeply attached. Over the next half century he gathered a vast library in his home, which became the center of intense intellectual activity and, after World War II, an institute for philosophical and historical studies.

Croce's intellectual interests underwent a constant development, from an early period of rather erudite studies in the late 1880s to the broader concerns of aesthetics and the nature of history starting in the 1890s. *Estetica (Aesthetics)* of 1902 became a standard school text. The antipositivist thrust became a central theme of his neoidealist philosophy, and he developed a lifelong antipathy for the place of science in the order of human knowledge. Between 1895 and 1900 he encountered and "overcame" Marxist theories (his *Materialismo storico ed economia marxista [Historical Materialism and Marxist Economy]* was published in 1900), ultimately rejecting Marxist determinism as "economistic reductionism." In 1905 he began to study and revise Hegel and the theory of the dialectic (*Ciò che è vivo e ciò che è morto della filosofia di Hegel [That Which is Living and That Which is Dead in the Philosophy of Hegel]*, 1907). Croce's theoretical studies of history and historical methodology, which stemmed from his wider philosophical concerns, were published before the Fascist seizure of power (*La storia ridotta sotto il concetto generale dell' arte [History Reduced Under the General Concept of Art]*, 1893; *Teoria e storia della storiografia [Theory and History of Historiography]*, 1917; *Storia della storiografia italiana del secolo XIX [History of Italian Historiography in the 19th Century]*, 1921), but in the 1920s he began to write what might be called "applied history," in response to the constraints and pretensions of the dictatorship.

Croce generally disdained participation in politics, but in 1910 he was made a senator and during the brief last government of Giovanni Giolitti (q.v.) in 1920-21 he served as minister of public instruction. Fascism forced him to assume increasingly more active responsibility. At first, Croce, like many other intellectuals— including his former collaborator Giovanni Gentile (q.v.)—viewed Fascism as a positive force that might reinvigorate Italy in the same way that he had been trying to deprovincialize Italian culture. But after the Matteotti Crisis (q.v.) he began to move into open opposition, although it was always an opposition motivated and sustained by philosophical categories rather than by political commitment. His first powerful act against Fascism came on May 1, 1925 when he issued his famous "Manifesto of Anti-Fascist Intellectuals" (q.v.) in response to Gentile's earlier manifesto of Fascist intellectuals. It may be that his manifesto was in fact directed more against Gentile than it was against Fascism, and it clearly expressed his liberal belief in the autonomy of culture from politics, but it did galvanize hundreds of prominent intellectuals against the regime and made him the symbol of cultural resistance.

Croce's role thereafter was that of the "quietist" anti-Fascist and the "serene" intellectual mentor to the generation of Italians that lived through the two decades of Fascist dictatorship. His deep, abiding faith in liberty and liberalism was expressed repeatedly—but always subtly and in highly intellectual terms—in the books he wrote, in the erudite pages of his prestigious philosophical journal *La*

Critica (whose circulation doubled in the 1930s), and in his informal teaching. Mussolini (who once boasted that he had never read a page of Croce's work) tolerated the philosopher and allowed him considerable freedom, despite the cultural opposition to Fascism that everyone knew he represented. When a group of Fascists broke into Croce's home in October 1926 and attempted unsuccessfully to destroy his library, Mussolini denied official Fascist responsibility and posted guards to protect him. On the one hand, the regime believed that his influence was restricted to small, scholarly circles and was therefore relatively harmless; on the other, Croce's reputation was so great that repressive action would have seriously damaged the regime's standing abroad. Cornelio Di Marzio (q.v.) expressed the dilemma best when he wrote in the 1930s, "We cannot not publish Croce." Instead, the regime did its best to ignore him, striking his books from the list of required school texts and allowing often vulgar criticism of his works in the Fascist press.

In a series of three important and influential historial works written during the Fascist period Croce skillfully emphasized his faith in "history as the story of liberty" and, by indirect implication, condemned Fascism: in his *Storia d'Italia dal 1871 al 1915 (History of Italy from 1871 to 1915)* (1928) and *Storia d'Europa nel secolo decimonono (History of Europe in the Nineteenth Century)* (1932) he praised the influence of classic liberalism in the progress of civilization, and in his *Storia come pensiero e come azione (History as Thought and As Action)* (1939) he reexamined the connection between the writing of history and political action. In fact, the year in which his controversial history of the Italian liberal state appeared, Croce in a sense took over the leadership of Italy's liberal movement following the death of Giolitti. On May 24, 1929, he spoke before the Senate, harshly criticizing the Lateran Pacts (q.v.) recently concluded and along with five other senators voted against their ratification. He did not return to the Senate.

Croce's political activity did not resume again until the fall of Mussolini and the Allied landings on the Italian mainland in 1943. He adhered to the reconstituted Liberal Party, serving as its president, endorsed the CLN—Comitato di Liberazione Nazionale (*see* COMMITTEE OF NATIONAL LIBERATION) union of anti-Fascist parties, and helped to establish the National Liberation Front of Italian Volunteers to fight against the "Nazi-Fascists." Throughout the crucial 1943-44 period Croce played a key role in the efforts to form a non-Fascist government, first under Pietro Badoglio (q.v.) and then under Ivanoe Bonomi (q.v.), serving as minister without portfolio under both. His liberal, promonarchist sentiments and his prestige led the Allies, the king, and the moderate Italian political leaders to look to him for advice and support, whereas his anti-Marxist and anticlerical sentiments divorced him from the Socialists, Communists, and the Christian Democrats that were rapidly gaining popular support. He served in the Consulta Nazionale (q.v.) and in the Constituent Assembly (*see* COSTITUENTE), and was appointed a senator for life. In 1944-46 he published a number of important political pamphlets and contributed significantly to the postwar debate on the nature of Fascism.

For further information see: Federico Chabod, "Croce storico," *Rivista storica italiana* 64 (1953); Charles F. Delzell, *Mussolini's Enemies* (Princeton: Princeton University Press, 1961); Antonio Gramsci, *Il materialismo storico e la filosofia di Benedetto Croce* (Turin: Einaudi, 1948); H. Stuart Hughes, *Consciousness and Society* (New York: Vintage Books, 1958); Giovanni Mastroianni, "La polemica sul Croce negli studi contemporanei," *Società* 4 (1958); Gaetano Salvemini, "La politica di Croce," *Il Ponte* 10 (November 1954); Cecil Sprigge, *Benedetto Croce, Man and Thinker* (Cambridge: Cambridge University Press, 1952); Nino Valeri, *Da Giolitti a Mussolini* (Florence: Parenti, 1956). Croce's complete works (*Opere*) have been published by Laterza.

PVC

CUCCO, ALFREDO (b. Castelbuono, Sicily, January 26, 1893). A Nationalist turned Fascist, Cucco held a degree in medicine. In the postwar period he became one of the most prominent exponents of right-wing nationalism in Sicily, serving as secretary of the island's Nationalist Association from 1919-23. A follower of Luigi Federzoni (q.v.) and an early supporter of Mussolini, he pushed the Nationalist movement into an alliance with the Sicilian landowners and the Mafia (in 1921 he and Pietro Lanza di Scalea founded the conservative Partito Agrario Siciliano), and was behind the Nationalist merger with Fascism. He led numerous *squadrista* (q.v.) expeditions and founded and directed *La Fiamma* (Palermo, 1919-25).

Cucco emerged on the national scene in 1923 when Mussolini made him a federal secretary (until 1927); the next year he was a member of the PNF's (see PARTITO NAZIONALE FASCISTA) *direttorio* (directorate), of the Fascist Grand Council (q.v.), and a deputy. Cucco faded into obscurity in the following decade, directing *Sicilia Nuova* (Palermo) and teaching medicine at the University of Rome.

With the reshuffling of the Fascist party and the government in May 1943, Cucco reemerged once again, first as vice secretary of the PNF under Carlo Scorza (q.v.). During the Salò Republic (*see* ITALIAN SOCIAL REPUBLIC) he was undersecretary for popular culture.

For further information see: *Chi è?* (1936); A. Cucco, *Non volevamo perdere* (Bologna: Cappelli, 1950); Giuseppe C. Marino, *Partiti e lotta di classe in Sicilia* (Bari: De Donato, 1976).

PVC

CULTURE. The relationship between culture and Fascism has been viewed largely from the perspective of the relationship between intellectuals and the Fascist regime. But the growing debate over the period of the 1930s has suggested a somewhat different approach. The question of culture may be seen in a number of different ways: (a) the degree to which cultural life (as expressed in the emergence of intellectual centers such as universities, journals, and academies) was either autonomous of or dependent on the dictatorship; (b) the new form assumed by culture in a mass society, in which culture also comes to mean customs and collective behavior; (c) the regime's cultural policy; (d) the creation of a cultural plan by the Fascist intelligentsia aimed at the development of a new ruling class.

It cannot be said that the Fascist regime forcefully channeled culture in a precise, well-defined direction; nor can we speak only of a "long voyage" through Fascism in which intellectuals moved steadily toward an anti-Fascist position. In reality it is more accurate to consider the existence only of a general plan for organizing an intellectual consensus through cultural agencies. The most important goal of this plan was to obtain subservience to the regime in exchange for the relative autonomy of artistic and cultural forms—but not of content.

As Asor Rosa has observed, Fascism was "an imperfect totalitarianism"; that is, a dictatorship without the homogeneity and ideological rigidity of Nazism. Rather, Fascism had poorly defined contours and was an accumulation of tendencies tied together in an unstructured way by obedience to the demands of Fascist ideology. Rationalist architecture (*see* ARCHITECTURE) may serve as an instructive example: it was one of the best manifestations of Italian cultural maturity and creativity and demonstrated the degree to which Italian intellectuals were open to the wider currents of European thought. It was also opposed to the so-called "*stile littorio*" (Lictoral Style) that today is identified with the extreme bad taste of Fascism. Yet rationalists like Giuseppe Pagano (q.v.), Edoardo Persico (q.v.), and Giuseppe Terragni (q.v.) dedicated their work to Mussolini and the PNF (*see* PARTITO NAZIONALE FASCISTA), and Fascism embraced it without being aware that its highly intellectual consciousness could eventually result in an anti-Fascist ideological consciousness. The same point can be made regarding the cinema (q.v.), which the regime attempted to control externally through an organizational structure without ideological content (although there were some notable exceptions); propaganda newsreels apart, fictional films may be viewed in isolation from the political context in which they were made. But it can also be argued that the young generation of Italians encountered politics while being nurtured by motion pictures, and they created subversive cells in the underground of the film clubs.

The universities provide still another example of this point: while it is true, as Norberto Bobbio believes, that Italian academic culture was largely impervious to Fascistization, it was in continual dialectic between culture and cultural policy, between autonomous intellectual development and external pressures. The most illuminating case is that of the university groups, such as the GUF (Gruppi Universitari Fascisti) organizations (*see* YOUTH ORGANIZATIONS), which produced numerous journals, student newspapers, some syndical reviews, and other publications of considerable autonomy.

Therefore, an analysis of culture must come to terms with the ambiguous and contradictory character of the Fascist intellectual world—ambiguity and contradictions that are contained in the very slogans of the regime, such as "bourgeoisie" and "revolution," which may be understood in different and opposing ways. Fascism cannot be understood as a parenthesis unassociated with the traditional values of Italian culture; instead, it was a manifestation endemic to elements latent in the country and that have strongly influenced the transformation of Italian society.

In his *Lectures on Fascism*, Palmiro Togliatti (q.v.) coined the phrase "mass-based reactionary regime" (*regime reazionario di massa*) to describe the Fascist system. The regime, in fact, had a great impact on the development of Italian society, which in the wake of more advanced industrial countries, was assuming an increasingly mass nature. At the same time, however, these potentially healthy changes were used by Fascism to create a general consensus with the help of censorship, repression, Special Tribunals (*see* SPECIAL TRIBUNAL FOR THE DEFENSE OF THE STATE), and other similar means. It is therefore necessary to speak of a nascent "cultural industry" in Italy that manufactured mass culture. The process was accelerated by the communications media: from microphones, radios, and loudspeakers that filled the town squares with the Duce's voice, to the photography used to project his image, and from wall posters to cartoons. Fascism stressed, of course, the press, radio, and cinema in its intervention on the level of mass society.

In the realm of cultural policy, two initiatives must be examined: the development of "Fascist doctrine" and the *Enciclopedia Italiana* (q.v.). The search to develop an official doctrine reflected the needs of a Fascism not fully established as a regime. Doctrine enabled Fascism to abandon its antistate, subversive ideology (Fascism as "movement"). The man who presided over this development was Giovanni Gentile (q.v.), who had authored the "Manifesto of Fascist Intellectuals" (*see* MANIFESTO OF ANTI-FASCIST INTELLECTUALS) and was the principal figure in cultural policy until the Concordat (*see* LATERAN PACTS) of 1929.

Catholic influences, which after 1929 were strongly in the regime's cultural thinking, had a major impact on the *Enciclopedia* project. The latter signalled a new phase in the relationship between Fascism and culture, and was in fact the first real effort to regiment and organize an intellectual consensus. But in the years that followed, the most important figure in this effort was Giuseppe Bottai (q.v.). His constant involvement with left wing corporativist journals and literary-university reviews reflected a certain liberalizing and modernizing tendency within Fascism. As a result, even on the level of cultural policy it may be accurate to view Bottai as the "planner of the 1930s" (as he was called because of his economic-bureacratic ideas).

On another level culture can be seen as the development and implementation of a new mentality within the ruling elite of the regime: that is, a current that sought to establish a cultured managerial bureaucracy as the future leadership of the nation (perhaps either with or without Fascism). In the plans for cultural transformation of the Bottai faction, there was a new concept for the exercise of power that encountered the heavy bureaucratic and clientele infrastructure of the regime. The Ministry of Popular Culture (q.v.) was the most exasperating example of this structural opposition to the Bottai approach.

One cannot explain Fascism's rapid drive toward the crisis of war by the failure of the plan to develop a new ruling class. Nevertheless, the attempts to open Fascist culture to wider European currents (such as occurred in the case of Bottai's journal *Il Primato*) must be at least noted, especially in the context of a postwar period that has been less than ideal.

For further information see: N. Bobbio, "La cultura e il fascismo," in *Fascismo e società italiana* (Turin: Einaudi, 1973); G. Luti, *La letteratura del ventennio fascista* (Bari: Laterza, 1972); L. Mangoni, *L'interventismo della cultura* (Bari: Laterza, 1974); A. Asor Rosa, *Storia d'Italia* 4, 2 (Turin: Einaudi, 1975).

VZ

CURIEL, EUGENIO (b. Trieste, December 11, 1912; d. Milan, February 24, 1945). An anti-Fascist militant, Curiel studied engineering and then physics at the Universities of Florence and Padua, where he received his degree in 1933. From then until 1938 he was an assistant at the latter university, but he was fired after the passage of the racial laws. As a student Curiel developed anti-Fascist sentiments that were reinforced by his studies of Marx, Croce, and Gentile. In 1933-34 he became an active anti-Fascist, believing that intellectuals should establish contact with the workers. He wrote for *Il Bo*, the student newspaper at Padua, and established contact with the Communist party in exile during a trip to France. In Milan, after he left teaching, Curiel worked with the underground and was arrested in June 1939. Condemned to five years confinement on the island of Ventotene, he carried on propaganda among the other prisoners. After his release by the Pietro Badoglio (q.v.) government in 1943, he returned to Milan and worked with the Communist party in organizing the resistance. He was for a period editor of the clandestine edition of *L'Unità* (Milan) and of the party's *La nostra lotta*. He also organized the Fronte della Gioventù group (Youth Front) and was a member of the central committee of the Communist party. Shortly before the liberation of the north, Curiel was shot by a Fascist squad.

For further information see: EAR (2); MOI (2); F. Frassati, ed., *Scritti di Eugenio Curiel*, 2 vols. (Rome: Riuniti, 1973); Marino Panzanelli, "L'attività politica di Eugenio Curiel, 1932-1943," *Storia Contemporanea* 10, 2 (April 1979):253-96.

PVC

D

DALLOLIO, ALFREDO (b. Bologna, June 21, 1853; d. Rome, September 20, 1952). An armaments production coordinator in 1923-39 and previously minister for arms and munitions between 1917 and 1918, Mussolini appointed Dallolio president of the Committee for Preparation of National Mobilization in January 1923. Renamed the Committee for Civil Mobilization in October 1925, it theoretically regulated armaments industries and allocated materials (except petroleum.) The military, preferring independent competition, resisted Dallolio's efforts. Nonetheless, he effectively directed munitions manufacture during the Ethiopian War (q.v.), after becoming head of the new General Commissariat for War Production (COGEFAG—Commissariato Generale per Fabbricazione di Guerra) in July 1935. After 1937 Dallolio faced fierce Army-Navy struggles over scarce resources. Exasperated by Mussolini's unrealistic militarism and the German alliance, Dallolio resigned in August 1939, though remaining an active senator.

For further information see: *Corriere della Sera*, September 21, 1952; Fortunato Minniti, "Protagonisti dell'intervento pubblico: Alfredo Dallolio," *Economia pubblica* 6 (June 1976): 209-219.

BRS

DALL'ORA, FIDENZIO (b. Palermo, February 20, 1879). Chief logistician for the Ethiopian campaign (*see* ETHIOPIAN WAR). Federico Baistrocchi (q.v.) chose Dall'Ora, a Fascist sympathizer since 1922, as quartermaster general for East Africa in September 1934. After arrival in Eritrea in January 1935, Dall'Ora confirmed criticisms of Emilio De Bono's (q.v.) inadequate preparations. Nonetheless, they collaborated well, Dall'Ora creating the infrastructure to absorb the huge influx of men and material Mussolini dispatched to Massawa. Dall'Ora guaranteed Mussolini readiness by October 1935, thereafter expediting the flow of munitions that won the war. He ignored Pietro Badoglio's (q.v.) retreat order on January 22, 1936, preventing disaster, and organized the motor column with which Badoglio seized Addis. Dall'Ora commanded Italy's only armored corps between 1938 and 1940 and became a senator in October 1939.

For further information see: Fidenzio Dall'Ora, *Intendenza in A.O.* (Rome: Istituto nazionale fascista di cultura, 1937); Giorgio Rochat, *Militari e politici nella preparazione della campagna d'Etiopia* (Milan: Angeli, 1971).

BRS

D'ANNUNZIO, GABRIELE (b. Pescara, March 12, 1863; d. Gardone Riviera, March 1, 1938). D'Annunzio was one of the most important Italian literary figures and a major element in the political-cultural origins of Fascism.

He studied at the Collegio Cicognini in Prato from 1874 to 1881 and then attended classes at the university of Rome. His earliest literary influence was the poet Giosuè Carducci. By 1882 he had already published *Primo Vere* and *Canto Novo*, both of which exhibited the decadent sensualism that characterized his most important works, especially the successful *Il Piacere* (1889). The themes of unfettered hedonism and eroticism that marked his novels also ran through his personal life, for he was the center of some of Rome's most notorious fin de siècle scandals. By 1893 D'Annunzio had discovered the philosophy of Friedrich Nietzsche, and although the superman concept became a central theme in his work and his life, it is doubtful that he fully understood its implications.

D'Annunzio entered politics for the first time in 1897, when he was elected to the Chamber of Deputies on an extreme right-wing ticket. In 1900 he shocked the public by moving over to the extreme left wing of the Socialist party in the first of many such grandiose gestures. But his Socialist phase was short-lived, for within a few years he had moved over to the Nationalists, a position marked by his poems *Canzoni del gesta d'oltremare*.

In 1914-15 D'Annunzio was one of the most influential and provocative of the interventionists. His speeches, rallies, and demonstrations drew huge crowds and galvanized thousands of Italians behind the war. He volunteered for combat and on numerous occasions risked his life in a series of heroic gestures, with the result that he lost an eye and was repeatedly decorated. In August 1918 he flew over the enemy capital of Vienna to drop propaganda leaflets. At the end of the war D'Annunzio's popularity was at its peak, and his remarkable ability to attract the enthusiastic and blind loyalty of men found him the focus of veteran adulation. In September 1919 he collected a group of veteran volunteers at Ronchi, near Trieste, and occupied the city of Fiume (q.v.). During the year that he ruled in that city he issued the so-called "Charter of Carnaro" (*see* CARNARO, CHARTER OF) for his government and implemented many of the public rituals and choreography— salutes, uniforms, war cries and so on—that Mussolini would later copy. Mussolini in fact made himself D'Annunzio's chief spokesman in Italy and raised funds for the poet-soldier but privately resented his popularity. When D'Annunzio was forced out of Fiume by General Enrico Caviglia (q.v.), he planned a march on Rome but Mussolini preempted him. He retired to his villa at Gardone Riviera (which he renamed the Vittoriale degli Italiani) and fitted it with rich and sumptuous furnishings. In August 1922 he gave an influential speech in Milan endorsing Fascism and Mussolini. In 1924 the king awarded D'Annunzio the title Prince of Monte Nevoso after the signing of the treaty of Rome with Yugoslavia, which made Fiume Italian. In 1926 Mussolini became honorary president of the commission for the publication of a national edition of D'Annunzio's works, a project later completed in 1937 in forty-nine volumes. Mussolini pronounced the poet Italy's greatest living writer and showed him deference and respect while, for his part, D'Annunzio came to regard Mussolini as an heroic figure. In 1937 he was named president of the Royal Academy.

For further information see: Renzo De Felice, *D'Annunzio politico* (Rome-Bari: Laterza, 1978); Renzo De Felice and Emilio Mariano, ed., *Carteggio D'Annunzio-Mussolini* (Milan: Bompiani, 1971); Michael A. Ledeen, *The First Duce* (Baltimore: Johns Hopkins, 1977); Nino Valeri, *D'Annunzio davanti al fascismo* (Florence: Le Monnier, 1963).

PVC

D'ARAGONA, LUDOVICO (b. Cernusco sul Naviglio, Milan, May 5, 1876; d. Rome, June 17, 1961). A labor organizer and Socialist politician, D'Aragona was a Socialist activist as a young man and served as administrative secretary of the Camera del Lavoro (q.v.) in Milan. By 1918 he had sufficiently established his reputation as a labor leader and became secretary-general of the Confederazione Generale del Lavoro (CGL) (q.v.), a post he held until 1925. A year later D'Aragona was elected a Socialist deputy and as a member of the Italian Socialist party's (Partito Socialista Italiano—PSI) (q.v.) right wing collaborated closely with Filippo Turati (q.v.), Claudio Treves (q.v.), and Giuseppe Modigliani (q.v.). During the "Occupation of the Factories" (q.v.) in September 1920, D'Aragona opposed the PSI's position and ignored the political importance of the strikes in deference to the possibility of assuming syndical control of the factories. In 1921 D'Aragona, who had previously worked to initiate contact between Mussolini and the worker's movement, persuaded a number of right-wing Socialists to support a pacification pact (*see* PACIFICATION PACT) with the Fascists, thus weakening any Socialist offensive against Fascism. Later he prevented the Alleanza del Lavoro (q.v.) from being represented in the national council of the Confederazione Generale del Lavoro and in 1922 failed to support a general strike called by the Alleanza to protest Fascist violence. Excluded from the Socialist party in 1922, in October 1925, after having declared himself in favor of some measure of cooperation with the regime, D'Aragona resigned as secretary-general of the Confederazione Generale del Lavoro and founded the Associazione Nazionale Studio.

After the war D'Aragona resumed his political activity and served in the Constituent Assembly (*see* COSTITUENTE) and became a member of Partito Socialista Democratico Italiano. In the second Alcide De Gasperi (q.v.) ministry D'Aragona was appointed minister of labor and was later made a senator.

For further information see: EAR (3); MOI (2).

MSF

DE AMBRIS, ALCESTE (b. Licciana Nardi, Massa-Carrara, September 15, 1874; d. Brive, France, December 9, 1934). Early in his life De Ambris broke with his middle-class traditions, abandoned his legal studies, and joined the PSI (*see* PARTITO SOCIALISTA ITALIANO). By 1898 he had been jailed twice for subversive activities. Rather than submit to a third jail term, he fled Italy in 1898, stopping at Marseille before he sailed to Brazil.

In Brazil he published a newspaper, *L'Avanti*, and helped to organize unions for

Italian immigrants. The Brazilian government, disturbed by his union activities, expelled him in 1903. When he fled Italy in 1898 De Ambris had been an inexperienced, idealistic youth; he returned a mature, successful labor organizer. In 1903 he became secretary of the Savona Chamber of Labor. He remained there until 1905, when he went to Rome in order to assist Enrico Leone, the editor of *Il sindacato operaio*, the first conspicuously revolutionary syndicalist (*see* SYNDICALISM) newspaper in Italy.

In February 1907 he became secretary of the Parma Chamber of Labor and from then until he went into exile for the third and last time in 1923 the workers of Parma provided him with his primary base of support in Italy. By 1907 De Ambris had become convinced that the PSI and the CGL (*see* CONFEDERAZIONE GENERALE DEL LAVORO) were incapable of establishing workers' control in Italy. In November 1907 he established a federation among the Chambers of Labor, the National Resistance Committee, which supported his program of violence and direct action. He published a paper, *L'Internazionale*, and used it to encourage constant, almost daily, strikes and direct action against the capitalist structure. He combined, in a rudimentary form, the ideas of Marx and Georges Sorel into a confusing utopian vision in which the myth of the general strike was the central element. He never, however, forged a link between his ideas and the practical politics of the Socialists. As De Ambris came to recognize in 1914, the strikes and demonstrations of the revolutionary syndicalists were not a substitute for disciplined political action. In particular, the myth of the general strike led to the fallacious belief in the inevitability of the revolution and directed the workers' attention to strike tactics rather than to a strategy for revolution.

Following the failure of the general strike in the agricultural areas around Parma, which he led, De Ambris again fled to Brazil. He returned to Switzerland in 1911 and from there helped to establish the USI (Unione Sindacale Italiana). In 1913, in order to gain immunity from prosectuion, De Ambris stood for election to the Chamber of Deputies. On October 26, 1913, the workers of Parma elected him, and he returned to his native land. The strikes of "Red Week" in June 1914 convinced De Ambris that the workers needed a single revolutionary strategy. Thus he moved to form an alliance with the revolutionary wing of the PSI. Before he and Mussolini could forge an alliance, however, the outbreak of the war convinced both of them that the war could become the revolution.

On August 18, 1914, De Ambris announced his support for Italian intervention. After that date he began haltingly to elaborate a confused doctrine of corporativism (*see* CORPORATIVISM AND THE CORPORATIVE STATE) that renounced an essential ingredient of revolutionary syndicalism, the class struggle. He remained a revolutionary, but only within the context of the capitalist system. Thus he joined Republicans, Socialists, Anarchists, and Freemasons in October 1914 in the Fascio Rivoluzionario d' Azione Interventista (*see* FASCI DI AZIONE RIVOLUZIONARIA). By 1917 he was even willing to collaborate with the Nationalists and Social Democrats in the Fascio Parlamentare di Difesa Nazionale (q.v.). During the war De Ambris also established an independent revolutionary syndicalist organization, the Comitato Sindacale Italiano, which the UIL (Unione Italiana del Lavoro) (q.v.) absorbed in 1918.

De Ambris became secretary-general of the UIL in March 1919 and at the same time gave guarded support to Mussolini's new Fasci di Combattimento (q.v.). In October 1919, however, he left the UIL in order to join with Gabriele De Annunzio (q.v.) in Fiume (q.v.). De Ambris, who had always believed that the revolution would be made with the Army, not against it, saw in D'Annunzio's actions the opportunity to spread the revolution throughout Italy. Although the Fiume regime did not foment the revolution, it did present De Ambris with a platform from which he could spread his corporativist ideas. His most spectacular success was the promulgation of the Charter of Carnaro, (*see* CARNARO, CHARTER OF), the corporativist constitution of the D'Annunzio regime.

Following the regime's collapse, De Ambris returned to Parma and the Chamber of Labor reinstated him as secretary in June 1921. Disillusioned by Mussolini's failure to support D'Annunzio and by Fascist attacks against UIL institutions, he became firmly anti-Fascist and organized the workers in Parma into militia units in order to protect their city from Fascist attacks. He also tried to win support for his corporativist ideas, but without D'Annunzio behind him, he had little success. In February 1923 he recognized that he could not continue the political struggle in Italy, and he went into exile for the last time. The Fascists stripped him of his citizenship in September 1926, and he remained in France, a publisher of anti-Fascist tracts, until his death.

For further information see: Renzo De Felice, *Mussolini il rivoluzionario* (Turin: Einaudi, 1965); Renzo De Felice, *Sindacalismo rivoluzionario e fiumanesimo nel carteggio De Ambris—D'Annunzio, 1919-1922* (Brescia: Morcelliana, 1966); Orietta Lupo, "I sindacalisti rivoluzionari nel 1914," in *Rivista Storica del Socialismo* 10 (n.d.).

CLB

DE BONO, EMILIO (b. Cassano d'Adda, Milan, March 19, 1866; d. Verona, January 11, 1944). A soldier by profession, De Bono played a key role in some of the most important events of the Fascist period. In 1878 he attended the Military College of Milan and then the Military School. By 1897 he had reached the rank of captain, and in 1912 was appointed Chief of the General Staff of the Department of Libya, an assignment which marked his first encounter with colonial administration. De Bono saw much action in the Italo-Turkish War and welcomed the onset of World War I as a means of personal redemption. He served in the Trincea region but as a result of a personality conflict with a superior officer—a problem which plagued him throughout his career—he was transferred to the Albanian front. Later in the war De Bono was sent to the Grappa area, where he helped repulse a savage Austrian attack. He was awarded a medal for his actions and composed the famous Songs of Monte Grappa.

De Bono considered joining Gabriele D'Annunzio's (q.v.) Fiume (q.v.) expedition in 1919 but finally decided against the idea. After two years of inactivity and after making contacts with various political parties, De Bono joined the Fascist party. He believed that only the Fascists would accommodate his desire for high office. Moreover, although unfamiliar with politics, De Bono believed the Fascists to be the strongest political force in Italy. Although relatively unknown by the Fascist leadership, De Bono was selected a Quadrumvir (q.v.) for the March on Rome (q.v.). In this post he was supposed to coordinate and control the seizure of power. As preparations progressed, De Bono's role as a Fascist gained in importance. He became the most obvious representative of what seemed to be a military conspiracy to overthrow the government. Moreover, De Bono's links with members of the royal family, specifically the duke of Aosta (*see* SAVOIA, EMANUELE FILIBERTO DI, DUKE OF AOSTA) and the queen mother, strengthened his position. Although symbolically important, De Bono's presence had little effect on the events of October 28-30 as he found himself in relative isolation and with little control over events in Rome.

Once Mussolini had assumed power, De Bono hoped that he would be made minister of war but due to his obscurity he was passed over for the position. Instead he was appointed director general of public security and some months later became the first commander of the Fascist Militia (q.v.). In these positions De Bono tried to control the violence initiated by intransigent and dissident Fascists. De Bono's failure to halt the disorder culminated in the murder of Giacomo Matteotti (*see* MATTEOTTI CRISIS) in June 1924. Accused of complicity in the murder, De Bono was forced to resign from both of his posts and was subsequently indicted by the Italian Senate. Although under heavy pressure, he remained silent and maintained that he was innocent. He also refused to implicate other Fascist officials, thus saving Mussolini's government further embarrassment. In June 1925 De Bono was found innocent of all the charges against him. The decision marked the definitive end of the Matteotti Crisis and ended all hope of a legal overthrow of the Fascist regime.

As a reward for his loyalty De Bono was appointed governor of Tripolitania, a post of relative obscurity and of little importance in the context of Fascist foreign policy. De Bono's appointment, however, foreshadowed Mussolini's future colonial policy. Most of De Bono's activities in Tripolitania were of little importance except for his constant but unsuccessful campaign to crush the native rebellion. As governor De Bono was attacked for maladministration of the colony and alleged financial illegalities. Nevertheless, in December 1928 he was nominated undersecretary of state in the Ministry of the Colonies and in September of the following year was appointed minister of the colonies. In this position De Bono was a major factor in formulating Fascist policy toward Ethiopia, the climax of which was the Italian invasion on October 3, 1935.

Between 1929 and 1935 De Bono sought to undermine relations between Italy and Ethiopia and tried to persuade Mussolini of the feasibility of a military action against the African nation. Between 1933 and 1934 De Bono and Mussolini secretly discussed invasion plans, and in December of 1934 they were finalized. De Bono was to lead the troops, an assignment that he hoped would provide a glorious climax to his military career. In January 1935 he was appointed high commissioner for East Africa, a move that signalled the coming of the war with Ethiopia (*see* ETHIOPIAN WAR). As the time for the conflict drew near, De Bono began to recognize that the war was to be a test of Fascism's strength and the will of the Italian people. For ten months he directed all the technical preparations, and on October 3, 1935, he led the Italian troops into Ethiopia. De Bono's campaign was marked by uncertainty and caution as well as decisive victories over the outmanned Ethiopians. But Mussolini wished the campaign to proceed at a quicker pace, and De Bono's refusal to obey the Duce's order to advance, as well as unfavorable reports concerning his activities, caused his dismissal. He was replaced by his rival, Pietro Badoglio (q.v.), and although he was immediately promoted to the rank of marshal, De Bono was very bitter about Mussolini's decision to remove him.

For the remainder of his career De Bono was relegated to honorary or ceremonial posts, but his reputation suffered further decline as a result of his feud with Alessandro Lessona (q.v.), minister of Italian Africa, over the cost of a highway that De Bono had built while in Africa. The feud gained nation-wide attention and threatened to split the ranks of the Fascist party. Although the dispute came to an indecisive conclusion, it greatly damaged the relationship between Mussolini and De Bono, for Mussolini was unwilling to aid the old marshal.

De Bono objected both to Mussolini's ever-deepening servitude to Hitler and to his war policies. Although appointed to several honorary positions (such as inspector of the overseas armies and commander of the southern armies), De Bono took no active role in the war. By July 1943 he no longer believed that Mussolini was capable of leading Italy to victory. At the July 25 meeting of the Fascist Grand Council (q.v.), De Bono voted for Dino Grandi's (q.v.) order of the day, which called for Mussolini's removal. De Bono merely wanted a change in the country's military leadership, not the overthrow of the Fascist state, but he failed to comprehend the political ramifications of Grandi's order.

On October 4, 1943, De Bono was arrested for his part in the coup against Mussolini and was brought to Verona to stand trial with the other captured conspirators. Although he protested his loyalty to Mussolini, the guilty verdict pronounced against him was predetermined by the political atmosphere in Verona. On January 11, 1944, De Bono was executed.

For further information see: Emilio De Bono, *La guerra come e dove l' ho vista e combattuto io* (Milan: Mondadori, 1935); Emilio De Bono, *La preparazione e le prime operazioni* (Rome: Istituto Nazionale Fascista di Cultura, 1937); Monte S. Finkelstein, "Emilio De Bono," in *Uomini e volti del fascismo*, ed. Ferdinando Cordova (Rome: Bulzoni Editore, 1980); Giuseppe Rossini, *Il delitto Matteotti tra*

Viminale e l'Aventino: Dagli atti del processo De Bono davanti all'Alta Corte di Giustizia (Bologna: Il Mulino, 1966).

MSF

DE BOSIS, LAURO (b. Rome, December 9, 1901; d. Tyrrhenean Sea, October 3, 1931). An anti-Fascist intellectual who died tragically at an early age, De Bosis had an Italian father and an American mother. He had a degree in chemistry but dedicated himself to literature and poetry. A liberal politically, he moved from an early sympathy for Fascism to a staunchly anti-Fascist position in 1928. Between 1924 and 1930 he visited the United States, taught at Harvard, and was secretary of the Italy-America Society, a Fascist propaganda agency. In 1930, after his conversion to anti-Fascism, he and Mario Vinciguerra organized the underground newspaper *Alleanza Nazionale*.

In October 1931 he took off from a Marseilles airport for a clandestine flight over Rome and dropped anti-Fascist leaflets. On his return to France, however, he ran out of fuel and crashed into the sea. The "Lauro De Bois Chair" in Italian Civilization was established at Harvard in his honor by his fiancee, Ruth Draper, and was first filled by Gaetano Salvemini (q.v.), who had counseled De Bosis before his flight.

For further information see DSPI; EAR (2); Lauro De Bosis, *The Story of My Death* (New York: Oxford University Press, 1933).

PVC

DE CAPITANI D'ARZAGO, GIUSEPPE (b. Milan, February 15, 1870; d. Paderno Dugnano, 1945). Minister of agriculture under Mussolini, De Capitani was a lawyer and a member of the right wing of the Liberal party. He served in Parliament from 1913 to 1929 and adhered to Fascism in 1922. He was undersecretary of the treasury in the first Facta (*see* FACTA, LUIGI) government in 1922, and, although nominated undersecretary for public instruction in the second Facta cabinet, he refused the appointment. Mussolini made him minister of agriculture in October 1922, a position he held until July 1923. De Capitani was made a marchese in February 1923 and for a time returned to private business in Milan, for which he was one of the principal spokesmen. He served as *Podestà* (q.v.) of Milan from 1928 to 1929, was made a senator in 1929, and from 1938 to 1943 was president of the Italian federation of savings banks.

For further information see: *Chi è?* (1936); DSPI; NO (1928).

PVC

DE GASPERI, ALCIDE (b. Pieve Tesino, Trentino, April 3, 1881; d. Sella Valsugana, August 19, 1954). An Italian statesman who played a major role in the formation of the Christian Democratic party and who served as premier of Italy from 1945 to 1953, De Gasperi was born in Austria-Hungary.

De Gasperi received his secondary schooling in Trent and his university education at the University of Vienna, where he specialized in philosophy and philology. As a student in Vienna (1900-1905), he was active in the Catholic social movement, and in 1902, while visiting Rome for an audience with Pope Leo XIII, he met representatives of the Christian Democratic movement of Italy. He joined the Trentine Popular party (Partito Popolare Trentino), which stood for the administrative autonomy of the Trentino and the application of the principles of social Catholicism to the socioeconomic problems of the day. In 1911 De Gasperi was one of the Popularists elected to the Austrian Parliament. During World War I he devoted much of his time to the plight of refugee Italians who had been forced by the Austrian authorities to leave their homes and live in camps.

After Italy's annexation of the Trentino under the Treaty of St. Germain (1919), De Gasperi became active in Don Luigi Sturzo's (q.v.) Popular party (Partito Popolare Italiano—PPI) (q.v.). Whether as head of the Popularists in the Chamber of Deputies, to which he had been elected in 1921, or as editor of the Catholic paper *Il Nuovo Trentino*, he opposed Fascism. Because of his participation in the Aventine Secession (q.v.) he was deprived of his parliamentary seat in November 1926, and in the following year he was arrested on the ground of attempted clandestine expatriation. Though sentenced originally to four years of imprisonment, he served only a year and a half. In 1929 he entered the employment of Pope Pius XI as a cataloguer in the Vatican library, rising to the position of secretary by 1939.

In 1942 after the Italian Army had suffered decisive defeats in Africa and the Balkans, De Gasperi took the initiative in reviving the Popular party, which was now renamed the Christian Democratic party. In December 1945 he became the first Christian Democratic premier; he was to preside over eight consecutive ministries lasting eight and a half years. His first ministries were coalitions, which included Communists and Socialists. In May 1947 De Gasperi expelled the Communists and their left-wing Socialist allies from his ministry. For purposes of governing he subsequently favored the quadripartite solution, that is, a government made of up Christian Democrats, Liberals, Social Democrats (right-wing Socialists), and Republicans.

In foreign affairs De Gasperi aligned Italy with the West. Italy accepted the Marshall Plan, joined NATO, and became a member of the European Coal and Steel Community. De Gasperi's domestic policy favored stabilization of the lira, a mixed economy, and extension of land proprietorship. The most comprehensive reform enacted was agrarian reform, a measure long advocated by Christian Democrats, but which cost De Gasperi the support of the landowning Liberals. In party councils De Gasperi represented the center, and he played a mediating role between the right and left wings of his party. Because of the absence of a well-developed party machinery, he was willing to accept the aid of the Catholic Church and especially of Catholic Action (*see* AZIONE CATTOLICA ITALIANA) in electoral contests. He was, however, opposed to integralism and resisted even Pope Pius XII when he thought that the autonomy and integrity of the party were at stake. He saw the Christian Democratic party as a party of the center that would move eventually to the left. In the summer of 1953 following the failure of the Christian Democrats and their allies to secure a majority in the parliamentary elections, De Gasperi considered a Centro-Sinistra government with Pietro Nenni (q.v.) and the left-wing Socialists, but Nenni's continuing ties with the Communists were an insuperable obstacle to such a coalition. His premiership terminated, De Gasperi became secretary of the Christian Democratic party, a post he held until his death in August 1954. He is buried in Rome in the Church of San Lorenzo Fuori le Mura.

For further information see: Giulio Andreotti, *De Gasperi e il suo tempo* (Milan: Mondadori, 1956); Eliza Carrillo, *Alcide De Gasperi, the Long Apprenticeship* (Notre Dame: University of Notre Dame Press, 1965); Maria Romana Catti De Gasperi, *De Gasperi uomo solo* (Milan: Mondadori, 1964).

ECa

DELCROIX, CARLO (b. Florence, August 22, 1896). One of the best known Fascist propagandists, Delcroix studied law before World War I and in 1915 he volunteered for combat after a vigorous interventionist campaign. In 1917 he lost his sight and both his hands as a result of an accidental explosion and in 1919 became an ardent follower of Mussolini. During the years before the March on Rome (q.v.) Delcroix was a tireless propagandist, giving countless speeches and traveling extensively on behalf of the Fascists. He developed a reputation as one of the most effective public speakers in the country, and his following among war veterans was especially useful to Mussolini.

In 1924 Delcroix became the president of the national disabled veterans organization (the Associazione Nazionale Mutilati e Invalidi di Guerra), a post he held until 1943. He served as a deputy in Parliament during that same period and was a member of the National Council of Corporations. His numerous books were popular bestsellers during the 1920s. In 1953 Delcroix was again elected to Parliament, this time on the monarchist ticket.

For further information see: *Chi è?* (1936); DSPI; EAR (2); NO (1928); C. Delcroix, *I dialoghi con la folla* (Florence: Vallecchi, 1922); C. Delcroix, *Un uomo e un popolo* (Florence: Vallecchi, 1928).

PVC

DE MARSANICH, AUGUSTO (b. Rome, April 13, 1891). Fascist ideologue and bureaucrat, De Marsanich began his career as a journalist, writing for *La Stampa* (Turin) and for *Il Lavoro Fascista* (Genoa), the paper of Fascist syndicalism that he later directed. He fought in World War I and was a Fascist deputy from 1929 to 1943. De Marsanich was active in the Fascist syndicalist movement and headed the legal office of the PNF (Partito Nazionale Fascista) (q.v.). He was a close friend and collaborator of Giuseppe Bottai (q.v.) and until 1933 wrote frequently for *Critica Fascista* as a follower of Bottai's revisionism (q.v.). De Marsanich held various positions in the Corporate system. He was president of the Syndical Confederation of Commerce and in December 1934 was made vice president of the Corporation of Building Trades. He served as a deputy from 1929 to 1934 and from January 1935 to February 1943 was undersecretary for communications. He adhered to the Salò Republic (*see* ITALIAN SOCIAL REPUBLIC), where he was president of the Società Alfa Romeo and the Banco di Roma. In the postwar period he was a founder and secretary of the neo-Fascist MSI—Movimento Sociale Italiano (q.v.).

For further information see: *Chi è?* (1936); DSPI; Alexander J. De Grand, *Bottai e la cultura fascista* (Rome-Bari: Laterza, 1978); A. De Marsanich, *Civiltà di masse* (Florence: Vallecchi, 1940); *I senatori e deputati del terzo parlamento repubblicano* (Rome: Navicella, 1958).

PVC

DE MARSICO, ALFREDO (b. Sala Consilina, Salerno, May 29, 1888). A Fascist legal expert and minister, De Marsico was a professor of law at various Italian universities, including Rome, and a criminal lawyer. He was an active Fascist deputy from 1924 to 1939, a propagandist for the regime, and he published widely. A member of the PNF (Partito Nazionale Fascista) (q.v.) directory and the Fascist Grand Council (q.v.), in February 1943 Mussolini appointed him minister of justice. De Marsico took part in the Grand Council meeting of July 24/25, 1943 and helped Dino Grandi (q.v.) draft the motion against Mussolini.

For further information see: *Chi è?* (1936); *Chi è?* (1948); NO (1928).

PVC

DEMOGRAPHIC POLICY. Fascist population policy evolved in the years immediately after the consolidation of Mussolini's power and was closely tied to a number of the regime's other key programs, including ruralization and agriculture, land reclamation, migration, and even foreign policy.

Mussolini had been influenced by the writings of Italian demographer Corrado Gini (q.v.) as well as by the ideas of Oswald Spengler and Richard Korherr, all of whom had discussed the concept of the decadence of Western nations in terms of declining birth rates and shrinking populations. In his famous "Speech of the Ascension" (May 26, 1927) Mussolini established the main lines of his demographic policy for the first time: he argued that the Roman Empire had fallen because of depopulation, and that racial strength and physical health were basic to a reinvigorated Italian people and a dynamic nation and announced the dual aims of "demographic power" and "rurality." He blamed the "pernicious tendencies" of modern urban civilization for the low birthrate in some European nations and in some areas of Italy, and extolled the countryside, where the uncontaminated virtues of rural peasant life had produced more children. The overcrowded metropolis was, according to the regime, a major source of physical and moral corruption, which raised the spectre of "vacant cradles" throughout the country.

Mussolini demanded the increased growth of Italy's population and argued that national territory could sustain many more millions of people—he even declared that his aim was a population of sixty million by the 1950s. Hence, a carefully orchestrated propaganda campaign was launched in 1928 against urbanism—"empty the cities" became a widespread slogan of the period—designed to slow down urban growth and reinforce rural values of family, motherhood, and children (this campaign reached its culmination in a 1934 law against urbanization).

This policy of ruralization responded to a number of ideological currents within Fascism, particularly the "populist" ideas of the Florentine intellectuals Curzio Malaparte (q.v.) and Ardengo Soffici (q.v.), both of whom were important figures in the Strapaese (q.v.) movement of the 1920s, which posited an idealistic-populist rural doctrine against the modernist tendencies of Futurism and other elements of Fascism. In addition, the regime's land reclamation program of Bonifica Integrale (q.v.) and its attempts to increase the productivity of Italian agriculture were in part aimed at making rural life more attractive to farmers.

The themes of demographic growth, ruralism, and agricultural reform had their impact on the question of internal migration and external emigration. The regime officially tried to discourage and prevent the migration of peasants from the countryside to the cities and from poorer regions to more productive areas. In 1926 a permanent Committee on Internal Migrations was created within the Ministry of Public Works, and in 1928 a commissariat for Migrations and Internal Colonization was established. But despite laws limiting internal freedom of movement, domestic migration actually increased in the 1930s (an average of one million people a year moved), largely from the south to the north.

Emigration abroad, which since the 1880s had drained Italy of millions of its citizens, had been encouraged by the pre-Fascist liberal governments as a means of getting rid of excess, unemployed population in the southern areas of the country. At first Mussolini opposed emigration as a sign of national weakness and criticized the liberal regimes for having abandoned its agrarian labor force to foreign countries, but in 1923-24 alone more than 765,000 Italians left. Although the figures dropped sharply after the imposition of foreign immigration quotas, in 1927 the Ministry of Foreign Affairs estimated that approximately nine million Italians were living abroad. Hence, by the end of the decade the regime reversed itself and declared that the presence of Italians around the world in such large numbers represented a sign of demographic and "racial" strength for Italy. The expansion of Italians abroad was therefore converted into a "demographic imperialism" that reinforced Mussolini's expansionist foreign policy. Similarly, one current of Nationalist ideology represented by Enrico Corradini (q.v.) had espoused the theory of Italy as a proletarian nation whose strength lay in the vitality and expansion of its people in the struggle against plutocracies. Ironically, the rationale used by Mussolini for territorial aggrandizement was overpopulation. In this context Mussolini attempted to establish close and permanent ties between Italians living in foreign countries in order to maintain their loyalty to the mother country. A vast propaganda campaign was therefore launched, and the regime backed the creation of Fascist organizations abroad for this purpose (the so-called Fasci all'Estero, [q.v.]).

The effort to increase Italy's population by driving up the birth rate intensified in the mid-1930s, especially because of the adverse impact of the depression. In order to stimulate births, the regime offered financial bonuses to veterans who married, put a tax on bachelors, extended loans to young newlyweds, and gave out medals and prizes to large families. Programs to improve health and hygiene were also set up to lower infant mortality and ensure healthier mothers (*see* FASCI FEMMINILI).

During the Fascist period Italy's population did increase modestly, from approximately 38,450,000 in 1921 to an estimated 44,900,000 in 1940, but it is doubtful that Fascist policies had a significant impact on that increase.

For further information see: Philip V. Cannistraro and Gianfausto Rosoli, "Fascist Emigration Policy in the 1920s," *International Migration Review* (Winter 1979); Renzo De Felice, *Mussolini il duce* (Turin: Einaudi, 1974); Corrado Gini, *I fattori demografici dell' evoluzione delle nazioni* (Turin: Bocca, 1912); Richard Korherr, *Regresso delle nascite*, preface by B. Mussolini (Rome: Littorio, 1928); Edward R. Tannenbaum, *The Fascist Experience* (New York: Basic Books, 1972); Anna Treves, *Le migrazioni interne nell'Italia fascista* (Turin: Einaudi, 1976).

PVC

DE NICOLA, ENRICO (b. Naples, November 9, 1877; d. Torre del Greco, October 1, 1959). A well-known legal expert and anti-Fascist politician, De Nicola served in Parliament from 1909 to 1924 as a member of the constitutional left and was president of the Chamber of Deputies from 1920 to 1923. Prior to the seizure of power, De Nicola was undersecretary for colonies (1913-14) and then for the treasury (1919). During the Fascist regime, De Nicola abandoned political activity and practiced law, and despite his nomination as a senator in 1929, he took no part in parliamentary life.

After the armistice of September 1943 De Nicola served as a member of the southern Committee of National Liberation (q.v.) and proposed the important compromise by which King Victor Emmanuel III (q.v.) retired in favor of his son, Umberto II (q.v.), who in turn became the lieutenant general of the realm.

In June 1946 De Nicola was elected provisional president of the Italian Republic by the Constituent Assembly (*see* Costituente) and in January 1948 became the first president under the new constitution. De Nicola also served in the Senate and was president of the Italian high court from 1956 to 1958.

For further information see: DSPI; EAR (2); Charles F. Delzell, *Mussolini's Enemies* (Princeton: Princeton University Press, 1961).

MSF

DE PINEDO, FRANCESCO (b. Naples, February 16, 1890; d. New York, September 2, 1933). De Pinedo began his career as a naval officer serving in the

Italo-Turkish War and in World War I. In 1917 he earned his pilot's license. In 1925 he completed a flight of fifty-five thousand kilometers in a Savoia 16-ter flying boat baptized "Gennariello" that touched on three continents and took 260 flying hours. His itinerary was Sesto Calende-Melbourne, Melbourne-Tokyo, and Tokyo-Rome. In 1927 he and Carlo Del Prete, flying a Savoia Marchetti S55 baptized "Santa Maria," crossed the Atlantic and parts of South and North America before returning to Italy in a journey that took 279 hours and 40 minutes of flying time and covered 43,820 kms. During the expedition, however, the "Santa Maria" was destroyed when it caught fire while moored on Roosevelt Lake, Arizona, the victim of a careless attendant. De Pinedo completed the trip in the "Santa Maria II" sent from Italy. In 1928 and 1929 De Pinedo helped to organize and participated in two mass training flights to the western Mediterranean (Rome-Los Alcazares, Spain) and to the eastern Mediterranean (Rome-Odessa). Promoted to general in 1929, he became deputy Air Force chief of staff. De Pinedo eventually fell victim to a rivalry with Italo Balbo (q.v.), Air Force undersecretary, and abandoned active service in February 1933. After a period as air attaché in Buenos Aires, De Pinedo planned a new distance record flight from New York to Baghdad in hopes of reviving his fortunes. While attempting to take off on this record flight, he was killed when his heavily loaded plane crashed on September 2, 1933.

For further information see: Francesco De Pinedo, *Un voli di 55,000 chilometri* (Milan: A. Mondadori, 1926); Francesco De Pinedo, *Il mio volo attraverso l'Atlantico e le due Americhe* (Milan: U. Hoepli, 1928).

CGS

DE PIRRO, NICOLA (b. Nocara, Cosenza, April 24, 1898). A cultural bureaucrat and publicist, De Pirro took a degree in law but retained an abiding interest in theater and music. He served as secretary-general of the Fascist Association for Entertainment in the 1920s and promoted the motion picture industry as an area of government intervention. In 1933 he was a director for the regime's radio programs among peasants (the Ente Radio Rurale) and in 1935 entered the Ministry of Press and Propaganda as director of theater. In this capacity he presided over the various efforts to popularize and Fascistize the Italian theater. He wrote for many cultural journals, was codirector of the journal *Scenario*, and a member of the National Council of Corporations.

For further information see: *Chi è?* (1936); Philip V. Cannistraro, *La fabbrica del consenso* (Rome-Bari: Laterza, 1975); Leopoldo Zurlo, *Memorie inutile* (Rome: Ateneo, 1952).

PVC

DE RUGGIERO, GUIDO (b. Naples, March 23, 1888; d. Rome, December 29, 1948). An historian, philosopher, and anti-Fascist, De Ruggiero took a degree in law but turned to the study of philosophy under the influence of Giovanni Gentile (q.v.) and neoidealist currents. Before World War I he held strongly nationalistic views and was an interventionist, collaborating with *L'Idea Nazionale*. After the war, however, he moved decisively toward a new liberalism, supporting F. S. Nitti (q.v.) and writing for Piero Gobetti's (q.v.) *Rivoluzione Liberale*. A moderate anti-Fascist, by the end of 1924 he had joined Giovanni Amendola's (q.v.) Unione Democratica Nazionale.

In 1925 his *History of European Liberalism* appeared. It became a liberal text for many younger Italians and posited the crisis of liberalism as the abandonment of universal values. The reprinting of this volume in 1941 brought his dismissal as a professor, but during the brief forty-five days that Pietro Badoglio (q.v.) was in power in 1943 he was made president of the University of Rome. When the Nazis occupied the city, he went underground and helped found the Partito d'Azione (q.v.). In June 1944 Ivanoe Bonomi (q.v.) appointed him minister of public instruction, and he was a member of the national Consulta (*see* CONSULTA NAZIONALE).

For further information see: DSPI: EAR (3); G. De Ruggiero, *Storia del liberalismo europeo* (Bari: Laterza, 1925); G. De Ruggiero, *Storia della filosofia*, 16 vols. (Bari: Laterza, 1918-48).

PVC

DE SANCTIS, GAETANO (b. Rome, October 15, 1870; d. Rome, April 9, 1957). An historian and anti-Fascist, he taught ancient history at the University of Turin from 1900 to 1929, and Greek history at Rome from 1929 to 1931. In addition to his teaching activities and scholarly writing, De Sanctis was director of *Rivista di Filologia Classica* and on the staff of Giovanni Gentile's (q.v.) *Enciclopedia Italiana* (q.v.). He was one of the eleven or twelve professors who in November 1931 refused to take the Fascist university oath (*see* UNIVERSITY OATH), thereby losing his teaching position and pension. To Education Minister Balbino Giuliano (q.v.), who urged him to reconsider, he wrote, "I have given many lessons to young people, but the best one is that which I am about to give." In 1934 Gentile fired him from the *Enciclopedia*, and in October he refused to take a similar oath as a member of the prestigous association of scholars, the Accademia dei Lincei, from which he was then expelled. After World War II he was reinstated at the University of Rome and made president of the *Enciclopedia Italiana* (1947-54). In 1950 he was named a senator.

For further information see: *Chi è?* (1948); EAR (1); Charles F. Delzell, *Mussolini's Enemies* (Princeton: Princeton University Press, 1961).

PVC

DE STEFANI, ALBERTO (b. Verona, October 6, 1879; d. Rome, January 15, 1969). A Fascist minister and professor, De Stefani taught in a number of universities, specializing in economics and finance. He served in World War I and in 1921 became a member of the PNF—Partito Nazionale Fascista (q.v.). In that same year he was elected to the Chamber of Deputies and participated in *squadristi* (q.v.) attacks against the Socialists. He was interim minister of the treasury in December 1922 and then minister of finance, a position he held until July 1925.

As minister De Stefani sought to restore Italy to an important role in the international economy and to reduce government interference in private enterprise. He therefore followed what was basically a capitalist approach to economic problems, trying to stimulate investment by reducing government laws and taxes, reducing trade restrictions, allowing free competition, and bolstering the lira. Although he produced a budget surplus and helped the Italian textile industries, his policies alienated leaders of the armaments, metal, and chemical industries, who opposed his free-trade ideas and his refusal to use government subsidies of private enterprises. In July 1925 he was forced to resign after his efforts to halt speculation in the stock market and in foreign currencies.

Between 1925 and 1943 De Stefani held a number of minor posts. He was Italy's representative at the Dawes Conference on German reparations payments in London and a member of the National Council of Corporations. On July 24, 1943, he attended the meeting of the Fascist Grand Council (q.v.) and voted for the Dino Grandi (q.v.) motion against Mussolini. He was condemned to death in absentia at the Verona Trials (q.v.), and a postwar trial for Fascist crimes absolved him.

For further information see: *Chi è?* (1936; 1948); DSPI; NO (1928); Alberto De Stefani, *Fuga del tempo* (Perugia: Donnini, 1948).

MSF

DE VECCHI, CESARE MARIA (b. Casale Monferrato, November 14, 1884; d. Rome, June 23, 1959). The shaven bullet head and belligerent mustachios of De Vecchi were among the most conspicuous ornaments of the regime, of which he incarnated the conservative clerico-monarchical tendency. De Vecchi fought with distinction in World War I (in 1933 he received the title "di Val Cismon" after the site of one of his exploits). He joined the Turin *fascio* in 1919 and soon dominated it. He resisted the movement's transformation into a party in September-October 1921. Appointed (along with Italo Balbo [q.v.] and Emilio De Bono [q.v.]) to command the Fascist Militia (q.v.) in August 1922, he served as one of the quadrumvirs (q.v.) directing the March on Rome (q.v.). He maintained contacts with the monarchy throughout, and in order to avoid a clash between Fascism and the Army attempted to delay the March and imprison Mussolini in an Antonio Salandra (q.v.) cabinet. Victor Emmanuel III (q.v.) resolved De Vecchi's conflict of loyalties by accepting Mussolini as prime minister on October 29.

Monarchist figurehead and undersecretary for war pensions in the new government, De Vecchi embarrassed Mussolini with political gaffes, which included public approval of the extreme Turin Fascist violence of December 1922. Mussolini dismissed him in May 1923, and in October De Vecchi accepted the governorship of Somalia (the most distant post of responsibility the regime had to offer). He organized the colonial forces there and disarmed the southern tribes by early 1925.

After visiting Rome to obtain further funds (and, incidentally, to discuss plans for an eventual assault on Ethiopia), he attacked the northern sultanates of Obbia and Mijjurtine. Despite initial success, he had to request reinforcements and barely survived Pietro Badoglio's (q.v.) demands for his removal. After the completion of pacification in February 1927 De Vecchi pushed outposts across the ill-defined Ethiopian border. He left Somalia in June 1928.

Restored to favor, he served as minister to the Holy See beginning on June 7, 1929 and apparently exacerbated the 1931 conflict between Church and regime over control of youth by clashing personally with Pius XI. Mussolini gave De Vecchi another chance, however, and in the January 1934 "change of the guard" appointed him minister of national education with the mission of subjugating Italian cultural life. De Vecchi applied himself bombastically to "Facist cultural land reclamation," but his lack of subtlety and intellectual standing proved disadvantageous. When he volunteered in November 1936 to govern the Dodecanese, Mussolini accepted.

On Rhodes De Vecchi was in his element. Styling himself "Gubernator," he roared about the island, requiring all to greet his passage with the Fascist salute, and made serious efforts to denationalize the Greek inhabitants. He also met frequently and ostentatiously with the other surviving quadrumvirs in order to demonstrate opposition to Mussolini's racial and foreign policies.

After Italy's entry into the war, De Vecchi bombarded Rome with messages alleging (largely imaginery) Greek collusion with the British fleet. He also gave orders that, along with a Navy directive, produced the unprovoked submarine attack on the obsolete Greek cruiser *Helli* on August 15, 1940. Once Mussolini did launch the Greek war on October 28, 1940, De Vecchi was less enthusiastic. His forces were by then short of supplies, and he was engaged in a running battle with Badoglio and the Navy and Air staffs over prerogatives and missions. At the end of November De Vecchi flew to Rome and resigned in protest.

Resignation proved a personal disaster; Mussolini refused to employ him elsewhere until 1943, and the public judged he had deserted his post. He remained a member of the Fascist Grand Council (q.v.), and at the July 24-25, 1943 meeting defended the Army against charges that it, not the regime, was responsible for defeat. He voted for Dino Grandi's (q.v.) motion, went into hiding, and subsequently escaped to South America; the Verona Tribunal (*see* VERONA TRIALS) condemned him to death in absentia. He returned to Italy ten years later and joined the MSI—Movimento Sociale Italiano (q.v.), which he attempted to influence in a clerico-monarchist direction.

For further information see: C. M. De Vecchi's unreliable "Una sconcertante storia del fascismo: Mussolini vero," serialized in *Tempo*, November 1959—March 1960; Ruggero Fanizza, *De Vecchi, Bastico, Campioni. Ultimi governatori dell' Egeo* (Forlì: S.A.C.-Valbonesi, n.d.).

MK/BRS

DIAZ, ARMANDO (b. Naples, December 5, 1861; d. Rome, February 29, 1928). Victorious Army Chief of Staff from 1917-1919, Diaz, influenced by his only son, a Fascist since 1921, believed Fascism could benefit the Army. During October 27-28, 1922, Diaz informed King Victor Emmanuel III (q.v.) that "the Army will do its duty but it would be better not to put it to the test" by ordering resistance to a Fascist takeover. For this crucial service Mussolini made Diaz war minister, promising him extraordinary powers and prevention of proposed radical Fascist military reforms. Diaz accepted small budgets but unrealistically expanded the Army. While disliking the Militia (q.v.), Diaz lent his prestige to Mussolini's government, delaying his resignation, despite ill-health, until after the April 1924 elections. Diaz remained an active senator and became Italy's first marshal in November 1924. He fought Antonino Di Giorgio's (q.v.) reforms but accepted the Pietro Badoglio (q.v.)-Ugo Cavallero (q.v.) Army reorganization.

For further information see: Giorgio Rochat, *L'esercito italiano da Vittorio Veneto a Mussolini* (Bari: Laterza, 1967).

BRS

DI GIACOMO, GIACOMO (b. Osimo, Ancona, November 23, 1885). A Fascist syndicalist and bureaucrat, Di Giacomo took a law degree and volunteered for combat in World War I. He joined the Fascist movement in 1919 and dedicated himself to organizing intellectuals and artists into Fascist trade unions. A member of the Rome *fascio* and the Militia (q.v.), he wrote widely on syndicalism and Fascism throughout his career. In 1924 he was a judge for the military tribunal in Rome, from 1927 to 1930 represented Italy on the international labor commission of the League of Nations, and was elected to Parliament in 1929 and 1934. In the late 1920s he was secretary-general of the National Federation of Intellectual Unions and in the 1930s became president of the Confederation of Professionals and Artists.

For further information see: *Chi è?* (1936); *Chi è?* (1948); NO (1928); Philip V. Cannistraro, *La fabbrica del consenso* (Rome-Bari: Laterza, 1975).

PVC

DI GIORGIO, ANTONINO (b. San Fratello, Palermo, September 22, 1867; d. Palermo, April 17, 1932). A controversial war minister, a successful general, and a Nationalist deputy from 1913 to 1921, Di Giorgio was kept from command between 1919 and 1924 by his factious personality and reformist military thinking. On Armando Diaz's (q.v.) advice Mussolini appointed Di Giorgio war minister in April 1924, after his reelection as independent deputy. Di Giorgio planned radical Army reorganization with reduced peace-time troop strength and an increased officer and NCO corps, hoping to spend resultant savings on modern equipment and training. The Carabinieri (*see* POLICE AND INTERNAL SECURITY) and Militia (q.v.) would provide internal security. In a crisis reserves would mobilize behind small frontier forces. Di Giorgio backed Mussolini during the Matteotti Crisis (q.v.) and, while disliking the MVSN—Milizia Volontaria per la Sicurezza Nazionale (*see* MILITIA), gave it one hundred thousand rifles in June 1924. Di Giorgio presented his reforms in November-December 1924, but senior generals, led by Gaetano Giardino (q.v.), opposed them. They feared a reduced Army would lose political power, especially to the Militia. While Di Giorgio's support helped him greatly, Mussolini realized Di Giorgio had alienated Army leadership. Roberto Farinacci (q.v.) opposed Di Giorgio for his hostility to the MVSN. In April Mussolini unexpectedly proposed a compromise but Di Giorgio refused and resigned. Di Giorgio was corps commander at Florence from 1925 to 1926, then in Sicily until 1928, when he retired, protesting Cesare Mori's (q.v.) arbitrary anti-Mafia measures.

For further information see: Antonino Di Giorgio, *Scritti e discorsi vari* (Milan: Albrighi, Segati, 1938); Giorgio Rochat, *L'esercito italiano da Vittorio Veneto a Mussolini* (Bari: Laterza, 1967).

                                                                                                             BRS

DI MARZIO, CORNELIO (b. Pagliara dei Marsi, December 6, 1896). One of the most important cultural bureaucrats in the Fascist regime, Di Marzio came to Fascism as a Nationalist ideologue. He held a degree in literature and philosophy, volunteered for combat in World War I, and in 1919 was editor of the Nationalist newspaper *L'Idea Nazionale*. In 1920 Di Marzio founded and directed the Fascio di Combattimento (q.v.) in L'Aquila and was a special envoy for *Il Popolo d'Italia*. Although he at first favored the fusion of the Italian Nationalist Association (q.v.) with the PNF—Partito Nazionale Fascista (q.v.), he became disillusioned with Mussolini's cultural rhetoric and with the totalitarian regime, and through numerous positions in the government and the party he sought to temper the negative impact of the dictatorship on Italian cultural life.

Di Marzio served a brief stint as commercial attaché at Constantinople, from 1926 to 1927 was secretary-general of the Fasci all'Estero (q.v.), and was a member of the PNF directorate, the Fascist Grand Council (q.v.), and the National Council of Corporations (*see* CORPORATIVISM AND THE CORPORATIVE STATE).

In the 1930s Di Marzio played a central role in the cultural policies of the regime. He wrote widely for numerous newspapers and journals, including Giuseppe Bottai's *Critica Fascista*, was the author of several plays, and spoke frequently on the radio. But his most important role was as secretary-general of the Confederation of Professionals and Artists in 1935-36 and 1939-43. He gave his official support to many of the most promising and avant-garde writers, artists, and intellectuals of the period, frequently protecting them from the harsh censorship policies of the regime and often providing outlets for their work when the more intransigent *gerarchi* (leaders) opposed them. He worked closely with Antonio Bragaglia's (q.v.) Teatro degli Indipendenti, sponsored exhibits of modern and

Jewish artists at the Confederation's Galleria di Roma, and in the mid-1930s published an outspoken newspaper called *Il Meridiano di Roma*, which was eventually suppressed by the regime.

For further information see: *Chi è?* (1936); Philip V. Cannistraro, *La fabbrica del consenso* (Rome-Bari: Laterza, 1975).

PVC

DINALE, NEOS (b. Mirandola, Modena, December 26, 1901). A Fascist bureaucrat and prefect, Dinale took a degree in accounting and was a volunteer in World War I, serving as an officer in the Alpini. He joined the Fascist movement in 1919 and collaborated with *Il Popolo d'Italia*, of which his father, Ottavio Dinale (q.v.), was an editor. In 1922-23 he went to South America, where he organized *fasci* among Italian immigrants and in 1925 became a press censorship official in Mussolini's Press Office. In 1934-35 Dinale was made director of the Italian Press Division of the Ministry of Press and Propaganda; subsequently he entered the prefectural system, first as prefect of Macerata (1935-37), then in Savona (1937-43), and Vicenza (February-August 1943). In September 1943 Dinale was reappointed prefect in Vicenza by German military officials and kept that position under the Salò Republic (*see* ITALIAN SOCIAL REPUBLIC).

For further information see: *Chi è?* (1936); Philip V. Cannistraro, *La fabbrica del consenso* (Rome-Bari: Laterza, 1975).

PVC

DINALE, OTTAVIO (b. Marostica, Vicenza, May 20, 1871; d. Rome, March, 1958). A revolutionary syndicalist and Fascist journalist, Dinale taught literature in a local *ginnasio* (advanced secondary school) in Mirandola as a young man and quickly gravitated to the Socialist party. He wrote widely in Socialist and syndicalist newspapers, organized strikes and peasant agitation in the province of Modena, and helped establish the provincial federation of peasant leagues. His tactical and ideological intransigence brought him into conflict with the party, however, and in 1902 he was expelled. By 1905 he had become a major syndicalist figure and the founder of the newspaper *La Lotta Proletaria*. In 1909 he moved to Nice, where he edited the influential *La Demolizione*.

Dinale met Mussolini as early as 1903-1904, when both men were in Switzerland, and they joined forces during the Interventionist Crisis in 1914-15 (q.v.). Dinale was an early member of Mussolini's Fascio Rivoluzionario d'Azione Internazionalista (*see* FASCI DI AZIONE RIVOLUZIONARIA) and one of the first collaborators and editors of *Il Popolo d'Italia*. He fought in World War I as a volunteer, stood as a candidate for Parliament as a Republican in 1921, but then quickly adhered to Fascism and remained an intimate friend and confidant of Mussolini. In the 1920s he entered the prefectural system as prefect of Nuoro from December 1926 to July 1928, of Potenza from July 1928 to August 1930, and of Salerno from May to August 1930. He worked as a journalist during the 1930s.

For further information see: *Chi è?* (1936); MOI (2); O. Dinale, *Quarant' anni di colloqui con lui* (Milan: Ciarrocca, 1962); Renzo De Felice, *Mussolini il rivoluzionario* (Turin: Einaudi, 1965); Alceo Riosa, "Dinale e le lotte agrarie nel Modenese," *Nuova Rivista Storica* (1969).

PVC

DISSIDENTISM. A term used to describe the phenomenon that gave rise to the so-called "crisis of Fascism" between late 1922 and late 1923, dissidentism can be divided into two kinds: (1) a breakdown of discipline and central authority among disgruntled Fascists on the local level, and (2) ideological-tactical disagreement over the role of the PNF—Partito Nazionale Fascista (q.v.) and its relationship to the government and over the very future of Fascism itself.

Generally speaking, the first type of dissidentism assumed the form of a vast and divisive struggle for power in the provinces among the local Fascist leaders. Innumerable quarrels and conflicts broke out especially in the northern and central regions of Italy, quarrels that sometimes had a political and economic basis but more often than not represented efforts of one leader to impose his personal authority over another. The causes of these internecine struggles varied from area to area, but certainly the sudden influx of new, often opportunist adherents to the Fascist movement following the March on Rome (q.v.) increased the competition for patronage and local power and frustrated many of the older Fascists "of the first hour." Then, too, the combative spirit of rural squadrism (*see* SQUADRISTI), whose violence had been given free reign during the struggle for power, had been unexpectedly stifled when Mussolini came to office without a real revolution; in these circumstances many long-standing, pre-1922 local antagonisms easily reemerged. This personalized dissidentism was widespread and may be illustrated by the case of the old *squadrista*, Gino Calza-Bini of Lazio, who attacked the headquarters of the Rome *fascio* because it was controlled by his opponents, or by the bitter struggle in Piedmont between the forces of Cesare Forni and Raimondo Sala on the one hand and of Edoardo Torre on the other.

The second variety of dissidentism was much more complex and significant, for it represented a genuine political movement that gave rise to "dissident Fascism." Here the causes also included the fusion between the PNF and the Italian Nationalist Association (q.v.) in 1923; the dissolution of the Fascist squads and the incorporation of the Blackshirts into the new Fascist Militia (q.v.) under the control of the regular army; the openly declared opposition to Freemasonry, which caused a real split between many local interests and Fascist activists tied to those interests; and the absorption into Fascism of many minor, local, political parties (the Sardinian and Sicilian independence movements, the republicans, and others). These events combined with or created a series of ideological disputes that brought into question the very nature of Fascism. For example, Alfredo Misuri, Gaetano Lumbroso, and Ottavio Corgini represented a conservative type of dissidentism that wanted to see the restoration of authoritarian government and had opposed the original creation of the PNF; they and their followers now demanded the dissolution of the party and an end to its interference in local affairs. They were closely associated with powerful agrarian interests who opposed the Fascist unions and the corporative (*see* CORPORATIVISM AND THE CORPORATIVE STATE) policies of the regime. Opposed to this group was the radical intransigent dissidentism of local leaders like Aurelio Padovani of Naples, who attacked Mussolini's tendency to compromise with pre-Fascist elites and the parliamentary system. Padovani was especially bitter about the influx of Nationalists into the movement, whom he identified with the local, non-Fascist power elites and clientele politics, and he denounced the imposition of government authority over the party. Unlike Misuri, however, Padovani represented the rural petty bourgeoisie attitude against big business and landowners.

Dissidents of all varieties were ultimately brought under control by Mussolini in one way or another—some were expelled or suspended from membership in the PNF, others were coopted into the regime, and some became the victims of more severe measures. Ultimately, however, dissidentism was destroyed as a result of the extension of Mussolini's personal dictatorship over the party and the state and by his deliberate policy of imposing the government's authority over the PNF apparatus, a process that culminated during and immediately after the Matteotti Crisis (q.v.). By 1923-24 one form of a genuinely doctrinal dissidence had been transformed into a cultural-ideological Revisionism (q.v.) that persisted into the 1930s.

For further information see: Renzo De Felice, *Mussolini il fascista* (Turin: Einaudi, 1966); Adrian Lyttelton, *The Seizure of Power* (London: Weidenfeld & Nicolson, 1973).

PVC

DOLFIN, GIOVANNI (b. San Pietro Valdastico, Vicenza, November 26, 1902). Mussolini's private secretary in the Salò Republic (*see* ITALIAN SOCIAL REPUBLIC) Dolfin was a lawyer by profession. He held a number of local Fascist party posts in the 1920s, was federal secretary of Vicenza, and an officer in the Militia (q.v.). In 1934 he was elected to Parliament, where he remained until Guido Buffarini-Guidi (q.v.) brought him into the prefectural system. He served as prefect of Enna from 1938 to 1940, of Foggia from 1940 to 1943, and of Ferrara from February-September 1943.

When Mussolini moved his government to Salò in October 1943, Buffarini-Guidi secured Dolfin's appointment as the dictator's private secretary. His office (located in a house near the Villa Feltrinelli on Lake Garda) was a particularly difficult one because Mussolini's son, Vittorio, had established a "political secretariat" through which all appointments and callers had to pass. Hence, Dolfin's position had considerably less authority than previous secretaries. In the spring of 1944 Dolfin was transferred to the Foreign Ministry. His diaries are an important source for the history of the Salò period.

For further information see: *Chi è?* (1936); F. W. Deakin, *The Brutal Friendship* (New York: Harper and Row, 1962); G. Dolfin, *Con Mussolini nella tragedia* (Milan: Garzanti, 1950).

PVC

DONATI, GIUSEPPE (b. Faenza, 1890; d. Paris, August 16, 1931). An anti-Fascist journalist, while a student at the Istituto di Studi Sociali Cesare Alfieri in Florence, he came under the influence of the intellectuals of Giuseppe Prezzolini's (q.v.) *La Voce*. Inspired by Gaetano Salvemini (q.v.), he fought against the Giolittian (*see* GIOLITTI, GIOVANNI) system. He was also associated with Romolo Murri in the Christian Democratic movement, assisting Murri in the organization of the Lega Democratica. He succeeded Murri as the director of the League in 1911.

When the Popular party (Partito Popolare Italiano—PPI) (q.v.) was formed in 1919, he did not join it immediately because he considered its platform too moderate. He founded the Christian Democratic party (Partito Democratico Cristiano Italiano) and sought election to Parliament. The failure of his party at the polls brought him into the Popular party. Don Luigi Sturzo (q.v.), the political secretary of the Popular party, entrusted him with the editorship of what became the party organ, *Il Popolo*. As editor, he upheld the right of Italian Catholics to political autonomy and opposed any identification between Church and party. He held the Fascist regime responsible for the assassination of Don Giovanni Minzoni (q.v.) and Giacomo Matteotti (*see* MATTEOTTI CRISIS), but during the Aventine Secession (q.v.) he urged the opposition deputies to return to Parliament. In 1925, as Fascism consolidated itself, *Il Popolo* was suppressed, and Donati went into exile. He lived at various times in Paris, London, and Malta.

While in exile Donati directed two anti-Fascist publications, first the *Corriere degli Italiani* (Paris, 1926) and then *Il Pungolo* (Paris, 1928-30). Critical of the Anti-Fascist Concentration (*see* ANTI-FASCISM) formed by Italian leftists in exile, he led a rather isolated existence.

For further information see: Lorenzo Bedeschi, *Giuseppe Donati* (Rome: Cinque Lune, 1959); G. Donati, *Scritti politici*, ed. G. Rossini, 2 vols. (Rome: Cinque Lune, 1956).

ECa

DONINI, AMBROGIO (b. Lanzo, Turin, August 8, 1903). An historian, militant Communist, and anti-Fascist, Donini spent the years 1928 to 1945 in exile in France, Belgium, Spain, and the United States. In Paris he was editor of *La Voce degli Italiani* (1937-39), and in New York he directed *Unità del Popolo* (1939-44). During these years as one of the *fuorusciti* (q.v.), Donini occasionally went back to Italy clandestinely on missions for the Communist party. In 1942 Donini, together with Giuseppe Berti (q.v.), Vittorio Vidali, and Mario Montagnana, founded the Alleanza Internazionale Garibaldi (*see* GARIBALDI, ALLEANZA INTERNA-

ZIONALE) in opposition to the Mazzini Society (q.v.). He taught at a number of American colleges and in 1945 returned to Italy and became director of the Communist publishing house L'Unità. He was ambassador to Poland from 1949 to 1954, a member of the party's central committee, and president of the Istituto Gramsci and of the Editori Riuniti.

For further information see: EAR (1): MOI (2).

PVC

DOPOLAVORO. The Dopolavoro, or Fascist after-work organization, was the principal means by which Mussolini's regime regulated the leisure hours of the adult working population. Cutting across all sectors of the society, its activities comprised virtually everything that in the 1920s and 1930s was defined as "mass culture," from bocce games to movies and radio listening. Exploiting social roles and needs outside of the workplace, the Dopolavoro circles built up a huge membership by the late 1930s, appealing especially to workers, peasants, and salaried employees who, because of their previous organizational traditions and bad economic treatment under Fascism, were not easily persuaded to support the regime by an explicitly political appeal.

The idea of a special institution for managing worker spare time had technocratic origins in the philanthropic projects of Mario Giani (d. 1930), a Turinese industrial engineer and former director of Italian Westinghouse, who claimed contemporary United States social engineering projects as the inspiration behind his plans to study and resolve the problem of worker leisure. The first "circles for worker uplift" were set up by the Fascist syndicalists in 1923-24 to compete with still surviving Socialist recreational and cultural circles. On May 1, 1925, these were removed from syndicalist control and unified under the Opera Nazionale Dopolavoro (OND), a semiautonomous state agency supervised by the Ministry of the National Economy and temporarily under the presidency of the duke of Aosta (*see* SAVOIA, AMEDEO DI, DUKE OF AOSTA). From May 1927, when the PNF seized control of the OND, replacing Giani with party stalwart Enrico Beretta, the network of local groups was gradually extended nationwide. During the early depression years, under Achille Starace's (q.v.) attentive leadership, the OND's local operations were vastly expanded as a way of undercutting the Fascist unions and to reinforce the party's own influence over social groups outside of its own middle-class constituency. By 1939 the OND supervised a total of twenty-three thousand local groups, about a third of which were pre-Fascist in origin, including many former Socialist mutual aid and cooperative societies. The others consisted of Dopolavoro Aziendali or enterprise Dopolavoro managed by private employers, several hundred well-equipped centers for civil servants, and the numerous municipal and village clubhouses built directly for the OND under the auspices of the provincial PNF (Partito Nazionale Fascista) (q.v.) federations. With a May 24, 1937 law designed to tighten central control over this far-flung organization, the government incorporated the whole structure into the national state administration. Although the PNF continued to supervise operations until the fall of the regime—except for a brief period of syndicalist control in 1939-1940—the legal status of the OND as a state institution, together with its functions as a social service agency, allowed it to survive with greatly reduced powers under the postwar Italian Republic as the Ente Nazionale Assistenza Lavoratori (ENAL).

Intervention in the domain of leisure time allowed the Fascist regime to contact and, in so far as possible, to "remake" the working population on at least three levels. First, the hierarchically organized national bureaucracy took over the forms of working-class associational life so closely associated with the Socialist and democratic labor movements of the pre-Fascist era. All recreational pastimes identified as popular and potentially subversive—from choral singing to plebian bocce—were subjected to the scrutiny of "technical consultants" in the bureaus of the OND's national office in the old Chamber of Labor in Rome, their social purposes assessed in light of a new national interest, and their specific practice brought into line with an overall national directive. This appropriation of formerly class-specific activities by means of incessant publicity, promotional efforts to engage groups in Fascist events outside of the neighborhood, and the imposition of new rules and regulations on previously spontaneous activities, broke down group solidarity and opened the way for groups to be influenced by the goals of the national state. Second, by vigorously promoting new mass leisure habits—movie-going, radio-listening, mass sports, and outings, as well as small-scale installment buying—the Dopolavoro circles conveyed the impression that the wants being stimulated by an emerging consumer market were actually being satisfied by benign government intervention. In this way the regime partially compensated for its own severe compression of wages, satisfying demands for radios and other consumer durables that if left unfulfilled would have deprived it of an important vehicle of propaganda and social communication. Finally, the Dopolavoro circles were centers for the dissemination of a Fascist "low culture"—the so-called *cultura dopolavoristica*. This was a mix of petty bourgeois social images, popular and folk rituals, and populist political motifs whose content was escapist rather than overtly propagandistic.

Fostering pastimes of suprising blandness and eschewing overtly ideological appeals, the regime thus managed to bring within the ranks of its leisure organization over 3.5 million Italians by 1939: a majority of the salaried employees in the nation; nearly 40 percent of the industrial workforce; a quarter of the eligible peasants. In the late 1930s some Fascists would be increasingly critical of the unwieldiness of this capillary organization and of its depoliticizing effects, especially as it became apparent that the military preparedness of Italian citizens was not at all commensurate with the regime's imperialist ambitions. Nevertheless, the initial aims of the regime, that of eliminating the oppositional Socialist "state within a state," bringing the working population into the organizational purview of the modern state, and blunting social tensions in a period of intense economic crisis, were largely achieved by such organizational policies.

For further information see: Victoria de Grazia, *The Culture of Consent: The Mass Organization of Leisure in Fascist Italy* (New York and London: Cambridge University Press, 1981); Palmiro Togliatti, *Lectures on Fascism*, trans. D. Dichter (New York: International Publishers, 1976).

VDG

DOUHET, GIULIO (b. Caserta, May 30, 1869; d. Rome, February 15, 1930). A Fascist aviation theorist, Douhet commanded Italy's first aviation battalion from 1912 to 1915 and then served on the general staff from 1915 to 1916. Revolted by Luigi Cadorna's (q.v.) meatgrinder tactics, Douhet sent critical reports to government officials, which Carabinieri (*see* POLICE AND INTERNAL SECURITY) intercepted. Consequently imprisoned, Douhet was freed after the Battle of Caporetto (q.v.). He retired in 1919, founding the newspaper *Il Dovere* and joining the PNF (Partito Nazionale Fascista) (q.v.) In 1921 Douhet's *Il Dominio dell'Aria* appeared. Seeking alternatives to trench warfare, Douhet argued for an independent force of strategic bombers. These would win wars alone, by apocalyptically fire-bombing and gassing enemy cities. There could be no defense. Realizing his violent nature had created many enemies, Douhet refused Mussolini's offer to be aviation commissioner but his fervent Fascism and friendship with Italo Balbo (q.v.) and Giovanni Battista Caproni (q.v.) made Douhet powerfully influential over the Regia Aeronautica (*see* AIR FORCE). Douhet's ideas encouraged Balbo and Giuseppe Valle (q.v.) to reject interservice cooperation, develop gas weapons, neglect antiaircraft defenses and emphasize bombers over fighters. Italian resources, however, were inadequate to create the air force Douhet envisioned.

For further information see: Giulio Douhet, *Scritti inediti* (Florence: Scuola di Guerra Aerea, 1951); and the bibliography in Claudio G. Segrè, "Douhet in Italy: Prophet Without Honor?," *Aerospace Historian* 26 (June 1979): 69-80.

BRS

DUCE. The word *duce* (leader) is from the Latin *dux*, and was the form of address for Mussolini during the Fascist regime. It was first used by the Arditi (q.v.) and veterans who rallied to Mussolini in 1919 and was occasionally employed for that purpose even during the last years of World War I. Later, after Mussolini came to power, the word became an official title—prime minister of Italy and duce of Fascism—that signified his identification both as the head of the Fascist movement and as the leader of a reinvigorated Italian people.

The term quickly entered the Fascist political vocabulary and assumed a variety of functions, especially to advance the cult of the authoritarian leader after 1926. Mussolini's entrance into a room or his appearance on a balcony was announced with the command, "Salute the Duce!" (equivalent to the Nazi "Heil Hitler!"). Mass demonstrations that were organized in the 1930s were usually accompanied by rhythmic shouts of "Du-ce! Du-ce! Du-ce!" The word was stenciled on the walls of countless houses throughout the Italian countryside along with Mussolini's famous axioms; the press was instructed to print it in bold-face letters.

Beyond the ritualized choreography surrounding it, the word *duce* conveyed a series of carefully developed propaganda images associated with Mussolini as leader. The qualities projected were those of the omniscient, selfless, heroic Duce who was more than human in his prowess: the depersonalized Duce who was always right, the remarkable man of extraordinary talents—statesman, warrior, airplane pilot, race car driver, athlete, writer, peasant, and so on—the man who shaped Italy's destiny.

For further information see: Dino Biondi, *La fabbrica del Duce* (Florence: Vallecchi, 1967); Philip V. Cannistraro, *La fabbrica del consenso* (Rome-Bari: Laterza, 1975).

PVC

DUDAN, COUNT ALESSANDRO (b. Verlicca, Spalato, 1883; d. Rome, 1957). An irredentist journalist and Fascist bureaucrat, Dudan took a law degree and became a foreign correspondent in Vienna for the Nationalist paper *La Tribuna* (1907-15). During his years in the Austro-Hungarian capital he carried on intense propaganda against Austrian control of "unredeemed Italy," and in World War I he traveled extensively on behalf of the Italian cause. In 1918-19 he was an editor for Rome's *Il Messaggero* and joined the Fascist movement in 1919. One of the founders of the Roman *Fascio*, he served on the executive committee of the PNF (Partito Nazionale Fascista) (q.v.). He was elected in November 1921 and was an administrative secretary in 1924. Dudan also was a member of the committee that negotiated the fusion with the Italian Nationalist Association (q.v.) in 1923 and was expelled by the Masons for having participated in the Fascist Grand Council (q.v.) session that declared Fascism and Freemasonry incompatible. Dudan served in the Chamber of Deputies from 1921 to 1934 and was then made a senator.

For further information see: *Chi è?* (1936); DSPI; NO (1928; 1937).

PVC

DUMINI, AMERIGO (b. St. Louis, Missouri, 1896; d. Rome, 1968). A Fascist Blackshirt (*see* SQUADRISTI) and assassin, Dumini was active in 1921-22 in a series of bloody punitive expeditions in Arezzo and Sarzana. After Mussolini's seizure of power, he worked for the Ministry of Interior and was sent to France to uncover anti-Fascist activity among the exiles. Although Dumini held no actual position in the government, he maintained an office in Cesare Rossi's (q.v.) quarters in the Palazzo Viminale. For a time he directed *La Sassaiola Fiorentina* (Florence), in which he wrote particularly crude and violent articles. In Rome in 1923 he took part in the attacks against former prime minister Francesco S. Nitti's (q.v.) villa and against Giovanni Amendola (q.v.).

In 1924 Dumini was charged with watching Giacomo Matteotti (*see* MATTEOTTI CRISIS), and in June he participated in the kidnapping and murder of the Socialist deputy. Dumini was recognized as having been the driver of the automobile in which Matteotti was taken to his death; he was tried in March 1926 but received only a five year prison sentence, of which he served only one.

Dumini was captured by partisans in July 1945 in Piacenza. After another trial he was imprisoned in 1947 and released in 1956.

For further information see: Amerigo Dumini, *Diciassette colpi* (Milan: Longanesi, 1951).

PVC

ECONOMIC POLICY. See **AUTARCHY; DE STEFANI, ALBERTO; IN-DUSTRY; QUOTA NOVANTA; VOLPI DI MISSURATA, COUNT GIUSEPPE**.

EDUCATIONAL POLICIES. Upon taking power the Fascist movement had no fixed ideas on educational policy, yet, ironically, the first major reform of the regime, defined by Mussolini as "the most Fascist reform," dealt with the educational system. The man responsible for this curious situation was Giovanni Gentile (q.v.), who was appointed minister of public instruction in the first Fascist government. Thus, the Gentile reform of May 6, 1923 was the work of conservative elitists and philosophical idealists who had been crusading for changes in the schools long before Fascism began its march to power. Those who had gathered around Gentile in the Fascio dell'Educazione Nazionale were determined that the schools should become vehicles by which the young could approach the realm of the spirit through real communication between teacher and student in the act of learning. Obviously such an aim involved only the best students and centered on the university-oriented humanistic curriculum with philosophy as its unifying discipline. Gentile's reform disregarded nursery and elementary schooling (leaving them to the gifted Giuseppe Lombardo Radice) in order to concentrate on the middle schools, the classical *ginnasio-liceo*, whose program emphasized philosophy, Latin and history. Scientific education was entrusted to a newly created *liceo scientifico*, again with a stress on Latin and the humanities. Teacher-training institutes were established on the middle school and university level, but, here again, psychology and pedagogical method were subordinated to philosophy.

Gentile hoped that by rigidly separating technical and professional education from the classical courses which led to the university and by severely restricting those who might attempt the classical program education would be returned to its true purpose of elite formation. To achieve this latter aim Gentile established a system of extremely rigorous state examinations, conducted by boards made up of representatives of the Ministry of Public Instruction, which the student had to pass at the end of the *liceo*.

As for the teaching faculties and administrators on the various levels of the system, the reform worked in two directions. The size of the administrative staff was reduced, and many institutions were consolidated in the interest of economy and efficiency. But within the system the authority of the rector or headmaster was increased. On the whole, however, the reform left intact the autonomy of the university over its own affairs and the apolitical nature of the student-professor relationship.

Gentile's reform seriously discriminated against the empirical social sciences, the natural sciences, modern languages, and modern teaching methods. It drastically cut the number of students progressing to the universities. Finally, the reform's concern for humanistic studies had little to do with Fascism, but responded rather to a liberal conservative vision of society, which was Gentile's own.

The government was soon deluged with complaints from parents about the impediment that the state examination placed in the way of upward mobility. Although Catholics gained mandatory religious instruction on the elementary school level and official recognition for the Catholic University of Milan, the Church disliked Gentile's elimination of the Catholic content of religious instruction on the higher levels. Finally, the reform failed to purge the universities of those hostile to the regime and offered no adequate instrument for Fascism to wage the cultural battle within the intellectual elite except by the indirect method of creating chairs of corporative law and economy.

Immediately after Gentile's departure from the government in 1924 his reform was subjected to piecemeal dismantling. In 1925 Pietro Fedele (q.v.), one of Gentile's successors, eased restrictions on the state examination. Religious instruction was extended in a gesture to win Church support. In 1931 the government attempted to purge the hostile and lukewarm from the universities by imposing a loyalty oath, but only eleven professors refused to take it.

To compensate, Fascism created parallel structures of party-controlled youth groups. In 1926 the Opera Nazionale Balilla for youths from six to eighteen and in 1930 the Fascio Giovanile del Littorio for those from eighteen to twenty-one were formed. A separate organization for university students, the Gruppi Universitari Fascisti (GUF), existed in all university centers and was under the direct control of the secretary of the Fascist party, but its membership was small and unenthusiastic. Whereas coordination between the lower schools and party organizations was fairly close, it became less so on the higher levels. It was not so much that the universities were centers of resistance to Fascism but that they were still strongly conditioned by pre-Fascist liberal culture.

Problems began to accumulate rapidly, made worse by instability of leadership at the Ministry of Education (Gentile, Alessandro Casati [q.v.], Pietro Fedele, Giuseppe Belluzzo [q.v.], Balbino Giuliano [q.v.], Cesare Maria De Vecchi [q.v.], and Giuseppe Bottai [q.v.] held the office for varying periods). After bottoming out in the 1920s the number of students in the middle schools increased rapidly after 1930. Between 1931 and 1939 enrollment doubled in the *ginnasio-liceo* and tripled in the teacher-training schools. By 1933-34 university enrollment returned to 1922 levels and rose rapidly thereafter. Pressure on professional and white-collar employment under depression economic conditions was intense and involved the very constituency which Fascism had tried to please, if in no other way than by an enormous expansion of bureaucratic employment.

Giuseppe Bottai's appointment in 1936 as minister of national education was expected to mark a major change. Many of his collaborators at the ministry were influenced by American and German theories that stressed the total formation of the child over traditional categories of knowledge. These new views only partially answered Fascism's desire to make the educational system respond to its mass-based and rural orientations. It was also expected that Bottai would find a way to reduce pressure on the overcrowded classical and teacher-training programs by reviving professional and technical education below the university level.

Bottai held the post of minister from 1936 to 1943. During this time two notable changes took place. In 1938 the racial legislation was applied to the schools, depriving many Jewish students of educational opportunities. In 1939 Bottai proposed the Carta della Scuola (*see* SCHOOL CHARTER), which was intended to be the major Fascist reform of the educational system. Although there were some innovations such as the extension of common schooling to a somewhat later age, the use of manual labor projects as an educational tool on all levels, and the establishment of new technical institutes, the overall impact of the reform was minimal, due in part to the outbreak of the war and to the resistance of Italian families who refused to abandon traditional routes to upward mobility.

On the whole Fascism had greater success in reaching the masses outside of the educational system through its use of radio and film and by means of parallel organizations like the Dopolavoro (q.v.). This factor symbolized Fascism's inability to win the cultural battle against the older traditional liberal culture.

For further information see: G. Giraldi, *Giovanni Gentile: filosofo dell' educazione, pensatore politico, riformatore della scuola* (Rome: Armando, 1968); Dina Bertoni Jovine, *La scuola italiana dal 1870 ai nostri giorni* (Rome: Editori Riuniti, 1967); L. Mineo-Paluello, *Education in Fascist Italy* (London: Oxford University Press, 1946).

AJD

EINAUDI, LUIGI (b. Carru, Cuneo, March 24, 1874; d. Rome, October 30, 1961). An economist, politician, and writer, Einaudi studied law in Turin and attached himself to Socialist ideology as a young man. Between 1896 and 1900 he collaborated on *La Stampa* in Turin and in 1900 began to work with Luigi Albertini (q.v.) on *Corriere della Sera*. In these years Einaudi espoused liberal economic theories, including proposals for worker organizations and trade unions based on an English model and at the same time attacked the Italian government's protectionist policies. In 1908 he became the director of *La Riforma Sociale*, in which he expounded on his economic theories. Made a senator in 1919, during the Fascist period Einaudi taught at the University of Turin and did not openly oppose the regime. In 1935 he founded *Rivista di Storia Economica* and for the remainder of the Fascist era wrote extensively.

After Mussolini's fall in 1943, Einaudi was forced to hide from the Germans and fled to Switzerland. He returned to Italy after the war and served in the Consulta Nazionale (q.v.), as a deputy to the Constituent Assembly (*see* COSTITUENTE), as governor of the Bank of Italy, and as a minister of the budget and interim minister of finance and the treasury in the fourth Alcide De Gasperi (q.v.) cabinet. In 1948 he was elected president of the Republic, a position he held until 1955.

For further information see: EAR (2); Luigi Einaudi, *Lo scrittorio del presidente* (Turin: Piccola Antologia, 1956); *Lezioni di politica sociale* (Turin: Einaudi, 1949); *Il buongoverno* (Bari: Laterza, 1954).

MSF

ENCICLOPEDIA ITALIANA. One of the most important cultural products of the Fascist regime, the *Enciclopedia Italiana* was conceived and launched by the wealthy industrialist Giovanni Treccani in 1925. The purpose of the project was to produce a complete, scholarly, and up-to-date compendium of human knowledge and world civilization, with particular emphasis on Italy's contributions, which would rival similar foreign reference works such as the *Encyclopaedia Britannica*. Moreover, Treccani intended his project as proof that Fascism was supportive of culture. He received the patronage of King Victor Emmanuel III (q.v.) and eventually of Mussolini—the latter believing that the *Enciclopedia* would add greatly to Fascist Italy's international prestige.

The project was placed under the overall direction of Giovanni Gentile (q.v.), the most eminent Fascist intellectual, and he ultimately secured the collaboration of more than twenty-five hundred Italian and foreign experts. Gentile was determined to maintain a high level of scientific accuracy and selected contributors for their expertise rather than their political views. As a result, among the writers were to be found numerous intellectuals and scientists (such as Francesco Ruffini [q.v.], Federico Chabod [q.v.], Adolfo Omodeo, and Enrico Fermi [q.v.]) of clear anti-Fascist persuasion, including eighty-five signers of Benedetto Croce's (q.v.) "Manifesto of Anti-Fascist Intellectuals" (q.v.) and some of the university professors who refused to take the loyalty oath to Fascism. Gentile no doubt regarded himself as the patron of Italy's intellectuals and defended the project against the bitter criticisms of Fascist party officials. Mussolini, who occasionally reviewed and edited some of the more important entries himself, supported Gentile against these accusations in the interest of maintaining the cultural prestige of Fascism in world opinion.

The *Enciclopedia Italiana*, the first volume of which appeared in 1929, has subsequently undergone several revisions and is still published. But the original edition remains a useful source of information on some aspects of the Fascist period (the famous article on "Fascism" coauthored by Gentile and Mussolini appeared in it) and is a striking example of the lack of rigid cultural controls under Mussolini's regime.

For further information see: Renzo De Felice, *Mussolini il duce* (Turin: Einaudi, 1974); G. Turi, "Il progetto dell'Enciclopedia Italiana: l'organizzazione del consenso fra gli intellettuali," *Studi Storici* 13, 1 (January-March 1972); Giocchino Volpe, "Giovanni Gentile e l'Enciclopedia Italiana," in *Giovanni Gentile, La vita e il pensiero* 1 (Florence: Sansoni, 1948).

PVC

ERCOLE, FRANCESCO (b. Spezia, May 1, 1894). A former Nationalist intellectual and Fascist minister, Ercole took a degree in law and became a professor of legal history. In 1924 he transferred to the University of Palermo, where he was professor of modern history and president. Ercole had been a prominent member of the Italian Nationalist Association (q.v.) since 1913, and as a member of its central committee had opposed its fusion with the PNF (Partito Nazionale Fascista) (q.v.) in 1923. Nevertheless, once Mussolini came to power he accommodated himself easily to the Fascist regime. He became one of the directors of the Palermo *fascio* and was president of the Unione Sindacale Fascista di Palermo.

In 1925 Mussolini appointed him to the so-called Committee of Eighteen to recommend constitutional reforms (*see* PARLIAMENT), and in the late 1920s Ercole was made a director of the Istituto Nazionale Fascista di Cultura (*see* ISTITUTO NAZIONALE DI CULTURA FASCISTA). He was elected to Parliament for the first time in 1929, and in July 1932 Mussolini appointed him minister of national education, a post he held until January 1935. As a minister Ercole made no major innovations in educational policy but was instructed to administer the regime's existing programs and provide a period of normalization in which Italian youth could adapt to Fascism. He was the subject of harsh criticism from many young intellectuals and anti-Fascists, and even Benedetto Croce (q.v.) attacked him directly in an article published in the *Quaderni di Giustizia e Libertà* (*see* ANTI-FASCISM) in November 1933.

After his dismissal as minister in 1935, Ercole returned to the University of Palermo as president. After 1943, he was one of the few intellectuals who went north with Mussolini to Salò (*see* ITALIAN SOCIAL REPUBLIC) and adhered to the new regime. He held a number of minor posts there, including director of *Nuova Antologia* and administrator of Gabriele D'Annunzio's (q.v.) former residence at the Vittoriale.

For further information see: *Chi è?* (1936); NO (1928); Renzo De Felice, *Mussolini il Duce* (Turin: Einaudi, 1974); F. Ercole, *Dal Nazionalismo al fascismo* (Rome: De Alberti, 1928); F. Ercole, *Genesi e carattere constituzionale dello stato fascista corporativo* (Rome: GUF, 1930).

                                                                                                    PVC

ETHIOPIAN WAR. Italian troops invaded Ethiopia on October 3, 1935, moving southward from the colony of Eritrea and northward from Italian Somaliland. It was to be a colonial conquest—there was no declaration of war. The war was over in seven months; the poorly equipped Ethiopian troops were defeated by the utterly superior Italian firepower and military organization. On May 5, 1936, after Emperor Haile Selassie (q.v.) had fled, and before mud from the seasonal rains in the highlands or the economic sanctions imposed in Europe by the League of Nations could stop the advance, Italian forces entered the capital city of Addis

Ababa. On May 9, 1936, Mussolini proclaimed an empire in East Africa. "Italy has its empire at last," he said, "a Fascist empire."

It was Mussolini's war. As first conceived in 1932 in the Ministry of Colonies under Emilio De Bono (q.v.), the plan was for a gradual penetration in which Italian colonial forces would move slowly southward from Eritrea, establishing bases of military strength against which the Ethiopians would throw themselves in vain. This continued pressure, it was thought, would result in progressive political disintegration in the decentralized empire, with the Italians taking over administrative control from local authorities. The prospect of military action brought the Army staff into the planning, and they envisioned a different sort of war. Instead of a localized, almost static process of penetration, the Army Chiefs in 1934 planned in terms of a major offensive war on a European scale. Artillery and air power would be used in a constant, crushing advance towards a decisive military victory. At the end of 1934 Mussolini rejected the colonialists' idea of an Ethiopian campaign in favor of the military's idea of a full-scale war and turned the whole campaign to his political purposes. His government would do what liberal governments had not: avenge Adowa, found an empire (purportedly for immigration and development), make Italy an African and Mediterranean power of consequence, and, at the same time, renew the stalled Fascistization of the Italian people.

The major problem was how to minimize European interference. Mussolini knew neither Britain nor France had a vital interest in maintaining Ethiopia's independence. But neither could turn a blind eye to the invasion or disassociate it from European concerns, as Ethiopia was a member of the League of Nations, founded precisely to prevent aggression against its members. Furthermore, this invasion was not a limited colonial action of the old style but rather a war of modern means and European magnitude against an apparently innocent and backward people. It was soon realized that even in the anxious and depression-ridden years of the mid-1930s the English still maintained a substantial popular sympathy for the Ethiopians.

Yet Mussolini judged correctly that neither Britain nor France wanted to go to war (or to blockade, or to close the Suez Canal) to stop an Italian conquest, even though for many in Geneva this was a test case of the League's capacity to enforce its system of collective security. Cautiously, the League imposed limited economic and financial sanctions (loans and imports were prohibited, arms and certain war-related materials embargoed). These sanctions were meant to work over time, progressively to wear down Italy's fighting capacity over the two years it was estimated the war would run.

But sanctions were limited, slow to work, and only partially supported. The United States never joined the boycott. In the short run, stockpiling and strict regulation of the economy allowed Italy to absorb these irritations without damage to the African campaign. Mussolini played on British and French fears in his threat of a European war should sanctions be extended to oil. He also won time by encouraging reconciliationist hopes that some sort of negotiated settlement was possible. War and diplomacy were thus closely related. Success on the battlefield would end the threat of prolonged or possibly intensified opposition; if any settlement short of total conquest were necessary, the more Italy held the more Italy could claim.

Hence the criticism of Emilio De Bono's (q.v.) conduct of the first stage of the northern campaign, his war of slow advance, of position, of subversion. De Bono's archrival in the Ministry of Colonies, Alessandro Lessona (q.v.), told him in October: "Either Italy wins the war in a few months or it is lost." Lessona's ally against De Bono was Pietro Badoglio (q.v.). To him De Bono was a Fascist functionary, not a knowledgeable military leader, and surrounded in the field by irresolute colonial officers. In October, after the first unopposed advance, De Bono estimated no forward movement was possible for another two months. For Badoglio this was defeatism—the objective of the northern armies should be a rapid strategic offensive to force the battles that would destroy the empire.

On November 12, increasingly anxious that his war not bog down, Mussolini gave Badoglio the northern command. If Badoglio succeeded, the burden of sanctions and international opposition would lift; if he failed, it would not be a failure of Mussolini's man but of the army, and of his main rival.

It was not much easier for Badoglio than it had been for De Bono to put the northern army in motion. Roads had to be built, supply routes established—and thousands of workers were sent from Italy. Then, in mid-December, Ethiopian forces under Rases Kassa, Seyum, and Mulugeta opened a strong counteroffensive against the Italian line. These were anxious and uncertain days in Rome, as pressure for settlement and talk of an oil embargo was increasing also at this time. By the end of the month the sense of siege lifted dramatically. Britain and France, pursuing a negotiated settlement outside the League, contrived a plan to carve up the empire, two parts to be annexed directly to the Italian colonies, another to be the exclusive sphere of Italian economic penetration, and the remainder to be supervised by the League, in which, however, it was assumed Italian influence would prevail. The revelation of these secret proposals, seemingly at cross-purposes to sanctions, stunned the League. Italy, it seemed, was being rewarded for its aggression. The two leaders of the League were going behind the organization. Disavowal of the Hoare-Laval proposals by the British government in the face of a storm of popular criticism did nothing to repair devastated morale in Geneva. Thereafter cooperation between British and French became increasingly problematic, both with regard to sanctions and Italy and with regard to any common strategy dealing with European security. The disarray of the collectivist front dissolved most of the international threat to Italy. Leaderless and disheartened, the League postponed further action. Oil was never embargoed. And at this time, in the beginning of January 1936, it was clear that while the Italian forces were not ready to renew the offensive, the Ethiopians could not break their line. The counteroffensive was turned back decisively—air power and poison gas were used to throw the Ethiopian troops into confusion and retreat. Badoglio was emboldened, learning that in the face of such opposition the Ethiopians could not carry through on the initial advantages of attack.

Meantime Mussolini intensified his domestic mobilization. In his contempt of the liberal preachings of the League and his awareness of the feebleness of purpose of the Western democracies, his government engineered a vast propaganda campaign, fueling resentment toward the dog in the manger attitude of satiated colonial powers against Italy's expansionary needs. This gave rise to xenophobia and reenforced the government's calls for autarchy and antisanctionist controls. December 18, 1935 was the "day of faith," the "wedding-ring day," of emotion-ladened donation ceremonies; the royal family associated itself with the national sacrifice; members of the clergy called for national unity. But it was the generals who won the empire, and beginning at the end of January they won it fast and won it sure. Some four hundred thousand men were sent to East Africa with modern equipment such as the Ethiopians did not possess: 254 airplanes, 30,000 trucks and tractors, thousands of rifles, machine guns, and field pieces together with 4.2 million artillery rounds and 845 million cartridges. A well-developed field command was tied together by two hundred radios and thirty thousand field telephones, which intercepted every Ethiopian message. By themselves the Ethiopians stood no chance.

The main offensive came on the northern front. In the south, in Somalia, Rodolfo Graziani (q.v.), intensely bitter at his secondary position, was kept on short rations. At first ordered by Badoglio to stand on the defensive, the record of Graziani's repeated appeals direct to Mussolini for supplies and permission to move forward show the personalized, manipulative nature of Mussolini's authority. Graziani got away with ignoring chains of ministerial command because Mussolini, to keep control, encouraged rivalry and discord among his commanders. He gave Graziani permission to advance, and on January 20, 1936 Graziani advanced to Negelli, destroying the southern army of Ras Desta, but bad weather and lack of supplies held him up thereafter. It was not until May 8 that his troops arrived at his main objective, Harar—by then Badoglio was in Addis Ababa.

In February Badoglio began the long-awaited "battles of annihilation." Comparing himself to Napoleon, commanding the strongest armed force ever mounted in a colonial campaign, and using artillery and air power and gas to disperse the poorly trained Ethiopian troops, Badoglio's northern command defeated Ras Mulugeta's dug-in troops at Amba Aradam, destroyed the men of Rases Kassa and Seyum in the second battle of Tembien, and then, firing fifty thousand artillery shells and 10 million cartridges, routed Ras Imru's twenty-five thousand Ethiopians in the second battle of the Shire. By the first of March the Ethiopian northern front was broken. There remained only the army of the emperor himself, waiting fatalistically for a final stand at Mai Chew. On March 31 that battle was joined; the next day it was over, the emperor's forces in retreat, the survivors drenched with bombs and gas as they fled to the shore of Lake Ashangi.

The crushing victory at Mai Chio proved wrong all European assumptions of a long war. No organized force stood between Badoglio and Addis Ababa. There was celebration in Italy. The drama of the victories, the heavy doses of patriotic propaganda, the small cost in Italian life (fewer than three thousand Italians died in the war), the apparent overcoming of international opposition, the sense of successfully standing "against the world," brought forth as close a popular consensus, couched in nationalist terms, as Mussolini's regime would ever realize.

Haile Selassie knew all was lost. The empire was disintegrating. He had the choice of withdrawal to the west to mount guerilla resistance or flight abroad. On the advice of his advisers he boarded a British ship for exile, knowing, as he had known throughout the conflict, that Ethiopia's cause would be won or lost by the extent of support it had in Europe. The emperor's departure solved the great problem of how to deal with his authority. It was what permitted Mussolini to announce on May 9, 1936 that "Ethiopia is Italian" and what made continued international measures against Italy futile. Taking advantage of Western irresolution and division, on March 6 Hitler had remilitarized the Rhineland. Eyes turned now to Germany. No one wanted to worry further about Ethiopia. Sanctions were raised on July 4, 1936. To base a state's security on the League made no sense. There was a general retreat from collective security, moves into neutrality, isolation, regional groupings, or appeasement.

There remained for Mussolini the two problems of what to do with his new empire and how to deal with the isolation of Italy in foreign affairs. He had no creative solution for the first problem because he cared little. There was no serious attempt to settle or develop the land. The colonial history of Ethiopia is marked primarily by brutal repression of guerilla opposition. For the second problem the old strategy of playing a "pendulum" between Germany and Britain no longer worked. The Spanish Civil War (q.v.) revealed and the Axis (*see* AXIS, ROME-BERLIN) confirmed that Italy's capacity to go it alone was increasingly limited. In allying with Hitler, Mussolini lost his initiative, and Italy became an appendage of the superior power and purpose of Nazi Germany.

For further information see: G. W. Baer, *Test Case: Italy, Ethiopia, and the League of Nations* (Stanford: Hoover Institution, 1976); R. De Felice, *Mussolini il Duce* (Turin: Einaudi, 1974); A. Del Boca, *La guerra d'Abissinia, 1935-1941* (Milan: Feltrinelli, 1965); G. Rochat, *Militari e politici nella preparazione della campagna d'Etiopia: Studio e documenti 1932-1936* (Milan: Angeli, 1971).

GWB

EVOLA, GIULIO (b. Rome, May 19, 1898; d. 1974). A writer, painter, and philosopher, Evola played a relatively unimportant role in the official life of the Fascist regime, but his ideas were often influential. He came from an old, well-connected Roman family and dabbled in various philosophical movements, including the occult, phenomenology, mysticism, and psychology. He wrote poetry, tried his hand at painting, directed the journals *La Torre* and *UR*, and was influential in the introduction of the Dada art movement into Italy. He never held a government or PNF (Partito Nazionale Fascista) (q.v.) post.

Evola was particularly active in propagating racial theories and in the early 1930s was in contact with a number of Nazi officials, including Alfred Rosenberg. He was denounced by Fascist ideologues, who disapproved of his racial ideas and his connections with the Germans, but by the time Mussolini had decided to launch his own racial program (*see* ANTI-SEMITISM), Evola had begun to separate his racial philosophy from that of the Nazis. Evola described his racism as "spiritual" in nature, as opposed to the "materialistic" or biological racism of Hitler's regime, and Mussolini, who read Evola's books on the subject, was clearly influenced by this concept.

After the July 1943 coup against Mussolini, Evola adhered to the Salò Republic (*see* ITALIAN SOCIAL REPUBLIC) (he had been in Germany at the time of the coup) but was frequently critical of its policies. After World War II Evola continued to write and was active in the postwar neo-Fascist movements, particularly in the effort to create an international fascism based on racial theories.

For further information see: *Chi è?* (1936); *Chi è?* (1948); Renzo De Felice, *Storia degli ebrei italiani sotto il fascismo* (Turin: Einaudi, 1961); Renzo De Felice, *Fascism: An Informal Introduction To Its Theory and Practice* (New Brunswick, N.J.: Transaction Books, 1976); Angelo Del Boca and Mario Giovana, *Fascism Today* (New York: Pantheon, 1969); G. Evola, *L'Uomo come potenza* (Rome: Atanor, 1926); G. Evola, *Imperialismo pagano* (Rome: Atanor, 1928); G. Evola, *Rivolta contro il mondo moderno* (Milan: Hoepli, 1935); G. Evola, *Il mito del sangue* (Milan: Hoepli, 1937); G. Evola, *Sintesi della dottrina della razza* (Milan: Hoepli, 1941).

PVC

"EXCEPTIONAL DECREES." The term "Exceptional Decrees" refers to the group of laws, decrees, and police measures issued in November 1926 in order to enact what Mussolini termed his "Napoleonic Year"—the creation of the Fascist dictatorship. The measures, which followed an assassination attempt on Mussolini by Tito Zaniboni (q.v.), were intended to eliminate the last traces of the legal anti-Fascist opposition in Italy. On November 5, the Council of Ministers announced or recommended a series of acts that dissolved all political parties (other than the PNF [Partito Nazionale Fascista] [q.v.]) and anti-Fascist organizations, suppressed anti-Fascist newspapers, cancelled all passports, adopted *confino* (domestic exile) for political criminals, and created a political police force (*see* POLICE AND INTERNAL SECURITY). The next day these measures were inserted into a new "Single Text of Laws on Public Security" (Royal Decree n. 1848; a new text was issued by Royal Decree n. 773 on June 18, 1931).

On November 9 the Fascist majority in the Chamber of Deputies declared the seats of the 120 anti-Fascist deputies who had participated in the Aventine

Secession (q.v.) annulled. The same day Mussolini presented to the Chamber a bill creating the Special Tribunal for the Defense of the State (q.v.).

For further information see: EAR (3); Paola Carucci, "L'organizzazione dei servizi di polizia," *Rassegna degli archivi di stato* (January-April 1976); Renzo De Felice, *Mussolini il fascista* (Turin: Einaudi, 1967); Charles F. Delzell, *Mussolini's Enemies* (Princeton: Princeton University Press, 1961).

RAM

EXPURGATION OF FASCISM, HIGH COMMISSION FOR. The elimination of Fascism from the political and economic life of Italy was one of the stated objectives of both Italian anti-Fascist groups and Allied leaders throughout World War II. However, neither the Allies nor successive wartime Italian governments achieved great success in their efforts to purge Fascism. First, no one could agree on a definition of what Fascism was or who was a Fascist. In addition, the protection of certain individuals and interests with Fascist connections by conservatives frustrated all efforts to "purify" Italy.

Prior to the invasion of Italy, both the United States and Great Britain committed themselves to a thorough purge of Fascists and of Fascist institutions. However, Allied leaders had only vague notions of what constituted Fascism. Mussolini, his closest associates, and such institutions as the Militia (q.v.) were clearly Fascist and marked for elimination. Instructions provided to AMG (*see* ALLIED MILITARY GOVERNMENT) officers at the time of the invasion specified certain political organizations and individuals as subject to immediate removal, and AMG carried out its responsibilities quickly and efficiently. However, final action on all purge-related matters was left to the Italian government. Prior to June 10, 1944, that government was led by King Victor Emmanuel III (q.v.) and Marshal Pietro Badoglio (q.v.), two of Mussolini's closest collaborators. As a result, little was done during the first nine months of the liberation. It was only under the combined pressure of Allied officials and anti-Fascists within his second government that Badoglio took a modicum of action. In May 1944 the prime minister established a committee to draft a decree law to deal with Fascism.

When the conservative Ivanoe Bonomi (q.v.) replaced Badoglio, the purge finally received some impetus. Decree law 159 (July 27, 1944) set up four commissions to deal with the cancellation of sentences of political prisoners, the punishment of Fascist crimes, the defascistization of the state administration, and the confiscation of wealth acquired through Fascist connections. Each of these commissions operated under its own commissioner. Special committees were also formed within each government department to clean house.

Count Carlo Sforza (q.v.) was appointed the first high commissioner for the purge of Fascism. Under Sforza's leadership the purge showed considerable vigor in dealing with lesser figures of the Mussolini regime, collaborationists, and defeatist generals. Nevertheless, leftist critics were impatient with the slowness with which the judicial process worked. In addition, opponents of Sforza charged that the high commissioner was settling past political scores. In November 1944

Sforza resigned. Bonomi placed the purge machinery in the prime minister's office. Thereafter the purge moved more slowly.

After the liberation, demands for a reckoning with powerful economic interests who had collaborated with Mussolini mounted and under the Ferruccio Parri (q.v.) government, the purge process showed renewed vigor. Socialist Pietro Nenni (q.v.) was appointed high commissioner. Conservative interests, however, were able to protect endangered industrialists and in November 1945 the Liberal party forced Parri out of power. Alcide De Gasperi (q.v.), the Christian Democrat who replaced Parri as prime minister, showed little interest in the vigorous prosecution of Fascists.

One of his first acts was to announce the termination of the purge. Six months later a broad amnesty, marking the establishment of the Italian Republic, was approved by the government. This amnesty, proposed by Communist party chief Palmiro Togliatti (q.v.), resulted in the release of thousands of convicted Fascists and signaled the end of the "purge."

For further information see: EAR (2).

JEM

F

FACCHINETTI, CIPRIANO (b. Campobasso, January 13, 1889; d. Rome, February 17, 1952). A writer, politician, and anti-Fascist, Facchinetti joined the Republican party (*see* PARTITO REPUBBLICANO ITALIANO) and as a young man edited *Il Secolo* in Milan. He fought in World War I and after the conflict helped found Lega Italiana per la Società delle Nazioni and directed the paper *Italia del Popolo* in Milan. He was elected a deputy in 1924 and later participated in the Aventine Secession (q.v.). Deprived of his parliamentary rights in 1926, Facchinetti fled to France where he became secretary of the Partito Repubblicano all'Estero. Arrested by the Germans, he was sent to prison and was not released until Mussolini's fall. In November 1944 he returned to Rome and later became a member of the Party of Action (*see* PARTITO D'AZIONE). After the war he served in the Consulta Nazionale (q.v.), as a deputy in the Constituent Assembly (*see* COSTITUENTE), and as a senator. He was also minister of defense in the second and fourth Alcide De Gasperi (q.v.) governments and later rejoined the Republican party.

For further information see: EAR (2); Elena Aga-Rossi, *Il movimento repubblicano, Giustizia e Libertà, e il partito d'azione* (Bologna: Cappelli, 1969); Charles Delzell, *Mussolini's Enemies* (Princeton: Princeton University Press, 1961).

MSF

FACTA, LUIGI (b. Pinerolo, Turin, November 16, 1861; d. Pinerolo, November 5, 1930). Prime minister from February to October 1922, because of weakness and perhaps personal ambition, Facta played an important role in failing to prevent Mussolini's accession to power.

Facta was a member of the Chamber of Deputies from 1892 to 1924. Always in the shadow of Giovanni Giolitti (q.v.), he served in the latter's governments of 1903-05, 1906-09, 1911-14, and 1920-21. He served also under A. Fortis (1905-06), L. Luzzatti (1910-11), and V. E. Orlando (q.v.) (1919) as a perennial lieutenant of Giolitti, whom he followed into political abstention during Italy's participation in World War I, which Giolitti opposed strenuously. When Giolitti's return to office in February 1922 was blocked by the opposition of the Popular Party (*see* PARTITO POPOLARE ITALIANO), Facta assumed the premiership in what was interpreted as an expedience intended to prepare the way for his mentor. During the following eight months, Facta's government proved unable to contain the ever-increasing violence of Fascist squads, thereby losing the confidence of the king and all political parties. The crisis spawned in early October by an imminent Fascist "March on Rome" (q.v.) occasioned various solutions, all predicated on the inclusion of Mussolini in a government led by Giolitti, Antonio Salandra (q.v.), or Facta himself. On October 28, with the Fascist march in motion, Facta was pressed by several members of his government to ask the king to sign a decree proclaiming a state of siege. Perhaps because Facta was not emphatic enough, more probably because Victor Emmanuel III (q.v.) feared a civil war, the request was rejected. Upon Facta's resignation the same day, Salandra was given the mandate to form a new government. But Mussolini, encouraged by the failure to declare a state of siege, refused to serve under Salandra, whereupon, on October 29 the king offered the mandate to Mussolini rather than Giolitti who, according to some writers, had been misled by Facta as to the realities of the situation in Rome.

After the advent of Fascism, Facta lapsed into political obscurity. In September 1924 he accepted an appointment to the senate from Mussolini.

For further information see: Antonio Repaci, *La marcia su Roma: Mito e realtà,* 2 vols. (Rome: Canesi, 1963); Carlo Sforza, *Contemporary Italy* (New York: E. P. Dutton, 1944); Marcello Soleri, *Memorie* (Turin: Einaudi, 1949).

SS

FALDELLA, EMILIO (b. Maggiora, Novara, March 5, 1897; d. September 9, 1975). An intelligence officer and Army general, Faldella was an Alpini officer from 1915 (including battalion commander at age twenty) before joining SIM (*see* SERVIZIO INFORMAZIONI MILITARI) in 1929. He directed SIM's Ethiopian Section, from 1935 to 1936, supervising negotiations with Haile Selassie (q.v.), and then organized plots to kidnap or murder him. Faldella next headed SIM's Second Section (foreign armies evaluation) until a brief appointment as Italian commander in Spain, from September to December 1936. Made Mario Roatta's (q.v.) Chief of Staff, Faldella planned the Malaga and Guadalajara (*see* GUADALAJARA, BATTLE OF) operations in the Spanish Civil War (q.v.), directing C.T.V. (Corpo di Truppe Volontarie, or Voluntary Troops Corps) headquarters during the March 18-19, 1937 debacle. After expiation as C.T.V. Fifth Regiment commander, from April 1937 to October 1938, Faldella entered the War Ministry. Angering Ubaldo Soddu (q.v.) by questioning Army preparedness, Faldella was transferred to the Third Alpini, commanding it in the French campaign in June 1940. Following Soddu's downfall, Roatta placed Faldella on the Army General Staff. Promoted to brigadier, Faldella was Alfredo Guzzoni's (q.v.) Chief of Staff in Sicily in May-August 1943. Under Raffaele Cadorna (q.v.), Faldella tried to capture Mussolini for trial in April 1945. Faldella wrote several military histories obscuring ties between the Army and Fascism.

For further information see: Franco Bandini, *Gli italiani in Africa* (Milan: Longanesi, 1971); John Coverdale, *Italian Intervention in the Spanish Civil War* (Princeton University Press, 1975); Emilio Faldella *Lo sbarco e la difesa della Sicilia* (Rome: L'Aniene, 1956).

BRS

FARA, GUSTAVO (b. Ort, Novarese, September 18, 1859; d. Nervi, February 24, 1936). A Fascist general, after his retirement from the army Fara organized

Fascist squads in Genoa. Fearing royal opposition, he urged delay of the March on Rome (q.v.) but commanded the central column. Appointed Militia (q.v.) commander in Liguria, then MVSN (Milizia Volontaria per la Sicurezza Nazionale) (*see* MILITIA) inspector general, Fara became a senator in 1938.

                                                                                                                        BRS

FARINACCI, ROBERTO (b. Isernia, Molise, October 16, 1892; d. Vimercate, April 28, 1945). An intransigent Blackshirt (*see* SQUADRISTI) leader and Fascist hierarch, Farinacci moved with his family to Tortona in 1900 and in 1908 to the city that would eventually become his permanent stronghold, Cremona.

Dropping out of school in the fall of 1909, he obtained a job as telegraph operator with the Italian State Railways and also began to take an active part in politics under the wing of Cremona's deputy and leader of the Socialist party's "reformist" faction, Leonida Bissolati (q.v.).

When World War I broke out Farinacci quickly became the leader of the interventionist agitation in the city and the province of Cremona, and in December 1915 he joined the Army and served in the front lines for almost a year, until early in 1917 when he was sent on indefinite leave. By the time the war ended Farinacci was undeniably a major power on the Cremona political scene and looking for ways of expanding his grip on the city and its surroundings.

In mid-January 1919 he decided to abandon his mentor, Bissolati, and join Mussolini. Two months later he was among the seventy men who with Mussolini founded the Fasci di Combattimento (q.v.) at Piazza San Sepolcro (*see* SANSEPOLCRISTI), and shortly afterwards the Fascio di Combattimento of Cremona was officially organized with Farinacci as its political secretary.

The next three years, which were the formative ones for the Fascist leadership, saw the emergence of Farinacci as a vocal and visible apostle of Fascist verbal and physical violence. Whether championing the Nationalist agitation over Dalmatia, or defending the rights and property of landowners against tenants and sharecroppers, Farinacci time and again led his Fascist squads in "punitive expeditions" against "Bolsheviks."

Farinacci also redoubled his efforts toward greater notoriety through the printed media, replacing the prewar *La Squilla* with *La Voce del Popolo Sovrano,* and then changing once more the title of his newspaper to *La Voce del Fascismo Cremonese.*

With the beginning of 1921 Farinacci resigned his railroad job, and in May he was elected with Mussolini and thirty-three other Fascist candidates to the Chamber of Deputies.

Concentrating on further expanding his power in his own domain, Farinacci started a new daily, *Cremona Nuova,* and using it as a platform of propaganda and intimidation, while also intensifying the activities of his *squadristi,* he launched a full-scale campaign that soon gave him control of the political and economic organizations in the province of Cremona.

In the summer of 1922 Farinacci was made a consul general of the newly organized Fascist Militia (q.v.), and on October 27, while the Fascist columns were converging on Rome, Farinacci, with his *squadristi*, obtained the surrender of the Cremona army garrison and gained complete control of the city.

The prompt legalization of the Fascist insurrection did not alter Farinacci's position as the de facto ruler of Cremona, nor did his behavior as the self-appointed censor of Fascist political purity.

Farinacci's conception of the PNF (Partito Nazionale Fascista) (q.v.) was a truly revolutionary one, envisaging for the party a dominant role in forcibly shaping the nation into a monolithic Fascist state governed by an intransigent elite for the alleged benefit of the laboring masses.

In expounding this view, the *ras* (q.v.) of Cremona was not only irrepressible, but he had a considerable following among the more intransigent Fascist activists, of whom he in fact was the unofficial leader. Farinacci was undoubtedly effective in supporting Mussolini during the crisis created in 1924 by the Matteotti (*see* MATTEOTTI CRISIS) affair and in pushing him to take the repressive actions foretold by the speech of January 3, 1925. One of these actions was the appointment of Farinacci as secretary-general of the PNF.

On his arrival in Rome on February 23, 1925 to take up his new duties, the *ras* of Cremona issued a proclamation spelling out the various problems to which he wanted prompt solutions: muzzling of the press, control of banks, "Fascistization" of the bureaucracy, establishment of Fascist syndicalism, and abolition of secret societies, meaning Freemasonry. These aims, of course, were in addition to others that Farinacci had already advocated, such as the elimination of the parliamentary opposition, the subjugation of the veterans' associations, and the "purification" of party membership rolls. There is no doubt that during this crucial period Farinacci was indeed instrumental, directly or indirectly, in steering the course of the government as well as of the party, so that when he left office the Fascist dictatorship was well established.

Mussolini, however, soon realized that he had to eliminate or somehow neutralize Farinacci and his more unruly followers who, by their revolutionary activism and terroristic tactics, stood in the way of the "normalization" at which Mussolini aimed in order to justify and strengthen his personal dictatorship.

It was probably Farinacci's arrogance and his demagoguery and histrionics during the trial of Matteotti's killers held at Chieti in March 1926, where Farinacci acted as defense attorney for the main defendant, which decided Mussolini to tolerate no longer his defiance and insubordination; accordingly, on March 30, 1926, the Fascist Grand Council (q.v.) named a new secretary-general of the party to replace Farinacci.

The next few months saw Farinacci trying to maintain himself in the spotlight on the national political scene, but he soon had to realize that Mussolini's position by now was too strong and that the scattered extremist pockets could never hope to succeed against the organized forces of the state.

Thus, from the summer of 1926 to the fall of 1933, Farinacci's activism in defense of Fascist orthodoxy was perforce limited to editorializing in *Il Regime*

Fascista, the daily which had replaced *Cremona Nuova.*

Despite his virtual banishment from public life, however, Farinacci's life was far from unpleasant. In December 1923, he had managed through fraudulent means to obtain a law degree and was therefore soon able to embark on a legal career, which his political connections and influence peddling eventually made extremely lucrative.

Determined as ever to fight against the transformation of revolutionary Fascism into a bourgeois establishment, Farinacci continued throughout this period to write and speak without restraint and to complain periodically but vainly to Mussolini for various imagined or real grievances against the party leadership and of government policies that he considered harmful to the true spirit of Fascism.

In November 1933 a meeting between Mussolini and Farinacci finally took place in Rome, and on January 15, 1934, Mussolini made Farinacci again a member of the Fascist Grand Council and also a state minister.

Four months after the attack on Ethiopia (*see* ETHIOPIAN WAR), Farinacci joined the bomber squadron commanded by Galeazzo Ciano (q.v.). He was only on active duty for four weeks, however, because early in April 1936, while fishing with grenades in a lake near Dessie, he lost his right hand in an explosion.

During the next two years Farinacci again and again took it upon himself to spotlight, both in articles in *Regime Fascista* and in lengthy letters to Mussolini, many of the problems facing Italy and Fascism, from the lack of preparedness of the Italian Army and Navy to the profiteering and disorganization besetting Italy's newborn empire in East Africa.

Early in 1939 Farinacci was appointed president of the Legislative Committee on the Judiciary in the Chamber of Fasci and Corporations (*see* PARLIAMENT) which replaced the elective Chamber of Deputies. A few months later he was made a lieutenant general in the Fascist Militia, and in the same year he was also allowed to publish a three-volume *History of the Fascist Revolution.*

It became obvious at this time that Farinacci was fascinated by the Nazi regime, because he felt that Hitler and his followers had succeeded in pursuing and establishing in Germany the kind of revolution that Farinacci had always envisaged as the true goal of Fascism, and which in Italy, to his great chagrin, Mussolini and his closer collaborators had allowed to degenerate into a bourgeois dictatorship.

Once the racial laws (*see* ANTI-SEMITISM) were proclaimed in Italy in the fall of 1938, Farinacci soon became the acknowledged leader of the anti-Semitic crusade Mussolini had seen fit to unleash to propitiate Hitler. At the Fascist Grand Council meeting of December 7, 1939, Farinacci was the only member who insistently, though vainly, proposed that Italy enter the war on the side of Germany.

Early in 1941 Farinacci asked to be recalled to active duty despite his mutilation, and the Duce appointed him inspector general of the Militia contingents in Albania.

At the Grand Council meeting on July 24, 1943, Farinacci submitted his own resolution, which urged the continuation of the war on the side of Germany and hinted at the need to dismiss or arrest the dissident hierarchs and form an intransigently pro-German government.

On July 25 Farinacci took refuge in the German embassy, and from there he was spirited to the headquarters of Field Marshal Albert Kesselring (q.v.) at Frascati and flown to Munich. There the Nazi leaders allowed him to broadcast from Radio Munich a series of messages to the Italian people extolling German armed might and urging resistance against the Allied "invaders."

After Mussolini's liberation and the formation of his puppet government at Salò (see ITALIAN SOCIAL REPUBLIC), Farinacci resumed the role of a strictly local chieftain, actually ruling the city and province of Cremona on behalf of the Germans.

By the end of April 1945, as German resistance in the Po Valley was collapsing, Farinacci attempted to escape to Switzerland but was captured by partisans and after a summary trial was executed by a firing squad.

For further information see: Harry Fornari, *Mussolini's Gadfly* (Nashville: Vanderbilt University Press, 1971); Guido Nozzoli, *I ras del regime* (Milan: Bompiani Editore, 1972).

HDF

FASCI ALL'ESTERO. Early in Mussolini's regime the Fascists attempted to organize Italians living in other countries into politically oriented Fascist organizations known as the Fasci all'Estero (Fasci Abroad). Although the first groups were created independently of the PNF (Partito Nazionale Fascista) (q.v.) as early as 1920-21 in the United States and Latin America, a central bureaucracy under official party control was established in Rome late in 1922—known as the Segreteria Generale dei Fasci all'Estero. Its first secretary was the Blackshirt (see SQUADRISTI) leader Giuseppe Bastianini (q.v.), who directed it with ideological fervor until he was replaced first by Cornelio Di Marzio (q.v.) in 1926 and then by Piero Parini (q.v.) in 1928.

Party leaders like Bastianini wanted the Fasci all'Estero to serve as the instrument for the spread of Fascism, but career diplomats in the Foreign Ministry opposed the introduction of ideological interference into the conduct of Italy's foreign policy. Mussolini, cautioned by the diplomats, took a middle position and publicly proclaimed that Fascism "was not for export." When Dino Grandi (q.v.) became minister of foreign affairs in 1925, he sided with the diplomats and insisted that the *fasci* assume a secondary place to more traditional diplomatic methods, but he also began to shift the emphasis from a policy focused on militant Fascists living abroad to one centered on the mass of Italian immigrants. At the first congress of the Fasci all'Estero (Rome, 1925) Mussolini emphasized the absolute subservience to the diplomatic corps and defined their function as the maintenance of Italianità among immigrants. After the dismissal of Bastianini, the *fasci* became increasingly under the control of the Foreign Ministry. A new statute in January 1928 obliged the *fasci* to respect the laws of their host countries and to refrain from all political activity; it also centralized the chain of command from Rome and stipulated that each local *fascio* was dependent on the direct authority of the Italian diplomatic representative (generally a consul) in each foreign city. Later that year the headquarters of the *fasci* in Rome actually came under the control of the Foreign Ministry and was thenceforth called the Direzione Generale degli Italiani all'Estero. Its major activity was thereafter the dissemination of cultural propaganda abroad. While the numerical strength of the *fasci* had expanded quickly in the years up to the Ethiopian War (q.v.), they registered a decline in the late 1930s: 150 in January 1923, 580 in 1929, 775 in 1935, and 487 in 1939.

For further information see: Giuseppe Bastianini, *Gli italiani all' estero* (Milan: Mondadori, 1939); Alan Cassels, *Mussolini's Early Diplomacy* (Princeton: Princeton University Press, 1970); Piero Parini, "I fasci all'estero," in *Il Decennale* (Florence: 1929); Enzo Santarelli, "I fasci italiani all'estero," in *Ricerche sul fascismo* (Urbino: Argalia, 1971).

PVC

FASCI DI AZIONE RIVOLUZIONARIA. The major organizational network of the extreme interventionist left in 1914-15, the *Fasci*, developed out of the Fascio Rivoluzionario d'Azione Internazionalista, which was formed in October 1914 to promote Italian intervention in World War I. The organization was spearheaded by revolutionary syndicalists, who, given the frustration they had experienced in the Italian labor movement, had been considering a new political grouping for several years. The "Red Week" strikes of June 1914 had suggested the possibility of new political alignments, and when the European war broke out, the syndicalists hoped to unite the extreme left in support of intervention. They failed, however, to carry a majority in the Unione Sindacale Italiana, which opted for the neutralism of the anarchist Armando Borghi (q.v.), so a group of them— A. O. Olivetti (q.v.), Filippo Corridoni (q.v.), Michele Bianchi (q.v.). Massimo Rocca (q.v.), Cesare Rossi (q.v.), and others—organized a new, specifically interventionist organization. They issued a manifesto addressed "to the workers of Italy" on October 5 and later that month met in Milan with those endorsing the manifesto to form the Fascio Rivoluzionario d'Azione Internazionalista. Bianchi was made political secretary, while Olivetti's review *Pagine Libere*, which renewed publication on October 10, served as the de facto organ of the movement.

Though it attracted few workers, the *fascio* did bring together a variety of interventionist leftists. A number of Mazzinian republicans were active in the movement, and, especially with Mussolini's espousal of intervention in November, a small but important minority of Socialists and ex-Socialists also became involved— including Mussolini himself. In December Socialist party sections in Milan and elsewhere declared participation in the *fasci* incompatible with party membership. Meanwhile, Mussolini's interventionist daily, *Il Popolo d'Italia*, which began publication November 15, 1914, became the major journalistic focus for the entire interventionist left.

In December, the original *fascio* became the Fasci di Azione Rivoluzionaria, a network of local interventionist cells. A national coordinating congress was held in Milan on January 24-25, 1915, with speeches by Olivetti, Mussolini, Alceste De Ambris (q.v.), and others, and by the end of February, there were 105 *fasci* with a total of about 9,000 members. They held interventionist rallies on the local level, while a central coordinating committee remained in operation in Milan, organizing national demonstrations on April 11 and especially during the "Radiant Days" of May 1915, in the context of the ministerial crisis accompanying Italy's decision for intervention. The demonstrations spearheaded by Corridoni in Milan were especially imposing. Though it was by now committed to intervention, the Antonio Salandra (q.v.) government remained quite hostile to the May demonstrations and to revolutionary interventionism in general.

With the declaration of war on May 24, the revolutionary interventionists closed ranks behind the government. There had been some earlier feeling that revolutionaries should participate in the war only in irregular Garibaldian units, as in the wars of national unification, but now most were happy to serve in the regular army. The *fasci* promptly dissolved as their members were either called to service or volunteered.

At first the statements of these interventionists accented Socialist orthodoxy: they called the workers to an idealistic crusade against German militarism and imperialism. Since a German victory would seriously threaten the European liberal context essential for a Socialist future, the proletariat could not afford to remain indifferent. These accents remained, but as the working class proved unresponsive and as the movement's composition grew more heterogeneous, new national-populist and antiparliamentary themes became more prominent. Addressing the national meeting of the *fasci* in January, Olivetti insisted that even without the workers, he and his fellow interventionists were creating something new, transcending ordinary politics, and linked to Mazzinian populism and idealism. There was occasionally even a kind of adventurism: the war would be a shot in the dark that, for better or for worse, would shatter the present impasse. Despite these heterodox notes, however, the revolutionary interventionists were not converging with the right-wing interventionists of the Italian Nationalist Association (q.v.), nor were they advocating a patriotic commitment to the Italian nation as presently constituted. They were still thinking in terms of revolutionary change in Italy, and they generally refused to collaborate with the Nationalists even in organizing interventionist rallies. Nor did the Nationalists have much use for them.

The *fasci* could not take credit for Italy's decision to intervene, and neither did they convince the bulk of the workers to embrace the war. But the movement was of major importance in bringing together frustrated leftists determined to develop new strategies, and in putting them in contact with alienated, nonproletarian, young people who were just becoming politically active. At Ferrara, for example, the movement brought together older syndicalists like Sergio Panunzio (q.v.), who headed the local *fascio*, and young dissidents like Italo Balbo (q.v.) and Dino Grandi (q.v.). These new alignments would survive the war.

For further information see: Renzo De Felice, *Mussolini il rivoluzionario* (Turin: Giulio Einaudi, 1965); David D. Roberts, *The Syndicalist Tradition and Italian Fascism* (Chapel Hill: University of North Carolina Press, 1979); Brunello Vigezzi, *L'Italia di fronte alla prima guerra mondiale,* I (Milan and Naples: Riccardo Ricciardi, 1966).

DDR

FASCI DI COMBATTIMENTO. The earliest local organizational cells of Fascism, the Fasci di Combattimento made their inauspicious entrance onto the Italian political scene in the spring of 1919. The first *fascio* was founded in Milan on the evening of March 21, 1919, by Mussolini and a tiny gathering of ex-Socialists, syndicalists, and war veterans. Initially Mussolini designed the *fascio* to express and embody not a precise political project, but rather a state of mind, a pervasive mood of postwar discontent and undirected revolt. With their informal structure and highly flexible program the *fasci* spread from Milan to some seventy other cities and towns of Italy, where they provided a point of reference for a small and heterogeneous mix of revolutionary interventionists, ex-servicemen, Futurist intellectuals, petty bourgeois employees and shopkeepers, and a few men of property. Despite a couple of well-publicized actions, such as the assault on the headquarters of the Socialist daily *Avanti!*, the *fasci* made scant headway and remained a marginal movement with little following or influence. By the end of 1919 the number of *fasci* had fallen to thirty-one, with a total membership of 870.

The fortunes of the *fasci* changed drastically in the winter of 1920-21, when the Fascist movement took the lead in the armed terrorist reaction against the Socialist party and the trade unions. By the end of 1921 the number of *fasci* jumped to 830, while membership rose to 249,036. The transformation of Fascism into a mass movement also meant that the *fasci* ceased to be organizations exclusively of displaced men and professional adventurers, attracting instead a huge influx of recruits from a much wider range of social groups. The altered character of the *fasci* was most evident in the countryside where they developed largely as a crude class reaction of agrarian capitalists and prosperous peasants to the Socialist leagues. At the same time, the *fasci* evolved more systematic organizational structures to deal with their growing membership and responsibilities. Within each *fascio* the old informality and egalitarianism gave way to a disciplined hierarchy and clearer division of labor, with armed squads for the all important punitive expeditions and separate sections to handle the problems of information, financing, transportation, and health.

The key to the tremendous growth and popularity of Fascism during 1921 and 1922 (*see* map series, "Fascism in Italy") lay chiefly in the local roots and orientation of the Fasci di Combattimento. Until the March on Rome (q.v.), new *fasci* arose primarily as a result of initiatives and problems on the provincial or municipal level. This parochial focus allowed each *fascio* to tailor its appeals and policies to fit the particular need and concerns of its immediate constituents. Thus, in the highly volatile border areas of Trieste and Venezia Giulia, for instance, the *fasci* emerged as an ultra-patriotic movement, defending the newly won "integrity of the nation" against the supposed subversion by Slavs and Communists. Conversely, in the "red provinces" of the Po Valley, the *fasci* gave little attention to nationalist and irredentist issues, devoting themselves instead to the more pressing task of destroying the powerful Socialist chambers of labor, cooperatives, and trade unions. This single-minded adaptation to local conditions proved strikingly effective in the short run. In many areas the *fascio* supplanted the chamber of labor and the prefecture as the dominant authority in the province, becoming a virtual "state within the state" with near total control over all aspects of public life.

Yet the very success of the *fasci* on the provincial level led to serious problems for the advance of Fascism as a coherent and unified force on the national level. Responsive to local rather than national imperatives and directly financed by their local supporters, the *fasci* tended increasingly to escape from effective control by Mussolini and the central leadership of the movement in Milan. As Mussolini recognized, the growing independence of the *fasci* undermined his personal authority over Fascism, reduced his margins for parliamentary maneuvering in Rome, and increased the risk of eventual state intervention and repression against the movement. In the fall of 1921 the Duce attempted to limit the freedom of the *fasci* and to change their status, when the movement was transformed into a political party with an official program and a formal hierarchical structure. However, prior to the March on Rome (q.v.), Mussolini's control over the *fasci* stemmed primarily from his ability to arbitrate and manipulate the bitter and often violent rivalries between local bosses, military and political leaders, and rural and urban organizations.

After the March on Rome in October 1922 the relative automony of the *fasci* became less a source of strength for Mussolini than an obstacle to his effective consolidation of power within the framework of established liberal parliamentary institutions. As the need to combat adversaries became less pressing, the *fasci* developed into focal points of dissension and internal rivalries which intensified confusion and instability, antagonizing influential conservative interests and obstructing the Duce's efforts to restore the authority of the state. While the *fasci* provided the backbone of mass support for Mussolini during the Matteotti Crisis (q.v.) of 1924, he wasted no time in bringing them under control after the formation of the dictatorship in January 1925. Indeed, the new authoritarian state marked the end of local autonomy for the *fasci*, as the locus of power shifted definitively from the provinces to Rome. In the period between 1926 and 1928 large numbers of Fascist activists were absorbed into the state administration, and Mussolini's prefects and *federali* seized control of all appointments in the increasingly bureaucratized *fasci*. With few meaningful functions to perform, militancy and morale in the *fasci* declined, and they lapsed into a state of inertia in which they remained for the duration of the regime.

For further information see: Renzo De Felice, *Mussolini il rivoluzionario* (Turin: Einaudi, 1961); Adrian Lyttelton, *The Seizure of Power: Fascism in Italy, 1919-1929* (London: Weidenfeld & Nicolson, 1972); Roberto Vivarelli, *Il dopoguerra in Italia e l' avvento del fascismo* (Naples: Istituto italiano per gli studi storici, 1967).

ALC

FASCI FEMMINILI. The Fasci Femminili, or women's auxiliaries of the Fascist party, were the mainstay of the regime's mass organization of women. The first groups out of which the *fasci* grew were formed in late 1920 at the initiative of a few middle-class women during the *squadristi* (q.v.) campaigns against the left. Before the March on Rome (q.v.) they attracted little support, either from prominent bourgeois feminists or from the Fascist party leadership itself, which always remained deeply suspicious of feminist activism in any form. As the Fascist movement shifted to the right after 1920, it tactically reversed its June 1919 affirmations of support for women's suffrage and equal right to hold political office. The preliminary guidelines on "women's groups" published on January 14, 1922 underscored the traditionalism of the movement's conception of women's roles in the Fascist "revolution." Thus women were allowed to attend meetings and rallies and encouraged to support the movement by undertaking charitable work, promoting propaganda, assisting the sick and wounded, and serving as godmothers or *madrine* to the newly founded Fasci di Combattimento (q.v.). But they were specifically barred from taking any political initiatives. Neglected by the party leadership, the *fasci* grew slowly in the 1920s, increasing from a membership of forty thousand in 1925 to just over one hundred thousand in 1930. Strengthened by the merger of the nationalist women's groups in 1923 and by the suppression of competing women's groups like the democratic Associazione per la Donna in 1926, the Fascist auxiliaries began publication of the *Giornale della Donna* (1924) and *Vita Femminile* (1926); by the late 1920s they also exercised a strong influence over editorial policy at the national *Almanacco delle Donne*. Yet efforts by their secretary, Elisa Majer Rizzioli, to formulate a "Fascist feminism" or at least to increase their autonomy of action by founding an Opera Assistenziale Femminile Fascista failed in the face of strong party opposition. The organizations always remained firmly under PNF (Partito Nazionale Fascista) (q.v.) control, a transmission belt both nationally and locally for directives formulated by a male leadership to carry out the regime's reactionary demographic and social policies.

From the early 1920s, Fascist ideologues developed what might be called an "integral anti-feminism" that identified the woman as pillar of the family and the family as the pillar of the authoritarian state. Propagandists cited population growth as an indicator of national strength and an excuse for imperialist expansion; they underscored the danger to male pride and the unemployment possibilities of competition from women workers, especially those in bureaucratic posts; finally they indicted feminism, however reformist in scope, for subverting the hierarchical relations of family and gender. From the mid-1920s, under the slogan "le donne a casa" ("woman into the home"), the regime passed a series of measures to strengthen the Italian family, to protect working mothers, and to remove women from the work force. The first measure, passed in 1925, established the Opera Nazionale di Maternità ed Infanzia (ONMI) to supervise children's and mothers' welfare. In May 1929 the regime passed a law for the care of working mothers that provided for maternity leaves and birth insurance; that same year it also imposed a special tax on bachelors. From 1933 on it provided for family paycheck supplements and for special loans, prizes, and subsidies for families with numerous offspring. At the same time, the regime approved legal and contractual measures which established sex quotas discriminating against women in many sectors of public service and ratified huge wage differentials between men and women workers. These patriarchal measures were powerfully supported by the Vatican, especially by Pius XI, who in his encyclical *Casti Connubi* of December 1930 blamed the weakening of paternal authority for the breakdown of the modern family, urging women to return to the home and family, where they would find a true equality in their roles as wives and mothers.

To support the regime's campaigns to "improve the race," the women's auxiliaries, in addition to defending the virtues of patient domesticity and prolific maternity against a barren feminist "flapperism," took part in a whole range of volunteer work. Women Fascists served on the local committees of the ONMI and in the party-administered children's vacation hostels. Female party cadres, trained in the party School for Social Work at San Gregorio a Celio, were responsible for organizing home economics courses for women workers who, the regime feared, were neglecting the art of homemaking at the very moment when austerity measures demanded a maximally efficient household administration. With the onset of the depression, the women's *fasci* were mobilized to assist the party relief agencies. In the mid-1930s they were also called on to promote the campaign against the League of Nations's sanctions against Italy, at the high point of which, on December 18, 1935, tens of thousands of women exchanged their gold wedding rings for tin bands. Finally, during the war the Fascists sent care packages to the armed forces, succored widows and orphans, and assisted refugees.

Notwithstanding their highly propagandized social responsibilities, the women's auxiliaries were also subordinated to a highly centralized bureaucratic apparatus and subject to an indifferent, if not antagonistic, male officialdom. Consequently, they were prevented from conducting the kind of inventive organizing campaign that was necessary to extend their following, largely because of the newness to politics of most of their constituents and the inconsistencies of Fascist policies toward women. Thus the auxiliaries were prevented from engaging in any of the reform campaigns for suffrage, educational, and property law reform that were typical of postwar bourgeois feminism. At the same time, they were constrained by the need to justify the regime's own opposition to giving women full voting rights, its attempts to limit the areas of education open to women, the laws penalizing abortion, and its accord with the Church on marriage and divorce, all measures that affected middle-class as well as working-class women.

The difficulties of organizing women under a regime that, in addition to damaging working-class women, undermined the economic security and personal freedom of bourgeois women as well, were reflected in the very slight growth of the *fasci* through the early 1930s. In 1935 the Fasci Femminili still had only four hundred thousand members nationally, as compared to the PNF's nearly two million. The only other women's organization tolerated by the regime, the two-decades-old Catholic Women's UDCI (Unione delle Donne Cattoliche Italiane), was always more active and as late as 1927 had more than double the membership of the Fascist groups.

Not until the mid-thirties did the Fasci Femminili begin to lose their upper-middle-class character. In keeping with its effort to "reach out to the people," the PNF called for the establishment of women's groups alongside all of the men's *fasci* in 1932. Subsequently, as the PNF itself developed a more total view of mass organizing, it sought to establish a presence among marginal groups, setting up the Massaie Rurali (rural housewives) for peasant women in 1935 and the Operaie e Lavoranti a Domicilio (domestic women workers) for female industrial and domestic workers in 1937. By 1940 these claimed enrollments of eight hundred and forty-five thousand and 1.65 million respectively. Even so, these new additions did not substantially change Fascism's profoundly ambivalent attitude toward the public organization of women as distracting from what propagandists considered their primary role: as mothers in the household. While in the end the public implications of working women's private roles and their evident presence in the economy—where in 1936, they made up 28 percent of the workforce in industry, 38 percent in agriculture, and 34 percent in the tertiary sector—justified the overcoming of such prejudices, the women's organizations continued to bear all of the marks of traditional Fascist attitudes. In its failure to differentiate women by social class and in its view of women's primary social functions as the charitable and educational extensions of child-raising and nurturing, the regime inevitably undercut its own efforts to mobilize public support from women. That this ambivalent attitude persisted even after the regime finally established special groups for peasant and proletarian women was demonstrated not only in the very name of the organization for peasant women (the "rural housewives"), which in effect denied the status of most as farm laborers, but also by the very slight resources and organizational talents it devoted to this constituency as a whole.

For further information see: Alexander De Grand, "Women under Italian Fascism,"*Historical Journal* 19, 4 (1976); Maria-Antonietta Macciocchi, *La donna 'nera': Consenso femminile e fascismo* (Milan: Feltrinelli, 1976); Piero Meldini, *Sposa e madre, Ideologia e politica delle donne e della famiglia durante il fascismo* (Rimini-Florence: Guaraldi, 1975); Chiara Saraceno, "La famiglia operaia sotto il fascismo," *Annali Feltrinelli* 20 (Milan, 1980).

VDG

FASCIO LITTORIO. The symbol of the Fascist movement, the *fascio* (Latin, *fascis*) was in ancient Rome the bundle of rods bound with an ax with a projecting blade. They were carried by minor Roman officials known as Lictors who went before the chief magistrates to clear the way during processions, and represented authority. In Italian the word *fascio*, meaning 'group' or 'association' (literally 'bundle'), was commonly used in politics—particularly on the Left—long before Mussolini adopted it for his movement. During the Fascist regime the *fascio* became the official emblem of the state (decree-law n. 2061, December 12, 1926).

For further information see: *Enciclopedia Italiana* 14 (Milan: Treccani, 1932): 846-47; Amerigo Montemaggiori, *Dizionario della dottrina fascista* (Turin: Paravia, 1934).

PVC

FASCIO PARLAMENTARE DI DIFESA NAZIONALE. Following the disaster of Caporetto (*see* CAPORETTO, BATTLE OF) in 1917, Italy was rampant with recriminations and accusations against "neutralists," "defeatists," and "subversives" who were blamed for what had been clearly a military crisis. The Fascio Parlamentare di Difesa Nazionale was created in December 1917 by interventionists and Nationalists who had been vigorous advocates of Italian entry in the war (*see* INTERVENTIONIST CRISIS 1914-1915) and sought to create a united front of all of those parliamentary forces which continued to support the war effort and who now demanded a national rededication to victory. The founders of the *fascio* were Maffeo Pantaleoni and Giovanni Preziosi (q.v.), and within a few months they had secured the adherence of more than 150 deputies, 90 senators, and political leaders from a wide range of parties and political persuasions— including Antonio Salandra (q.v.), Mussolini, Luigi Federzoni (q.v.), and Enrico Corradini (q.v.). The *fascio* was the most important of numerous such organizations that appeared in the aftermath of Caporetto, and while it included spokesmen for the democratic and socialist-syndicalist forces, its leadership was in the hands of the Nationalist right.

For further information see: Renzo De Felice, *Mussolini il rivoluzionario* (Turin: Einaudi, 1965); Adrian Lyttelton, *The Seizure of Power* (London: Weidenfeld and Nicholson, 1973); L. Pulla and G. Celesia di Veglissio, *Memorie del Fascio di Difesa Nazionale* (Bologna: Cappelli, 1932).

PVC

FASCISM.
1. Origins. World War I produced changes and crises in all of Europe, and while these changes assumed different dimensions in each country, they also possessed common characteristics and affected all areas of life, economic and ethical, social and political. The origins of Fascism are inseparably linked to the changes that took place in Italy. Without the reference point and the historical perspective of World War I it is not possible to understand Fascism.

It cannot be denied that in prewar Italy Fascism was already evident in certain psychological and cultural attitudes and even in certain concrete events (as early as the 1908 Parma riots, and during the strikes of "Red Week" in 1914, there were examples of protest against the 'absenteeism' of the state and even of bourgeois 'self-defense' against proletarian violence). These attitudes and manifestations, however, cannot be viewed as "Fascist seeds destined to germinate in the postwar period," as some have claimed. In fact, it is difficult to argue that Fascism would have germinated at all without the war.

Rather than emphasize the manner in which Italy entered the war, it is necessary to examine its consequences. These became apparent in the immediate postwar period and sparked many significant changes. On one level Italy had demonstrated the vitality of its political-national identity in the war itself, and on another level it had shown how this vitality served the interests of a small segment of society (those who had led the Risorgimento or unification) but did not correspond to the interests of the other sectors. Hence, in order to understand the nature of Fascism and the reasons for its rise, it is necessary to distinguish the various facets of the postwar Italian crisis and to determine their role in the situation that in less than four years gave way to Fascism.

The postwar Italian economy was characterized by a deep crisis caused by the strains of the war. Agricultural production was first reduced, then reversed into overproduction, which led to agricultural and industrial price inflation. Industry was immobilized; factories were outdated and could not be rebuilt without large amounts of capital. Productive capacity was greater than demand, and there was no foreign market. The state employed strict regulations, and unemployment was widespread. As a result, these economic difficulties were accompanied by an enormous increase in class struggles, with numerous uprisings, strikes, and factory and land seizures. The outcome was a great strengthening of the working class movement and a large increase in blue collar wages, contrasted with a small increase in white collar wages.

On the social level relatively small sectors of the population, at one time insignificant, now demanded participation in the political life of the nation. A new system of electing representatives to Parliament in relation to the population favored the Communist and Socialist parties, as well as the new Popular party (*see* PARTITO POPOLARE ITALIANO)—none of which represented the Risorgimento tradition or the values of the old ruling class. Moreover, a strong demand for political participation came, not from small sectors of the population, but from the already established lower middle class, which felt threatened by the "rise of the masses" and the consequently diminished political impact of the middle class. The most apparent postwar social crisis was the deepening of the division between state institutions and the needs of the people.

Culturally there was a major reaction against Positivism and a widespread acceptance of nationalism, activism, elitism, and skeptical relativism. But two phenomena are most significant: the fanatical belief of the masses in an ideology that might bring them social and political equality, and a growing disbelief in the old, traditional cultural system. As a result, a deep struggle ensued over traditional values and the social order they represented and mistrust of parliamentary democracy grew.

Politically, the synthesis of all these crises (far more comprehensive than that expressed by the division between the "legal" and the "real" Italy) focusd on three areas:

1. on the parliamentary level, an "anarchic government assembly" was unable to exercise its authority and equally incapable of expressing either an effective majority or a consistent alternative;

2. on the governmental level, a group of ministers existed that had neither the prestige nor the ability to initiate effective legislation and that was unable to promote respect for or carry out its responsibilities;

3. at the organizational level, there was a chronic instability in the political system, which clearly ignored the demands of those groups opposed to the system, groups that were unable to put their own differences aside.

Only in this context is it possible to understand the origin and success of Fascism. Founded in Milan on March 23, 1919, on the sole common denominator of a variety of prewar subversive experience, during the 1920-21 period Fascism was numerically and politically irrelevant and exhibited contradictions that were ultimately similar to trends and phenomena occurring within both the Left and the Right.

Within two years, however, Fascism took on sudden political and numerical strength and came to power. Until then Fascism had been an exclusively urban phenomenon, but it now found increasing support in rural, agricultural areas.

In order to understand this transformation, one must consider various factors. Historians and sociologists agree that at the end of 1920 the tension and mobilization of the masses, together with the capacity of the left to fight and dominate the national scene, had begun to diminish. The outbreak of Fascism, therefore, interrupted a process of integration similar to that occurring in other countries. In this light the Fascist counterrevolution would have been nothing more than a kind of "vendetta" against those who had made the Italian middle classes live in the nightmare of revolution for two years. There is no doubt that this spirit also existed among the *squadristi* (q.v.); it is difficult, however, to argue that this was the mainspring of the movement. At the end of 1920 the decline of "Bolshevism" was much less apparent to Italians than it may seem today, and the failure of the "Occupation of the Factories" (q.v.) did not suggest that the capacity for violence and eventual success had lessened on the part of the left. The key to the situation lay elsewhere. At the level of class struggle, the mainspring of Fascism was not so much the fear of a "Bolshevik" revolution as it was the fact that the working-class organizations had the ability to overthrow the traditional economic structure and impose limitations on the ownership of property. But the discussion cannot be limited to the level of class struggle. For many years other material interests, ingrained principles, and traditional values had been harmed without any protection by the state. The first major gain for Fascism came when those who considered these interests and values important perceived Fascism as a substitute for the "absent" state. Without this consensus, Fascism would have remained merely *squadrismo*, without support, with few followers, and an irrelevant political factor, or only the insignificant guardian of a few limited interests.

An important factor to bear in mind is the extreme violence that accompanied the class struggle in those agrarian regions where Fascism manifested itself and which was far greater than in industrial zones. In these agricultural areas the class struggle affected a larger number of people more directly and more violently than in the cities, especially where a strong system of peasant leagues existed and where many of the earlier gains of the peasant movement were under attack. While the landowners as a whole had been adversely affected by the class struggle, only certain segments of the rural laborers had benefited, depending on their classification. Hence, Fascism represented an element of strength for the former and of weakness for the latter. This diversity explains why Fascism began to rise suddenly in the countryside but not in the cities: whereas it had the unanimous support of the landowning class, the industrialists remained cautious because they were better able to protect their own interests and generally did not fully agree with Fascist policies, even after the March on Rome (q.v.).

The last important factor to consider is the composition of the *fasci*, which took shape in 1920-21. They increased their ranks by opening themselves up to all social classes, but their strength lay especially with the lower middle class, a fact that explains their limited penetration in more traditional areas where the petty bourgeoisie were not of the modern variety and therefore more fully integrated. One of the enduring characteristics of the PNF (Partito Nazionale Fascista) (q.v.) was that it gave to certain sectors of the lower middle class a sense of participation in the social and political life of the nation, particularly to those who no longer recognized the legitimacy and competency of the traditional ruling class to govern; in addition, the party also maintained the political autonomy of the lower middle class with respect to other political forces.

In addition to its social character, Mussolini's ability and opportunism made Fascism into something more than just *squadrismo*. In the summer of 1922, after the failure of the "legalitarian strike" (*see* ALLEANZA DEL LAVORO), Fascism won a social victory but still remained largely irrelevant at the parliamentary level. In fact, there were many indications that its political consensus had been stretched thin and that in the eyes of the middle classes the violence of its rank and file had made Fascism the real cause of social instability; there were also those who believed that Fascism had made possible the collaboration of the Liberal democrats, the Popular Party, and the reformist Socialists. All this occurred at the very moment when Fascism was faced with the problem of satisfying the masses that had flocked to its ranks and when the ruling classes still believed it impossible to govern in opposition to Fascism. In fact, many considered it wise to incorporate Fascism into the system, which needed reinvigoration, in order to eliminate the antisystem thrust of Fascism. This was the logic of Giovanni Giolitti (q.v.), Antonio Salandra (q.v.), V. E. Orlando (q.v.), Luigi Facta (q.v.), and even of F. S. Nitti (q.v.), who were willing to make Fascism a part of the government but not willing to give Mussolini power as prime minister. At this point Mussolini's strategy was twofold: (1) to play on the subversive elements within his movement and its desire for a show of force that, once put to the test, would certainly fail, but if maintained within the limits of a threat would precipitate the situation to his advantage; (2) to turn the various political groups against each other and take advantage of the fear of a renewed civil war. Hence, the March on Rome was a military bluff but a political success because the ruling class continued to misunderstand the nature of Fascism, believing that once in power it could be "constitutionalized."

Today this misunderstanding and this illusion may appear absurd. It is necessary to note, however, that if—as Palmiro Togliatti (q.v.) suggested in his *Lezioni sul fascismo* in 1935—"it is a serious error to believe that in 1920, or after the March on Rome, Fascism had a preestablished plan for a dictatorship of the kind that was later established," then it is also logical to ask whether the destiny of Fascism and of Italy was decided on October 28, 1922, or later, during the struggle between the potentially constitutional component of Fascism and its subversive, lower-middle-class element. If this is so, then it is evident that the attitude of the ruling class in 1922, if not excusable, appears at least more comprehensible.

2. The Regime. The twenty years of Fascist rule in Italy was a single unit and responded to a precise logic. One can, however, distinguish four successive phases that must be examined individually in order to grasp their overall logic and not to arrive at an interpretation that renders impossible the understanding of its links with the real Italian situation and how it differed from other fascisms. These four periods are: 1922-25, 1925-29, 1929-36, and 1936-43.

The first period, from the March on Rome to Mussolini's speech of January 3, 1925, saw the stabilization of Fascist power and was characterized by the construction of a relationship between Fascism and the traditional ruling class.

Mussolini's coming to power in October 1922 was the result of a compromise between the Fascists and the traditional ruling class of Italy. Therefore, until 1925 Mussolini's government was something of a coalition in which the old ruling class attempted to keep as much power as possible from the Fascists by maintaining control of important institutions, especially the armed forces. This compromise was strengthened at the outset of 1925 when much of the ruling class preferred to support Mussolini after the Matteotti Crisis (q.v.) rather than face the unknown or risk the danger of a show of force. For the ruling class, increasingly identified with the so-called "*fiancheggiatori*" (supporters) of Fascism, this compromise was not to make substantial changes in the system but merely to reorganize and revitalize it. The most ideal solution for them would have been for Fascism—in exchange for the inclusion of its elite in an enlarged power base—to strengthen the executive branch and deemphasize the democratic practices that had come into existence over the last few years. But this prospect was unacceptable to the Fascists, or at least to a large section of the old, pre-1922 Fascists, who not only desired more participation, but who saw themselves as an alternative to the traditional ruling class. The old-guard Fascists also objected to many aspects of the very system that they had wanted to democratize to their advantage but which the traditional ruling class wanted to maintain. Thus, during the entire first period there took place a struggle between the "intransigents" (who demanded a "second wave") and the "supporters" (who wanted "normalization"), a struggle that created many difficulties for Mussolini and retarded efforts to drain power from traditional strongholds and infuse more power into the Fascist party. The trust and sympathy of a large part of the traditional ruling class dissipated, but during the Matteotti Crisis Mussolini won because the intransigents remained loyal to him and induced the ruling class to continue along the path of compromise. Between Mussolini and a "leap into darkness" the supporters of Fascism chose Mussolini, hoping to repeat earlier efforts to constitutionalize Fascism, but now merely trying to save the essential structure of the pre-Fascist system while hoping to absorb Mussolini and Fascism into it.

The second phase, which went from Mussolini's speech on January 3, 1925, to the plebiscite of 1929, saw the progressive construction of the Fascist regime. The essential steps in the process were the dissolution of all non-Fascist parties and organizations; the "Exceptional Decrees" (q.v.); the "constitutionalization" of the Fascist Grand Council (q.v.); the introduction of a new electoral system (*see* PARLIAMENT); the creation of the Fascist syndical structure; and finally the conclusion of the Lateran Pacts (q.v.) in 1929. Other equally essential measures included the political liquidation of the Fascist party (*see* PARTITO NAZIONALE FASCISTA), the breaking up of the National Confederation of Fascist Unions (*see* ROSSONI, EDMONDO), and the "Quota Novanta" (q.v.) policy. Only if one takes into account all these elements is it possible to understand the character that the regime assumed in those years and the role that Mussolini played.

Seen from the perspective of the end of Fascism in 1943, the regime only superficially "Fascisticized" its supporters, for in reality the revolutionary content of Fascism was defused, and it became the tool of traditional conservatives. Although the regime was draped in a Blackshirt (*see* SQUADRISTI) and was transformed in an authoritarian manner, it remained fundamentally the old traditional regime. For the moment, Fascism was largely a form without substance, though an oppressive and poisonous form, and only much later did it succeed in acquiring substance. Thus those who benefited most from the compromise were the old ruling elites, since Fascism merely assumed the role of administering and balancing a series of conservative interests (those very interests, it should be noted, against which the early petty bourgeois element of revolutionary Fascism had revolted). The mythological worshiping of Mussolini as the Duce (q.v.) who would lead Italy to greatness acted as the cement that reinforced the regime's structure. But in a society in transition such as Italy's, the equilibrium was destined to collapse at the first crisis, as it did on July 25, 1943 when, in the face of military disaster, both Fascism and the regime crumbled. What remained was (1) the Italian Social Republic (q.v.), in which the old, intransigent Fascists deceived themselves into believing they could return to the social program of 1919 and tried to take revenge on the "supporters" for leading Fascism to its defeat, and (2) a large part of the old ruling class which, divesting itself of its Blackshirt, tried and in part succeeded in placing its own heavy blame on Fascism while depicting itself as the victim.

But this factual account is only a partial one, for during the second and especially during the third phase the compromise and the equilibrium that rested on it increasingly worked in favor of Fascism. It is therefore possible to posit a double hypothesis: (1) that without the external factor of World War II the Fascist regime would not have collapsed; and (2) that its evolution would have been in a populist direction that would have slowly weakened the old ruling class to the advantage of the new Fascist elite and would have created a social order characterized by the dominance of government intervention in the private sector, with the consequent formation of a new ruling class different from the previous one but also very different from the one envisioned by the Fascists.

Mussolini transformed the PNF from a party in the usual sense of the word into a large organization of mass control because he perceived the need to dispose of the old, unstable Fascist movement and to satisfy those who wanted from him the restoration of order and discipline. But he was also moved by another logic: the need for an instrument that allowed him to permeate the state (to which the PNF was subordinated) in order to control society, create a consensus, and mold new generations free from all other influences (particularly that of the Church). In contrast to the old, conservative-authoritarian regimes, which attempted to exclude the masses from active participation in political life, Fascism sought to mobilize them and give them a sense of a common spirit and a common involvement in the revolutionary process. There was a deliberate effort always to keep the masses in direct contact with the Duce, who assumed a charismatic quality because he was able to translate their aspirations into action and forge a collective faith in a better national future. The masses were to feel themselves part of a moral community with its own ideals, its own acceptable models of behavior, and its own hierarchical structure. The Fascist regime would thus become a legitimate source of power that would not require continual recourse to coercion to maintain its authority. Through the instruments of mass policy (schools, propaganda, the party, and so on) Fascism would therefore free itself from the shackles of compromise with the old ruling class and could render its power increasingly autonomous, especially from the ever-present economic power of the ruling class. The ultimate victory would be symbolized by Fascism's ability to overcome its most difficult and decisive test —the acceptance of a successor for Mussolini.

All the important Fascist initiatives of the 1929-36 period, even those that may appear contradictory, must be viewed from this perspective and in the context of the above-described elements.

In the 1929-36 period it is clear that the crisis over Azione Cattolica Italiana (q.v.) in 1931 was caused by the Fascist determination to monopolize the educational formation of Italian youth and, to a lesser extent, to alleviate the political consequences of the Lateran Pacts (q.v.). Mussolini, after viewing the collapse of the Spanish monarchy, was convinced that the support of the Church was neither essential nor trustworthy. In the same way the 1929 policy of ruralization was clearly inspired by two concerns: the desire to generate consensus among the peasantry and the lower middle class, and to restrain the economic power of big industries (which in the 1930s was frequently done through direct state intervention in the economy). Finally, in its search for consensus, the regime sought approval of its actions through the Ethiopian War (q.v.).

The key to the above-mentioned problems may be found in the nature and limitations of Fascist consensus. Until the military catastrophe of 1942, Fascist consensus was widespread, even among workers and peasants, and especially among the young. This is not surprising if one considers the prevailing atmosphere in the country and its slow social development. Through the regime a new political-bureaucratic class evolved that contained elements of proletarian and lower-middle-class origins, an achievement attributable directly to Fascism.

Three other aspects of Fascist consensus must be noted: (1) it reached its highest point in the mid-1930s, but in later years it declined and was often met with resigned indifference; (2) its essential characteristic was the energetic action of the Duce, who gained support among the masses for his nonaristocratic, popular background, while Fascism itself often was viewed in a negative light apart from Mussolini; (3) given the nature of the regime, its elements of force, the international situation, and the balance of its components, it was practically impossible for Fascism to enlarge its consensus through domestic programs alone. Hence, for Mussolini and for Fascism it was necessary to make the regime more totalitarian (*see* TOTALITARIANISM) in order to force the mechanism of consensus and quicken the pace of mass integration. This process was linked to the realization of an energetic foreign policy that would give Fascism the moral and cultural support of the middle classes as well as create economic and social consensus among the masses. Only in this way could Fascism have survived and won a victory over the traditional ruling classes.

The Ethiopian War cannot be viewed exclusively in the light of the politics of consensus; it must also be seen as the result of Mussolini's conception of international relations, of Italy's role in the world, and of how that role could be realized. This does not, of course, mean that there was no link between consensus and the Ethiopain War—on the contrary, it succeeded in galvanizing the entire nation. Subsequent initiatives were less and less popular, however, either because they were more dangerous or because of the latent hostility among Italians for Nazi

Germany. Thus, in 1935-36 the dynamism of Italian policy became a reality because Italy acted at a favorable moment in international affairs, but later that dynamism and that success represented only a facade. Ultimately, Mussolini found himself increasingly tied to Germany, a fact that corresponded neither to his own foreign policy aims nor to the needs of domestic policy. His intimate ties with Hitler and the growing threat of a European war seriously weakened the regime's consensus. At the same time, the determining presence of Nazism on the European scene gave international affairs an ideological imprint that it had not had and with which the Fascist regime increasingly identified itself, thus losing its distinctiveness. All this explains Mussolini's indecision in 1939-40 when Hitler launched World War II, Italy's initial "non-belligerency," and his decision to intervene only when he believed Germany was about to win. Mussolini feared that he would be excluded from the postwar political and territorial rearrangement of Europe and would be subject to Hitler's resentment for not having observed the Axis (*see* AXIS, ROME-BERLIN) alliance.

These observations concerning the last two stages in the history of the Fascist regime demonstrate that the determining factor in Mussolini's decisions was not the relationship between politics and economics, nor the prevalence of the latter over the former, but rather—as Franz Neumann has observed—pure politics. Similarly, the source of Fascist foreign policy, which became the chief characteristic of Fascism as the years went by, was not the logic of expansion but Fascism's survival as a political reality.

3. The Italian Social Republic. From a political-historical point of view, it is difficult to say whether the RSI (Repubblica Sociale Italiana) (*see* ITALIAN SOCIAL REPUBLIC) represented the continuation of or a break from Fascism. This is especially true if we consider two circumstances: the fact that from the very first the RSI could not be autonomous from German power and that any future it might have had in the event of a Nazi victory was doubtful at best; and the fact that Mussolini's personal position was greatly reduced from what it had been once, and his now almost powerless presence created ambiguities and uncertainties that virtually confined the evolution of Fascism to the personal drama of Mussolini. On the basis of this premise, we may examine the elements of continuity and discontinuity contained in the RSI with respect to Fascism of the 1920s. One element of continuity was nationalism, or a particular variety of nationalism that was peculiar to the republican Fascists. It was fundamentally of a romantic-knightly character, which stressed national honor, adhesion to agreements and comradeship, and was anti-English and frequently anti-American, but seldom anti-Russian. This is explained by the fact that the nationalism of the RSI was antidemocratic and nourished a myth concerning youthful versus old and decadent nations; the most important element, however, was the lower-middle-class revolutionary spirit of early Fascism. In the beginning this spirit was antiproletarian and anticapitalistic, and it had seen corporativism (*see* CORPORATIVISM AND THE CORPORA-

TIVE STATE) as an alternative to both capitalism and communism—but Mussolini had ultimately sacrificed it on behalf of the *fiancheggiatori*.

The coup of July 25, 1943, while seen as a tragedy, was also a moral victory because it confirmed the true enemy of Fascism to have been the *fiancheggiatori*—the monarchy, the military, the old ruling class, and the capitalists—who deceived and betrayed Mussolini. Hence, the return to the 1919 origins of Fascism and the "vendetta" against all *fiancheggiatori*.

These are the basic elements of continuity, but it should be noted that they also represent, from the political-ideological perspective, elements of novelty. The same can be said for those factors which divided the RSI from the earlier Fascism, factors that derived from the military collapse of the regime and the knowledge that, even with a German victory, Fascism would never recapture the charismatic rapport it had once had with the nation. These new elements, however, were such that they may be regarded as points of rupture between historic Fascism and post-World War II neo-Fascism (*see* MOVIMENTO SOCIALE ITALIANO, MSI). Among these elements, however, was the acquisition of a European dimension for Fascism that was conceived neither in terms of the Universal Fascism (q.v.) of the 1930s nor according to the Nazi view of hegemony, but rather through a common commitment to the survival of Europe and its civilization against anti- or non-European forces.

G. L. Mosse and T. Kunnas, two of the most perceptive scholars of fascist ideology and of its social-cultural origins, have clarified the relationship between fascist ideology and the moral, cultural, and existential crisis of Europe in the interwar period. In particular they stressed the fascist efforts to construct the "complete man" and the basic desire to transcend the historical present, to offer an alternative to the crisis of European civilization, and to revive a sense of community in the national consciousness. In the various historical fascisms and among some individual fascist intellectuals, these ambitions assumed different forms. But they were presented as possible future realities in contrast to the reality of the crisis of European civilization. Many different results were possible—the cyclical millennium of Nazism, or the capacity of the young to effect worldwide transformation through Fascism—but they all offered a future that appeared to many to be worth fighting for.

With the military and political defeat of Fascism, this attitude changed profoundly, transformed into the conviction that European civilization was destined to decay. The result was a tragic sense of pessimism without which it would be impossible to understand the reality of the RSI and its later influence on the neo-Fascist movements: either a prevailing sense of death, or a kind of love-hate attitude toward Soviet Russia, which was seen as either the vindication of Fascism or as the last, temporary halt to the degeneration of European civilization.

4. The Fascist Phenomenon. Until the early 1930s few observers saw fascism as anything but a strictly Italian phenomenon. Except for the Marxists of the Third

International, who viewed fascism as the last reactionary form of a dying capitalist system, most explained it as a specific Italian reality: Fascism emerged because of the weaknesses of Italian institutions, the inadequacy of Italy's ruling class, and the postwar political-social upheavals. There were even those who believed that Fascism was the result of the peculiar Italian national character. Others pointed out how Fascism could be a model for those Eastern European nations that lacked liberal traditions and were socially and economically underdeveloped.

After Hitler came to power in Germany, fascist and quasi-fascist movements appeared in many countries. Fascism was regarded by some as a model that transcended capitalism without falling into communism. But the Spanish Civil War (q.v.), the Pact of Steel (q.v.), and World War II destroyed any illusion that fascism could be a "third way." The tendency thereafter was for observers to emphasize the common elements of nationalism, class reaction, and terrorism, while ignoring differences among fascisms. For fifteen years, therefore, fascism was viewed as a politico-ethical problem that caused the world's most destructive war. This explains why, after the disappearance of fascist regimes at the end of the war, the discussion concerning fascism (except in Spain, where fascist tendencies were transformed into a conservative-authoritarian regime) was conditioned by some of the same opposing ideological debates over which the war itself had been fought. In one respect fascism became a comprehensive category increasingly deprived of references to historical fascism and used as a political label to define political adversaries; in another respect, fascism was studied from a series of new perspectives, less conditioned by "classical" interpretations which emphasized the national characteristics of each fascism, thus downplaying the common elements previously stressed.

In the "classical" interpretations, liberals, radicals, and communists perceived the causes of fascism on cultural and political levels and confronted the problem of post-fascism in a similar manner. For the liberals (B. Croce [q.v.], F. Meinecke, G. Ritter, G. Mann, H. Kohn, and others) fascism was a moral sickness, a loss of conscience on the part of all European social classes, and had distant roots: the mobilization of the masses in the French and industrial revolutions; the belief in happiness, profit, and power; the dissolution of traditional social ties; the rejection of reason and the praise of life and power by many currents of modern philosophy. The crisis caused by World War I galvanized and provoked fascism into being.

The radicals (E. Vermeil, P. Viereck, D. Mack Smith, and others) saw fascism as the inevitable consequence of a series of weaknesses inherent in the historical development of particular countries. These weaknesses were linked to the frustration over, and the fragility of, the retarded development and late realization of national independence: the middle classes had failed to develop except in "pathological" ways and therefore sought conservative alliances and antidemocratic structures in order to assert their dominance and exclude the masses from political participation. Thus fascism had been the logical result of antipopular reaction and the actual continuation of authoritarian-imperialist traditions.

For many Marxist and Communists, fascism was a product of capitalist society, the concrete manifestation of antiproletarian reaction on the part of capitalism to save itself. This interpretation, however, has been articulated in many different and less schematic forms (especially by L. Trotsky, R. Lowenthal, P. Togliatti [q.v.], and others) and has been widely acepted even by non-Marxist historians.

Another interpretation, widely accepted especially in the United States and West Germany, sees fascism as the result of the atomization of modern society and the social disintegration caused by World War I—that is, a response to a society characterized by the central role of the masses and of modern technology, a "totalitarianism" aiming to reconstruct the social fabric on the basis of an elementary ideology and the use of terror in order to create a sense of community and new forms of organization to meet the social and economic needs of mass society.

In the last thirty years other theories have arisen, particularly among social scientists, which have taken the discussion in new directions. Many of these interpretations took their lead from the works of W. Reich, E. Fromm, and K. Mannheim in the 1930s and 1940s. Generally, however, they coincide with recent psychological, sociological, and socioeconomic theories. They offer a positive contribution in explaining the relationship between fascism and mass society, and therefore the attitudes of various sectors of the social body toward fascism. But they also have had a negative impact when they attempt to offer all-encompassing interpretations of fascism and build "models" removed from the concrete history of individual countries. An example of this is the case of those sociologists and political scientists (influenced by the theory of W. Rostow concerning the stages of economic development) who have placed the discussion within the framework of "modernization," with the result that fascism is removed from its geographical, cultural, and historical contexts; a model is thus constructed in which vastly different experiences and regimes are thrown together, including the developing nations of Latin America and the Third World.

However important the contributions of the social sciences have been to the development of the theory of fascism, the major contributions have come from systematic, detailed research carried out in West Germany, the United States, and Italy. These studies have become increasingly important as more sources are made available and as historians are less preoccupied with their own political views. The discussion of fascism is today certainly less ambiguous than it once was. On the one hand, these studies have confirmed fascism to have been a complex, single phenomenon, either because it can be defined within precise geographical and chronological boundaries (Europe between the wars), or because it is connected to specific socioeconomic conditions and changes, to a special elitist cultural temperament, and to the concept of power relations within nations and among states. On the other hand, they have tended to stress two new facts which run counter to earlier views: first, that in individual fascisms national peculiarities, and especially the degree of the "nationalization of the masses," were of such decisive importance as to make impossible a single theory regarding fascist movements or regimes; and second, that the historical origins of fascism cannot be found only in right-wing cultural and political traditions, but rather were very often born out of the radicalism of the left that stemmed from the French Revolution. The mass-based fascist regimes were therefore profound departures from the traditional authoritarian-conservative systems, and the new political style of fascism proposed completely new objectives: the transformation of crowds into masses organized in a political movement that had the stamp of a secular religion.

For further information see: Alberto Aquarone, *L'Organizzazione dello stato totalitario* (Turin: Einaudi, 1966); F. W. Deakin, *The Brutal Friendship* (New York: Harper & Row, 1962); Renzo De Felice, *Mussolini*, 5 vols. to date (Turin: Einaudi, 1965-81), *Interpretations of Fascism* (Cambridge: Harvard University Press, 1977), and *Fascism: An Informal Introduction* (New Brunswick, N.J.: Transaction Books, 1976); A. James Gregor, *The Fascist Persuasion in Radical Politics* (Princeton: Princeton University Press, 1974); Adrian Lyttelton, *The Seizure of Power* (London: Weidenfeld and Nicolson, 1973); George L. Mosse, *The Nationalization of the Masses* (New York: Fertig, 1974); Ernest Nolte, *Die Krise des liberalen Systems und die faschistischen Bewegungen* (Munich: Deutschen Taschenbuch-Verlag, 1968); Luigi Salvatorelli and Giovanni Mira, *Storia d'Ialia nel periodo fascista* (Turin: Einaudi, 1964); Enzo Santarelli, *Storia del regime fascista*, 3 vols. (Rome: Riuniti, 1973); Attilio Tamaro, *Due anni di storia, 1943-1945* (Rome: Tosi, 1948), and *Venti anni di storia, 1922-1943* (Rome: Tosi, 1953); Angelo Tasca, *The Rise of Italian Fascism* (New York: Fertig, 1966); Palmiro Togliatti, *Lectures on Fascism* (New York: International Publishers, 1976); Gioacchino Volpe, *Storia del movimento fascista* (Milan: Istituto di studi di politica, 1939); Stuart J. Woolf, ed., *The Nature of Fascism* (New York: Random House, 1968).

RDF

FASCIST GRAND COUNCIL. In theory the highest organ of the Italian state and of the Fascist regime, the Grand Council was originally created as a consultative body of the PNF (Partito Nazionale Fascista) (q.v.) on December 15, 1922, and met for the first time in Rome on January 12, 1923, a few months after Mussolini came to power. Although it discussed and approved many important issues over the next five years, it functioned without any legal status until Alfredo Rocco (q.v.) drafted a bill on the "Ordinamento e attribuzioni del Gran Consiglio del Fascismo" ("Organization and Functions of the Grand Council of Fascism"). The law, (n. 2693), containing fifteen articles, was approved by the Chamber of Deputies on December 9, 1928.

The 1928 law declared that the head of government (Mussolini) was president of the Grand Council and called it into session at will. Its meetings were to be secret and no quorum was necessary. The secretary of the PNF acted as the council's secretary. Three categories of membership existed: the four Quadrumvirs (q.v.) of the March on Rome (q.v.) (Emilio De Bono [q.v.], Cesare Maria De Vecchi [q.v.], Italo Balbo [q.v.], and Michele Bianchi [q.v.]), who were members for life; certain high officials of government such as the ministers of foreign affairs, justice, interior, finance, and so on, the presidents of the Senate and Chamber of Deputies, the commander of the Militia (q.v.), the members of the PNF Direttorio, the presidents of the Royal Academy of Italy (q.v.), the Special Tribunal for the Defense of the State (q.v.), and the national confederations of workers and employers; and those individuals who, because of exemplary service to the regime, might be appointed by Mussolini. All members were above the law, but membership could be revoked at any time. Given the nature of these membership criteria, over the years part of the composition of the Grand Council changed from time to time according to the wishes of Mussolini. In actual fact, Mussolini controlled the Grand Council absolutely and designed it as an instrument for his personal dictatorship.

The powers and attributes of the council were in theory vast: it selected the list of candidates for election to the Chamber of Fasces and Corporations (*see* PARLIAMENT); it drew up the statutes of the PNF and appointed the party's secretary and vice secretaries as well as members of its Direttorio; it was supposed to present lists of candidates when ministerial posts became vacant; it was supposed to maintain a list of successors to Mussolini in the event of his death, but in fact only one name—that of Costanzo Ciano (q.v.)—was ever included; it was supposed to deliberate on questions regarding the succession to the throne; and it was to be consulted on all important matters of government and party policy.

During the life of the regime the Fascist Grand Council deliberated on many of the vital policy decisions, but its role was largely a propagandistic one and was designed to maintain the appearance of a consultative body that combined party and state attributes in a "consensus dictatorship."

The penultimate meeting of the Grand Council took place on December 7, 1939 when it declared Italy's "nonbelligerency" in World War II, and Mussolini did not call it into session again until its last meeting on the evening of July 24, 1943. That meeting, which resulted in the fall of Mussolini and the collapse of the regime, was demanded by a group of discontented Fascist leaders headed by Dino Grandi (q.v.), Giovanni Giuriati (q.v.), Giuseppe Bottai (q.v.), and Galeazzo Ciano (q.v.). During that final session, many of its members leveled open criticism at Mussolini for the responsibility of the war, and its unsuccessful military conduct, while Mussolini attempted to defend himself and maintained a rather unconcerned attitude. The final segment of the meeting, which carried over until 2:30 A.M. on July 25, resulted in the adoption by a majority of members (nineteen in all) of a motion by Grandi that called for the de facto restitution of the constitutional prerogatives of the king as commander in chief of the armed forces. Later that day Mussolini visited Victor Emmanuel III (q.v.) in an effort to reconfirm the king's confidence in his leadership, but he was arrested. The king's action, taken after highly secret discussions between his aide the Duke of Acquarone (*see* ACQUARONE, PIETRO, DUCA D'), anti-Fascists and dissident Fascists, and military leaders, seized upon the Grandi motion as proof that the Fascist leadership had rejected Mussolini. Yet the Grand Council "decision" had no actual legal or constitutional implications, and it is ironic that the very body that Mussolini had used to reinforce his dictatorship provided the setting for his downfall.

For further information see: Alberto Aquarone, *L'organizzazione dello stato totalitario* (Turin: Eianudi, 1965); G. Bianchi, *25 luglio: crollo di un regime* (Milan: Mursia, 1963); F. W. Deakin, *The Brutal Friendship* (New York: Harper and Row, 1962); G. D. Ferri, *La funzione di governo e il Gran Consiglio del Fascismo* (Rome: Athenaeum, 1941).

PVC

FASCIST PARTY. See **PARTITO NAZIONALE FASCISTA**.

FAVAGROSSA, CARLO (b. Cremona, November 22, 1888). Nominally responsible for the Italian war economy in World War II as head of COGEFAG (Commissariato Generale per Fabbricazione di Guerra in General Commissariat [later Undersecretariat and Ministry] for War Production), Favagrossa first distinguished himself in Spain, reorganizing the supply service of the Italian forces after Guadalajara. In August 1939 he took over COGEFAG after the resignation of its first chief, Alfredo Dallolio (q.v.). Like many of the regime's military leaders, Favagrossa exaggerated to Mussolini Italy's (admittedly great) unpreparedness, then acquiesced to intervention in May 1940 after the French collapse made a short war seem likely. Favagrossa controlled raw materials allocation, but not weapons procurement, and despite chaotic results refused to demand full centralization, perhaps fearing that his already overworked organization would collapse. Favagrossa served until the Pietro Badoglio (q.v.) government suppressed his ministry in January 1944.

For further information see: Carlo Favagrossa's not entirely reliable *Perchè perdemmo la guerra, Mussolini e la produzione bellica* (Milan: Rizzoli, 1946); Fortunato Minniti, "Aspetti organizzativi del controllo sulla produzione bellica in Italia (1923-43)," *Clio* (October-December 1977): 305-40.

MK

FEDELE, PIETRO (b. Minturno, Caserta, April 15, 1873). Fascist minister of education, Fedele taught history at the University of Rome and wrote on the history of southern Italy and Rome from the fall of the Roman Empire to the Renaissance. An interventionist, Fedele worked mainly to keep up the morale of the peasants and workers in Campania. Fedele was elected a deputy on the Nationalist list in 1919. He joined the PNF (Partito Nazionale Fascista) (q.v.) in September 1924 and on January 8, 1925 succeeded Giovanni Gentile (q.v.) as minister of public instruction, a post he held until July 9, 1928. Fedele sought to Fascisticize further all levels of the educational system, but rather than modifying Gentile's reforms, Fedele left them intact during his term in office. In 1925, Fedele supported the law dismissing university professors from their posts if their loyalty to the state was questioned. Fedele also initiated the excavations at Ercolano and helped found the Royal Academy of Italy (q.v.). He became a senator on December 22, 1928, and a minister of state in April 1933. In the 1930s he was the president of the government printing office, the Poligrafico di Stato.

For further information see: *Chi è?* (1936); NO (1927); Luigi Salvatorelli and Giovanni Mira, *Storia del Italia nel perido fascista* (Turin: Einaudi, 1964).

MSF

FEDERZONI, LUIGI (b. Bologna, September 27, 1878; d. Rome, January 24, 1967). Luigi Federzoni was an important Fascist minister and former prominent Nationalist. Educated at the local university under Giosuè Carducci, he majored in letters. Using the anagram "Giulio de Frenzi," he wrote novels, short stories, and essays on contemporary art and was literary critic and political commentator for several newspapers.

Federzoni attracted wide attention and established contacts with the Nationalist ideologue Enrico Corradini (q.v.) with his *L'Italianità del Gardasse* (1909). Published in the supercharged atmosphere resulting from Austria's outright annexation of Bosnia, it underlined the threat that Teutonic penetration of the Lake Garda border region posed for Italy. Federzoni was on the preparatory committee of the Florence Nationalist Congress, which organized the Italian Nationalist Association (q.v.) on December 5, 1910. He was elected to the central committee of the association and was on the founding board of the Nationalist Roman weekly, *L'Idea Nazionale*. He attained national stature through the 1913 campaign undertaken against freemasonry in public life.

Disagreement with Sidney Sonnino (q.v.) over the coalition ticket for the general elections of 1913 provoked Federzoni's resignation from Sonnino's *Giornale d'Italia* of Rome and his declared candidacy for the first electoral college of Rome. Backed by Nationalists, Catholics, and disaffected Right Liberals, Federzoni defeated the incumbent Socialist, Antonio Camponozzi, and the radical, Scipione Borghese. He espoused a pro-Libyan, conservative program. Federzoni held the seat until the 1923 fusion with Fascism, proving himself a great vote-getter.

Volunteering in 1915, Federzoni served both as an Army artillery and as an air force bombardier officer, receiving three decorations for gallantry. Against the background of stalemated peace negotiations and ineffectual governmental leadership, Federzoni articulated the Nationalists' maximum expectations. A mutuality was struck with Fascist deputies. Federzoni's name was linked with several potential conspiracies, but all were denounced by him as baseless.

Federzoni was not enthusiastic over fusion with Fascism, believing merger was premature. Still, he, along with Corradini and Maurizio Maraviglia (q.v.), signed the Pact of Union and presented to Mussolini the members of the last central committee of the association at the Chigi Palace meeting in Rome on March 7, 1923.

Federzoni labored for Fascism as minister of colonies (October 28, 1922-June 5, 1924; November 6, 1926-December 18, 1928) and minister of interior (June 6,

1924-November 5, 1926). His stint as colonial chief was distinguished by the imaginative thrust and coordinating skills with which he strengthened Italian rule and initiated plans for the economic development and settlement of Italy's colonial empire.

Appointed minister of interior immediately after the Matteotti assassination (*see* MATTEOTTI CRISIS), Federzoni's presence as a Fascist of Nationalist origins was designed to restore support for the regime and to introduce a statist type of control of anti-Fascists and Fascist extremists. The decree laws of July 10, 1924 and December 31, 1925 intimidated the press, making the editor or managing director of publications legally accountable for all printed matter. Federzoni later defended his action, citing the emergency situation, recalling his prudent and impartial implementation, and pointing to the alleged indiscriminate censorship of Liberal ministries. His pleadings notwithstanding, prefects were instructed to seize organs considered subversive while advised to use caution and private persuasion with hostile constitutional mouthpieces. In the interests of discipline, professionalism, efficiency, and tighter governmental supervision, elective communal administrations and councils were replaced by the Podestà (q.v.) and a Consulta, both appointive. The public security forces of the country were reorganized and reinvigorated. Federzoni's ministry pushed much health and social welfare legislation, from maternity assistance and protection of infancy to measures to combat diseases.

Although Federzoni gained Mussolini's respect for his industry and abilities, he did not win his confidence nor that of the Fascist hierarchs. Envy over his experience, competence, uneasiness over possible personal ambition, his Nationalist derivations and strong support of the monarchy, together with his highly ambiguous and meddlesome maneuverings during the March on Rome (q.v.) and his repeated insistence to prefects that Fascist violence be curbed and all citizens and officials comply with the law, made him suspect and contemptible in major Fascist circles. Mussolini conceded to distrust and resentment and moved Federzoni away from sensitive posts, although he continued to draw on Federzoni's visibility. Federzoni served as a senator (November 28, 1928-43), president of the Senate (April 20, 1929-March 15, 1939), and president of the Royal Academy of Italy (q.v.) (March 7, 1938-1943).

Federzoni was late in facing up to Italy's increasingly difficult situation. The isolation of the Crown, the Pact of Steel (q.v.), racial laws, and disastrous World War II were sobering realities. At the July 24-25 session of the Fascist Grand Council (q.v.), Federzoni voted for Dino Grandi's (q.v.) majority resolution restoring active command to the king. One doubts Grandi would have submitted the proposal without Federzoni's tacit complicity.

Condemned to death in absentia by the Fascist tribunal in Verona (*see* VERONA TRIALS), Federzoni was later tried by the Italian Supreme Court of Justice for his service to Fascism. Convicted, he was sentenced to life imprisonment on May 28, 1945 and received amnesty in December 1947. He left Italy for Portugal, where he accepted the chair of Italian literature at the University of Coimbra.

For further information see: Vittorio Cian, *Luigi Federzoni* (Piacenza: Porta, 1924); Alexander J. De Grand, *The Italian Nationalist Association and the Rise of Fascism in Italy* (Lincoln: University of Nebraska Press, 1978); Francesco Gaeta, *Nazionalimo italiano* (Naples: Edizioni Scientifiche Italiane, 1965); Raffaele Molinelli, *I nazionalisti italiani e l'intervento* (Urbino: Argalia, 1973).

RSC

FERMI, ENRICO (b. Rome, September 29, 1901; d. Chicago, November 28, 1954). Among scores of eminent twentieth-century physicists, Fermi alone stood in the first rank in both theory and experiment. Recognized as a prodigy while still a boy, he received his Ph.D., magna cum laude from the University of Pisa at the age of twenty-one in 1922. After two years of post-doctoral study in Germany and Leiden he returned to Italy and in 1927 was awarded a professorship in theoretical physics at the University of Rome.

Fermi had developed a system of quantum statistics in 1926, and in 1927 he developed a statistical model of the atom. Building on the theoretical work of Wolfgang Pauli and the discovery of the neutron by James Chadwick in 1932, he studied the emission of particles from atomic nuclei (nuclear beta decay) and postulated a new basic subatomic force (weak interaction) for which he introduced a new constant (Fermi constant). In the mid-thirties he began bombarding various elements with neutrons to produce artificial radioactivity and discovered that slowing the neutrons by passing them through paraffin greatly increased the induced radioactivity.

Fermi's wife, the former Laura Capon, was Jewish, and the racist policies of Fascism were becoming increasingly abhorrent to them, if not actually dangerous. In 1938 he was awarded the Nobel prize in physics. Accompanied by his wife and two children, he journeyed to Stockholm to receive the award, and instead of returning to Italy, went to New York where a position was awaiting him at Columbia University. In 1939 the discovery of nuclear fission by Otto Hahn in Berlin elicited a rush of investigation among physicists. Fermi led a group at Columbia which proved that the fissionable isotope of uranium was U^{235} rather than the more plentiful U^{238}. When British and American scientists began a concerted effort to produce an atom bomb, it was Fermi's group, working now at the University of Chicago, that produced the first self-sustaining nuclear chain reaction (December 2, 1942). Later Fermi played a leading role in Robert Oppenheimer's research group, which developed the trigger, put the pieces together, and tested the first atom bomb in July 1945 at Los Alamos, New Mexico. Fermi received a Congressional Medal of Merit in 1946.

After the war Fermi continued his theoretical and experimental research at the University of Chicago's newly created Institute for Nuclear Studies. A few days before his death, he received the first Fermi Award of the Atomic Energy Commission.

For further information see: *Dictionary of American Biography*, Supplement Five (New York, 1977); *Dictionary of Scientific Biography* 4 (New York, 1970-80); Emilio Segrè, *Enrico Fermi, Physicist* (Chicago: University of Chicago Press, 1970).

MMV

FERRARI, FRANCESCO LUIGI (b. Modena, 1891; d. Paris, March 2, 1933). A leading figure in the Partito Popolare Italiano (PPI) (q.v.) and an anti-Fascist, Ferrari became a Catholic militant at an early age, and in 1919 he helped to organize the party's Modena section. His opposition to Fascism was such that he was beaten by *squadrista* (*see* SQUADRISTI) groups on numerous occasions, as a result of which he eventually died, but he worked tirelessly to prevent the Popolari from cooperating with the Fascists. In 1922 he founded Domani d'Italia, a Catholic left-wing movement. He was eventually forced to flee Italy and settled in Paris, where he established the review *Res Publica* and participated in anti-Fascist activities. After the Lateran Pacts (q.v.) he organized an air drop of propaganda materials attacking Fascism and denounced the agreements.

For further information see: EAR (2); Charles F. Delzell, *Mussolini's Enemies* (Princeton: Princeton University Press, 1961).

MSF

FERRARI, GIUSEPPE FRANCESCO (b. Lerici, La Spezia, March 28, 1865). Army Chief of Staff between April 1923 and May 1925, conservative but acquiescent, Ferrari supported both Armando Diaz (q.v.) and Antonino Di Giorgio's (q.v.) army reorganizations but sought control over the Militia (q.v.). After losing his post to Pietro Badoglio (q.v.), Ferrari received first the Turin and later the Milan Army command and an Army Council seat. When Badoglio's powers were reduced, Ferrari returned as Chief of Staff (February 1927-February 1928). He unsuccessfully requested larger forces to face France and Yugoslavia, control of colonial military operations, and an effective staff for Badoglio. Dismissed after opposing Ugo Cavallero's (q.v.) planned subordination of the general staff to the War Ministry, Ferrari became a senator (March 1928), returned to the Turin Army command (1930-33), and then retired, becoming Senate vice president in 1936.

For further information see: Giovanni De Luna, *Badoglio: Un militare al potere* (Milan: Bompiani, 1974).

BRS

FERRERO, GUGLIELMO (b. Portici, Naples, July 21, 1871; d. Mount Pelerin, Switzerland, August 3, 1942). An historian and anti-Fascist, Ferrero studied criminology and sociology at the University of Pisa and then at Turin, where he joined the Socialists. Ferrero became interested in civil institutions and called for radical reforms in the court and prison systems. He supported Italy's intervention in World War I on the side of the Allied powers, and from its beginning opposed Fascism because of his democratic ideology. After the death of Matteotti (see MATTEOTTI CRISIS), Ferrero and Giovanni Amendola (q.v.) organized the National Union of Liberal and Democratic Forces and helped prepare its first and only congress, held in June 1925. Under constant surveillance, Ferrero was forced to leave Italy in 1930 and emigrated to Switzerland, where he taught history at the University of Geneva. Although he remained distant from any direct anti-Fascist initiatives, Ferrero remained in contact with anti-Fascists in Europe until his death.

For further information see: DSPI; MOI (2).

MSF

FERRETTI, LANDO (b. Pontedera, Pisa, May 2, 1895). A Fascist deputy and bureaucrat, Ferretti took a degree in law and literature from Pisa and worked as a journalist. A fervent interventionist, he volunteered for combat in World War I and after the conflict worked for the Italian administration in the Trento region. Ferretti had an abiding interest in sports (q.v.) and in Milan he codirected the *Gazzetta dello Sport* from 1919 to 1924, was an editor for *Il Secolo* (Milan) from 1924 to 1926, and also served as an editor for *Il Corriere della Sera* (Milan) from 1927 to 1928. He served as president of the Italian Olympic Committee from 1925 to 1928.

Ferretti took part in the March on Rome (q.v.), and thereafter held numerous posts in the regime. A member of the Fascist Grand Council (q.v.), a deputy in Parliament (q.v.) from 1924 to 1943, and an officer in the Militia (q.v.), he was head of Mussolini's Press Office from 1928 to 1931. In that latter position he helped to increase and extend the regime's control of the press and establish some of Fascism's important cultural policies.

During the Salò Republic (see ITALIAN SOCIAL REPUBLIC), Ferretti was on the staff of *Il Corriere della Sera* and worked for radio propaganda. In 1953 he was elected a senator on the neo-Fascist MSI (see MOVIMENTO SOCIALE ITALIANO) and was later reelected.

For further information see: NO (1937); Philip V. Cannistraro, *La fabbrica del consenso* (Rome-Bari: Laterza, 1975); *I deputati e senatori del terzo parlamento repubblicano* (Rome: La Navicella, 1958).

PVC

FINOCCHIARO-APRILE, ANDREA (b. Palermo, June 26, 1878; d. Palermo, January 15, 1964). A pre-Fascist Italian politician and leader of the post-World War II Sicilian Separatist Movement (q.v.), Finocchiaro-Aprile studied law and in 1913 was elected to Parliament (q.v.). In 1919-20 he served as undersecretary of war and undersecretary of the treasury. He participated in the Aventine Secession (q.v.) but retired from overt political activity during the Fascist regime. Between 1943 and 1948 Finocchiaro-Aprile helped to establish and led the Separatist

Movement in Sicily that demanded complete independence from Italy. In October 1945, after issuing a declaration to the San Francisco Conference calling for Allied assistance for Sicily, he was arrested and confined to the island of Ponza. He was released early in 1946 and elected as a Separatist deputy to the Constituent Assembly (*see* COSTITUENTE). Later he was elected to the first Sicilian Regional Assembly.

For further information see: Andrea Finocchiaro-Aprile, *Il movimento indipendentista siciliana* (Palermo: Libri Siciliani, 1966); Giuseppe Carlo Marino, *Storia del separatismo siciliano* (Rome: Riuniti, 1979).

MSF

FINZI, ALDO (b. Badia Polesine, Rovigo, April 20, 1891; d. Rome, March 24, 1944). Mussolini's closest adviser between 1922 and 1924, Finzi flew with Gabriele D'Annunzio (q.v.) over Vienna in September 1918 and later joined him at Fiume (q.v.). After abandoning D'Annunzio Finzi was elected a Fascist deputy in 1921 and became Mussolini's intimate. During the Fascist takeover of Milan in August 1922 Mussolini and D'Annunzio barely restrained Finzi from revolution. After accompanying Mussolini during the March on Rome (q.v.), Finzi became interior undersecretary and then a member of the Fascist Grand Council (q.v.) (December 1922). Named aviation vice-commissioner in January 1923, Finzi obtained large air budgets, striving for a Fascist service. He also gained a reputation for corruption. Sugar interests financed Finzi's newspapers, *Corriere del Polesine* and *Corriere Italiano*. As interior undersecretary, Finzi curbed provincial Fascism while directing Mussolini's "cheka" (secret squad of assassins) against anti-Fascists. Although close to the Vatican, Finzi prevented Mussolini's alliance with the Popolari (*see* PARTITO POPOLARE ITALIANO) in April 1923. He helped direct the elections of April 1924, retaining his seat, but resigned his other offices in June, accused of involvement in Matteotti's (*see* MATTEOTTI CRISIS) disappearance. Finzi privately implicated Mussolini but escaped punishment. Although he was Jewish, after 1938 Finzi's earlier service protected him from anti-Semitic legislation (*see* ANTI-SEMITISM) until Aldo Vidussoni (q.v.) expelled him from the PNF (Partito Nazionale Fascista) (q.v.) for "indiscipline" in November 1942. Finzi aided partisans in the Castelli-Romani (September 1943-March 1944) until his arrest by the Germans. They murdered him at the Ardeatine Caves (*see* ARDEATINE CAVES MASSACRE).

For further information see: Renzo De Felice, *Mussolini il fascista* (Turin: Einaudi, 1966); Robert Katz, *Death in Rome* (New York: Macmillan, 1967); Meir Michaelis, "Il Generale Pugliese e la difesa di Roma," *La Rassegna Mensile di Israel* 27 (June-July, 1962); Alessandra Staderini, "Una fonte per lo studio della utilizzazione dei'fondi segreti': la contabilità di Aldo Finzi (1922-1924)," *Storia Contemporanea* 10, 4-5 (October 1979).

BRS

FIUME. Fiume is on the northeast Adriatic coast of the Istrian peninsula, presently in the territory of Yugoslavia. Its position made it an important port as well as an industrial center. Given its location, Fiume was populated not only by Croats, but also by a large number of Italians. In 1905 the Italian population organized a nationalist association, Giovane Fiume, in reaction to the influx of Croats and Hungarians into the area. The presence of the Italian population provided Rome with the basis for a request to annex the city at the Paris Peace Conference, although the Pact of London (1915), signed prior to Italy's entry into World War I, ignored the question. The Italians were opposed by President Woodrow Wilson, who wished to make Fiume a free city. Wilson's rigid stance, as well as that of V. E. Orlando (q.v.) and Antonio Salandra (q.v.), caused the Italian delegates to withdraw from the conference. The crisis came to a climax when the Allies dissolved the Consiglio Nazionale Fiumano, which in 1918 had proclaimed the city's annexation to Italy, and F. S. Nitti (q.v.) ordered the withdrawal of Italian troops that had occupied the city by Orlando's orders in 1918. This was followed by Gabriele D'Annunzio's (q.v.) invasion of Fiume (September 1919) and the organization of the Regency of Carnaro. According to the Italo-Yugoslav Treaty of Rapallo (November 1920), Fiume was declared a free city, and approximately a month later D'Annunzio and his followers were forcibly expelled from Fiume after threatening armed resistance. The elections of April 1921 gave a majority to the Autonomist party, but in 1922 the Fascists forced its leaders to resign. In January 1924 the annexation of Fiume to Italy was formalized, thus ending any question of possession that still existed. Occupied by the Germans during World War II, the city was liberated by Yugoslav partisans and incorporated into Yugoslavia in 1945.

For further information see: DSPI; R. Albrecht-Carrie, *Italy at the Paris Peace Conference* (New York: Columbia University Press, 1938); Michael A. Ledeen, *The First Duce* (Baltimore: Johns Hopkins, 1977).

MSF

FOA, VITTORIO (b. Turin, September 18, 1910). An anti-Fascist political figure, Foa took a degree in law. In the 1930s he became a member of the Turin group of Giustizia e Libertà and wrote anti-Fascist articles for the clandestine press. In May 1935 he was arrested by the Fascist police and sentenced to fifteen years in prison by the Special Tribunal for the Defense of the State (q.v.). After the fall of Mussolini in 1943, Foa was freed and made contact with the Partito d'Azione (q.v.), which he represented in the Piedmontese Committee of National Liberation. He was also a member of the CNL (Committee of National Liberation) (q.v.) for Northern Italy, a position he held until the end of the war. He was made undersecretary for reconstruction in the Ferruccio Parri (q.v.) government, was elected to the Constituent Assembly (*see* COSTITUENTE) and served as a deputy from 1948. After the collapse of the Partito d'Azione, Foa

joined the Partito Socialista Italiano d'Unità Proletaria (*see* PARTITO SOCIAL-
ISTA ITALIANO).

For further information see: EAR (2).

MSF

FOREIGN AFFAIRS, MINISTRY OF. In 1922 all but two of Italy's top
diplomats agreed to serve Mussolini. As a conservative institution the Foreign
Ministry accepted Fascism as a bulwark against Bolshevism; moreover, it sub-
scribed sufficiently to the Nationalist argument that Italy's wartime victory had
been mutilated in the peace settlement to consider using Mussolini to frighten other
powers into concessions. Mussolini, however, intended to be his own man. The
Foreign Ministry was moved from the tranquil and aristocratic Palazzo della
Consulta to the Palazzo Chigi on a busy corner suited to Mussolini's demagogic
exercises, and the Duce himself assumed the foreign affairs portfolio from 1922 to
1929 and again from 1932 to 1936.

Mussolini's omnipresence notwithstanding, the professionals at the Palazzo
Chigi worked with him comfortably at first. There was broad agreement about the
goals of Italian foreign policy—the assertion of Italian rights in the Adriatic and
Eastern Mediterranean (specifically, sovereignty over Fiume (q.v.) and the Dodecanese
Islands), the extension of Italy's influence in the Balkans (via an Albanian
protectorate), and the absorption of Ethiopia into an African empire (the accom-
plishment of which by war in 1935-36 was endorsed by the Foreign Ministry from
the sidelines) (*see* ETHIOPIAN WAR). On the other hand, the career diplomats
did have qualms about Mussolini's methods. Traditionally cautious to a fault, they
feared his belligerence exhibited in the Corfu Crisis (q.v.) of 1923, his propensity
to take sides simplistically, as in his blanket espousal of peace treaty revisionism in
a notorious speech of 1928, and his conspiratorial nature, which led him to employ
secret diplomatic agents behind the back of his ambassadors. It was distaste for this
Fascist style of diplomacy, rather than its content, which in 1926 drove Salvatore
Contarini (q.v.), secretary general of the Foreign Ministry and dean of the
professionals, to resign. Contarini's departure was followed soon by the abolition
of the old guard's command post within the Palazzo Chigi—the secretary-generalship
itself. This all seemed to pave the way for the ascendency of Dino Grandi (q.v.),
appointed undersecretary of foreign affairs in 1925 and foreign minister in 1929.
Grandi was ostensibly Mussolini's man, chosen to bring the foreign ministry to
heel. Yet it was Contarini who had brought Grandi into the Palazzo Chigi,
deeming him "malleable." Grandi did prove astonishingly receptive to the professionals' tutelage. Indeed, his dismissal in 1932 came about because Mussolini now
adjudged him insufficiently Fascist and too Anglophile.

Partly through the intermediacy of Grandi, then, the modus vivendi between the
Palazzo Chigi and Fascism endured into the 1930s. But gradually the integrity and
influence of the Foreign Ministry were eroded. In 1924 a reform of recruitment and
promotion procedures was intended to open up a diplomatic career to talent instead

of birth, although, like other Fascist promises to democratize Italian life, there was more sound than substance to the changes. Naturally, new recruits tended to be the products of Fascist training and to fill the shoes of an old guard depleted by normal attrition as well as the occasional resignation. An ominous portent occurred in 1928 when the Foreign Ministry's entrance requirements were waived to allow the appointment of a number of Fascist party members to the consular corps. It was significant, too, that in 1932 several senior Italian diplomats were given new postings abroad, just as planning for the Ethiopian War began in Rome.

The end of the career diplomats' effective role in decision-making can be dated from June 11, 1936, when Galeazzo Ciano (q.v.) became foreign minister. Within a year Ciano would boast of having broken with the past to create a truly Fascist foreign policy. Certainly, Italy's international record during the last years of the Fascist era broke every precept of the traditionalists. Instead of friendship with Britain as the dominant naval power, the new Fascist foreign policy widened the gulf with Anglo-Saxon democracy that had been created by the Ethiopian crisis; instead of a circumspect fence-sitting in international quarrels, Mussolini enunciated the special Rome-Berlin Axis (see AXIS, ROME-BERLIN); instead of national interests conceived in narrow, materialist terms, Fascist diplomacy now swathed itself in the grandiloquence of a new Roman Empire and justified expensive intervention in Spain on ideological grounds. All this ambitious overcommitment resulted in the Anschluss (q.v.) of 1938, which placed German troops on the Brenner Pass; the Pact of Steel (q.v.) of 1939, which tied Italy to Nazi Germany in an offensive military pact; and ultimately the fatal lurch into war in June 1940. Needless to add, the functionaries of the Palazzo Chigi were given minimal roles to play in these events. They have been called shadows, since diplomatic business was funnelled through Ciano's cabinet staffed by party members, while policy was determined by the Duce's caprice.

Only fleetingly in these years was a career diplomat able to interpose any obstacle to the Fascist juggernaut. In August 1939 the ambassador in Berlin, Bernardo Attolico (q.v.), was instrumental in preventing Mussolini from joining in Hitler's war at the outset, although even this temporary success was due less to the Foreign Ministry than to Ciano, who belatedly urged caution on the Duce in dealing with Nazi Germany. For his efforts, Attolico was dismissed shortly after at the behest of the Germans. Ciano himself lost his post in February 1943 in a cabinet reshuffle induced by the total failure of Fascist foreign and military policy. Mussolini once more took over the Foreign Ministry with another Fascist, Giuseppe Bastianini (q.v.), as undersecretary. Much of Bastianini's time was expended in unavailing efforts to persuade Mussolini to cut his losses and make a separate peace. Contact was established between the Palazzo Chigi and the Allies, but the Foreign Ministry officials bided their time until the collapse of the Fascist regime in July 1943. Thereupon they threw in their lot with the king; only one diplomat of any prominence followed Mussolini to Salò (see ITALIAN SOCIAL REPUB-LIC). The survival and reemergence of the old guard was manifested in the appointment of Raffaele Guariglia (q.v.), a career diplomat of twenty years' standing, as foreign minister in Italy's first post-Fascist government.

Despite the years of Fascistization, the Foreign Ministry had succeeded in retaining a measure of self-identity. In this it provided a microcosm of the enduring Italian power structure at large.

For further information see: Luigi Ferraris, *L'amministrazione centrale del Ministero degli esteri* (Florence: Biblioteca della Rivista di studi politici internazionali, 1955); F. Gilbert, "Ciano and his Ambassadors," in Vol. 2, *The Diplomats*, eds. G.A. Craig and F. Gilbert (Princeton: Princeton University Press, 1953); Raffaele Guariglia, *Ricordi 1922-1946* (Naples: Edizioni scientifiche italiane, 1950); H. Stuart Hughes, "Early Diplomacy of Italian Fascism," in Vol. 1, *The Diplomats*, eds. G. A. Craig and F. Gilbert (Princeton: Princeton University Press, 1953).

AC

FORGES DAVANZATI, ROBERTO (b. Naples, February 23, 1880; d. Rome, 1936). A well-known Fascist publicist and political figure, Davanzati took a degree in law and began a career first as a syndicalist in 1906 and then as a leader of the Italian Nationalist Association (q.v.). He also fought in World War I. An active journalist, he cofounded and directed *Idea Nazionale* (Rome) and then directed *La Tribuna* (Rome). Although he opposed the Nationalist fusion with Fascism in 1923, he held numerous posts in the Fascist regime: he was secretary of the PNF's (Partito Nazionale Fascista) (q.v.) provisional Direttorio in 1924, a member of the Fascist Grand Council (q.v.), president of the Society of Authors and Publishers, and a member of numerous cultural organizations. He was made a senator in 1934. In 1933 he created one of the most popular radio programs of the period, "Cronache del Regime," which he hosted during the Ethiopian War (q.v.) until his death.

For further information see: *Chi è?* (1936); DSPI; NO (1928); Philip V. Cannistraro, *La fabbrica del consenso* (Rome-Bari: Laterza, 1975).

PVC

FORTUNATO, GIUSTINO (b. Rionero in Vulture, Potenza, 1848; d. Naples, July 23, 1932). A political writer and anti-Fascist, Fortunato was a deputy from 1880 to 1909, when he was made a senator. During the governments of Francesco Crispi (1889-91, 1893-96) and Luigi Pelloux (1899-1900) Fortunato defended free speech and civil liberties against government repression, and later he and Benedetto Croce (q.v.) were leaders of the Liberal democratic movement. Fortunato was especially interested in the problems of southern Italy and steadfastly defended southern Italians from the charges that they were inferior. He argued that the backward condition of the south was the result of the government's protectionist policies and the system of clientele politics. After Mussolini came to power Fortunato helped to reorganize the Liberal party (q.v.) in 1925 and wrote *Nel regime fascista* (1927), a valiant attack against Mussolini's government.

For further information see: EAR (2); E. Gentile, ed., *Carteggio di G. Fortunato*, 2 vols. (Bari-Rome: Laterza, 1975).

MSF

FORZANO, GIOVACCHINO (b. Florence, November 19, 1884). A playwright and Fascist supporter, Forzano originally studied medicine but then decided on a career in journalism. In Florence he founded the journal *Cirano* and later edited *La Nazione*. Prior to the Fascist era, Forzano wrote numerous novels, plays, and operettas. He supported the Fascist regime through his work, and it is believed that some of his plays in this period were inspired and partially written by Mussolini. In 1933 Forzano wrote and directed the film *Camicia nera*, an achievement regarded as his most important contribution to the Fascist state. He adhered to the Salò Republic (*see* ITALIAN SOCIAL REPUBLIC) in 1943.

For further information see: *Chi è?* (1948); Edward R. Tannenbaum, *The Fascist Experience* (New York: Basic Books, 1972).

MSF

FOSCHI, ITALO. A Fascist bureaucrat and prefect, Foschi was a lawyer by profession and had been a member of the Italian Nationalist Association (q.v.) since 1911 and secretary of the Rome section from 1918 to 1923. He was a volunteer in World War I, and with the fusion of the Nationalists in the PNF (Partito Nazionale Fascista) (q.v.) in 1923 he became secretary of the Rome *fascio*. In June 1924 Mussolini appointed him to the national directory of the PNF in an effort to built a moderate consensus in the party, but he was forced to resign as Rome secretary in October 1925 after the Fascists attacked the headquarters of the Freemasons.

In 1928 he was secretary of the *fascio* of Spezia and the next year his long career as a prefect began: Macerata (1929-31), Pola (1931-33), Taranto (1934-36), Treviso (1936-39), and Trento (1939-43). He adhered to the Salò Republic (*see* ITALIAN SOCIAL REPUBLIC) and held his last post as prefect of Belluno from November 1943 to April 25, 1945.

For further information see: NO (1928; 1937); Renzo De Felice, *Mussolini il fascista* (Turin: Einaudi, 1966); Adrian Lyttelton, *The Seizure of Power* (London: Weidenfeld and Nicolson, 1973).

PVC

FOUGIER, RINO CORSO (b. Bastia, Corsica, November 14, 1894; d. Rome, April 25, 1963). The last chief of staff of the regime's Air Force, General Fougier succeeded Francesco Pricolo (q.v.) on November 15, 1941, and served until July 1943. He had earlier commanded the air expeditionary force (Corpo Aereo Italiano) which joined the Luftwaffe bombardment of Britain from October 1940 to January 1941; the inadequacy of its equipment and crew training compelled its withdrawal.

MK

FOUR POWER PACT. Called the "Patto Mussolini" in the regime's propaganda, the Four Power Pact was the Duce's principal diplomatic initiative of 1933. He had foreshadowed it in his Turin speech of October 1932 and delivered a draft to the Germans, French, and British in mid-March 1933, after the Geneva Disarmament Conference produced a deadlock. The draft affirmed the desire of the four powers to collaborate in the spirit of earlier international agreements to contemplate peaceful revision of the World War I peace treaties, to accord Germany "equality of rights" in armaments, and to collaborate on colonial questions. The agreement was to run for ten years with automatic renewal. The Italian draft (in the words of Robert Vansittart of the British Foreign Office) "subsequently endured a diplomatic orgy of niggling metamorphoses, till everyone but the author was slightly sick of its six articles." The final version, from which the French banished overt references to revision and promises of "equality of rights," was meaningless enough to satisfy all. The powers initialed it in Rome on June 7 and signed it on July 15. Only Italy and Britain ratified it on (August 31 and September 16 respectively); Germany's dramatic exit from the Disarmament Conference and the League of Nations (October 14) revealed the Pact's hollowness and effectively killed it.

Diplomats and diplomatic historians have tended to see the Pact as a revival of the nineteenth-century great-power concert to deal with the breakdown of the League, which world depression, the Manchurian crisis, and Hitler's coming to power produced. Mussolini's aims, however, were not so conventional. He proposed the Pact less as a means of crisis management in the general interest and more as a way to avoid a French preventive war against Hitler, which would have placed Fascist Italy in an embarrassing position both diplomatically and ideologically. Thereafter Mussolini proposed to use the Pact to bypass the small League powers and tap National Socialist dynamism for Italian expansionist purposes, exploiting his position as Hitler's "tamer" to extort concessions from the West while diverting German energies from the Danube to the Polish corridor. Hitler's refusal to suffer the tutelage of France and Britain or of his fellow-dictator put Mussolini on notice that he would eventually have to choose between Germany and the West.

For further information see: Fulvio D'Amoja, *Declino e prima crisi dell'Europa di Versailles* (Milan: Giuffre, 1967); Giancarlo Giordana, *Il patto a quattro nella politica estera di Mussolini* (Corregio: Arnaldo Forni, 1976); Jens Petersen, *Hitler-Mussolini* (Tübigen: Niemayer, 1973).

MK

FRANCE, INVASION OF. The invasion of France by Italian forces in mid-June 1940, ordered by Mussolini solely to merit a share in Germany's victory, was a failure that demonstrated Italy's complete military unpreparedness.

No immediate hostilities on the part of Italy followed Mussolini's declaration of war against Britain and France on June 10, 1940. On June 15 Mussolini ordered an all-out attack against France, only to be told that such action would require twenty-five days preparation. Fearing a French collapse before his forces were in the field, Mussolini then ordered more limited offensive operations by the Italian armies along the Alpine frontier. Before the orders could be carried out, they were cancelled because of news that the French had requested armistice terms from the Germans.

Hitler and Mussolini met in Munich on June 18-19 to discuss the armistice. Hitler refused joint Italo-German negotiations with the French and Mussolini's demand for an Italian takeover of the French fleet. Returning to Rome, Mussolini once again ordered action by Italian forces. After further indecision, on June 21 the Fourth Army launched a frontal assault across the Little Saint Bernard Pass. On June 22 the First Army, with Nice its target, also attacked.

The result was almost total failure. Italian forward movement halted at the first sign of French resistance and made no dent in massive French fortifications. At most, Italian troops moved several miles into French territory, capturing only the border towns of Modane, Briançon, and Mentone. Italian casualties numbered 631 dead, 2,631 wounded and 1,141 taken prisoner. By comparison the French suffered only 37 dead and 42 wounded.

The reasons for the Italian military debacle were obvious. The military command lacked unity and was plagued by Mussolini's vacillation. Planning for the operation was virtually nonexistent. This was evidenced by the fact that Italy lost one-third of her merchant marine fleet when it was caught in foreign ports and that many of the Italian wounded were victims of frostbite caused by fighting in the Alpine snow in summer uniforms and cardboard boots.

Despite the Italian disaster, armistice talks began at Villa Incisa near Rome on June 23, and on June 24 the Italo-French armistice was signed. The truce called for the occupation of French territory then held by Italian forces and demilitarization of a fifty-mile area along Italy's European and North African borders with France. These were minimal demands, particularly in light of Mussolini's requirements expressed earlier to Hitler for Italian occupation of territory to the Rhone River and of Corsica, Tunisia, and France's North African naval bases and were prompted by the Italian army's poor showing.

For further information see: Giorgio Bocca, *Storia d'Italia nella guerra fascista* (Bari: Editori Laterza, 1969); Emilio Faldella, *L'Italia e la seconda guerra mondiale* (Rocca San Casciano: Cappelli, 1960); and Denis Mack Smith, *Mussolini's Roman Empire* (New York: The Viking Press, 1976).

MFL

FRASSATI, ALFREDO (b. Pollone, Vercelli, September 28, 1868; d. Turin, May 21, 1961). A journalist and politician, Frassati was the director of *La Stampa* (Turin) from 1900 to 1920, and supported the policies of Giovanni Giolitti (q.v.). Although he became a senator in 1913 and favored Italian participation in the war against Libya, he rejected intervention in World War I. From 1920 to 1922 he was ambassador to Berlin but was dismissed by Mussolini because of his anti-Fascist attitudes. In 1926 he was finally forced to relinquish his controlling interest in *La Stampa* and withdrew from journalism. From 1930 to 1943 Frassati directed the industrial combine, Italiana Gas, a position he held even after the war. After 1945 he returned to work for *La Stampa* and was a member of the Senate.

For further information see: EAR (2); Luciana Frassati, *Alfredo Frassati* (Rome: Edizione di Storia e Letteratura, 1978).

MSF

FREDDI, LUIGI (b. Milan, June 12, 1895). A Fascist squad leader and cultural bureaucrat, Freddi was self-educated. In his youth he flirted with nationalism and was a follower of F. T. Marinetti (q.v.). He became a fervent interventionist in 1914 and was arrested for participating in violent demonstrations. In 1915 he joined the staff of Mussolini's *Il Popolo d'Italia* for which he later was an editor (1920-22). Freddi fought as a volunteer in World War I and in March 1919 joined the Fascist movement.

In 1919 Freddi organized a Blackshirt squad (*see* SQUADRISTI) outside of Milan, led a number of particularly bloody attacks against Socialists, and was arrested for the outbreak of a serious incident in Lodi. He was briefly a D'Annunzian (*see* D'ANNUNZIO, GABRIELE) legionnaire in Fiume (q.v.) in 1920. In the same year he founded the Fascist youth organization, Avanguardie Giovanili, and became its secretary and director of its newspaper, *Giovinezza* (Milan). He was a member of the PNF (Partito Nazionale Fascista) (q.v.) executive committee (a provisional *direttorio*) in 1923-24 and was head of the PNF press office in 1922. In 1927 he became vice-secretary of the Fasci all'Estero (q.v.). Freddi's most important contribution, however, was as director of the Direzione Generale per la Cinematografia in the Ministry of Popular Culture (q.v.), a position he held from 1934 to 1940. In this capacity he organized the Italian cinema (q.v.) under government control and turned the cinema into a valuable propaganda and cultural arm of the regime. His goal of creating a genuine state cinema was frustrated by Mussolini, and in 1940 he founded and was president of Cinecittà, a modern film studio that was ultimately taken over by the regime and still functions today.

For further information see: *Chi è?* (1936); NO (1937); Luigi Freddi, *Il Cinema* 2 vols. (Rome: Arnia, 1949); Philip V. Cannistraro, *La fabbrica del consenso* (Rome-Bari: Laterza, 1975).

PVC

FREE ITALY. The term "Free Italy" (or "Italia Libera") represents a number of autonomous groups formed by Italian anti-Fascist exiles around the globe in the general attempt to defeat Mussolini and to shape postwar Italy. The various proponents of "Free Italy" generally agreed on the need for a form of government-in-exile.

The Free Italy movement was born amid the dispersion of Italian political activists in the interwar period. Although never a dominant position, sentiments in favor of a government-in-exile existed within the Giustizia e Libertà (*see* ANTI-FASCISM) group in Paris and—with the Nazi invasion of France—spread with the exiles to Switzerland, Mexico, the United States, and England. Mussolini's entry into the war induced the British to encourage moderate anti-Fascist groups including the "Free Italy" and "Italia Libera" groups in Algeria, Morocco, Tunisia, Egypt, South Africa, Australia, South America (Chile, Argentina, Ecuador, Venezuela, Colombia, Paraguay, and Peru) and Canada (Montreal and Toronto). The British recognized and subsidized a nascent Free Italy Committee under the direction of Carlo Petrone, an obscure Catholic monarchist. But in 1941 Paolo and Piero Treves (*see* TREVES, PAOLO) led a factional revolt by Republicans markedly to the left of Petrone and in July reorganized as the Free Italy Movement. As a result the British withdrew their subsidy and adopted a policy of benign neglect.

In 1941 the impetus of the Free Italy organization moved from London to New York, where it was supported by some members of the Mazzini Society (q.v.), most notably Carlo Sforza (q.v.). The attack on Pearl Harbor provoked an interest in "free" movements, and for over a year the U.S. State Department gave the idea a sympathetic hearing. President Roosevelt finally dropped the idea in response to the objections of the British authorities and the U.S. War Department. The hopes of Sforza and others for recognition of a Free Italy were finally laid to rest when on September 3, 1943 the Allies signed an armistice with King Victor Emmanuel III (q.v.) and Marshal Pietro Badoglio (q.v.).

For further information see: Charles F. Delzell, *Mussolini's Enemies: The Italian Anti-Fascist Resistance* (Princeton: Princeton University Press, 1961).

CLK

FRUSCI, LUIGI (b. January 16, 1879). A colonial general and governor, Frusci served in Eritrea from 1917 to 1927, headed the Colonial Ministry's military office from 1927 to 1929, and was commander in Somalia from 1929 to 1932. Frusci returned to Somalia (January 1935-October 1936) leading the native corps under Rodolfo Graziani (q.v.). Later Frusci served in Spain as division commander from May 1937 to June 1938. After commanding the Twentieth Corps in Libya, Frusci became governor of Amhara in January 1939, gaining limited success against the guerrillas. Appointed military commander of northern Ethiopia in June 1940, Frusci faced widespread rebellion when his forces invaded the Sudan. Frusci responded indecisively to British counterattacks after January 1941, though his subordinates resisted heroically at Keren (q.v.). Abandoning Asmara in April, Frusci joined the viceroy at Amba Alagi to surrender in May.

For further information see: Emilio Canevari, *La guerra italiana* (Rome: Tosi, 1948); Luigi Frusci, *In Somalia sul fronte meridionale* (Bologna: Capelli, 1936).

BRS

FUORUSCITI. The *fuorusciti* were anti-Fascist political exiles from a broad spectrum of parties and ideologies who relocated in the diaspora of the Fascist era. Of medieval origin, the term *fuorusciti* was reintroduced as a contemptuous epithet by the Fascists. Although criticized as ineffectual escapists by some Liberal and Catholic "quietists" who chose to remain in Italy, the *fuorusciti* developed a sense of identity and pride forged by both the hardships and the common political commitment they shared.

Two notable political exiles, the former premier F. S. Nitti (q.v.) and the Popolari (*see* PARTITO POPOLARE ITALIANO) leader Don Luigi Sturzo (q.v.), had left Italy earlier, but as Mussolini's repression intensified after January 1925, political emigration accelerated. Giovanni Amendola (q.v.), the Aventine leader, and journalist Piero Gobetti (q.v.) fled to France, as did *Il Popolo* editor Giuseppe Donati (q.v.) and Florentine professor Gaetano Salvemini (q.v.), two of the thirteen *fuorusciti* deprived of Italian citizenship and property in 1926. In the face of the ban against political parties and the failure of the king to oppose Mussolini, many others relinquished any hope of successful opposition within Italy. Those who left for France in 1926 and 1927 included Alberto Cianca (q.v.), Giuseppe Modigliani (q.v.), Pietro Nenni (q.v.), Randolfo Pacciardi (q.v.), Egidio Reale (q.v.), Giuseppe Saragat (q.v.), Carlo Sforza (q.v.), Alberto Tarchiani (q.v.), and Filippo Turati (q.v.).

Outside Italy the *fuorusciti* both adhered to old party allegiances and attempted to create supraparty structures. The Communist, Socialist, and Republican exiles reorganized their parties in Paris. And in 1927 Socialists and Republicans created the Anti-Fascist Concentration (*see* ANTI-FASCISM) which gathered regularly at Turati's Paris home and published the weekly *La Libertà*. Dissatisfied with the existing groupings, and in disagreement with the passive methods of the Concentration, a number of Republicans and Democratic Socialists—including Ernesto Rossi (q.v.), Ferruccio Parri (q.v.), Riccardo Bauer (q.v.), Emilio Lussu (q.v.), Salvemini, Tarchiani, and the wealthy young Florentine Jew Carlo Rosselli (q.v.)—formed Giustizia e Libertà (*see* ANTI-FASCISM). Led by the brilliant Rosselli, the *giellisti* engaged in audacious deeds to propagandize Fascist repression and to support opposition within Italy. After Rosselli's assassination by Fascist agents in 1937, Giustizia e Libertà declined rapidly.

The Spanish Civil War (q.v.) heightened ideological disagreement among the *fuorusciti*. The *giellisti* and the Italian anarchists formed the Italian ("Rosselli") Legion, which fought in support of the Catalan anarcho-syndicalists. Meanwhile the Italian Social-Communists, operating under the popular front strategy, formed the Garibaldi Battalion in support of the loyalists, entrusting leadership to the non-Marxist Republican, Randolfo Pacciardi. Thousands of *fuorusciti* fought in Spain, the survivors gaining experience in guerrilla tactics that proved useful during the Armed Resistance (q.v.).

The final phase of migration began with the passage of anti-Semitic laws (q.v.) and continued through the fall of France. Many Communists and their Socialist collaborators in the popular front in France were arrested, interned, and extradited to Italy where they were imprisoned. The *fuorusciti* who escaped France dispersed to England, Switzerland, Egypt, Mexico, South America, and the United States.

By 1940 New York had become the center of activity among the *fuorusciti*. Salvemini, Sforza, Max Ascoli (q.v.), Giuseppe Borgese (q.v.), and others founded the Mazzini Society (q.v.) to develop a program of anti-Fascist propaganda and moral protest that they hoped would influence Allied policy on the "Italian question." They largely failed to win popular following, and their split on the issue of support for American policy marked the last hope for a consolidated anti-Fascism among the *fuorusciti*.

A number of *fuorusciti* returned home by joining the Allied invasion of Italy, including Tarchiani, Cianca, Sforza, Aldo Garosci (q.v.), Leo Valiani, and PCI (Partito Comunista Italiano) (q.v.) leader Palmiro Togliatti (q.v.). Several, including Tarchiani and Sforza, joined the first postwar governments. But for most of the exiles, the experience had been long and difficult and the ultimate rewards, few. For most the satisfaction with the results of the 1946 institutional referendum (*see* REFERENDUM OF 1946) was offset by their disillusionment with the rise of forces they believed had abetted Fascism.

For further information see: Aldo Garosci, *Storia dei fuorusciti* (Bari: Laterza, 1953); Vera Modigliani, *Esilio* (Milan: Feltrinelli; 1946); Massimo Salvadori, *Resistenza ed azione* (Bari: Laterza, 1951); Gaetano Salvemini, *Memorie di un fuoruscito* (Milan: Feltrinelli, 1960).

CLK

FUTURISM. The first major Italian arts movement of the twentieth century, Futurism was the product of F. T. Marinetti (q.v.), who issued his famous "Futurist Manifesto" on February 2, 1909. He called for the violent rejection of the historical and cultural past and the celebration of modern life as manifested in the Industrial Revolution. Assuming purposefully dramatic postures, Marinetti urged the destruction of museums, academies, and libraries; the exploits of his early followers were deliberately meant to shock the bourgeois public. This rebellion against traditional rules and themes in the arts and literature was intended to make culture more responsive to modern society.

In calling for the overthrow of the past, Futurism advocated violence ("anarchy") as a necessary ingredient of change. Futurist works focused on the theme of speed and dynamic motion and set forth the first machine aesthetic. Part of a wider European revolution in the arts, Futurism must be seen in the context of such movements as Fauvism, Cubism, and Expressionism, although each had its own theoretical concerns. By 1912 Futurism had influenced all of Europe and had become one of the dominant styles in Italian painting, sculpture, architecture, theater, and literature.

Members of the original Futurist group included Carlo Carrà (q.v.), Umberto Boccioni, Giacomo Balla (q.v.), Luigi Russolo, Gino Severini, and Antonio

Sant'Elia. Some of its major advocates perished in World War I, and by the end of the war the movement had virtually died out. The so-called "second Futurism" of the 1920s lacked the originality of the earlier experience and represented a modern style frequently employed by second-rate artists for political or commercial purposes. Important figures like Carrà and Severini had left the movement and gone on to other styles, and although Marinetti attempted to resurrect Futurism in 1926-29 in new, abstract forms called "Aeropittura" (aerial painting) and "Aeropoesia" (aerial poetry), the movement was giving way to new cultural ideas.

In 1919, when the Fasci di Combattimento were founded, Marinetti joined with Mussolini in a political enterprise that exhibited a number of common characteristics, especially a generic radical orientation and a growing concern for cultural nationalism. Mussolini welcomed the cultural prestige that Marinetti brought to Fascism, but over the next twenty years Futurism and Fascism grew further apart rather than closer together.

For further information see: Peter R. Banham, *Theory and Design of the First Machine Age* (London and New York: Praeger, 1960); Enrico Crispolti, *Il mito della macchina e altri temi del futurismo* (Rome: Celebes, 1969).

JH

G

GABBA, MELCHIADE (b. Milan, August 20, 1874). A colonial general and staff officer, Gabba served as commander in Eritrea from 1921 to 1927 and as Prince Umberto's (*see* UMBERTO II) adjutant from 1932 to 1935. Initially against the Ethiopian War (q.v.), Gabba became Emilio De Bono's (q.v.) Chief of Staff in March 1935 and was retained by Pietro Badoglio (q.v.). With Alessandro Lessona (q.v.) Gabba prepared Mussolini's abortive proposal for partitioning Ethiopia in April 1936. Rodolfo Graziani's (q.v.) Chief of Staff from May to July 1936, then Third Army commander until August 1938, in March 1939 Gabba became a senator. His knowledge of Ethiopia and military planning contributed greatly to Italian victory.

For further information see: NO (1937).

BRS

GALBIATI, ENZO (b. Monza, May 25, 1897). The last Fascist commander of the Militia (q.v.), and a squadrist (*see* SQUADRISTI) leader from 1919, Galbiati's Fascist crimes brought him eleven months imprisonment. In October 1922 during the March on Rome (q.v.), Galbiati's Monza squads guarded Mussolini at *Il Popolo d'Italia* offices in Milan. With Aldo Tarabella, a Blackshirt leader, Galbiati led the consuls to Mussolini on December 31, 1924, demanding he crush the opposition or the Militia would act. For this and other indiscipline Mussolini expelled Galbiati from the Militia and PNF (Partito Nazionale Fascista) (q.v.) in the summer of 1925. However, Mussolini rehabilitated him in 1926. Galbiati subsequently served as MVSN (Milizia Volontaria per la Sicurezza Nazionale) commander in Perugia, Varese, and Turin. In 1933 he became Rome's Militia group commander. During the Ethiopian War (q.v.), Galbiati was seriously wounded while leading the "Vittorio Veneto" Legion. After recovery he was inspector of the university Militia. Galbiati commanded Blackshirt units in the Alpine and Greek campaigns. Mussolini appointed him MVSN Chief of Staff on May 25, 1941. That autumn Galbiati created the "M Battalions" for security duties, but military exigencies and Mussolini's orders sent them to war. By late 1942 Galbiati sensed growing internal unrest. He had obtained German aid to form the "M Division" to protect Mussolini, but it was unready by July 1943. Galbiati also failed to gain Carlo Scorza's (q.v.) cooperation. Galbiati supported Mussolini at the final Grand Council (q.v.) meeting, but quietly surrendered the Militia on July 26 and was arrested in August. Freed by the Germans, Galbiati rallied to Mussolini but received no new position.

For further information see: F. W. Deakin, *The Brutal Friendship* (New York: Harper & Row, 1962); Enzo Galbiati, *Il 25 luglio e la MVSN* (Milan: Bernabo, 1950).

BRS

GAMBARA, GASTONE (b. Imola, December 10, 1895; d. Rome, February 28, 1962). Ciano's chief military confidant and a favorite of Mussolini's, Gambara served with the Alpini in World War I, in the Libyan pacification, and as Ettore Bastico's (q.v.) divisional chief of staff in Ethiopia. He made his name in Spain as chief of staff of the Italian expeditionary force under Bastico. With G. Ciano's (q.v.) support he supplanted Bastico's successor, Mario Berti (q.v.), in October 1938 in time to lead the final campaign in Catalonia and remained on in Spain as ambassador until recalled in early May 1940 to command the breakthrough force in a proposed attack on Yugoslavia. Pietro Badoglio (q.v.) succeeded in relegating Gambara to a corps on the Riviera; there the general met with indifferent success in the brief French campaign.

Ciano's influence finally secured Gambara an active corps in Albania in February 1941, but the March offensive demanded by Mussolini and prepared by Ugo Cavallero (q.v.), Carlo Geloso (q.v.), and Gambara proved a bloody failure. However, Gambara had earned Cavallero's esteem and was soon in North Africa as chief of staff to Rodolfo Graziani's (q.v.) successors, Italo Gariboldi (q.v.) and Bastico, and as commander of the Italian mobile corps operating alongside Rommel, with whom Gambara repeatedly quarrelled. He also fell out with Cavallero, who removed him in March 1942, following insubordinate behavior and an embezzlement scandal among Gambara's subordinates (the general was not personally implicated).

After the 1943 armistice (q.v.), Gambara handed over Trieste to the Germans and subsequently rallied to Mussolini, serving as chief of staff of the Salò (*see* ITALIAN SOCIAL REPUBLIC) army until March 12, 1944, when the Duce removed him for excessive pessimism. Despite abject pleas and a belated request to join the party (January 1945), Gambara failed to secure new employment.

For further information see: *Corriere della Sera*, February 28, 1962.

MK

GANDOLFO, ASCLEPIA (b. Oneglia, Liguria, July 22, 1864; d. Rome, August 31, 1925). A Fascist general, Gandolfo was commander at Fiume (q.v.) in September 1919, secretly assisted Gabriele D'Annunzio (q.v.), then retired in 1920 to organize the Blackshirts (*see* SQUADRISTI), and stood unsuccessfully as a Fascist parliamentary candidate in May 1921. After helping direct the March on Rome (q.v.), Gandolfo became prefect of Cagliari in December 1922, absorbing the Sardinian Action party into the PNF (Partito Nazionale Fascista) (q.v.) and reducing autonomy tendencies. Mussolini appointed him MVSN (*see* MILITIA) commander on December 1, 1924. After January 3 Gandolfo's MVSN suppressed the opposition while he subdued rebellious Militia consuls on Mussolini's orders. Mussolini rejected Gandolfo's proposals to expand Militia powers.

For further information see: Renzo De Felice, *Mussolini il fascista* (Turin: Einaudi, 1966 and 1968); Adrian Lyttelton, *The Seizure of Power* (New York: Scribner's, 1973); Giorgio Rochat, *L'esercito italiano da Vittorio Veneto a Mussolini* (Bari: Laterza, 1967).

BRS

GARIBALDI, ALLEANZA INTERNAZIONALE. An anti-Fascist organization established in Mexico City in November 1941, its founders included a wide array of exiles from all political parties, but the group was dominated by Communists. The central committee of the Alleanza was headed by Francesco Frola and Mario Montagnana, and Ambrogio Donini (q.v.) represented them in New York. The group had been established in opposition to the Mazzini Society (q.v.), which refused to accept Communists, at the same time that an agreement for unity of action had been reached in Paris among leaders of the Socialist and Communist parties and Giustizia e Libertà. Its program called for combined action against the Axis (*see* AXIS, ROME-BERLIN) and the creation of a democratic government in Italy after the war, the formation of a Comitato Nazionale in exile representing all parties, and direct action in Italy and abroad.

For further information see: EAR (1); Charles F. Delzell, *Mussolini's Enemies* (Princeton: Princeton University Press, 1961); Aldo Garosci, *Storia dei fuorusciti* (Bari: Laterza, 1953).

PVC

GARIBOLDI, ITALO (b. Lodi, April 20, 1879; d. Rome, February 9, 1970). A governor of Libya and later an ARMIR (Armata Italiana in Russia) commander, Gariboldi led the "Sabauda" Division in Ethiopia and directed the motorized column that seized Addis. After being Rodolfo Graziani's (q.v.) chief of staff (July 1936-December 1937), Gariboldi received command of the Trieste Corps in June 1938 and of the Fifth Army facing Tunisia in September 1939. Gariboldi took temporary command of the Tenth Army between November and December of 1940 and suffered the initial defeat before Mario Berti's (q.v.) return from sick leave. Nonetheless, Gariboldi replaced Rodolfo Graziani in February 1941 until Ugo Cavallero (q.v.) removed him in July for inept dealings with Rommel. After nine months staff duty Gariboldi became Italian commander in Russia (*see* RUSSIA, ITALIAN FORCES IN), apparently for seniority reasons alone, arriving there in July 1942. Lacking equipment and crippled by Gariboldi's shortcomings, the Italians were crushed by the Soviet Stalingrad offensive. Gariboldi led the survivors home in March 1943. The Germans arrested Gariboldi in September 1943. The Special Tribunal for the Defense of the State (q.v.) sentenced him to ten years imprisonment for dereliction in January 1944.

For further information see: Ufficio storico dell'Esercito, *L'opera dell'esercito*, III-VI (Rome: Istituto Poligrafico dello Stato, 1949-74).

BRS

GAROSCI, ALDO (b. Meana di Susa, Turin, August 13, 1907). An active participant in Giustizia e Libertà (GL) (*see* ANTI-FASCISM) and in the Partito d'Azione (q.v.), Garosci ultimately became the most persistent historian of the exiled resistance. As a law student at the University of Turin he led a student demonstration against the government's promulgation of the ecclesiastical laws of

1926. Four years later he and Mario Andreis organized the Turin chapter of Giustizia e Libertà and produced the clandestine periodical *Voci d'Officina*. In 1932 Garosci escaped to Paris, where he began to collaborate with Carlo Rosselli (q.v.) in the weekly *Giustizia e Libertà* and to act as corresponding secretary for GL. While serving as a volunteer in the Rosselli column in the Spanish Civil War (q.v.), Garosci was wounded in combat. He returned to France, where he supported Rosselli and remained a Social Democrat through the decline of GL and the assassination of Rosselli.

When the Nazis invaded France in 1940, Garosci joined the last wave of exiles in their escape to the United States. There he worked with Gaetano Salvemini (q.v.) and others in producing anti-Fascist propaganda, particularly in editing— with Bruno Zevi, Enzo Tagliacozzo, and Renato Poggioli—the *Quaderni Italiani*.

In September 1943 Garosci returned to Italy, where he participated in the war of liberation as a leader of the Partito d'Azione. He joined the Allied forces during the Salerno landing (q.v.) and in the Anzio (q.v.) offensive of January 1944. After the fall of the Partito d'Azione Garosci served as a director of the daily *L'Italia Socialista* and contributed to *Il Mondo*. After the war he obtained the chair of modern history at the University of Turin and published his major works on anti-Fascism, which remain definitive sources.

For further information see: Aldo Garosci, *Vita di Carlo Rosselli* (Florence: Vallecchi, 1973); Aldo Garosci, *Storia dei fuorusciti* (Bari: Laterza 1953).

CLK

GASPARRI, CARDINAL PIETRO (b. Ussita, Macerata, May 5, 1852; d. Rome, November 18, 1934). Papal secretary of state from 1914 to 1931, and chief Vatican negotiator for the Lateran Pact (q.v.), Gasparri had risen in the Church hierarchy from humble origins. A brilliant student, he taught in Paris at the Institut Catholique for twenty years before being sent to Latin America as apostolic delegate. In 1901 he returned to Rome as secretary of the Congregation for Extraordinary Ecclesiastical Affairs. He was made a cardinal in 1907, and Pope Benedict XV appointed him secretary of state in 1914.

Gasparri tended to associate with the progressive elements in the Vatican, but in 1919 he was alarmed over the Italian political situation—particularly the dramatic rise of the Socialist party. When Don Luigi Sturzo (q.v.) proposed the formation of the Italian Popular Party (*see* PARTITO POPOLARE ITALIANO), Gasparri endorsed it. Nevertheless, over the next several years his dislike of the Popolari grew steadily, and when in 1924 the Fascists endangered Sturzo's life, the cardinal welcomed the opportunity to send him to London and bring about the dissolution of the party.

Gasparri had long desired to arrange a settlement of the "Roman Question" with the Italian government, and therefore welcomed Mussolini's overtures. Gasparri proved to be a cautious and able negotiator in the long discussions that led to the

Lateran Pact that he and Mussolini signed in 1929. He was especially insistent on obtaining recognition for the pope's sovereignty over the Vatican City.

For further information see: A. Martini, *Studi sulla questione romana e la conciliazione* (Rome: 5 Lune, 1963); Giovanni Spadolini, "Il Cardinale Gasparri e la questione romana," *Nuova Antologia* (October 1971); F. M. Taliani, *Vita del cardinale Gasparri* (Milan: Mondadori, 1938).

PVC

GAVIGNIN, ANTONIO (b. Venice, October 3, 1901). A political figure and anti-Fascist, Gavignin was self-educated and as a young man pursued a journalism career. He became a militant anti-Fascist and was a member of Giovane Italia, a forerunner of Giustizia e Libertà (q.v.). In 1929 Gavignin was sentenced to seven years imprisonment for his activities. After the liberation he edited *Il Gazzettino* in Venice and became a member of the Italian Socialist Party (*see* PARTITO SOCIALISTA ITALIANO). For a time he served as vice-mayor of Venice.

For further information see: A Gavignin, *Vent'anni di resistenza al fascismo* (Turin: Einaudi, 1957).

MSF

GAYDA, VIRGINIO (b. Rome, August 12, 1885; d. Rome, March 14, 1944). Mussolini's principal journalistic mouthpiece for almost twenty years, beginning in February 1921 Gayda served as managing editor of *Il Messaggero* (Rome), converting it (in his own words) "from the liberal-democratic paper it was into a lively and combative organ at the service of the Fascist movement," and defending the regime during the Corfu Crisis (q.v.) and Matteotti Crisis (q.v.). In 1926 Gayda took over *Il Giornale d'Italia* and made it into a major semi-official organ that, unlike much of the party press, appealed to and influenced well-informed middle-class opinion. Author of a never-ending deluge of propaganda works, Gayda was assiduous in justifying the regime's claims on Yugoslavia and France and adept at alternately vituperating Germany (1934) or celebrating the Axis (1936-43) and wooing Britain (1938) or demanding her destruction (1940). Mussolini dismissed him in early 1943. After the fall of the regime he took refuge in the Japanese embassy. U.S. bombing killed him in March 1944.

For further information see: NO (1937).

MK

GAZZERA, PIETRO (b. Bene Vagienna, Cuneo, December 11, 1879; d. Cirie, Turin, June 30, 1953). A war minister and colonial governor, Gazzera was Pietro Badoglio's (q.v.) protégé. He followed a rigidly conservative policy after becoming war undersecretary in November 1928 and war minister in September 1929, though he unsuccessfully attempted to modernize Army artillery. Dismissed when Mussolini became war minister, in July 1933 he was made a senator. Appointed governor of Galla and Sidama in August 1938, Gazzera faced persistent insurgency. After the British invasion of Southern Ethiopia in February 1941 Gazzera assumed the defensive to protect colonists and pin down enemy forces. Aided by weather and terrain, he resisted until July 1941, serving as acting governor general for six weeks.

For further information see: Emilio Canevari, *La guerra italiana* (Rome: Tosi, 1948); Pietro Gazzera, *Guerra senza speranza* (Rome: Tipografia Regionale, 1952).

BRS

GELOSO, CARLO (b. Palermo, August 20, 1879). A member of the PNF (Partito Nazionale Fascista) (q.v.) from 1921, General Geloso was one of the major war criminals whose extradition the Ethiopian government unsuccessfully sought after 1945. He served in Libya, in World War I and then in the Ministry of Colonies and on the Somali front in 1935-36. Governor-general of Galla-Sidamo province from June 1936, his methods drove the previously loyal Galla tribe to a revolt that he attempted to quell with "bloody repressions," which even Roberto Farinacci (q.v.) judged "often disproportionate and unjustified." Mussolini relieved him in July 1938.

Geloso succeeded Alfredo Guzzoni (q.v.) in December 1939 as commander of Italian forces in Albania, but in May-June 1940 G. Ciano (q.v.) apparently had him replaced by Visconti Prasca, when Geloso showed insufficient enthusiasm for the attack on Greece the foreign minister was promoting. Paradoxically, in July 1940 Geloso drafted a plan for just such an attack at the request of his close associate, Mario Roatta (q.v.); the draft subsequently evolved into the Army staff plan of October 1940. Geloso then commanded the Eleventh Army in the improvised Albanian winter campaign (November 1940-April 1941). He held the vital port of Valona, although the March offensive that he, U. Cavallero (q.v.), and G. Gambara (q.v.) prepared for Mussolini failed. Geloso subsequently served as military governor in Greece until May 1943. Surprisingly, he opposed anti-Jewish measures, and at one point ordered the Athens synagogue guarded against pro-German Greek students.

For further information see: NO (1937).

MK

GEMELLI, EDOARDO AGOSTINO (b. Milan, January 18, 1878; d. Milan, July 15, 1959). From a well-to-do family, Gemelli received a strongly lay education. After classical studies in Milan, he graduated in medicine from the University of Pavia in 1902. Experiencing a religious crisis, Gemelli entered the Franciscan order at Rezzato (Brescia) in November 1903 and was ordained in 1907. A man of action as well as culture, and a skillful administrator, in 1908 Gemelli founded the *Rivista di Filosofia Neoscolastica*, a journal designed to rally Italian Catholic culture against the positivism and the growing neo-idealism of Benedetto Croce (q.v.) and Giovanni Gentile (q.v.). In 1914 he also founded the journal *Vita e Pensiero*. His spirit of Catholic struggle against modernism was also reflected in his pamphlet, *Il Programma del Partito Popolare Italiano: Com'è e come dovrebbe essere* (1919), written with Filiberto Olgiati, in which Don Sturzo's (q.v.) Popular party (*see* PARTITO POPOLARE ITALIANO) was attacked for its lack of confessional emphasis. In 1921 he established the Università Cattolica del S. Cuore in Milan. As a Fascist sympathizer Gemelli saw in the Lateran Pact (q.v.) the means of effecting the triumph of Catholic culture. He supported the corporate state (*see* CORPORATIVISM AND THE CORPORA-TIVE STATE), the Ethiopian War (q.v.), and the Fascist intervention in the Spanish Civil War (q.v.). In a speech at the University of Bologna in 1939 Gemelli proclaimed his own anti-Semitism, receiving the admiration of Roberto Farinacci (q.v.).

He dedicated the last days of his life to psychological studies.

For further information see: *Agostino Gemelli francescano* (Milan: Vita e Pensiero, 1959); Giorgio Rumi, "Padre Gemelli e l'Università Cattolica," in Giuseppe Rossini, ed., *Modernismo, fascismo, comunismo* (Bologna: Il Mulino, 1972).

SR

GENTILE, GIOVANNI (b. Castelvetrano, Trapani, May 30, 1875; d. Florence, April 15, 1944). One of the most important philosophers in modern Italy and a major figure in the Fascist regime, Gentile took a degree in philosophy from the *Scuola normale* of Pisa in 1896. While undertaking a critical reappraisal of Kant and Hegel he also investigated the philosophical writings of Marx, and the latter reinforced his aversion toward materialism and naturalism. He collaborated with Benedetto Croce (q.v.) in the publication of *La Critica* for almost twenty years and became a leading proponent of Italian neoidealism, which he developed in an original manner as the theory of "actualism." Gentile later broke with Croce over deep ideological and political disagreements. He held the chair in philosophy at the University of Palermo, Pisa, and after 1917 at Rome.

Politically a right-wing Liberal, he moved toward nationalism and became active during the Interventionist Crisis (q.v.). Between 1914 and 1920 Gentile defined the fundamental elements of his political thought, especially his theory of the "ethical state": the state is the authority that represents the universality of all moral will and through which moral values become civil law. Self-realization can best be fulfilled through integration into society and into the nation (the state is the juridical embodiment of the nation). Hence, for Gentile Fascist totalitarianism (q.v.) offered the best possibility for the actualization of his essentially authoritarian views.

Gentile therefore became a convinced supporter of Fascism (although he did not formally join the PNF [Partito Nazionale Fascista] [q.v.] until June 1923) and its most authoritative ideologue. He was made a senator in November 1922 and served as minister of public instruction from October 1922 to July 1924, implementing a major educational reform (*see* EDUCATIONAL POLICIES). In September 1924 Mussolini appointed him head of the Commission of Fifteen (and in January 1925 to the Commission of Eighteen) for parliamentary reform (*see* PARLIA-MENT). In the aftermath of the Matteotti Crisis (q.v.), Gentile began to hope that the regime could be contained within the context of a constitutional-authoritarian state. This position resulted in the beginning of recurrent attacks against him by Fascist intransigents. A member of the Fascist Grand Council (q.v.) from 1923 to 1929, founder and president of the Istituto Nazionale di Cultura Fascista (q.v.), general editor (1926-44) of the Giovanni Treccani *Enciclopedia italiana* (q.v.), and director of the *Giornale critico della filosofia italiana*—all these positions made him the major arbiter of Fascist cultural policy in the 1920s.

From 1929 until June 1943 Gentile took no further active role in politics and was increasingly isolated within the regime. Nevertheless, his great intellectual prestige was a valuable asset to Mussolini and his philosophical theories served as ideological justifications for Fascism and the dictatorship (in April 1925 he had drafted the famous "Manifesto of Fascist Intellectuals" [*see* MANIFESTO OF ANTI-FASCIST INTELLECTUALS] as a cultural defense of Fascism). The 1932 article on Fascism in the *Enciclopedia* that appeared under Mussolini's name was clearly derived from Gentile's work—he in fact drafted sections of it—and reinforced the philosopher's image as the official thinker of the regime. But his attacks against the Lateran Pacts (q.v.) of 1929 and his condemnation of the pope's philosophical attitudes brought him severe criticism from clerical Fascists, and his works were placed on the papal Index.

Gentile emerged from political retirement with his Campidoglio speech of June 24, 1943—the so-called "Discorso agli italiani"—in which he called upon all Italians to rally behind Fascism in the moment of supreme national crisis. After a period of uncertainty he adhered to the Salò Republic (*see* ITALIAN SOCIAL REPUBLIC) and became president of the Royal Academy of Italy (q.v.) and director of *Nuova Antologia*. The most important intellectual to remain loyal to Mussolini, he became the target of partisan hatred. On April 15, 1944, Communist "Gappisti" (special partisan groups) shot and killed him in his automobile as he was entering his villa in Florence. While the Communist party accepted responsibility for the act, the Tuscan branch of the anti-Fascist coalition CLN—Comitato di Liberazione Nazionale (*see* COMMITTEE OF NATIONAL LIBERATION) disassociated itself from the assassination. Many anti-Fascist intellectuals deplored his death.

For further information see: Eugenio Garin, *Cronache della filosofia italiana* (Bari: Laterza, 1955); G. Gentile, *Guerra e fede* (Naples: Ricciardi, 1919); *Che cos'è il fascismo* (Florence: Vallecchi, 1925); *Fascismo e cultura* (Milan: Treves, 1928); *Giovanni Gentile: Vita e pensiero*, 9 vols. (Florence: Sansoni, 1948-61); A. James Gregor, *The Ideology of Fascism* (New York: Free Press, 1969); Henry S. Harris, *The Social Philosophy of Giovanni Gentile* (Urbana: University of Illinois Press, 1960).

PVC

GIANNINI, ALBERTO (b. Naples, 1885; d. Rome, 1952). An anti-Fascist journalist, Giannini was editor of *Il Messaggero* (Rome) and *Paese* (Rome) in 1922, and in 1924 together with Alberto Cianca (q.v.) he founded *Il Becco giallo*, a satirical, clandestine publication that was suppressed in 1926. Giannini went to Paris, where he directed *La Tribuna d'Italia* and then returned to Italy and switched loyalty to the Fascist regime. He then republished *Il Becco giallo* as a journal attacking the anti-Fascist exiles.

For further information see: DSPI; Alberto Giannini, *Memorie di un fesso* (Milan: Corbaccio, 1941).

PVC

GIARDINO, GAETANO (b. Monferrato, January 24, 1864; d. Turin, November 21, 1935). A victorious Fourth Army commander in June-November 1918, Giardino hoped Fascism would lead to military dictatorship and as military commander of central Italy encouraged the March on Rome (q.v.). He was governor of Fiume (q.v.) from September 1923 to January 1924, resigning to protest the annexation terms. Giardino attempted to succeed Mussolini in December 1924. Senate leadership of opposition to Antonino Di Giorgio's (q.v.) reforms was Giardino's last political success, though he received the rank of marshal in June 1926.

For further information see: Giorgio Rochat, *L'esercito italiano da Vittorio Veneto a Mussolini* (Bari: Laterza, 1967).

BRS

GIL (GIOVENTÙ ITALIANA DEL LITTORIO). See YOUTH ORGANIZATIONS.

GINI, CORRADO (b. Motta di Livenza, Treviso, May 23, 1884). A Fascist demographic expert, Gini attended the University of Bologna, where he later taught statistics, and then was a professor at the University of Cagliari and at Padua (he founded the *Istituto di statistica* at the latter).

During the Fascist regime Gini held numerous minor posts and represented Italy on foreign missions, including the 1925 war debts conference. He was a member of the famous Commission of Eighteen (1924-25) for the reform of Parliament (q.v.), but his most important influence was in the field of demographic policy (q.v.). He based his work on the research and writing that had been produced in France, and Mussolini read and admired his theories about the "old age" of nations. He also served as president of the Società Italiana di Genetica e Eugenica.

For further information see: *Chi è?* (1936); *Chi è?* (1948); NO (1937); Adrian Lyttelton, *The Seizure of Power* (London: Weidenfeld & Nicolson, 1973).

MSF

GINZBURG, LEONE (b. Odessa, April 4, 1909: d. Rome, February 5, 1944). An anti-Fascist intellectual, Ginzburg was born in Russia but became a naturalized Italian and lived in Turin, where he studied and taught modern literature at the university. During the Fascist era Ginzburg lost his teaching position when he refused to take an oath of loyalty to the regime. In 1934 he was arrested and imprisoned for his work with Giustizia e Libertà, but his prison sentence was shortened by an amnesty. Upon his release he resumed his anti-Fascist work and in 1940 was interned in a village in the Abruzzi region. After the fall of Fascism he became one of the organizers of the Party of Action (*see* PARTITO D'AZIONE) and the partisan group, Giustizia e Libertà. He also became director of the Action party's newspaper in Rome, *Italia libera*, but in November 1943 he was arrested by the police and sent to prison where he died.

For further information see: DSPI; EAR (2); *Scritti politici e letterari di Leone Ginzburg* (Turin: Einaudi, 1955).

MSF

GIOLITTI, GIOVANNI (b. Mondovì, October 27, 1842; d. Cavour, July 17, 1928). Prime minister of Italy from the turn of the century to World War I and perhaps the most important Italian statesman since Count Camillo di Cavour, Giolitti's political career has been the subject of much controversy. He took a law degree from the University of Turin in 1860 and entered government service. In 1882 he was elected to the Chamber of Deputies, appointed to the Consiglio di Stato, and then served as minister of the treasury under Prime Minister Francesco Crispi.

Giolitti became premier for the first time in May 1892, but he was forced to resign over a financial scandal involving the Bank of Rome in December 1893. He returned to the government in February 1901 as minister of interior under Giuseppe Zanardelli in the wake of the reactionary administrations of Antonio di Rudinì and Luigi Pelloux and the constitutional crises they had engendered. From November 1903 to March 1914 Giolitti virtually dominated Italian politics, whether as prime minister during three lengthy cabinets or in temporary "retirement," so that the entire period has come to be known as the "Giolittian era."

Giolitti proved to be a master politician, forging a solid majority out of the often confused Italian parliamentary spectrum and utilizing the prefectural system and patronage to sustain an intricate and often corrupt network of local clientele power bases (as a result of which Gaetano Salvemini [q.v.] dubbed him the "ministro della mala vita"). Yet his domestic policies encouraged industrial-economic development, and he presided over significant social and political reforms—including a wide extension of suffrage—that have led some scholars to speak of the period as "Italian democracy in the making." In addition, Giolitti was determined to relax the social-political tensions and the government repression of previous years; instead, he viewed the working-class and peasant struggles of the 1890s as symptoms of deep-seated injustices and economic backwardness and followed a policy of carefully tempered government "tolerance," in which social and economic protests were allowed to play themselves out "within the limits of the law," at least in comparison to events of the Crispi-di Rudinì-Pelloux period. He saw the moderate Socialists as the source of potential political support and as a means of controlling the working class and skillfully coopted ("constitutionalized") them into Parliament (q.v.) and the political system of the Liberal state.

Giolitti's foreign policy was geared to the maintenance of the Triple Alliance, but he held out the possibility of Italy's rapprochement with France. The rising strength of the Nationalist movement forced his hand in pushing Italy into war with Turkey over Libya in 1911-12, but he opposed Italian intervention in World War I. Nonetheless, despite his belief that Italy was unprepared for a major conflict, once it was clear that the king and the Liberal leadership were intent on war, he abandoned his opposition.

Giolitti made a political comeback following his famous Dronero speech of October 12, 1919, in which he criticized those responsible for the war and proposed a reform program designed to win support from the liberal right and the liberal left. He served as prime minister for the last time from June 1920 to July 1921, and in many ways he held the key to the postwar political situation. But while he was able to conclude the Treaty of Rapallo with Yugoslavia against Nationalist objections and successfully defused the "Occupation of the Factories" (q.v.) in September 1920 it was clear that Giolitti was a "prisoner of the past" and seriously misjudged both the revolutionary temper of postwar Italy and the nature of Fascism.

His attitude toward Fascism was ambiguous at best: after the May 1921 elections in which Fascists sat in Parliament for the first time, he characterized the movement as an example of "youthful exuberance," and believed—in the great, earlier tradition of Giolittian politics—that he could "tame" and "constitutionalize" them by legal representation in Parliament. Hence, rather than restrain their violence by force, he adopted a negative, noninterventionist policy that corresponded to his prewar method of governing. As a result of what A. William Salomone has called his "crypto-transformistic policies adopted in the face of rising fascism" (Angelo Tasca [q.v.] went so far as to call him the "John the Baptist" of Fascism), Giolitti was the major example of the Italian Liberal leadership whose shortsightedness and misjudgments did much to pave the way for the Fascist seizure of power (*see* LIBERAL PARTY).

Giolitti lived long enough to see the installation of Mussolini's dictatorship and to regret his mistakes. In 1923 he chaired a special parliamentary commission that approved the so-called "Acerbo Law" (*see* ACERBO, GIACOMO), by which the Fascists won control of the Chamber of Deputies. He refused to ally himself with Mussolini during the election that followed and was shocked by the Fascist violence. During the Matteotti Crisis (q.v.) in 1924 Giolitti refused to join the Aventine Secession (q.v.) of anti-Fascists and remained in Parliament, but in

November he formally withdrew his support from the government. His last political act, four months before his death, was to speak out in the Chamber against the 1928 Fascist electoral law.

For further information see: Gabriele De Rosa, ed., *Giolitti e il fascismo* (Rome: Cinque Lune, 1957); Giovanni Giolitti, *Memorie della mia vita*, 3rd ed. (Milan: Garzanti, 1945); A. William Salomone, *Italy in the Giolittian Era* (Philadelphia: University of Pennsylvania Press, 1960); Nino Valeri, *Da Giolitti a Mussolini* (Florence: Parenti, 1956).

PVC

GIULIANO, BALBINO (b. Fossano, January 4, 1879; d. Rome, 1958). A Fascist minister and professor, Giuliano began his career in 1919 as a Nationalist after serving in World War I. He went over to Fascism in 1923 and was elected a deputy the next year. Undersecretary of public instruction from July 1924 to January 1925 and minister of national education from September 1929 to July 1932, Giuliano was made a senator in 1934. During the 1930s he was also a professor of philosophy at the University of Rome.

A follower of Giovanni Gentile (q.v.), as minister of education he did little to change the character of Italian schools and universities. It was under his direction that the loyalty oath was forced on university professors (*see* UNIVERSITY OATH) and that the government began publishing its own textbooks and censoring others. In the late 1930s he held numerous cultural positions in the regime.

For further information see: *Chi è?* (1936); DSPI; NO (1937); Balbino Giuliano, *Elementi di cultura fascista* (Bologna: Zanichelli, 1929).

PVC

GIULIETTI, GIUSEPPE (b. Rimini, March 21, 1879; d. Rome, June 20, 1953). A syndicalist organizer and supporter of Gabriele D'Annunzio (q.v.), Giulietti was a sailor in his early days. In 1909 he began his political career by founding the Federazione Italiana dei Lavoratori del Mare to represent seamen. Under his tireless leadership the federation became quite strong, and its many successful strikes resulted in important benefits for its members.

An ardent interventionist, he associated with Mussolini in 1915, helping to gather funds for *Il Popolo d'Italia*. In 1915 he joined with Mussolini in establishing the Fascio di Azione Rivoluzionaria (q.v.), and later that year volunteered for naval service.

After the war Giulietti resumed his syndical organizing, but became an ardent follower of D'Annunzio after the latter's expedition to Fiume (q.v.). In October 1919 he led the highjacking of the *Persia*, an Italian cargo ship ladden with arms and munitions destined for the White Army in Russia, and delivered the equipment to D'Annunzio, thereby establishing a long relationship between the two men. In January 1920 he proposed that D'Annunzio lead a march on Rome.

His syndical ties and activities made him at first an enemy of the Fascists, and in September 1922 he was almost killed by a group of *squadristi* (q.v.). In October 1922 he signed an accord with Mussolini that guaranteed the existence of the seamen's federation. Two years later D'Annunzio renounced his support of Giulietti, and in 1926 he was arrested by the Fascists on charges of having misappropriated the federation's funds. He was exiled to Sardinia, where he remained under close observation, despite the fact that he was declared innocent. Forced by a lack of financial resources to appeal to Mussolini, he returned to Italy and was active in various propaganda activities for the regime.

After the fall of Fascism Giulietti resumed direction of the federation, and in 1948 he was elected a deputy for the Republican party (q.v.).

For further information see: MOI (2); Ferdinando Cordova, *Arditi e legionari dannunziani* (Padua: Marsilio, 1969); Michael A. Ledeen, *The First Duce* (Baltimore: Johns Hopkins, 1977).

MSF

GIUNTA, FRANCESCO (b. S. Piero, Siena, March 21, 1887; d. Rome, 1971). A parliamentary deputy and Fascist leader, Giunta practiced law in Florence before World War I. He volunteered for combat in 1915 and in 1919 organized the Associazione Nazionale dei Combattenti in Milan, for which he led raids against the Socialists. In that same year he established ties with Mussolini, who sent him to Venezia Giulia to assume control of the Fascist movement in that region. In November 1920 he cofounded *Il Popolo di Trieste*, which he directed for three years, and sparked an uprising in Venezia Giulia on behalf of Gabriele D'Annunzio's (q.v.) Fiume (q.v.) expedition. He was arrested for this action but quickly released. In 1921 he was a deputy from Trieste, a seat he held until 1939. In March 1922 Giunta led a small assault on Fiume, whose status was still uncertain, and forced the surrender of the local government.

During the March on Rome (q.v.) Giunta commanded a group of three thousand Blackshirts (*see* SQUADRISTI) and seized control of Trieste. In January 1923 he was secretary of the Fascist Grand Council (q.v.) and in October was made the political secretary of the provisional Direzione Nazionale of the PNF (Partito Nazionale Fascista) (q.v.). In April 1924, however, Mussolini and his closest associates decided that Giunta's leadership of the party stood in the way of Mussolini's control over Fascism, and he was dismissed. While he presided over the party Giunta was responsible for its growth and for numerous assaults against anti-Fascists. As vice-president of the Chamber of Deputies in 1924, he replied to Matteotti's (*see* MATTEOTTI CRISIS) accusations against Fascist illegalism. In December 1927 he was made undersecretary of state for the president of the Council of Ministers, a position he held until July 1932.

For further information see: *Chi è?* (1936); DSPI; NO (1928; 1937); Renzo De Felice, *Mussolini il fascista* (Turin: Einaudi, 1966); Adrian Lyttelton, *The Seizure of Power* (London: Weidenfeld and Nicolson, 1973).

MSF

GIURIATI, GIOVANNI (b. Venice, August 4, 1876; d. Rome, 1970). A Fascist political figure and minister, Giuriati took a degree in law and was an active leader of the "irredentist" movement, aimed at obtaining Austrian-controlled lands for Italy, and in 1913 he founded the "Trento and Trieste" association for that purpose. Giuriati was an interventionist in 1914-15, and a volunteer in World War I. In 1919 Giuriati joined Gabriele D'Annunzio's (q.v.) expedition to Fiume (q.v.) and served as his cabinet chief for four months.

In 1921 he was elected a deputy and joined the PNF (Partito Nazionale Fascista) (q.v.), led a number of *squadrista* (*see* SQUADRISTI) raids, and participated in the March on Rome (q.v.). In 1923 Mussolini appointed him minister of liberated lands, and from 1925 to 1929 he was minister of public works. Giuriati was president of the Chamber of Deputies from 1929 to 1934, after which he became a senator. He served as secretary of the PNF from October 1930 to December 1931 and attempted to follow Augusto Turati's (q.v.) policy of creating a small, select party.

A member of the Fascist Grand Council (q.v.), Giuriati voted against Mussolini in the July 1943 meeting and was condemned to death in absentia by the Verona tribunal (*see* VERONA TRIALS). After the war another court tried and absolved him of Fascist crimes.

For further information see: *Chi è?* (1936); DSPI; NO (1937); Michael A. Ledeen, *The First Duce* (Baltimore: Johns Hopkins, 1977).

PVC

GIUSTIZIA E LIBERTÀ. See **ANTI-FASCISM**.

GOBETTI, PIERO (b. Turin, June 19, 1901; d. Paris, February 15, 1926). A leading political and social thinker and anti-Fascist, Gobetti displayed great intellectual capacity as a young man and frequented the University of Turin. Inspired by Gaetano Salvemini (q.v.), he and a group of friends established the review *Energie Nuove* in Turin. In 1919 he helped organize the Fascio di educazione nazionale and was committed to the broadening of civil liberties, including proportional representation, the franchise for women, and reform of public administration. He was greatly influenced by the left-wing political developments in Turin, especially by the work of Antonio Gramsci (q.v.), with whom he became close friends. He was a literary critic for *L'Ordine Nuovo* for a time.

In February 1922 Gobetti published the first issue of his influential *Rivoluzione Liberale*. He had the support and cooperation of men from many different political positions, including Giovanni Amendola (q.v.), Luigi Einaudi (q.v.), Guido Dorso, and Luigi Salvatorelli (q.v.). *Rivoluzione Liberale* sought to involve the masses in the renovation of Italian political life. It assumed a staunch anti-Fascist position, and he was arrested in February 1923. After several arrests he opened a publishing house to issue important political and social studies and was under constant police observation. By 1924 he had come to realize that the working-class movement was the only hope for overthrowing Fascism. In June of that year his house was assaulted by *squadristi* (q.v.). After the Matteotti (*see* MATTEOTTI CRISIS) murder Gobetti called for Mussolini's resignation, and he supported the Aventine Secession (q.v.). He remained attached to the legalistic approach of the opposition and believed that the intellectual classes would assume the leadership of the working classes to restore a democratic government.

Gobetti became a prime target of the Fascists, and in September 1925 he was severely beaten by *squadristi*. The injuries he suffered resulted in his death the next year in Paris.

For further information see: P. Bagnoli, *Il risorgimento eretico di Piero Gobetti* (Florence: Cooperativa Universitaria, 1976); *Opere complete di Piero Gobetti* (Turin: Einaudi, 1969).

MSF

GONZAGA, PRINCE MAURIZIO (b. Venice, September 21, 1861; d. Rome, March 24, 1938). An Army general, Militia commandant, senator, Florence corps commander, and war hero, Gonzaga opposed Antonino Di Giorgio's (q.v.) reforms but supported Mussolini during the Matteotti Crisis (q.v.). After consulting the king and Armando Diaz (q.v.), he accepted command of the MVSN (*see* MILITIA) in September 1925. He and Luigi Federzoni (q.v.) proposed uniting the Militia and Army to discipline the former and politicize the latter. Mussolini, however, preferred an independent MVSN, and in September 1926 he dismissed Gonzaga and assumed Militia command himself. The king made Gonzaga Marquis of Vodice in December 1932 for his wartime exploits.

For further information see: NO (1937).

BRS

GOTHIC LINE. The third of the major World War II defensive positions set up by the Germans in their efforts to retard the northern advance of the Allied forces in Italy, the Gothic Line derived its name from a captured German map. Although later German maps named it the "Green Line," the Allies continued to use the earlier designation.

The line followed roughly the major mass of the Apennine Mountains as they spread out north of Florence. From the area of Massa and Carrara on the west coast it ran through Borgo a Mozzano, north to Pretta, then south again to Vernio, east to Casaglia, southeast through San Godenzo to Sevravalie, and swung in a semicircle through Valsavignone up to Pesaro. It was, therefore, not a straight east-west line but one which curved to take advantage of every physical obstacle. Almost 2,400 machine gun posts, 480 antitank, mortar, and assault gun positions, and over 120,000 meters of barbed wire bristled along this barrier, which was backed by crack and experienced German troops and six Italian divisions from Mussolini's Salò Republic (*see* ITALIAN SOCIAL REPUBLIC). But effective German air cover was lacking.

Originally Hitler had intended soon after the Allied landing at Salerno to pull all of his forces in Italy back to this defensive line. Albert Kesselring's (q.v.) stubborn resistance in southern Italy led Hitler to move reinforcements and materiel southward. The fighting at the so-called Winter Line and Gustav Line (q.v.) had already taken a heavy toll of both German and Allied forces before operations opened against the Gothic Line on August 25, 1944. The battles that followed were the most costly of the Italian campaign. The German line on the Adriatic was breached in October, but the Allied drive for Bologna met heavy resistance and had to be broken off late in December. This key city was not captured until April 21, 1945, marking the completion of preparations for the final drive into northern Italy. A week later SS General Karl Wolff (q.v.) signed the agreement surrendering German forces in Italy, but Kesselring, who had become Supreme Commander of the German forces in Western Europe, did not ratify this agreement until after the death of Hitler on May 1.

For further information see: Douglas Orgill, *The Gothic Line. The Italian Campaign, Autumn, 1944* (New York: W. W. Norton & Company, Inc., 1967); G. A. Shepperd, *The Italian Campaign, 1943-45. A Political and Military Reassessment* (New York: Praeger, 1968).

ERB

GRAMSCI, ANTONIO (b. Ales, Cagliari January 23, 1891; d. Rome, April 27, 1937). Gramsci was from a family of moderate means but observed the poverty of his native Sardinia firsthand as a child. In 1911 he won a scholarship and attended the University of Turin, where he studied under Luigi Einaudi (q.v.) and others. In Turin he joined the local Socialist party section and contributed to its newspaper. He later wrote a column for *Avanti!*, in addition to theater reviews. In 1917 Gramsci was elected secretary of the Turinese Socialist section.

Along with a number of friends who were to become major leaders of Italian communism—Palmiro Togliatti (q.v.), Angelo Tasca (q.v.), and Umberto Terracini (q.v.)—Gramsci founded *L'Ordine Nuovo*, a weekly review of Socialist culture. The journal, which would become a daily in 1921, discussed the important issues of the period, especially the possible transformation of the factory councils into an Italian version of the Soviet Councils. Gramsci criticized reformist gradualism and the failure of the Maximalist (*see* PARTITO SOCIALISTA ITALIANO) wing of the Socialist party, led by G. M. Serrati (q.v.), to take advantage of the revolutionary situation that he believed existed in Italy. Gramsci then helped constitute and lead the "Communist faction" within the Socialist party with the approval and support of the Third International and Lenin. At the 1921 Congress of Livorno, the Communists broke away from the Socialists and formed the Italian Communist party (*see* PARTITO COMUNISTA ITALIANO).

In 1922 Gramsci went to Moscow, where he met Lenin and participated in the labors of the Third International. He and his companion, Giulia Schucht, also had two children during this period. After a stay in Vienna in 1923, Gramsci moved to Rome in May 1924, having been elected to the Chamber of Deputies.

The three years from 1921 to 1924 were intense ones for Gramsci as he worked hard to create a cadre of leaders, to steer the Communist party away from the more extreme positions of Amadeo Bordiga (q.v.), and to obtain the blessing of the Third International, whose policies he frequently sought to modify. His writings are an invaluable source for the history of Italy during the period when Fascism was becoming dominant in Italy. Gramsci also was instrumental in founding *L'Unità* and in selecting the name, which recalled Gaetano Salvemini's (q.v.) old newspaper.

In 1924 and 1925 Gramsci participated in the national protest against the Matteotti murder (*see* MATTEOTTI CRISIS), which nearly toppled Mussolini. The Communist deputies, however, broke away from the Aventine (*see* AVENTINE SECESSION) and reentered the Chamber of Deputies, where Gramsci denounced Mussolini. Gramsci actively participated in the clandestine preparation of the Third Congress of the Communist party held in Lyons in 1926, which saw another duel between Gramsci and Bordiga. On November 8, 1926, the Fascists arrested Gramsci, who was eventually tried by the Fascist Special Tribunal (*see* SPECIAL TRIBUNAL FOR THE DEFENSE OF THE STATE) and sentenced to twenty years' imprisonment.

In delicate health even as a child, Gramsci suffered greatly during his imprisonment because of the unhealthy conditions. He came close to death several times, and the ordeal would ultimately kill him.

Although he had a very difficult time obtaining books and other materials, Gramsci wrote voluminously in prison. His prison correspondence has won him a place as one of the masters of that literary form, and his *Prison Notebooks*, smuggled out by Tatania Schucht, Giulia's sister, and partially published in a number of volumes, have established him as Italy's major Marxist philosopher and as a thinker of international stature. In addition to presenting his Marxism, Gramsci's *Prison Notebooks* range widely over the major problems of Italian culture and society and enunciate the main cultural themes debated in Italy after World War II.

Alarmed by Gramsci's deteriorating health, Tatania Schucht campaigned for his release. This activity led to the formation of an international committee that pressured the Fascist government. Gramsci was transferred from Turin to a prison hospital in Formia and then to Rome. His sentence was reduced, but he died three days after its expiration.

For further information see: John M. Cammett, *Antonio Gramsci and the Origins of Italian Communism* (Stanford, Calif.: Stanford University Press, 1967); Martin Clark, *Antonio Gramsci and the Revolution that Failed* (New Haven: Yale University Press, 1977); Giuseppe Fiori, *Antonio Gramsci* (New York: Dutton, 1971.

SD

GRANDI, DINO (b. Mordano, Bologna, June 4, 1895). One of the most important leaders of Fascism and a major figure in the formulation of Fascist foreign policy, Grandi was the son of a modest landowner of liberal-Mazzinian

ideas. A number of intellectual currents influenced his early development, including the ideas of Alfredo Oriani, Giuseppe Mazzini, Romolo Murri, Antonio
Fogazzaro, Andrea Costa, and the journal *La Voce* (Florence). After completing
classical studies he graduated with a degree in law. His first political experiences
came as a member of the Catholic Lega Democratica Nazionale (National Democratic League); his earliest journalistic experience was on the staff of the newspaper *Il Resto del Carlino*, where he was greatly influenced by Mario Missiroli
(q.v.). In November 1914 he joined the *Fasci di Azione Rivoluzionaria* (q.v.).
During the Interventionist Crisis, 1914-15 (q.v.), his major work was with the
nationalist-liberal weekly *L'Azione*, of which he was practically the editor in chief
for a time. During World War I he saw active service in the Alpine units, winning
several decorations for valor and reaching the rank of captain. Once demobilized,
he returned to Bologna, where he practiced journalism and law. He was also an
organizer for an independent trade union of clerks, for the anti-Giolittian (*see*
GIOLITTI, GIOVANNI) liberal group of Giovanni Borelli and Alberto Giovannini,
and for the Fascio delle Forze Economiche. He joined the Fascist movement—of
which he had been critical at first—only in September 1920, after an attempt had
been made on his life.

Grandi's career as a Fascist was extremely rapid. In the Fascio di Combattimento
(q.v.) of Bologna he emerged as the leader of the Mazzinian-syndicalist current
and director of the newspaper *L'Assalto*. At the first congress of the *fasci* of Emilia
and the Romagna (April 1921) he was appointed regional secretary and therefore
also became a member of the national directorate of the movement. The same year
he was elected a deputy to Parliament, but his election was invalidated because he
was under legal electoral age. The Pacification Pact (q.v.) between the Fascists
and the Socialists and Confederazione Generale del Lavoro (CGL) (q.v.) was the
cause of his first clash with Mussolini, who advocated the pact vigorously.
Grandi's position differed from that of the agrarian *squadristi* (q.v.) and was
dictated above all by his fear that the pact would be made at the expense of the
Fascist unions. Nevertheless, in July and August 1921 he became the major force
behind the opposition to Mussolini and created the impression of wanting to
challenge his leadership. The high point of the disagreement came at the congress
of the Po Valley Fascists who were opposed to the pact, held at Bologna on August
16. Grandi realized quickly, however, that it would not be possible to use the
popularity of Gabriele D'Annunzio (q.v.) to undermine Mussolini's position. Ten
days later, at the national Fascist congress in Milan, Grandi continued to oppose
the pact but assumed a middle ground between the extremist supporters of
Mussolini and the agrarian *squadristi* who were bitterly hostile to the pact. Behind
this position was his decision not to remain a prisoner of the hopeless, intransigent
policies of the *squadristi*, and his awareness that Fascism could not survive
without Mussolini.

Grandi accepted Mussolini's leadership in spite of a new source of disagreement
that arose between them: Mussolini's decision to transform the Fascist movement

into a party (*see* PARTITO NAZIONALE FASCISTA). Grandi believed that this move would compromise the future of Fascism, which he understood essentially as "the soul and conscience" of a new "national democracy" that was to cement the masses to the national state. Grandi argued this thesis in Rome on November 8, 1921 at the third national Fascist congress (see Grandi's *Le origini e la missione del fascismo* [Bologna: Cappelli, 1922]), but without breaking with Mussolini. In fact, the congress ended with a formal reconciliation and an agreement between the two men: Grandi, although voting against the creation of the party, did not push his opposition further and agreed to become a member of the new party directorate; Mussolini declared the Pacification Pact superseded by events and "buried."

In 1922 Grandi underwent an important change in two ways: he moved toward a moderate-legalitarian position vis-à-vis the earlier Fascist platform; and he concluded that Fascism, while a necessity for Italy in that historical moment, was a transitory phenomenon. The March on Rome (q.v.) saw him nominally chief of staff of the Quadrumvirs (q.v.), but he concentrated his activity in Rome—where he had made contacts with the royal court—in order to achieve a cabinet headed not by Mussolini but by either Antonio Salandra (q.v.) or, preferably, Vittorio E. Orlando (q.v.), with Fascist participation. These maneuvers provoked Mussolini's wrath and a period of political isolation that lasted until the 1924 elections. A formal inquiry into his political conduct, however, absolved him.

In the April 1924 parliamentary elections Grandi was reelected a deputy and was then chosen vice-president of the Chamber of Deputies. In June, with the outbreak of the Matteotti Crisis (q.v.), he sided completely with Mussolini, convinced of his personal innocence. Hence, he was included in the Fascist party directorate. When Mussolini was forced to relinquish the ministry of interior to Luigi Federzoni (q.v.), Grandi was also named undersecretary (July 5, 1924). According to the Fascist intransigents, he was supposed to keep the "untrustworthy" Federzoni under control; actually, however, the two men collaborated closely and Grandi fully supported Federzoni's action in keeping the extremist Fascists in check. Once Roberto Farinacci (q.v.) was made secretary of the Fascist party, Grandi was removed from the interior ministry and named undersecretary at the foreign ministry (May 14, 1925).

As undersecretary in the foreign ministry (*see* FOREIGN AFFAIRS, MINISTRY OF) Grandi's autonomy was extremely limited, for the major problems were handled directly by Mussolini. His principal task was actually to reorganize and "Fascisticize" the ministry and deal with a series of special questions, such as relations between the Fasci all'Estero (q.v.) and the ministry. In the second half of 1925 Grandi played a major part in overcoming Mussolini's reluctance to accept the logic of the Locarno conference (which Grandi always considered the high point of Mussolini's foreign policy and the point of reference from which not to deviate) and intervened personally in the signing of the subsequent accord.

On September 12, 1929, Mussolini appointed Grandi minister of foreign affairs. In that capacity he sought to give Fascist foreign policy that unity and consistency of goals and that realism of action that it had lacked. In this way he hoped to realize two basic goals: the end of French hegemony on the continent and the creation of a vast Italian colonial empire in Africa. This aim had to be achieved without a European war, which he believed Italy could not survive and which would be a general catastrophe that would benefit only communism. The natural scene for this policy was to be the League of Nations, through which Italy would pursue peace, disarmament, and the extension of the League to other countries (such as the Soviet Union) in order to weaken French hegemony and to create conditions in which Italian claims would be considered. For this purpose Italy would act as the "determining weight" between France and Germany, without prejudicing her autonomy and freedom of action vis-à-vis the other powers. This would make her the arbiter of the diplomatic situation. Grandi pushed hard in this direction (in June 1932 he even went so far as to endorse the Herbert Hoover plan for disarmament) and in 1931-32 there were signs that France might make colonial concessions to Italy.

Nevertheless, by early 1932 Grandi's policies were encountering growing difficulties: viewed with suspicion because of his excessively anti-French stance and because of a series of indiscrete actions in the internal affairs of Austria and Yugoslavia, he began to lose credibility in the chanceries of Europe. Moreover, many Fascists considered his policies too supportive of the League of Nations and insufficiently "Fascist." Finally, the growing success of the Nazis in Germany induced Mussolini to consider a more dynamic foreign policy and began to drive France and England closer together, a fact which made it difficult to extract substantial colonial concessions from Paris. These factors ultimately led Mussolini to reassume personal control of the ministry of foreign affairs on July 20, 1932.

Grandi was then named ambassador to London, a post he held until July 1939. The seven years he spent in London were of decisive importance in his personal and political evolution: in what was then the heart of world politics, and in close contact with the British ruling circles (with which he established lasting personal relations on the highest levels), he acquired a new awareness of international realities as well as of the effective possibilities (and the limits and risks) of Italian policy. As a result, he developed an increasingly critical attitude toward Mussolini's policies (especially after the conquest of Ethiopia and the formation of the Axis)—but an attitude that did not prevent him from remaining psychologically tied to Mussolini, whose presence at the head of the Fascist state he considered necessary and whose realism he hoped would prevent irreparable mistakes. Grandi's activity in London (in a strictly diplomatic sense, but also through contacts with political circles and the press) in support of Rome's policies was intense and, in the long run, quite fruitful. It was not unusual for him to go beyond the letter of official instructions and to modify, or even disregard, them. He also assumed the responsibility for personal initiatives of which Rome was either not informed or was only told as a fait accompli, and sometimes in terms different than the truth. Such initiatives frequently gave Italy significant temporary advantages which, had they been exploited fully, could have brought Fascist foreign policy results very different from those it obtained.

Grandi had a decisive role in the Ethiopian War (q.v.): the Hoare-Laval Plan (q.v.) substantially reiterated an agreement that Grandi had worked out with British undersecretary for foreign affairs Robert Vansittart; moreover, if sanctions were not extended to oil and other strategic raw materials, it was due in great part to Grandi's initiative in arranging a tacit understanding with London during the German remilitarization of the Rhineland—which he accomplished by ignoring Mussolini's instructions concerning the Italian position toward Hitler's actions. (At the end of the war Mussolini thought of recalling Grandi from London, but reconsidered in view of his skill in presenting Italy's position before the Spanish Nonintervention Committee). Even more important, however, was his role in the period from the second half of 1936 to the Munich Conference (q.v.). Grandi was, in fact, the real architect of the Italo-English rapprochement: the "Gentleman's Agreement" of January 2, 1937, which mutually guranteed the status quo in the Mediterranean, and the "Easter Accords" of April 16, 1938, which settled specific issues in the Red Sea area, secured British recognition of the conquest of Ethiopia, and contained assurances that Italy had no further ambitions in Spain. Grandi was also behind Prime Minister Neville Chamberlain's request that Mussolini use his influence to resolve the Czech crisis of 1938.

All this explains why Grandi was held in high esteem in English conservative circles; it also explains the hostility toward him from the Nazis, the pro-German Italians, and from Galeazzo Ciano (q.v.), who saw Grandi above all as his most serious competitor for the succession to Mussolini's leadership. Despite these hostilities and Mussolini's recurrent distrust of him, Grandi succeeded for a time in maintaining his position, largely by playing on Mussolini's vanity and offering protestations of his loyalty and admiration for the Duce. Because of these tactics, Grandi later appeared to many to be an opportunistic and shadowy figure, and to Mussolini's extremist followers a traitor.

Grandi did not deny that a careful tactical approach to Germany could reinforce Italy's "determining weight" and her bargaining power between London and Paris, but he was convinced that in case of a European war Italy's place was on the Anglo-French side. Even after the signing of the Pact of Steel (q.v.), he continued to think Italy could switch sides at the last minute (as she had done in 1915) and to hope that he could be the architect of a new "Treaty of London" (similar to the one that brought Italy into World War I). For these reasons Grandi considered it vital that he not lose his post in London. But his tactics did not ultimately prevent his recall once Mussolini, having signed the Pact of Steel, decided to change the nature of relations with England and had to show proof—by recalling Grandi—of his friendship for Germany.

While recognizing his anti-German position, Mussolini would not deprive himself of Grandi's collaboration. On July 12, 1939 Grandi was therefore named minister of grace and justice, and on November 30 he was also made president of the Chamber of Fasces and Corporations (*see* PARLIAMENT). In the first of these positions Grandi had a decisive role in the final stages of the preparation of the new codes of civil law and procedure and navigation, for which he used non-Fascist and Jewish legal experts and for which he was nominated professor of civil law at the University of Rome (which he declined). It was during this period that King Victor Emmanuel III (q.v.) demonstrated the first signs of his esteem and confidence in Grandi, later reinforced by granting him the Collar of the Annunziata and the title of count of Mordano.

During the crisis of August-September 1939 that led to the outbreak of World War II, Grandi worked closely with Ciano to keep Italy out of the conflict. At the September 1 meeting of the Council of Ministers he took an anti-German posture, arguing that Italy could denounce the alliance with Germany because Hitler had disregarded the obligation not to start a war before 1943. In a letter of April 21, 1940 containing the same argument, Grandi made another attempt to keep Mussolini from a precipitous decision. But later, in the face of the unexpected and total military collapse of France, even Grandi was converted over to the idea of intervention.

When hostilities began against Greece in October 1940 (*see* GREECE, INVASION OF), Mussolini sent Grandi—with many other leaders and ministers—to fight on the Greek-Albanian front. He was named governor of Greece at the end of the campaign, but he turned down the post. The dramatic experience of the war against Greece was a decisive moment for him: it was at this point that Grandi began to see the necessity of restoring to the king his complete constitutional prerogatives and of taking Italy out of the war.

The practical possibility of realizing this plan, however, presented itself only after the fall of Tunisia (May 1943) and above all after the Allied landing in Sicily (July 10, 1943). Through a group of senators to whom he had ties, Grandi sought to arrange a meeting of the Senate in secret session, before which Mussolini would report on the situation. But although the Duce blocked the move, it helped to induce him to call the Fascist Grand Council (q.v.) into session. It was then that Grandi seized the initiative to deal with the situation by presenting a motion to the Grand Council on the night of July 24-25, 1943—a motion that called for the de facto restitution of the king's prerogatives as commander-in-chief of the armed forces. Grandi's motion obtained nineteen votes against the five cast for the motion of Fascist party secretary Carlo Scorza (q.v.) (*see* APPENDIX I). Grandi immediately informed the king of the outcome, suggesting the formation of a government of national unity headed by Marshal Enrico Caviglia (q.v.). Grandi's intention was for the new government to confront the inevitable German reaction with arms (and, if necessary, to provoke it) in order to present the Allies with the fait accompli of a complete Italian turnabout and thereby to avoid an unconditional surrender (*see* CASABLANCA CONFERENCE). But the king did not accept this proposal and instead replaced Mussolini with Marshal Pietro Badoglio (q.v.). Grandi then asked Badoglio to send him immediately to Madrid in order to make contact with Sir Samual Hoare, the British ambassador to Spain, to discuss an armistice. Only in mid-August did Grandi go to Portugal, but his mission had been predestined to fail by the fact that the Badoglio government had already made contact with the Allies. It is revealing, however, that on September 29, 1943, as the so-called "Long Armistice" (*see* ARMISTICE) was being signed in Malta, Badoglio asked the Allies (in the king's name) to permit Grandi to reenter Italy and to approve his inclusion in a new government. Although well received by the English, the request was vetoed by the Americans. Thus ended Grandi's political career.

At the Verona Trials (q.v.) in January 1944 Grandi, who was considered the person most responsible for the July 25 coup (for Mussolini's attitude toward Grandi see his *Storia di un anno: Il tempo del bastone e della carota*, in which an entire chapter is devoted to Grandi), was condemned to death in absentia by the Italian Social Republic (q.v.). In 1947 he was also tried in absentia by a special court under the aegis of the High Commission for the Expurgation of Fascism (q.v.), but he was fully acquitted. He did not return to Italy for a number of years. From Portugal he went to San Paolo, Brazil, where he engaged in a series of successful legal and business ventures (through the Organizzazione Techint firm founded in Argentina by Agostino Rocca, in which Grandi was a vice-president). He returned to Italy in the 1950s, and in the Albareto Modenese area he established a model agricultural enterprise. He now lives in Bologna.

For further information see: Renzo De Felice, *Mussolini il fascista* (Turin: Einaudi, 1966-68); Renzo De Felice, *Mussolini il duce* (Turin: Einaudi, 1974-81). No biographical study of Grandi exists. A large part of his private archive has been preserved, which includes his diaries and the memoirs written in Portugal in 1944.

RDF

GRAY, EZIO MARIA (b. Novara, October 9, 1885; d. Rome, February 8, 1969). A Fascist journalist and deputy, Gray was among the founders of the Italian Nationalist Association (q.v.) in 1910. He strongly endorsed the Italo-Libyan War of 1911-12 and covered the conflict as a correspondent, and he was an interventionist and soldier in World War I. Elected to Parliament in 1919, Gray founded the *fascio* of Novara in 1920. He served on the PNF's (*see* PARTITO NAZIONALE FASCISTA) Direttorio Nazionale in 1924-25, was a member of the Fascist Grand Council (q.v.) in 1925-26, and traveled widely overseas on government missions. In the late 1920s and 1930s he was a bureaucrat in various government agencies, including the Dante Alighieri Society, and was also a radio commentator. In 1943 he was vice-president of the Chamber of Fasces and Corporations (*see* PARLIAMENT).

During the Salò Republic (*see* ITALIAN SOCIAL REPUBLIC) Gray was a journalist and directed the *Gazzetta del Popolo* (Milan). Although condemned to death after the war, he received amnesty. In the postwar period Gray was an active leader of the neo-Fascist MSI (*see* MOVIMENTO SOCIALE ITALIANO) party and a deputy.

For further information see: *Chi è?* (1936); EAR (2); NO (1937); Angelo Del Bocca and Mario Giovana, *Fascism Today* (New York: Pantheon, 1969).

PVC

GRAZIANI, RODOLFO (b. Follettino, Frosinone, August 11, 1882; d. Rome, January 11, 1955). The regime's foremost colonial general, Army Chief of Staff, and future defense minister of the Italian Social Republic (q.v.) emerged from World War I as the Army's youngest colonel. In August 1921 he accompanied Giuseppe Volpi (*see* VOLPI DI MISURATA, COUNT GIUSEPPE) to Tripolitania and distinguished himself in the savage war with the Arabs that followed. By June 1928 he commanded all forces in Tripolitania and in February 1930 became vice-governor of Cyrenaica after Pietro Badoglio (q.v.) failed to pacify the Senussi through negotiations. In July Graziani launched a brutal campaign planned by Badoglio. He imprisoned the nomad population in camps (sixty thousand died), sealed the Egyptian border with wire, and hunted the "rebels" relentlessly. Badoglio declared Cyrenaica pacified in January 1932.

Graziani returned to Italy to command the Udine Army corps in April 1934, but in February 1935 he was appointed governor of Somalia. He expanded the role of the southern front in the ensuing Ethiopian War (q.v.) far beyond that originally planned by establishing a direct relationship of personal Fascist fealty to Mussolini. In January 1936 Graziani destroyed Ras Desta's army at Ganale Doria and in April began an offensive through the Ogaden that reached Harar on May 8. Two weeks later Graziani, now a marshal, replaced Badoglio as viceroy of Ethiopia.

By February 1937 Graziani had eliminated the remnants of Haile Selassie's (q.v.) armies. However, on February 19 he narrowly escaped assassination in Addis Ababa. Always quick to suspect conspiracies, Graziani reacted savagely. He allowed a massacre in the capital, incarcerated thousands, then, with Mussolini's approval, he launched an extermination campaign in the countryside. By August Graziani believed he had crushed all resistance. Instead, his brutality provoked general revolt. Despite savage reprisals and massive use of poison gas, rebellion spread. Mussolini announced Graziani's replacement by the duke of Aosta (*see* SAVOIA, AMEDEO DI, DUKE OF AOSTA) in November. Graziani left Ethiopia in January 1938, after attempting to remain as military commander. He had caused a quarter of a million Ethiopian deaths.

After almost two years in eclipse, Graziani returned to power as Army Chief of Staff in place of Alberto Pariani (q.v.) on October 31, 1939. In rivalry with Badoglio and Ubaldo Soddu (q.v.), he supervised the Army's preparation and agreed to go to war on the tacit condition that it be short and involve no fighting. After Italo Balbo's [q.v.] death in Libya on June 28, 1940, Badoglio and Mussolini transferred Graziani there as theater commander, while keeping him as Chief of Staff (Mario Roatta [q.v.], his deputy, ran the staff). Contrary to expectations, Graziani did not immediately thrust forward into Egypt to take advantage of British weakness as he had been ordered; instead, the marshal complained repeatedly of equipment and supply deficiencies. Only ferocious prodding and Mussolini's personal assumption of responsibility compelled Graziani to advance sixty miles in September to Sidi el Barrani. He then refused to move further.

The British counteroffensive of December 9, 1940, surprised his forward units and swiftly destroyed them. Graziani frittered away his remaining forces in a piecemeal defense of a series of untenable positions, while blaming Mussolini and Badoglio for the disaster in hysterical telegrams to Rome. After the destruction of the remaining Italian forces in Cyrenaica at Beda Fomm (February 5-7, 1941), Graziani retired to private life, pleading nervous collapse. Mussolini convened a board under Grand Admiral Paolo Thaon di Revel (q.v.) to investigate Graziani's conduct; the findings were unflattering, but no action resulted.

Graziani nevertheless remained the most reliably Fascist of Italy's high military figures, and Mussolini considered putting him in Vittorio Ambrosio's (q.v.) place in the July 24-25, 1943 coup against Mussolini. After the armistice Graziani vented his hatred at Badoglio by becoming defense minister and Chief of Staff in the Fascist republic. He presided ineffectually over the savage civil war of 1943-45, in constant rivalry with the other Fascist and German power centers in northern Italy. He received a nineteen-year sentence as a war criminal, but served only until May 1950, then became honorary president of the neo-Fascist MSI (*see* MOVIMENTO SOCIALE ITALIANO).

For further information see: R. Graziani, *Ho difeso la patria* (Milan: Garzanti, 1947); Giorgio Rochat, "La repressione della resistenza araba in Cirenaica nel 1930-31," *Il Movimento di Liberazione in Italia* 110 (January-March 1970); Giorgio Rochat, "L'attentato a Graziani e la repressione italiana in Etiopia nel 1936-37," *Italia Contemporanea* 118 (January-March 1975).

MK/BRS

GRAZIOLI, FRANCESCO SAVERIO (b. Rome, December 18, 1869; d. Florence, February 20, 1951). A Fascist general, after rising from major to lieutenant-general in six years (1912-18), Grazioli became interallied commander at Fiume (q.v.) (December 1918-August 1919). With the Duke of Aosta (*see* SAVOIA, EMANUELE FILIBERTO DI, DUKE OF AOSTA) and Gaetano Giardino (q.v.), Grazioli aided Gabriele D'Annunzio's (q.v.) seizure of Fiume. As Army Deputy Chief of Staff (November 1919), then as director of Military Schools (1920) and member of the Army Council (November 1921), Grazioli unsuccessfully advocated mobile warfare. Considering Fascism a modernizing force, he assured Mussolini of Army support before the March on Rome (q.v.). Armando Diaz (q.v.) exiled him as Verona Corps commander (March 1923), but Mussolini made Grazioli Pietro Badoglio's (q.v.) Deputy Chief of Staff (May 1925). Grazioli helped Badoglio and Ugo Cavallero (q.v.) reorganize the Army but failed to modify Badoglio's conservatism. After Grazioli's post was abolished (February 1927) he became Bologna Army commander and a senator in December 1928. Grazioli gained Mussolini's permission to criticize Badoglio's ideas but his attempts to take over the armed forces with Giovanni Giuriati (q.v.), Italo Balbo (q.v.), and Roberto Farinacci (q.v.) failed. Grazioli commanded the four divisions sent to the Brenner Pass in July 1934. Retired in November 1935 because of his age, he became inspector of premilitary and postmilitary training and continued to write military history and theory.

For further information see: Carlo De Biase, *L'aquila d'oro* (Milan: Borghese, 1969); Renzo De Felice, *Mussolini il Duce* (Turin: Einaudi, 1974); Giorgio Rochat, *L'esercito italiano da Vittorio Veneto a Mussolini* (Bari: Laterza, 1967).

BRS

GREECE, INVASION OF. The October 28, 1940 attack on Greece was both a partial fulfillment of Mussolini's hegemonic Mediterranean program and a response to German expansion in the Balkans. After the April 1939 occupation of Albania, Mussolini envisaged "jumping on Greece at the first opportunity" and ordered the creation of an Albanian road network to support the attack. In August 1939 he directed Pietro Badoglio (q.v.) to prepare plans for invasions of both Yugoslavia and Greece. However, entry of Great Britain and France into the German-Polish conflict dictated Italian abstention, and Mussolini settled for a rapprochement with the Greek regime, a rapprochement the Duce and G. Ciano (q.v.) saw as a means of making Greece a satellite without war. The Greeks, in close contact with London, evaded closer Italo-Greek ties. Rome temporarily lost interest.

However, Ciano revived Italian designs in April and May of 1940. After Carlo Geloso (q.v.), the Army commander in Albania, showed a lack of enthusiasm for an immediate attack, Ciano apparently secured his replacement with the more ductile Sebastiano Visconti Prasca (q.v.). Casare Maria De Vecchi (q.v.) repeatedly accused the Greeks of collusion with the British Navy in June and July, and Ciano and Francesco Jacomoni (*see* JACOMONI DI SAN SAVINO, FRANCESCO) produced imaginary Greek border provocations. Ciano urged Mussolini to move even before the expected German invasion of England gave Italy freedom in the Mediterranean.

At the unofficial Rome Council of War Mussolini summoned in mid-August, Visconti Prasca undertook to carry out a coup de main in Epirus. However, the Italian propaganda buildup, the Navy's sinking of the Greek cruiser *Helli* (August 15, 1940), and simultaneous Italian requests for cooperation in an invasion of Yugoslavia alerted Hitler, who conveyed to Rome through both diplomatic and military channels his displeasure at Italian deviations from the paramount strategic aim of laying Britain low. Badoglio and Mario Roatta (q.v.) disciplined Visconti Prasca for jumping channels, and in September Mussolini temporarily consigned resolution of the Greek (and Yugoslav) questions to the "peace table."

However, following the Brenner Conference with Hitler on October 4, Mussolini tentatively revived the Greek enterprise. Hitler's move into Romania (October 12) ended Italian pretensions of Balkan domination and appeared to be a betrayal to

Mussolini, despite a cursory German warning earlier that the step was coming. In retaliation he ordered preparations to launch the Army's "Contingency 'G'" operation to seize Epirus on October 26. At a Palazzo Venezia Council of War on October 15 he secured Badoglio's reluctant approval; Visconti Prasca promised "shattering success." Technical objections from Badoglio resulted in a two-day postponement until October 28. Later the generals claimed that Ciano and Mussolini had assured them Albanian irredentist uprisings in Epirus and bribery in Athens would secure a walkover. At the time, however, all shared what Ubaldo Soddu (q.v.) described as "the conviction... that the enemy was devoid of serious military qualities."

Visconti Prasca's offensive, begun with a mere four divisions in the principal thrust, collapsed swiftly under torrential rains (Mussolini refused postponement), Greek resistance around Janina, and Greek counterattacks from Macedonia. Soddu replaced Visconti Prasca in overall command on November 9, assumed the defensive, and presided over a precipitate withdrawal that gave up almost a third of Albania and culminated in the request on December 4, for a "political intervention" to halt the Greeks. Mussolini instead sent Ugo Cavallero (q.v.), who reorganized Italian forces and broke the logistical bottleneck at Durazzo and Valona. The Greeks continued to advance slowly but failed to break through. However, the Italian offensive that Cavallero, Geloso, and Gastone Gambara (q.v.) launched at Mussolini's insistence on March 9 failed with heavy casualties. Italy's war "parallel" to that of Germany was in shambles; the Greek fiasco, along with Taranto (*see* TARANTO, ATTACK ON) and the North African disaster, produced an internal crisis and resulted in the German military aid that reduced Italy to satellite status.

Hitler's April 1941 assault on Yugoslavia and Greece allowed Mussolini to claim victory, but that victory was purely German: the Greeks initially refused to surrender to Italy, and German troops briefly barred the Italians from crossing into Greece. Ultimately, Italy received Western Greece as an occupation zone. The Greeks regarded their occupiers (*makaronades*) with amusement.

For further information see: Mario Cervi, *The Hollow Legions. Mussolini's Blunder in Greece, 1940-1941* (Garden City, N.Y.: Doubleday, 1971); Martin van Creveld, *Hitler's Strategy, 1940-1941. The Balkan Clue* (Cambridge: Cambridge University Press, 1973).

MK

GRONCHI, GIOVANNI (b. Pontedera, Pisa, September 10, 1887). President of the Republic of Italy from 1955 to 1962, Gronchi obtained a degree in letters in 1910 and taught in middle schools between 1910 and 1915. He was also active in the Christian Democratic movement, organizing rural and urban workers into Christian (so-called "White") unions. A volunteer during World War I, he won a silver and two bronze medals.

Gronchi was a founder of the Italian Popular Party (*see* PARTITO POPOLARE ITALIANO), adhering to its left wing. Continuing as a labor leader, he brought to the Popular party the votes of Christian workers. In the first Mussolini ministry, which was a coalition, he served as undersecretary for industry and commerce. When the Turin congress of the Popular party adopted an anticollaborationist resolution (April 1923), Gronchi resigned from Mussolini's government. Until deprived of his electoral mandate in 1926, he participated in the Aventine Secession (q.v.) as a protest against Fascist involvement in the murder of Giacomo Matteotti (*see* MATTEOTTI CRISIS). During the years of Mussolini's dictatorship, he engaged in commercial and industrial activities.

Between 1943 and 1944 Gronchi was involved in the anti-German resistance and assisted Alcide De Gasperi (q.v.) in establishing the Christian Democratic party as the successor to the Popular party. From June 1944 to July 1946 he was minister of industry and commerce. In 1946 he was elected to the Constituent Assembly (*see* COSTITUENTE), and in 1948, following the parliamentary elections, he became president of the Chamber of Deputies. He was considered a member of the left wing of the Christian Democratic party.

In 1955 Gronchi was elected president of the Republic of Italy. He believed that the president should play an active rather than a passive role in the formulation and execution of government policy. He advocated the greater integration of the masses into the government and the implementation of the social program of the constitution. In foreign affairs he was an exponent of detente and of close U.S.-European ties. After the completion of his term of office, he became a senator for life.

For further information see: G. Gronchi, *Per la storia della Democrazia Cristiana; una politica sociale, Scritti e discorsi scelti (1948-1954)* (Bologna: Il Mulino, 1962); G. Gronchi, *Per una democrazia cristiana e popolare, 1919-1926* (Rome: Cinque Lune, 1975); Giancarlo Vigorelli, *Gronchi: Battaglie d'oggi e di ieri* (Florence: Vallecchi, 1956).

ECa

GUADALAJARA, BATTLE OF. Mussolini suffered major political humiliation during the Spanish Civil War (q.v.) when the Corpo di Truppe Volontarie (Voluntary Troops Corps) was repulsed attempting to seize Guadalajara in March 1937. Commanded by Mario Roatta (q.v.), the CTV advanced on Guadalajara in what the Italians believed was part of a pincer movement to isolate Madrid. Learning the Nationalists would not attack, Roatta visited Franco to gain permission to withdraw. The CTV halted near Brihuega. In Roatta's absence International Brigade units counterattacked on March 18. The poorly trained Italian Militia (q.v.) broke in disorder. Enraged by Western press descriptions of a "Spanish Caporetto," Mussolini resolved to fight until victory restored Fascist honor.

For further information see: John Coverdale, *Italian Intervention in the Spanish Civil War* (Princeton University Press, 1975).

BRS

GUARIGLIA, RAFFAELE (b. Naples, February 19, 1889; d. Rome, April 27, 1970). A career diplomat, Raffaele Guariglia was foreign minister in Pietro Badoglio's (q.v.) first government, in which post he helped arrange the armistice of September 3, 1943.

In 1909, following legal studies, Guariglia entered the foreign service, serving as vice-consul and embassy secretary before heading a ministry bureau in 1920. He later served as an expert at various international conferences and became director general for Europe, the Levant, and Africa and a close associate of Foreign Minister Dino Grandi (q.v.).

In 1932 Guariglia went to Madrid as ambassador. He returned to Rome in 1935 as chief of the Special Office on the Ethiopian Question. He later became Italy's ambassador to Argentina (1936-38), France (1938-40), the Holy See (1941-42), and Turkey (1942-43).

As foreign minister (July 1943-February 1944) Guariglia urged military collaboration with the Allies before the announcement of the armistice in order to prevent Italy from becoming a major battleground.

Guariglia tendered his resignation from the Foreign Service upon the demise of the monarchy and later was elected to the Senate as a member of the National Monarchist party.

For further information see: Raffaele Guariglia, *Ricordi 1922-1946* (Naples: Edizione scientifiche italiane, 1949).

MFL

GUF (GIOVENTÙ UNIVERSITARIA FASCISTA). See **YOUTH ORGAN-IZATIONS**.

GUGLIELMOTTI, UMBERTO (b. Perugia, February 12, 1892). A Fascist journalist and deputy, Guglielmotti won numerous medals for combat in World War I. A Nationalist, he was an editor for *Idea Nazionale* before and after the war, secretary general of the Italian Nationalist Association (q.v.), and supported the fusion with the Fascists in 1923. After working with *La Nazione* (Florence), *La Tribuna* (Rome), and *Il Resto del Carlino* (Bologna), in 1924 he was made head of the PNF (Partito Nazionale Fascista) (q.v.) press office, and founded *Roma Fascista* in 1932. He held numerous party and government posts, including secretary general of the Fascist union of journalists, and was elected to Parliament in 1929. In 1936 he became director of *La Tribuna*, was a radio commentator during World War II, and in the Salò Republic (*see* ITALIAN SOCIAL REPUB-LIC) was director of a special radio and press propaganda agency.

For further information see: *Chi è?* (1936); NO (1937); Philip V. Cannistraro, *La fabbrica del consenso* (Rome-Bari: Laterza, 1975).

PVC

GUSTAV LINE. One of two defensive lines established by Field Marshal Albert Kesselring (q.v.) to stop the Allied advance northward in Italy during the fall and winter of 1943 was the Gustav Line. The southernmost of the two lines was called the Bernhardt or Winter Line and was based on high points surrounding the town of Mignano. The Gustav Line was based on the Garigliano River and included the heights surrounding the monastery of Monte Cassino (q.v.).

The stubborn defense of the German troops in this area encouraged Hitler to provide reinforcements rather than ordering a withdrawal far to the north of Rome, as had been originally planned. The rugged terrain slowed the advance of the Allies as the heavy artillery needed to reduce the German positions became mired in mud and aerial bombardment proved ineffective. German emplacements were sheltered by both natural and artificial caves. After a winter of ineffective fighting, the decision was made and executed on February 15, 1944, to bomb the famous monastery of Monte Cassino, considered a strategic observation point if not a German stronghold, in one of the most bitterly contested areas of the Gustav Line. Even then German defense of the Gustav Line continued to pose serious problems for the Allied Forces until late in May 1944.

For further information see: Peter Calvocoressi and Guy Wint, *Total War: The Story of World War II* (New York: Pantheon Books, 1972); G. A. Shepperd, *The Italian Campaign, 1943-45. A Political and Military Re-assessment* (New York: Praeger, 1968).

ERB

GUTTUSO, RENATO (b. Bagheria, Palermo, January 2, 1912). Guttuso was an anti-Fascist, realist painter, social polemicist, and member of the Italian resistance (*see* RESISTANCE, ARMED). His studies began in Rome in 1931 with adherence to the Roman School, an antiacademic expressionist movement, and its rebellion against the reactionary "neoclassicism" of the Fascist period. In 1932 and 1934 he participated in the collective exhibits in Milan, joining the anti-Fascist movement, Corrente. His first important work, *La Fuga dall'Etna* (1938-39) constitutes a homage to Pablo Picasso's *Guernica* and anticipates the major elements of his future paintings: orchestrated composition, violent color, and a radically cut perspective contained within a rigorously unified design.

During the German occupation of northern Italy, he served in the resistance and published a book of bitterly anti-German drawings, *Gott Mit Uns* (1945). Following World War II Guttuso continued developing Socialist themes in a series of paintings featuring proletarians such as seamstresses and cart drivers. His political stance was formalized as a member of the Nuova Secessione Artistica Italiano (1946), which the following year became the Fronte Nuovo delle Arti (1947), a group that gathered together diverse stylistic and poetic tendencies under the banner of social consciousness (a form of social realism). Themes of social-political inspiration and criticism dominated his art until 1956, at which time experimentation brought about an expressionistic incursion into his rigid realism and introduced autobiographical material.

For further information see: M. Gendel, "Guttuso: A Party Point of View," *Art News* 57 (April 1958); S. Hunter, "Two Contemporary Italians: Guttuso and de Chirico," *Arts Magazine* 43 (November 1950); G. Marchiori, "Momento di Guttuso," *Emporium* 106 (November 1947).

MCG

GUZZONI, ALFREDO (b. Mantua, April 12, 1877). One of the regime's more competent generals, Guzzoni served in Eritrea in 1935-36, and commanded the improvised expeditionary corps that seized Albania on April 7, 1939. He remained on in charge of the occupation forces until December 5, 1939, and at Mussolini's orders prepared the first Italian plan for a land attack on Greece (the plan did not underestimate the Greeks quite so grossly as the Geloso-Roatta-Visconti Prasca plan actually implemented in October 1940) (*see* GREECE, INVASION OF). In June 1940 Guzzoni commanded the Fourth Army in the brief and abortive French campaign. On November 29, 1940, Mussolini appointed him undersecretary for war and deputy chief of the Comando Supremo (q.v.) in place of Ubaldo Soddu (q.v.). Until his resignation in May 1941 after a series of clashes with Ugo Cavallero (q.v.), Guzzoni provided what little strategic direction the Italian war effort possessed and helped negotiate the arrangements for German intervention in North Africa. Unprepossessing in appearance, he was, in the words of the German military attache, "a practical soldier." Guzzoni later commanded the unsuccessful defense of Sicily against the Allies in July 1943.

For further information see: NO (1937).

MK

HAILE SELASSIE I (b. Ejärsa Goro, July 23, 1892; d. Addis Ababa, August 27, 1975). Emperor of Ethiopia from 1930 to 1974, Haile Selassie was given the name Tafari Makonnen. His father, Ras ("duke" or "prince") Makonnen, a cousin of Emperor Menelik II (reigned from 1889 to 1913), visited Italy in 1889-90 for the ratification of the Treaty of Ucciali. Orphaned in March 1906, young Tafari was educated in Addis Ababa, served briefly as governor of some districts of Sidamo, and in 1910 was appointed governor of Harar. A rivalry developed between Tafari and Menelik's grandson and prospective successor, Lij Iyasu. From Menelik's death in December 1913 until September 1916, a coup d'etat removed Iyasu from power, placed Menelik's daughter Zawditu on the throne, and brought Tafari to national prominence as ras and prince regent. It was widely believed that he was Zawditu's heir apparent.

Having been exposed to Western education in his youth, Ras Tafari was regarded as a progressive and modernizer. In 1923, after initial opposition from Italy but ultimately with Italian sponsorship, Ethiopia was admitted to membership in the League of Nations. Three years later Tafari made a tour of Europe, visiting Italy and a half dozen other countries. As prince regent he strongly opposed European attempts to keep alive the Tripartite Italo-Franco-English agreement of 1905-1908, which provided for the partition of Ethiopia into European colonial spheres in the event of the collapse of the Ethiopian government. Most of his effort in the 1920s was devoted to consolidating his political base within the often confusing politics of Ethiopia. When Zawditu died in early 1930, Tafari consolidated his influence. On November 2, 1930, he was crowned emperor and took the throne name Haile Selassie I (literally, "Power of the Trinity").

In the early 1930s Haile Selassie strengthened Ethiopia's defenses, particularly along the border with Italian Eritrea, in anticipation that trouble with Fascist Italy would be inevitable. When the Italian invasion of Ethiopia began, Haile Selassie's main line of defense was in the diplomatic arena. Within Ethiopia he was strongly criticized for not appearing on the battlefield against the Italian invaders until the final stages of the war. After the decisive battle of Mai Chio, when the fall of Addis Ababa became imminent, Haile Selassie fled the country, ostensibly to present the Ethiopian case before the League of Nations in Geneva. There, on June 30, 1936, he delivered his widely publicized (and just as widely ignored) speech warning that only collective security could protect small nations against the growing power of aggressive nations like Fascist Italy. From mid-1936 until mid-1940 Haile Selassie lived in exile in Bath, England.

Italian entry into World War II offered exiled Ethiopians the opportunity to persuade Great Britain to invade Ethiopia from the Sudan and from Kenya. On January 20, 1941, Haile Selassie returned to Ethiopia with the invading Ethiopian and British troops. On May 5, 1941, he reentered Addis Ababa, five years to the day after it had fallen to the Italian Army. Among his first acts as reinstated emperor was a proclamation urging all Ethiopians to protect individual Italians stranded in Ethiopia; remarkably, few acts of violence were committed against Italians in newly liberated Ethiopia.

In the postwar period Haile Selassie was determined to wrest control of the former Italian colony of Eritrea from its British occupiers. In 1952 he succeeded in federating Eritrea with Ethiopia under a single crown. He was less successful in preventing the return of Italy to Somalia as trustee-administrator under United Nations auspices. By 1963 Haile Selassie emerged as a major figure in the creation of the Organization of African Unity and as a world leader. Behind the scenes, however, there was increasing disaffection from the newly educated classes that he had helped create. Once known as a modernizer and progressive, he became regarded in Ethiopia as an obstacle to greater progress and development. When disillusion spread to the military, his days were numbered. Despite reconciliation with Italy and the symbolic restitution to Ethiopia of various items looted by the Fascists, the emperor could no longer capitalize on his earlier image. Indeed, the memory of the emperor who fled the country rather than die on the battlefield resurfaced. Adding to the erosion of his prestige was the revelation that the government had attempted to cover up a disastrous famine in Wollo province. Beginning in February 1973 the emperor yielded to one demand after another from the military, from striking workers, and from students. The "creeping coup" evolved into a full-scale military revolution. On September 13, 1974, Haile Selassie was deposed and placed under house arrest.

For further information see: Richard Greenfield, *Ethiopia, A New Political History* (New York: Praeger, 1965); R. L. Hess, *Ethiopia, The Modernization of Autocracy* (Ithaca, New York: Cornell University Press, 1970); Leonard Mosley, *Haile Selassie: The Conquering Lion* (Englewood Cliffs, N.J.: Prentice Hall, 1965). Haile Selassie I, *The Autobiography of Emperor Haile Selassie I: "My Life and Ethiopia's Progress", 1892-1937* (London: Oxford University Press, 1976).

RLH

HASSELL, CHRISTIAN ALBRECHT ULRICH VON (b. Anklam, Germany, November 12, 1881; d. Plötzensee Prison, Berlin, September 8, 1944). German ambassador in Rome between 1932 and 1938, Von Hassell was born into the Pomeranian nobility, and was married to the daughter of Grand Admiral Alfred von Tirpitz. His diplomatic career began before World War I but was interrupted by military service. Seriously wounded in 1914, he was a domestic administrative officer until the end of the war.

In 1919 Von Hassell returned to the diplomatic service with his first post that of counselor of the embassy and chargé d'affaires in Rome, where he served for two years. In 1921 he became consul general in Copenhagen, in 1926 ambassador to Denmark, and in 1930 ambassador to Yugoslavia, before returning to Rome as ambassador in 1932. He served in that post until early in 1938, when he was recalled and retired after differences with Hitler.

Von Hassell, therefore, served over seven years in Italy, a country which he greatly liked and respected. He honored Italy's cultural achievements (he was a scholar of Dante) and respected the Italian way of life. Although he believed Italy and Germany had common interests due to their central European geographical position and worked for their cooperation in international affairs, he opposed the Anti-Comintern Pact (q.v.) of 1937 as a military alliance likely to lead to war. As a consequence, he was recalled from Italy on February 4, 1938, being replaced by Hans-Georg Viktor von Mackensen (q.v.).

In the period that followed von Hassell became one of the leaders of the German resistance movement, serving it in efforts to contact British and American officials and convince them of its seriousness and its rational objectives. Von Hassell was one of those arrested after the unsuccessful assassination attempt on Hitler on July 20, 1944. He was tried by the infamous People's Court, convicted, and executed at Plötzensee Prison in Berlin.

For further information see: biographical sketch by Friedrich Baethgen in *Neue deutsche Biographie*, 12 vols. (Berlin: Duncker und Humblot, 1969), 8:44-46; Christian Albrecht Ulrich Von Hassell, *Vom andern Deutschland, Aus den Nachgelassenen Tagebüchern, 1938-1944* (Zürich: Atlantis Verlag, 1947); Hugh Gibson, ed., *The Von Hassell Diaries, 1938-1944. The Story of the Forces Against Hitler Inside Germany as Recorded by Ambassador Ulrich von Hassell* (New York: Doubleday, 1947).

ERB

HAZON, AZOLINO (b. July 20, 1883; d. Rome, July 19, 1943). Hazon was a Carabinieri general who served Pietro Badoglio (q.v.) ruthlessly as Carabinieri commander in Ethiopia, from 1935 to 1936, and continued under Rodolfo Graziani (q.v.). Despite failure to prevent the February 1937 attempt on Graziani's life, Hazon regained his confidence by brutal interrogations, mass executions, and murderous administration of concentration camps. Angered by Alessandro Lessona's (q.v.) creation of the rival Polizia Africana Italiana, Hazon accused Lessona and his cousins, Vincenzo De Feo and Alessandro Pirzio Biroli (q.v.), the governors of Eritrea and Amhara, of treason, insubordination, and incompetence. Hazon resurrected corruption charges against Ugo Cavallero (q.v.) in December 1937, hoping to keep Graziani as military commander to the new viceroy, the duke of Aosta (*see* SAVOIA, AMEDEO DI, DUKE OF AOSTA). Repatriated, Hazon became Carabinieri vice-commandant after Graziani's appointment as Army Chief of Staff. By 1942 Hazon was the king's major source of intelligence, while he plotted with Carmine Senise (q.v.) and G. Ciano (q.v.). In November Hazon began planning Mussolini's substitution by Badoglio. After promotion to Carabinieri commandant on February 28, 1943, Hazon began preparing Mussolini's overthrow until he was killed by an American bombing raid on Rome. Hazon's successor, Angelo Cerica, directed the coup.

For further information see: Paolo Puntoni, *Parla Vittorio Emanuele* (Milan: Aldo Palazzi, 1958); Giorgio Rochat, "L'attentato a Graziani e la ripressione italiana in Etiopia nel 1936-37," *Italia Contemporanea* 26 (January-March 1975); Alberto Sbacchi, "I governatori coloniali in Etiopia," *Storia Contemporanea* 8 (December 1977).

BRS

HOARE-LAVAL PLAN. The Hoare-Laval Plan (named after British foreign Secretary Sir Samuel Hoare and French foreign minister Pierre Laval) of December 7-8, 1935 for the redistribution of Ethiopian territory in Italy's favor and for bringing the war between Italy and Ethiopia to an end has given rise to much controversy. On the one hand, it is contended that after the submission of Mussolini's military directive of December 30, 1934, to his service chiefs it was Mussolini's aim to conquer the whole of Ethiopia and to annex the entire country. The military preparations taken in 1935 appeared to support this view. On the other hand, Mussolini and the British and French governments, whose territories also adjoined Ethiopia, expressed themselves in favor of a compromise. On the occasion of his visit to Mussolini in Rome in late June 1935 Anthony Eden proposed that Ethiopia should be given the port of Zella in British Somaliland; Italy in exchange should have large areas of the Ogaden in Ethiopia, which was mostly desert and occupied by Moslem Somali tribes. In August the British went a step further. They were now prepared to allow an Italian economic sphere of influence in Ethiopia. The British proposals and the even more radical ones made by Laval in August were far from satisfying to Mussolini.

Before and after the outbreak of hostilities on October 3, 1935, Mussolini made demands in London and Paris on the following lines. First, there should be outright annexation by Italy of the non-Amharic areas of the country. These lay mainly south of the Great Rift and were conquered by Menelik II late in the nineteenth century. Second, Ethiopia should cede to Italy those areas in eastern Tigre adjoining Eritrea that had been already occupied by Italian forces by the middle of November 1935. Third, the right should be granted to Italy to build a road running preferably east of Addis Ababa through Harar, to Italian Somaliland. Fourth, Ethiopia should in return be allowed a port, preferably at Assab in Eritrea with a road to Dessie or, alternatively, the port of Zeila in British Somaliland. The reconstituted Ethiopian state should be disarmed and be converted virtually into an Italian Protectorate. Late in October the British government rejected Mussolini's proposals. But toward the end of November, when there was a real threat of war if sanctions were extended to include oil, British undersecretary for foreign affairs Robert Vansittart, as well as the British service chiefs, pressed the cabinet to agree on a compromise. They argued that the concentration of the Italian fleet in the Red Sea and the Mediterranean was considerably greater than had been anticipated earlier in the crisis and that the British warships sent to these waters were especially vulnerable to air attacks by long-range Italian bombers.

The British could not calculate on gaining military support from France. Laval had in fact concluded military agreements with Italy in the previous summer. Although the British had been given pledges of military aid early in December from Yugoslavia, Greece, and Turkey, these powers were so absorbed by domestic problems or were pursuing goals which were not related to Ethiopia, that the material aid expected was negligible. The terms of the pledges were not made public and thus failed to act as a deterrent.

Early in December Vansittart and Dino Grandi (q.v.) worked out the terms of a possible agreement which were studied by Hoare and Laval on December 7-8 in Paris. Instead of granting nominal independence to Tigre and its falling under effective Italian control as envisaged by Vansittart and Grandi, Italy was to gain (under the Hoare-Laval Plan) a small strip of the Tigrean highlands in the east and large tracts of the adjoining Danakil desert. The Ethiopians were to be granted Assab. Instead of acquiring the highlands near Harar with control over the sources of the Shebelli River and its tributaries as demanded by Grandi, Italy was to annex that part of the Ogaden wedged between British and Italian Somaliland. This area was of little or no economic value apart from water wells near Wal Wal. The area below eight degrees latitude, well to the south of the Haras highlands, and east of the thirty-five degree meridian was to be reserved for Italian expansion and colonization. Although Italian forces had far from occupied this extensive area in the south, its mainly Galla and Somali inhabitants were thoroughly hostile to Amharic rule. Hence, it can be contended that the Hoare-Laval Plan was not so flagrantly contrary to the principle of self-determination as is generally assumed. The fact, however, that the partial dismemberment of Ethiopia was discussed after Italy had committed an act of war caused an uproar among those states whose future security depended on the Covenant of the League. For this and other reasons the plan has been described as the death warrant of the League of Nations.

It is debatable whether Mussolini was prepared to accept the plan unless radical amendments were made to it in Italy's favor. He was certainly under pressure from his own advisers to compromise. But he could not ignore a change in the fortunes of the war. He had hoped for victories. Yet on December 15 the Ethiopians counterattacked and by December 18, the day when the British government disowned the plan, certain strong points in Southern Tigre were reoccupied by the Ethiopians. As a result Mussolini did not define his attitude to the plan, but he waited. That it was rejected by the British and the Ethiopians and not by Mussolini, greatly enhanced his prestige at home. Since Italian acceptance was also expected and feared by Hitler, its rejection rendered it easier for Germany and Italy to draw closer together in subsequent months.

For further information see: R. De Felice, *Mussolini il Duce* (Turin: Einaudi, 1974); Rosaria Quartararo, "Le Origini del piano Hoare-Laval," *Storia Contemporanea* 8 (1977); E. M. Robertson, *Mussolini as Empire-Builder: Europe and Africa*

1932-36 (London: St. Martin's, 1977); James C. Robertson, "The Hoare-Laval Plan," *Journal of Contemporary History* 10, 3 (July 1975).

EMR

HOST-VENTURI, GIOVANNI (b. Fiume, June 25, 1892). A supporter of Gabriele D'Annunzio's (q.v.) Fiume (q.v.) expedition and a Fascist minister, from his youngest days Host-Venturi was active in politics in his birthplace. He worked for Fiume's unification with Italy and at one point was forced to flee the city because of his politics. During World War I he served in the Italian Army in the Piave sector, and his extensive knowledge of the Austrian zones greatly aided the Italian forces. In November 1918 Host-Venturi entered Fiume at the head of his troops and claimed the city for Italy.

After the Italian government withdrew the troops from the area, Host-Venturi went to Venice, where he met with Gabriele D'Annunzio and helped plan the latter's seizure of Fiume. He participated in the March from Ronchi and served as the Regency of Carnaro's (*see* CARNARO, CHARTER OF) diplomatic representative.

During the Fascist period Host-Venturi served as secretary of the Federazione Fascista in Fiume and was consul of the Carnaro legion in the Fascist Militia (q.v.). He became a deputy in 1934 and from January 1935 to October 1939 was an undersecretary in the Ministry of Communications. From October 1939 to February 1943 he was minister. Prior to the July 24-25, 1943, meeting of the Fascist Grand Council (q.v.) Host-Venturi urged Mussolini to take decisive action against the conspirators.

For further information see: *Chi è?* (1936); NO (1937); F. W. Deakin, *The Brutal Friendship* (New York: Harper & Row, 1962); Giovanni Host-Venturi, *L'impresa fiumana* (Rome: Volpe, 1976).

MSF

I

IACHINO, ANGELO (b. San Remo, 1889). Commander of the battle fleet from December 8, 1940, to April 5, 1943, Admiral Iachino led at Matapan (*see* MATAPAN, BATTLE OF) and in the first and second battles of the Sirte (December 17, 1941; March 22, 1942). Although competent, his British opponents, Cunningham and Vian, outclassed him, despite Italian superiority of force in the Sirte battles.

MK

INDUSTRY. During all of 1919 and most of 1920 Fascism received little sympathy or support from Italian industrialists, who considered the still infant movement little better than Bolshevism. Its initial program, in fact, included: an eight-hour workday, the participation of workers in factory management, syndical organization in public industry and services, a progressive tax on capital, and confiscation of 85 percent of war profits. Only in the spring of 1920—because of the renewed strength of the Socialist movement and the new Fascist policy of defending the middle classes—did industries begin to give financial help to the Blackshirt squads (*see* SQUADRISTI), progressively increasing their contributions after the "Occupation of the Factories" (q.v.) in September. These subsidies, however, remained sporadic and limited and did not involve the national organization of industrialists known as the Confindustria (Confederazione Generale dell'Industria Italiana), which viewed the Fascists as a movement of uncertain ideological thrust and led by men with subversive backgrounds. The Confindustria therefore regarded Fascism only as a means for restoring "normalcy" to the old liberal system.

After the Rome congress of 1921 Mussolini began to obtain wider industrial support because he could thenceforth be seen as a more legitimate leader than the dangerous *ras* (q.v.) and because his personal position was now characterized by an essentially liberal economic-financial platform. At the same time the Fascist leadership decided to exploit this financial assistance, but with the explicit understanding that they would not become the servants of the industrialists.

In October 1922 Confindustria, speaking through its president, Antonio S. Benni (q.v.), and its secretary, Gino Olivetti (q.v.), endorsed the formation of a government headed by one of the distinguished Liberal statesmen (Giovanni Giolitti [q.v.], Antonio Salandra [q.v.], or V. E. Orlando [q.v.]), but one in which the Fascists could be included in such a way as to neutralize and contain them and restore economic and social order to the nation. But when Mussolini remained adamant about forming his own government, they consented to a coalition cabinet under his leadership, hoping to achieve the same aim. Between 1922 and 1925 the economic policy of Finance Minister Alberto De Stefani (q.v.) created an ever wider level of industrial support for the Mussolini regime, mainly because of its laissez-faire attitude, which encouraged new investments; its fiscal measures; its restructuring of trade tariffs; the abolition of many wartime taxes and inheritance laws; and the almost total reduction of the state deficit. With a worldwide increase in productivity and trade and the decline of social agitation, there began to take place in Italy an expansion of industrial activity, which, in spite of the crisis caused by the reevaluation of the lira in 1927 (*see* QUOTA NOVANTA), increased the index of manufactured goods from fifty-four in 1921 to ninety in 1929 (with a 1938 base of one hundred). In addition, unemployment was reduced from three hundred and eight-two thousand at the end of 1922 to one hundred and twenty-two thousand in 1925; national income rose from 95 billion lire (1938 prices) in 1921 to 124 billion, 600 million lire in 1929; and savings increased to 8.6 percent of the national income. Although the growth rate could not reach the levels of the Giolittian era, the postwar crisis had been overcome, and this enabled Mussolini to take credit for having "saved" the economy and obtain the support of the Confindustria (despite tensions caused by the lack of complete "normalization" and the demands of the Fascist syndicalists).

Ever since the March on Rome (q.v.), Edmondo Rossoni (q.v.), secretary general of the Confederation of Fascist Corporations, had been making three basic demands for the organization of the nation's productive forces: a monopoly for the Fascist unions; the abolition of the so-called *commissioni interne* controlled by the CGL (Confederazione Generale del Lavoro) (q.v.) and their substitution by Fascist *fiduciari di fabbrica* (factory agents); and the creation of owner-manager corporations and the destruction of the Confindustria. These demands had been accompanied by agitation and polemics against capitalism and "plutocracy," especially in the metal-worker strikes of the spring of 1925, which had been encouraged by the Fascist press and organized even with the participation of the Socialist-run Federation of Italian Metal Workers (Federazione Italiana Operai Metallurgici—(FIOM). The industrialists naturally rejected these demands, arguing that they were dangerous to economic and trade-union freedom and not really applicable because of the small Fascist following among workers. During the Matteotti Crisis (q.v.) the industrialists assumed a watch-and-wait attitude and considered the possibility of supporting the Aventine opposition (*see* AVENTINE SECESSION) in order to preserve their interests against the danger of Fascist syndicalism. But without any other real alternative, the Confindustria decided to back Mussolini, largely because they considered him the only man capable of controlling the political situation and the Fascist movement. In exchange for this support the industrialists obtained in July 1925 the end of union agitation and the substitution of De Stefani and Cesare Nava (q.v.), ministers of national economy, with Count Giuseppe Volpi di Misurata (q.v.) and Giuseppe Belluzzo (q.v.), two of the most respected figures in finance capital.

The hopes for "normalization" were diminished between 1925 and 1927, a period in which Mussolini—skillfully maneuvering between opposing forces—

succeeded in creating the fundamental institutions of the Fascist state and subordinating to government authority the apparatus of his own movement as well as his *fiancheggiatori* (supporters). Obviously, neither economic policy nor the unions escaped this process, for he used Rossoni's organization to pressure the industrialists into agreement with his position in exchange for the destruction of Rossoni's "integral syndicalism," in which the Duce never believed anyway. The Palazzo Vidoni Pact (q.v.) of 1925, which confirmed the earlier Palazzo Chigi Pact (q.v.) of 1923, the syndical law of April 1926 (*see* ROSSONI, EDMONDO), the creation of the Ministry of Corporations (*see* CORPORATIVISM AND THE CORPORATIVE STATE) in July 1926, and the promulgation of the Carta del Lavoro (*see* CHARTER OF LABOR) in April 1927 were all steps in this direction—for if they did not satisfy the intransigent syndicalists and corporativists, they certainly did not satisfy the industrialists. These new measures and institutions were inspired by Mussolini's (and Alfredo Rocco's [q.v.]) corporativist ideas, which aimed simply at bringing the productive forces of the nation under the authority and control of the state. The legal recognition of only one Fascist organization for "each kind of business and each category of worker," with the power to impose collective contracts; the creation of labor courts (*magistrature del lavoro*) empowered to settle disagreements; the absolute prohibition of strikes and lockouts; and the compulsory hiring of workers from the *Uffici di collocamento* (employment offices)—all these measures were accepted reluctantly by industrialists, who were now increasingly frightened by a potentially dangerous Fascist totalitarianism (q.v.).

The obvious advantages to the industrialists notwithstanding—the defeat of Rossoni's policies, the strengthening of management, the restoration of "order" in the factories, and the continued existence of the Confindustria as an autonomous entity—Mussolini had fully realized his aim: the industrialists had been forced into his regime and, although they were still powerful and able to impose some conditions, had to maneuver within the political and legal order of the Fascist state. The events surrounding the "battle for the lira" in 1926-27 demonstrated clearly that Mussolini was capable of imposing major decisions on them for purely political purposes. When the financial and industrial critics openly opposed his stabilization policies, Mussolini responded by mobilizing the PNF (Partito Nazionale Fascista) (q.v.) and its press against the Italian "plutocracy," which he accused of being guilty of blocking the restoration of the country's economic health. But once he had won the struggle, he granted the industrialists fiscal concessions and wage reductions, did not oppose the creation of large trusts, imposed further restrictions on Fascist unions, and once again (in September 1929) vetoed the *fiduciari di fabbrica*. The *sbloccamento* or breaking up of Rossoni's syndical organization and its subdivision into a number of individual confederations (one for each branch of the economy) in November 1928 further reassured the industrialists. By the end of 1929 relations between industrialists and the regime were solidly established.

On the other hand, by the end of 1929 the effects of the world economic crisis began to overturn the entire national economy. The production index dropped from ninety to seventy-seven in 1931-32, while unemployment rose to seven hundred and fifteen thousand in 1933. Corporativist theorists proclaimed the end of liberal economics and looked forward to the beginning of a state-planned and regulated economy through the corporations. There were even those, like Ugo Spirito (q.v.), who demanded the expropriation of capital and the creation of the "proletarian corporations." The industrialists, who refused to accept any undermining of the economic system, sought to reduce production and employment, cutting wages, consolidating industries to divide up the markets, fixing prices, and coordinating production. State intervention was welcomed only when public funds were used to save particularly hard-hit industries.

Mussolini, who was unwilling to implement revolutionary solutions, did create the National Council of Corporations in 1930 and finally established the corporations themselves in 1934, but in general his emergency measures were essentially similar to Roosevelt's policies under the New Deal. Worker salaries were cut 15 percent, while a whole series of government-assistance programs—including public works (q.v.) projects and *bonifica* (q.v.)—were established. Moreover, in an effort to obtain the fullest possible consensus, the regime permitted widespread mergers and concentrations of ownership. Indeed, in June 1932 it even set up *consorzi obbligatori* (obligatory industrial consortia) in which the government had to approve all new industrial plants and the expansion of existing ones. These policies had long-term negative results because they were not based on the logic of modernization and rationalization. Rather, they froze what was essentially a backward economic structure and advanced the formation of monopoly cartels that discouraged technological development. The decrease in competition was particularly counterproductive in view of the limited size of the Italian market.

Two public agencies were created to save banks and crucially affected industries: the Istituto Mobiliare Italiano (IMI) on November 13, 1931, which was to control credit; and the Istituto per la Ricostruzione Industriale (IRI) on January 23, 1933. IRI was by far the more radical solution, for it purchased all the shares of stock in industrial, agricultural, and real estate companies previously held by banks. (The banking law of 1936 prohibited banks from extending long-term credit to industrial concerns.) Although the industrialists fully expected a return to "normalcy" and to private enterprise after the crisis had passed, Mussolini had successfully created an instrument for the permanent intervention of government in the economy. By 1939 IRI controlled a series of firms representing 44.15 percent of the capital of Italian stock values and 17.80 percent of the total capital of the country—hence, the Fascist government controlled a proportionally larger section of national industry than any other government in Europe except the Soviet Union.

The Ethiopian War (q.v.) and the League of Nations sanctions against Italy in 1935-36 combined to convince Mussolini of the necessity of making Italy self-sufficient. For that purpose he adopted a regulating plan for production that favored state intervention, the drastic limitation of imports and exports, and the reorientation of trade heavily toward Italy's new German ally. Industrialists were critical of these policies, favoring instead a return to normal conditions and rapprochement with the Western powers. They expected that a return to conventional trade patterns would mean regaining much needed raw materials and energy sources as well as the recapturing of central and southwestern European markets that had been lost to the Germans during the war. Many entrepreneurs feared that Italy would become an economic satellite of Germany and its superior industrial system. Faced with Mussolini's unbending determination to pursue his policy of autarchy (q.v.), the industrialists were forced to give in and accept concessions. In October 1936 Mussolini therefore approved the request of financiers to reduce by 40.9 percent the intrinsic value of the lira vis-à-vis the 1927 parity (which had not been changed during the depression despite the fact that foreign currencies had been devalued). In general, the industrialists began to understand that they were progressively losing their autonomy as economic needs were subordinated to political requirements that were becoming increasingly more dangerous.

On the eve of World War II Fascist economic policy was able to claim the following results: an increase in the production of manufactured goods which reached an index of 109; the growth of the national income to 146 billion lire in 1938; the overtaking between 1936 and 1940 of the percentage of agriculture (29.4 percent) in the gross national product by industry (34.1 percent) for the first time in the history of Italy; and the reduction by 1938 of the importation of raw materials to 88 percent of the 1928 level, and of semifinished and finished products to 60 percent and 52 percent respectively (with a consequent reduction in the trade deficit of 776 million lire in 1938).

These "successes," however, must be seen in the context of the persistence of a number of traditional weaknesses and imbalances in Italian industry: the disparity between north and south and from region to region; the decline in private consumption, whose per capita level was lower than in 1929; the low productivity of labor; exceedingly high production costs for domestically made goods (which were also frequently of inferior quality). To these problems must be added the drastic reduction of exports and the resulting decline in foreign currency holdings and the fact that Italian industrial production increased between 1929 and 1939 by only 15 percent, a lower rate of increase than the corresponding growth averages of other industrial-agrarian countries in Western Europe. Poor government planning and inefficient corporate bureaucracy greatly hindered the mobilization of industrial resources and energies.

On June 10, 1940, Italy entered World War II substantially unprepared and in a clearly inferior position, given the evident disproportion between her material and technical resources and those of the other great powers. As is well known, Mussolini made the decision to intervene convinced that a quick German victory would follow. The industrialists were torn between their anti-German feelings and the prospect of a victory that would have resulted in the redistribution of world markets in favor of the Axis powers (*see* AXIS, ROME-BERLIN)—but in any case they were by then unable to oppose Mussolini's political decisions in any meaningful way.

Although sustained by a major financial and productive effort (fed by German supplies that were never sufficient to meet Italy's needs and that declined steadily during the war), the Italian war effort operated in a condition of clear inferiority and was unable to deal with the needs of the situation.

The defeat and collapse of Fascism was accelerated by the growing division between Mussolini and the industrialists. The latter became determined to separate their fate from that of the regime, to keep their holdings intact as much as possible from the destruction of the war, and to permit the transfer of political power with the least possible damage to the socioeconomic balance of the country. Thus, they supported Pietro Badoglio's (q.v.) "normalization" program and the later hostility toward the Italian Social Republic (q.v.), which seemed on the verge of implementing the aspirations of the Fascist left wing through the "socialization" law of February 12, 1944. The measure provided for the following: (1) the establishment of direct responsibility of private businessmen vis-à-vis the state, which had the power to substitute them as industrial executives; (2) the nationalization of those industries crucial to the economic and political independence of the nation or which furnished raw materials, energy, and necessary services; (3) the participation of workers in the management of factories and businesses through elected councils, whose members could also participate in the election of company executives. In this situation, one in which they feared that Mussolini's search for a third alternative to capitalism and communism might give way to extremist solutions, the industrialists decided to sabotage the socialization law by raising all possible obstacles to its implementation while awaiting the arrival of the Allied armies. In this they were aided both by the Germans, who opposed the socialization program as detrimental to war production, and by the open hostility of the workers, who had been incited by anti-Fascists and refused to believe the promises of the regime that had oppressed them for so long. By April 1945 the law had affected only a few dozen companies, and Mussolini's belated decision to socialize all industries starting on April 26 obviously came to nothing.

For further information see: M. Abrate, *La lotta sindacale nella industrializzazione dell'Italia* (Milan: Angeli, 1967); P. Ciocca and G. Toniolo, eds., *L'economia italiana nel periodo fascista* (Bologna: Mulino, 1976); R. De Felice, *Mussolini il rivoluzionario* (Turin: Einaudi, 1965); idem, *Mussolini il fascista* (Turin: Einaudi, 1966-68); idem, *Mussolini il duce* (Turin: Einaudi, 1974); P. Grifone, *Il capitale finanziario in Italia* (Turin: Einaudi, 1971); F. Guarneri, *Battaglie economiche* (Milan: Garzanti, 1953); S. La Francesca, *La politica economica del fascismo* (Bari: Laterza, 1972); P. Melograni, *Gli industriali e Mussolini* (Milan: Longanesi, 1972); R. Romeo, *Breve storia della grande industria in Italia* (Bologna: Cappelli, 1975); R. Sarti, *Fascism and the Industrial Leadership in Italy* (Berkeley: University of California Press, 1971); S. Setta,

"Potere economico e Repubblica sociale italiana," *Storia Contemporanea* 8 (June 1977).

PN

INTERLANDI, TELESIO (b. Chiaramonte, Ragusa, October 20, 1894). A prominent Fascist journalist, Interlandi took a law degree and entered journalism as a staff member of *Giornale dell' Isola* (Palermo). In 1921-22 he edited *La Nazione* (Florence) and from 1923 to 1924 he worked on *L'Impero* and produced poems and literature. Loyal to Mussolini and a Fascist extremist, in 1924 he established the newspaper *Il Tevere* (Rome) as the unofficial mouthpiece of Mussolini, through which he expressed unrestrained and intransigent views, including anti-Semitism. His paper had an important influence on cultural life, for the positions it assumed were known to have reflected the regime's official views. In 1943 Interlandi was arrested by the Pietro Badoglio (q.v.) government, was subsequently freed by the Germans, and followed Mussolini north to the Salò Republic (*see* ITALIAN SOCIAL REPUBLIC), where he was again active in journalism. He was also in charge of propaganda for invaded territories under the Ministry of Popular Culture (q.v.).

For further information see: *Chi è?* (1936); NO (1937); Philip V. Cannistraro, *La fabbrica del consenso* (Rome-Bari: Laterza, 1975).

PVC

INTERVENTIONIST CRISIS, 1914-1915. The outbreak of World War I in Europe in August 1914 opened a prolonged period of stress and tension in Italy that culminated with the declaration of war against Austria-Hungary on May 23, 1915. The internal divisions that resulted from the almost ten months of the interventionist crisis proved more severe in Italy than elsewhere in Europe, so severe that throughout the war, even after the disaster of Caporetto (*see* CAPORETTO, BATTLE OF), the Italians could not create a united internal front. The severity of the internal divisions stemmed from the interventionists' refutation of the Giovanni Giolitti (q.v.) system and their desire to prevent a Socialist revolution.

Although four principal political and ideological currents formed the interventionist movement, it was more compact than its diverse origins indicate. Most of the interventionists came from the ranks of the defeated. Since the turn of the century those from the left, the democratic and revolutionary interventionists, had lost a series of battles to the Socialist party (Partito Socialista Italiano—PSI) (q.v.) and the CGL—Confederazione Generale del Lavoro (q.v.). Those from the right, the nationalist and liberal interventionists, had lost to Giolitti. The members of each of these groups believed that Italy was in crisis and that only a war could release Italy from the "moral crisis" into which Giolitti and the Socialists had plunged her.

Thus much of the interventionist crisis was a repeat of the struggle of the past ten years with, however, the important distinction that between August 1914 and May

1915 the interventionists moved the struggle outside of the traditional legal rules and boundaries. Led by Gabriele D'Annunzio (q.v.), Mussolini, and Filippo Corridoni (q.v.), the interventionists took their message directly to the people. The used the *piazza* to glorify the use of violence by staging mass rallies, and they urged the masses to use violence not only to punish the guilty, but also to influence the decisions of the government.

The government leaders, Antonio Salandra (q.v.) and Sidney Sonnino (q.v.), had a similar aim. They wanted to create a new conservative force that, strengthened by a victorious war, could eliminate the Giolittian majority in the Parliament and halt the advance of socialism. From early in August, therefore, Salandra worked to provide Italy with a "little war" or a diplomatic triumph, and he pursued his goal without consulting Parliament. From the formation of his second government on November 5, Parliament sat only until December 12, then recessed until February 18, 1915. It then sat only from that day until March 22 when it recessed until May 20, too late for Giolitti's neutralist majority to prevent the declaration of war. Thus Salandra and Sonnino, aided by the interventionist agitators of the *piazza*, deprived the neutralist majority in Parliament and in the country of its rights and pushed Italy into the war.

By early 1915 the industrial bourgeoisie, who had direct or indirect links to war production, began to support the interventionist cause. As Antonino di San Giuliano, foreign minister, and Sonnino had recognized in 1914, these industrialists did not wish to lose their markets (real or potential) in the Balkans or in the colonies. In addition, the industrialists recognized that a war would provide not only investments and profits, but also the means to weaken the working-class organizations. Many members of the industrial bourgeoisie therefore saw the war as an opportunity to reverse the political and economic directions of the Giolittian system, to cut the links between the working-class organizations and the masses, and to return management to its dominant position in the factory and in the society.

Thus a minority of the people and a minority of the politically organized imposed intervention and war on the Italian people. The majority of the population, the Socialists, the workers, the Giolittians, the peasants, and the Catholics, all rejected the interventionist arguments and remained neutralist and antiwar throughout the crisis. The neutrality of the workers and peasants explains why the leaders of revolutionary and democratic interventionism lost their traditional links with the masses. Alceste De Ambris (q.v.), for example, lost the USI (Unione Sindacale Italiana) and Mussolini lost the PSI (Partito Socialista Italiano) (q.v.) because neither could convince a majority from these organizations to follow them into interventionism. Without their traditional base of support, both men moved to the right, and faced with the political realities of 1915, they reluctantly accepted the hegemony of Salandra.

The alliance of Salandra's government, the military, and the bureaucracy with the principal interventionist groups defeated the neutralist majority because the Giolittians and the Socialists refused to collaborate, even when their stubbornness meant victory for the interventionists. After he issued his famous *parecchio* letter on February 1, 1915, in which he argued that "quite a lot" could be obtained from Austria-Hungary, Giolitti lost much of his maneuverability because the letter bound him to negotiations with Austria-Hungary. Thus the PSI refused to support him, since his position compromised their insistence on absolute neutrality. The interventionists at the same time increased their ferocious attacks against Giolitti for his "opportunism." Finally, the *parecchio* letter also strengthened Salandra's position because it restricted Giolitti to negotiations with Austria-Hungary. Salandra meanwhile continued to play both sides as he talked to the Austrians about compensation and to the members of the Triple Entente (England, France, and Russia) about intervention.

The agitation of the interventionists reached its peak during the "radiant days" of May. In a series of antiparliamentary, anti-Giolittian demonstrations, the interventionists took advantage of the passivity of the members of Parliament to weaken fundamentally the constitutional government. In the crisis precipitated by Salandra's resignation on May 13 all the interventionist forces, fearful that Giolitti might return to power and repudiate the Treaty of London, exploded in widespread demonstrations that continued until the king requested Salandra to form a new government. The ferocity of the demonstrations frightened the king and apparently convinced Giolitti that there would be a civil war if he returned to power.

Hence Giolitti refused to form a government and the king, concerned about the interventionists' shouts of "war or revolution," turned again to Salandra and his war cabinet. On May 20 the Chamber of Deputies granted exceptional powers to the new government and the Senate concurred the following day. Two days later, on May 23, Italy notified Austria-Hungary that a state of war would exist between the nations the next day. At the same time Italy severed diplomatic relations with Germany, but stopped short of a declaration of war.

After almost ten months of struggle, the interventionists had finally won. They had brought Italy into the war, had destroyed the Giolittian system, and had crippled the constitutional position of the Parliament. Between August 1914 and May 1915, the conservatives, with an increasing awareness of the consequences of their actions, joined with the revolutionary interventionists in extra-legal maneuvers that ominously foreshadowed their postwar alliance that would fuse conservative ideas and revolutionary direct action into the Fascist movement.

For further information see: Alberto Asor Rosa, "L'intervento 1914-1918," in *Storia d'Italia*, IV, 2, *Dall' unità a oggi* (Milan: Einaudi, 1975); Giorgio Candeloro, *Storia dell' Italia moderna*, VIII (Milan: Feltrinelli, 1978); Ernesto Ragionieri, "La grande guerra e l'agonia dello stato liberale," in *Storia d'Italia*, IV, 3, *Dall' unità a oggi* (Milan: Einaudi, 1976); John Thayer, *Italy and the Great War, Politics and Culture, 1870-1915* (Madison, Wis.: University of Wisconsin Press, 1964); B. Vigezzi, *L'Italia di fronte alla prima guerra mondiale*, I, *L'Italia neutrale* (Milan: Ricciardi, 1966).

CLB

ISTITUTO NAZIONALE DI CULTURA FASCISTA. One of the Fascist regime's agencies of cultural propaganda, the Istituto (originally called the Istituto Nazionale Fascista di Cultura) had its origin in the PNF (Partito Nazionale Fascista) (q.v.) national congress of June 1925. The philosopher Giovanni Gentile (q.v.) proposed the Istituto as a response to the challenge of the anti-Fascist intellectuals, led by Benedetto Croce (q.v.), who charged that Fascism was anticulture (*see* "MANIFESTO OF ANTI-FASCIST INTELLECTUALS"). The specific aim of the Istituto was to create an organic national consciousness based on Fascist values, and this was to be achieved through a vast network of provincial and regional branches under PNF control. These branches would conduct propaganda, "popular" educational and cultural programs, and political indoctrination.

The official goal of the Istituto was to promote the cultural life of the working classes and integrate them into a national experience, but despite the fact that by 1941 it had more than two hundred thousand members, only twelve thousand were workers; the majority were students, teachers, and professionals.

The actual direction of the Istituto was in the hands of capable men like Giorgio Masi (head of the PNF propaganda office), Arturo Marpicati (q.v.), Piero Rancicci, and later the technocrat Camillo Pellizzi (q.v.). Giovanni Gentile was its president, but over the years it came increasingly under the control of the Ministry of Popular Culture (q.v.). After the Ethiopian War (q.v.), the Istituto was reorganized, and in 1937 its name changed from the National Fascist Institute of Culture to the National Institute of Fascist Culture. It fully endorsed the regime's racial policies and during World War II greatly increased its functions in order to bolster the home front morale—in 1942 alone it sponsored several thousand public lectures as well as films, concerts, art exhibits, and recreational activity. With the collapse of the regime in 1943, the Istituto ceased to exist.

For further information see: Philip V. Cannistraro, *La fabbrica del consenso* (Rome-Bari: Laterza, 1975).

PVC

"ITALIA"—FLOTTE RIUNITE (ITALIAN LINE). The Italian Line was formed in January 1932 by a combination of the shipping companies Lloyd Sabauda, Navigazione Generale Italiana, and Cosulich. The objective of the minister of communications, Costanzo Ciano (q.v.), was to reduce wasteful competition during the world depression at a moment when the superliners *Rex* of the NGI and *Conte di Savoia* of Sabauda were nearing completion. In 1936 there was additional state intervention and Cosulich was more closely integrated into the organization, which was renamed "Italia"—Società Anonima di Navigazione. The Italian Line was then placed with the Lloyd Triestino, Adriatica, and Tirrenia in Finmare, the shipping group of the state holding company IRI (Istituto per la Ricostruzione Industriale [*see* INDUSTRY]).

The 880-foot *Rex* (51,062 tons) and the 860-foot *Conte di Savoia* (48,502 tons) were Italy's major entry into the North Atlantic competition at a time when ocean travel was still in its heyday. Both ships were magnificent, if costly, symbols of prestige for the Fascist regime. They were also intended to be more successful than the older ships of the line in diverting the tourist trade toward the more temperate Mediterranean route. The *Conte di Savoia* was the first passenger liner fitted with gyrostabilizers to reduce roll, and had in the Colonna Room, modelled after the Palazzo Colonna, one of the most sumptuous public halls afloat. The larger *Rex* was expected to capture the Blue Ribbon of the Atlantic for the fastest crossing, and Mussolini himself was present when she left Genoa on her maiden voyage on September 27, 1932. The results, however, must have brought great satisfaction to anti-Fascist exiles, for off the Spanish coast two of her three turbogenerators failed and, instead of setting a record, the *Rex* was forced to wait at Gibraltar for spare parts, while numbers of irate passengers disembarked for alternate arrangements. The *Conte di Savoia* also suffered mechanical difficulties on her maiden voyage in November 1932 and arrived in New York a day late.

Both ships overcame their initial difficulties, and in August 1933 the *Rex* did capture the Blue Ribbon with a record crossing—the only Italian ship ever to do so. She held the record, however, for only a short time before it was won by the French Line's *Normandie* in May 1935. Nevertheless the *Rex* and *Conte di Savoia* were for several years possibly the most familiar representatives of Italy for many Americans, particularly New Yorkers. Heavily advertised with lavish pictures emphasizing the size of their then novel outdoor pools and Lido decks, they were undoubtedly attractive showpieces for the Fascist regime, although they supposedly never showed a profit. Both were sunk by Allied air attacks during the war.

For further information see: Nicholas T. Cairis, *North Atlantic Passenger Liners since 1900* (London: Ian Allen, 1972); Francesco Ogliari and Lamberto Radogna, *Transporti Marittimi di Linea*, II: *Dall' Adriatico Destinazione Oriente e Americhe* (Milan: Cavallotti Editore, 1975).

PGH

ITALIA LIBERA. An anti-Fascist underground organization composed chiefly of Republican war veterans, Italia Libera was founded in Florence in June 1924 after the Matteotti Crisis (q.v.) erupted. Among those who adhered to and directed its activities were General Decio Garibaldi, Raffaello Rossetti, Carlo Rosselli (q.v.), and Ernesto Rossi (q.v.). It maintained a highly secret organization in Florence (where it had about two hundred members) and inspired branches in other cities throughout northern and central Italy, promoting street demonstrations and pasting up wall posters demanding a restoration of civil liberties. Although suppressed in 1925, many of its adherents later joined Giustizia e Libertà (*see* ANTI-FASCISM).

For further information see: EAR (2); Charles F. Delzell, *Mussolini's Enemies* (Princeton: Princeton University Press, 1961); Luciano Zani, *Italia Libera* (Bari: Laterza, 1976).

PVC

ITALIAN NATIONALIST ASSOCIATION. The Italian Nationalist Association was formed in December 1910 by Enrico Corradini (q.v.) and Luigi Federzoni (q.v.), who forged a heterogeneous coalition of sentimental irredentists and national imperialists into one of the most important anti-Socialist and antidemocratic forces in twentieth-century Italy and one which exercised a decisive influence on Fascism. Never aspiring to a mass following, the Italian Nationalist Association exerted its control through larger political movements and by cultivating close ties with heavy industry.

In its emergence as a significant political force, the Nationalist Association was aided by the patriotic fervor and class polarization caused by the Libyan War of 1911 and by the inability of traditional Italian liberalism to organize the new mass electorate created by the manhood suffrage law of 1912. The Nationalists also understood the inadequacy of traditional authoritarian repression in this situation. Their position, as outlined in 1913 and 1914 by Alfredo Rocco (q.v.), the future legal architect of the Fascist regime, on the pages of the *Idea Nazionale*, the major Nationalist newspaper, eschewed racial or mystical appeals in favor of a program designed to elicit an immediate, positive response from certain industrial and agrarian interests. In included the creation of state sponsored cartels for production and marketing, heavy doses of tariff protection, an expansionist colonial policy, state control of worker unions, elimination of the political function of the Socialist party, and a greatly strengthened executive authority.

During the elections of 1913 the Nationalists managed to elect several deputies including their leader, Federzoni, by an open appeal for Catholic support. The rapid conversion of the Nationalists from a pro-Triple Alliance (Germany, Austria-Hungary, Italy) position to one favoring the Triple Entente (England, France, Russia) ended the alliance with the neutralist clericals but offered an opportunity to join with democratic and left-wing, prowar parties in an attempt to impose entry into World War I on the neutralist parliamentary majority and a reluctant country. Not only did the Nationalists help create an outlook in wartime Italy that identified victory with the total realization of the expansion program in Dalmatia, Albania, the Adriatic Sea, and Africa, but they also contributed to the development of the productivist ideology that emphasized class collaboration and the maintenance of social hierarchies in an all-out effort to win the war. Benito Mussolini, probably influenced by this campaign, began to expound similar ideas in his *Il Popolo d'Italia* in 1917.

In 1919 and 1920 the Nationalist Association found itself swamped by the revolutionary tide, but it again maneuvered to find a movement through which it might propagate its ideas. It turned first to the patriotic veterans' associations and then to the Fascists. The Nationalists felt their ties to the industrialists, agrarian interests, and the monarchy would allow them to play a pivotal role in the emerging conservative coalition. For the most part, Mussolini avoided the Nationalists' overtures. However, the association was influential during the crisis of October 27-28, 1922, which led to the appointment of Mussolini as prime minister. Yet their calculation had been that the crisis would lead to the appointment of Antonio Salandra (q.v.), the leader of the conservatives since 1914, as chief minister and dominant political figure. The Nationalists only belatedly adjusted to Mussolini's government when Salandra faced Mussolini's absolute refusal to cooperate. As a result, the Nationalists were in a weak position to exert much influence in the first Fascist government. Federzoni received the less important colonial ministry instead of the foreign office that he desired.

The March on Rome (q.v.) brought the Nationalists an unexpected success in southern Italy, where the association rapidly became a serious rival/ally of the Fascists. But because they had never sought a mass base, the Nationalists were willing to trade off their newly won following for influence within the PNF (Partito Nazionale Fascista) (q.v.). Protracted negotiations led to the merger of the two parties in March 1923. Unlike their German counterparts, the Italian Nationalists negotiated with the Fascists on relatively equal terms and represented a major bridgehead of conservative elitists within the Fascist party.

Although the association ceased to be an independent party after 1923, its real victory came in June 1924, after the murder of Giacomo Matteotti (*see* MATTEOTTI CRISIS). The involvement of several of Mussolini's close associates forced the prime minister to appoint Federzoni as his minister of interior. Despite rumors that the Nationalists would join other conservatives to displace Mussolini, they followed their traditional policy of maneuvering from within. This strategy was confirmed when Mussolini stabilized his power in January 1925 but appointed Alfredo Rocco as his minister of justice. The emergence of Federzoni and Rocco, just as the initial moves were made to establish full dictatorship, gave to the regime its statist, traditionalist, authoritarian character, which limited the role of the PNF and markedly distinguished Italian Fascism from German Nazism.

For further information see: Alexander De Grand, *The Italian Nationalist Association and the Rise of Fascism* (Lincoln, Nebraska: The University of Nebraska Press, 1978); Franco Gaeta, *Il nazionalismo italiano* (Naples: Edizioni scientifiche, 1965); Paolo Ungari, *Alfredo Rocco e l'ideologia giuridica del fascismo* (Brescia: Morcelliana, 1966).

AJD

ITALIAN SOCIAL REPUBLIC (RSI). The Italian Social Republic (Repubblica Sociale Italiana), Mussolini's government in northern Italy between September 1943 and April 1945, remains controversial. Commonly known as the Salò Republic, after Mussolini's residence on Lake Garda, the RSI has been damned as camouflage for brutal German occupation and praised as the pure expression of Fascist idealism. In fact, the RSI reflected many of the contradictory strains within Fascism (which Mussolini's earlier regime had suppressed) as well as Mussolini's attempt to vindicate his reputation. Its ultimate reality, however, was German control.

After Mussolini's downfall in July 1943, Alessandro Pavolini (q.v.), Renato Ricci (q.v.), Roberto Farinacci (q.v.), and Giovanni Preziosi (q.v.) fled to Germany. Thus, the nucleus for a reconstituted but extremist Fascist government existed prior to Mussolini's liberation in September. Flown to Munich, Mussolini reluctantly agreed to form a new government. He hoped to restore Fascism's 1919 radical social program and prevent German and extremist dominance of northern Italy. Nonetheless, under German pressure he appointed Pavolini as secretary of the new Republican Fascist party (Partito Fascista Repubblicano) and Ricci as Militia (q.v.) commander.

On September 18 Mussolini announced the formation of the RSI, promising to "Annihilate the parasitic plutocracies, and finally make labor the object of our economy and the indestructible foundation of the State." Mussolini also declared he would "Take up arms once more alongside Germany. . . and the other allies," "eliminate the traitors. . . of July 25," and reorganize the armed forces around the Militia.

Implementation of this contradictory program was beyond Mussolini's power. While loyalty to Germany, a desire for vengeance, or appeals to Fascist honor attracted the squadrists (*see* SQUADRISTI), thugs, and romantics mobilized by Pavolini and Ricci, these notions repelled the mass of the population and many moderate Fascists. Basing the RSI on the working class contradicted German plans to force maximum production from Northern Italian industry and agriculture and to use Italian workers in Germany as virtual slaves. It also alarmed the Swiss financiers that the RSI needed for capitalization.

Hoping to reestablish an army, Mussolini persuaded Rodolfo Graziani (q.v.) to become national defense minister. But Graziani insisted on an apolitical armed force, feuding bitterly with Ricci. The result was the formation of a small regular army to be trained in Germany, a Republican National Guard (Guardia Nazionale Repubblicana) under Ricci, plus a number of autonomous Fascist forces such as the Decima Mas and Muti Legion.

Added to these obstacles was Hitler's refusal to release Italian soldiers imprisoned in Germany for Graziani's forces, relegation of RSI forces to antipartisan and police operations against fellow-Italians, and annexation of Italian territory by Germany and Croatia.

Mussolini's creation of a government dominated by F. M. Barracu (q.v.) as undersecretary of the Ministerial Council, Guido Buffarini-Guidi (q.v.) as interior minister, and Fernando Mezzasomma (q.v.) as popular culture minister conflicted with Pavolini's intention to dominate the RSI. At the first meeting of his government on September 29 Mussolini stated objectives including reconquest of national territory, summoning of a constituent assembly to create a single-party federal republic, and determination "to resolve the social question."

At the November 1943 PFR Verona Congress, which Mussolini did not attend, Pavolini elaborated this program in an eighteen-point manifesto, heavily influenced by the ex-Communist Nicolò Bombacci (q.v.). The RSI would have an anticapitalist, collective, labor-based economy with a single national union, workers councils, profit-sharing, land reform, public housing, and wage and price controls. Elections, civil rights, and private property were guaranteed but so was official Catholicism and anti-Semitism. A European community and exploitation of Africa were foreseen as postwar developments.

The RSI's reality proved much harsher. The congress itself adjourned to launch a punitive expedition against anti-Fascists in Ferrara. The congress also demanded a Special Tribunal for the Defense of the State (q.v.), which condemned Galeazzo Ciano (q.v.), Emilio De Bono (q.v.), Giovanni Marinelli (q.v.), Luciano Gottardi, and Carlo Pareschi in January 1944. By then Ricci's Republican National Guard and other Fascist formations were terrorizing the countryside and searching for partisans, Jews, and deserters. When Mussolini's Ministerial Council approved nationalization and socialization of essential industries in January 1944 his RSI government counted for little against Pavolini's PFR and the Germans. Mussolini, guarded by the SS like a prisoner and physically and mentally exhausted, was nearly impotent. Mussolini's attempts to demonstrate independence from the Germans and undercut Communist strength among the workers failed.

His visits to Hitler in April and July 1944 to gain support for his concepts, better treatment for Italian workers and prisoners in Germany, and return of German-annexed territories accomplished little; though four regular Army divisions trained for Graziani in Germany did return between July and December 1944. More significantly, Pavolini ordered a mass compulsory conscription of squadrists from the PFR in July, creating Black Brigades (Brigate Nere) for antipartisan operations and further alienating the population.

The danger of an Axis (*see* AXIS, ROME-BERLIN) collapse in August-September 1944 stirred Mussolini to feeble attempts at a separate peace with the West. But after these efforts failed, and buoyed by a temporary German resurgence, Mussolini made a last sally to create support for the RSI. In Milan in December 1944 Mussolini offered collaboration with non-Fascist groups. That winter he ordered a number of socialization measures to maintain a minimal standard of living. In February 1945 the RSI decreed socialization of large industries, though most workers abstained from voting for the necessary labor councils. The same month Mussolini allowed creation of the collaborationist Republican National Socialist Groupment (Raggruppamento Nazionale Repubblicano Socialista), though it was suppressed in March after violent opposition from Pavolini and Farinacci.

By April 1945 the RSI controlled little more than Milan. Fascist attempts to make a last stand there or in the Valtellina were impeded by the German command, which was seeking a separate Italian surrender to the Allies. Mussolini's discovery of these negotiations prompted his flight from Milan. When he departed on April 25, 1945, the RSI's existence ceased.

For further information see: Bernard Berenson, *Rumor and Reflection* (New York: Simon and Schuster, 1952); Silvio Bertoldi, *Salò* (Milan: Rizzoli, 1976); Giorgio Bocca, *La repubblica di Mussolini* (Bari: Laterza, 1977); Renzo De

Felice, "La Repubblica Sociale Italiana," in *Trent'anni di storia politica italiana* (Turin: ERI, 1967); Ernst Nolte, *Three Faces of Fascism*, Part Three (London: Weidenfeld and Nicolson, 1965); Giorgio Pisano, *Storia della guerra civile in italia (1943-1945)* (Milan: FPE, 1966); Enzo Santarelli, *Storia del fascismo* (Rome: Riuniti, 1973).

BRS

J

JACINI, COUNT STEFANO (b. Milan, November 3, 1886; d. Milan, May 31, 1952). A political figure and economist, Jacini was lay president for almost twenty years of the Church missionary organization known as the Opera Bonomelli per l'Assistenza agli Emigrati. He was a member of the Catholic "modernist" movement that sought to put the Church in the center of social reform, and in 1919 he joined the Partito Popolare Italiano (q.v.). From 1919 to 1926 Jacini was a Popolare deputy in Parliament, but he lost his seat because of his participation in the Aventine Secession (q.v.) against Mussolini. During the Fascist period he devoted himself to historical research but in 1943 joined the anti-Fascist movement, first as a member of the Committee of National Liberation (q.v.) and then as president of that organization in northern Italy. After World War II he served as minister of war (June-December) in the Ferruccio Parri (q.v.) cabinet and as a member of the Costituente (q.v.). In 1948 he was made a senator.

For further information see: DSPI; Philip V. Cannistraro and Gianfausto Rosoli, *Emigrazione, Chiesa e Fascismo* (Rome: Studium, 1979); Gabriele De Rosa, *Storia del movimento cattolico in Italia: II, Il Partito Popolare Italiano* (Bari: Laterza, 1966); Stefano Jacini, *Il regime fascista* (Cernusco sul Naviglio: Garzanti, 1947).

PVC

JACOMONI DI SAN SAVINO, FRANCESCO (b. Reggio Calabria, August 31, 1894). Galeazzo Ciano's (q.v.) man in Tirana from 1936 to 1943, Jacomoni served as Pompeo Aloisi's (q.v.) assistant in Bucharest (1923-26) and Durazzo (1926-27), then as vice-chief of the Cabinet of the Ministry of Foreign Affairs from 1927 to 1936. He married the daughter of General Ugo Cavallero (q.v.) and secured the title "di San Savino" with the general's help in December 1937. In Tirana he supervised the accelerated penetration of Albania, which led to Italian occupation on April 7, 1939. That event, which Jacomoni prepared by bribing numerous Albanian chieftains, brought his own elevation to governor (Luogotenente Generale del Re in Albania).

In 1940 Jacomoni was a central figure in the planning of the attack on Greece (*see* GREECE, INVASION OF) and encouraged Ciano to press for action, lest the Germans forestall Italian designs. At the Rome meeting of October 15 at which Mussolini announced his definitive decision to attack, Jacomoni showed himself less convinced than Ciano that the Greeks would not fight; nevertheless he later reported enthusiastically on his arrangements to bribe Greek notables, disrupt the Greek rear, and create bogus border incidents to justify Italy's "lightning military intervention." The enterprise's miserable collapse shook Jacomoni's standing, but Mussolini avoided making scapegoats of the civilians involved because their failure reflected on himself. Political turbulence and guerrilla warfare in Albania caused Jacomoni's recall in favor of Alberto Pariani (q.v.) in March 1943.

For further information see: Francesco Jacomoni's unreliable *La politica dell'Italia in Albania* (Bologna: Capelli, 1965); *I documenti diplomatici italiani*, nona serie, 5 (Rome: Istituto Poligrafico dello Stato, 1965).

MK

JUNG, GUIDO (b. Palermo, February 1, 1876; d. Palermo, 1949). A financial expert and Fascist deputy, Jung held a number of regional banking positions. A Nationalist, he was an interventionist and soldier in World War I. He was a member of the Italian delegation to the Paris Peace Conference and to the various postwar reparations conferences and organized the Banco di Roma and the Banca Nazionale di Credito in 1923. Elected a deputy in 1924, he served in Parliament until 1938. Mussolini made him minister of finance in 1932 (to 1935), and after the fall of Mussolini in 1943 he was again minister of finance under Pietro Badoglio (q.v.) and finally Ministro di Scambi e Valute until June 1944.

For further information see: *Chi è?* (1936); DSPI; NO (1937).

PVC

KAPPLER, HERBERT (b. Stuttgart, 1907; d. Soltau, February 9, 1978). A German security officer stationed in Rome during World War II, Kappler played a key role in some of the most horrible episodes of the Nazi occupation in Italy. He trained as an espionage and security expert in Germany and came to Rome in 1939 as an SS lieutenant colonel and head of the SD (Sicherheitsdienst) (Security Service) in the Italian capital, where he worked closely with the Fascist police and the German embassy.

In 1943 Kappler helped organize the German rescue of Mussolini from Gran Sasso led by Otto Skorzeny (q.v.). But the most notorious and controversial of his actions came in 1944 when Kappler planned and led the mass arrests and deportation of Roman Jews to Germany (after the extortion of gold from the Jewish community), and the subsequent organization of the Ardeatine Caves Massacre (q.v.). After the war Kappler was held by British authorities, who turned him over to the Italians for trial in 1947. The next year he was tried by the Military Tribunal of Rome and sentencd to life imprisonment. After spending many years in prison on the island of Gaeta, he escaped in 1977 and died at his home in West Germany.

For further information see: Robert Katz, *Death in Rome* (New York: Macmillan, 1967); *New York Times*, February 10, 1978.

PVC

KEREN, BATTLE OF. The site of the most conspicuous Italian defensive success of World War II, Keren Pass was the western gateway to Eritrea, located in terrain which guaranteed the Italian Army's World War I tactics and weapons maximum effectiveness. Under the command of Generals Carnimeo and Orlando Lorenzini (q.v.), Italian and colonial troops doggedly resisted superior British and Indian forces from February 3 to March 27, 1941, markedly slowing British occupation of Italian East Africa.

For further information see: Alberto Bongiovanni, *La fine dell'impero* (Milan: Mursia, 1974); Giuseppe Pizzorno, "Da Cassala a Cheren," *Rivista Militare* 15 (April 1959).

MK

KESSELRING, ALBERT (b. Marktsteft, November 30, 1885; d. Munich, 1960). The German field marshal who was Supreme Commander Southwest of the German armies in Italy from November 6, 1943 to March 11, 1945, Kesselring was brought up in Bayreuth in Bavaria. From the first he sought a military career. By 1906 he was a lieutenant in the Bavarian artillery and during World War I became a general staff officer at division and corps levels. After the war he moved into the German regular Army (Reichswehr). His administrative talents brought him into service with the general staff.

With the organization of the German Air Force after 1933 Kesselring moved into this new arm of the German military, passed pilot training, and gained rapid promotions in rank. By 1938 he was a full general and commander of German Air Fleet One. With the outbreak of World War II he took part in the campaigns against Poland and on the Western Front, obtaining the rank of general-field marshal in 1940. After a brief experience on the Eastern front, he was transferred to Italy on December 1, 1941. His command there included all air activities in North Africa as well as Italy. His optimism and determination led Hitler to appoint him Supreme Commander-Southwest after the fall of Mussolini and the Italian defection from its alliance with Germany.

Kesselring's command of German forces during the Allied campaign in Italy underscored his persistence, his ingenuity, and his outstanding command of military tactics. But the development of the Italian resistance movement (*see* RESISTANCE, ARMED) confronted him with a type of warfare that he considered illegal and immoral. His most controversial action involved retaliation against a Communist guerrilla exploit against German SS soldiers in Rome (*see* ARDEATINE CAVES MASSACRE) on March 23, 1944. Although Kesselring was able to secure some moderation of Hitler's demands for reprisals, he ordered the execution of ten Italians for every German soldier killed.

Kesselring was tried in February 1947 for his part in this action and on charges that he had also been responsible for the death of 1,078 other unarmed persons in later actions against Italian guerrillas. Although condemned to death, the sentence was commuted to life imprisonment, and he received amnesty in October 1952, finishing his life in a villa near Munich, where he died in 1960.

For further information see: Robert Katz, *Death in Rome* (New York: Macmillan, 1967); Kenneth Macksey, *Kesselring: The Making of the Luftwaffe* (New York: David McKay Company, Inc., 1978); G. A. Shepperd, *The Italian Campaign, 1943-45. A Political and Military Re-Assessment* (New York: Praeger, 1968).

ERB

KOCH, PIETRO (b. Benevento, August 19, 1915; d. Rome, June 5, 1945). The leader of a notorious Fascist group operating against anti-Fascists, Koch (who had a German father) was a lieutenant in the Italian Army. He was an agent on the staff of the equally infamous Mario Carità (q.v.) band in Florence before moving to Rome after the German occupation in 1943. In Rome he received authorization from Police Chief Tullio Tamburini (q.v.) to establish a "special service" to repress the anti-Fascist resistance. While he operated under the command of the Fascist police, he worked closely with the Nazis. With his staff of unscrupulous agents and informants, Koch rounded up Italians for deportation to German labor camps, sent Jews to extermination camps, and arrested and tortured anti-Fascist partisans. His headquarters were located first in the Pensione Oltremare (Via

Principe Amedeo 2), then in the Pensione Jacarino (Via Romagna 30). He played a key role in the Ardeatine Caves Massacre (q.v.) of 1944.

After the liberation of Rome Koch transferred his operations to Milan. He was arrested after the end of the war, condemned to death by the Italian High Court of Justice, and executed.

For further information see: EAR (2); Carlo Francovich, *La resistenza a Firenze* (Florence: Nuova Italia, 1961); A. Troisio, *Roma sotto il terrore nazifascista* (Rome: Mondini, 1944).

PVC

L

LABRIOLA, ARTURO (b. Naples, January 22, 1873; d. Naples, June 23, 1959). The first leader of the revolutionary syndicalist (*see* SYNDICALISM) current in Italian socialism, Labriola combined modern Marxism and preindustrial populism in devising a strategic alternative to reformism. His Neapolitan background shaped his conception of Italian problems, but he looked for solutions to industrialization and the emerging industrial proletariat. In 1902 he moved from Naples to Milan, where he founded *Avanguardia Socialista*, the first Italian syndicalist periodical, as an instrument in the struggle against reformist socialism. He felt that the reformists, with their emphasis on parliamentary politics and their complicity in the Giolittian (*see* GIOLITTI, GIOVANNI) system, would undermine the capacity of the proletariat to develop new values and institutions. Thus he began to emphasize the role of an autonomous labor movement in creating socialism.

Although he favored the Libyan War and Italian intervention in World War I, Labriola continued to view Italian problems in relatively orthodox terms, and thus he did not share in the redefinition of syndicalism that led many of his colleagues to corporativism (*see* CORPORATIVISM AND THE CORPORATIVE STATE). Italy, he decided, would not be ready for syndicalism until her bourgeois revolution had been completed, so he began working for reforms to undermine the power of the monarchical and protectionist forces in the Italian state. He won election to the Chamber of Deputies as an independent Socialist in 1913.

After the World War I, Labriola served as minister of labor in Giolitti's government of 1920-21 and then joined the reformist Partito Socialista Unitario, founded in 1922. He was quite hostile to Fascism, which he portrayed as a postwar bourgeois reaction in a relatively backward country. His participation in the Aventine Secession (q.v.) cost him his parliamentary seat in 1926, and he went into exile in France the next year.

Labriola returned to Italy in December 1935 during the Ethiopian War (q.v.). He had long been concerned about Italy's position in the Mediterranean, and he approved of Mussolini's turn to a more aggressive foreign policy. However, he remained apart from active politics and after World War II served first as a deputy in the Constituent Assembly (*see* COSTITUENTE) and then as a senator in the Republic.

For further information see: Arturo Labriola, *Spiegazioni a me stesso* (Naples: Rispoli, 1945); Dora Marucco, *Arturo Labriola e il sindacalismo rivoluzionario in Italia* (Turin: Fondazione Luigi Einaudi, 1970); Alceo Riosa, *Il sindacalismo rivoluzionario in Italia* (Bari: De Donato, 1976).

DDR

LANTINI, FERRUCCIO (b. Desio, Milan, August 24, 1886). A Fascist bureaucrat and minister, Lantini took a degree in business and spent a number of years abroad in commercial activity. Upon returning to Italy, he settled in Genoa and became active in the Nationalist-Irredentist movement, participating in the 1911 campaign against the pacifists who wanted to keep Italy out of war with Turkey. He was an interventionist and fought in World War I.

Lantini formed close ties with important business interests in Genoa, especially with banking firms and the Odero shipbuilding company. With their backing he established the first of a series of *fasci* in the city in April 1919 and, after overcoming numerous rivals, became secretary in 1921. He was appointed to the PNF's (Partito Nazionale Fascista) (q.v.) first central committee in that year, in January 1923 served as high commissioner for Liguria, and in April was a member of the executive committee (*giunta esecutiva*). He was elected a deputy in 1924, serving until 1939. In 1927 Lantini demonstrated his loyalty to Mussolini by renouncing his former associate and friend Gerardo Bonelli, who was a leading dissident in Genoa, and in 1929 he was rewarded by membership in the Fascist Grand Council (q.v.).

In 1932 Lantini was appointed president of the Confederazione Nazionale di Commercio; this was followed two years later by the presidency of the Istituto Nazionale per le Esportazioni, a position he owed to his business connections. In January 1935 Mussolini brought Lantini into the government as undersecretary in the Ministry of Corporations (*see* CORPORATIVISM AND THE CORPORATIVE STATE), and then in June 1936 made him minister. Lantini was a member of the 1936 commission chosen to recommend the restructuring of the Chamber of Deputies (*see* PARLIAMENT).

For further information see: *Chi è?* (1936); NO (1928; 1937); Adrian Lyttelton, *The Seizure of Power* (London: Weidenfeld & Nicolson, 1973).

PVC

LANZA DI SCALEA, PRINCE PIETRO (b. Palermo, October 20, 1863; d. Rome, October 16, 1938). A cabinet minister and political figure, Lanza di Scalea began his political career in 1897 as a parliamentary deputy from Serradifalco in Palermo. Lanza di Scalea held this seat until 1929 but during these years also served as an undersecretary in the Foreign Ministry in the second Sidney Sonnino (q.v.) ministry (1909-10), the Luigi Luzzatti ministry (1910-11), and the fourth Giovanni Giolitti (q.v.) cabinet (1911-14). During the first Luigi Facta (q.v.) government in 1922 Lanza di Scalea was selected to be minister of war and from July 1924 to November 1926 was minister of colonies. Although he did not play a leading role in the Fascist regime, in 1929 Lanza di Scalea was made a senator and served as vice -president of the Senate.

For further information see: *Chi è?* (1936); DSPI; NO (1937).

MSF

LANZILLO, AGOSTINO (b. Reggio Calabria, August 31, 1886; d. Milan, March 13, 1952). An important Fascist publicist from the revolutionary syndicalist tradition, Lanzillo was most influential during the formative period from 1918 to

1922, although he was also a member of the Commission of Fifteen (later Eighteen) established in 1924 to design new institutions. Despite a personal relationship with Georges Sorel, he was attracted to the labor movement as an expression of societal autonomy and initiative, not because of an interest in myth and violence. Lanzillo was an active interventionist, an important contributor to *Il Popolo d'Italia*, and a member of the central committee of the Fasci di Combattimento in 1919-20. His *La disfatta del socialismo*, published in 1918, was one of the most influential revolutionary interventionist considerations of the impact of the war, the limits of orthodox socialism, and the need for political alternatives.

Though a full participant in the doctrinal transition from revolutionary syndicalism (q.v.) to Fascist corporativism (*see* CORPORATIVISM AND THE CORPORATIVE STATE), Lanzillo maintained a relatively independent and critical posture within the regime. He objected to the coercive features of Alfredo Rocco's (q.v.) syndical law of 1926 in a forceful speech in the Chamber of Deputies. Long a vehement free-trader, he was especially critical of the move toward autarchy (q.v.) in the 1930s, when his independent posture led to serious trouble with Fascist party authorities. But while less influential than some other corporativists, Lanzillo continued to publicize his relatively open and pluralistic corporativist conception. He also pursued an academic career in economics, serving as rector of the Istituto Superiore di Economia e Commercio di Venezia beginning in 1935.

For further information see: Agostino Lanzillo, *La disfatta del socialismo* (Florence: Libreria della Voce, 1918); idem, *Le rivoluzioni del dopoguerra* (Città di Castello: Il Solco, 1922); David D. Roberts, *The Syndicalist Tradition and Italian Fascism* (Chapel Hill: University of North Carolina Press, 1979).

DDR

LATERAN PACTS. The Lateran Pacts were signed on February 11, 1929, between the Holy See and the Mussolini government after two and one-half years of secret negotiations. The pacts included three documents: a political treaty recognizing the sovereign independence of the Holy See; a concordat that regulated Church-State relations within Italy; and a financial convention that compensated the Vatican for the losses it suffered as a consequence of the unification of Italy in the nineteenth century.

Negotiations between the Vatican and the Mussolini government began in August 1926. Francesco Pacelli represented the Vatican and Domenico Barone the government. Both men were extremely able negotiators who, over the years of almost daily discussions, developed a close working relationship that played a significant role in bringing about the Lateran Pacts. Pacelli practiced law and had personal ties to the Vatican as the brother of Monsignor Eugenio Pacelli, who was at that time Apostolic Nuncio to Germany and later became Pope Pius XII (q.v.). Barone was a member of the Council of State, the most important administrative court in Italy. He had served both Liberal and Fascist Italy on important legal and constitutional commissions. Pacelli was assisted by Monsignor Borgongini-Duca, secretary for the Congregation of Extraordinary Affairs, and the cardinal secretary of state, Pietro Gasparri (q.v.). Both Mussolini and Pope Pius XI (q.v.) were directly involved in the negotiations.

Agreements in principle on the three documents—treaty, concordat, and financial convention—were arrived at by the spring of 1927, but the official Lateran Pacts were not signed for another year and a half. This delay can be explained by Mussolini's major concern over the nature and extension of sovereignty insisted on by Pope Pius XI in order for the Holy See to have an independence recognized in international law. Mussolini's dilemma was to grant this sovereignty without appearing to endanger Italian national interests. Both King Victor Emmanuel III (q.v.) and important elements within Fascism would have opposed the conciliation between Church and State if it seemed Mussolini were granting more to the Vatican than former Liberal governments had been willing to do. While ensuring that Italian national interests as perceived by the Fascists and the king were guaranteed in any agreement, Il Duce had to do so without frightening Pope Pius XI into breaking off negotiations and leaving the resolution of the issues between Church and State to his successor.

Mussolini was willing to grant the Holy See sovereignty over the Vatican territory that had remained in its possession since 1870. He sought, however, to limit even this sovereignty to one based on the spiritual and not the temporal power of the Holy See. Consequently the new papal territory would be bound to neutrality and excluded from all international competition. The pope had to recognize Rome as the capital of Italy under the House of Savoy and in doing so renounce all temporal claims on Italy resulting from the conquest of the Papal States in 1870. Reluctantly the pope accepted these limitations. The issue that delayed negotiations involved the extent of papal territory beyond the land held by the Vatican since 1870. Pope Pius XI insisted on sovereignty over the Villa Doria Pamphili, located behind the Janiculum. This extension of territory with sovereignty was politically impossible for Mussolini to grant.

In order to pressure the pope into renouncing Villa Doria Pamphili and yet to avoid his breaking off negotiations completely, Mussolini adopted a carrot and stick tactic. He granted important concessions in the concordat that gave the Church in Italy a privileged position by allowing religious education in the secondary schools, granting civil recognition to religious marriages, and guaranteeing full autonomy to Catholic Action (*see* AZIONE CATTOLICA ITALIANA). While conceding on these important points, Mussolini threatened to disband youth groups under Catholic Action at two important stages in the negotiations in January 1927 and April 1928. His purpose was to show the pope that only through a concordat tied to a treaty would it be possible to protect Catholic Action. Without these legal guarantees for Catholic Action, one of the aims of Pius XI's pontificate, the Christian education of the young, would be seriously endangered.

This tactic worked, for despite misgivings Pope Pius XI continued the negotiations. In November 1928 he finally gave up all claims to Villa Doria Pamphili.

Negotiations quickly came to a conclusion, despite the death of Mussolini's chief negotiator, Domenico Barone, a month before the treaties were signed. The Lateran Pacts were enthusiastically received in Italy and throughout the Catholic world. By them Mussolini had consolidated his support at home and won international prestige for Fascist Italy. In return for this victory, Mussolini paid an enormous price by granting the Church a privileged position in Italy. The protection granted to Catholic Action became an especially bitter issue between Church and State over the next two years and created a serious conflict between Pope Pius XI and Mussolini in 1931.

Pope Pius XI also gained important benefits from the conciliation. Through the concordat the Church won a privileged place in Italian society and protection for Catholic Action, which became the only organization outside Fascism permitted to exist. The financial convention generously indemnified the Holy See and saved it from bankruptcy. The treaty granted to the Holy See the sovereign independence that it perceived as essential to its spiritual mission. The danger to this mission only appeared with time. Because of the Lateran Pacts the papacy often seemed more allied to totalitarian Fascism than to democracy as the two movements headed toward a collision course in the 1930s. With the emergence of democracy in Italy after World War II and the new openness in the Church brought about by Pope John XXIII and Vatican II, a concordat based on privileges and tied historically to Fascism became an embarrassing liability.

For further information see: Carlo Alberto Biggini, *Storia inedita della conciliazione* (Milano: Garzanti, 1942); D. A. Binchy, *Church and State in Fascist Italy* (London: Oxford University Press, 1941); Angelo Martini, *Studi sulla Questione Romana e la conciliazione* (Rome: Edizioni Lune, 1963); Francesco Pacelli, *Diario inedito della conciliazione con verbali e appendice di documenti*, ed. by Michele Maccarone (Città del Vaticano: Libreria editrice, 1959).

ACO

LAZZARI, COSTANTINO (b. Cremona, January 1, 1857; d. Rome, December 26, 1927). One of the principal leaders in the Italian Socialist movement, Lazzari was raised in Milan by his maternal grandparents. Constrained by poverty, he left school at the age of fifteen and worked as an apprentice in a wholesale firm. He became active in the Milanese labor movement in the early 1880s by joining the Circolo Operaio Milanese. Through the counsel of Osvaldo Gnocchi-Viani, a lawyer-journalist who acted as a patron for this "workers circle," he was introduced to current Socialist theories. In 1883 Lazzari, together with a group of workers from the Circolo Operaio, founded the Lega dei Figli del Lavoro (League of the Sons of Labor), which became the Partito Operaio Italiano (Italian Worker party) in 1884. Lazzari served as the editor of the party's weekly newspaper, *Fascio Operaio*, and established a reputation as a militant Socialist and an effective labor organizer. The government dissolved the Partito Operaio in June 1886 because of its success in organizing labor unions and promoting strike activity. The party leaders, including Lazzari, were arrested and received prison sentences varying from two to nine months.

In 1891 Lazzari joined with other Milanese labor leaders in organizing the Camera del Lavoro (Chamber of Labor), which served as a model for similar institutions established throughout Italy during the next two decades. The Lazzari also collaborated with Filippo Turati (q.v.) in the founding of the Lega Socialista Milanese (Milanese Socialist League) in 1889. This alliance between the leaders of the Partito Operaio and Milanese Socialist intellectuals served as the nucleus around which the Italian Socialist Party (Partito Socialista Italiano—PSI) (q.v.) was formed. Lazzari composed the statutes for the new party and participated in the party's founding congress at Genoa in 1892. He held positions on the party's provisory committee in 1891, the central committee from 1892 to 1895, the executive commission from 1895 to 1897, and served as administrator of the official party newspaper, *Lotta di Classe*, from 1893 to 1896. He accepted employment in 1896 as a sales representative for a Milanese wholesale firm. His frequent business travel allowed him the opportunity to engage in party organizing activity throughout northern and central Italy. As a result of his political activities Lazzari was arrested and imprisoned following episodes of popular unrest in 1894 and 1898.

Within the Socialist party Lazzari represented the "revolutionary intransigent" faction. As an implacable critic of the existing political and economic order, he opposed the reformist tendencies in the party. In order to combat the influence of reformism, he allied with the revolutionary syndicalists (*see* SYNDICALISM) in the party led by Arturo Labriola (q.v.) and served as administrator of the syndicalist newspaper, *Avanguardia Socialista*, from 1903 to 1906. Despite his avowed opposition to the reformist majority in the party, Lazzari did not follow the syndicalists when they broke from the party in 1907. Instead in 1911 he founded a new Socialist newspaper, *La Soffitta*, and used his skills as a party organizer to strengthen the revolutionary faction in the party.

With the victory of the revolutionary intransigents at the Socialist Party National Congress at Reggio Emilia in 1912, Lazzari assumed the position of political secretary of the party. His seven-year tenure as political secretary coincided with a dramatic increase in the party membership, from twenty-eight thousand in 1912 to more than seventy thousand in 1919. As political secretary he recommended Mussolini for the prestigious and influential position of editor of the party newspaper, *Avanti!*, in 1912. When Mussolini publicly deviated from the official party position of absolute neutrality during the World War I intervention crisis (q.v.), Lazzari personally submitted the request to the Milanese Socialist Federation that Mussolini be expelled from the party.

Under Lazzari's leadership the Socialist party gained international recognition during the war for promoting and participating in the Socialist peace conferences held at Zimmerwald in 1915 and Kienthal in 1916. Lazzari's dictum, *nè aderire, nè sabotare* (neither support nor sabotage), defined the party's official attitude in regard to the Italian war effort. This neutral stance provided a compromise that preserved party unity during the war but left the party in a politically ambiguous and isolated position. Accused by the government of undermining the nation's war effort, Lazzari was arrested in January 1918 and held in prison for the duration of the war.

At the Socialist Party National Congress held in 1919, Lazzari broke with the revolutionary faction (Maximalists) over the issue of political violence. Despite his belief in the necessity and inevitability of the Socialist revolution, he refused to endorse the use of violence as an integral part of the party's political program. Though his political influence in the party declined in the postwar period, Lazzari remained active in party politics. He was elected to the Chamber of Deputies in 1919 and served in this capacity until 1926. In 1921 he represented the Socialist party at the Communist International Congress in Moscow, but was unsuccessful in his attempts to gain the party's admittance into the Third International. As a noted Socialist leader and outspoken opponent of the Fascist government, Lazzari was the target of harassment and in one instance was assaulted by a Fascist group on the steps outside the Parliament. Fearful of future assaults and possible imprisonment, he made two attempts to leave the country clandestinely in 1927, but in both attempts the police arrested him at the border. Because of his age and ill-health he was not imprisoned but forbidden to travel beyond the city limits of Rome. He lived his last years in abject poverty and died in 1927 after a long illness. Though not noted as an intellectual, Lazzari wrote a number of articles and political tracts on revolutionary socialism, including: *La necessità dell politica socialista in Italia* (1902), *I principi e metodi del Partito socialista italiano* (1911), and *I proletari socialisti nella politica parlamentare* (1922).

For further information see: Luigi Ambrosoli, *Nè aderire nè sabotare* (Milan: Avanti!, 1961); Felice Anzi, *Il Partito operaio italiano* (Milan: A.N.S., 1933); Costantino Lazzari, "Memorie," *Movimento operaio* 4 (July-August 1952): 598-633; (September-October 1952): 789-837; Italo Toscani, *Costantino Lazzari* (Rome: Morara, 1921).

                                                                                          MH

LESSONA, ALESSANDRO (b. Rome, September 9, 1891). After serving as Armando Diaz's (q.v.) personal secretary from 1918 to 1919 Lessona became head of the War Ministry Cabinet from 1920 to 1921. Despite his claims, Lessona only joined the PNF (Partito Nazionale Fascista) (q.v.) after October 1922. He rose through Genoa's Fascist organization, gaining election to the Camera in 1924, serving on a mission to Albania in 1925, holding the leadership of the Ligurian Fascist Federation in 1926, and receiving an appointment as Savona's Federale and Militia Consul in 1927. Lessona became National Economy undersecretary in July 1928 with responsibility for fishing. He was then appointed colonial undersecretary in September 1929. Lessona served Emilio De Bono (q.v.) faithfully until he departed for Eritrea in January 1935, and Lessona took over, under Mussolini's nominal ministership. He endorsed Rodolfo Graziani's (q.v.) projected Somali offensive and, after inspecting Eritrea with Pietro Badoglio (q.v.), supported De Bono's replacement in November 1935. Lessona returned in March 1936 to unsuccessfully attempt negotiations with Haile Selassie (q.v.), and then entered Addis with Badoglio. Named colonial minister in June 1936, Lessona instructed the reluctant Graziani to replace native rulers with Italian officials, to create a huge garrison of native troops and Militia (q.v.) under Colonial Ministry control and to prepare Ethiopia for massive exploitation. Lessona ordered resistance crushed brutally, bypassing Graziani to deal directly with provincial governors. Graziani complained to Mussolini, whose respect for Lessona diminished as he schemed with Italo Balbo (q.v.) against G. Ciano (q.v.) and Achille Starace (q.v.) and feuded publicly with De Bono in February 1937. In August 1937, after Italian cruelty sparked massive revolt in Amhara, which was ruled by Lessona's cousin, Alessandro Pirzio Biroli (q.v.), Lessona and Graziani exchanged recriminations. Lessona gained Graziani's substitution by the duke of Aosta (*see* SAVOIA, AMEDEO DI, DUKE OF AOSTA) and Ugo Cavallero (q.v.) before losing his post in November 1937. He became a history professor at Rome University. In 1948 Ethiopia accused Lessona of war crimes.

For further information see: Alessandro Lessona, *Un ministro di Mussolini racconta* (Milan: Edizioni Nazionali, 1973); Giorgio Rochat, *Militari e politici nella preparazione della campagna d'Etiopia* (Milan: Angeli, 1971); Alberto Sbacchi, "Italian Colonialism in Ethiopia 1936-1940" (Ph.D. diss., University of Illinois at Chicago Circle, 1975).

BRS

LEVI, CARLO (b. Turin, November 19, 1902; Rome, January 4, 1975). A painter and writer, Levi received a medical degree in Turin and was very well known as an artist. He was part of the avant-garde "Group of Seven" painters. As a result of his anti-Fascist activities, he was arrested and confined to Lucania in southern Italy from 1935 to 1936. For two years he served as codirector of the newspaper *Nazione del Popolo* (Florence), then director of *L'Italia Libera* (Rome). In 1943 he was named senator of the Communist party. His literary fame began in 1945 with the novel *Christ Stopped at Eboli* (*Cristo si è fermato a Eboli*), in which he described the antiquated world of the Calabrian peasants and condemned the archaic social structure on which middle-class predominance is based. It is a work that is rich in poetry, sentiment, moral passion, and common sense. The mere description of the state of things generated a spontaneous indignation against the Fascist regime, against a social system based on ignorance and hypocrisy. This novel was followed by *Paura della libertà* (1946), *L'orologio* (1950), and travel related books: *Le parole sono pietra* (1953) about Sicily, *Il futuro ha un cuore antico* (1956) about Russia, published again in 1964 with the title, *Tutto il miele è finito*, and finally: *La doppia notte dei tigli* (1956) about Germany.

For further information see: P. Pancrazi, *Scrittori d'oggi* 4, 6 (Bari: Laterza, 1946-53); C. L. Ragghianti, *Carlo Levi* (Florence: Edizioni Universitaria, 1948); E. Falqui, *Prosatori e narratori del Novecento italiano* (Turin: Einaudi, 1950); *Novecento letterario*, 4th and 5th series (Florence: 1954-57); G. Trombatore, in *Scrittori del nostro tempo* (Palermo: Manfredi, 1959); issue dedicated to Carlo Levi in *Galleria* (May-December 1967).

WEL

LIBERAL PARTY. An ill-defined term employed to refer to the loosely joined coalitions of parliamentary factions that dominated Italian political life from the time of unification to 1919. Although differing over many domestic issues, these various Liberal factions (Left, Center, and Right) were in general agreement on the desirability of preserving constitutional government, the monarchy, and private property. Hence the Liberals' distinction from the Republican party, which opposed monarchy as a matter of principle; from the Socialist party, with its Marxist ideology; and least so from the Radical party, champion of universal suffrage and anticlericalism, but otherwise not too distant from the Liberal left.

For more than a decade before 1914, Giovanni Giolitti (q.v.), leader of the Liberal left, pursued a program of socioeconomic reforms intended to coopt the Radicals and domesticate the Socialists. Giolitti's major opponent in the ranks of liberalism was Sidney Sonnino (q.v.), usually characterized as of the Right but too complex a figure to fit neatly under any political label. Antonio Salandra (q.v.), Sonnino's frequent political ally, was more distinctly conservative; and it was Salandra who, owing to the caprices of politics, found himself prime minister in 1914. In concert with Sonnino, by May 1915 Salandra determined Italy's intervention in the war, despite the opposition of Giolitti and the majority of Parliament. The less-than-happy conduct of the war, the strains it imposed on a country still divided between interventionists and neutralists, and the dissatisfaction with the real and alleged failures of V. E. Orlando (q.v.) and Sonnino at the Paris Peace Conference produced a situation with which the fragmented ranks of Italian liberalism proved unable to cope.

It is argued by some writers that the Liberals were primarily responsible for the postwar paralysis of government that was certainly one of the root causes of the rise of Fascism. But the crisis that began in 1919 afflicted not only the Liberals; it was a crisis of a parliamentary system they no longer controlled. The elections of 1919 produced two mass formations outside the liberal orbit: the Socialist party with 156 seats and the Catholic Popular party with 100 seats in a Chamber of 508 seats. A disorganized assortment of Liberals, Democrats, Radicals, and Republicans garnered approximately 220 seats. Inasmuch as the Socialists talked of revolution and refused to collaborate with any "bourgeois" party, and given the Popularists' insistence that they would support no government except on their terms, the vicissitudes experienced by all postwar governments before Mussolini came to power acquired an aspect of inevitability.

F.S. Nitti's (q.v.) sensible attempts to repair the country's shattered economy in 1919-20 were frustrated by the hostility of the Liberal and Nationalist Right, the revolutionary posture of the Socialists, and the loss of the Popularists' support. Unquestionably, Nitti's inability or unwillingness to deal forcefully with Gabriele D'Annunzio's (q.v.) seizure of Fiume (q.v.) in 1919 did not redound to the credit of a liberal state that failed to punish an act of mutiny which, three years later, served as the model for a greater mutiny. But that same state, under Giovanni Giolitti's direction in 1920-21, did have the vigor to oust D'Annunzio from Fiume. It did have the initiative to try to revitalize liberalism with a grand program of reforms that might have spared Italy the "experiment" with Fascism, had the development of this program not been obstructed by the factious Socialists and the ambitious Popularists personally hostile to Giolitti. Admittedly, Giolitti made the mistake of thinking that he could domesticate the Fascists in 1921 as he had domesticated some of the prewar Socialists; however, the notion that the inclusion of Fascists in Parliament and even in the government might moderate the course of Fascism was shared not only by Giolitti, Salandra, Orlando, and other Liberal leaders, but by some Socialists and Popularists as well. Sixteen months of well-intentioned but ineffectual governments under Ivanoe Bonomi (q.v.) and Luigi Facta (q.v.) in 1921-22 converted this notion into a general conviction, the ultimate consequence of which was the creation of a coalition government led by Mussolini. The hope, not altogether groundless, that Fascism could be tamed by the responsibility of power waxed and waned in 1923 and the first half of 1924. It vanished completely during the crisis of the Aventine Secession (q.v.) late in 1924, when the last bulwark of the liberal state, the king, proved as weak as in October 1922. By 1925, when Fascism assumed an openly dictatorial aspect, all that the former paladins of liberalism could offer was a verbal opposition which, however futile, was not entirely lacking in courage.

For further information see: Benedetto Croce, *A History of Italy, 1871-1915*, trans. by C. M. Ady (Oxford: Clarendon, 1929); Christopher Seton-Watson, *Italy from Liberalism to Fascism, 1870-1925* (London: Methuen, 1967); Adrian Lyttelton, *The Seizure of Power: Fascism in Italy, 1919-1929* (New York: Scribner's, 1973).

SS

LIBYA (TRIPOLITANIA AND CYRENAICA). The Ottoman provinces of Tripolitania and Cyrenaica became Italian possessions at the conclusion of the Italo-Turkish War of 1911-12. Patriotic rhetoric and a sensational newspaper campaign had described Libya as a "terra promessa" (promised land) for Italy's emigrants who were forced to settle in foreign lands. Italians soon found that they had acquired sovereignty over two vast desert territories, totally lacking in natural resources and thinly populated by a hostile Moslem population—scarcely an emigrant's paradise. Nevertheless, for nearly thirty years, until the defeat of the Axis (*see* AXIS, ROME-BERLIN) marked the end of Italian rule, Italy worked to create a "fourth shore" (to add to Italy's Tyrrhenian, Adriatic, and Sicilian shores), a single colony, along the lines of Algeria, that would become an integral part of the mother country and would provide opportunities for emigrants to settle as small landowners.

Following the initial conquest, Liberal regimes, preoccupied with World War I and then with Italy's postwar domestic crisis, made little attempt to establish control over the entire territory or to undertake colonization. When the Fascists came to power in 1922, they embarked immediately on a campaign of military conquest. The repression took nearly a decade. Although Tripolitania was peaceful by 1924, the Sanusi-led rebellion in Cyrenaica lasted until 1931 and was particularly ferocious. According to official Italian figures, the population of Cyrenaica declined from two hundred twenty-five thousand in 1928 to one hundred forty-two thousand in 1931. Moreover, the livestock, the chief means of livelihood of the indigenous population, was decimated.

Under the governorships of Count Giuseppe Volpi (q.v.) between July 1921 and July 1925, General Emilio De Bono (q.v.) between July 1925 and December 1928, and Marshal Pietro Badoglio (q.v.) between January 1929 and December 1933, the Italians experimented with various programs of land grants and subsidies to attract investors and colonists. Despite ever larger subsidies and increasing government regulation, the results remained unsatisfactory. Large plantations (devoted to almonds, olives, and vineyards), worked by Libyan labor, developed instead of a small landholder's paradise.

During the last half dozen years of Italian rule, however, the outlines of a "fourth shore" began to emerge. Thanks to peaceful internal conditions, the eagerness of the Fascist regime to finance the colony's development, and the personal energy and influence of the flamboyant Italo Balbo (q.v.), governor from 1934 to 1940, the colony flourished. Colonization companies, financed by the government and by social welfare organizations, were entrusted with programs of intensive land settlement. Balbo himself presided over two mass migrations of colonists (twenty thousand in October 1938 and an additional ten thousand a year later) chosen primarily from the Po Valley and the Veneto. Communications improved vastly with the completion of a 1,800-kilometer border-to-border highway inaugurated in 1937. Tripolitania and Cyrenaica were united administratively into one territory known as Libya with a single governor located in Tripoli. Socially and culturally the coastal regions became an extension of Italy, as tourists flocked to special events such as car races and air rallies or to visit the newly excavated archeological sites of Sabratha and Leptis Magna. By 1939 the transformation was given legal recognition when the four coastal provinces of Tripoli, Misurata, Benghazi, and Derna were incorporated into the kingdom of Italy.

The transformation of Libya, however, was very costly to the mother country. The colony never came close to self-sufficiency and remained heavily dependent on subsidies from Italy. Nor were the Italians successful in dealing with the indigenous Libyans, on whom they depended for labor. By 1940 the Italian population numbered about one hundred and ten thousand in contrast to a Libyan population of about eight hundred thousand. The failure of a "separate but equal" policy became clear when World War II broke out. Many Libyans rallied to the Sanusi banner once again (in alliance with the British), and the Libyans rejected any claims for even a limited period of postwar Italian trusteeship over Tripolitania. Nevertheless, a sizeable Italian colony remained in Tripoli until its final expulsion in 1970.

For further information see: F. Malgeri, *La guerra libica* (Rome: Edizioni di Storia e Letteratura, 1970); E. E. Evans Pritchard, *The Sanusi of Cyrenaica* (London: Oxford University Press, 1949); Giorgio Rochat, "La repressione della resistenza araba in Cirenaica," in *Il movimento di liberazione in Italia* 110 (1973); Claudio G. Segré, *Fourth Shore: the Italian Colonization of Libya* (Chicago: University of Chicago Press, 1974).

CGS

LITERATURE. World War I, with its suffering and atrocities, generated a very rich literature in which the most acclaimed writers of the time utilized lyricism as a highly effective mode of self-expression. But together with the inevitable war stories, the mainstream of Italian literature of the time was characterized by a spiritual void caused not only by the obvious tragedies of war but, more importantly, by the intellectual and social crisis of the prewar period, a crisis that was unresolved and in fact actually aggravated by the war.

The result was not only a lack of poetry but a lack of genuine feeling, a lack of style and faith in humanity. The new generation of poets, in an effort to deny literary tradition and the past, defined existence as an end in itself and man only in relation to himself rather than as a part of a much larger reality as the Romantics had believed. The young poets thus resigned themselves to a new rhetorical historicism duly integrated and developed wherein each "fact" in itself constituted only the surface of a richer and deeper experience. Hence, any whimsical idea was futuristically reduced to its impulsive reality, thereby becoming a symbol and a kind of gospel truth capable of moving the masses and creating a new social or political ideology.

Intellectual anarchism was fast becoming a part of Italian culture, producing a sharp decline in individual responsibility. Similarly, the literature of the period produced a light and loquacious impressionism, completely devoid of any harmonious construction or composition. In the specific case of literary technique, great importance was given to the bare world stripped of all constructive or logical ties and valid above all as a musical suggestion.

Among the many works of this period, the novel *Rubè* (1921) by Giuseppe Antonio Borgese (q.v.) is an excellent example of the passage from intellectualism to the rhetorical postwar historicism. Filippo Rubè is the symbol of his times: he is weak and uncertain, he reacts impulsively to any stimulus, he wavers with every gust of wind and is exposed to every temptation. He lacks a solid character and firm moral fiber. Rubè is continuously bombarded by an extraordinary variety of stimuli and lives almost exclusively by breaking and crumbling.

Rubè justly represents the repudiation of tradition and the extreme desire for something new at any cost. In the culture of the time, as in the novel, there was a tendency to explore every world and every unknown idea. This led to the discovery of German Romanticism. Spiritualism, idealism, and pragmatism were rejected in favor of the new ideas and experience of reviews such as *Leonardo*, *La Voce*, *Lacerba*, and *La Ronda*, all of which had the collaboration of renowned authors such as Giovanni Papini (q.v.), Borgese, and Giuseppe Prezzolini (q.v.). While these journals proclaimed responsibilities and upheld a credo, there appeared to be an ideological void and a profound intellectual anarchy, a rejection of tradition without any alternative to take its place.

Benedetto Croce (q.v.), although partly responsible for that attitude, tried to hold back the irrationality of the times with his review, *La Critica*, and through his constant work as a patient and scrupulous thinker.

With respect to literary culture during the years immediately following the rise of Fascism, there was among writers and poets, notwithstanding a few exceptions, a silence, a seemingly deliberate nonproductivity. They would write so-called *capitoli* (chapters) or *frammenti* (fragments), or editorial-page articles in daily newspapers. They preferred to isolate themselves in the techniques of style and form (the only freedom conceded by the regime) in order to suggest what they could not openly state. Many preferred to write works far removed from politics, such as travel diaries.

In 1922 there appeared a new direction in literature, one that had been already gradually prepared for in the preceding years. Conformism and rhetorical historicism were replaced by a widespread "moralism," already evident in Riccardo Bacchelli's *Lo sa il tonno* (1923), a novel rich in humanity, reason, and good sense. Also in 1923 Bruno Cicognani's *Velia* introduced a new Florentine narrative style with the restoration of the historical perspective as an essential element of human life. The writers of the time were versatile and revealed a moral conscience that was altogether missing just a few years earlier. Typical examples are *Il Lettore provveduto* (1923) by Cesare Angelini and *Ossi di seppia* (1924) by Eugenio Montale (q.v.). Mario Moretti wrote *Il Trono dei poveri* in 1928, which described an enchanted fantasy world; the same year brought *La Coscienza di Zeno* by Italo Svevo, only later fully understood and valued. Svevo's work accepts moral reality without appeals to sentiment or reason.

Together with the beginning of Luigi Pirandello's (q.v.) major works in 1929 came Alberto Moravia's (q.v.) novel, *Gli Indifferenti* (*The Indifferent Ones*), a strong reaction to the conformism of earlier years and a key book in the interpretation of Moravia as a narrator. Nineteen-thirty marked the beginning of a new period in literature that lasted until 1936, in which the moralism of the preceding years deepened, resulting in two new currents of thought: (1) Freudianism, which discovered the world of the unconscious, a private world that went far beyond the historic and economic world; and (2) existentialism, which coldly demonstrated the defeat of reason and the superiority of existence over thought.

In the 1930s literature began to reflect a mistrust of the politics and the history that had provoked a useless war and the advent of Fascism. This skepticism was matched by a sense of overpowering reduction of the self due to the oppressive omnipresence of the state and its authority in all aspects of society. Writers therefore felt nullified by the totalitarian state on one side, and plunged into an existentialist nothingness on the other. Such negativeness and mistrust paradoxically produced a richer, more sincere, and moral literature. In the complete destruction of the political and social world, only one possible element remained: the sovereignty of the word of one finite human being over the world.

Thus, the literary works of the 1930s overturned the rapport between historical totality and the individual, a rapport that was established by rhetorical historicism and reinforced by Fascism. Works such as Corrado Alvaro's (q.v.) *Gente di Aspromonte* (1930), Salvatore Quasimodo's *Acque e terre* (1930), and Vincenzo Cardarelli's *Il Sole a picco* (1929) created a new integral humanism and depicted the salvation of the individual within the ruins of society.

The year 1931 produced Giovanni Papini's *Gog*, a series of grotesque caricatures, and Elio Vittorini's (q.v.) *Piccola borghesia*, which depicted the vanity of the provincial and prefectural world.

In 1933 Giuseppe Ungaretti (q.v.) wrote *Sentimento del tempo* in which he assembled his poems from 1919 to 1932 in an attempt to give a meaning to time. In 1934 Angelo Gatti's *Le Massime e i caratteri* offered an open programmatic moralism, while Carlo Emilio Gadda's *Il Castello di Udine* presented a lively war narrative, and Aldo Palazzeschi published a strong and powerful masterpiece, *Le Sorelle Materassi*.

A major turning point in literature appeared in the shift from moralism to "hermeticism." Literary moralism presented a negative world. It had in fact denied politics and idealistic history, as well as the theory of a gratuitous world capable of every abundance; it even denied the consolation of death. And yet the emphasis was not on the refusal of these things. On the contrary, it was a powerful affirmation of a new philosophical literary credo: an opening toward providence in history and a window to the soul in the psychology of the individual.

In the philosophy of those years, the accord attempted by Croce between Hegel (the state worshiper) and Vico (the Catholic) was inadequate. So too was the subsequent formation of an existentialist right and a Marxist left. It appeared more urgent to refute the ambitions of idealism and the absolute of history, claiming instead the faith of a human and worthy survival in time.

Massimo Bontempelli (q.v.), in *Gente del tempo* (1937), proposed this new prospective by combatting the stereotyping of idealistic historicism and proclaiming providence as a leading force beyond immediate events. Similarly, in *Il Mulino del Po* (1938), Riccardo Bacchelli openly pronounced morals to be beyond history, nature beyond morals, and God beyond nature. A parallel scale of religious order led the individual to the first and last essence of man: his soul. Ungaretti achieved through poetry what Bacchelli had achieved through prose. In

Vita d'un uomo, Allegria, and *Il Dolore* he expressed the freedom from history and above all the lyrical presence of the soul in the terrestial adventure.

In conjunction with the works of Bacchelli and Ungaretti, the journal entitled *Il Frontespizio* helped to diffuse the new poetic credo throughout Italy. Under the direction of Piero Bargellini, who knew how to find a happy formula for the diffusion and comprehension of hermeticism, *Il Frontespizio* had collaborators who claimed to be preoccupied with the ideology and the philosophy of Catholicsm. But the poetry of "Ermetismo" remained nevertheless obscure, and the word became synonymous with closed, airtight, and incomprehensible.

Carlo Bo tried to clarify the poetry of "Ermetismo" with his essay entitled *La Letteratura come vita* (1938), in which he confronted the new poetry with the absolute morality of literature as life, which could also imply the Catholic revelation without the metaphysical promise of the eternal and the divine. Thus poetry was the ultimate revelation of individual essence, a new secular religion.

But the most sensational episode, the boldest proclamation of "Ermetismo," was made by Luigi Pirandello. By proposing in theater the theory of relativity and especially the incommunicability of man, he sought the absolute validity of the word, the inner communication between writer and reader, and an understanding deeper than that entrusted to the temporary and fickle figure of the human character. Because of this, theater did not aspire to be, nor could it be, either an isolated adventure and spectacle or an accusation of society resolved through political and social reforms; rather, it had to be a *rite* for the discovery of the truth, a religious and theological inquest aimed at finding the ultimate reasons for life and the word.

This intuition of "Ermetismo" was repeated by other playwrights: Ugo Betti, in *Frana allo scalo nord* (1937), portrayed the quest for a judgment, an authority that was somehow superior to man; Bontempelli, in *Gente nel tempo*, described the ultraterrestial substance of time; Cesare Zavattini, in *I Poveri matti*, knowingly merged fantasy and humanity in an implicit condemnation of social egoism; Bacchelli, in the first volume of *Il Mulino del Po*, marked out a balance between history, morality, and nature; and finally Eugenio Montale, in *Le Occasioni* (1939), sketched a kaleidoscope of life images in which the power and amplitude of a divine gaze seemed to possess his human world.

From 1940 to 1945 two distinct literary tendencies developed. The first consisted of writers who clearly attempt to detach themselves from the then present world situation such as Mario Moretti with *La Vedova di Fioravanti*, Vasco Pratolini (q.v.) with *Via dei magazzini*, and Giani Stuparich with *Ritorneranno*.

The other literary current is richer and historically motivated. Unlike the first current, it is characterized by a new realism that, taking a cue from the realism of Verga, Capuana, and Fogazzaro, proposed a deprovincialization of Italian culture, a major involvement in politics on the part of writers, and a new contract with reality (hence the term neorealism) implying the search for a new narrative language.

The main writers of this new literary current (limited to the years 1940-45) were: Elio Vittorini who published *Conversazioni in Sicilia* (1941) and *Uomini e no* (1945); Cesare Pavese, who wrote *Lavorare stanca* (1936, followed by an appendix in 1940) and *Paesi tuoi* (1941); and Alberto Moravia who wrote *Quasi un secolo* (1940) and *Napoli, guerra e pace* (1945).

Other notable authors were: Francesco Jovine, Vitaliano Brancati, Guido Piovene, and finally Carlo Levi (q.v.), who contributed to the essay production during postwar realism. Levi, in his famous *Cristo si è fermato a Eboli* (*Christ Stopped at Eboli*) (1945) exemplifies with a clear and precise realism one of postwar Italy's deepest wounds: the existence of two Italys, the north and the south, historically and socially divided by radically different heredities, cultures, traditions, and inveterate customs. Levi's book served to clarify the groundwork for the resolution of one of the gravest crises of contemporary Italy.

For further information see: Francesco Flora, *Storia della letteratura italiana* (Milan: Mondadori, 1966); Mario Fubini and Ettore Bonora, *Antologia della critica letteraria* (Turin: Petrini, 1961); Natalino Sapegno, *Compendio di Storia della letteratura italiana* (Florence: Nuova Italia, 1964).

WEL

LOCATELLI, ANTONIO (b. Bergamo, August 19, 1895; d. Lekempti, June 26, 1936). An aviator and unique winner of three gold medals, Locatelli won his first gold medal in Gabriele D'Annunzio's (q.v.) squadron in 1918. He joined D'Annunzio at Fiume (q.v.) and then departed for flying exploits in South America. Locatelli was elected to the Chamber of Deputies as a Fascist in 1924. That same year he unsuccessfully attempted to fly over the North Pole. After criticizing government aviation policies, Locatelli abandoned national politics in 1929, though Mussolini appointed him *Podestà* (q.v.) of Bergamo in 1933. Locatelli won his second gold medal for daring reconnaissance flights over the Somali Front in 1936. He died fighting at Lekempti, where he had flown an occupation force, and was granted a posthumous third gold medal.

For further information see: I. Mencarelli, *Cenno biografico su Antonio Locatelli* (Rome: Ufficio storico dell' Aeronautica militare italiana, 1970).

BRS

LOJACONO, VINCENZO (b. Palermo, July 8, 1885). A Fascist diplomat, Lojacono took a law degree from the University of Palermo in 1906 and the next year began his career in the foreign service as a member of the Italian legation in London. In 1909 he became secretary of the legation, a post he held until his transfer to Lisbon in 1913. When World War I broke out, he volunteered for service, was wounded, and was decorated.

After the war he resumed his diplomatic career, becoming minister plenipotentiary in 1923. In March 1924 he was appointed director of internal affairs in the Foreign Ministry and two years later was placed in charge of Italian laborers working abroad. In 1929 he was appointed ambassador, serving in Ankara from 1932 to 1934. Later he was transferred to China, Brazil, and Belgium and remained in the foreign service after World War II.

For further information see: *Chi è?* (1936; 1948); NO (1937); *Annuario diplomatico del regno d'Italia* (Rome: Ministry of Foreign Affairs, 1937).

MSF

LONGANESI, LEO (b. Ravenna, August 30, 1905; d. Milan, September 27, 1957). An editor, writer, and painter, Longanesi took a degree in law and entered journalism. He founded *Il Toro*, *Il Dominio*, *L'Italiano*, and other newspapers. An admirer of Mussolini in the early days of the regime, he began to move away from Fascism by the late 1930s. *L'Italiano*, which he published from 1927 to 1946, was a literary-political review with tendencies toward the Strapaese (*see* STRACITTÀ/ STRAPAESE) movement. Longanesi never quite lost his individualism, despite the fact that it was he who coined the phrase "Mussolini is always right," and in 1926 had published *Il vademecum del perfetto fascista*. After World War II he founded the Longanesi publishing house and wrote widely on a number of topics. In 1950 he and Indro Montanelli founded the right-wing journal *Il Borghese*.

For further information see: EAR (2); *Il meglio di Leo Longanesi*, ed. M. Monti (Milan: Ronda, 1958).

WEL

LONGO, LUIGI (b. Fubine Monferrato, Alessandria, March 15, 1900). A leading Communist organizer, Longo studied at technical schools, but his education was interrupted by World War I. He served at the front as a soldier, and then his conversion to socialism began. In 1920 he joined the Socialist Youth Federation in Turin and became the group's secretary, participating in the "Occupation of the Factories" (q.v.) of northern Italy in September. Longo collaborated with Antonio Gramsci (q.v.) on *L'Ordine Nuovo* and became increasingly more radical. He joined the Italian Communist party (*see* PARTITO COMUNISTA ITALIANO) upon its creation in 1921 and was assigned the task of organizing armed squads to fight Fascist violence in Turin.

Longo was sent to Moscow by the party to represent Italy at the Third International, and after the Fascist seizure of power he began actively to organize anti-Fascist groups and published *La Voce della Gioventù*. Arrested in May 1924, he was released and then severely beaten by Fascists the next year. He returned to Moscow again in 1926 and sided with Stalin against the Trotskyites, and then went to Paris and Switzerland on party missions. In 1933 he was elected to the central committee of the Communist International and the next year helped to negotiate the Pact of Unity with the Socialists.

Among the first anti-Fascists to go to Spain to fight Franco, he joined the Garibaldi Brigade and was wounded in action. After the Spanish Civil War (q.v.), he went to Paris but was arrested by the French and not freed until August 1943.

Returning to Rome, Longo attempted to achieve a unity of action among all anti-Fascist forces. He took part in the defense of Rome against the Germans in September and then became leader of the Communist political and military activites in northern Italy for the rest of the war.

After World War II Longo became vice-secretary of the Communist party and was elected to the Constituent Assembly (*see* COSTITUENTE) and to Parliament on numerous occasions. Upon the death of Palmiro Togliatti (q.v.) in 1964, Longo became secretary-general of the party, a position he held until 1972.

For further information see: MOI (3); Paolo Spriano, *Storia del partito comunista italiano*, 5 vols. (Turin: Einaudi, 1967-75).

MSF

LORENZINI, ORLANDO (b. Guardistallo, Pisa, May 3, 1890; d. March 17, 1941). Lorenzini commanded Askaris and then armored car units in Libya (q.v.) almost continuously from 1913 to 1934, before transfer to East Africa. His leadership in the December 1935-January 1936 crisis and the Danakil expedition in March 1936 brought Lorenzini counterguerrilla assignments in central and northern Ethiopia between 1936 and 1940. After leading Askaris in the Somaliland Campaign in August 1940, and leading the resistance at Agordat in January 1941 he was promoted to brigadier. He animated the Keren (q.v.) defense. Lorenzini's death shattered Askari morale. A Christian mystic, yet implacable counterinsurgency commander, he became a legend in Ethiopia. Lorenzini received a posthumous gold medal.

For further information see: Paolo Caccia Dominioni, *Askari K 7* (Milan: Longanesi, 1966); *Corriere della Sera*, March 19, 1941.

BRS

LUCE, ISTITUTO NAZIONALE. A government-controlled film agency that produced the Fascist regime's newsreels and documentaries, LUCE (L'Unione Cinematografica Educativa) had its origins in a private film company created in 1923 known as the Sindacato di Istruzione Cinematografica, which the government began to subsidize almost immediately. In 1924 the Sindacato was transformed into the Istituto LUCE, and the next year it was made a state agency under the presidency of Marchese Giacomo Paulucci di Calboli Barone (q.v.) and the direction of Luciano De Feo. A decree of 1926 required all movie theaters in Italy to show a LUCE film at all public showings of commercial films.

The LUCE newsreels, known as Cinegiornali, were similar to those shown in other countries during the same period but had the requisite degree of Fascist rhetoric about the accomplishments of the regime. They also heavily emphasized sports. The documentaries, which also concentrated on the major achievements and themes of the regime, were often better produced but not nearly as successful as their Nazi equivalents in Germany. Among the most outstanding examples of Fascist documentaries were *Il cammino degli eroi* (Italy's Ethiopian conquests),

La battaglia del grano (the Fascist wheat production program), and *Il Decennale*, which described Fascism's transformation of Italy after ten years in power.

For further information see: Philip V. Cannistraro, *La fabbrica del consenso* (Rome-Bari: Laterza, 1975); Edward R. Tannenbaum, *The Fascist Experience* (New York: Basic Books, 1972).

PVC

LUSSU, EMILIO (b. Armungia, Cagliari, December 4, 1890; d. Rome, March 5, 1975). A militant Sardinian republican, Lussu dedicated his long political career to a program of democratic radicalism based on the struggle of the workers, land reform, and regional autonomy. Born to a family of landowners, he took a law degree and was wounded and decorated for courage in World War I.

He returned to Sardinia where he launched his political career. In 1921, as leader of the Sardinian Party of Action, he won election to the Chamber of Deputies, where he worked for social and economic reform and the creation of a popularly based democratic republic.

Always an energetic anti-Fascist, he boldly accused Mussolini and the Fascists of killing Matteotti (*see* MATTEOTTI CRISIS). He was arrested for forcefully defending himself when a gang of squadrists (*see* SQUADRISTI) attacked his house in Cagliari in October 1926. Despite being acquitted after thirteen months of preventive detention, he was confined to the Lipari Islands on the express orders of Mussolini. There he planned anti-Fascist strategy extensively with Carlo Rosselli (*see* ROSSELLI, CARLO and ROSSELLI, NELLO), (q.v.), with whom he was daringly rescued in July 1929.

Lussu escaped to Paris where he helped found Giustizia e Libertà (*see* ANTI-FASCISM). As a leader of GL, he committed himself to the ideological Left, championing the causes of republicanism, regional atuonomy, and a European federation. He hoped ultimately to convert GL to a proletarian movement that would replace the Socialist party (*see* PARTITO SOCIALISTA ITALIANO), which he denounced in 1934 as a "handful of mercenary brigands."

In 1935 he withdrew from GL in a dispute with Carlo Rosselli, arguing the need for a revolutionary, democratic, Socialist party with a paramilitary arm to arouse and lead the proletariat. He moved to Switzerland to recover from aggravations of his war wounds and the hardships of prison life.

The assassination of the Rosselli brothers in 1937 brought Lussu back into active politics. He resumed his radical leadership role in GL, continuing to pursue his democratic revolutionary idealism by sponsoring a union of Republicans, Socialist, and Communists on behalf of the proletariat.

With the outbreak of World War II, he and his wife, Joyce Salvadori, organized a clandestine center at Marseilles for the emigration of political exiles. At the fall of France he fled with his wife to London where he attempted—and failed—to persuade the British to withdraw support of Pietro Badoglio (q.v.), the king, and Fascist dissidents and to guarantee Italian territorial integrity in return for guerrilla insurgency in Sardinia. In exile he continued to pursue his political agenda through GL, travelling to the U.S., Portugal, Switzerland, and France.

In July 1943 Lussu reentered Italy where he organized a GL nucleus and led the partisan resistance in Rome. He emerged as a radical leader in the Party of Action (q.v.) and after liberation served as a minister in the governments of Ferruccio Parri (q.v.) and Alcide De Gasperi (q.v.).

He continued to lead the leftist Socialists away from cooperation with Christian Democracy until 1968. His poor health forced him to retire from the Senate and from the cause of militant democratic radicalism to which he had devoted his public life.

For further information see: EAR (2); Charles F. Delzell, *Mussolini's Enemies* (Princeton: Princeton University Press, 1961); Emilio Lussu, *Marcia su Roma e dintorni* (Turin: Einaudi, 1945); Emilio Lussu, *Partito d'Azione e gli altri* (Milan: Mursia, 1968); Emilio Lussu, *Diplomazia clandestina* (Florence: Nuova Italia, 1956).

CLK

M

MACCARI, MINO (b. Siena, November 24, 1898). A journalist and Fascist supporter, in July 1924 Maccari helped found *Il Selvaggio* in Florence. *Il Selvaggio* adopted a satirical tone and was one of a number of Florentine journals that were critical of Mussolini's attempt to legalize Fascism and restrain its more violent and revolutionary tendencies. For many years *Il Selvaggio* was a mouthpiece for intransigent Fascists and in the late 1920s was one of the main organs of the Strapaese (*see* STRACITTÀ/STRAPAESE) literary movement of which Maccari was a leading figure. Supported by Curzio Malaparte (q.v.), Ardengo Soffici (q.v.), and Leo Longanesi (q.v.), the Strapaese movement sought to produce a true Fascist literature. It extolled the values and nature of rural society, glorified populist Fascism, and praised the purity and power of provincial *squadrismo* (*see* SQUADRISTI).

Although he helped edit both *La Stampa* and *Il Popolo d'Italia*, Maccari's main interest remained *Il Selvaggio*, which continued publication under his leadership until 1943. In the 1930s and 1940s, *Il Selvaggio* satirized many Fascist institutions and personages and became popular with anti-Fascists. Many writers not favored by the regime contributed to the journal. During these years Maccari voiced his disapproval of Nazi militarism and ideology and was especially contemptuous of Nazi racial policies, an attack he continued even after the Fascist government had adopted its anti-Semitic legislation.

For further information see: *Chi è?* (1936; 1948); EAR (3); Adrian Lyttelton, *The Seizure of Power* (London: Weidenfeld and Nicolson, 1973).

MSF

MACKENSEN, HANS-GEORG VIKTOR VON (b. Berlin, January 26, 1883; d. Konstanz, Germany, September 28, 1947). German ambassador to Italy from 1938 to 1943, Mackensen was the son of the field marshal of World War I. He completed his doctorate in law in 1918 at the University of Berlin and had a brief period of military service during the war. By 1919 he was already launched upon a diplomatic career. He spent the years between 1923 and 1926 as counselor of the embassy in Rome. This was followed by service in Belgium, Albania, Spain, and Hungary before he was appointed in 1938 to replace Christian Albrecht Ulrich von Hassell (q.v.) as the German ambassador in Rome.

Mackensen was the typical old-line diplomat, serving as the messenger of the regime at home and having little apparent effect upon the policies either of Germany or Italy. The real decisions were made by Hitler and Mussolini, and Mackensen was one of the ceremonial attendants and rapporteurs of the preparations for them and their aftermaths. It is apparent that he did not fully grasp the divisions in Italian politics under Mussolini nor the Italian resentment at German domination. Mussolini's major cabinet change, the "changing of the guard" in 1943, caught him by surprise, and the development of the anti-Mussolini movement in the months that followed found him failing to provide his government with adequate warnings. Although Roberto Farinacci (q.v.) conveyed to him some of the proposed plans of the conspirators against Mussolini on July 21, 1943, Mackensen concluded incorrectly that they planned only a reinvigoration of the war effort.

Mackensen considered Mussolini "a personal friend" as well as an ally of Germany and believed that his fall from power marked the end of the Fascist era. Mackensen's replacement with Rudolf Rahn (q.v.) signified the intention of the Nazi regime to exercise a much more rigorous control over Italian politics than had been possible under a rather colorless professional diplomat.

Mackensen was arrested by the French in 1945 but was not brought to trial.

For further information see: F.W. Deakin, *The Brutal Friendship. Mussolini, Hitler and the Fall of Italian Fascism* (New York: Harper & Row, 1962).

ERB

MAFAI, MARIO (b. Rome, February 10, 1902; d. Rome, 1965). Mafai was an Italian painter and cofounder with Scipione (*see* SCIPIONE [GINO BONICHI]) of the expressionistic Roman school, whose work, especially from the mid-thirties on, developed veiled anti-Fascist themes. Early in his training Mafai was expelled from the Academy of Fine Arts in Rome. Marriage to Antonietta Raphael, a young artist just returned to Italy, brought exposure to the latest innovative movements in Europe. Under her influence Mafai broke completely with the monumental official academic Italian painting. With his friend and fellow artist, Scipione (Gino Bonichi), he espoused a visionary, lyric, poetic, expressionist style that characterized the so-called Roman school. Landscapes, flowers, and nudes provided the subject matter.

Mafai exhibited for the first time in 1928 at the Circolo di Roma, at the first Quadriennale, and the XVIII Biennale of Venice. He won the Premio Bergamo in painting.

A new theme, subtly subversive in the imperial-Fascist climate, was introduced by Mafai's "demolition" paintings such as *Demolizione in via Ripetta* (1935). These studies of buildings with floors, interiors, and the exposed skeletal structure in the process of being dismembered evoked lost lives and values. The destruction of the older working-class neighborhoods to make way for a new, ideal imperial city provided a visual metaphor that Mafai used to imply a destruction of human values. In answer to his critics Mafai wrote in 1940 that he believed it better to begin with more recent roots (the nineteenth century in his case) than the Roman period. The statement places him stylistically and ideologically in opposition to the classic revival proposed in Fascist ideology.

World War II and the German occupation awakened in Mafai a spirit reminiscent of Goya, which manifested itself in a series of scenes and dramatic tortures (the *Fantasies*, 1941-43). These scenes offer a lyric examination of human cruelty and suffering under Fascism.

For further information see: Giuseppe Marchiori, "Artisti Contemporanei: Mario Mafai," *Emporium* 92 (September 1940); Antonio Santangelo, "Mario Mafai," *Emporium* 95 (April 1942).

MCG

MAGISTRATI, MASSIMO (b. Gallarate, July 5, 1899; d. Rome, 1970). A career diplomat and brother-in-law of Galeazzo Ciano (q.v.), Magistrati held an important post in the Berlin embassy during the critical years between 1934 and 1940.

Following law studies, Magistrati served in the Italian embassies in Peking, Rio de Janeiro, Geneva, and Algiers before becoming embassy counselor in Berlin. In that post, because of his close relationship with Ciano, he served as an observer and sounding board for the foreign minister. Magistrati also was a confidant of Hermann Goering and served as a conduit for the Italians to that German leader.

In February 1940 Magistrati went to Sofia as minister. Ciano briefly considered him for the Berlin embassy vacated by Bernardo Attolico (q.v.) later that year, but the Germans specifically rejected him. In 1943 Magistrati was reassigned as Italian minister in Berne.

Magistrati continued his diplomatic career after the war, representing Italy in international organizations and as ambassador to Turkey and the UAR and as head of the Political Office of the Foreign Ministry.

For further information see: Massimo Magistrati, *L'Italia a Berlino* (Milan: Arnaldo Mondadori Editore, 1956).

MFL

MALAPARTE, CURZIO (b. Prato, June 9, 1898; d. Rome, July 19, 1957). An early Fascist and intellectual, Malaparte (born Kurt Eric Suckert) volunteered for service in World War I and was decorated. After the conflict he had a short-lived diplomatic career as an aide to the Italian ambassador in Poland, but in 1921 he returned to Italy and joined the PNF (PARTITO NAZIONALE FASCISTA) (q.v.). He participated in the March on Rome (q.v.) as a member of the Florentine *squadristi* (q.v.).

In 1924 he founded *La Conquista dello Stato* (Florence), a weekly review that expressed the attitudes of the intransigent, provincial Fascists against the normalizing tendencies of Mussolini. He frequently criticized Mussolini for his moderating policies and glorified the "purity" of the early *squadrismo*. In February 1925 Minister of Interior Luigi Federzoni (q.v.) confiscated *La Conquista* and thereafter it became more measured and careful in its criticisms.

During the 1920s Malaparte was a leading intellectual in the regime, especially in advocating the elimination of foreign influences from Italian life. He rejected Futurism (q.v.) as being too modern and international and became the advocate of

Fascist populism. Perhaps more than any other writer of the period, he expressed the contradictory nature of Fascism, and his reactionary, antimodern themes foreshadowed the future development of much of Fascist ideology. He became a leader of the Strapaese (*see* STRACITTÀ/STRAPAESE) movement in the late 1920s. As one of the so-called "wild ones" of the populist tendency, Malaparte led an adventurous life, fighting many duels and carrying on numerous polemics.

He was editor of *La Stampa* from 1929 to 1931. He then transferred to Paris, where he wrote several important works, including *Tecnica del colpo di stato*, and attacked leading Fascist personalities such as Italo Balbo (q.v.). When he returned to Italy in 1933 he was sentenced to a year of confinement on Lipari and Ischia but managed to be released after the intervention of G. Ciano (q.v.).

In 1937 Malaparte founded the literary review *Prospettive* and during World War II was a correspondent for *Corriere della Sera* in Africa, France, and Russia. He was arrested for his Fascist activities in July 1943 after Mussolini's fall but was released and served as a liason between the Allied troops and the Corpo Italiano di Liberazione. His books were placed on a list of forbidden publications in the Salò Republic (*see* ITALIAN SOCIAL REPUBLIC). He sought to join the Communist party after the war and returned to journalism.

For further information see: *Chi è?* (1948); EAR (3); Adrian Lyttelton, *The Seizure of Power* (London: Weidenfeld & Nicolson, 1973).

MSF

MALETTI, PIETRO (b. Castiglione delle Stiviere, Mantua, May 24, 1880; d. Abu Nibeiwa, Egypt, December 9, 1940). One of Rodolfo Graziani's (q.v.) most trusted subordinates in the suppression of Arabs and Ethiopians, General Maletti exemplified the Fascist colonial fighting soldier. At Debra Libanos (Shoa Province) in May 1937 he massacred several hundred Coptic monks and deacons whom Graziani suspected of complicity in an attempt on his life in the previous February. Maletti by his own account killed over fifteen thousand "rebels" and destroyed over fifty-six thousand habitations between March 28 and June 1, 1937, alone.

Although he was, in Graziani's words, an "old wolf of the desert," Maletti got his motorized Libyan brigade group lost during the march on Sidi el Barrani (September 1940), giving the British more time to make their escape. He died during the surprise British counteroffensive, which caught much of his armor parked outside his perimeter and unready for action.

MK

MALLADRA, GIUSEPPE (b. Turin, September 22, 1863; d. Verona, June 7, 1940). A colonial general and Enrico Caviglia's (q.v.) Chief of Staff between 1919 and 1921, Malladra was also military commander in Tripolitania (*see* LIBYA [TRIPOLITANIA AND CYRENAICA]) under his friend Emilio De Bono (q.v.) from July 1925 to July 1926. Malladra conquered no territory but disciplined his troops sternly, preparing them for later operations. Following war scares, Pietro Badoglio (q.v.) dispatched him on a study mission to East Africa, in July and August of 1926, hoping to gain control over colonial military operations. Malladra informed Mussolini that war with Ethiopia was inevitable. He advised invasion from Eritrea by two hundred thousand troops, with heavy use of artillery, aircraft, and poisonous gas. Badoglio rejected Malladra's proposals as extravagant, but they influenced Mussolini's planning. Malladra commanded the Salerno and Verona divisions between 1926 and 1927 and became a senator in March 1939.

For further information see: Giorgio Rochat, "La Missione Malladra e la responsibilità della preparazione militare in Africa Orientale nel 1926," *Il Risorgimento* 22 (October 1970).

BRS

MANGANELLO. The term refers to the large wooden clubs with rounded heads and often reinforced with iron wielded by the *squadristi* (q.v.) against the enemies of Fascism. The *manganello* became a symbol of the Fascist Blackshirts and their violence, particularly in the bloody "punitive expeditions" between 1919 and 1921. After having been beaten, the victims were administered castor oil and left in the *piazze* and public streets as lessons to others who would oppose the Fascists. In the period after the establishment and consolidation of the regime, the club became something of a venerated relic of the revolution and was referred to in Fascist literature as the *santo manganello*. Cartoons, posters, and commercial advertisements of the 1920s and 1930s often pictured *manganelli* in various forms, even *manganellini* as baby rattles.

For further information see: EAR (3); Ernesto Rossi, *Il manganello e l' aspersorio* (Florence: Parenti, 1958).

PVC

"MANIFESTO OF ANTI-FASCIST INTELLECTUALS." During the first three years of his ministry, Benito Mussolini concentrated on politics. After the series of events that began with the murder of Giacomo Matteotti (*see* MATTEOTTI CRISIS) and ended with Mussolini's defiant speech on January 3, 1925, Fascism proceeded to bring under its control all groups within Italy. To the philosopher Giovanni Gentile (q.v.), Mussolini's first minister of education, fell the task of aligning intellectuals behind the regime. At the end of March 1925 Gentile convened a Convegno per la Cultura Fascista (Conference on Fascist Culture), also called the Convegno per le Istituzioni Fasciste di Cultura (Conference of Fascist Cultural Institutions), at Bologna. Its purpose was to demonstrate that no conflict existed between Fascism and culture, or as the still extant opposition press pointed out, between "the cudgel and culture."

Some four hundred of Italy's leading intellectuals accepted the invitation, but only two hundred and fifty actually attended. Among those who formally addressed the assembly were Giuseppe Bottai (q.v.) and Balbino Giuliano (q.v.), each later to serve Mussolini as minister of education; the painter Ardengo Soffici (q.v.); Tommaso Sillani, journalist and founder of the *Rassegna Italiana*; and the economist and statistician Corrado Gini (q.v.).

At the end of the meeting the delegates issued a "Manifesto of Fascist Intellectuals," which appeared in the press on April 21. It was a curious document, reflecting perhaps the divergent points of view of its sponsors. Among its signers appeared respected and well-known names: Gino Arias, Roberto Cantalupo (q.v.), Vittorio Cian, Francesco Coppola (q.v.), Enrico Corradini (q.v.), Francesco Ercole (q.v.), Filippo Tommaso Marinetti (q.v.), Ugo Ojetti (q.v.), Sergio Panunzio (q.v.), Giuseppe Pirandello, Alfredo Rocco (q.v.), Giuseppe Saitta, Arrigo Solmi (q.v.), Ugo Spirito (q.v.), Giovanni Treccani, Lionello Venturi (q.v.), and Gioacchino Volpe (q.v.).

A few days later on May 1, Benedetto Croce (q.v.) and Giovanni Amendola (q.v.) responded with a countermanifesto, which first appeared in the pages of Amendola's *Il Mondo* and later was reprinted in Croce's *La Critica*. Entitled an "Answer from Italian Writers, Professors, and Journalists to the Manifesto of Fascist Intellectuals," it ridiculed the Fascist document as "a schoolboy's exercise . . . an incoherent and bizarre mixture" of conflicting ideas, and it went on to remind Italians that the men who had fought to create a modern Italy had been inspired by a belief in truth, justice, and liberty, without which there can be no progress.

Among the original forty-one signers of the Croce-Amendola "Manifesto of Anti-Fascist Intellectuals," as it came to be called, were to be found some of Italy's best minds and creative artists, men and women like Sem Benelli (q.v.), Guido De Ruggiero (q.v.), Luigi Einaudi (q.v.), Guglielmo Ferrero (q.v.), Giustino Fortunato (q.v.), Tommaso Gallarati-Scotti, Arturo Carlo Jemolo, Luigi Salvatorelli (q.v.), and Matilde Serao. In subsequent issues of May 10 and 12 *Il Mondo* published additional signatures of many others, who, upon reading the Croce-Amendola statement, wished to join the protesters publicly. These included Luigi Albertini (q.v.) and Alberto Albertini, Corrado Barbagallo, Piero Calamandrei (q.v.), Epicarmo Corbino, Panfilo Gentile, Michelangelo Schipa, Adriano Tilgher, Silvio Trentin (q.v.), Gaetano Salvemini (q.v.), Gaetano Mosca, Sibilla Aleramo, and Tino Luzzatto.

In reviewing the subsequent position vis-à-vis Fascism of the signatories of both manifestos, it becomes evident that as Fascism tightened its controls over Italy, there was some shifting of allegiances. Early supporters of Fascism became disenchanted and withdrew their public adherence. Inversely, others became reconciled or resigned to the reality of Fascist power and made their peace, at least outwardly, with the regime. But the "Manifesto of Anti-Fascist Intellectuals" represented an important and significant moment not only in the history of Italy but in the struggle to defend the intellectual's right to freedom of thought against regimentation.

For further information see: Emilio R. Papa, *Fascismo e cultura* (Padua: Marsilio, 1974).

EPN

MARAINI, ANTONIO (b. Rome, March 5, 1886). An artist and Fascist supporter, Maraini received a law degree before embarking on his career as an artist. He became well known for his numerous works, which adorned buildings throughout Italy. Although a parliamentary deputy from 1934 to 1939, Maraini's most important positions during the Fascist era were those he held in the artistic fields. He was a member of the National Council of Corporations, the Corporation of Professionals and Artists, and the National Council of the Union for Fine Arts. In 1930 Maraini became the secretary-general of the Venice Biennale and two years later was appointed president of the National Union of Fine Arts. Maraini helped transform the Venice Biennale into a nationalistic exhibition and an instrument through which Fascist culture would be glorified. By 1942 the Biennale had literally become a showplace for Italian and German art.

For further information see: *Chi è?* (1936; 1948); Lawrence Alloway, *The Venice Biennale 1865-1968* (Greenwich, N.Y.: New York Graphic Society, 1968); Philip V. Cannistraro, *La fabbrica del consenso* (Rome-Bari: Laterza, 1975); Fernando Tempesti, *Arte dell'Italia fascista* (Milan: Feltrinelli, 1976).

MSF

MARAVIGLIA, MAURIZIO (b. Paola, Cosenza, January 15, 1878; d. 1955). A journalist, Nationalist, and Fascist supporter, Maraviglia began his political activism as a Socialist in his youth. He received a degree in law and served for a short time in the Ministry of Public Instruction. By 1910 he had become a Nationalist and, with Enrico Corradini (q.v.), Luigi Federzoni (q.v.), and Roberto Forges Davanzati, he helped establish the Italian Nationalist Association (q.v.). In December of that year he participated in the first Nationalist congress and was on the staff of *Idea Nazionale*. He was an interventionist and volunteered for combat in World War I.

After 1922 Maraviglia took part in negotiations for the fusion of the Nationalist Association and the PNF (Partito Nazionale Fascista) (q.v.) and in 1923, after their successful outcome, was made a member of the Fascist Grand Council (q.v.). In 1924 he was elected a deputy (until 1939), when he became a senator. He was associate director of *La Tribuna*, a member of the National Council of Corporations (*see* CORPORATIVISM AND THE CORPORATIVE STATE), and taught the history of Fascist doctrine at the University of Perugia. After the fall of Fascism, he was tried but acquitted of Fascist crimes.

For further information see: *Chi è?* (1936; 1948); NO (1937); Alexander De Grand, *The Italian Nationalist Association and the Rise of Fascism* (Lincoln: University of Nebraska Press, 1978).

MSF

MARCH 1943 STRIKES. The strikes that occurred in northern Italy during March of 1943 were the result of efficient anti-Fascist action and mounting discontent and unrest among Italy's working classes. The strikes signalled the beginning of the end of the Fascist dictatorship and set the background for the fall of Mussolini four months later.

By early 1943 Mussolini's war effort was going from bad to worse, with a series of major military defeats and severe Allied bombings of the Italian mainland itself. The civilian population suffered under the dual pressures of the air raids and the rapidly deteriorating economic situation—supplies, food, clothing, energy, and transportation were all scarce and continually rising prices combined with fixed wages meant that the average Italian worker was consuming only one-third of the calories necessary for good nutrition.

By the end of 1942 several localized strikes were breaking out each month. Anti-Fascist organizers, especially Communists, sought to exploit the unrest. Communist workers, led by Leo Lanfranco, Giuseppe Alciati, Umberto Massola, Giovanni Roveda and others prepared the workers for strikes in Turin and Milan, the two chief industrial cities, and the first strike occurred on March 5. Within a week forty-seven separate strikes hit the major factories, and by the end of the month the number had risen to almost two hundred and fifty.

Mussolini's beleaguered regime reacted with mass arrests and attempts to appease the workers with vague promises, and in April Mussolini had to grant substantial wage increases. Although the strikes came to an end, the implications were profound: the strikes were the first working-class action on a massive scale since the creation of the Fascist dictatorship, and their success established a dangerous precedent. Moreover, they demonstrated the weakness of the government and its increasing inability to control the domestic situation. The fall of Mussolini in July 1943 was, in one sense, the logical outcome of the strikes.

For further information see: EAR (3); Charles F. Delzell, *Mussolini's Enemies* (Princeton: Princeton University Press, 1961); Umberto Massola, *Marzo 1943* (Rome: Edizioni di Cultura Sociale, 1950); Giorgio Vaccarino, "Gli scioperi del marzo 1943," *Aspetti della resistenza in Piemonte* (Turin: Istituto della Resistenza in Piemonte, 1950).

PVC

MARCH ON ROME. The projected military occupation of Italy's capital city by the Fascist squads, the March on Rome was a central event in a larger crisis of public order and parliamentary government that culminated in Mussolini's accession to power in October 1922. The precedent and inspiration for such an undertaking came in part from the armed occupation of Fiume (q.v.) by Gabriele D'Annunzio (q.v.) and his legionnaires in September 1919. Within the Fascist movement the idea was reinforced in the summer of 1922 by the temporary occupation of various provincial capitals, which won important political concessions and apparently demonstrated the weakness of the government. Not surprisingly, the chief exponents of the March on Rome were the militant Fascist leaders, Michele Bianchi (q.v.) and Italo Balbo (q.v.) and their *squadristi* (q.v.) in the Po Valley, who wanted a violent seizure of power that would sweep away, in one decisive stroke, the debris of the parliamentary regime.

Mussolini's personal reservations about an assault on the state did not diminish until the beginning of October 1922, after D'Annunzio had agreed to demobilize his legionnaires and the government had failed to respond to the Fascist occupation of Trento and Bolzano. At a meeting in Milan on October 16 the Duce and the top Fascist leaders made the decision to march on Rome. The actual plan for the march was drawn up at a secret meeting in a Neapolitan hotel on October 24. The plan involved three stages: the occupation of public buildings throughout northern and central Italy, the concentration of three columns of Blackshirts on the main roads leading to Rome and their convergence on the capital, and the forceful occupation of the ministries in the event of armed government resistance.

From its inception the March on Rome had little chance of success as a strictly military operation. The city of Rome was defended by a force of twelve thousand men under the command of the loyal General Umberto Pugliese (q.v.). As previous encounters had clearly demonstrated, the *squadristi* lacked the training, discipline, arms, and supplies to challenge and defeat the regular army. The events of October 27 and 28 pointed up the strategic shortcomings of the Fascist mobilization: caught in torrential autumn rains, many Fascists failed to reach their points of concentration outside of Rome, and those who did, arrived poorly armed and lacked food. In the provinces the Blackshirts initially appeared to fare somewhat better. In Perugia, Cremona, Alessandria, and in almost all the provincial capitals of the Veneto, the squads seized public buildings and acquired notable quantities of arms. These successes, though, remained unconnected and localized. Moreover, in all the great northern cities the authorities maintained control of the situation without much difficulty.

The real importance of the March on Rome lay not on the military plane, but rather in its psychological and political effects. Above all, it did succeed in creating a climate of confusion and the impression of the widespread collapse of the state, which the Duce exploited in his negotiations with Liberal politicians and the monarchy. For the Fascist mobilization was only part of a two-pronged strategy that also involved simultaneous intrigue and negotiation with other political forces. As his squads were massing in various points of the peninsula, Mussolini displayed an apparent willingness to compromise, thereby sharpening divisions within the Liberal camp and undermining the determination of the caretaker government to offer serious resistance. The indecisiveness of the Luigi Facta (q.v.) government found dramatic expression in its failure to take immediate countermeasures to prevent the occupations and to arrest the leaders of the movement. In the critical period between October 28 and 29 the partial success of the Fascist tactics in the provinces raised the prospect of a long and bloody civil war, for which the army commanders, with their pro-Fascist sympathies, displayed scant enthusiasm. Since most Liberal leaders were resigned to Mussolini's participation in any future government, the burden of the crisis and mounting disorders fell on the frail shoulders of the king. Anxious about the reliability of the army and the designs on the throne of his pro-Fascist cousin, the Duke of Aosta (*see* SAVOIA, AMEDEO DI, DUKE OF AOSTA), Victor Emmanuel III (q.v.) decided to revoke the decree of martial law on October 28. Although the king did not immediately realize it, his decision put Mussolini in a commanding position and led influential industrial leaders and military officials to support an immediate invitation to the Fascist leader to form a government as the only resolution to a rapidly deteriorating situation. In this context Mussolini arrived in Rome by train on the morning of October 30 and presented himself to the king who made him the prime minister.

Thus the March on Rome was neither the revolution claimed by Fascist propagandists nor a mere piece of mass choreography or a simple military failure as some anti-Fascist historians have written. Rather it must be placed within Mussolini's broader political strategy, which had as its chief aim the winning of power. Significantly, the ambiguity of the March on Rome, "a violent movement prepared by political intrigue and legitimized by royal investiture," would deeply influence Mussolini's subsequent efforts to consolidate his new power.

For further information see: Renzo De Felice, *Mussolini il fascista* (Turin: Einaudi, 1961); Adrian Lyttelton, *The Seizure of Power: Fascism in Italy, 1919-1929* (New York: Charles Scribner's Sons, 1973); A Repaci, *La marcia su Roma* (Rome: Canesi, 1963).

ALC

MARCONI, GUGLIELMO (b. Bologna, April 25, 1874; d. Rome, July 20, 1937). A prominent inventor and scientist, Marconi attended secondary schools in Florence and Livorno. He was interested in physics at an early age and became an expert on wireless transmissions, gaining worldwide fame for his numerous discoveries. By 1922 he had perfected a system by which messages could be sent any distance around the world, had won the Nobel Prize in physics, and had been made a senator. During World War I he was an officer in the Italian Army and was sent on diplomatic missions, including to the Paris Peace Conference in 1919.

Marconi embraced the Fascist movement and the regime, and in 1928 he accepted the presidency of the National Research Council. The next year he was made a marchese (primarily because his contributions to the radio had made him a prestigious international figure), and in 1930 he became president of the Royal Academy of Italy (q.v.). In the latter capacity he was also a member of the Fascist Grand Council (q.v.). His career under Fascism was typical of a large number of major intellectuals who sold their prestige to the regime for honors and recognition.

For further information see: *Chi è?* (1936); DSPI; EAR (2); *Annuario della Reale Accademia d'Italia* (Rome: Royal Academy, 1938).

MSF

MARINELLI, GIOVANNI (b. Adria, Rovigo, October 18, 1879; d. Verona, January 11, 1944). One of the most prominent of the "Fascists of the first hour," a supporter of Mussolini, and an important Fascist leader, Marinelli came out of the syndical-socialist tradition. An accountant by profession, he was active in the Milan labor movement before World War I and held membership in the executive committee of the Milanese Chamber of Labor. Marinelli was a fervent interventionist in 1914-15 (*see* INTERVENTIONIST CRISIS, 1914-1915) and, together with Michele Bianchi (q.v.), Alceste DeAmbris (q.v.), and Mussolini, founded the *fasci interventisti* (*see* FASCI DI AZIONE RIVOLUZIONARIA) in 1915. Although prevented from serving in the army because of a sight defect, he was extremely active in domestic propaganda during World War I.

Marinelli was among the founders of the Fascist movement in 1919, having attended the Piazza San Sepolcro (*see* SANSEPOLCRISTI) meeting of March 23, and having served as a member of its central committee. Mussolini appointed him administrative secretary of the PNF (Partito Nazionale Fascista) (q.v.) in November 1920, a position he held with a few interruptions for more than twenty years. In this capacity he was instrumental in establishing the party's organizational structure and raising the funds necessary for its growth. Despite his bureaucratic visage, Marinelli was also active in organizing the Blackshirt squads (*see* SQUADRISTI) and was repeatedly involved in violent encounters with Socialists, for which he was arrested several times.

Always intent on solidifying Mussolini's position over the PNF, in 1924 Marinelli became part of a provisional party directorate of four men that included Cesare Rossi (q.v.), Roberto Forges Davanzati (q.v.), and Alessandro Melchiori (q.v.), in an effort to undermine PNF secretary Francesco Giunta (q.v.) and the Revisionists (*see* REVISIONISM).

Marinelli's control over the party apparatus was temporarily interrupted as a result of his complicity in the Matteotti Crisis (q.v.). Although the details of his involvement are uncertain, the evidence suggests that he may well have ordered the attack on Matteotti, and he was certainly a key figure in its planning. He was dismissed from his post as PNF administrator after pressure from the moderates in Mussolini's cabinet and in June 1924 was arrested. Mussolini released him (along with Rossi and Filippo Filipelli) in order to prevent major revelations about the crime, and in December 1925 he was named inspector general of the party. He was reinstated as administrator in March 1926, thereafter holding that post until 1943.

Marinelli was elected to the Chamber of Deputies in 1929 and in May 1935 was appointed to the Fascist Grand Council (q.v.). It was in this capacity that he played his last important role in the history of Fascism. During the July 1943 meeting of the Grand Council, Marinelli supported the Dino Grandi (q.v.) motion against Mussolini, for which he was arrested by Fascist agents in October. Taken north to Verona (*see* VERONA TRIALS) Marinelli was tried for high treason and, along with G. Ciano (q.v.) and Emilio De Bono (q.v.), was executed in January 1944.

For further information see: DSPI; EAR (3); NO (1928; 1937); Renzo De Felice, *Mussolini* (Turin: Einaudi, 1965-74).

                                                                                                          PVC

MARINETTI, FILIPPO TOMMASO (b. Alexandria, Egypt, December 12, 1876; d. Bellagio, December 2, 1944). The founder and leader of Italian Futurism (q.v.), Marinetti was the son of wealthy Milanese parents. He studied in Paris, where he was highly influenced by French intellectual currents, especially the Symbolists. Marinetti hoped to found a similar movement in Italy through *Poesia*, a literary magazine he edited in 1905.

In response to what he saw as a need for Italy to move into the industrial world, Marinetti wrote the first Futurist manifesto on February 20, 1909. The initial Futurist statement proposed to destroy things of the past represented by such historic institutions as museums, libraries, and academies and to venerate speed, which represented the essence of modern industrial life. Marinetti hailed the racing car and airplane as more beautiful than classical statues and suggested that real beauty was found only in struggle.

While Marinetti's heroes included non-Italians—the French Symbolists as well as German philosopher Nietzsche—and Futurist interests were international, Marinetti became increasingly nationalistic in outlook. He participated actively in the interventionist campaign (*see* INTERVENTIONIST CRISIS, 1914-1915) and was arrested in 1914 and twice in 1915. The interventionist struggle brought him into contact with Mussolini. Marinetti fought in World War I, and by 1918 a Partito Politico Futurista had been announced by his followers. He attended the San Sepolcro meeting (*see* SANSEPOLCRISTI) in March 1919 at which the Fasci di Combattimento were founded, and was an unsuccessful candidate for Parliament on the Fascist ticket in November. Marinetti's political ideas were vague and ill-defined, but he did find areas of correspondence in some of Mussolini's radical rhetoric.

After Mussolini came to power Marinetti hoped that he would adopt Futurism as the regime's official artistic movement, but he was disappointed. Marinetti, an internationally known figure, gave the regime considerable prestige and he was heaped with honors, including membership in the Royal Academy of Italy (q.v.) in 1929. Mussolini, for his part, gave lip service to Futurism and extolled it as an example of Italy's creative genius, but Futurism did not always meet the cultural needs of the regime. Moreover, in the 1920s Futurism had already entered its "Second Generation" phase and lacked much of its earlier originality and verve. In the 1930s Marinetti's constant propaganda efforts for Futurism were often tolerated as the antics of an excitable and flamboyant poet. By the end of the decade, however, his polemics with anti-intellectual Fascists like Roberto Farinacci (q.v.) caused Mussolini some consternation, especially when Marinetti openly defended modern art and Jewish painters against the regime's anti-Semitic policies (*see* ANTI-SEMITISM).

Marinetti volunteered for service in the Russian campaign during World War II and adhered to the Salò Republic (*see* ITALIAN SOCIAL REPUBLIC), where he was president of the Royal Academy. His death in 1944 was the occasion for a major state funeral.

For further information see: Philip V. Cannistraro, *La fabbrica del consenso* (Rome-Bari: Laterza, 1975); Renzo De Felice, *Mussolini* (Turin: Einaudi, 1965); M. Drudi and T. Fiore, *Archivi del futurismo* (Rome: De Luca, 1958).

JH

MARINI, MARINO (b. Pistoia, February 27, 1901). One of the major figures in European sculpture of the twentieth century, Marino Marini studied painting and sculpture at the Accademia in Florence; he presently resides in Milan. During his formative years in the second decade of this century, he became acquainted with the artists of the Scuola Metafisica, the Italian branch of Surrealism, but remained aloof from any specific commitments to their ideals. Of his own volition he rejected the romantic and naturalistic art of the late nineteenth century, a point of view coincidentally taken by the Fascist regime. But as a tremendously culti-vated figure, who travelled to Paris and elsewhere in Europe many times between 1919 and 1938, he absorbed the impact of the international modern movement rather than standing aloof from it as many Italian artists had done. He derived the unique quality of his work—familiarity combined with timelessness—from the broad basis of sources he chose to emulate: the impressionism of Medardo Rosso, the realism of ancient Roman portrait busts, and the static volumes of Egyptian and Etruscan sculpture. Aside from his famous horse-and-rider series, which was inspired by the memory of peasants escaping from war-stricken lands, his subjects were strictly traditional, as in the case of his male and female nudes. In other words, there was no concession in his work to contemporary political events, and he was never under pressure to devote his resources to proselytizing for the state. His growing international reputation helped secure the first prize for sculpture in the prestigious II Quadriennale in Rome in 1935—dramatic proof that an artist untouched by the policies of Mussolini could nevertheless achieve success on Italian soil during the Fascist period.

For further information see: Filippo De Pisis, *Marino Marini* (Milan: Conchiglia, 1941); Lamberto Vitale, *Marino Marini* (Milan: Ulrico Hoepli, 1937).

RN

MARPICATI, ARTURO (b. Ghedi, Brescia, November 9, 1891). A Fascist bureaucrat and intellectual, Marpicati took a degree in letters from the University of Florence and taught in a *liceo* in Fiume (q.v.). A nationalist interventionist in 1914-15 (*see* INTERVENTIONIST CRISIS, 1914-1915), he fought as a volun-teer in World War I and joined Gabriele D'Annunzio's (q.v.) expedition to Fiume in 1919. Upon his return to Italy he adhered to the Fascist movement and wrote for *Il Popolo d'Italia* and Fascist journals. After the March on Rome (q.v.), Marpicati taught literature at the University of Rome and held a number of posts in the Fascist regime. He was federal secretary of Fiume in 1928-29, a member of the PNF (Partito Nazionale Fascista) (q.v.) directorate in 1930, party vice-secretary from 1931 to 1934, and a member of the Fascist Grand Council (q.v.) until 1934.

Marpicati directed the Istituto Nazionale di Cultura Fascista (q.v.) for a time in the 1930s and was then chancellor of the Royal Academy of Italy (q.v.) until 1938, when he became a member of the important review body, the Council of State (Consiglio di Stato).

For further information see: *Chi è?* (1936); EAR (3); NO (1937).

PVC

MARRAS, EFISIO (b. Cagliari, August 2, 1888). A military attaché in Berlin from 1936 to July 1939 and from November 1939 to September 1943, General Marras acted as intermediary between those unequal and uncomfortable partners, the Italian and German armed forces. His fundamentally anti-German attitude checked the facile enthusiasms of the wartime ambassador, Dino Alfieri (q.v.). After the 1943 armistice the Germans imprisoned Marras and then turned him over to the Salò Republic (*see* ITALIAN SOCIAL REPUBLIC), under which he had refused service. He escaped to Switzerland and was later Army Chief of Staff (1950-54) and Italian representative to NATO.

For further information see: Michele Lanza, *Berlino, Ambasciata d'Italia, 1939-1943* (Rome: Mondadori, 1946).

MK

MARTINI, ARTURO (b. Treviso, August 11, 1889; d. Milan, March 22, 1947). Martini was a prominent Italian sculptor who combined an acute expressionist sensibility with classical (Etruscan and Roman) influences. A modern artist with strong Fascist ties, Martini was a leader in the Novecento (Twentieth Century) Movement (q.v.) sponsored by Margherita Sarfatti-Grassini (q.v.), Mussolini's mistress.

Martini left school at thirteen to work as a goldsmith's apprentice and later in a ceramic factory. These early experiences left him with an artisan's command of materials. At first self-taught, he eventually studied in Treviso and Venice, and then in Munich with Adolf Hildebrand, mastering the decorative art nouveau style. A trip to Paris in 1914 brought him in contact with Amedeo Modigliani and Umberto Boccioni.

He joined the Valori Plastici group in Rome, helped lead the Novecento movement in Milan, and throughout the 1920s achieved critical acclaim with a series of appealingly expressive genre sculptures such as *Pisan Woman* (*La Pisana*), 1928, *Maternity* (*Maternità*), 1929, and *Seated Boy* (*Raggazzo Seduto*), 1930. He received the grand prize for sculpture at the First Quadriennale in Rome for *Woman in the Sun* (*Donna al Sole*). He was appointed professor of sculpture at the Brera Acadamy in Milan in 1941.

During the 1930s he submitted readily to the monumental grandiloquence of Fascism: the low reliefs in the Palace of Justice in Milan (1936) and a monument for Tito Minniti are examples from this period. These works are executed with a plastic aggressiveness lacking in prior works.

Paralleling the war and the collapse of the Fascist regime, Martini entered a period of severe self-searching and questioning of the values that he had explored in a lifetime of work. He finished by renouncing sculpture and expressed his personal and philosophic reasons in *La scultura, Lingua Morta*. His best sculptures, however, belie his final polemic: they speak a universal tongue that is lyric, poetic, and human.

For further information see: Giulio Argan, *Martini* (New York: Universe Sculpture Series, 1959); Massimo Bontempelli, *Arturo Martini* (Hoepli: Milan, 1939); Arturo Martini, *La scultura, Lingua Morta* (Verona: Bodoni, 1948).

MCG

MARZABOTTO. The scene of one of the worst Nazi reprisals in Italy, Marzabotto is a village approximately twenty kilometers south of Bologna. Prior to the Fascist period Marzabotto's local administrations were dominated by Socialists and Communists, and during the war the town became openly anti-Fascist. The partisan organization Stella Rossa operated in the area and constantly committed acts of sabotage. Nazi reprisals against the town and the surrounding district began in May 1944 but reached their height between September 29 and the end of the first two weeks in October. At least 1,830 persons were murdered, including members of the partisan group and numerous women and children. In 1949 Luigi Einaudi (q.v.), then president of the republic, awarded the village a gold medal. Two years later, Walter Reder, the officer responsible for the massacre, was brought to trial and sentenced to life imprisonment.

For further information see: EAR (3); Charles Delzell, *Mussolini's Enemies* (Princeton: Princeton University Press, 1961); Renato Giorgi, *Le stragi di Marzabotto* (Bologna: 1954).

MSF

MASCAGNI, PIETRO (b. Livorno, December 7, 1863; d. Rome, 1945). The most important Italian musical composer during the Fascist period, Mascagni permitted Mussolini to use his considerable prestige for propaganda purposes in return for numerous honors and awards. Mascagni studied at the Conservatory of Milan and was a conductor before gaining international fame as the composer of *Cavalleria Rusticana* (1890), *Le Maschere* (1901), and other operas written in the verismo tradition. During the 1930s Mascagni appeared in numerous Fascist ceremonies, encouraged Mussolini to create a state-controlled theater, and was made a member of the Royal Academy of Italy (q.v.) in 1929. After the permanent departure of Arturo Toscanini (q.v.) in 1931, Mascagni's position as the most notable living figure in Italian music (*see* MUSIC) was secured, and he presided over the regime's official musical events. He bitterly attacked modernism in music, including such "foreign" imports as jazz, and his last opera, *Nerone* (1935), was widely praised by official propaganda (the regime originally planned to hold its inaugural performance in the Colosseum before a mass audience to celebrate its "Roman" theme). During the last years of World War II Mascagni spent much of his time imploring Mussolini to protect his villa from attack.

For further information see: *Chi è?* (1936); NO (1937); Philip V. Cannistraro, *La fabbrica del consenso* (Rome-Bari: Laterza, 1975).

PVC

MATAPAN, BATTLE OF. The second major Italian naval disaster of World War II (after Taranto), the Battle of Matapan took place on March 28, 1941. In response to German insistence that the Navy assert itself, Arturo Riccardi (q.v.) ordered Angelo Iachino (q.v.) to sortie with the *Vittorio Veneto* and cruiser forces in search of British convoys bound for Greece. The British, forewarned through decryption of the operations order, sallied secretly from Alexandria and intercepted. British aerial torpedo strikes slowed the *Vittorio Veneto* and stopped the cruiser *Pola* (later sunk). The cruisers *Zara* and *Fiume,* detached to aid the *Pola,* then fell victims in night action to the main British fleet. Matapan confirmed the Italian naval leadership's inferiority complex vis-à-vis the British, and ensured that only the Luftwaffe would offer serious opposition to British evacuation from Greece and Crete.

For further information see: Ufficio storico della Marina Militare, *Le azioni navali in Mediterraneo* (Rome: Istituto Poligrafico, 1970).

MK

MATTEOTTI CRISIS. One of the most crucial turning points in the history of Fascism, the crisis began on June 10, 1924, with the kidnapping of Giacomo Matteotti, a reformist Socialist deputy. On May 30 Matteotti had given a speech in the Chamber of Deputies attacking the elections of April 6, which had taken place under the so-called Acerbo Law (*see* ACERBO, GIACOMO). The election had been marked by numerous incidents of violence and intimidation on the part of the Fascists, and Mussolini's list of candidates had won the two-thirds majority called for in the Acerbo measure. From his seat in the Chamber, Matteotti had uncompromisingly exposed the illegalities and violence of the *squadristi* (q.v.) and declared that Mussolini's government did not enjoy the support of the Italian people.

Matteotti (b. Fratta Polesine, Rovigo, May 22, 1885) came from a prosperous family and had graduated from the University of Bologna in law. He had been active in the Po Valley as a Socialist organizer, had traveled extensively in Europe, and had been first elected to Parliament in 1919. He soon distinguished himself as one of the most dedicated and dangerous enemies of Fascism, and his exposure of Fascist illegalism had been characterized by a studied use of figures and statistics that made his arguments all the more compelling.

His speech of May 30 had been met with bitter denunciations from Fascist deputies and suggestions that violent revenge be taken against him, including a remark by Mussolini himself to that effect. On June 10 a group of Fascists led by

A. Dumini (q.v.), and including Albino Volpi, A. Poveromo, G. Viola, and A. Malacria kidnapped him as he was on his way to Parliament, beat him severely, and killed him. His body, buried on the outskirts of Rome, was not found until the middle of August, but it was immediately assumed that he had been the victim of Fascist violence. No direct link to Musslini could be established, although it was common opinion that orders to deal with Matteotti had come from the highest levels of the government. Demands for Mussolini's resignation came from the opposition parties and Carlo Sforza (q.v.), then a senator, called for his immediate arrest. The Duce was denounced in Parliament (q.v.) and public demonstrations were organized in the streets and *piazze*. The government appeared to be on the brink of collapse during the first days of the crisis, and Mussolini feared the intervention of the king.

Mussolini's reaction was to dismiss all those subordinates suspected or accused of collusion in the crime, including Emilio De Bono (q.v.), minister of interior. His appointment of Luigi Federzoni (q.v.) to that post reassured those who believed that Fascism could be moderated and controlled. Mussolini's position improved after his meeting with the king on June 17, and the king's failure to act crippled the opposition from the outset. But the anti-Fascists refused to adopt the same violent methods used by Mussolini, and at the end of the month the opposition deputies withdrew from the Chamber and declared themselves representatives of the people. This so-called "Aventine Secession" (q.v.) became the most important aspect of the Matteotti Crisis, for its "moral," legalistic stance symbolized the failure of many Italian political leaders to understand the nature of Fascism. Mussolini quickly undercut the effectiveness of the Aventine by securing a vote of confidence from the Senate after a conciliatory speech to that body, and a few days later he remade his cabinet by appointing a number of politicians from the opposition parties.

Throughout the summer of 1924 the Aventine carried out a vigorous press campaign against the government, and industrial-military elements also began to denounce Mussolini. In November Giovanni Giolitti (q.v.), who had supported the government, declared his opposition and some members withdrew from the Fascist majority. Mussolini therefore embarked on a course of conciliation and moderation, announcing on November 20 that the revolutionary phase of Fascism was over. This policy, however, was rejected by the dissident Fascists, who called for a "second wave" of violence to destroy all the opposition. These intransigents were largely provincial *squadristi* (q.v.) who feared that Mussolini would sell them out to protect himself. This would-be revolt within his own ranks finally persuaded Mussolini to take decisive action, and in December it was rumored that Militia (q.v.) members were planning to stage a coup against him.

Pressure on Mussolini mounted in December with the publication of the Cesare Rossi (q.v.) "Memoriale," which implicated Mussolini in the Matteotti murder. Four days later he was confronted by a group of thirty-three Militia consuls, who threatened Mussolini personally and demanded action against the anti-Fascists.

Hence, on January 3, 1925, he went before Parliament and in his most important public speech, assumed the complete responsibility for all political, moral, and criminal activity that had occurred in Italy since taking office. His speech ended with the promise that the entire situation would be clarified within forty-eight hours. Within days of his speech, the "second wave" of Fascist violence was unleashed against the opposition, and the Fascist dictatorship began to emerge.

For further information see: Renzo De Felice, *Mussolini il fascista* (Turin: Einaudi, 1966); Adrian Lyttelton, *The Seizure of Power* (London: Weidenfeld & Nicolson, 1973); Giuseppe Rossini, *Il delitto Matteotti* (Bologna: Mulino, 1966).

MSF

MATTIOLI PASQUALINI, COUNT ALESSANDRO (b. Cingoli, Macerata, March 1, 1863; d. Cingoli, 1943). An Italian diplomat and minister of the royal household, Mattioli Pasqualini took a law degree from Bologna and entered the Foreign Ministry. He served as attaché in Berlin from 1885 to 1891, then as legation secretary and consul at Copenhagen until 1894, when he returned to Berlin. He was then consul general in Hungary, Chile, and Brazil.

In November 1909 Mattioli Pasqualini was made minister of the royal household, a position he held until being replaced by the Duke d'Acquarone (q.v.) in 1939. During World War I he served as the king's representative to the chiefs of staff. He was made a senator in 1913 and an ambassador in 1923. During the Matteotti Crisis (q.v.) he played a careful and limited role in efforts to form a government of national unity and refused to vote in the Senate debate.

For further information see: *Chi è?* (1936); NO (1937); *Annuario diplomatico del Regno d'Italia* (Rome: Ministry of Foreign Affairs, 1937).

PVC

MAZZINI SOCIETY. Founded in New York in 1939 on the ideals of liberty, republic, and social justice postulated by the nineteenth-century patriot Giuseppe Mazzini, the Mazzini Society became the major wartime organization of anti-Fascist exiles. Fascist anti-Semitic laws, the fall of France, the Battle of Britain, waning British support, and a series of organizational failures among anti-Fascists in England produced a migration of *fuorusciti* (q.v.) to America in 1939-40. This last wave of refugees added considerable political experience and intellectual leadership to the small but enthusiastic and capable band of Italian anti-Fascists in the United States.

Gaetano Salvemini (q.v.), Harvard professor and passionate opponent of Fascism, provided the initiative and the conceptual framework, and adapted the principles of Giustizia e Libertà (*see* ANTI-FASCISM) to the American setting. Salvemini was joined at the two initial Mazzini Society meetings in 1939 by Lionello Venturi (q.v.), Roberto Bolaffio, Michele Cantarella, Renato Poggioli, Max Ascoli (q.v.), Giuseppe Borgese (q.v.), and others. They constructed the society's constitution, a series of broad objectives designed to blend the Italian and anti-Fascist agenda of the *fuorusciti* with the interests of the United States: (1) to inform the American public about real conditions inside Italy; (2) to combat Fascist propaganda in the United States; (3) to "defend" American democratic institutions against totalitarianism (q.v.); (4) to assist Italian political refugees who sought asylum and work in America; (5) to establish contact between anti-Fascist intellectuals and American liberals; (6) to cooperate with the organizations of other nationalities in the struggle against dictatorship, and, most importantly, (7) to undertake educational and cultural activities in the Italian-American communities; that is, to mold Italian-Americans into an effective pressure group on the "Italian question."

Italy's entry into the war brought significant changes to the organization. In the face of escalating conditions, the Mazzini Society aligned itself more directly with American policy and redoubled its efforts. Ascoli was elected president and Alberto Tarchiani (q.v.), secretary. With about one thousand members and forty branches, the society sponsored meetings, rallies, marches, and radio broadcasts. Members wrote anti-Fascist tracts for the society's weekly, *Nazioni Unite*, and for other publications, the most strident of which was Giuseppe Lupis's *Il Mondo*. They exposed Fascist activities in the United States and railed at Italian-American "pre-Pearl Harbor Fascists." And persistently they trumpeted the Salveminian theme that the Allies must distinguish the Italian people from the Fascist regime.

As the war continued conflicts arose that would ultimately split the society. Past party loyalties and antipathies reemerged. Liberals found anarchists embarrassing in their quest for credence in diplomatic circles; anarchists, in turn, fought tenaciously against collaboration with Stalinists; Salveminian radicals opposed both Communists and Catholics. By the summer of 1942, when the annual convention was held, the Communist issue provoked an open confrontation culminating in the resignation of the Republican Randolfo Pacciardi (q.v.). The pro-American Ascoli liberal coalition prevailed, rejecting Communist membership and placing power more clearly in control of the labor union forces of Luigi Antonini.

The growing influence of Antonini and the increasing dependence of the Mazzini Society on the State Department and the Roosevelt administration led to Salvemini's departure. The Antonini group, with ties to the pro-Fascist publisher Generoso Pope, solicited support from prominent Italian-Americans recently converted from their Fascist sympathies. Salvemini profoundly objected to this course and withdrew from the organization he had founded. Salvemini's supporters in the society joined him in public criticism of the government's policy of including former Fascists on important liberation committees. During the last two years of World War II the organization became almost totally an Italian-American group and ceased to represent the exiled anti-Fascists, focusing its efforts largely on relief measures and postwar Italian issues.

For further information see: Charles Delzell, *Mussolini's Enemies* (Princeton: Princeton University Press, 1961); John P. Diggins, *Mussolini and Fascism*

(Princeton: Princeton University Press, 1972); Maddalena Tirabassi, "La Mazzini Society," in Giorgio Spini, Gian Giacomo Migone, and Massimo Teodori, eds., *Italia e America dalla Grande Guerra a Oggi* (Venice, 1976).

                                                                                    CLK

MECOZZI, AMEDEO (b. Rome, January 17, 1892; d. Rome, November 2, 1971). An Air Force general, aviation theorist, and a World War I ace, Mecozzi received command of the Seventh Fighter Group in 1927, where he developed air warfare theories antithetical to Giulio Douhet's (q.v.). Mecozzi advocated developing fighter-bombers for coordinated tactical air strikes in combined aeronaval and ground support operations. He argued Italy's resources could not support Douhet's concepts, which grossly exaggerated strategic bombing's effectiveness. Instead, many opportune assaults on enemy forces could achieve what attempting a knockout blow against civil-industrial targets could not. Mecozzi developed his concepts in numerous publications and as commander of the Seventh Assault Aircraft Group between 1931 and 1934, the Fifth Assault Wing between 1934 and 1936, the Fifth Air Assault Brigade between 1936 and 1937, and an air sector commander in Somalia between 1937 and 1938. But underpowered aircraft and Giuseppe Valle's (q.v.) fear that interservice cooperation meant Air Force subordination crippled Mecozzi's efforts. Italian experiences between 1940 and 1943 generally vindicated Mecozzi's ideas.

For further information see: Giuseppe D'Avanzo, *Ali e poltrone* (Rome: Ciarrapico,1976); Armando Silvestri, "La vita e le idee dell'aeronautica nelle pagine della rivista," *Rivista Aeronautica* 49 (March 1973).

                                                                                    BRS

MEDA, FILIPPO (b. Milan, January 1, 1869; d. Milan, December 31, 1939). A Catholic political leader and attorney, Meda took degrees in literature and law in 1891. He collaborated actively with the newspaper *Osservatore Cattolico* and took over as its director in 1902, using it to pressure Pope Pius X to lift the *"non expedit"* prohibition against Catholic participation in elections in June 1905.

Meda was elected to Parliament in 1909 and became director of several other papers, including *Unione*, which became the political organ of Italian Catholics in 1912 as *L'Italia*. Meda was a neutralist in 1914-15 (*see* INTERVENTIONIST CRISIS, 1914-1915), but in 1916 he accepted appointment as minister of finance in the Paolo Boselli government. He remained in that position under V. E. Orlando (q.v.), and in 1920 was minister of the treasury under Giovanni Giolitti (q.v.).

In the postwar period Meda became a leading figure in the new Partito Popolare (*see* PARTITO POPOLARE ITALIANO) and was reelected in 1921. The following year he twice refused the king's offer to become prime minister. After Mussolini came to power, Meda was isolated and ignored by the Fascists. During the Matteotti Crisis (q.v.) he turned against the government and in 1925 undertook the legal defense of Alcide De Gasperi (q.v.), who had been arrested by the

Fascists. Although he did not assume an openly anti-Fascist posture, he did maintain a dignified separation from the regime and its activities.

For further information see: DSPI; EAR (3).

PVC

MELCHIORI, ALESSANDRO (b. Ancona, October 12, 1901). A Fascist Blackshirt, journalist, and PNF (Partito Nazionale Fascista) (q.v.) bureaucrat, Melchiori's activities as a *squadrista* (*see* SQUADRISTI) centered in and around Brescia, whose *fascio* he founded in 1919. He was involved in numerous and violent confrontations with Socialists, including a particularly bloody clash in Lodi, and extended his operations to Milan, Verona, and Cremona. In 1920 Melchiori joined Gabriele D'Annunzio (q.v.) at Fiume (q.v.) as a legionnaire, returned to Italy in 1921, and worked closely with Italo Bresciani (q.v.). He was a correspondent for *Il Popolo d'Italia* and drew increasingly closer to Mussolini's position within the Fascist movement. In April 1924 Mussolini appointed him one of the four members of a provisional directory—along with Cesare Rossi (q.v.), Roberto Forges Davanzati (q.v.), and Giovanni Marinelli (q.v.)—designed to undermine the position of the Fascist Revisionists (q.v.). In August, during the Matteotti crisis (q.v.), Melchiori was named to the larger directory under the PNF secretaryship of Roberto Farinacci (q.v.) and subsequently served as vice-secretary. Melchiori was a consul in the Militia (q.v.) , director of its official journal *Milizia Fascista*, president of the Associazione Nazionale Bersaglieri, and in 1929 was elected to Parliament.

For further information see: *Chi è?* (1936); NO (1928; 1937).

PVC

MESSE, GIOVANNI (b. Mesagne, Brindisi, December 10, 1883; d. Rome, December 18, 1960). Mussolini's finest general, a royal aide (1923-27), assistant division commander in Ethiopia, assistant inspector and then division commander of *celeri* (cavalry and *bersaglieri*) (1937-39), Messe was deputy commander of the Albanian invasion. He commanded the *Celeri* Corps between June and December 1940. Messe's defense of Valona against the Greeks (December 1940-February 1941) brought him command of the Italian Corps in Russia. Messe's corps fought well, despite equipment shortages and German abuse. After opposing Mussolini's expansion of the corps to army strength and disagreements with the new commander, Italo Gariboldi (q.v.), over strategy, Messe obtained relief in November 1942. Messe took command of Italian forces in Tunisia in February 1943, delaying Montgomery's advance. He surrendered on May 13, after being promoted to marshal.

For further information see: Giovanni Messe, *La guerra al fronte russo* (Milan: Rizzoli, 1964); Giovanni Messe, *La mia armata in Tunisia* (Milan: Rizzoli, 1960).

BRS

MEZZASOMA, FERNANDO (b. Rome, August 3, 1907; d. Dongo, April 28, 1945). Partito Nazionale Fascista (q.v.) bureaucrat and Fascist minister in the Salò Republic (*see* ITALIAN SOCIAL REPUBLIC), Mezzasoma studied economics and joined the party as a young man in 1921. He was active in the Fascist university movement, Gioventù Universitaria Fascista (GUF) (*see* YOUTH ORGANIZA-TIONS), edited its Perugia newspaper, *L'Assalto*, and in 1930 became vice-president of the Scuola di Mistica Fascista (*see* MISTICA FASCISTA) in Milan. Rising quickly in the party under Achille Starace (q.v.), Mezzasoma in 1935 was transferred to Rome where he became vice-secretary and then secretary of GUF. During World War II he worked as director of internal propaganda for the Ministry of Popular Culture (q.v.) and immediately offered his services to the Nazis after the German occupation of Rome in 1943.

An intransigent Fascist, Mezzasoma was fanatically loyal to Mussolini and went north to Salò (*see* ITALIAN SOCIAL REPUBLIC), where he was made minister of popular culture. He imposed a hardline policy on newspapermen and intellectuals and along with party secretary Alessandro Pavolini (q.v.) was intent on destroying all Fascist "traitors" and anti-Fascists. At the end of the war he was captured by partisans while attempting to escape to Switzerland and executed. On April 29, 1945, his body was hung in Piazzale Loreto in Milan with those of Mussolini and other Fascist leaders.

For further information see: EAR (3); Philip V. Cannistraro, *La fabbrica del consenso* (Rome-Bari: Laterza, 1975).

PVC

MEZZETTI, OTTORINO (b. Rome, November 30, 1877). A colonial general and governor, Mezzetti served ably in Tripolitania (*see* LIBYA [TRIPOLITANIA AND CYRENAICA]) from 1917 both as military commander (January-July 1921) and in combat operations alongside Rodolfo Graziani (q.v.). Transferred to Cyrenaica in December 1926, Mezzetti became military commander (May 1927-January 1929) under Attilio Teruzzi (q.v.). Deploying large motorized columns and airpower, Mezzetti achieved high body counts and linked Cyrenaica to Tripolitania (January-May 1928), but he failed to eliminate the Senussi. After repatriation Mezzetti was frequently ill, though he commanded the Salerno Division (1930) and the Naples Military District (June 1935-December 1937). On Graziani and Teruzzi's recommendation Mussolini appointed him governor of revolt-torn Amhara in December 1937. Mezzetti's vitality had declined. He proved incompetent, quarreling with Ugo Cavallero (q.v.), hindering his commanders, and suffering numerous defeats. Removed in January 1939, Mezzetti became a senator that March.

For further information see: Ottorino Mezzetti, *Guerra in Libia* (Rome: Cremonese, 1933).

BRS

MICHELUCCI, GIOVANNI (b. Pistoia, January 2, 1891). An architect, city planner, and university professor, Michelucci's most well-known contribution to the architecture of this era was to head the team of architects who designed the Florence train station (1932) in the rational style. He was editor of a monthly journal, *La Nuova Città*, from 1946 to 1956, which centered on town planning, architecture, and interior design.

For further information see: Franco Borsi, *Giovanni Michelucci* (Florence: Le Monnier, 1966).

JH

MILITIA. After stormy Party discussions in December 1922, Mussolini transformed the PNF (Partito Nazionale Fascista) (q.v.) Blackshirts (*see* SQUADRISTI) into the state security forces, the Voluntary Militia for National Security (Milizia Volontaria per la Sicurezza Nazionale). Officially created on February 1, 1923, the MVSN remained divided between units controlled by a commandant under Mussolini and those controlled by local Militia commanders who fought centralization. The Army appreciated relief from security duties but feared rivalry for funds and power. Mussolini responded by placing generals in high MVSN posts, which Militia commanders resented. Militia discipline improved by June 1924, but the Matteotti Crisis (q.v.) revived Blackshirt violence. Mussolini barely prevented Militia coup attempts in June and December 1924, while generals demanded MVSN suppression. After January 1925 Mussolini used the state bureaucracy, the Army, and empty promises to restore MVSN obedience. Mussolini profited from Militia violence against anti-Fascists during Roberto Farinacci's (q.v.) PNF secretaryship, while Farinacci reduced regional Militia independence. Mussolini became MVSN commandant in September 1926, though chiefs of staff actually were in command. The Militia evolved into three groups that were only formally united. Most Militia units remained under local control but discipline was tightened. Creation of the Interior Ministry's Pubblica Sicurezza (*see* POLICE AND INTERNAL SECURITY) force and scant funds permitted little activity except premilitary-postmilitary training. Special Militia groups under ministerial control guarded railways, highways, ports, borders, forests, political prisoners, and Mussolini. A few Blackshirt battalions and artillery batteries performed military and colonial service. Active duty Militia officers enjoyed rapid promotion, creating serious army resentment. While Mussolini rejected suggestions for Army-Militia amalgamation, he allowed increasing Army domination of active MVSN units. The Fascist nature of the Militia declined under deliberate Army neglect. Mussolini's desire for "proof that the venture has popular support" required MVSN participation in the Ethiopian War (q.v.). After the first Blackshirt battalions in Eritrea proved useless, Mussolini authorized Army organization of Militia divisions, many of whose members were non-Fascist conscripts or Army personnel. Eventually six Blackshirt divisions served in Ethiopia. They fought adequately but frequently clashed with the Army. The MVSN reorganized in

October 1936 as a predominantly military force, but independent operations in Spain and Ethiopia failed due to poor organization. In 1939-40 Blackshirt battalions were attached to Army infantry divisions, and four Militia divisions were formed. The divisions were destroyed in Libya between December 1940 and February 1941. The Army vetoed creating new Militia units, though they grudgingly accepted the new "M" battalions for overseas duty. Combat requirements retarded strengthening of internal security units until Germany helped establish the "M" division in May 1943. Poor Militia-party coordination and MVSN bungling prevented a response to Mussolini's arrest. Placed under Army command, the MVSN was formally abolished by King Victor Emmanuel III (q.v.) on December 6, 1943.

Mussolini reestablished the Militia in the Salò Republic (see ITALIAN SOCIAL REPUBLIC) on September 16, 1943, and renamed the Republican National Guard (Guardia Nazionale Repubblicana) on November 20. GNR attempts to incorporate the Army failed and it assumed police and anti-partisan duties. Militia-party differences over military discipline versus political enthusiasm returned. The party created the Black Brigades (Brigate Nere) in July 1944 as its own antipartisan force, surpassing the GNR in atrocities and attracting many GNR members. Both forces collapsed in April 1945.

For further information see: Alberto Aquarone, "La Milizia volontaria nello stato fascista," La Cultura 2 (May and June 1964); Giulio Lenzi, Diari Africani (Pisa: Giardini, 1973); Adrian Lyttelton, The Seizure of Power (London: Weidenfeld & Nicolson, 1973); Giampaolo Pansa, L'esercito di Salò (Verona: Mondadori, 1970).

BRS

MINISTRY OF POPULAR CULTURE. The chief propaganda agency of the Fascist regime, the purpose of the Ministry of Popular Culture was to impose a totalitarian control over all areas of Italian cultural life and to create a government monopoly on the manufacture and dissemination of information. The ministry evolved out of Mussolini's Press Office, which at first concerned itself only with the censorship and distribution of news. The Press Office was run successively by Cesare Rossi (q.v.), Giovanni Capasso Torre (see CAPASSO TORRE DI CAPRARA, GIOVANNI), Lando Ferretti (q.v.), Gaetano Polverelli (q.v.), and Galeazzo Ciano (q.v.). Until Ciano assumed the post, the office was simply and unimaginatively run, consisting of the preparation of detailed deviations from government instructions. When Ciano took over in 1933 he added radio and motion pictures to the areas under his jurisdiction, so that the activities and authority of the office expanded greatly. In September 1934, on the example of Nazi Propaganda Minister Joseph Goebbels, the Press Office was replaced by a new Undersecretariat for Press and Propaganda, which also took control of tourism, music, theater, and literature; in June of the next year it was elevated to a full ministry. The period of the Ethiopian War (q.v.) greatly extended the ministry's work, for the regime launched its most important, systematic propaganda campaign to date. When Ciano was transferred to the Foreign Ministry in 1936, Dino Alfieri (q.v.) became minister of press and propaganda and proceeded to incorporate all remaining aspects of cultural life into the ministry's cumbersome bureaucracy. Alfieri's tenure in office also saw the imposition of a rigid conformity and administrative control over intellectuals, artists, and creative people in general. In the late 1930s the ministry concentrated largely on the manipulation and expansion of the mass media in a program designed to integrate Italians of all social classes into the national experience. As a consequence, in May 1937 Mussolini officially renamed the office the Ministry of Popular Culture, which Italians sarcastically dubbed "Minculpop." In 1939 Alessandro Pavolini (q.v.) succeeded Alfieri as minister and led the regime's internal propaganda effort during World War II, until he too was replaced at the beginning of 1943 by Gaetano Polverelli.

In spite of the regime's stated goals of producing a "revolutionary" Fascist culture, however, the Ministry of Popular Culture realized few of its programs, and it failed to achieve the same degree of control that Goebbels's effective propaganda had imposed on Nazi Germany. Newspapers and motion pictures continued to remain in private hands, thus subject to market demands and escapist tendencies, while only radio was nominally run by a semipublic agency. Inefficient, unsophisticated censorship techniques were responsible for the appearance of many unorthodox—and at times even anti-Fascist—cultural products, and bureaucratic duplication combined with jurisdictional disputes to prevent a full implementation of Mussolini's "totalitarian" goals. The ministry was officially dissolved by the Pietro Badoglio (q.v.) government in July 1944, but had been reconstituted by Mussolini in the Salò Republic (*see* ITALIAN SOCIAL REPUBLIC) under the direction of Fernando Mezzasoma (q.v.)

For further information see: Philip V. Cannistraro, *La fabbrica del consenso: Fascismo e Mass Media* (Rome-Bari, 1975); Edward R. Tannenbaum, *The Fascist Experience: Italian Society and Culture, 1922-1945* (New York: Basic Books, 1972).

PVC

MINZONI, DON GIOVANNI (b. Ravenna, June 29, 1885; d. Argenta, August 23, 1923). From a fairly well-do-do family, Minzoni was, like many young men of his day, influenced by the political and social ideas and the democratic thought of Romolo Murri, who broke with the abstentionist position of Catholic intransigents. After being ordained in September 1909, he arrived at his parish in Argenta, a small and strongly anticlerical village in the province of Ferrara.

In February 1916 Minzoni was elected archpriest of San Niccolò and in July was drafted into the Army. On his request he was sent to the front as a military chaplain, where he earned a silver medal.

After his discharge in March 1919, he returned to Argenta and dedicated himself to economic and social reforms and to educational programs. He promoted cooperatives through the Unione Professionale Cattolica and worked for the growth of white (Catholic) leagues. Although at first he avoided involvement with the Partito Popolare Italiano (q.v.), in the spring of 1923 he joined the party as an openly defiant anti-Fascist act; he also supported the Catholic daily, *Il Popolo*, after the Catholic newspapers of the Grasoli chain went over to Fascism.

During the last months of his life he intensified his activity in Catholic youth organizations, creating in July 1923 an Argenta branch of the Associazione degli Esploratori Cattolici, a group that strongly displeased the Fascists.

After repeated efforts to stop his intransigent and uncompromising anti-Fascist statements, Minzoni was fatally beaten by two Fascists from the nearby town of Casumaro di Cento in a public street of Argenta.

For further information see: Lorenzo Bedeschi, *Don Minzoni: Il prete ucciso dai fascisti* (Milan: Bompiani, 1973); Gabriella Fanello Marcucci, *Don Minzoni* (Bari: Paoline, 1974); Giovanni Minzoni, *Diario di don Minzoni*, ed. L. Bedeschi (Brescia: Morcelliana, 1965); Giovanni Minzoni, *La crisi di un prete: Memorie, 1910-1915* (Florence: Vallecchi, 1967).

SR

MISSIROLI, MARIO (b. Bologna, November 25, 1886; d. Rome, November 29, 1974). A journalist, Missiroli began his career by working on the Bolognese weekly *Don Chisciotte* and by publishing numerous political essays. In 1917 he directed the Liberal periodical *Il Tempo* and a year later became director of *Il Resto del Carlino* in his home town. In 1921 Missiroli ran *Il Secolo* but was forced to resign after he wrote a number of anti-Fascist articles. In the 1930s Missiroli changed his attitude and supported the regime through his writings but never held any major posts. After the war he directed *Il Messaggero* in Rome and *Corriere della Sera* in Milan.

For further information see: EAR (3); Mario Missiroli, *La politica estera di Mussolini* (Milan: Industrie Grafiche, 1939).

MSF

MISTICA FASCISTA. An ideological current within Fascism that emerged in the 1930s, the proponents of "Fascist mysticism" were chiefly the younger ideologues who rejected the idea that Fascism could have a coherent and rational philosophical basis—as opposed to the older ideologues like Giovanni Gentile (q.v.) and Giuseppe Bottai (q.v.), and to the young, "leftist" ideologues like Ugo Spirito (q.v.). Instead, the Mistica Fascista movement sought to provide ideological support for Mussolini's personal dictatorship by propagating with almost religious fervor the myth of the Duce (q.v.) and the necessity for fanatical faith, obedience, and violence.

In April 1930 a school was set up in Milan (known as the Scuola di Mistica Fascista Sandro Mussolini) to train and indoctrinate Italian youth in the values of the movement. The school was part of the PNF's (Partito Nazionale Fascista) (q.v.) university youth group, GUF (Gioventù Universitaria Fascista (see YOUTH ORGANIZATIONS), and became an agency of the party. Vito Mussolini, the son of Arnaldo Mussolini (q.v.), was the president of the school, Fernando Mezzasoma (q.v.) was vice-president, and Nicolò Giani, director. The school, which in 1940 had about 169 members, was jointly financed by the PNF and the government, and by the late 1930s had come increasingly under the authority of the Ministry of Popular Culture (q.v.). It organized public debates, published pamphlets and the journal *Dottrina Fascista*, and gave courses in doctrine.

For further information see: Daniele Marchesini, *La scuola dei gerarchi* (Milan: Feltrinelli, 1976).

PVC

MODIGLIANI, GIUSEPPE E. (b. Livorno, October 28, 1872; d. Rome, October 5, 1947). A Socialist leader and anti-Fascist, Modigliani joined the Socialist party at its inception. He studied law at Pisa, was a youthful contributor to F. Turati's (q.v.) *Critica Sociale*, and was active in numerous local Socialist organizations. Elected to Parliament in 1913, Modigliani was a vociferous opponent of intervention (see INTERVENTIONIST CRISIS, 1914-1915) in World War I and during the conflict worked for the restoration of peace (he participated in the Zimmerwald and Kienthal conferences). After the Communist split from the PSI (Partito Socialista Italiano) (q.v.) in 1921, he joined with Turati, Claudio Treves (q.v.), and others in the foundation of the Partito Socialista Unitario and became a determined anti-Fascist. Forced to leave Italy in 1925 after a number of violent Fascist assaults against him, he went to Paris and, with Turati, Treves, Giuseppe Saragat (q.v.), and Pietro Nenni (q.v.), helped to reconstitute the Socialist movement. An active participant in the Concentrazione Antifascista (see ANTI-FASCISM), he edited *Rinascita Socialista* and was instrumental in recreating Socialist unity. He made a lengthy speaking tour of the United States and polemicized with Carlo Rosselli (see ROSSELLI, CARLO and ROSSELLI, NELLO) over anti-Fascist strategy.

With the outbreak of World War II and the Nazi invasion of France, Modigliani made his way to Switzerland with the help of Joyce Lussu, where he resumed his anti-Fascist work. In October 1944 he returned to Italy, joined the PSIUP (Partito Socialista Italiano di Unità Proletaria), and represented that party in both the Consulta Nazionale (q.v.) and the Constituent Assembly (see COSTITUENTE). In 1947 he adhered to Saragat's newly created PSLI (Partito Socialista dei Lavoratori Italiani).

For further information see: DSPI; EAR (2); MOI (3).

PVC

MOMBELLI, ERNESTO (b. Turin, July 12, 1867; d. Florence, February 24, 1932). A colonial governor and general, Mombelli headed Italian forces in Turkey between 1921 and 1923, then commanded the Rome division. He became Governor of Cyrenaica (*see* LIBYA [TRIPOLITANIA AND CYRENAICA]) in May 1924. Lacking resources, Mombelli abandoned large counterinsurgency operations for smaller mobile patrols. He reduced some Senussi strongholds and occupied the Jarabub Oasis (February 1926), but failed to cripple guerrilla activities despite using mustard gas. Mombelli departed in November 1926 to become Army Deputy Chief of Staff in February 1927 under G. F. Ferrari (q.v.). Mussolini wanted him as Ferrari's successor but Mombelli declined, pleading exhaustion. Instead he received the corps commands at Udine (1928-32) and Florence.

For further information see: *Corriere della Sera*, February 25, 1932; E. E. Evans-Pritchard, *The Sanusi of Cyrenaica* (Oxford: Clarendon Press, 1949).

BRS

MONARCHY. See **REFERENDUM OF 1946; SAVOIA, AMEDEO DI, DUKE OF AOSTA; SAVOIA, EMANUELE FILIBERTO, DUKE OF AOSTA; SAVOIA-AOSTA, ADMIRAL LUIGI AMEDEO, DUKE OF THE ABRUZZI; UMBERTO II; VICTOR EMMANUEL III.**

MONDOLFO, UGO GUIDO (b. Senigallia, Ancona, June 26, 1875; d. Milan, May 23, 1957). An educator and journalist, Mondolfo participated directly in Italian politics before and after the Fascist era. After taking a degree in letters from the University of Bologna, he began his teaching career while completing a law degree in Siena. As a Socialist party member in Florence in 1895, he began contributing to numerous Socialist journals including *Il Domani* and *La Ricossa*. For these activities he was brought before a military tribunal.

In 1910 he moved to Milan, where he continued his teaching and journalistic efforts and entered public life. In 1914 he ran successfully for communal councilman, and in 1918 the mayor of Milan appointed him assessor for city planning and private buildings. He continued to contribute to *Critica Sociale*, the review that he directed from 1920 until it was suppressed by the Fascist government.

During the Fascist era Mondolfo taught secondary school in Italy until the passage of the racial laws. As a Jew he was prohibited from teaching in 1938 and in 1940 was placed in confinement in the province of Pesaro. He fled to Switzerland, where he remained until August 1943 when he reentered Italy.

In the postwar era Mondolfo participated in Italian politics as a member of the democratic left. Elected to the Chamber of Deputies (*see* PARLIAMENT) in 1948 as a PSU (Partito Socialista Unitario) deputy, he later moved to the PSDI (Partito Socialista Democratico Italiano), where he remained in the left wing of the party in opposition to the policies of Giuseppe Saragat (q.v.). He then broke decisively with the PSDI, joining Ferruccio Parri (q.v.), Piero Calamandrei (q.v.), and others in opposing the "fraudulent" election law of 1953. In 1956, the year before his death, Mondolfo returned to local politics, winning reelection as communal councilman of Milan.

For further information see: EAR (3): MOI (3).

CLK

MONTALE, EUGENIO (b. Genoa, October 12, 1896). One of the major Italian poets of the twentieth century, Montale studied classics at Genoa and was an infantry officer in World War I. From 1929 to 1939 he was director of the Vieusseux Library in Florence, a position he had to give up because of his refusal to join the PNF (Partito Nazionale Fascista) (q.v.). Thereafter he lived in Milan and served as editor for *Il Corriere della Sera*, specializing in literary criticism.

Montale's poetry confronted both the artist's place in life and the psychological impact of historical events, and his work is an example of how a creative intellectual under Fascism could do his own work without compromising his integrity. Although his poetry was often self-sustaining and transcended the arid climate of Fascism, he was not a hermetic writer, and especially with his volume *Le Occasioni* (1939) he directly faced the political crisis of World War II. In 1962 Montale was awarded the Feltrinelli prize and in 1967 was made a senator.

For further information see: *Enciclopedia Italiana* (Rome: Treccani, 1948); Eugenio Montale, *Poesie/Poems*, trans. G. Kay (Edinburgh: Edinburgh University Press, 1964); Edward R. Tannenbaum, *The Fascist Experience* (New York: Basic Books, 1972).

PVC

MONTE CASSINO. Monte Cassino is an ancient Benedictine monastery overlooking the Liri Valley southeast of Rome. During the latter months of 1943 German forces fortified the monastery as an observation post from which to direct counterattacks upon Allied forces advancing on Rome. Four separate battles comprised the struggle for control of the monastery, the first commencing on January 24, 1944, by elements of the U.S. Second Corps. After eighteen days of bitter fighting and heavy casualties, the Allies were forced to disengage.

In mid-February the Allies concluded that saturation bombing was the only means of dislodging the enemy and dropped over 1,500 tons of high explosives. Despite the monastery's destruction, the Germans fought on: instead of being housed in the monastery they were positioned in underground passages between the rock walls, shielded from the effects of the bombing.

The third assault on the monastery began on March 15 by New Zealand and Indian infantry divisions under the command of Lieutenant General Sir Bernard Freyberg. On March 23 Freyberg was forced to withdraw because of abnormally high casualties. At this point both sides paused to recover after months of fighting that had ended in a statemate. The Allies opted to wait until spring to continue their offensive when they could utilize their greatest assets, air superiority and armor.

Finally, on May 18, after suffering over four thousand casualties, the monastery was captured by the Twelfth Polish Lancers. The struggle for Monte Cassino remains a classic example of defensive warfare.

For further information see: F. A. Sheppard, *The Italian Campaign, 1943-45* (New York: Praeger, 1968).

WAJ

MONTEVIDEO CONGRESS. The Montevideo Pan-American Anti-Fascist Congress of August 17-18, 1942, was an attempt by Carlo Sforza (q.v.) and other *fuorusciti* (q.v.) to publicize and win Allied endorsement of the Free Italy (q.v.) program. Attended by 1,500 delegates and supported by the Mazzini Society (q.v.) and the U.S. Department of State, the congress elected Sforza leader by acclamation and proceeded to adopt his program for Italy. The program consisted of (1) election of an Italian constituent assembly for the purpose of adopting a new constitution as soon as Italy was liberated; (2) creation of a "democratic and social republic" to replace the monarchy; (3) recognition of an Italian National Committee headed by Sforza; (4) organization of an Italian Legion under Randolfo Pacciardi (q.v.); and (5) European federation.

A period of ambiguous relations between Sforza and Allied leaders followed Sforza's expression of willingness to accept Communist participation and the U.S. State Department's implicit support of Sforza at Montevideo. The conference did succeed in focusing attention—positive and negative—on Sforza's program. Among those objecting were the Salveminian (*see* SALVEMINI, GAETANO) faction, who argued that such an Allied commitment would limit the freedom of action of the Italian people. Winston Churchill, comfortable in maintaining the House of Savoy, objected to Sforza's republican agenda.

Essentially, the Montevideo Congress failed to win American support because Sforza's program offered little military advantage at the cost of premature political commitment. In 1943, when the Allied invasion justified part of the Montevideo program, President Franklin D. Roosevelt endorsed the participation of exile leaders in the liberation of Italy.

For further information see: Charles Delzell, *Mussolini's Enemies* (Princeton: Princeton University Press, 1961); James E. Miller, "Carlo Sforza e L'evoluzione della politica Americana verso l'Italia 1940-1943," *Storia Contemporanea* 7 (December 1976); Carlo Sforza, *L'Italia dal 1914 al 1944 quale io la vidi* (Rome: Mondadori, 1945).

CLK

MORANDI, GIORGIO (b. Bologna, July 20, 1890; d. Bologna, June 18, 1964). One of Italy's finest painters of the twentieth century, Morandi studied at the Academy of Fine Arts in Bologna. He lived in relative seclusion, rarely leaving the city. Between 1918 and 1920 Morandi joined the ranks of the Scuola Metafisica, whose imagery was based on the subconscious and supernatural. However, he worked apart from the two leaders of the movement, Giorgio de Chirico and Carlo D. Carrà (q.v.) and carried on a brief flirtation with Futurism (q.v.) as well. His greatest admiration was reserved for the French post-Impressionist master Paul Cézanne, who had willfully chosen isolation in Provence and had dedicated himself to solving specific formal problems within a limited range of subjects. Morandi knew Cézanne's work in reproduction only; unlike many artists of the modern movement who readily acknowledged the cultural ascendancy of Paris, Morandi never left Italy for the requisite pilgrimage to the capital of the art world. From 1922 he developed a unique idiom, like that of Cézanne, limited to a repertory of mute geometric volumes chosen from the traditional subject categories of still life and landscape. His works resemble the products of the Cubist movement and much later twentieth-century art in their concentration on formal elements alone, with no reference to contemporary events. Nor were any verbal statements regarding meaning issued by the painter. His work remained traditional in one major respect: his study of color and shape was always carried out in representational terms rather than via the abandonment of subject matter, as was the case in the work of the Dutch painter, Piet Mondrian, the closest modern counterpart to Morandi.

Morandi's native Bologna was a powerful influence on his choice of subjects as well as color. The subtle tonalities of his palette reflect the red brick and terra cotta of both the town and its environs. But no influence was exerted by the social activity of the city, which at times was a base in the discussion of the alliance between Fascism and the arts (for example, the Bologna Congress of Fascist Intellectuals in 1925). Morandi's abandonment of artistic connections with the nineteenth century and his strong sense of self-discipline might both be interpreted as a response to Mussolini's demands for artists. But in fact Morandi was anti-Fascist and never had any intention of putting his talents to work for the state. His career demonstrates to what extent a great artist, possessing aloofness and restraint, could live in Italy without bowing to Fascist doctrine. Nevertheless, his international reputation secured for him a subsidy from the regime as well as high public esteem.

For further information see: James Thrall Soby and Alfred H. Barr, Jr., *Twentieth-Century Italian Art* (New York: The Museum of Modern Art, 1949); Lamberto Vitali, *Morandi: Catalogo Generale, 1913-1947* (Milan: Electa, 1977).

                                                                                                                          RN

MORAVIA, ALBERTO (b. Rome, November 28, 1907). An important twentieth-century writer, Moravia's first novel, *Gli Indifferenti* (*The Indifferent Ones*) (1928), was an instant success in Italy and a major turning point in Italian literature under Fascism. Moravia wanted to portray the baseness, corruption, and moral emptiness of the bourgeoisie and the hollow atmosphere of life under Fascism. Although this theme was carefully disguised in plot and language, a contemporary dispute erupted that saw some Fascist critics, including Arnaldo Mussolini (q.v.), bitterly attack Moravia and others like F. T. Marinetti (q.v) and Massimo Bon-tempelli (q.v.) defend the work as a masterpiece of modern literature.

Other works of this period were *Le Ambizioni Sbagliate* (1935), *La Mascherata* (1941), and *La Speranza* (1944), in which Marxism and Freudianism are viewed positively as elements that would reform bourgeois corruption, and a series of stories: *La Bella Vita* (1935), *L'Imbroglio* (1937), *I Sogni del Pigro* (1940), *L'Amante Infelice* (1943), and *L'Epidemia* (1944). In *Agostino* (1945) Moravia succeeded in giving a very poetic description of a young adolescent's crisis during his years of sexual discovery and development. Another masterpiece was the novel *La Romana* (1947), followed by *La Disobbedienza* (1948), *L'Amore Coniugale* (1949), *Il Conformista* (*The Conformist*, 1951), *Il Disprezzo* (1954), *Racconti Romani* (1954), and finally *La Ciociara* (1957), an outstanding work in which Moravia described the Nazi persecution and vicissitudes of postwar Italy. In this novel he rid himself of all former intellectualism. *La Ciociara* is followed by essay novels including *La Noia* (1960), *L'Automa* (1962), *L'Attenzione* (1965), *Una Cosa è una Cosa* (1967), and *Io e Lui* (1971). Moravia acts as a strict moralist and through his narrative attempts to solve the problems posed by contemporary ideologies. The same strict morality is present in the dramatic works including *L'Intervista* (1966), *Il Mondo è quello Che è* (1966), *Il Dio Kurt* (1968), and *La Vita è un Gioco* (1969).

Of all Moravia's writings, the most significant are his novels and short stories. In these the writer described a world void of moral light, one that is tired, indifferent, and made up of superficial social conventions, a world in which the various characters search in vain to fill their spiritual emptiness with the illusion of sexual or monetary conquest.

For further information see: E. De Michelis, *Introduzione a Moravia* (Florence: Nuova Italia, 1954); E. Fulqui, *Prosatori e narratori del Novecento italiano* (Turin: Einaudi, 1950); F. Longobardi, *Moravia* (Florence: Nuova Italia, 1969); G. Pullini, *Il romanzo italiano del dopoguerra*, (Milan: Schwarz, 1961).

WEL

MORGAGNI, MANLIO (b. Forlì, June 3, 1879; d. Rome, July 25, 1943). A Fascist journalist and bureaucrat, Morgagni was an interventionist (*see* INTERVENTIONIST CRISIS, 1914-1915) and early supporter of Mussolini. In November 1914 he became the first business administrator for *Il Popolo d'Italia*, a position he held until it was given to Arnaldo Mussolini (q.v.) in 1919. A "fascist of the very first hour," he took part in the March on Rome (q.v.), and was a member of the directorate of the Milan *fascio*. He founded and directed the *Rivista Illustrata del Popolo d'Italia*, and in 1943 he became president and director of the regime's official news agency, Agenzia Stefani (q.v.).

He held a number of local posts (including vice-Podestà [q.v.] of Milan) in the 1920s and 1930s and was widely known as a profiteer. A fanatical Fascist journalist, when Mussolini fell from power in 1943, Morgagni committed suicide.

For further information see: *Chi è?* (1936); NO (1937); Philip V. Cannistraro, *La fabbrica del consenso* (Rome-Bari: Laterza, 1975).

PVC

MORGARI, ODDINO (b. Turin, November 16, 1865; d. Sanremo, November 1944). An anti-Fascist exile, Morgari was one of the pioneers of Italian socialism. He was elected a deputy from Turin in 1897 and continued to serve the Socialist party (PSI—Partito Socialista Italiano) (q.v.), and then the Unitarian Socialist party (PSUI-Partito Socialista Unitario Italiano) in Parliament until the Aventine Secession (q.v.). As an exponent of "integralism," in 1906 Morgari attempted to conciliate the rifts between syndicalism (q.v.) and reformism. Briefly in 1908 he served as editor of *Avanti!*

During World War I Morgari gained fame as the "socialist diplomat" because of his far-flung travels to keep international socialism alive. Although he was elected to the International Socialist Commission at the Zimmerwald Conference, Morgari nonetheless broke with Socialist orthodoxy by flirting ingenuously with the Henry Ford Peace Mission.

When the reformists were expelled from the PSI in 1922, Morgari joined the PSUI. After the assassination of Matteotti (*see* MATTEOTTI CRISIS) he became an anti-Fascist exile in France. There he collaborated on the *Corriere degli Italiani*. When the PSI was reconsolidated in 1930, Morgari was elected administrative secretary. In 1939 Morgari, together with Giuseppe Saragat (q.v.) and Angelo Tasca (q.v.), replaced Pietro Nenni (q.v.) as director of *Nuovo Avanti*. A year later Morgari was granted permission to return to Italy because of poor health.

For further information see: Renata Allio, "Oddino Morgari Socialista," *Bolletino storico-bibliografico subalpino* 68 (1970); Gaetano Arfè, *Storia dell' Avanti!*, 2 vols. (Milan: Edizioni Avanti!, 1956-58); Giuseppe Calciano, "Appunti e documenti sull'attività internazionale di Oddino Morgari," *Rivista storica del socialismo* 10, 32 (1967).

NGE

MORI, CESARE (b. Pavia, January 1, 1872; d. Udine, July 5, 1942). A career prefect, Mori started out as a provincial police chief (*questore*) and was responsible for coordinating all police action in the lower Po Valley. He became deeply involved in the campaign against peasant agitation and as a reward for his work was promoted to prefect in 1920. From February 1921 to August 1922 Mori was prefect in Bologna and in an effort to maintain tranquility, followed a policy of firmness toward both the Fascists and the local underworld. As a result of Fascist opposition to his policies, Mori was forced out of his post and sent to Bari.

In June 1924 Mori was transferred to Sicily, where he became prefect of Trapani for a short time. Mussolini then appointed him prefect of Palermo, a post he held until his retirement from active political life in July 1929. During his term he carried on an unrelenting struggle against the Sicilian Mafia. Mori used illegal trials, torture, and forced exile as a means to destroy the criminal organization that Mussolini correctly recognized as a threat to Fascist domination in Sicily. Although he had some temporary success, Mori failed to eliminate the Mafia because he made no changes in the island's social or economic conditions. During his term in Sicily Mori was made a senator (December 1928) and later received an honorary law degree from the University of Palermo.

For further information see: NO (1937); Giacomo de Antonellis, *Il Sud durante il fascismo* (Manduria: Lacaita, 1977); Renzo De Felice, *Mussolini il fascista* (Turin: Einaudi, 1966); Arrigo Petacco, *Il Prefetto di ferro* (Milan: Mondadori, 1975).

MSF

MOSCONI, ANTONIO (b. Vicenza, September 9, 1866; d. Rome, 1955). A Fascist minister, Mosconi received a law degree from the University of Padua and began his administrative career in 1890 by serving in the prefecture of Vicenza and then as cabinet chief of the Ministry of Post and Telegraph. In 1911 Mosconi became a prefect and during the Libyan War served in the Ministry of the Interior. In 1913 Mosconi became chief secretary of the president of the Council of Ministers and six years later became the prefect of Trieste, a post he held until 1922. While in this position, Mosconi, who became a senator in October 1920, encouraged the Fascists in Trieste and aided in the conquest of the area by Mussolini's supporters. Between 1922 and 1928 Mosconi held a number of relatively insignificant posts, but in July 1928 he was made minister of finance. As minister Mosconi headed the Italian delegation to The Hague Conference on reparations in 1929-30. Mosconi lost his post in July 1932 and after that date was relegated to minor positions within the Fascist bureaucracy.

For further information see: *Chi è?* (1936); DSPI; NO (1937).

MSF

MOSTRA DELLA RIVOLUZIONE FASCISTA. For the tenth anniversary of the March on Rome (q.v.), Mussolini organized a huge exhibition in 1932 known as the Mostra della Rivoluzione Fascista. It was directed by Dino Alfieri (q.v.) and Luigi Freddi (q.v.). Housed in the renovated Palazzo degli Esposizioni on the Via Nazionale in Rome, it commemorated the struggle for power between 1919 and 1922 in room after room of memorabilia, posters, artifacts, sculpture, and paintings. The fallen Blackshirt martyrs (*see* SQUADRISTI) had a shrine dedicated to them, Mussolini's headquarters in Milan was recreated, and important episodes in the period 1919-22 depicted. The *squadristi* were dubbed the "old guard" (Vecchia Guardia) and took turns as honor guards on the front steps of the building. Mussolini insisted on an essentially modern style of architecture for the exhibit and the building renovations (the Palazzo had a series of huge *Fasci* [*see* FASCIO LITTORIO] erected before it), so that the Mostra was enshrined in a combination of Futurist-Novecento modernism. While on one level the exhibit was a massive propaganda effort, on another it was a symbol that the heroic era of Fascist violence and *squadrismo* had passed into history.

For further information see: Dino Alfieri and Luigi Freddi, *Mostra della Rivoluzione Fascista* (Bergamo: Arti Grafiche, 1933); Philip V. Cannistraro, *La fabbrica del consenso* (Rome-Bari: Laterza, 1975).

PVC

MOTION PICTURES. See **CINEMA**.

MOVIMENTO SOCIALE ITALIANO (MSI). A neo-Fascist party, the MSI was founded in Rome on December 26, 1946, by a group of former Fascists who had participated in the Salò Republic (*see* ITALIAN SOCIAL REPUBLIC). This group included Giorgio Almirante (q.v.), who was chosen its first secretary, Roberto Mielville, Arturo Michelini, and Giorgio Pini (q.v.). Within a brief time other ex-Fascists, such as Rodolfo Graziani (q.v.), Junio Valerio Borghese (q.v.), and Cesare Maria De Vecchi (q.v.) had joined the MSI.

Almirante pushed the party toward an aggressive, violent orientation and bitter anti-Communism. In 1950, however, he was replaced by Augusto De Marsanich (q.v.), who advocated a centrist, moderate stance in view of the electoral failures experienced under Almirante's leadership. De Marsanich began to create electoral alliances with other right-wing political forces, especially the Monarchist party. By 1954 the MSI was experiencing internal fractionalization and De Marsanich was forced to give up control of the party to Michelini, whose policy was the insertion of the MSI in the Italian parliamentary system. An intransigent wing led by Almirante developed, and in 1956 the so-called "Ordine Nuovo" organization broke from the party and set up its own squads. In 1969 with the death of Michelini, Almirante returned to the head of the party.

The MSI has developed an elaborate structure over the years that includes a large number of branches and affiliated organizations. In the mid-1970s it had an official national membership of four hundred thousand (although other sources put the total at less than that) and more than four thousand local sections. In national parliamentary elections the MSI has registered some success: from five hundred and twenty-five thousand votes in 1948 (six deputies and one senator) to three million votes in 1972 (fifty-six deputies and twenty-three senators).

While the MSI has not represented a major threat to Italian democracy, it has on occasion been able to influence the formation of cabinets and has caused considerable violence, which has created an atmosphere of great tension. In the regional administrative elections of 1970, the MSI succeeded in placing members in almost all the provincial councils and elected representatives in more than half of the communal governments (its strongest regional base appears to be in the south).

For further information see: Angelo Del Boca and Mario Giovana, *Fascism Today* (New York: Pantheon, 1969); Giuseppe Gaddi, *Neofascismo in Europa*

(Milan: La Pietra, 1974); Peter Rosenbaum, *Il nuovo fascismo* (Milan: Feltrinelli, 1975).

PVC

MUNICH CONFERENCE. A conference among leaders of Great Britain, France, Germany, and Italy, the Munich Conference, held on September 29-30, 1938, temporarily solved the German-Czech crisis and preserved a precarious European peace.

The crisis was precipitated by Hitler's intransigence in regard to returning the Sudeten German population of Czechoslovakia to the Reich. Two efforts by British Prime Minister Neville Chamberlain to head off the crisis by offering Hitler return of parts of the Sudetenland failed, as Hitler raised his demands. The failure of Chamberlain's second conference with Hitler led both sides to military preparations, with a German mobilization ordered for September 28.

Mussolini meanwhile supported Hitler's case by statements in *Informazione Diplomatica* on September 13, an open letter to the British representative in Prague on September 15, and speeches in which he pledged military aid to Germany and demanded a plebiscite for the Sudetenland.

On September 28 Chamberlain proposed a conference to both Mussolini and Hitler to settle the Sudeten question and specifically requested Mussolini to intervene. Mussolini's intervention made the Munich Conference possible. He immediately requested Hitler to postpone hostilities for twenty-four hours. Hitler accepted. Mussolini then rejected the British proposal of a conference including the Czechs and proposed to Hitler that only representatives from France, Britain, Germany, and Italy attend. Hitler again accepted and allowed Mussolini to choose the site.

The conference convened the following day with Chamberlain, Georges Bonnet, Hitler, and Mussolini representing the parties. Because of the haste, the conference lacked agenda and organization, allowing Mussolini to take charge. He alone seemed comfortable, largely because only he had a useful knowledge of the others' languages. The working paper of the conference was a memorandum produced by Mussolini, arranged in advance by telephone with the German Foreign Ministry and in person with Hitler, who joined Mussolini on his train for the last miles into Munich.

The final agreement satisfied all German demands. Germany occupied all of the Sudetenland by October 7 and the agreement's boundary commission ceded to Germany all areas where the German population outnumbered other populations, whether or not they held an absolute majority. The solution disrupted Czechoslovakia's fortifications, industry, and railway systems. It further provided for the settlement of the Polish and Hungarian minority questions, with which the Italians became involved.

Following Munich Mussolini was widely hailed in Italy and abroad for saving the peace. His international reputation reached a high point as his moderation and reasonableness were compared to Hitler's bullying stance. The Munich Conference also led to some tangible advantages for Italy, as Britain (and later France) finally recognized the Italian Empire. Munich further convinced Mussolini of the moral and military weakness of the Western democracies and deluded him about his control over Hitler, a delusion shattered by the German takeover of the rump state of Czechoslovakia in March 1939.

For further information see: Mario Donosti, *Mussolini e l'Europa* (Rome: Edizioni Leonardo, 1945); Elizabeth Wiskemann, *The Rome-Berlin Axis* (New York: Oxford University Press, 1949).

MFL

MUSIC. An overall view of the musical developments in Italy from the beginning of the twentieth century until 1945 reveals stylistic trends in musical composition in two major directions. The first emerging style of musical composition, exhibited by a group of composers known as "La generazione dell '80" (The Generation of 1880), can generally be described as neoclassic. The second style, which began to surface in the mid-1930s, can be described as twelve-tone. A third group of Italian composers evolved in the late 1940s whose works are also immersed in the twelve-tone style and on occasion exhibit a more progressive outgrowth of that style, abstract pointillism.

"La generazione dell '80" consisted of Alfredo Casella (1883-1947), Ildebrando Pizzetti (1880-1968), Gian Francesco Malipiero (1882-1973), and Ottorino Respighi (1879-1936). These composers, assisted by the musicologist Fausto Torrefranca, initiated a break with the nineteenth-century musical tradition in both the instrumental-symphonic and vocal-operatic mediums. "La generazione dell '80" believed that verismo opera was no longer effective and that a renaissance of Italian music was possible only through the assimilation of the spirit and style of great instrumental Italian masters of the past such as Girolano Frescobaldi, Antonio Vivaldi, and Arcangelo Corelli.

Italian verismo opera was represented primarily by Giacomo Puccini (1858-1924). The most successful Italian opera composer during the early twentieth century, his fame was established by such works as *Madame Butterfly*, *Tosca*, *Gianni Schicchi*, and *Turandot*. Puccini, together with Pietro Mascagni's (1863-1948) (q.v.) *Cavalleria Rusticana* (1890), and Ruggiero Leoncavallo (1858-1919), with his *I Pagliacci* (1892), presented an alternative to the operatic tradition established by Wagner. Instead of presenting an historical or exotic world of myth as did Wagner, they introduced realism (verismo) in Italian opera. The verismo tradition was characterized by the selection of a libretto that displayed the average human being acting extremely under the impulse of primitive emotions. This move to verismo occurred under the influence of Emile Zola and the French realist school of writers, whose rather brutal French novels of contemporary life began to appear in the 1870s.

All members of "La generazione dell '80" insisted on a break with the musical traditions of the immediate past and demanded an art exclusively nurtured in Italy and free from the influences of German romanticism and French impressionism. They also supported the Italian neoclassic musical tradition, which meant their musical style of composition would have a tonal, harmonic foundation and they would utilize Renaissance and/or Baroque forms and compositional techniques and devices. Breaking from the past also committed them to establishing a new vocal-operatic style as well as a new instrumental-symphonic style, and they reacted strongly against the veristic opera tradition.

Two characteristics of "La generazione dell '80," the belief in an art exclusively Italian and free from foreign influences and their break with the immediate past (verismo), rendered their cultural traditions compatible with the nationalist thrust of Fascism. Fascism, in addition to espousing cultural autarchy (q.v.), also viewed itself as making an intellectual and cultural break with the past.

Alfredo Casella, who supported the perpetuation of the Italian musical tradition, was for the most part a neoclassicist and thereby can be construed as a nationalist. While his instrumental works prior to World War I display the influences of Gustav Mahler, Richard Strauss, Claude Debussy, and Maurice Ravel (and he was also aware of the musical activities of Arnold Schoenberg and Igor Stravinsky), he held steadfastly to the ideals of Italian art. For a time, from 1922 to 1927, he embodied the trends established in music in the Fascist period and was musical spokesman for the regime. But in 1927 when Mussolini received a group of musicians to demonstrate he was supportive of contemporary Italian musicians, Casella was not present. He had become associated with an intelligentsia that disassociated itself from the Fascists. I. Pizzetti, who became more reactionary each year, was designated as spokesman for the Fascists. Casella was greatly influenced by F. T. Marinetti's (q.v.) Futurist manifesto. It kindled his patriotism since it argued that Italy could produce art of its own that could compete with the modernism of other nations.

Of all members of "La generazione dell '80" G. F. Malipiero was perhaps the most prolific. He wrote several works for stage and a large number of instrumental and orchestral works. As early as 1904 he began transcribing works of Renaissance and early Baroque composers such as C. G. A. Monteverdi and Frescobaldi, whose polyphonic practices ultimately influenced his own compositional style. In 1913 he went to Paris, where he absorbed the techniques of musical impressionism that utilized parallel chord formations, juxtapositions, and amplified tonal harmonies. It was also during 1913 that he met Casella, with whom he established a long-standing friendship.

Three compositions are representative of Malipiero's first period and illustrate impressionist and neoclassic influences. The first is *Pause del Silenzio I* (1917), which is similar in ferocity to Stravinsky's *Rite of Spring* and reveals something of an impressionist influence. An opera entitled *Sette Canzone* (1918-19) contains influences of Gregorian chant, folk song, and preclassical Italian music. Malipiero's operas, unlike those of the veristic school, exclude dramatic activity: action and characters are not developed. Lyricism is the prime factor of Malipiero's operas.

The third work is a theater piece entitled *San Francesco d'Assisi* (1920-21), which reveals Malipiero's debts to Gregorian chant, to Monteverdi, and to Renaissance music in general.

Representative of his second period are works illustrating the use of neoclassic techniques. In his opera *Toreno Notturno* (1929), the central idea is epitomized by a *canzone del tempo* that utilizes a repeated pedal tone and a descending scalic bass. *Favola del Figlio Cambiato* (1934), also a stage work, illustrates Monteverdi's influence on Malipiero. His first and second symphonies (1936 and 1937) are modeled on Italian sinfonie of the seventeenth and eighteenth centuries and display a characteristic Baroque concertante treatment of woodwinds and brass.

In 1939 he became the director of the Liceo Musicale Benedetto Marcello in Venice, and his stature as a composer was recognized as he was named a member of various international academies.

Ildebrando Pizzetti, the third member of "La generazione dell '80," is the least known among the group. He worked with musicologist Giovanni Tebaldini, the pioneer of Italian musicology, and became interested in early Baroque music and Gregorian chant. He was on the faculty at the Conservatory of Parma (1907-08) and of the Conservatory of Florence (1908-24), and was appointed the director of the Istituto Musicale Cherubini from 1917 to 1924. From 1924 to 1926 he was also director of the Milan Conservatory. In 1927 Mussolini designated him musical spokesman of the Fascist regime. He later moved to Rome and occupied the chair of composition at the Accademia St. Cecilia from 1936 to his retirement in 1960. On December 17, 1932, Pizzetti joined the reactionaries and signed a manifesto published in several Italian newspapers attacking the more forward musical trends of the time. He received the Mussolini Prize in 1932 for his work supporting the regime. Pizzetti reacted against Puccini and Mascagni.

His stature as a major composer became apparent with the opera *Fedra* (1915). The compositional techniques used here established the basic musical tendencies that were to underlie his music dramas and made a clean break with his predecessors. He evolved a kind of declamation involving dramatic recitative and arioso, examples of which can be found in *Debra e Jaele* (1915-21). His subsequent operas added little to what was achieved in *Debra e Jaele*. The three orchestral preludes *Per l'Edipo Re di Sofocle* (1903) reflect the melodic autonomy and rhythmic flexibility of plainsong. His *Concerto dell'Estate* (1928) consists of three movements reflecting the experiences of summer and night, while *Rondo Veneziano* (1929) symbolizes the pride and splendor of Venice. From about 1923 onward Pizzetti became more reactionary and continued composing in a neoclassic musical style.

Ottorino Respighi (1879-1936) also belonged to "La generazione dell '80." With the exception of Puccini, Respighi was the most prominent Italian composer in the first third of the twentieth century. This was due in part to the performance of his two symphonic poems, *The Fountains of Rome* (1914) and *The Pines of Rome* (1924), given by Arturo Toscanini on his concert tours in Italy, Europe, and the

United States. His compositions are very structured and exhibit a tendency toward design rather than color.

Respighi's mature period can be divided into two parts: the Roman and the Gregorian periods. The first part lasted from 1916 to 1926 and was characterized by a sumptuous and a highly colored sensuality. *The Fountains of Rome* and *The Pines of Rome* are representative of this era. The *Concerto Gregoriano* for violin (1922) and *Concerto in Modo Inisolodico* for piano (1924) anticipate his concentration on Gregorian chant and modality. One of his last works, an opera entitled *La Fiamma* (1933), makes use of both Gregorian and Byzantine liturgial chant. His overall style of musical composition was eclectic in that he borrowed from Debussy, Strauss, Nikolai Rimsky-Korsakov, and to a lesser degree from Giacomo Puccini.

In 1913 he was appointed instructor in composition at the Academy of Santa Cecilia in Rome, and ten years later he was appointed its director. He resigned in 1925, however, because of musical commitments that necessitated frequent absences from Italy. He was elected a member of the Royal Academy of Italy (q.v.) on March 23, 1932.

Concurrent with the development of the neoclassicism of "La generazione dell '80" was the excursion of a few Italian musicians into the Futurist movement. Originally Futurism (q.v.) was an anti-intellectual movement of intellectuals that issued its first manifesto from Paris in 1909 and sought adherents in Italy. It represented the rebellion of the young against the old and supported the mystique of the machine in a society that advocated humanism. The Italian musical reflection of Futurism can be seen in a letter written by Luigi Russolo entitled "The Art of Noises" (March 11, 1913) to Balilla Pratella while listening to a performance of Pratella's *Musica Futurista*:

The first musical sounds were an astonishing discovery—it was sacred. Initially the chord did not exist—music in the Middle Ages was horizontal, not vertical. Today we approach the music of noise. Music parallels the multiplicity of machines. (Noise is equated with dissonant chords of the twentieth century). Musicians' sensibility is now being renewed working with noise, which gives a new sense of pitch and rhythm. We musicians construct new instruments and challenge young musicians to listen to noises.[1]

The Futurists Russolo and Pratella initially moved away from the use of tonality and advocated the use of "sound-noise" as contrasted to "La generazione dell '80" who defended the use of tonality by encouraging Italian artists to return to the use of Renaissance and particularly Baroque musical styles. From a political perspective initially the Futurists appear outside the nationalist sphere because nationalist musicians generally supported tonality. In his later career Pratella became disassociated from the Futurists because he began to use folk songs in his works.

The Futurists maintained their distance from "La generazione dell '80" even into the early thirties. Such statements as the following were written by F. T. Marinetti and Maestro Guintini:

We condemn music for music's sake. . . . We condemn imitation of classical music. In art, every return is a defeat or disguised impotence. We condemn the use of popular songs which has led such inspired spirits as Pratella and Malipiero away. . . . We condemn imitations of jazz and negro music. Italian musicians be futurists. . . . arousing pride of living in the great Italy of Mussolini.[2]

Despite the ostensible lack of support of nationalism (by writing tonally oriented music), the Futurists managed to survive easily in Fascist Italy.

During several years of the Fascist regime the critic Guido Gatti published a magazine, *Il Pianoforte*, and subsequently, *Rassegna Musicale*, which attempted to help Italian musicians maintain knowledge of international musical developments. Gatti was successful in this venture because he understood the incapacity of the regime to understand the intuitions of the musicians. These magazines were bulwarks of information for those who did not subscribe to the regime. However, in the Italian musical world the effect of those publications was not seen until the mid-1930s.

The next generation of Italian musicians illustrates the transition that began taking place in the late thirties and early forties in Italy from the use of neoclassic style to the use of twelve-tone style of musical composition. It was with these works that Italy began to participate in the mainstream of current European developments. This generation is represented by Luigi Dallapiccola (1904-75) and by Goffredo Petrassi (b. 1904), who represented major exponents of serial technique in Italy. Dallapiccola's style was initially influenced by sixteenth-century polyphony as well as the composers from the more traditional style, Casella and Malipiero, until the mid-1930s. His early works are characterized by modal-diatonic writing of preclassic derivation though without neoclassical or baroque qualities. He attended the 1935 International Society for Contemporary Music Festival in Prague where he heard Anton von Webern's Concerto, Opus 24. This exposure to Webern and the so-called "hermetical" movement in contemporary Italian poetry initiated his transition to twelve-tone musical techniques. His major works of this period are both operas, *Volo di Notte* (1937-39) and *Il Prigioniero* (1944-48). Both offer theatrical presentations of modern subjects, the first offering action symbolic of a machine taking possession of men, the second portraying the horror of psychological and political tyranny, and may establish Dallapiccola as the most important modern opera composer since Berg.

Goffredo Petrassi's musical development was influenced in his early period by Casella and Paul Hindemith. His style was characterized by use of various kinds of diatonic writing with rhythmic interest predominantly. He was influenced somewhat by neoclassicism but used baroque forms in the Concerto for Orchestra (1934). His use of the concerto principle, a baroque technique, is evident in that thematic ideas are allotted to different instrumental groups. The *Coro di morti* (1941), whose subject is the countryside brutalized by war, *Psalm IX*, and *Magnificat* are representative of his best works. During the late 1940s Petrassi began a gradual approach to dodecaphony.

Throughout the beginning of the second period in Italy's musical development a number of foreign contemporary works were found on musical programs. In 1935, however, because the League of Nations imposed sanctions against Italy, the music of foreign musicians was banned. In 1938 Italy passed anti-Semitic legislation that initiated the censoring of all music and performances by Jewish musicians. Several prominent musicians, including Dallapiccola and Toscanini, opposed the anti-Semitic campaign. Some musicians were forced into exile, others of this period wrote musical compositions critical of various events and aspects of society caused by the Fascist regime: for example, Luigi Nono's *Canto* based on letters of fugitives captured and condemned to death, Dallapiccola's *The Prisoner* (1948), and Petrassi's *Coro dei morti* (1941).

The third generation of Italian musicians represents the movement of Italian music into the more avant-garde realm of European musical activity.

The younger Italian composers (those born after 1910) can be divided into two groups. The first group consists of Aldo Clementi, Domenico Gaccero, Ennio Morricone, Carlo Prosperi, Vittorio Fellegara, and Nicolò Castiglioni. Generally speaking, works by these composers can be characterized by describing them as stopping short of extending serialization into all dimensions of a given work.

The second group of Italian composers of this younger generation uses serialization through all aspects of their works. Camillo Togni, for instance, treats the minute details of his works in a serial fashion. The most radical tendency that is an outgrowth of serialism, abstract pointillism, is found in the works of Luciano Berio, Bruno Maderna, and Luigi Nono. Maderna and Berio have also been active exponents of the electronic music studio. They were able to use the Studio di Fonologia in Milan, which Radio Italiana put at their disposal.

The musical developments which occurred in Italy between 1910 and 1945 are similar to those that happened elsewhere in the musical world; namely, the use of neoclassicism and impressionism and twelve-tone and avant-garde compositional styles. The length of the period of neoclassicism and impressionism (ca. 1910-35) was perhaps fostered by the Fascist regime's emphasis on nationalism and a determination to remove outside influences from Italy. With the weakening of the regime and the growing resistance of musicians to submit to Fascist oppression, the reintegration of Italians into the European mainstream of musical composition began. While all aspects of Italian cultural life were influenced to some degree by Fascist policy, music appears to have escaped major regimentation. In theory the Ministry of Popular Culture (q.v.) was supposed to have controlled music, but other areas of artistic creativity suffered more severe regimentation. Musicians were most directly affected by required membership in the Fascist Union of Musicians.

For further information see: William W. Austin, *Music in the Twentieth Century* (New York: Norton, 1966); Nicholas Slominsky, *Music Since 1900* (New York: Coleman-Ross, 1949); Arnold Whittall, *Music since the First World War* (London: Dent, 1977).

1. Quoted in Nicholas Slominsky, *Music Since 1900*, 3rd ed. (New York: Coleman-Ross, 1949), 642.
2. *In Stile futurista* (August 1934), quoted in Slominsky, *Music Since 1900*, 662.

JCG

MUSSOLINI, ARNALDO (b. Dovia, Predappio, January 11, 1885; d. Milan, December 21, 1931). The younger brother and confidant of the Italian dictator, Arnaldo was the only man in whom Mussolini had full confidence and trust. An elementary schoolteacher by training, Arnaldo spent the 1903-04 period in Switzerland working as a manual laborer before returning to Italy. He was communal secretary of Taglimento. In 1917, after the Battle of Caporetto (*see* CAPORETTO, BATTLE OF), he joined the Army as an infantry officer, and when the armistice came he went to work for his brother in Milan as a staff member of *Il Popolo d'Italia* (q.v.). In November 1922, after Mussolini became prime minister, Arnaldo was made director of the newspaper, a position he held until his death. Devoted to his brother and family, extremely loyal, devoid of personal ambition, and reflective in character, Arnaldo never held an official post in the Fascist government. Instead, he translated Mussolini's views and policies into editorial opinion in the columns of *Il Popolo d'Italia*, while frequently contributing articles of his own on subjects that interested him—particularly on Church matters and cultural questions. Under his direction the paper became the most authoritative press organ in Italy, for Arnaldo was in daily contact with the Duce and was known to reflect his ideas. He alone appears to have been able to exercise a moderating influence on the dictator, and his sudden death in December 1931 had a considerable impact on Mussolini's personality. It made his isolation from human contact complete and increased the Duce's tendency to rely only on himself, hence contributing to the egocentric solitude in which Mussolini was enclosed during the 1930s.

For further information see: Arnaldo Mussolini, *Scritti e discorsi*, 5 vols. (Milan: Alpes, 1937); Benito Mussolini, *Vita di Arnaldo* (Milan: Alpes, 1932).

PVC

MUSSOLINI, BENITO (b. Dovia, Predappio, July 29, 1883; d. Giulino di Mezzegra, April 28, 1945). The founder of Fascism and dictator of Italy, Mussolini was born in the Romagna region into a family of very modest means. His father, Alessandro, a Socialist and a participant in the first Socialist International, had a considerable influence on his development. Having completed his studies to qualify for an elementary school teaching certificate, in July 1902 Mussolini emigrated to Switzerland, where he remained until November 1904. The Swiss experience was an extremely important one for him: it immersed him fully in the world of socialism; exposed him to the ideas of Georges Sorel, Louis Blanqui, Friedrich Nietzsche, Vilfredo Pareto (q.v.), and Gustave Le Bon, which were to become critical elements in his own brand of socialism (characterized by idealism, voluntarism, and elitism); and had a great impact on his political development in general.

Expelled from Switzerland, he returned to Italy to serve in the military. After a brief period teaching in Tolmezzo, he moved to Oneglia in 1908 as a teacher and became director of the Socialist weekly, *La Lima*. Returning to the Romagna, he took part in Socialist agitation and then went to the Austrian-controlled region of Trento to undertake political and trade union work and to direct the newspaper *L'Avvenire del lavoratore*. During this period, in which he collaborated actively with the patriotic agitator Cesare Battisti, he was influenced by the Florentine journal *La Voce*, which published his *Il trentino visto da un socialista* (1911). Austrian authorities expelled him from the Trentino in September 1909, and Mussolini then settled in Forlì. There he founded the newspaper *La lotta di classe* and became the head of the local Socialists, whom he led in campaigns against the Italo-Turkish War and for which he was imprisoned. In less than three years he emerged as one of the most significant new leaders of the revolutionary wing of Italian Socialism (*see* PARTITO SOCIALISTA ITALIANO), which at the Congress of Reggio Emilia (July 1912) assumed control of the party. At the congress Mussolini played an important role in the expulsion of the right-wing reformists and was elected to the party's directorate. That November he was named director of *Avanti!*, the party's official newspaper. As one of the most prominent and popular party leaders, Mussolini—thanks in part to his journalistic talents—spearheaded a violent polemic against the leftist reformists, the leaders of the Confederazione Generale del Lavoro (q.v.), political alliances with democratic forces, and the freemasons. He was the center of a political current that sought to create around the party a unity of all subversive forces of the Left. His position, articulated in the journal *Utopia*, which he founded in 1913, evoked wide consensus, especially among the young and the intellectuals on the fringes of party life. On the other hand, he encountered the growing and bitter opposition of the reformists, and some of the old revolutionary leadership questioned his ideas.

The outbreak of World War I saw Mussolini assume a rigidly neutralist and internationalist stance (*see* INTERVENTIONIST CRISIS, 1914-1915). But two factors led him to fear that the Socialist party would isolate itself politically and flounder in inactivity: the collapse of the second Socialist International; and the demand of some subversives and especially of many revolutionary syndicalists (*see* SYNDICALISM)—Enrico Corradini (q.v.), Alceste De Ambris (q.v.), and others—for a "revolutionary war." It was out of this situation that Mussolini's "crisis" arose, a genuine crisis but ambiguous in the way it appeared, and typical of his character—basically insecure and hesitant in taking initiative for making major decisions. As a result, he lent himself to accusations of betrayal by his party and provoked uncertainty even among those who agreed with his position. Mussolini's political-ideological crisis took concrete form in his article "Dalla neutralità assoluta alla neutralità attiva e operante" ("From absolute neutrality to active and working neutrality"), with which he broke from the party's official neutrality stance on the war. Mussolini was forced to resign as director of *Avanti!*, and on November 15 he founded his own daily newspaper, *Il Popolo d'Italia* (q.v.), which was financed at first by a group of industrialists interested in weakening the Socialist party and then also by the French, who sought to promote Italian intervention. As a result, he was expelled from the party.

Mussolini's newspaper was an important element in the left-wing and democratic interventionist campaign. After Italy entered the war in May 1915 and Mussolini was drafted into the army, its importance declined, but it grew substantially again after the battle of Caporetto (q.v.), which radicalized his anti-Socialist and nationalist sentiments.

At the end of the war Mussolini focused his political action on the disaffected war veterans (*trinceristi*) and the elite fighting groups such as the Arditi (q.v.) and the Futurists (*see* FUTURISM). He attempted unsuccessfully to forge an alliance of former interventionists (a "Constituency of Interventionism"), but it was too heterogeneous in composition. Then, on March 23, 1919, at Piazza San Sepolcro (*see* SANSEPOLCRISTI) in Milan he founded the Fasci di Combattimento (q.v.). Its program was partly leftist, partly productivist (*see* CORPORATIVISM AND THE COPORATIVE STATE) and partly in defense of the "values of war" and the "rights of Italy." Despite their activism and their initial support for Gabriele D'Annunzio (q.v.) and the seizure of Fiume (q.v.), the Fasci did not grow significantly and were severely defeated in the 1919 elections. Their fortunes began to rise toward the end of 1920 as a result of several factors: the altered political climate in Italy; Mussolini's tactical collaboration with Giovanni Giolitti (q.v.) during the last stage of the Fiume crisis (in 1921 the Fasci di Combattimento took part in Giolitti's "national bloc"); the abandonment by the Fasci of the leftist elements in their original program, which allayed the fears and secured the growing consensus of the middle class; and, above all, their spread from the cities to the countryside with the violent anti-Socialist action of *squadrismo* (*see* SQUADRISTI). Mussolini's role in this new situation was decisive: despite many difficulties and severe internal disputes—especially because of the Pacification Pact (q.v.) of 1921—and because of numerous compromises, he was able to give the Fasci (which he transformed into a political party in November 1921) new possibilities and a large degree of political autonomy. This permitted him, through a skillful political game combined with the threat of insurrectional action—a "March on Rome" (q.v.)—to be brought to power by King Victor Emmanuel III (q.v.) and to be accepted quickly by a large part of the liberal-democratic leadership, who believed they could "constitutionalize" and absorb Fascism.

Mussolini's first cabinet (formed on October 30, 1922) was a coalition government that included Popolari (*see* PARTITO POPOLARE ITALIANO), social democrats, liberals (*see* LIBERAL PARTY), and nationalists (*see* ITALIAN NATIONALIST ASSOCIATION). The 1924 elections and the Matteotti crisis (q.v.), however, represented a turning point. Using the most intransigent form of *squadrismo*, which he had once tried to temper, and a complex system of political compromises and adjustments with the old ruling class, Mussolini laid the basis of the Fascist regime with his speech of January 3, 1925. He had overcome an initial series of difficulties and remained in power only because of the king's unwillingness to act and the political ineptness of the Aventine Secession (q.v.). In 1929, with the Lateran Pacts (q.v.) and a national plebscite that sought to demonstrate popular consensus for Fascism, the regime was solidly established. From that moment Mussolini's actions assumed new, wider dimensions, extending from the domestic politics that had previously preoccupied him, to other areas: the ideological elaboration of Fascism (his "Dottrina del fascismo" was published in 1932); the cautious development of the corporate state (*see* CORPORATIVISM AND THE CORPORATIVE STATE); the formation of a new Fascist ruling class; and, with increasing emphasis, the formulation of a foreign policy that sought to exploit Italy's "decisive weight" in the European balance and the possibility that it offered for Italy to maneuver between the Anglo-French and the Germans—all in order to give Italy a "true" colonial empire and Mediterranean hegemony.

Out of this policy there emerged the conquest of Ethiopia in 1935-36 (*see* ETHIOPIAN WAR), unquestionably one of Mussolini's great successes despite the negative consequences it was to bear. In one sense the war began to reduce the flexibility of his foreign policy and signalled the progressive movement toward Nazi Germany (*see* AXIS, ROME-BERLIN)—the Italian intervention in the Spanish Civil War (q.v.), pushed by Foreign Minister Galeazzo Ciano (q.v.) even more than by Mussolini, had a significant influence on the growing association with Germany. In another sense, the war transformed the basic insecurity of the Duce (q.v.) into an excessive belief in his own political abilities at the very moment when the first symptoms of his physical decline had begun to manifest themselves.

To all this must be added that after the Ethiopian War Mussolini underwent a decisive phase of ideological evolution and involution influenced by the writings of the nationalist Alfredo Oriani, the demographer Richard Korherr, and the philosopher Oswald Spengler, as well as by the ideas of the nineteenth-century patriots Giuseppe Mazzini and Vincenzo Gioberti which he garnered from both Oriani and Giovanni Gentile (q.v.). This process led him to believe that Europe and the world were undergoing a profound "crisis of civilization" from which would emerge a "new civilization" characterized by the rapid decline of countries like France and England and the rise of Germany, Japan, Russia, and Italy. In this view, Fascist Italy had to fulfill its own special "mission" by exercising its "moral primacy" over other nations, in addition to realizing its Mediterranean hegemony. In order to achieve this aim it was necessary, according to Mussolini, for the Italian people to free themselves from the negative constraints of "bourgeois mentality" and the Catholic Church and profoundly feel Italy's "historic mission." Hence Mussolini's attempts between 1937 and 1939 to produce a Fascist "cultural revolution" that would transform the Italians—and especially the young generations— and his recurrent proposals to eliminate the monarchy. Absorbed fully by these problems and certain that the regime faced no internal dangers, after the second half of 1936 Mussolini increasingly entrusted the supervision of domestic policies to his son-in-law Galeazzo Ciano (q.v.), to the party secretary Achille Starace (q.v.), and to the undersecretary of interior Guido Buffarini-Guidi (q.v.). Although he intended to maintain some degree of personal supervision over foreign affairs, Mussolini had even wanted to delegate his authority in that sphere, but mounting problems induced him to intervene repeatedly in Ciano's domain.

Despite his obvious political abilities, Mussolini found himself faced with numerous difficulties after mid-1936. On the international level he sought to control a situation determined increasingly by Hitler. He was torn on the one hand by his innate political realism, which made him fear both international isolation and the Germans, and on the other hand by his conviction that Italy had to participate in the great historic struggle that would usher in the "new civilization," and that only he could lead Italy through it successfully. He therefore tried in vain to delay his entry into World War II until after 1942-43, hoping thereby to prepare Italy more fully and to be in a position—rather than Hitler—to determine the political strategy, the timing, and the priorities of the war (he intended, for example, that France alone would be the enemy, leaving action against England for a later moment).

On the domestic level, the greatest problems for Mussolini stemmed from the opposition and hostility that his foreign policy and his efforts to create a "cultural revolution" encountered on all levels. These were not problems of decisive importance, for critics and opponents never succeeded in forming any credible alternative, and the consensus on which the regime was based, although weakening, was never in crisis. Unquestionably, however, they did lead him to impose on the regime and on Italian society a form of totalitarianism (q.v.) which he believed essential for the future of Fascism, for the creation of the Fascist "new man," and for the achievement of Italy's "historic mission" in the context of Europe's "new order" and "new civilization."

Mussolini's last, if ephemeral, success and moment of true popularity was the Munich conference (q.v.) of September 1938. The conclusion in the following spring of the Pact of Steel (q.v.) with Germany, while it would later prove to be decisive for the destiny of Fascism, was not the result of Mussolini's expectation of an imminent war. Rather, it was designed to guarantee him several more years of peace (again, until after 1942-43) during which he could make his political and military preparations and reinforce his position in the Mediterranean vis-à-vis France, England, and even Germany. This explains why, with the unanticipated outbreak of the war in September 1939, Mussolini vainly attempted a desperate mediation and why he stayed out of the conflict initially. And when, on June 10, 1940, he did decide that Italy would participate in the war, he convinced himself that it was "necessary" for Italy not to renounce the territorial advantages and the prestige connected to victory; he also saw the importance of not alienating Germany and the need for Fascism to prove itself in the "test" that was to "transform" the character of the Italian people.

At the outset he tried to give Italy's role in the war an autonomous and distinct character from Germany's—hence the so-called "parallel war." But the serious military setbacks that Italy suffered, especially in the Greek campaign of 1940-41 (*see* GREECE, INVASION OF), forced him to abandon this notion quickly and placed him in a growing condition of inferiority vis-à-vis Germany. After the military disasters in the East, however, Mussolini sought to persuade Hitler to make an accommodation with Russia in order to concentrate all Axis forces against the British and Americans. Moreover, shortly before the coup against him in July 1943, Mussolini also began to consider the possibility of disassociating Italy from Germany. The change in the military situation following the Allied invasion of Sicily finally led a group of major Fascist leaders to take the initiative and remove Mussolini from power in order to make possible Italy's withdrawal from the war. This plan, which took concrete form in the meeting of the Fascist Grand Council (q.v.) on the night of July 24-25, 1943, was conceived and guided by Dino Grandi (q.v.), with the cooperation of Giuseppe Bottai (q.v.), Luigi Federzoni (q.v.), Alfredo De Marsico (q.v.), and Galeazzo Ciano (q.v.).

After the Grand Council vote against him and his dismissal by the king, Mussolini was placed under arrest and taken first to Ponza, then to the island of Maddalena, and finally to the mountain stronghold of Gran Sasso. Following an attempt at suicide about which little is known, he was liberated from Gran Sasso by the Nazis and taken to Germany. He returned to northern Italy in October and created the Italian Social Republic (q.v.). It is difficult to determine to what extent this decision—which at first was not among his plans—was the result of German pressures and threats, of a blind "sense of honor," of motives of personal rancor, or of the illusory myth of an impossible "return to the origins" of Fascism. What is clear is that by then Mussolini was merely the shell, the ghost of himself, oscillating between moments of lucid awareness and self-delusion, between exaltation and depression, aggression and passivity. His former personality expressed itself only in journalistic polemics, yet it is revealing that in the Italian Social Republic Mussolini refused to resurrect *his* newspaper—his so-called "favorite child"—*Il Popolo d'Italia*.

On April 25, 1945, with the partisan forces in full insurrection and having been informed that the Germans were trying to arrange a surrender in Italy, Mussolini moved from Milan, where he attempted to negotiate with the Committee of National Liberation (q.v.), to Como. From there he joined a German column heading for Merano which was stopped by partisans from Dongo on April 27. Mussolini was recognized and arrested, and the next day was taken to the nearby village of Giulino di Mezzegra and summarily shot along with his lover, Clara Petacci (q.v.).

For further information see: Benito Mussolini's *Opera Omnia*, 44 vols., edited by Edoardo and Duilio Susmel: 1-36 (Florence: La Fenice, 1951-63); 37-44 (Rome: Volpe, 1978-80). Mussolini's other principal works are *Giovanni Huss il veridico*

(Rome: Podrecca, 1913); *Il mio diario di guerra, 1916-17* (Rome: Littorio, 1931); *Vita di Arnaldo* (Milan: Popolo d'Italia, 1932); *Parlo con Bruno* (Milan: Popolo d'Italia, 1941); *La mia vita* (written in 1911-12 but posthumously published in Rome: Faro, 1947); and his posthumous *Testamento politico* (Rome: Tosi, 1948). Mussolini's correspondence with his brother Arnaldo has been published by Duilio Susmel, ed., *Carteggio Arnaldo-Benito Mussolini* (Florence: La Fenice, 1954); Renzo De Felice and Emilio Mariano edited the *Carteggio D'Annunzio-Mussolini, 1919-1938* (Verona: Mondadori, 1971); Mussolini's *My Autobiography* (New York: Scribner's, 1928), published under the auspices of Richard W. Child and translated into numerous languages, was actually written by Arnaldo and only partially corrected by Mussolini; from 1921 on Mussolini kept a diary the fate of which is not known with certainty but which was probably destroyed, although various false versions are said to be in circulation.

The bibliography on Mussolini is vast. Starting points for a study of his life are Giorgio Pini and Duilio Susmel, *Mussolini l'uomo e l'opera*, 4 vols. (Florence: La Fenice, 1953-55), pro-Fascist in tone but useful for its narrative details; and Renzo De Felice, *Mussolini*, 5 vols. to date (Turin: Einaudi, 1965-81).

RDF

MUSSOLINI, RACHELE GUIDI (b. Salto, Forlì, April 11, 1892; d. Forlì, October 31, 1979). Mussolini's companion and wife for thirty years, "Donna Rachele" came from a peasant family of the Romagna. They met in 1908, when she was working as a domestic servant, and lived together after 1910. They were married in a civil ceremony in 1915 and a religious ceremony followed in 1925. The couple had five children: Edda (b. 1910), Vittorio (b. 1916), Bruno (b. 1918; d. 1941), Romano (b. 1927), and Anna Maria (b. 1929).

A simple, uneducated woman, she was generally ignored by Mussolini for long periods of time and frequently not informed of the most important political events. She either was unaware of or pretended not to know about her husband's romantic liaisons with other women, although in 1945 she did confront and denounce Clara Petacci (q.v.). Official Fascist propaganda extolled Donna Rachele as the model of the virtuous housewife and mother.

In September 1943 she was flown to Munich to join her rescued husband and then accompanied him back to Italy, where she lived at a villa in Gargnano on Lake Garda. In April 1945 she attempted to escape to Switzerland but was arrested on April 29. Interned in prison camps for several months, she was eventually released and returned to Forlì, where she opened a restaurant. Years later she received several government pensions.

For further information see: EAR (3); Rachele Mussolini, *La mia vita con Benito* (Milan: Mondadori, 1948) and *Mussolini: An Intimate Biography* (New York: Pocket Books, 1977).

JMP

MUTI, ETTORE (b. Ravenna, May 22, 1902; d. Fregene, August 23, 1943). First of four transitory wartime party secretaries, Muti replaced Achille Starace (q.v.) on October 31, 1939, and he in turn lost the job to Adelchi Serena (q.v.) a year later. Nothing in his previous career suggested political talent; for precisely this reason Galeazzo Ciano (q.v.) promoted his candidacy out of confidence that Muti would follow instructions "like a child." But Muti soon proved unruly, gleefully purged many of his predecessor's appointees, and apparently developed a taste for money. A freebooter by nature, he had fought as an Ardito (*see* ARDITI) in World War I, joined Gabriele D'Annunzio (q.v.) at Fiume (q.v.), helped lead the Fascists of Ravenna, and made a national name for himself as a bomber pilot in Ethiopia (as G. Ciano's co-pilot) and Spain. After Italy's intervention in World War II (a development he encouraged, despite ambivalence about the regime's German allies), Muti divided his time between the party and the more congenial task of leading air attacks on Gibraltar (cancelled because Franco refused staging airfields) and the Bahrein oil fields. In October 1940 Mussolini decided to dismiss him as "inept and corrupt" and replace him with someone more capable of mobilizing the home front for the lengthening war. Muti died while attempting escape after arrest on Pietro Badoglio's (q.v.) and Giacomo Carboni's (q.v.) orders in 1943; death made him a neo-Fascist martyr.

For further information see: G. Nozzoli, *I ras del regime* (Milan: Bompiani, 1972).

MK

MVSN. See **MILITIA**.

NASALLI ROCCA, COUNT SEVERIO (b. January 11, 1856; d. September 10, 1933). An army general, Fascist prefect and Podestà (q.v.), Nasalli Rocca served as Italian military attaché in Russia, then commanded the Fortieth Infantry in Bologna, and was a director of the Scuola di Guerra. He commanded a brigade and a division in Libya and was decorated. After 1919 he went to Trecate as prefectural commissar to quell Socialist activity, and then to Verona. On May 25, 1923, Mussolini sent him to Milan as the first Fascist prefect of that city. In September 1924 he was named president of the veterans' organization, Opera Nazionale dei Combattenti. He was sent by the PNF (Partito Nazionale Fascista) (q.v.) as special commissar to Vercelli and Spezia, and in 1927 was made a Podestà.

For further information see: NO (1927).

PVC

NASI, GUGLIELMO (b. Civitavecchia, February 21, 1879). A colonial general and governor, Nasi served in Tripolitania (*see* LIBYA [TRIPOLITANA AND CYRENAICA]), from 1919 to 1925, before becoming an attaché in Paris from 1925 to 1928. After commanding the Third Artillery and teaching at the War College, Nasi was Rodolfo Graziani's (q.v.) chief of staff in Cyrenaica from 1931 to 1934. Nasi succeeded Graziani as vice-governor from 1934 to 1935 and then became commander of Libyan troops from 1935 to 1936. Nasi took the Libya Division to Somalia, ably leading it in the Ogaden in April-May 1936. Named governor of Harar in June 1936, Nasi used the Moslems against the Copts, completing occupation by December. While more reasonable than Graziani, Nasi killed many Amharas on his orders between February and June 1937. Appreciated by Mussolini and the duke of Aosta (*see* SAVOIA, AMEDEO DI, DUKE OF AOSTA), Nasi gained appointment as senator in March and as vice-governor general in May 1939. Agreeing that force had failed, the duke and Nasi obtained approval for less brutal policies in July 1939 which nearly pacified the Empire by March 1940. After the war began, Nasi became Eastern Sector commander, directing the British Somaliland invasion in August 1940. Given the Western Sector in February 1941, Nasi retreated to the Gondar redoubt. Geography and summer rains assisting, Nasi resisted Commonwealth forces heroically until he surrendered the remnants of Italian East Africa in November 1941. Ethiopia accused Nasi of war crimes in 1948.

For further information see: *La guerra in Africa Orientale* (Rome: Ufficio storico dell'esercito, 1952); Alberto Sbacchi, "Italian Colonialism in Ethiopia 1936-1940" (Ph.D. diss., University of Illinois at Chicago Circle, 1975).

BRS

NATIONALISTS. See **ITALIAN NATIONALIST ASSOCIATION.**

NAVA, CESARE (b. Milan, October 7, 1861; d. November 27, 1933). A political figure and Fascist minister, Nava was originally an engineer. He was regarded as a financial expert and served as the president of the Banco Ambrosiano from 1897 to 1933. Nava was a deputy from 1909 to 1921 and served as an undersecretary of arms and munitions from May to September 1918 in the V. E. Orlando (q.v.) ministry. From June 1919 to March 1920 he was minister of *terre liberate* in the F. S. Nitti (q.v.) cabinet. In the period prior to the Fascist seizure of power, Nava belonged to the right wing of the Popular party (*see* PARTITO POPOLARE ITALIANO) and from 1922 to 1923 was among those who called for collaboration with the Fascists. Nava worked to purge the party of its left-wing members and his failure to do so led him to join in founding the Partito Nazionale Popolare in April 1923. Made a senator in 1921, in July 1924, in the midst of the Matteotti Crisis (q.v.), Nava was appointed minister of national economy, a post he held for only one year.

For further information see: DSPI; Adrian Lyttelton, *The Seizure of Power* (London: Weidenfeld & Nicolson, 1973).

MSF

NAVY. The least overtly Fascist of the armed forces, the Regia Marina remained wedded throughout the course of the regime to monarchical loyalties, a characteristic brand of nationalist expansionism and admiration for the British Royal Navy. The service emerged from World War I with two rival traditions: that of the battle fleet, which had seen no action, and that of the highly successful motor torpedo boat and underwater raiding forces. In the interwar period the latter tradition languished. The administrations of Grand Admiral Paolo Thaon di Revel (q.v.) between 1922 and 1925 and Admiral Giuseppe Sirianni (q.v.) between 1925 and 1933 emphasized cruisers and submarines. With the advent of Dominico Cavagnari (q.v.) in 1933, the Navy modernized two World War I battleships (*Cesare* and *Cavour*) and laid down two extremely well-designed modern battleships (*Littorio* and *Vittorio Veneto*). The submarine force also began rapid expansion even before Mussolini decided in January 1935 to go ahead in Ethiopia.

The Navy supported that decision and moved efficiently to provide shipping. When British opposition developed, some naval circles favored a surprise attack on Malta and Alexandria, but Cavagnari recognized that until the new battleships were ready, war meant disaster. In October 1935 he therefore urged on Mussolini a large-scale buildup directed against Britain to "secure our existence and the respect of our rights." In the next years, despite foreign exchange and raw material shortages, Cavagnari and Mussolini pressed the construction of an impressive program of light units. In 1937 they began modernization of two more older battleships (*Duilio* and *Doria*) and ordered construction of two additional *Littorio*-class ships (*Roma* and *Impero*). But Mussolini and the Air Force compelled the

Navy to renounce its intention of building a carrier, and Cavagnari defended the decision in a March 1938 budget speech. Yet despite promising experiments with frogman-guided torpedoes during the 1935-36 crisis, Cavagnari did not press their development.

The Navy participated vigorously in the Spanish Civil War (q.v.), supporting the conquest of the Baleares and conducting an anonymous submarine and surface campaign against the Republic's supply lines, which, according to Mussolini, sank almost two hundred thousand tons of shipping. After J. V. Borghese's (q.v.) attack on H.M.S. *Havock* (August 31-September 1, 1937), G. Ciano (q.v.) and Mussolini suspended action, while the British and French organized naval patrols against "piracy." However, Italian submarines continued to serve under Franco's nominal control and resumed attacking merchant ships in January 1938.

During the Munich crisis (*see* MUNICH CONFERENCE) the Navy partially mobilized, and in August 1939 it was the only service prepared in some sense for war. But in April 1940 Cavagnari was anything but bellicose and warned Mussolini that war might mean Italy's arrival at the peace table "without a fleet." Once France collapsed he acquiesced unenthusiastically and unnecessarily wrote off the possibility of surprise attacks on British bases or a landing on Malta (at that point lightly defended). The Navy's strategy was to hold the central Mediterranean with battleships and mine fields and to seek out the British with Italy's large submarine force. But British sonar and aircraft tended to find Italian submarines first. In a series of encounters and quasi-encounters (Punta Stilo, July 9; the sorties of August 31 and September 29; Cape Teulada, November 27, 1940) the battle fleet failed to close in on and destroy the British, despite superiority of force, particularly after *Vittorio Veneto* and *Littorio* came into service in August. On November 10, 1940, British torpedo bombers sank *Littorio, Duilio*, and *Cavour* at anchor in Taranto. The disaster produced Cavagnari's dismissal. His successor, Arturo Riccardi (q.v.), gave in to German insistence that the Navy take the offensive and lost three cruisers at Matapan. Only the long-neglected special weapons, particularly the frogman-guided torpedoes that sank the battleships *Valiant* and *Queen Elizabeth* at Alexandria (December 19, 1941), redeemed the navy's reputation.

Even after that exploit and the entry of Japan into the war had reduced the British to light units, the Navy confined its activities to protection of the North African convoys in the long attrition struggle around Malta. With Axis defeat at El Alamein and Allied landings in North Africa (October-November 1942), the Navy faced enemy superiority; deprived of air cover, it made no significant attempt to counter the Allied landings on Pantelleria and Sicily (June 11, and July 10, 1943) that caused the crisis of the regime. With the armistice most ships still in service joined the Allies. A German glider bomber sank the battleship *Roma* on its way to Bizerte (September 9, 1943). A few officers joined Salò (*see* ITALIAN SOCIAL REPUBLIC) but were unable to offer significant resistance to the Allies at sea.

For further information see: the extensive memoir literature and the multivolume official history, *La marina italiana nella seconda guerra mondiale* (Rome: Ufficio Storico della Marina Militare, 1950-   ).

MK

NAZISM. See **AXIS, ROME-BERLIN**.

NENNI, PIETRO (b. Faenza, Forlì, February 9, 1891; d. Rome, January 1, 1980). An outstanding Socialist leader, at seventeen years of age Nenni joined the Republican party (*see* PARTITO REPUBBLICANO ITALIANO) and in 1911, along with Mussolini, helped to promote a general strike in the Romagna area to protest the Libyan War. After having spent some months in jail for this activity, Nenni began to direct the journal *Lucifero* in Ancona. As he slowly moved to the left-wing of the Republican movement, Nenni became more concerned with syndical and worker problems and the Italian monarchy. In June 1914 he was one of the major promoters of "Red Week," which led to his arrest.

During World War I Nenni adhered to the interventionist (*see* INTERVENTIONIST CRISIS, 1914-1915) stance of the Republican party and collaborated with Mussolini on *Il Popolo d'Italia*. Nenni originally believed that the war would be a revolutionary experience that would benefit the working classes, but as the conflict progressed he became increasingly disillusioned. Nenni served in the military for a year and at the end of 1916 assumed direction of *Il Giornale del Mattino*, an interventionist journal in Bologna. After the war Nenni became dissatisfied with the Republican party's postwar programs and solutions, but rather than immediately attaching himself to a particular political movement, he entered a short period of ideological and political confusion. He was involved in founding the first Fascio di Combattimento (q.v.) in Bologna and at the same time supported worker and Republican movements. Most importantly, he began to drift from Mussolini's orbit to that of the Socialists.

In 1921 Nenni became a correspondent for *Avanti!* and at the end of 1922 was appointed the paper's chief editor. From this position he campaigned against the fusion of the Socialists with the Communists and sought to organize the growing anti-Fascist struggle by helping to direct the National Committee of Socialist Defense.

After Matteotti's (*see* MATTEOTTI CRISIS) death, Nenni supported the Aventine Secession (q.v.) and attempted to create an alliance with the reformists, liberal democrats, and the Popular Party (*see* PARTITO POPOLARE ITALIANO), a bloc that he believed would constitute the most valid alternative to Fascism. This theory caused Nenni's rupture with the Socialist party (*see* PARTITO SOCIALISTA ITALIANO) and his removal as director of *Avanti!*.

Fleeing to France, Nenni continued to work for the restructuring of the Socialist party and in 1934 supported the Pact of Unity with the Communist party (*see* PARTITO COMUNISTA ITALIANO). During his exile he served as the party's secretary and published his own paper, *Nuovo Avanti!* During the Spanish Civil War (q.v.), Nenni volunteered for the International Brigade and between 1939 and 1944 undertook clandestine activities in France and Italy. After Mussolini's fall Nenni criticized the *"svolta di Salerno"* (*see* TOGLIATTI, PALMIRO) and refused to collaborate with the Ivanoe Bonomi (q.v.) government. In 1945 Nenni was a candidate for the presidency of the Council of Ministers and at the end of the year served as vice-president in the first Alcide De Gasperi (q.v.) cabinet.

Nenni based his postwar political positions on the Pact of Unity until the Hungarian invasion of 1956. After that date Nenni led the Socialist party toward autonomy but in July 1960 helped form the first center-left government, in which he served as vice-president of the Council of Ministers and foreign minister. With the collapse of the center-left coalition and the almost constant divisions within the Socialist camp, Nenni temporarily withdrew from active politics. In the last decade of his life Nenni gradually resumed his participation within the Socialist party and became the organization's president.

For further information see: DSPI; MOI (3); Domenico Zucaro, ed., *Vento del nord* (Turin: Einaudi, 1978).

MSF

NEO-FASCISM. See MOVIMENTO SOCIALE ITALIANO (MSI).

NERVI, PIER LUIGI (b. Sondrio, June 21, 1891; d. Rome, January 9, 1979). One of the best-known and most important Italian architects of the twentieth century, Nervi trained as an engineer at the University of Bologna and graduated in 1913. The beginning of Nervi's career coincided with the rise of new directions in Italian architecture (*see* ARCHITECTURE). His Cinema Augusteo in Naples dates from 1927, the year of the founding of the Movimento Italiano per l'Architettura Razionale. But his first major commission, the Communal Stadium in Florence (1930-1932), was clearly outside the mainstream of the Fascist cultural Novecento Movement (q.v.), which advocated modernist reform according to neoclassical principles. With its emphasis on structure alone and its strong relationship to works of the International Style, especially Le Corbusier, such a building was essentially antinationalist and thus incompatible with a reactionary government. During the years of the ascendancy of Fascist architecture, from 1931 to 1937, most of Nervi's commissions were not for civic or governmental buildings, but for viaducts, bridges, silos, and the like. His closest association with Mussolini's regime came with the design of the hangars for the Italian Air Force (built between 1935 and 1941 at Orvieto, Orbetello, and Torre del Lago; all destroyed by the German Army) in which the major theme of his work was developed: namely, the ordering of prefabricated concrete units into lattice-like designs. The essence of Nervi's attitude toward architecture—that the logic of the exposed structure should be combined with aesthetics of the greatest simplicity and imagination—was achieved in his mature works, the Exhibition Hall, Turin (1948-49) and the Palazetto dello Sport, Rome (1960, in collaboration in Vitellozzi).

For further information see: C. G. Argan, *Pier Luigi Nervi* (Milan: Il Balcone, 1955); Ada Louise Huxtable, *Pier Luigi Nervi* (New York: Braziller, 1960); Pier Luigi Nervi, *Arte o scienza del costruire* (Rome: Bussola, 1945); Pier Luigi Nervi, *Costruire correttamente* (Milan: Ulrico Hoepli, 1954).

RN

NITTI, FRANCESCO SAVERIO (b. Melfi, July 19, 1868; d. Rome, February 20, 1953). Prime minister from June 1919 to June 1920, Nitti had the misfortune of coming to power at a time of intractable domestic crises. The advent of Fascism ended a career that never saw the fulfillment probable for a person of his exceptional talents.

A prolific writer, professor of financial sciences at the University of Naples, and member of the Chamber of Deputies from 1904 to 1924, his expertise in economic matters and prominence in the Radical party earned him the post of minister of agriculture, industry, and commerce in Giovanni Giolitti's (q.v.) government of 1911-14. After Giolitti's resignation in March 1914 Nitti abstained from the furious neutralist-interventionist controversy of 1914-15 (*see* INTERVENTIONIST CRISIS, 1914-1915), although he shared Giolitti's doubts on the wisdom of Italy's intervention in the war. In October 1917, during the Caporetto (*see* CAPORETTO, BATTLE OF) military disaster, Nitti became treasury minister in the newly-formed V. E. Orlando (q.v.) government, from which he resigned in January 1919 owing in part to his insistence on plans for a rapid conversion to a peacetime economy. As he had hoped, Nitti succeeded Orlando as prime minister (June 1919) and for the next year attempted to implement a program of national reconciliation and major socioeconomic reforms. But Gabriele D'Annunzio's (q.v.) seizure of Fiume (q.v.) in September 1919 faced Nitti with an act popular in Italy but opposed by the Allies; the results of the elections of November 1919 destroyed his hopes of collaboration with moderate Socialists and made him a captive of the Popular party (*see* PARTITO POPOLARE ITALIANO); his projected fiscal reforms alienated the conservatives but gained him no support from the Socialists, who talked of revolution. Reviled by the Right as a "renouncer" of the fruits of victory and by the extreme Left as the man who abolished the bread subsidy, Nitti resigned in June 1920.

Never a supporter of Fascism, until 1923 Nitti did not oppose "the experiment," which he felt should be allowed to run its course. The Fascists nevertheless sacked his home in November 1923. He left Italy in June 1924 and became a rallying figure among anti-Fascist exiles in France, where he was arrested by the SS in August 1943. Freed by Allied troops in 1945, Nitti returned to Italy, resuming his political activity first as a firm opponent of communism but in the last years of his life as a proponent of Italian neutrality in the cold war.

For further information see: Paolo Alatri, *Nitti, D'Annunzio e la questione adriatica, 1919-1920* (Milan: Feltrinelli, 1959); Alberto Monticone, *Nitti e la grande guerra, 1914-1918* (Milan: A. Giuffre, 1961); Francesco Saverio Nitti, *Rivelazioni: Dramatis personae* (Naples: Edizioni scientifiche italiane, 1948).

SS

NOBILE, UMBERTO (b. Lauro, Avellino, January 21, 1885; d. Rome, July 30, 1978). A designer and builder of airships, Arctic explorer, professor of aeronautical design (1926-55) at the University of Naples, and general in the Air Force, Nobile was best known for his airship explorations of the North Pole regions. In 1926 he built the airship *Norge* and together with R. Amundsen and L. Ellsworth he crossed the unexplored (approximately two thousand kms.) regions of the North Pole between the Pole and Alaska, flying over the Pole and discovering the Polar Sea. In 1928, in the airship *Italia* designed and commanded by him, he carried out long exploratory flights (one hundred and sixty-four hours) over unknown regions north of Greenland, Spitzbergen, and Siberia, flying over the Pole for a second time. On the return flight, however, the *Italia* crashed. After a series of dramatic rescue attempts that made international headlines, Nobile and a few of his crew were saved. On his return to Italy Nobile faced an official inquiry into the crash of the *Italia*. Partly for political reasons (Nobile had never supported Fascism), the inquest was unfavorable to him and Nobile resigned from the Air Force. From 1932 to 1936 he designed dirigibles in the Soviet Union and then taught in the United States (1939-42) before returning to Italy. After World War II he was vindicated and readmitted to the Air Force. He served as a deputy to the Constituent Assembly (*see* COSTITUENTE) (1946) for the Communist party.

For further information see: Wilbur Cross, *Ghost Ship of the Pole* (New York: W. Sloane Associates, 1960); Umberto Nobile, *In volo alla conquista del segreto polare (da Roma a Teller attraverso il Polo Nord* (Milano: Mondadori, 1928); Umberto Nobile, *"L'Italia" al Polo Nord* (Milano: Mondadori, 1930); Umberto Nobile, *Posso dire la verità* (Milano: Mondadori, 1945); Felice Troiani, *La coda di Minosse* (Milano: U. Mursia, 1964).

CGS

NOVECENTO MOVEMENT. Novecento, which literally means "twentieth century," was an artistic and literary movement centered in Milan during the 1920s. Although Novecento supported tradition, especially Roman elements, the group developed ideas in common with the Rationalists—representatives of the modern international movement—which caused contradictions within and about Novecento. Prominent members of Novecento included Margherita Sarfatti-Grassini (q.v.), Mussolini's mistress of the late 1920s; Mario Sironi (q.v.), painter and art critic for *Il Popolo d'Italia*; and Arturo Martini (q.v.), sculptor and former member of the Futurist movement (*see* FUTURISM). In literature its major advocate was Massimo Bontempelli (q.v.).

Novecento attempted to integrate the historical past, in particular the Roman, with a new modern Italian state inspired by those past glories. Hence, it supported the use of Roman themes and motifs indicating a cultural nationalism and rejected the international and Futurist styles that represented the immediate past and foreign influence. However, by supporting a "modernized" Romanism, confusion about the style resulted.

In February 1926 Mussolini addressed the opening of a Novecento exhibition and proclaimed the intimate relationship between art and politics. The Novecento's traditional basis caused many to hope that this style would become the official style of the Fascist regime. However, by the 1930s the by then modernized classical style of Novecento caused strong debate among party officials. Mussolini himself entered the fray to end the polemics. Novecento's appeal lay in its claim of a revolutionary synthesis of Romanism and modernity into a new Roman style capable of representing a renewed Italy.

Novecento, a journal directed by Bontempelli in Florence and then in Rome between 1926 and 1929, attempted to distinguish between aristocratic/Futurist and populist/Novecento philosophies.

For further information see: Philip V. Cannistraro, "Mussolini's Cultural Revolution: Fascist or Nationalist?" *Journal of Contemporary History* 6, 3-4, (July-October, 1972); Leonardo Venevolo, "Il novecento e l'architettura," *Edilizia moderna* 81 (December, 1963).

JH

O

OCCUPATION OF THE FACTORIES. Highlighting a period of economic and social unrest in Italy, the September 1920 occupation of the factories by Italian workers gave a dramatic demonstration of the strength and militancy of the labor movement during the years from 1919 to 1921—the so-called "Red Biennium." Italy in the postwar years suffered from an unprecedented economic crisis. The experience of the war, combined with uncontrolled inflation, industrial stagnation, unemployment, and food shortages, created an extremely volatile political climate. Moreover the political upheavals in Russia and Central Europe, watched intently by Italians, gave the prospect for revolution in Italy a sense of immediacy.

The transition to a peace-time economy was severe for all industrial workers, particularly the metalworkers. Although founded and directed by a moderate labor leader, Bruno Buozzi (q.v.), the Metalworkers' Union (FIOM, Federazione Italiana Operai Metallurgici) became increasingly militant in the postwar period. Following the failure of FIOM-industry negotiations on August 13, 1920, FIOM leaders, fearing possible lock-outs by proprietors, warned that they would use all means, including violence, to defend the right to work and to enter and remain in the factories. On August 30, after receiving notice of a lock-out at the Alfa-Romeo plant in Milan, FIOM ordered its members to occupy their factories. From Milan the occupations spread to Turin, Genoa, and then throughout the country. Union compliance was complete. Over 400,000 metalworkers participated by occupying foundries and assembly plants. An additional 100,000 workers from other unions supported the metalworkers by seizing control of chemical and rubber factories, breweries, and even ships in port. Although the action was widespread and affected establishments of all sizes and categories, it was centered in Italy's northern industrial triangle—Turin, Milan, and Genoa. In Turin alone, the occupations involved over 100,000 workers. With rare exceptions workers carried out their union's orders and maintained control of the factories without recourse to violence. Red flags were draped from factory windows. "Red guards," fledgling paramilitary groups inspired by the Russian example, patrolled the factories, maintaining discipline within and defending the workers against possible attacks from without.

The intention of FIOM leaders was to prevent further lock-outs, but the workers went beyond a simple "sit-down" strike by attempting to keep the factories operating normally. "Factory councils" were established to perform managerial functions—setting production schedules, restocking basic materials, and distributing finished goods. The success of the worker-directed operations varied greatly from factory to factory, but despite the absence of trained supervisory and technical personnel, and other formidable obstacles, some of the larger firms sustained production levels as high as 50 to 60 percent of average monthly rates.

Much to the horror of industrialists and the amazement of the Socialists, it appeared as if the revolutionary program of the Socialist party (*see* PARTITO SOCIALISTA ITALIANO)—the transfer of ownership and control of production to the workers—was actually being fulfilled. Angered and alarmed, the industrialists demanded that the government take immediate action to end the crisis. To their dismay Prime Minister Giovanni Giolitti (q.v.) refused to use force against the workers. Just as during Italy's first national general strike in 1904, he preferred to allow the extraordinary labor protest to run its course, avoiding if at all possible bloodshed and destruction of property.

While the factory occupations continued into their second and third weeks, Socialist and labor leaders argued bitterly over the nature and function of the "factory councils," and the proper course of action to pursue. Moderates from the Socialist party and the General Confederation of Labor (CGL) (q.v.) adamantly opposed any suggestion of exacerbating the revolutionary situation created by the factory occupations. Even the more militant Socialists, notably the Turin group led by Antonio Gramsci (q.v.) and Palmiro Togliatti (q.v.), were reluctant to promote full-scale revolutionary action, given the lack of preparation and uncertainty about the sentiment of workers outside the northern industrial centers.

By pressuring intransigent proprietors and appealing to moderates on all sides, Giolitti succeeded in bringing together representatives of FIOM, the CGL, and Confindustria (*see* INDUSTRY) on September 19. The negotiated settlement represented, in economic terms, a victory for FIOM. A twelve-member commission was established to resolve unsettled issues and to formulate labor legislation regarding "worker control" in the factories. FIOM members approved the agreement by referendum, and on September 27 began evacuating the factories. The workers returned to their posts on October 4, feeling somewhat betrayed by their leaders, and lamenting the "missed opportunity" for revolution. The disaffection of workers was reflected in the rapid decline of union membership and the faltering of the labor movement in 1921. Weakened internally, organized labor was even more vulnerable to the growing violence of the Fascist movement.

For the industrialists the occupation of the factories was a dismal, humiliating experience. Not only had the workers flagrantly violated the rights of property, but the government had failed to act forcefully to suppress the illegal action. The events of September confirmed their worse fears about the prospect of a Bolshevik-like revolution and the inability of the government to deal with that threat. Angry and vindictive, proprietors began searching anxiously for the means to protect their interests and found in Mussolini's Fascism an attractive political solution.

For further information see: Bruno Buozzi, "L'occupazione delle fabbriche," in *Almanacco socialista* (Paris: Partito socialista italiano, 1935); Christopher Seton-Watson, *Italy: From Liberalism to Fascism, 1870-1925* (London: Methuen and Co., 1967); Paolo Spriano, *L'occupazione delle fabbriche* (Turin: Einaudi, 1964).

MH

OJETTI, UGO (b. Rome, July 15, 1871; d. Florence, January 1, 1947). An art critic and writer, Ojetti was from an extremely wealthy family. He took a law degree from Rome in 1908 but had already begun a career in journalism, writing for *Il Corriere della Sera* (Milan) and other newspapers. He served on numerous government cultural commissions, fought in World War I, was president of the Royal Art Institute of Florence, and then president of the Consiglio Superiore delle Antichità e Belle Arti (High Council for Antiquities and Fine Arts). From March 1926 to November 1927 he was made interim director of *Il Corriere della Sera* during the regime's efforts to fascisticize that important paper. He was appointed to the Royal Academy of Italy (q.v.) in 1930.

Ojetti's fame derives chiefly from his position as the regime's quasi-official spokesman on cultural matters. He was a conservative aesthete whose innumerable articles on literature, art, and music had a considerable influence. The three journals he founded and directed, *Dedalo* (1920-33), *Pegaso* (1929-33), and *Pan* (1933-35), stood squarely against modernism in the arts, and he was a staunch opponent of the Novecento Movement (q.v.). His diaries are a useful source for the cultural history of Fascist Italy.

For further information see: *Chi è?* (1936); NO (1928; 1937); Ugo Ojetti, *Taccuini* (Florence: Sansoni, 1954); Edward R. Tannenbaum, *The Fascist Experience* (New York: Basic Books, 1972).

PVC

OLIVETTI, ANGELO OLIVIERO (b. Ravenna, June 21, 1874; d. Spoleto, November 17, 1931). A major corporativist theorist and Fascist publicist, Olivetti became active in Socialist circles while a university student in the early 1890s and gravitated to the revolutionary syndicalist (*see* SYNDICALISM) wing of the Socialist party (*see* PARTITO SOCIALISTA ITALIANO) by 1905. He was especially influential as publisher and editor of the notable syndicalist review, *Pagine Libere*, which appeared from December 1906 to December 1911, again from October 1914 to March 1915, and yet again from February 1920 to December 1922. After supporting the Libyan War of 1911-12, he promptly advocated Italian intervention (*see* INTERVENTIONIST CRISIS, 1914-1915) when the European war broke out in 1914. Indeed, he was a major force behind the Fascio Rivoluzionario d'Azione Internazionalista (*see* FASCI DI AZIONE RIVOLUZIONARIA), which became the leading organization of revolutionary interventionism.

Olivetti played a central role in the doctrinal revision that led from revolutionary syndicalism to corporativism (*see* CORPORATIVISM AND THE CORPORATIVE STATE), but since he was particularly hostile to political parties and parliamentary politics, he was skeptical about Fascism during its first years in power. He became an active Fascist publicist only during the Matteotti Crisis (q.v.) of 1924, when there seemed a chance of forcing Fascism beyond parliamentary compromise and on to a postliberal, corporativist order. He began contributing regularly to *Il Popolo d'Italia* in July and soon was named to the Commission of Fifteen (later Eighteen) (*see* PARLIAMENT) established to design new institutions.

Olivetti's conception required spontaneity and autonomy for the Fascist corporative groupings, and he was sharply critical of the bureaucratic and party interference that developed in practice. Writing in *La Stirpe* in 1931, for example, he warned that the Fascist corporative regime could end up nothing but "a superbureaucracy and a police state . . . completely devoid of social and historical meaning."

For further information see: A. O. Olivetti, *Cinque anni di sindacalismo e di lotta proletaria in Italia* (Naples: Partenopea, 1914); A. O. Olivetti, *Bolscevismo, comunismo e sindacalismo* (Milan: Editrice *Rivista Nazionale*, 1919); A. O. Olivetti, *Le corporazioni e la loro formazione naturale* (Rome: Edizioni del *Diritto del Lavoro*, 1928); David D. Roberts, *The Syndicalist Tradition and Italian Fascism* (Chapel Hill: University of North Carolina Press, 1979).

DDR

OLIVETTI, GINO (b. Urbino, September 5, 1880; d. Argentina, 1942). An industrial organizer and founder of the Confindustria (*see* INDUSTRY), Olivetti received a law degree in 1901 and entered private business. Although he did not actually hold major corporate positions of vital consequence, Olivetti was the most professional organizer of industrial interests in Italy. In 1906 he was the secretary of the Industrial League of Turin and during World War I served on numerous government commissions.

In 1919 he was elected to the Chamber of Deputies, where he remained until 1938. That same year he founded the national association of industrialists known as the Confederazione Generale dell'Industria Italiana or Confindustria and served as its secretary until 1933. In the weeks before the March on Rome (q.v.), Olivetti and other industrial leaders tried to convince Giovanni Giolitti (q.v.) of the necessity to channel Mussolini and Fascism into the government.

A staunch defender of owner management of factories and an opponent of the labor movement, Olivetti emerged as an outspoken critic of Fascist corporativism (*see* CORPORATIVISM AND THE CORPORATIVE STATE), which he feared would lead to worker control of factories. It was this position that induced Mussolini to secure his dismissal as secretary of Confindustria. An Italian Jew, with the passage of Fascist anti-Semitic laws in 1938 Olivetti was forced to emigrate to Argentina.

For further information see: *Chi è?* (1936); NO (1928; 1937); Roland Sarti, *Fascism and the Industrial Leadership in Italy* (Berkeley: University of California Press, 1971).

PVC

OPPO, CIPRIANO EFISIO (b. Rome, July 2, 1890; d. Rome, January 10, 1962). A painter, art critic, and deputy, Oppo was a Nationalist who began to

win fame as an artist on the eve of World War I. He studied at the Istituto di Belle
Arti in Rome, was first influenced by the post-Impressionists, and was a leader of
the "Secessione Romana" modern art movement. A member of the Venice Biennale
Art Festival commission, Oppo fought and was wounded in World War I and
joined the Fascist movement in 1919. From 1914 to 1925 he was an illustrator for
L'Idea Nazionale, and then art critic for *La Tribuna*. After World War I he hailed a
"return to order" in art and culture and was associated with the Novecento
Movement (q.v.). He served in various syndical positions in the 1920s and was a
deputy from 1929 to 1934. Like many of his fellow Nationalists, Oppo became
disillusioned with Fascism after Mussolini's dictatorship was consolidated, but he
remained strongly attached to Mussolini. He adhered to the Salò Republic (*see*
ITALIAN SOCIAL REPUBLIC) after 1943.

For further information see: *Chi è?* (1936); NO (1937); *Enciclopedia Garzanti
dell'Arte* (Milan: Garzanti, 1973).

PVC

ORANO, PAOLO (b. Rome, June 15, 1875; d. Padula, 1945). A former Socialist
and revolutionary syndicalist (*see* SYNDICALISM), Orano became one of the
major proponents of Fascist anti-Semitism in the 1930s. He took a degree in letters
at the University of Rome and in 1895 began a prolific career as a writer and
journalist. He joined the Socialist party (*see* PARTITO SOCIALISTA ITALIANO)
at the turn of the century and was on the editorial staff of *Avanti!*, the Socialist
daily. Moving toward the syndicalist movement, he resigned from *Avanti!* and
collaborated with *Gioventù Socialista*, along with Michele Bianchi (q.v.) and
Alceste De Ambris (q.v.). In 1907 he worked with *Lotta di Classe* in Milan, and
then with *Pagine Libere* of A. O. Olivetti (q.v.). Three years later he became
editor of *Lupa*, a syndicalist review with Nationalist tendencies published in
Florence. His break with the antimilitarist campaign came in 1911-12, when he
agitated for the Italo-Turkish War and joined the Italian Nationalist Association
(q.v.).

Orano volunteered for combat in World War I, serving in the Italian Military
Mission Abroad as a press agent. In 1919 he went to Sardinia, and was active in
local politics there, supporting the Partito Sardo d'Azione. He was elected to
Parliament in 1919, and wrote for Mussolini's *Il Popolo d'Italia*, having adhered
to the Fasci di Combattimento (q.v.). He joined the PNF (Partito Nazionale
Fascista) (q.v.) in 1922, and was a member of the commission that presented the
electoral reform bill of 1923 (the so-called Acerbo Law) (*see* ACERBO, GIACOMO).
In 1924 he was Rome editor for *Il Popolo d'Italia*.

During the 1930s Orano was president of the University of Perugia and an
outspoken advocate of Fascist colonial expansion. In 1937 he launched the
anti-Semitic campaign (*see* ANTI-SEMITISM) with the publication of a pamphlet
called *Gli Ebrei in Italia*, and two years later was made a senator. He died in a
concentration camp in 1945.

For further information see: *Chi è?* (1936); MOI (4); Renzo De Felice, *Sindacalismo rivoluzionario e fiumanesimo nel carteggio De Ambris-D'Annunzio* (Brescia: Morcelliana, 1966); Renzo De Felice, *Storia degli ebrei italiani sotto il fascismo* (Turin: Einaudi, 1961).

MSF

ORESTANO, FRANCESCO (b. Alia, Palermo, April 14, 1873). An intellectual and Fascist supporter, Orestano received his law degree in 1896 from the University of Palermo and his philosophy degree from the University of Leipzig in 1901. He taught at the University of Palermo and the University of Rome but in 1924 voluntarily retired from his profession. Orestano later was a delegate to international congresses on education and was considered the Fascist regime's official philospher in university circles. He also served as president of the Italian Philosophical Society and in March 1929 was appointed to the Royal Academy of Italy (q.v.).

For further information see: *Chi è?* (1936); NO (1937); *Annuario della Reale Accademia d'Italia, 1934-1937* (Rome: Reale Accademia d'Italia, 1938).

MSF

ORLANDO, VITTORIO EMANUELE (b. Palermo, May 19, 1860; d. Rome, December 1, 1952). Prime minister from October 1917 to June 1919, Orlando rallied Italy from the military catastrophe of Caporetto (*see* CAPORETTO, BATTLE OF) but foundered subsequent to his bitter dispute with President Woodrow Wilson and the Yugoslavs over Fiume (q.v.) and Dalmatia.

Orlando distinguished himself early in life with numerous works on jurisprudence, which won him a chair at the University of Rome (1901-31) and an international reputation. A member of the Chamber of Deputies from 1897 to 1925, he served in governments led by Giovanni Giolitti (q.v.) (minister of education, 1903-05; minister of justice, 1907-09), Antonio Salandra (q.v.) (minister of Justice, 1914-16), and Paolo Boselli (minister of interior, 1916-17). A liberal of the Left at first allied with Giolitti, Orlando broke with him by supporting Salandra's decision to enter the war in May 1915. After Salandra's fall in June 1916 Orlando became, next to Foreign Minister Sidney Sonnino (q.v.), the chief figure in Boselli's government, attempting for more than a year to reconcile the Giolittians, the Socialists, and the Catholics to a war they had opposed. He thus became suspect to the more uncompromising interventionists, who accepted reluctantly Orlando's accession to the premiership during the early days of the Caporetto disaster (October 29, 1917). Throughout 1918, the interventionists divided between those who demanded full implementation of the Entente's commitments made to Italy in the Pact of London (April 1915), primarily Sonnino, and the followers of L. Bissolati (q.v.), who were willing to compromise for the sake of amity with the future Yugoslav state. Orlando was inclined to Bissolati's views; but, unable to disown Sonnino, Orlando accepted Bissolati's resignation from the government in December 1918. Divided in its counsels, the Italian delegation at the Paris Peace Conference failed to persuade President Wilson to grant Italy part of the Dalmatian coast and Fiume (q.v.). After a futile withdrawal from the conference in protest against an appeal by Wilson directly to the Italian people (April 23, 1919), Orlando and Sonnino returned to Paris (May 6) but were unable to change Wilson's position. The country's immense agitation over the failure to acquire Fiume led to Orlando's fall in June 1919 followed in September by Gabriele D'Annunzio's (q.v.) seizure of the city.

With the culmination of Italy's postwar crisis in 1922, Orlando twice attempted in vain to form a grand coalition which, by including some Fascists, might lead them along the constitutional path. This same hope led Orlando to a vote of confidence in Mussolini's government in November 1922. With less confidence Orlando agreed to be included as a candidate in the Fascist-dominated list in the April 1924 general elections. Thoroughly disillusioned, he openly joined the opposition after Mussolini's truculent speech of January 3, 1925; and in August he resigned from the Chamber in protest against Fascist violence during local elections in Palermo. Six years later he retired from his university post to avoid compliance with a law, effective November 1, 1931, mandating an oath of loyalty (*see* UNIVERSITY OATH) to the Fascist regime by all professors. When the same requirement was applied to members of the Accademia dei Lincei in October 1934, Orlando refused to swear the oath. But a year later Orlando's sense of patriotism led him to support the Ethiopian venture (*see* ETHIOPIAN WAR). As an adviser to Victor Emmanuel III (q.v.), a similar sense of duty apparently led Orlando to support the king's dismissal of Mussolini from office on July 25, 1943.

In 1944 Orlando resigned his post at the University of Rome, returned to active politics as president of the Chamber of Deputies in June of the same year, and in June 1946 was elected to the Constituent Assembly (*see* COSTITUENTE). Two years later he was appointed to a lifetime seat in the Senate for services rendered to the nation.

For further information see: V. E. Orlando, *Discorsi parlamentari*, 4 vols. (Rome: Tipografia della Camera dei deputati, 1965); V. E. Orlando, *Memorie, 1915-1919*, Rodolfo Mosca, ed. (Milan: Rizzoli, 1960); Luigi Salvatorelli and Giovanni Mira, *Storia d'Italia nel periodo fascista*, new ed. (Turin: Einaudi, 1964).

                                                                                                    SS

OSSERVATORE ROMANO. The *Osservatore Romano* originated in 1861 because of the Vatican's need for a newspaper that would present its position on the issues at a time when the Church was coming under increasing attack from the secular forces of liberalism and Italian nationalism. The *Osservatore* never technically became the official newspaper of the Vatican, but in effect it served that function. The Vatican financed the paper, and the pope appointed its editor, who was answerable to the Holy Father or his secretary of state. The *Osservatore*

Romano is therefore an important source to use in understanding the Vatican's public position on issues affecting the Church in Italy and the world.

During the Fascist period the *Osservatore* played a role in shaping Catholic attitudes toward this movement. Before the advent of Mussolini to power in October 1922, the Vatican paper adopted a neutral attitude toward Fascism. Once Mussolini came to power this policy changed, resulting in the newspaper praising the Fascists for bringing a new era of harmony between Church and State after years of liberal government hostility toward the Church. The support for Fascism remained consistent until 1939 despite frequent editorials against the anticlerical extremists within the movement and occasional disagreements with official government actions that threatened the Church's influence over Catholic youth. With Mussolini's growing friendship with Hitler and the introduction of anti-Semitic legislation (*see* ANTI-SEMITISM) into Italy, the *Osservatore* reflected the Vatican's disillusionment with Mussolini.

The *Osservatore* appeared every evening except Sunday. Under the editorship of Count Giuseppe Dalla Torre (1920-60) the circulation of the newspaper increased dramatically, as it was the only reliable source of news in a country where freedom of the press was suspended during the Fascist period.

For further information see: Francesco Leoni, *L'Osservatore Romano: Origini ed evoluzione* (Naples: Guida editori, 1970); Giuseppe Dalla Torre, *Memorie* (Verona: Mondadori, 1965).

ACO

OVRA. See **POLICE AND INTERNAL SECURITY**.

P

PACCIARDI, RANDOLFO (b. Giuncarico, Grosseto, January 1, 1899). Anti-Fascist journalist and general secretary of the Italian Republican party (PRI—Partito Repubblicano Italiano) (q.v.), during World War I Pacciardi was a decorated officer in a Bersaglieri army unit. In 1921 he took a law degree at the University of Rome.

From the beginning of the Fascist movement Pacciardi made his opposition known. In 1923 he organized the Italia Libera (q.v.) movement, and in 1924 he served as defense counsel for a newspaper accused of slandering the Fascist leader Italo Balbo (q.v.). In 1926 Pacciardi was sought by the police but managed to escape to Switzerland, where he made contact with other exiles and began extensive propaganda efforts. In 1933, after pressure by the Italian government, Switzerland expelled Pacciardi and sent him to France after he had uncovered a Fascist spy ring.

When the Spanish Civil War (q.v.) broke out, Pacciardi organized and commanded a legion of anti-Fascists known as the "Garibaldi Battalion." By 1938 his legion numbered five thousand men and had become an integral part of the larger International Brigade. Wounded in the fighting for Madrid, Pacciardi went to France to recuperate, returning in time to direct the counterattack at the Battle of Guadalajara (q.v.), which inflicted a serious defeat upon the rebel forces led by Francisco Franco.

In 1938 Pacciardi journeyed to the United States in an attempt to enlist Italian Americans to fight with his legion. Before he could return to Spain, Franco's forces proved victorious and Pacciardi travelled to France to continue his anti-Fascist struggle. With the fall of France in 1940 he returned to the United States, where he renewed his efforts to form an Italian Legion. He believed that the legion would do more to entice the Italians to overthrow Mussolini than a full-scale invasion of the Italian mainland itself.

In October 1942 at the International Congress of Italians in Montevideo (*see* MONTEVIDEO CONGRESS), Uruguay, the Italian Legion was officially organized with Pacciardi as its head and Count Carlo Sforza (q.v.) as a principle supporter. With the Allied invasion of Sicily in July 1943, Pacciardi believed that he would shortly be returning to Italy. He condemned both the replacement of Mussolini with Marshal Pietro Badoglio (q.v.) and King Victor Emmanuel III (q.v.) for complicity in the Mussolini regime.

In May 1944 Pacciardi resigned from the International Honorary Board of the Free World Association in protest against Sforza and Alberto Tarchiani's (q.v.) joining of the Badoglio cabinet. In June, with the approval of the United States government, Pacciardi returned to Italy. By July the official organ of the PRI, *Voce Repubblicana*, resumed publication. In its initial editorial Pacciardi proclaimed that the PRI would combine leftist and Nationalist tendencies.

Pacciardi played an extremely important role in the formation of the postwar Italian government, serving as vice-premier and minister of the interior under Alcide de Gasperi (q.v.). His main concern centered around insuring that the postwar elections for Parliament were free and open. He served as a deputy in the Costituente (q.v.) and in the Chamber of Deputies. Pacciardi is now retired from public life and resides in Rome.

For further information see: DSPI; Charles F. Delzell, *Mussolini's Enemies* (Princeton: Princeton University Press, 1961).

WAJ

PACIFICATION PACT. The Pacification Pact, a short-lived truce between Socialists and Fascists, was formally signed on August 3, 1921. Its main objective was to check the *squadristi* (q.v.) violence that spread with increasing efficiency against working-class organizations after the bloody clash at Palazzo d'Accursio in Bologna on November 21, 1920. Essentially a parliamentary maneuver, this truce was encouraged by the Ivanoe Bonomi (q.v.) government and especially by Enrico De Nicola (q.v.), president of the Chamber of Deputies. Popolari, Communist, and Republican deputies were also invited to join the negotiations, but they refused. In signing the pact representatives of the General Confederation of Labor (CGL-Confederazione Generale del Lavoro) (q.v.), Italian Socialist Party (PSI-Partito Socialista Italiano) (q.v.), and Fasci di Combattimento (q.v.) pledged a mutual respect for economic organizations. They also agreed to end violent reprisals. The most significant concession, however, was made by the PSI: it disavowed the Arditi del Popolo (q.v.), thus disarming its members of more active means for resisting Fascist violence.

Local agrarian *fasci* proved less willing to disarm. Even before the pact was signed, a crisis developed within Fascism that prevented politically opportunistic leaders like Mussolini and Cesare Rossi (q.v.) from imposing discipline on their movement. Throughout 1920 and the spring of 1921 Mussolini had willingly used the *squadristi* to beat back the "Bolshevik threat." But after the election of thirty-five Fascist deputies, he decided that Fascists should also strive for power through parliamentary means by forging new alliances with Popolari, the CGL, and even the Socialists. *Squadristi* violence consequently had to be controlled. Rebellious *ras* (q.v.), however, resisted Mussolini's attempt to "parliamentarize" Fascism. At a meeting of the Fascist national council in mid-July 1921, they warned Mussolini that the Fascist rank and file would never accept pacification; soon afterwards, Pietro Marsich and Roberto Farinacci (q.v.) resigned in protest from the central committee. Mussolini nonetheless continued negotiating for the pact because he feared an anti-Fascist backlash. This fear was heightened by a brutal Fascist assault against Socialists at Sarzano on July 21. Following it, Mussolini warned that unless Fascists avoided excessive violence, they would face political isolation. For Mussolini, therefore, the Pacification Pact was a means both for regaining control over his movement and for achieving political legitimacy.

But instead of fulfilling these expectations, the pact merely intensified the rifts that had developed between the "two" Fascisms: the "old," ultrarevolutionary, collaborationist Milanese Fascism; and a new, reactionary, intransigent, agrarian Fascism. In defending the pact Mussolini evoked the ideals of Fascism's "first hour," but he quickly abandoned this tactic when confronted by the resistance of local *fasci* at a regional conference in Bologna on August 16. Two days later Mussolini resigned from the executive committee. He thus avoided responsibility for the pact's failure and prevented a Fascist schism. To regain control over the movement, Mussolini attempted to transform it into a party. This transformation was achieved at the Fascist congress in Rome (November 7-10, 1921). By agreeing not to discuss the pact at this time, Mussolini won a compromise and symbolic embraces from Dino Grandi (q.v.) and Marsich. Several days later, on November 15, 1921, the Pacification Pact was denounced by the Fascist central committee and *Il Popolo d'Italia*.

For further information see: Renzo De Felice, *Mussolini il fascista* (Turin: Einaudi, 1966); Antonio Gramsci, *Socialismo e fascismo: L'Ordine nuovo 1921-22* (Turin: Einaudi, 1971); Benito Mussolini, *Opera omnia di Benito Mussolini*, 36 vols., ed. Edoardo e Duilio Susmel, vols. 16 and 17 (Florence: La Fenice, 1972); Angelo Tasca, *Nascita e avvento del fascismo: L'Italia dal 1918 al 1922* (Florence: La Nuova Italia, 1950).

NGE

PACT OF STEEL. The Pact of Steel was a politico-military alliance signed in Berlin on May 22, 1939, between Nazi Germany and Fascist Italy by Joachim von Ribbentrop and Galeazzo Ciano (q.v.), the respective parties' foreign ministers.

Movement toward an Italo-German alliance began with the rapprochement following Germany's diplomatic support of Italy during the Italo-Ethiopian War (*see* ETHIOPIAN WAR) and the League of Nations economic sanctions. Ciano's visit to Hitler (October 1936) produced an unpublished agreement of views that Mussolini announced on November 1, 1936, as a Rome-Berlin "Axis" (*see* AXIS, ROME-BERLIN). The Axis was strengthened on November 6, 1937 by Italy's adherence to the Anti-Comintern Pact (q.v.).

By 1938 the Germans, particularly Ribbentrop, were anxious to negotiate a tripartite military pact among Germany, Japan, and Italy. This was proposed to Mussolini on October 28, 1938 but was rejected by him on Ciano's advice, because of German unpopularity among the Italians. The changing international situation prompted Mussolini to resurrect the concept in January 1939, but the Japanese then balked.

On May 6, 1939, Mussolini ordered Ciano, then meeting in Milan with Ribbentrop, to accept a dual alliance with Germany. Ciano had not prepared a draft for discussion, did not pursue substantive discussions on treaty provisions, and allowed the German Foreign Ministry to draft the final treaty with minimal input from the Italian side.

While the Italians believed that the pact and the discussions preceding it guaranteed several years of peace, it gave virtual carte blanche to Hitler's future moves. They key article provided that if either party "became involved in warlike complications with another Power or Powers, the other High Contracting Party would immediately come to its assistance as an ally and support it with all its military forces. . . ."

The Pact of Steel as signed also called for continuous contact between the parties on all questions of common interest and for immediate consultation on measures to be taken to protect threatened common interests. It further stated that should either party's security be threatened from without, the other would provide full political and diplomatic support to remove the threat.

Other articles provided for joint commissions on military collaboration and war economy; allowed for the conclusion of armistice and peace only by agreement of the parties; and recognized the importance of common policies toward friendly powers.

The pact was to last an initial term of ten years from signature. Included in the preamble was recognition of the parties' common frontier "fixed for all time," an important point in Italo-German relations. A secret protocol called for rapid implementation of the commissions and collaboration of press and propaganda services.

Ciano attempted to use Germany's failure to abide by the consultation clause as reason for Italy's nonbelligerency in September 1939, but the German leaders considered Italian nonaction a betrayal of the treaty. The pact was finally abrogated by the separate Italian armistice with the Allies in September 1943.

For further information see: Mario Toscano, *Le origine diplomatiche del patto d'acciaio* (Florence: G. C. Sansoni, 1956); Elizabeth Wiskemann, *The Rome-Berlin Axis* (New York: Oxford University Press, 1949).

MFL

PAGANO, GIUSEPPE (b. Trieste, 1896; d. Mauthousen, 1945). A major architect, Pagano worked within the Fascist system for over twenty years only to become disillusioned and to join the Resistance. He was captured by the Nazis and sent to a concentration camp, where he was killed in 1945.

Pagano distinguished between modern and monumental architecture and outlined the similarity among styles in all countries. In 1928 Pagano directed a show in Turin, which was a center for anti-Fascist cultural resistance and for which he built the Festival Pavilion in the functional style. By 1931 he was one of the major architects involved in the designing of the University City in Rome. Pagano's expressed philosophy stated that architecture could give meaning to political revolution. As director of *Casabella*, a major architectural journal, he criticized traditional architecture and called for an architecture that expressed Fascist ideals. In 1937 Pagano worked on designs for the Esposizione Universale di Roma (EUR) along with Marcello Piacentini (q.v.), Luigi Piccinatio, Ettore Rossi, and Luigi

Vietti. An early Fascist, he found favor with Mussolini until the late 1930s when Piacentini's monumental imperial style captured the Duce's imagination.

For further information see: Carlo Cresti, *Appunti storici e critici sull'architettura Italiana dal 1900 ad oggi* (Florence: G. & G., 1971); Luciano Patetta, *L'Architettura in Italia 1919-1943. Le Polemiche* (Milan: Cooperativa libraria universitaria del politecnico, 1972); Carlo Ludovico Ragghianti, "Ricordo di Pagano," *Metron* 44 (1952); Bruno Zevi, *Storia dell'architettura moderna* (Turin: Einaudi, 1955).

JH

PAINTING AND SCULPTURE. Painting and sculpture in Fascist Italy reflected the general social and political situation in Europe between the wars as well as the inconsistencies of the regime's cultural policies. The visual arts in Italy were not as effectively controlled by the state as they were in Hitler's Germany or Stalin's Russia. Mussolini's cultural aims were less defined than Hitler's, and there was a certain ambiguity in the relationship between government and the arts. Mussolini turned his attention to cultural matters only after he had consolidated power and silenced his critics following the Matteotti Crisis (q.v.). As early as 1922, however, the painter and critic Ardengo Soffici (q.v.) had outlined the ideal function of art in the Fascist regime as the expression of a political program. Fascist cultural policies were certainly tied to political goals, but there was never any one officially sanctioned style that was enforced during the life of the regime.

Mussolini's first significant pronouncement on art came in a speech at the opening of the group of Novecento (*see* NOVECENTO MOVEMENT) artists in Milan (February 1926), where he proclaimed the creation of a "hierarchy between politics and art." Implying that there should be reciprocal obligations between artists and political leaders, Mussolini set up a structure that provided both a means of government support for the arts and an instrument to exercise at least partial control over them. In 1925 the Royal Academy of Italy (q.v.) was established, an elite organization of the most illustrious artists and intellectuals of Italy. Membership in the academy was a great and lucrative honor, but participation compromised the intellectual independence of its members. On a broader level, Mussolini extended a certain control over the visual arts by the organization of artists into unions. Painters and sculptors enrolled in the union were required to be members of the Fascist party and to demonstrate "good political and moral conduct." Since membership in the union was necessary to work and exhibit, artists were highly dependent on the regime.

But in spite of the unions and other measures intended to control and channel artistic production, many artists continued to work in their own personal styles; officially disapproved, "decadent" works were displayed in small private galleries outside the state arts organization. Even within the official structure, deviance from government-approved standards was tolerated, and the Italian public could see examples of modern and avant-garde art at exhibitions sponsored by the

Confederation of Professionals and Artists under the direction of Cornelio Di Marzio (q.v.).

Mussolini's ambiguous cultural policies allowed a wide variety of styles to coexist in Fascist Italy. In the early years of the Fascist movement he was strongly identified with Futurism (q.v.). F. T. Marinetti (q.v.), the founder of Futurism, continued into the 1930s to urge Mussolini to adopt Futurism as the official style of the regime. Embracing the realities of the modern technological world and rejecting all connections with the past, the Futurists' famous declaration that "a speeding automobile is more beautiful than the Victory of Samothrace" was not in keeping with Mussolini's policy of normalization and his stress in the mid-1920s on traditional values. Even though artists experimented with Futurism well into the 1930s (these later Futurists, part of a movement called "Second Futurism," included Enrico Prampolini, Giovanni Korompay, and Pippo Oriani), the movement's ties with internationalism and its rejection of history were not appropriate to Fascism after the mid-1920s, when Mussolini was emphasizing Italy's Roman and Renaissance heritage.

As part of his program of normalization, an important aspect of which was the glorification of Italy's past, Mussolini endorsed the efforts of painters working in a modernized classical style, exhibiting together under the name Novecento. The group was associated with Margherita Sarfatti (q.v.), Mussolini's mistress and an important figure in the cultural life of Fascist Italy. Among the artists—some of them ex-Futurists—active in the Novecento were Anselmo Bucci, Mario Sironi (q.v.), Achille Funi, Ubaldo Oppi, Arturo Martini (q.v.), and Piero Marrussig. Like Futurism, Novecento art (characterized by severity, formal asceticism, and neoquattrocento qualities) was never adopted by the regime as an official style but by the 1930s had become widely identified with the formalism of public art.

While the Futurists and the Novecento painters grappled with the problem of producing an art valid for Fascism, the metaphysical painters instead turned inward for inspiration. The highly personal, introverted paintings of Giorgio De Chirico and Carlo Carrà (q.v.) evoke the emptiness of human life and a society without any meaningful direction. Carrà, who began his career as a Futurist, met De Chirico at the Military Hospital of Ferrara in 1916 and became interested in metaphysical painting, which formed the basis of later surrealistic art. Giorgio Morandi (q.v.) worked in the style of De Chirico and Carrà until 1920, when he returned to Bologna and worked in isolation on his poetic studies of still lifes and landscapes. The work of this group can be related to the hermetic movement in contemporary literature especially apparent in the writing of Luigi Pirandello (q.v.) and Giuseppe Ungaretti (q.v.).

The Strapaese movement (*see* STRACITTÀ/STRAPAESE), centered in Florence in the late 1920s and associated with the journal *Il Selvaggio*, was a literary and artistic current that considered its nationalistic provincialism the truest expression of the spirit of Fascism. The work of Ottone Rosai (q.v.) is the best representative example of this school. Certainly by the late 1920s such provincialism was officially encouraged; the Venice Biennale, traditionally a meeting place for international avant-garde art, was placed under state control as a showplace for officially acceptable works.

In the 1930s there were other responses to the reactionary tendencies of Novecento. Experiments with nonrepresentational art continued, and it was not until the passage of the racial laws in 1938 (*see* ANTI-SEMITISM) that abstract art— equated by right-wing Fascists with bolshevism and Jewish internationalism—was haphazardly suppressed. Mario Radici, Atanasio Soldati, and Manilio Rho were among those artists who maintained ties with modernistic currents beyond the Alps. The neoclassicism of Novecento painting was also spurned by Scipione (Gino Bonichi) (q.v.) and Mario Mafai (q.v.) in favor of a more personal, romantic style. Scipione is especially noted for his almost baroque visions of a decadent Rome of cardinals and prostitutes.

The situation in sculpture in Fascist Italy is analogous to that of painting, with both reactionary and progressive tendencies discernible. This extreme diversity of style can be illustrated by comparing an offical commission, such as the neo-Renaissance *Equestrian Statue of the Duce* (Bologna, Stadium) by Giuseppe Graziosi, with an abstract steel sculpture by Lucio Fontana. There are echoes of Futurist sculpture (particularly well represented by Ernesto Thayat) in much public sculpture of the Fascist era. The powerfully built, brutal athletes decorating the Stadium of the Marble Statues in the Mussolini Forum in Rome are a good example.

The absence of a definite policy addressing itself to cultural matters is well illustrated by the competitions for the Cremona and Bergamo prizes, both established in the late 1930s. The Cremona prize, founded by Roberto Farinacci (q.v.), the intransigent *ras* (q.v.) of that city and an outspoken critic of modern art, was restricted to obligatory themes (*The Battle for Grain* [q.v.], *Italy Listens to the Duce on the Radio*, and so forth) and was the most extreme interpretation of Soffici's concept of art as the expression of a political program. The Bergamo prize competition, instituted by Giuseppe Bottai (q.v.), minister of national education, instead attracted the most avant-garde wing of Italian artists, many of whom were later active in the Resistance. The 1939 prize was awarded to Renato Guttuso (q.v.), whose *Crucifixion* was a thinly disguised protest against Nazi persecution. Guttuso went on to become the leading artist of the Resistance. These two competitions typify the ambivalence of both Mussolini's cultural policies and of the entire artistic scene in Fascist Italy.

For further information see: Philip V. Cannistraro, *La fabbrica del consenso* (Bari-Rome: Laterza, 1975); Carla Lazagna, "La concezione delle arti figurative nella politica culturale del fascismo," *Il movimento di liberazione in Italia* 4, 89 (October-December 1967); Edward R. Tannenbaum, *The Fascist Experience* (New York: Basic Books, 1972); Fernando Tempesti, *Arte dell'Italia fascista* (Milan: Feltrinelli, 1976); Vito Zagarrio, "Il fascismo e la politica delle arti," *Studi Storici* 17, 2 (April-June 1976).

DB

PALAZZO CHIGI, PACT OF. A formal agreement between representatives of Italian industry and Fascist trade unions concluded on December 19, 1923, the pact signalled the defeat of Fascist syndicalism (q.v.) and the alliance between industrialists and Mussolini's regime.

The chief ideologue and leader of Fascist syndicalism, Edmondo Rossoni (q.v.), head of the General Confederation of Fascist Syndical Corporations, had been working to create what he called "integral syndicalism"—by which he meant the creation of mixed syndicates (or corporations) of workers and employers. But industrial leaders bitterly opposed the integral concept and feared the loss of their autonomy in such a system. Antonio Benni (q.v.), president of the Confindustria (Confederazione Generale dell'Industria Italiana) (*see* INDUSTRY) warned Mussolini in March 1923 that industry had supported Fascism because Mussolini agreed to maintain its independence. On November 15 the Fascist Grand Council (q.v.) issued a statement endorsing the autonomy of the Confindustria. Then, on December 19, Mussolini called together at Palazzo Chigi (Rome) both sides and forced an agreement whereby they promised to increase cooperation and to organize industrialists and workers, but separately. Although not expressly stated, implicit in the pact was the understanding that only Rossoni's confederation would be recognized as representing labor, hence undercutting the still free Socialist-oriented labor movement. A permanent committee of five members for each side was set up to ensure liaison.

The pact did not end the division between the Confindustria and the syndicalists, and the agreement fell apart during the Matteotti Crisis (q.v.). A subsequent agreement was negotiated in the Palazzo Vidoni pact (*see* PALAZZO VIDONI, PACT OF) of 1925.

For further information see: Renzo De Felice, *Mussolini il fascista* (Turin: Einaudi, 1966); Adrian Lyttelton, *The Seizure of Power* (London: Weidenfeld & Nicolson, 1973); Roland Sarti, *Fascism and the Industrial Leadership in Italy* (Berkeley: University of California, 1971).

PVC

PALAZZO VIDONI, PACT OF. In the two years following the conclusion of the Palazzo Chigi Pact (*see* PALAZZO CHIGI, PACT OF) of 1923, tensions between Italian industrialists and Fascist syndicalist leaders continued to surface. Edmondo Rossoni's (q.v.) hopes for the creation of an influential syndicalist movement had suffered a serious setback as a result of the agreement, and the Confindustria, representing Italian industry, retained a deep-seated suspicion and fear that the regime might yet seek to implement meaningful reform in labor-employer relations. A series of Fascist-instigated strikes in 1925 was intended to convince the industrialists of the wisdom of reaching a compromise with the syndicalists. In April Interior Minister Luigi Federzoni (q.v.) informed Antonio Stefano Benni (q.v.) that the government wanted an accommodation. The result was the Palazzo Vidoni agreement of October 2, 1925 between the Confindustria and Rossoni's syndical confederation.

The major element in the pact was the provision that all labor contract negotiations would take place exclusively between the Fascist syndicates and the Confindustria or its affiliates, hence explicitly giving Rossoni's trade unions the monopoly that the earlier Chigi pact had only implied. Non-Fascist labor unions could not engage in collective bargaining. But in order to obtain this concession from the industrialists, the syndicalists had to surrender a number of key demands: all workers' factory councils (*commissioni interne*) were abolished, and the so-called workers' agents (*fiduciari di fabbrica*) that Rossoni had hoped would replace the councils were vetoed. Hence, the authority of management over the factories was guaranteed. In addition, the syndicalists failed to secure an agreement that wage increments would be tied to the cost of living.

In the months that followed Mussolini imposed further concessions on both sides. The government made it clear that it intended to ban all strikes, while also setting up a system of labor courts that would settle disputes by compulsory arbitration. The Palazzo Vidoni pact was a pivotal event in the consolidation of the Fascist regime and in the history of labor-management relations, an event that represented the victory of both Fascism and the industrialists at the expense of the workers.

For further information see: Renzo De Felice, *Mussolini il fascista* (Turin: Einaudi, 1966); Adrian Lyttelton, *The Seizure of Power* (London: Weidenfeld & Nicolson, 1973); Roland Sarti, *Fascism and the Industrial Leadership in Italy* (Berkeley: University of California Press, 1971).

PVC

PANUNZIO, SERGIO (b. Molfetta, July 20, 1886; d. Rome, October 8, 1944). One of the most substantial and influential Fascist theorists, Panunzio began as a revolutionary syndicalist and ended up a major proponent of corporativism (*see* CORPORATIVISM AND THE CORPORATIVE STATE). He enjoyed a successful academic career, winning a chair on the political science faculty at the University of Rome in 1927, and he served the regime in a variety of posts, most notably as director of the first specifically Fascist institution of higher education, the Facoltà Fascista di Scienze Politiche at the University of Perugia. However, he was most important as a publicist, playing a central role in the debates surrounding each step toward a corporative system. In December 1925 the younger Fascist Curzio Suckert Malaparte (q.v.) credited Panunzio with having given Fascism its content and direction.

As a syndicalist, beginning in 1903, Panunzio was concerned not with violence, myth, and elitism, but with the socializing attributes of socioeconomic organization. When it became clear by 1910 that revolutionary syndicalism (q.v.) could make little headway in the Italian labor movement, Panunzio, with many of his syndicalist colleagues, began the evolution that led through interventionism to

Fascism. Along the way he came into close contact with Mussolini, and he contributed frequently to *Il Popolo d'Italia* during the war, but he developed his postwar revolutionary conception on his own, before linking his political aspirations to Fascism in 1921.

The thrust of Panunzio's mature corporativist conception was totalitarian, populist, and decentralizing. As a way of involving ordinary people more constantly and directly in public life, he proposed to organize society by economic sector and to diffuse legislative capacity into the resulting corporative groupings. The people would become more fully political, and the society would learn to govern itself, as the various corporative bodies absorbed the functions of the centralized bureaucracy and moved into areas that the liberal state had eschewed altogether, especially the political coordination of the economy. Panunzio's conception differed considerably from the elitist and coercive versions of corporativism proposed by Fascists like Alfredo Rocco (q.v.) and Carlo Costamagna (q.v.). He sought a more intense kind of political participation than the liberal suffrage system made possible; indeed, he portrayed Fascist corporativism as the only viable heir to the European Socialist tradition, after the revision of Marxism and the anomalies of the recent years of war and revolution.

Panunzio was a persistent critic of the defects that undermined the autonomy and initiative of the Fascist corporative bodies, but he continued until the fall of the regime to portray Fascism in grandiose terms, as the solution to a universal crisis of modern liberalism. Thus he ended up a mythmaker, giving Mussolini's dictatorship a veneer of revolutionary legitimacy.

For further information see: Sergio Panunzio, *La persistenza del diritto* (Pescara: Abruzzese, 1910) Sergio Panunzio, *Stato nazionale e sindacati* (Milan: Imperia, 1924); Sergio Panunzio, *Rivoluzione e costituzione* (Milan: Fratelli Treves, 1933); David D. Roberts, *The Syndicalist Tradition and Italian Fascism* (Chapel Hill: University of North Carolina Press, 1979).

DDR

PAPINI, GIOVANNI (b. Florence, January 9, 1881; d. 1956). A Nationalist intellectual and writer, Papini taught in Florence from 1902 to 1903. In 1903 he founded, with Giuseppe Prezzolini (q.v.), the influential review *Leonardo* (Florence), moving increasingly to the Nationalist cause. He was editor in chief for Enrico Corradini's (q.v.) journal *Il Regno*, revealing his disdain for democracy, his social Darwinist theories, and the advocacy of violence. He assumed an anti-Socialist position quite early and urged an imperialist expansion for Italy. In 1906 he began to write for *Il Giornale d'Italia* and later for *La Voce*, working closely with Prezzolini on the latter. In 1911 he and Giovanni Amendola (q.v.) established *L'Anima*, in 1913 he and Ardengo Soffici (q.v.) started *Lacerba*, and then during the Interventionist Crisis (1914-1915) (q.v.) he joined Mussolini's *Il Popolo d'Italia*.

As a major intellectual in the "revolt against positivism" at the turn of the century, Papini had earned an international reputation, publishing widely on a number of topics, including philosophy, religion, and literature. After Mussolini came to power he held a number of ceremonial positions, was appointed to the Royal Academy of Italy (q.v.) in 1937, and edited the important *Il Frontespizio*. He criticized Giovanni Gentile's (q.v.) attitudes toward school reform and Christianity and oscillated between Fascism, Futurism (q.v.), and Catholicism. He was a professor of literature at the University of Bologna after 1935 and then was president of the Renaissance studies center in Florence. In the late 1930s Papini was a spokesman for Fascist racial policies, although in 1942 he was vice-president of the Congress of European Writers (on Mussolini's orders) and defended European culture against Nazi pretensions.

For further information see: *Chi è?* (1936); Alexander J. De Grand, *The Italian Nationalist Association and the Rise of Fascism in Italy* (Lincoln: University of Nebraska, 1978); Edward R. Tannenbaum, *The Fascist Experience* (New York: Basic Books, 1972).

MSF

PARETO, VILFREDO (b. Paris, 1848; d. Celigny, Geneva, 1923). An important social and economic thinker, in 1893 Pareto was professor of political economy at the University of Lausanne. In the last years of the nineteenth century he collaborated on many journals, formulating his economic and sociological theories. In his work *Cours d'economie politique*, published in 1896-97, Pareto established himself as a supporter of free trade. During his Socialist period Mussolini read Pareto and while in Switzerland supposedly attended some of his lectures. Pareto's thoughts on the theory of elites, the importance of myths in government, the relationship between force and consent, as well as his disdain for parliamentary democracy and humanitarianism all influenced Mussolini and the development of Fascist ideology. In 1922 Mussolini made Pareto a senator, and prior to his death he worked on *Gerarchia*.

For further information see: DSPI; Herbert Finer, *Mussolini's Italy* (New York: Grosset & Dunlap, 1965); Adrian Lyttelton, *The Seizure of Power* (London: Weidenfeld & Nicolson, 1973).

MSF

PARIANI, ALBERTO (b. Milan, December 27, 1876; d. Malcesine, Verona, March 1, 1955). An Army Chief of Staff, Pariani directed the demarcation of the Italo-Austrian border between 1920 and 1924 and then headed the General Staff Operations Office from 1925 to 1926. As attaché and then chief of the military mission to Albania between 1927 and 1933, Pariani expanded Italian influence. This service and able command of the Brennero Division (June 1933-October 1934), especially during the Austrian Crisis, brought him a promotion to Deputy Chief of Staff. Pariani ran the General Staff effectively for Federico Baistrocchi (q.v.), expanding Army control over the Ethiopian campaign (*see* ETHIOPIAN WAR). He succeeded Baistrocchi as Chief of Staff and war undersecretary in October 1936. Yet together Pariani and Mussolini wrecked the Army. Pariani enthusiastically supported the Spanish Civil War (q.v.) and Mussolini's other expansionist dreams without sufficient resources. Ever-optimistic, Pariani accepted Mussolini's assurances of peace until Italy was ready to fight. He expanded the Army, creating smaller but more numerous divisions, publicly stressing Fascist spirit over materiel. Privately Pariani scrimped on training and infantry equipment to build weak, mechanized forces for *guerra di rapido corso*. He supported the Pact of Steel (q.v.), vainly hoping for German aid. Despite Pietro Badoglio's (q.v.) objections, Pariani prepared Libya for offensive war yet obediently followed Mussolini's orders to reinforce northern Italy and occupy Albania. The chaotic mobilization of August and September 1939 revealed Pariani's overextension. When Pariani encouraged Mussolini's bellicosity, interventionists and neutralists denounced him, provoking his dismissal in late October. But Mussolini rehabilitated him in March 1943 as Lieutenant General of Albania to suppress widespread insurgency. Named ambassador to Germany in September 1943, Pariani was arrested in northern Italy before reaching Berlin. Rearrested in May 1945 for pro-Fascism, he was acquitted in 1947.

For further information see: Lucio Ceva, "Un intervento di Badoglio e il mancato rinnovamento delle artiglierie italiane," *Il Risorgimento* 28 (June 1976); Enno von Rintelen, *Mussolini l'alleato* (Rome: Corso, 1952); John Sweet, *Iron Arm: The Mechanization of Mussolini's Army, 1920-1940* (Westport, Conn.: Greenwood, 1980); *L'Esercito italiano tra la 1ª e la 2ª guerra mondiale* (Rome: Ufficio stroico dell'esercito, 1954).

BRS

PARINI, PIERO (b. Milan, June 13, 1894). A journalist, Fascist, and diplomat, Parini was a "'28er"—one of the activists Dino Grandi (q.v.) imposed on the foreign service in 1928 to render it more Fascist. A friend of Filippo Corridoni (q.v.) and an interventionist, he served in World War I, joined the Milanese *fascio* in January 1920, and was a foreign correspondent for *Il Popolo d'Italia* from 1922 to 1927. In 1928 he entered the consular service, took over the Fasci all'Estero (q.v.) (the organization in charge of Fascist groups abroad), and by 1930 was responsible for all Italians abroad. On the Somali front in 1936 he commanded a unit allegedly equipped through contributions from the Italo-American community. After Ethiopia Parini's career languished. He lost his foreign ministry posts after he failed to handle G. Ciano (q.v.) with appropriate deference (September 1937) and financial irregularities in one of his organizations incurred Mussolini's ire (January 1938). In 1939 he reappeared as Jacomoni's (*see* JACOMONI DI SAN SAVINO, FRANCESCO) chief assistant in Albania, as "adviser" to the Albanian puppet council of ministers, and as inspector-general of the Albanian fascio; in 1940 he helped with the political preparation of the Greek enterprise (*see* GREECE, INVASION OF) and in 1941 became governor of the Ionian Islands. Much later Parini ran Milan for the Salò Republic (*see* ITALIAN SOCIAL REPUBLIC).

For further information see: NO (1937).

MK

PARLIAMENT. The legislative branch of the Italian government was established by the Piedmontese Statuto (constitution) granted by King Charles Albert in 1848. When the Kingdom of Italy was proclaimed in 1861, the Statuto became the constitution of the new nation. Under its provisions Parliament consisted of two chambers: the Senate, whose members were appointed by the king and served for life; and the Chamber of Deputies, whose members were elected by limited manhood suffrage according to electoral laws that were gradually broadened over the years.

Liberal party (q.v.) politicians dominated the Chamber of Deputies and controlled the government with clear majorities until after World War I; but in the November 1919 election (the first national election held in Italy on the basis of the greatly widened suffrage law of 1911) the Liberals suffered a serious setback. The Socialists suddenly became the largest party in the Chamber (156 seats), and the new Popular (Catholic) party (*see* PARTITO POPOLARE ITALIANO) came in second (100 seats).

The Fascist party had no more than thirty-five seats in the Chamber, but the Acerbo Law (*see* ACERBO, GIACOMO) of 1923 and the elections of 1924 gave Mussolini and his allies a two-thirds majority. Although the earliest Fascist program and many Fascist ideologues had called for far-reaching changes in the parliamentary structure, Mussolini did not try to implement them until after he had consolidated his power. In January 1925 the so-called "Commission of Eighteen" was appointed under Giovanni Gentile (q.v.) to suggest constitutional reforms. Among other things, the commission recommended changing representation in Parliament by permitting representatives of labor and management (for example, corporative representation) to sit in both chambers. No real substantive change in the Senate was ever made by Mussolini.

The question of parliamentary reform was debated over the next few years, especially among corporative ideologues, and the law of May 17, 1928 (n. 1019) created a new system of "election" for the Chamber of Deputies (whose members were reduced to four hundred). A list of one thousand candidates was prepared by the national syndical confederations and other selected public agencies; from this list the Fascist Grand Council (q.v.) selected the deputies, who were then approved by the electorate in a plebiscite. (Under the new law, the number of citizens eligible to vote was decreased from about 12.5 million to 9.5 million.)

The final alteration in the parliamentary structure came in the next decade. In 1936 a commission (composed of Costanzo Ciano [q.v.], Achille Starace [q.v.], Arrigo Solmi [q.v.], Giuseppe Bottai [q.v.], and Ferruccio Lantini [q.v.]) was appointed to recommend further changes, and the law of January 19, 1939 (n. 129) substituted the Chamber of Fasces and Corporations for the old Chamber of Deputies. The new Chamber consisted of people in the following categories: (1) members of the National Council of the Fascist party; (2) members of the National Council of Corporations; (3) members of the Fascist Grand Council; (4) the head of government (Mussolini). Participation in the Chamber ceased automatically with the end of membership in any of the four categories. This last, "revolutionary" reform brought about the definitive end of the concept of parliamentary government in Italy as it had been understood since unification. The election principle was completely abolished, and the Chamber became a meaningless institution with no real power, for the effective legislative power was now in the hands of the "government," or more precisely in Mussolini's hands.

For further information see: Alberto Aquarone, *L'organizzazione dello stato totalitario* (Turin: Einaudi, 1965); Celestino Arena et al., *La Camera dei Fasci e delle Corporazioni* (Florence: Sansoni, 1937); Italo Lunelli, *Riforma costituzionale fascista* (Milan: Treves, 1937); Alfredo Rocco, *La formazione dello stato fascista* (Milan: Giuffre, 1938); Herbert W. Schneider, *Making the Fascist State* (New York: Oxford, 1928).

PVC

PARRI, FERRUCCIO (b. Pinerolo, January 19, 1890). A leader of the military resistance (*see* RESISTANCE, ARMED) and Italy's first postwar prime minister, Parri personified the democratic idealism of the anti-Fascist resistance. He received his degree in 1913 and taught from 1914 to 1916. He then joined the Army and fought with great heroism in the trench warfare along the Alps.

Released from military service in 1919, Parri returned to teaching. By 1921 he was taking an active part in the opposition to Fascism, collaborating on *Il Corriere della Sera* and the anti-Fascist periodical *Il Caffè*. The Fascists retaliated by ousting Parri from his teaching post and from the staff of *Corriere*. In 1926 Parri aided the aging Socialist leader Filippo Turati (q.v.) to escape from Italy. He was arrested and imprisoned. From 1926 until 1930 and again in 1931-32, Parri was either in prison or confinement. After release from a second confinement in 1932, Parri remained politically inactive for a decade under the twin pressures of continuous police surveillance and the requirements of supporting his family. However, he kept up his contacts with other anti-Fascists and, after the collapse of the Mussolini regime in July 1943, he reemerged as a political leader.

From September 1943 to April 1945 Parri was a leader of the political and military resistance in northern Italy. He represented the Partito d'Azione (q.v.) within the Milan Committee of National Liberation for Northern Italy (CLNAI) —Comitato di Liberazione Nazionale per l'Alta Italia (*see* COMMITTEE OF NATIONAL LIBERATION) and was a senior military commander. In November 1944 Parri took part in a mission to Rome to coordinate military and political strategy with the Allied high command and the Italian government. The negotiations led to agreements that subordinated the CLNAI to the Allied high command in return for formal recognition of the CLNAI as the representative of the Italian government in occupied Italy.

Shortly after his return from Rome Parri was arrested (January 2, 1945) and spent the following two months in a German prison. He was released in Switzerland in March 1945 as a good faith gesture by German officials attempting to negotiate a military surrender in Italy. On April 13, 1945, Parri reentered Italy and shortly thereafter took part in the final victorious insurrections that liberated northern Italy.

Within a month of the conclusion of hostilities, Parri emerged as a compromise choice for prime minister. The Parri government (June 19 to November 24, 1945) was marked by the dissolution of the CLN (Comitato di Liberazione Nazionale) coalition that had guided the resistance. Parri's program of democratic reform was blocked by the parties of the right and received only lukewarm support from the two mass parties of the left. The major accomplishments of his five months in power, disarming the resistance and ensuring the continuity of political institutions, furthered a conservative political reconstruction. Parri's diplomacy associated Italy with the victorious Allied powers through the symbolic act of declaring war on Japan. His two major reform proposals, a more sweeping purge of Fascist organizations and individuals and currency reform, were blocked by the right and became the immediate causes of the fall of his government.

In November the Liberal party withdrew from the Parri government to block further reform efforts. This act had the support of the more powerful Christian Democrats (see CHRISTIAN DEMOCRACY), and Parri was forced to resign. Thereafter he continued to play an active role in Italian politics. In 1946 he was elected to the Constituent Assembly (see COSTITUENTE) and led the moderate wing out of the Partito d'Azione and then into the Republican party (see PARTITO REPUBBLICANO ITALIANO). In 1948 he was elected to the Senate. The following year he actively supported Italian membership in NATO. Throughout the 1950s and 1960s he took an active role in political movements, working for European unity and cooperation among leftist parties. In addition, he has been very active in promoting historical research on the resistance movements.

For further information see: Ferruccio Parri, *Scritti, 1915-75* (Milan: Feltrinelli, 1976); Enzo Piscitelli, *Da Parri a De Gasperi* (Milan: Feltrinelli, 1975); *L'Italia dalla liberazione alla repubblica* (Milan: Feltrinelli, 1977).

JEM

PARTITO COMUNISTA ITALIANO (PCI). The Italian Communist party was founded in January 1921 as a result of the confluence of Antonio Gramsci's (q.v.) leftwing Socialist Ordine Nuovo movement and Amadeo Bordiga's (q.v.) abstentionist faction. Joined by other, smaller groups, these leaders split off from the Socialist party during the Congress of Livorno when the Maximalist (revolutionary) majority refused to expel the reformists, an indispensable condition set by the Third International for Italian membership. The new party organized itself in Livorno, approving a program inspired by Bordiga and naming a central committee that had a leftist majority faithful to him. Between 1923 and 1926 there was a struggle between the Bordiga faction and the Third International, especially after Bordiga aligned himself with positions that resembled those of the losing Trotskyists. The Comintern favored Bordiga's Italian rivals, Antonio Gramsci and Palmiro Togliatti (q.v.), who defeated Bordiga at the party's third congress held at Lyons in 1926.

In the meantime the Fascists had tightened their control on Italy, passing legislation that transformed the country into a dictatorship. Mussolini arrested Gramsci and other Communist leaders and tried them before the Special Tribunal for the Defense of the State (q.v.) in 1927. The Communist party responded by going further underground in Italy and, spurred by Moscow, expelling dissidents. Bordiga and Angelo Tasca (q.v.), leaders of the left and right wings, were expelled. Furthermore, the Communists intensified their political isolation. They continued to attack the Socialists, whose influence they had sought to destroy in every way since 1921, and refused to cooperate with the Anti-Fascist Concentration (*see* ANTI-FASCISM).

With the rise of Hitler, however, international Communist policy changed. In July 1934 the Italian Communist party agreed to coordinate its actions with the Socialists and initiated a program of cooperation with the other popular parties. The basis for these alliances was opposition to the Italian invasion of Ethiopia, participation in the Spanish Civil War (q.v.) against the Fascists, and, most important, the crucial Communist contribution to the Italian Armed Resistance (q.v.). Concurrently with these actions came the theoretical formulation by Togliatti in 1944 of the so-called "new party," according to which the Communists would work with other political factions in seeking to install a progressive democratic regime in Italy. The fifth party Congress, held in Rome at the end of 1945, officially sanctioned these ideas, which, however, were already being applied. The Communist party participated in the CLN (Comitato di Liberazione Nazionale), or Committee of National Liberation (q.v.), and in the various coalition governments after the fall of Fascism until Alcide De Gasperi (q.v.) expelled the Communists from his cabinet in the spring of 1947.

With the postwar international climate dominated by the cold war between the United States and the Soviet Union, the Italian Communist party started a campaign designed to return itself to power by attracting supporters beyond those persons ideologically committed to Marxism. The campaign involved a series of political compromises that seemed contrary to the party's principles and failed to achieve its goal of winning a majority, although the party did become the largest Communist political organization in the West. During this period, for example, the Communists in the Constituent Assembly (*see* COSTITUENTE) supported insertion of the Lateran Pacts (q.v.) into the new Republican constitution, but the Church refused to be placated. In 1948 the Communists, in alliance with the

Socialists, lost the crucial general elections. This loss relegated the Communist party to a perpetual opposition role.

During the 1950s the Communist party was shaken by the denunciation of Stalin and by the Soviet invasion of Hungary. These events caused the loss of significant intellectual elements of the movement, led to uncertain attempts at liberalization within the party, and stimulated the progressive Socialist drift out of the Communist orbit. The party supported Khrushchev's policies and stressed the "Italian road to socialism," but it was caught between the demands for greater internal liberalization and the resistance of a significant percentage of the rank and file to modifying the party's iron discipline and its close relationship with Moscow. The debates that ensued on these topics, however, had little effect on the overall appeal of the Communists for the Italian voters and workers. The Communist vote increased progressively in the general elections, and the CGIL (Confederazione Generale Italiana del Lavoro) (q.v.), the Communist labor union, gained in power. In July 1960 the party's opposition to Tambroni, who was supported by the neo-Fascists (MSI-Movimento Sociale Italiano) (q.v.), contributed to the fall of that cabinet and won praise for the Communists. With the establishment of the center-left coalition, however, the Communists were again cut out of power. On the international plane, the Italian Communist party, under Togliatti's deft leadership, sided with the Russians against the Chinese.

When Togliatti died in 1964 a hero of the Resistance (see RESISTANCE, ARMED), Luigi Longo (q.v.) replaced him as party secretary, but Longo lacked Togliatti's political charisma. With the accession of Enrico Berlinguer came revitalization; greater independence from Moscow, decisively influenced by the Soviet Union's invasion of Czechoslovakia in 1968; and Eurocommunism. This latter movement, launched in the early 1970s, was an effort by the Italians to create a bloc of Western Communist parties capable of resisting Russian dominance, an attempt that appears to have failed because of the recalcitrance of the French Communist party. In domestic politics Berlinguer announced the "historic compromise," a policy of cooperation with the Christian Democrats. In a further bid to share power the Communists also accepted the NATO alliance. These policies appeared to be working as the Communist percentage of the vote increased significantly. Through the mediation of Aldo Moro, the Communist party became an unofficial partner in the governing coalition in 1978. However, Moro's assassination by terrorists, the hostility of the Socialists, reaction against the new situation from the Communist rank and file, and disillusionment with the scarce results of the experiment led to declines in the Communist vote, a new power relationship between the Christian Democrats and the Socialists, and the return of the Communist party to the opposition.

For further information see: Donald L. M. Blackmer, *Unity in Diversity: Italian Communism and the Communist World* (Cambridge, Mass.: M.I.T. Press, 1968); Direzione del Partito comunista italiano, *Il comunismo italiano nella seconda guerra mondiale* (Rome: Riuniti, 1963); Aurelio Lepre, *La formazione del Partito comunista d'Italia* (Rome: Riuniti, 1971); Paolo Spriano, *Storia del Partito comunista italiano*, 5 vols. (Turin: Einaudi, 1967-75).

SD

PARTITO D'AZIONE. A party of intellectuals of the radical democratic tradition, the Party of Action (P d'A) played a prominent role in the Armed Resistance (*see* RESISTANCE, ARMED) and in the political leadership of Italy in the period 1943-45. Lacking a mass base, it failed completely to influence postwar Italian politics.

Finding its inspiration in the Mazzinian heritage of the Risorgimento, the P d'A was created in Paris during the Fascist period, a product of the union of three basic elements: members of Giustizia e Libertà (*see* ANTI-FASCISM), the Liberal Socialists of Guido Calogero, and the radical Democrats of Ferruccio Parri (q.v.). It was never able completely to fuse these factions.

This covert "conspiracy of intellectuals" drafted a manifesto in May 1940. Police arrested several leaders, including Parri and Calogero, but failed to prove their conspiracy. In November 1942 Parri resumed his underground work with Ugo La Malfa and others, and in January 1943 they took the name Party of Action. They began to publish their clandestine journal, *L'Italia Libera* (Milan), which made public their political program: a secular state with republican institutions; local and regional autonomy; agrarian and industrial reform, including nationalization of electric power, antitrust laws, and factory councils; progressive taxation; administrative reform; mass education; development of the south; and European federation.

In the summer of 1943 the P d'A emerged to take a position, with five other parties, in the Rome Committee of National Liberation (CLN-Comitato di Liberazione Nazionale) (q.v.) with the P d'A's Sergio Fenoaltea as secretary. When Mussolini was toppled by the Fascist Grand Council (q.v.) in July, they adamantly refused to collaborate with the government of Marshal Pietro Badoglio (q.v.). At the end of Badoglio's "Forty Five Days" (July-September 1943), Parri convened the first P d'A congress in Florence where, under cover, they organized a military campaign. Under the command of Parri ("Zio Maurizio"), with their greatest strength in the Piedmont, the P d'A made a major contribution to the Resistance, second only to that of the Communists (PCI) (*see* PARTITO COMUNISTA ITALIANO). They participated in the 1945 insurrections in the northern cities. Their brigades— named "Rosselli," "GL," and "Italia Libera"—reflected their political tradition. Other commanders included Mario Andreis, Tancredi Galimberti, Dante Livio Bianco (q.v.), Franco Venturi, Cesare Gnudi, and Carlo Ragghianti.

Within the structure of the CLNs, the P d'A participated in two of the wartime cabinets. Although critical of the PCI for supporting Badoglio, they reluctantly joined his cabinet during the Lieutenant-Generalcy of the Realm, Alberto Tarchiani (q.v.) serving as minister of public works and Adolfo Omodeo as minister of education. They continued to participate in Ivanoe Bonomi's (q.v.) "Concert of

Six Parties," in which Alberto Cianca (q.v.) held a ministry without portfolio. In an apparent effort to broaden their base, they began to take a more radical position in favor of a "social republic."

In August 1944 internal conflicts began to surface. The party divided at its Cosenza conference, the right wing following La Malfa and the left, Emilio Lussu (q.v.). With the collapse of Bonomi's first government in November, the P d'A engaged in a series of disputes—with the CLN of upper Italy and the Allied Military Government (q.v.)—over the political goals of the Resistance and over Bonomi's successor. When the British blocked their candidate, Carlo Sforza (q.v.), in favor of the continuation of Bonomi, they boycotted the second Bonomi government.

Soon after the liberation of Italy, the P d'A achieved its highest political distinction. The CLN demanded Bonomi's replacement, and when a stalemate developed, Parri was named premier. He convened the Consulta Nazionale (q.v.) and pushed for an institutional referendum. But he quickly realized the limits of his power. Plagued by the rift in his own ranks, the interference of the Allies, and the ambitions of the three mass parties, Parri was toppled by the royalist Liberals and Christian Democrats within his cabinet.

The fall of Parri marked the ascendency of the Christian Democrats and ended the political power of the P d'A. Briefly their influence had greatly exceeded their numbers. In February 1946 the party split again, the left aligning with Pietro Nenni's (q.v.) Socialists, and the more moderate group (Parri, La Malfa, Sforza, Luigi Salvatorelli [q.v.] and others) generally joining the Republican forces of Randolfo Pacciardi (q.v.). The party's earlier, unsuccessful attempts to recruit from the left had alienated moderates. Liberal Democrats and Socialists had seldom agreed in their vision of the Italian future. But most damaging was the P d'A's utter failure to build a mass base. The 1946 elections—in which they won only 1.5 percent of the votes and seven seats—marked the demise of the P d'A.

For further information see: DSPI; Charles Delzell, *Mussolini's Enemies* (Princeton: Princeton University Press, 1961); Emilio Lussu, *Sul Partito d'azione e gli altri* (Milan: Mursia, 1968); Giuliano Pischel, *Che cosa è il Partito d'Azione?* (Milan: Tarantola, 1945); Carlo Ragghianti, *Disegno della liberazione italiana* (Pisa: Nistri-Lischi, 1961); Elena Aga Rossi, ed., *Il Movimento repubblicano, Giustizia e Libertà e il Partito d'Azione* (Bologna: Cappelli, 1969).

CLK

PARTITO NAZIONALE FASCISTA (PNF). In its attempt to exploit the immediate postwar climate of rebellion and discontent, the Fascism of 1919-20 defined itself as 'an anti-party movement,' denoting its repudiation of existing political structures and a discredited ruling class. Being self-consciously a 'movement' rather than a 'party' also permitted flexibility in tactics and program, facilitated the absorption of new members, and rationalized the elitism of the small fringe grouping of revolutionary syndicalists, interventionists, and exservicemen who represented the limited constituency of early Fascism.

The impetus behind the transformation of the movement into a party sprang from Fascism's rapid expansion after late 1920, particularly in the countryside and small towns of northern and central Italy. According to Fascist figures, an organization numbering 20,615 members in late 1920 had mushroomed into a mass movement of 249,036 members by the end of 1921.

Numbers alone did not explain the need for a more organized structure. If in general terms Fascism was benefiting from the violent middle-class reaction to the advances of socialism, the massive growth of 1920-21 was a localized affair, occurring largely beyond the control of the Milanese leadership and financed directly by agrarians and employers. Also, the dominance of the squads (*see* SQUADRISTI) within the provincial movement and the often coercive recruitment of a more heterogeneous membership, including agricultural workers, operated against the early urban Fascists and the existence of a genuine internal democracy and facilitated the concentration of powers in charismatic and authoritarian local bosses, the *ras* (q.v.).

The emergence of Fascism as a mass movement was both an opportunity and a challenge for Mussolini's leadership. It gave him considerable political leverage and prestige, but its continued illegality, its local perspective, and its independence from central controls reduced its effectiveness as an instrument for achieving power on a national level. Both the abortive Pact of Pacification (*see* PACIFICATION PACT) of the summer of 1921 and the contested moves toward the creation of a 'party', a label which in itself implied a centralized organizational structure and the formulation of serious long-term political aims, represented the first major steps in Mussolini's recurring campaign to reimpose control on the Fascist movement and to reassure conservative, right-wing interests.

Mussolini's defeat over the Pact of Pacification demonstrated the strength of provincial Fascist resistance to central directives that sought to restrain and channel the violent Fascist offensives in the localities. So although the Rome National Congress of November 1921 approved the formation of the Partito Nazionale Fascista against the opposition of many exponents of provincial Fascism, the first party statute of December was a compromise between Mussolini's desire for centralization and the power of entrenched local Fascist positions.

The directing agencies of the new party were the Central Committee and the Direzione, both elected by a national congress. The provincial federations and individual *fasci* and squads were directed to follow the political and administrative policies laid down by the central party organs, but the choice of squad commanders, secretaries, and directorates of federations and *fasci* was left to local initiative and congresses.

Between the Fascist assumption of power in October 1922 and the Matteotti Crisis (q.v.) of 1924, party organization was marked by a variety of short-term expedients and experiments. These often reflected the impact of tensions in the movement as a whole, which largely revolved around differing views of the party's role and status. Deprived of the unity imposed by the years of struggle, the party suffered a revival of its internal quarrels, exacerbated to the point of serious outbreaks of dissidence (*see* DISSIDENTISM) in 1923 by the influx of opportunistic, new members who contributed to extremist Fascist disorientation at the government's compromises with traditional political groupings. The major controversy between revisionism (q.v.) and intransigents in 1923-24 broadly corresponded to the split between urban and agrarian Fascism apparent in the movement since the rapid growth of 1920-21. Both tendencies agreed on the need for the Fascistization of personnel and institutions. But while the revisionists regarded an end to party illegality as the essential prerequisite for an orderly reform of the state, the intransigents feared that their provincial mass followings would disintegrate in conditions of normalcy and urged the extension of party controls over the state apparatus.

Mussolini's sympathies came to lie with the revisionists. In this light one consistent strand apparently informing changes in party organization was his attempt to limit the power and autonomy of the provincial party, to make it respond to his political strategy rather than help to determine it. But whatever damage an inherently unstable party was inflicting on Mussolini's hopes of constructing a wide base of consent for his government, the policy of disciplining the party could not be pursued unequivocally while it still represented the most effective means of retaining and consolidating Fascism's hold on the country. Any attempt to impose uniformity of procedures and directives would inhibit the provincial party's ability to master particular local circumstances.

Organizational changes at the center therefore often left untouched the real sources of power of the provincial party and did little to improve coordination between center and periphery or expressed the ambiguous compromise between revolutionary dynamism and normalization characterizing the early years of Fascism in government.

The establishment of the Fascist Grand Council (q.v.) in December 1922 as the supreme decision-making body of Fascism diminished the importance of the elective party Direzione, since the council was nominated and included both party and government figures and was therefore more likely to reflect Mussolini's wishes. At its second meeting in January 1925 the Grand Council effectively abolished the 1921 party statute by splitting the Direzione into two secretarial offices, one political and one administrative, the former to be run by a triumvirate. However, extremist provincial party pressures were satisfied by the council's creation of Alti Commissari (high commissioners), posts assumed by the *ras* and responsible for controlling party activity on a regional basis. They were abolished in April 1923 because they threatened to become a kind of informal *ras* council, more influential than the party Direzione itself.

In May 1923 the Direzione gave way to the Giunta Esecutiva (Executive Committee), which became the new directive organ of the party. But this organizational tinkering reflected a continued compromise, not a resolution of the party's position. Grand Council and central party directives urged party respect for state authority in the provinces; but the Giunta included Roberto Farinacci (q.v.) and other provincial bosses, and the so-called *fiduciari provinciali* (provincial trustees or overseers), responsible to the Giunta for party organization in the provinces, were elected by the directorates of provincial federations and thus reinforced the provincial party's position.

Both the 1923 party reforms officially sanctioned the involvement of local Fascist bosses in the party's administration, positions they exploited to consolidate their provincial strongholds and to perpetuate the uneasy dualism between party and state organs in the localities.

The revisionist crisis broke with the Giunta's expulsion from the party of Massimo Rocca (q.v.). Mussolini intervened to enforce the Giunta's resignation, and Rocca's expulsion was later commuted to a suspension. This move, however, did not anticipate a final break with the intransigents, although the complex maneuverings of the next few months indicated Mussolini's attempt to exclude the provincial bosses from the party leadership and to secure it for his own placemen. In October 1923 the Grand Council replaced the Giunta with a *Direttorio* (directorate) of five members, all to reside permanently in Rome, and established the party's hierarchy as the Grand Council, the Consiglio Nazionale (National Council, composed of Grand Council members and all provincial secretaries, elected by provincial congresses and approved by Mussolini), and the Direttorio Nazionale. The newly-appointed directorate was meant to be provisional, pending a National Council meeting planned for January 1924 that would suggest names from which Mussolini would choose a permanent *Direttorio*.

However, behind the screen of imminent parliamentary elections, Mussolini managed to maintain the provisional directorate in office and changed its composition even more in his favor in April 1924. This coincided with a Grand Council resolution making incompatible the simultaneous tenure of party and state office, which meant that the newly-elected deputies could not hold party positions, whether in the central *Direttorio* or as provincial secretary. Aimed directly at the local party bosses, this decision would involve the large-scale reappointment of provincial secretaries, a process which the central party leadership, now faithful to Mussolini, could attempt to influence.

The Matteotti Crisis intervened, and, by stripping the regime of its opportunistic support and making it dependent on hardcore provincial extremist Fascism, put an end to the admittedly uneven campaign to limit the party's independence between 1922 and 1924.

Roberto Farinacci, the leading exponent of provincial intransigence, was appointed party general secretary in February 1925. He was by temperament an authoritarian and a centralizer, distrustful of all discussion and dissent, whose monument to conformity was the last national party congress of June 1925. Farinacci brought a sectarian discipline to the party, dissolving and reconstituting *fasci* and federations, replacing *federali* (provincial secretaries), expelling hundreds of Fascists, and purging the Fascist press. He regarded the elimination of internal dissent as the means to establish the party as an all-powerful and all-present organ based on the impregnable positions of the local party bosses he patronized. Under Farinacci the general secretary became a genuinely prestigious and authoritative post elevated above the *Direttorio*, whose members were nominated by the secretary and whose role was purely consultative, a pattern he encouraged in the provinces. Organizationally, he gave each directorate member specific and well-defined functions in the party secretariat, which was divided into two branches, political and party matters, and corporations, and laid the foundations of a permanent central party bureaucracy.

These reforms revamping the general secretary's powers and developing a centralized party apparatus provided the essential basis for the assault by Farinacci's successors on the kind of party he epitomized. In the same self-defeating way Farinacci's demands for the enactment of repressive legislation in 1925-26 devalued the functions of political and social control informally exercised by the provincial party. Party excesses, culminating in the Fatti di Firenze of October 1925, in which intransigents unleashed a reign of terror against Freemasons, alienated respectable opinion and undermined Mussolini's strategy of creating the consensus he regarded as essential to the regime's survival. Now confident that the state machinery of repression was a more reliable and appropriate means of control than the party, Mussolini vigorously denounced illegal party methods and forced Farinacci to take action against the squads he himself had encouraged to revive.

In March 1926 Farinacci was replaced by A. Turati (q.v.) as party secretary. Turati's tenure of office was decisive in determining the party's role within a state that was supposedly Fascist or in the process of becoming so.

Farinacci had rationalized the party's role as the carrier of permanent revolution, the exclusive custodian of Fascist values responsible for defending the revolution against its enemies and infusing the political, social, and economic forces of the country with the Fascist spirit. In effect, this meant the perpetuation and extension of irregular party methods and the continued confusion and encroachment between party and state functions. Mussolini's totalitarian view, confirmed in a circular to the prefects of January 1927, was a single and indivisible state authority to which all other forces, and above all the party, were subordinated, implying a clear demarcation of party and state responsibilities.

Turati's tasks were therefore to impose a rigid centralized control on the party and to bring about the integration of the party into the Fascist state. The new party statute, approved by the Grand Council in October 1926, placed the *Duce* at the peak of the party hierarchy and established the Grand Council, where Mussolini's influence was now dominant, as the supreme organ of Fascism. Probably the most significant element of the statute was the abolition of elections within the party: the Grand Council appointed the party secretary and National Directorate; the party secretary appointed the *federali*, and the *federali*, the political secretaries of the local *fasci*.

The principle of hierarchical nomination of party posts from above directly threatened the compact provincial stronghold of the *ras* and anticipated Turati's concerted campaign between 1926 and 1929 to dismantle the substance and style of the intransigent party. On an organizational level Turati attempted to destroy the autonomy of provincial federations by insisting on conformity to centrally imposed standards of administration and financial accountability and the observance of precise procedures regarding the disciplining of party members. *Ras* rule had been marked by cavalier administrative practice masking corrupt and arbitrary conduct and the dispensing of a personal justice against personal and political opponents.

The extremist local Fascist press was purged, and federations were encouraged to establish official newspapers, whose tedium and monotony both contributed to and embodied the increasingly conformist atmosphere of the late 1920s. A new party broadsheet, the *Fogli d'Ordini*, conveyed central directives to the periphery. It was a mixture of exhortation, homily, and minute regulations on the staging of party ceremonies and the like.

Turati's more direct challenge to the intransigent party struck at the source of its power to arbitrate provincial affairs—the squads. In a drastic reshaping of party membership, at its height before the official closing of party rolls in 1927 but continuing into 1928-29, many thousands of exsquadrists and extremist Fascists were expelled from the party, their numbers swollen by the spontaneous defections of other disillusioned old members. There was a corresponding recruitment drive attracting to the party an influx of opportunists and white-collar public employees in particular, a more passive membership that mirrored the consensus at the basis of Mussolini's dictatorship.

The expulsion of squadrists went hand in hand with the central leadership's isolation of Farinacci, the destruction or domestication of his clientele in various parts of Italy, and the steady and sometimes spectacular removal of other party bosses.

Turati's party reforms satisfied Mussolini's essentially negative and instrumentalist view of the party. But Turati regarded them as preliminaries to undertaking the party's constructive functions within the Fascist state. These centered on the selection and preparation of the new Fascist ruling class to ensure the regime's continuity and development, which required party control of youth, and on a more general moralizing and indoctrinating role, the reformation of the Italian character and mentality so as to secure a positive commitment to the Fascist state. Turati's secretaryship saw the steady growth of so-called capillary organizations, extending the party's interests in youth activities, leisure, culture, sport, and social welfare, a trend accelerated under his successors.

Turati's view of the party's indispensable role would be embellished by party theorists and propagandists in the late 1920s and 1930s, glorifying the party as a quasi-representative institution that mediated between the masses and the regime, filtering government decisions downward and articulating popular needs and aspirations to the leadership.

But it was likely that the outcome of Turati's own reorganization prevented the party from effectively performing such tasks. The party was certainly disciplined and subject to centralized controls, but at the cost of removing or demoralizing its most combative members and leaders and of stifling internal debate and initiative. It was no accident that the slogan "the Duce is always right" was a product of the Turati era.

Normal party life in many areas came to be marked by apathy and absenteeism, only periodically galvanized by a strong provincial party leadership, which usually lacked the authority to impress itself on the membership or the population at large and became supinely dependent on the real arbiter of provincial affairs—the prefect (q.v.). There were exceptions, but the pattern of devitalization and bureaucratization established during Turati's secretaryship was merely reinforced rather than changed in the 1920s.

The party's subordination to the state was celebrated institutionally as well as in fact. In the 1929 party statute, the party secretary, who was appointed by royal decree on a proposal of the head of government, could participate in meetings of the Council of Ministers and sat on various other ministerial bodies. (The 1939 statute gave the party secretary the title and functions of a minister.) The National Directorate and *federali* were nominated by the head of government, making them even more like public officials.

Giovanni Giuriati (q.v.) replaced Turati as party secretary in September 1930 and immediately embarked on a revision of party membership apparently aimed at the lukewarm entrants recruited by Turati in 1926-27. The purge might have been Mussolini's sop to old Fascists dismayed by the effects of Turati's reorganization, and in some areas the remnants of intransigent networks temporarily spluttered into life. It seems likely, however, that many of the one hundred and twenty thousand whom Giuriati claimed to have disciplined, a figure that stupefied and alarmed Mussolini, were quickly rehabilitated before and after his replacement as secretary by Achille Starace (q.v.) in December 1931.

Turati and Giuriati had persisted against reality in upholding the concept of an elite party, as demonstrated by the theoretical closure of party rolls beginning in 1927, which restricted entry to graduates of the Fascist youth organizations. Starace's secretaryship, however, inaugurated the mass party, dissolving the distinction between party and nation. In celebration of the *decennale* (tenth anniversary of the Revolution [*see* Mostra della Rivoluzione Fascista]), party ranks were reopened beginning in October 1932. Membership leapt from 1,007,231 to 1,415,407 in October 1933, thereafter increasing more modestly to 1,851,777 in 1934 and 2,633,514 in 1939. The voluntary character of membership practically disappeared: decrees of 1932-33 made membership indispensable to gain employment in central and local public bodies.

The reopening of party ranks demonstrated Mussolini's confidence in the security of the regime and represented his final act of emancipation from the provincial movement that had brought him to power. Significantly, the 1932 party statute, while differing little in substance from its predecessors, described the party as "a civil militia at the orders of the Duce in the service of the Fascist state" and printed "Duce" in capital letters wherever it appeared in the text. Unlike all previous statutes, the 1932 version did not classify Mussolini among the party hierarchy: he was above and beyond the party, in no way deriving his authority from the party.

In this light Starace's secretaryship, lasting until October 1939, was not the cause but the culmination of an irretrievable process of depoliticization initiated under Turati, which conformed to Mussolini's basic wishes. Superficial and incompetent, Starace made grotesque attempts to inculcate a Fascist mentality that provoked cynicism both in and out of the party. As the party's impact on decision making declined, its administrative empire continued to expand. This guaranteed access to patronage and represented a kind of influence within the regime. But its supposed totalitarian function as a representative institution stopped short at ritual propaganda and regimentation of numbers. The experience of wartime, where popular support drained away from the regime and the party leadership was entrusted to callow youths like Aldo Vidussoni (q.v.), exposed the party's failure to form a new elite and act as an effective bridge between the state and the nation.

For further information see: A. Aquarone, *L'Organizzazione dello stato totalitario* (Turin: Einaudi, 1965); R. De Felice, *Mussolini il fascista* (Turin: Einaudi, 1966); A. Gambino, *Storia del PNF* (Milan: Garzanti, 1962); D. Germino, *The Italian Fascist Party in Power. A Study of Totalitarian Rule* (Minneapolis: University of Minnesota, 1959); A. Lyttelton, *The Seizure of Power. Fascism in Italy 1919-29* (London: Weidenfeld & Nicolson, 1973); S. Tranquilli (pseud. I. Silone), "Elementi per uno studio del PNF," *Lo Stato Operaio* (October 1927); "Borghesia, piccola borghesia e fascismo," *Lo Stato Operaio* (April 1928).

PM

PARTITO POPOLARE ITALIANO (PPI). The first mass-based political party of Catholic orientation in Italian politics, the Italian Popular party was launched in January 1919 in the midst of the postwar crisis. Its founder and first secretary, Don Luigi Sturzo (q.v.), had received prior authorization from Cardinal Pietro Gasparri (q.v.) to establish a party that would both support Christian principles and offer a safe alternative to the spectre of socialism. The PPI was to be independent of Catholic Action (*see* AZIONE CATTOLICA ITALIANA) and the Vatican and issued a twelve-point program of democratic, secular reform, which supported defense of the family, the fostering of small independent landholdings, the right to unionize, local autonomy, freedom and independence of the Church, proportional representation, women's suffrage, and the League of Nations.

The growth of the PPI was dramatic and changed the face of Italian politics. In the first postwar elections of November 1919 it won one hundred seats in the Chamber of Deputies (*see* PARLIAMENT), making it second only to the Socialist party's one hundred and fifty seats. Similarly, the Catholic or "White unions," represented in the Confederazione Generale Italiana del Lavoro (q.v.), had a million members by 1920. Prime Minister Giovanni Giolitti (q.v.), who had sponsored the Gentiloni Pact of 1913 that created an electoral alliance between Liberals and Catholics, brought the first Popolare minister into a national cabinet. However, in the 1921 elections Sturzo rejected Giolitti's "national block" of center and right parties and ran an autonomous campaign that increased the PPI's seats in Parliament. With the fall of the Ivanoe Bonomi (q.v.) government in 1922, the PPI refused to support another Giolitti ministry, with the result that Luigi Facta (q.v.) established a government that was unable to deal effectively with the rising Fascist threat. (The PPI contributed to the fall of Facta in August 1922.)

Mussolini's coming to power further weakened an already deeply divided PPI. As early as 1920 the Vatican had begun undermining the party in local electoral campaigns, and the ascension of Pius XI (q.v.) in January 1922 brought to the papacy an unsympathetic attitude. Moreover, clerico-Fascists who had opposed Sturzo and the radical program of the PPI increased their influence. Under Sturzo's leadership the Popolari had moved squarely into the anti-Fascist opposition, but at the Turin Congress in April 1923 the party approved its participation in Mussolini's cabinet.

Mounting pressure from the Vatican ultimately forced Sturzo to resign as party secretary on July 10, 1923, and without his leadership the party collapsed rapidly. During the debate in Parliament over the Acerbo Law (*see* ACERBO, GIACOMO), the party as a whole declared its intention to abstain in the voting, but a group of dissidents supported the bill and was immediately expelled. In the subsequent elections of 1924, Fascist violence against the Popolari peaked, and many anti-Fascist activists, including Don Giovanni Minzoni (q.v.), fell victim to *squadristi* (q.v.) brutality. The PPI was reduced to thirty-nine seats. During the Matteotti Crisis (q.v.) that followed the election, the Vatican issued an injunction against Catholic participation in the Aventine opposition (*see* AVENTINE SECESSION). Sturzo, who had been threatened by Blackshirts, was forced to leave Italy in October 1924, and Alcide De Gasperi (q.v.) resigned as political secretary in December 1925. The PPI ceased to exist in 1926 after the passage of the Exceptional Decrees (q.v.).

For further information see: Gabriele de Rosa, *Storia del Partito Popolare Italiano* (Bari: Laterza, 1958); Richard Webster, *Christian Democracy in Italy* (London: Hollis & Carter, 1961).

MSF/PVC

PARTITO REPUBBLICANO ITALIANO (PRI). The Italian Republican party traced its origins to the Mazzinian movement of the Risorgimento and its ideology to the works of Pierre Proudhon, Henri Saint-Simon, Carlo Pisacane, and Carlo Cattaneo. The party maintained a small but loyal following and a steadfast opposition to the monarchy throughout the Fascist era. In its broadest sense, the

Republican movement encompassed opponents of the House of Savoy from many political parties.

Republicans came into direct conflict with the nascent Italian Socialist party (*see* PARTITO SOCIALISTA ITALIANO) in the 1890s by appealing to some of the same constituent groups. The Republicans traditionally recruited from the laboring and artisan classes and from the regions of Latium, the Marches, Romagna, central Italy, and Sicily. They remained a small group during the period of the Liberal State, and those Republicans who advocated intervention in World War I generally supported the Allies.

The early Fascist movement included a large group of Republicans (for example, Italo Balbo [q.v.]), although a number of Republican activists like Guido and Mario Bergamo (q.v.) became quickly disenchanted with Fascist conservatism. But the initial confusion within Republican ranks during the postwar crisis quickly abated. Giovanni Conti and Olivero Zuccarini helped restore the PRI organization so that it recovered in time to join the early opposition to Mussolini. Victor Emmanuel III's (q.v.) failure to act severely damaged the claim of the House of Savoy to be protectors of the parliamentary state and thus strengthened the Republican position. In October and November 1922, immediately following the March on Rome (q.v.), the PRI condemned the monarchy for facilitating Mussolini's rise to power in its newspaper, *La Voce Repubblicana*, and from the floor of the Chamber.

Mussolini's consolidation of power once again produced disagreement within the PRI. The Conti faction rejected collaboration in favor of an intransigent position of autonomous ideological republicanism. The other group, under the leadership of Fernando Schiavetti (q.v.), Mario Bergamo, and Cipriano Facchinetti (q.v.) advocated direct political action to overthrow the Fascists. The latter group prevailed at the Trieste Congress (1922) and under the secretaryship of Schiavetti cooperated with Socialists, Popolari, and Constitutional Democrats in the Aventine Secession (q.v.). The interparty debate continued through the PRI Milan Congress (April 1925) and the PRI withdrawal from the Aventine (October 1925), interrupted only by the Exceptional Decrees (q.v.) of 1926.

The repression of opposition parties forced Republicans into exile and produced a regrouping in Switzerland (Randolfo Pacciardi [q.v.], Egidio Reale [q.v.], and Schiavetti) and France (Eugenio Chiesa, Mario Bergamo, Aurelio Natoli, and Facchinetti). The Republican *fuorusciti* (q.v.) participated actively in the anti-Fascist organizations in exile but had little success in resolving the internal divisions that had existed within Italy. Dino Zanetti was an enthusiastic member of the Italian League of the Rights of Man, the nonpartisan anticlerical society. In 1927 the PRI helped found the Anti-Fascist Concentration (*see* ANTI-FASCISM), partly over the opposition of the radical minority. One of the minority, Mario Bergamo, was replaced as secretary in 1928, and Schiavetti and Francesco Volterra continued to push for collaboration with the parties of the left.

But the first PRI Congress in exile (Lyon, 1928) confirmed the moderate position of the majority and its support for the concentration. Still, the conflicting currents continued to divide the party. In 1932 the PRI left the concentration in pursuit of the revolutionary program of Carlo Rosselli's (q.v.) Giustizia e Libertà (GL), only to return the following year.

The Spanish Civil War (q.v.) offered Italian Republicans the opportunity to fight Mussolini while saving the Spanish Republic. Many responded with dispatch, none more enthusiastically than Pacciardi. In October 1936 the PRI signed a pact with the Socialist and Communist parties creating an autonomous Italian Legion. It became the Garibaldi Battalion, one of the Comintern's international brigades. However, the PRI's relationship with the Socialists and Communists during the popular front era did not remain amicable. Under Pacciardi's command, the Garibaldi Battalion defeated Mussolini's troops in a week-long encounter at Guadalajara (*see* GUADALAJARA, BATTLE OF) in March 1937. In that same month the popular front recruited numerous Republicans into its Italian popular union. By August, after a bitter disagreement with Stalinists, Pacciardi resigned his command and returned to Paris to assume a leadership role in GL.

Pacciardi was among the *fuorusciti* who left Europe at the fall of France. In New York he championed a Free Italy (q.v.) legion that he hoped would accompany the Allies in liberating Italy. He was joined in the Mazzini Society (q.v.) by fellow Republicans Natoli, former editor of *La Voce Repubblicana,* and Carlo a Prato (q.v.), former Socialist and close associate of Gaetano Salvemini (q.v.). Pacciardi resigned from the Mazzini Society in 1942 when he was defeated in his call to recruit Communists into an Italian legion.

But the small contingent of Republicans continued to contribute to the anti-Fascist cause, and Republican ideals permeated all currents of anti-Fascism. In the Armed Resistance (*see* RESISTANCE, ARMED) of 1943-45, the Republicans generally remained outside the Committees of National Liberation (q.v.), which they suspected of a willingness to compromise with the monarchy. They formed several Republican fighting groups in the Romagna, the Marches, and Lombardy. In March 1944 the PRI was formally reconstituted within Italy, and they consistently won a small minority of seats in the postwar Parliaments. More significantly, they provided a continuity with the Mazzinian heritage and had worked with single-minded dedication against the monarchy through the entire Fascist period. In the institutional referendum of June 1946 the Italian electorate confirmed their position by choosing a Republican form of government.

For further information see: Giovanni Conti, *Il partito repubblicano dalle origini al momento attuale* (Rome: Libreria politica moderna, 1947); Renzo De Felice, "Il partito repubblicano nell'emigrazione antifascista,"*La Voce Repubblicana,* June 2, 1966; Bruno Di Porto, *Il partito repubblicano italiano* (Rome: Ufficio-Stampa del P.R.I., 1963); Santi Fedele, *Storia della concentrazione antifascista, 1927-1934* (Milan: Feltrinelli, 1976); Elena Aga Rossi, ed., *Il Movimento repubblicano, Giustizia e Libertà e il Partito d'Azione* (Bologna: Cappelli, 1969).

CLK

PARTITO SOCIALISTA ITALIANO (PSI). The Partito Socialista Italiano, or Italian Socialist party (the name it took at its third congress), was established in Genoa in August 1892. It assumed the structure of Italy's first modern political party when it was reorganized at the Congress of Parma in 1895. From the beginning, however, the PSI was lacerated by numerous political currents. The first important division was between "revolutionary intransigents" who opposed political alliances with democratic and republican groups and "reformists" who favored the formation of "popular party blocs." After the riots of 1898 the PSI cooperated with democrats, republicans, and liberals to block the passage of restrictive legislation in the Chamber of Deputies (see PARLIAMENT). In 1900 the PSI endorsed the reformists' Minimal Program. Proposed by Filippo Turati (q.v.), the Minimal Program committed the party to the idea of evolutionary political change through social and economic reforms. At the same time the Socialists retained the Maximal Program of 1892, which affirmed that the ultimate goal of the party was the emancipation of the workers and the socialization of property and the means of production. The coexistence of programs of revolution and reform made the party politically ambiguous and created internal contradictions that remained essentially unresolved. The reformists, led by Turati, dominated the PSI in the early 1900s. Their political orientation culminated in the vote of the Socialist deputies for the Giuseppe Zanardelli ministry in 1901 and the party's subsequent support for the government until 1903.

In 1904 a center-left coalition in the PSI succeeded in imposing a policy of intransigence, which emphasized the party's Maximal Program and rejected both tactical alliances with other parties and support for the government. Despite the party's intransigent directives, the Socialist deputies continued the reformist policies by forming political alliances and by voting in favor of the governments of Sidney Sonnino (q.v.) and Luigi Luzzatti. By 1905 the center-left coalition weakened and the leadership passed in 1906 to the center faction, which promoted compromise and party unity under the banner of "integralism." In 1908 Turati's reformists regained control and held it until the Congress of Reggio-Emilia in 1912, when the ultra-reformists led by Leonida Bissolati (q.v.) were expelled for supporting the government of Giovanni Giolitti (q.v.) during the Libyan War. The intransigent faction led by Giovanni Lerda, Costantino Lazzari (q.v.), Benito Mussolini, and Angelica Balabanoff (q.v.) won a majority at the Congress of Reggio-Emilia and assumed complete control of the party's executive body, the Directorate. Mussolini was appointed director of the party's official newspaper, *Avanti!*. His revolutionary propaganda in *Avanti!* contributed to the political unrest in Italy which culminated in "Red Week"—a national general strike and a series of local insurrections in June 1914.

The PSI advocated Italian neutrality when World War I began in 1914 (see INTERVENTIONIST CRISIS, 1914-1915) and expelled Mussolini when he urged intervention, but the party failed to halt the country's drift toward war in 1915. Officially the party remained neutral through the war, promoting the international peace conferences at Zimmerwald (1915) and Kienthal (1917) and urging its members neither to support nor sabotage the Italian war effort. On the local level Socialist revolutionaries ignored the official neutrality directives and carried out intense anti-war and anti-government campaigns which contributed to popular disturbances in northern and central Italy in 1915 and 1917.

After the war the divisions within the PSI worsened and further paralyzed its action. In 1919 the PSI, inspired by the Bolshevik Revolution in Russia, endorsed the position of the Maximalists. Led by Giacinto Menotti-Serrati (q.v.), then director of *Avanti!*, the Maximalists promoted the party's Maximal Program and went beyond the intransigent political line by advocating the use of political violence to achieve their goals. As a result of the November 1919 elections the PSI became the largest party in the Chamber of Deputies but failed to choose between parliamentarianism and force. During the "Red Biennium" (1919-1921) workers exacerbated the postwar political crisis with strikes and factory occupations (*see* OCCUPATION OF THE FACTORIES), but the moderate leadership of the Confederazione Generale del Lavoro (q.v.) generally tempered the militant labor activity. The Socialists were incapable of forcing a political solution in their favor and proved unable to cope with Fascist violence both in the street and on the governmental level.

In 1921 the left wing split off and formed the Partito Comunista Italiano (PCI) (q.v.). Increasing Fascist atrocities and Turati's attempts to curb them by reaching an understanding with the government caused the Maximalists to expel the reformists in 1922, with the latter founding the Partito Socialista Unitario (PSU). Thus divided, the Left was unable to oppose the March on Rome (q.v.) in October 1922. With the murder of Matteotti (*see* MATTEOTTI CRISIS) in 1924, the Left collaborated briefly in the Aventine Secession (q.v.) but proved unable to dislodge Mussolini, who succeeded in establishing a dictatorship that forced the major Socialist leaders into exile.

In Paris the reformist and Maximalist leaders cooperated in the Concentrazione Antifascista (*see* ANTI-FASCISM), and in July 1930 agreed to the political reunification urged by Pietro Nenni (q.v.) and Turati. The new party proposed cooperation with the Communists, but they refused. The Communists changed their attitude after Hitler's rise to power directly threatened the Soviet Union. They adopted the "popular front" tactic, thus making collaboration between Socialists and Communists impossible. The first unity pact between the two groups dates from 1934. The basis of cooperation included active military intervention during the Spanish Civil War (q.v.) and participation in the partisan struggle during the Armed Resistance (q.v.).

With the outbreak of World War II, the policy of unconditional support of the Allies, advocated by Nenni and Giuseppe Saragat (q.v.), won out over pacifist and critical tendencies within the party.

In July 1943 the party joined with Socialist groups within Italy, reorganized itself, and took the name of Partito Socialista Italiano di Unità Proletaria (PSIUP), strengthened its collaboration with the Partito Comunista Italiano (PCI), and participated in the government through the Committee of National Liberation (Comitato di Liberazione Nazionale, CLN). At the same time there was a heated discussion as to whether the party should fuse with the PCI or remain autonomous. The Twenty-fourth Congress of Florence (April 1946) failed to resolve the issue, and in January 1947 the anti-Communist Saragat broke away to establish the Partito Socialista dei Lavoratori Italiani (PSLI), which cooperated with the Christian Democrats and participated in cabinets. Another split occurred on the Right in 1949, this splinter group joining with the PSLI in 1951 to give birth to the Partito Socialista Democratico Italiano (PSDI).

The height of the PSI's pro-Communist phase was from 1949 to 1951, but currents favorable to the organization's independence never died out and became stronger in 1953. Party congresses after that date sanctioned a dialogue with the Christian Democrats, and international events hastened the process (for example, Destalinization and the Hungarian Revolution).

By 1959 the ties of the PSI (it had changed its name again) and the PCI had sufficiently loosened to allow preliminary discussion aimed at creating a new, center-left coalition consisting of the Christian Democrats, the Republicans, the Social Democrats, and the Socialists. The PSI first supported an Amintore Fanfani cabinet (1962-63) that included representatives of the other three parties and then, after obtaining the approval of the Thirty-fifth Congress (Rome, October 1963), joined Aldo Moro's cabinet in December 1963. This caused a split in the left wing (1964) led by Lelio Basso (q.v.) and the establishment of a new party that took the old name of the PSIUP. In 1966 the PSI and the PSDI reunited but split once more in 1971. In 1968 the center-left coalition fell apart, and all attempts to revive it failed. The PSI returned to its pro-Communist tendencies but by 1978 appeared to be turning against the PCI, fearful of being crushed between it and the Catholic party.

For further information see: Gaetano Arfè, *Storia del socialismo italiano* (Turin: Einaudi, 1965); Luigi Cortesi, *La costituzione del Partito Socialista italiano* (Milan: Avanti!, 1962); Luigi Cortesi, *Il Partito socialista italiano tra riforme e rivoluzione* (Bari: Laterza, 1969); Franco Pedone, ed., *Il Partito socialista italiano nei suoi congressi*, 4 vols. (Milan: Avanti!, 1963).

                                                                                    SD

PASELLA, UMBERTO (b. Orbetello, July 20, 1870). An early political secretary of the Fasci di Combattimento (q.v.), Pasella came out of the revolutionary syndicalist tradition. He was secretary of the Camera del Lavoro in Ferrara in 1907, substituted for Alceste De Ambris (q.v.) in Parma in 1908, and then went to Piombino in the same capacity. Active but not very successful in organizing strikes, he was arrested numerous times before World War I. In 1912 he moved to Milan, and in 1915 to Florence, where he was an interventionist (*see* INTERVENTIONIST CRISIS, 1914-1915).

During World War I Pasella returned to Milan and gravitated to Mussolini. He was present at the founding of the Fasci di Combattimento in March 1919. In the summer of that year the Segreteria Nazionale of the *fasci* was reorganized and he replaced Atillio Longoni as political secretary (he served with Eno Mecheri and Cesare Rossi [q.v.]), a position reconfirmed in May 1920 at the Milan congress of the *fasci*. Pasella served a valuable purpose for Mussolini, helping to attract many other syndicalists to the new movement.

At the Rome congress of the *fasci* in November 1921, Pasella was purged as secretary for a combination of political and personal reasons—most important of which was the fact that he bitterly disliked Cesare Rossi and was close to Mussolini's opposition in the movement.

Pasella was reinstated in the PNF (Partito Nazionale Fascista) (q.v.) in 1924, held a few minor posts in Milan thereafter, and reappeared again in the Salò Republic (*see* ITALIAN SOCIAL REPUBLIC) in a series of insignificant capacities.

For further information see: MOI (4); Renzo De Felice, *Mussolini il rivoluzionario* (Turin: Einaudi, 1965); Renzo De Felice, *Mussolini il fascista* (Turin: Einaudi, 1966).

PVC

PAULUCCI DI CALBOLI BARONE, MARCHESE GIACOMO (b. Caltagirone, October 12, 1887). An Italian career diplomat, Paulucci di Calboli took a law degree from Rome in 1909 and also studied in Berlin, Oxford, and Paris. He entered the diplomatic corps in 1915 as attaché in Bern and then attended the Paris Peace Conference as secretary of the Italian delegation. In 1919 he went to Tokyo and then returned to Rome, first as private secretary to Foreign Minister Tomasi della Torretta under the Ivanoe Bonomi (q.v.) government in 1921, then as cabinet secretary of the Foreign Ministry in the first Luigi Facta (q.v.) government.

Paulucci di Calboli represented the traditionalist, old guard of the Italian diplomatic service. His father-in-law, the Marchese Raniero Paulucci di Calboli (Giacomo married the Marchese's daughter and succeeded to the title), had been an ambassador and conservative aristocrat. It was a considerable surprise, therefore, when Mussolini made Paulucci di Calboli *chef de cabinet* of the Foreign Ministry in November 1922, an appointment that symbolized Mussolini's initial desire for some continuity in the conduct of Italy's foreign affairs. Paulucci di Calboli remained in that position until the Fascistization of the Foreign Ministry under Dino Grandi (q.v.) in 1927. He was then transferred to Geneva as vice-secretary-general of the League of Nations, where he remained until 1932.

In the 1930s he held numerous government and party positions and was especially active in the regime's film programs—he was, among other things, president of ENIC (Ente Nazionale Industrie Cinematografiche) and president and director of LUCE (q.v.).

For further information see: *Chi è?* (1936); NO (1937); *Annuario diplomatico del regno d'Italia* (Rome: Ministry of Foreign Affairs, 1937); Alan Cassels, *Mussolini's Early Diplomacy* (Princeton: Princeton University Press, 1970).

PVC

PAVELIĆ, ANTE (b. Herzegovina, June 14, 1889; d. Madrid, December 28, 1959). The head of Fascist-controlled Croatia during World War II, Pavelić was a lawyer who represented the Croatian State party in Parliament. He fled to Italy in 1928 and founded the Ustasha (insurrectionary) movement in 1929. As *poglavnik* (leader), he advocated an extreme nationalism calling for a "pure," independent Croatia. With the support of Mussolini's government Pavelić established a training center for terrorists at Borgotaro. He himself participated in the assassination of King Alexander, for which a French court sentenced him to death in absentia.

With the German invasion of Yugoslavia, the Independent State of Croatia was proclaimed on April 10, 1941, Pavelić having first agreed to an Italian protectorate and to the surrender of Dalmatian territory. Pavelić immediately instituted a policy of forced conversion to Roman Catholicism and of "purifying" Croatia racially, which led to the massacre of hundreds of thousands of Serbs, who were now labelled aliens. By June 1941 opposition to his brutality had sparked massive armed resistance. After the war Pavelić surfaced in Argentina, where he directed a new Ustasha movement until 1957. After an attempt on his life, he fled to Spain.

For further information see: Phyllis Auty, *Tito* (New York: McGraw Hill, 1970); Vladimir Dedijer et al., *History of Yugoslavia* (New York: McGraw Hill, 1974); Fitzroy Maclean, *Disputed Barricade* (London: Jonathan Cape, 1957); Stevan K. Pavlowitch, *Yugoslavia* (New York: Praeger, 1971).

WOO

PAVOLINI, ALESSANDRO (b. Florence, September 27, 1903; d. Dongo, April 28, 1945). A journalist, minister of popular culture, and Republican Fascist party secretary, Pavolini was an active squadrist (*see* SQUADRISTI) after joining the PNF (Partito Nazionale Fascista) (q.v.) in October 1920 and took part in the March on Rome (q.v.). Rising rapidly in Florentine Fascist organizations, Pavolini became a *federale* in 1929, while completing doctorates in law and political science. In 1932 Achille Starace (q.v.) appointed him to the PNF Directorate. Pavolini was elected to Parliament in March 1934, becoming president of the Confederation of Professionals and Artists and a member of the National Council of Corporations that October. Founding editor of *Il Bargello*, contributor to *Tevere* and *Critica Fascista*, Pavolini served as war correspondent for *Corriere della Sera* in Ethiopia while an observer in his friend's, G. Ciano's (q.v.), squadron. Ciano made him president of the International Trade Institute in February 1938. Pavolini sat in the Chamber of Fasces and Corporations (*see* PARLIAMENT). Mussolini named him minister of popular culture on October 31, 1939, to Ciano's satisfaction. Supervised by Mussolini, Pavolini directed Fascist propaganda, increasingly hindered by inept PNF leadership and news of Italian defeats. Mussolini dismissed him on February 6, 1943, and Pavolini became director of *Il Messaggero*. He escaped to Germany in September, helping persuade Mussolini to head the Salò Republic (*see* ITALIAN SOCIAL REPUBLIC). After Mussolini appointed him secretary of the Partito Fascista Repubblicano, Pavolini directed the creation of a new government, backing Renato Ricci (q.v.) against Rodolfo Graziani (q.v.) in favoring politicized armed forces. At the Verona Party Congress in November 1943 Pavolini dictated a program of socialism, elitism, and intransigence. He ensured the execution of Ciano and other "traitors" and ordered merciless antipartisan measures. When Ricci's National Guard proved unsuccessful, Pavolini drafted all available PFR members into the Brigate Nere, personally leading the first attack against the partisans. Pavolini was second only to Mussolini in the republic, thanks to German support, but he opposed those, like Guido Buffarini-Guidi (q.v.), who surrendered completely to Berlin. After witnessing the Fascist collapse in central Italy, Pavolini urged a last stand in the north to redeem PFR honor. Mussolini's impotence, local German hostility, and scarce resources thwarted Pavolini's efforts. He followed Mussolini in his flight from Milan, hoping to die fighting. Partisans wounded, captured, and executed Pavolini at Dongo.

For further information see: Silvio Bertoldi, *Salò* (Milan: Rizzoli, 1976); Alessandro Pavolini, *Disperata* (Florence: Vallechi, 1937); E. Saini, "Alessandro Pavolini: una tragedia italiana," *Settimo giorno* (July 30-August 27, 1959).

                                                                                          BRS

PEACE TREATY (1947). The conclusion of a peace between Italy and the victorious Allied states revolved around four major issues: border rectifications, reparations, colonies, and disarmament. Negotiations for a peace with Italy began at the Potsdam Conference (July 17-August 3, 1945). The United States government pressed for the earliest conclusion of a nonpunitive treaty with Italy. The Soviet Union, however, insisted that any treaty with Italy be tied to the conclusion of similar agreements with the three other defeated "exsatellite" states within its sphere of influence: Bulgaria, Romania, and Hungary. Agreement was reached that the preparation of draft treaties with the four states would be the first matter of business considered by a newly created Council of Foreign Ministers (CFM).

The first meeting of the CFM took place in London in September 1945. It bogged down on procedural questions. After the Allied powers resolved their differences at the Moscow meeting of foreign ministers (December 1945), negotiations on an Italian treaty again began, and in April the foreign ministers again met for another long and acrimonious series of discussions. The second CFM took place in Paris from April 25 to July 12, 1946, with a month recess in the middle. It made enough progress on the basic issues to call a twenty-one nation formal peace conference. At the peace conference (Paris, July 29-October 15, 1946) the smaller powers and the four "exsatellite" states were given the opportunity to comment on the foreign ministers' draft treaty and to suggest minor modifications. After approval of these draft treaties the CFM met again in New York (November 4-December 6, 1946) to complete work on the treaties. The treaties were then formally signed in Paris on February 10, 1947, and, after approval by the parliamentary bodies of the nations involved, final ratifications were deposited in Paris on September 15, 1947.

Negotiations over the Italian treaty within the CFM were marked by sharp clashes between the United States and the Soviet Union. The United Kingdom generally supported the American position, while France attempted to play the role of "honest broker." In order to secure a treaty, the Americans were obliged to make a series of concessions that greatly angered Italian public opinion. Nevertheless, the treaty was a relatively moderate document, which did not seriously damage the Italian economy or involve major or unjust territorial losses. Italy's border with France was slightly modified in favor of the French. Italy lost the greater portion of disputed borderlands in the Venezia Giulia area, including the cities of Fiume (q.v.) and Pola, to Yugoslavia, but retained Gorizia. Trieste and its surrounding area became a "Free Territory" administered by an Anglo-American and Yugoslav military government. In 1954 the areas occupied by the Western Allies—including the city of Trieste—were returned to Italy.

Italy was compelled to pay reparations totaling $360 million to the Soviet Union, Yugoslavia, Greece, Albania, and Ethiopia. The United States, United Kingdom, and France voluntarily renounced their claims against Italy. The size of Italy's armed forces was severely limited by the treaty, and Italy was obliged to turn a large portion of her fleet over to the victorious states to compensate them for ships lost in their wars. To soften the blow to Italian national pride, the United States and Great Britain returned their share of the ships to Italy for decommissioning and scrapping.

The major powers were unable to resolve the issue of final disposal of the Italian colonies. The United States held that the colonies were too great a burden for Italy's shattered economy to support and wanted them placed under a United Nations mandate. The Soviet Union claimed a mandate for itself. The United States rejected this claim for strategic reasons. The British were determined to strip Italy of its colonies. A final settlement of all of the issues involved took place only in 1949-50. Italy, however, was effectively stripped of the colonies and thus spared a debilitating postwar struggle with anticolonialist African nationalists.

Although the Italian government objected to all the major clauses of the treaty, it reluctantly signed the agreements as the price of ending the Allied occupation and the formal state of war that existed with the Allied powers.

For further information see: John W. Wheeler Bennett and Anthony Nicholls, *The Semblance of Peace* (New York: Norton, 1974); U.S.Department of State, *Foreign Relations of the United States*, 1945, vol. 1 and 1946, vols. 2-4 (Washington: Government Printing Office, 1967-72).

JEM

PELLIZZI, CAMILLO (b. Collegno, Turin, August 24, 1896). An intellectual of wide interests and great learning, Pellizzi was by profession a journalist, university professor, and literary critic with an abiding interest in theater and sociology. He was a prime example of that group of Fascist ideologues sometimes defined as the "new technocrats," and he belonged to the moderate wing within Fascism headed by Giuseppe Bottai (q.v.).

He fought in World War I after taking a law degree from Pisa and worked in England for long periods of time from 1920 to 1939, where he was professor of Italian literature and language at the University of London. This experience had a great impact on his intellectual development, for on the one hand it opened his thought to European currents and brought him into contact with important Fascist intellectuals, while on the other it convinced him that parliamentary democracy of the British type was outdated.

Pellizzi was intensely interested in the relationship between authority and the individual, a topic he explored in his book *Fascismo—Aristocrazia* (1925). The regime, he believed, had to transform the ruling class and establish a managerial elite capable of running the state in an efficient manner. His political thought evolved in reaction to the overall trends in Fascist cultural policy. First he supported the idea of a continuing revolution in which the state functioned as a "dynamo" stimulated by "aristocratic and creative revolutionary virtue"; then, as the regime concentrated on building state authority, he became increasingly interested in popular political education.

Pellizzi, who may be considered a protagonist of the regime's cultural policies, was a professor at the University of Pisa, signed Giovanni Gentile's (q.v.) "Manifesto of Fascist Intellectuals" (*see* MANIFESTO OF ANTI-FASCIST INTELLECTUALS) in 1925, taught Fascist doctrine at Messina and Florence, and from 1940 to 1943 was president of the Istituto Nazionale di Cultura Fascista (q.v.).

He possessed the appeal of a modern intellectual who was interested in the literary and artistic issues of his age (he participated, for example, in a famous debate over hermeticism (*see* LITERATURE) sponsored by Bottai's *Primato*), especially in ideological and sociological theories. In fact, in the postwar period he continued to study the sociological implications of theater, film, and literature.

For further information see: Camillo Pellizzi, *Problemi e realtà del fascismo* (Florence: Vallecchi, 1924); Camillo Pellizzi, *Fascismo-Aristocrazia* (Milan: Alpes, 1925); Camillo Pellizzi, *Una rivoluzione mancata* (Milan: Longanesi, 1949).

VZ

PENNAVARIA, FILIPPO (b. Ragusa, August 6, 1891). A Fascist minister and deputy, Pennavaria was a Nationalist during his student days and took a law degree from the University of Rome. In May 1915 he volunteered for combat in World War I and was wounded and decorated. In 1919 he returned to Sicily and organized anti-Socialist actions and became a strong Fascist spokesman. He established the island's Associazione dei Combattenti and directed a number of *fasci* in the Syracuse region. In 1922 Mussolini made him *fiduciario* for the PNF (Partito Nazionale Fascista) (q.v.) in Sicily, and he sat in Parliament as a deputy from 1921 to 1939.

During the Matteotti Crisis (q.v.) in 1924-25, Pennavaria was made secretary of the Fascist parliamentary majority, and from November 1926 to July 1932 served as undersecretary in the Ministry of Communications. In addition to these activities, he was vice-president of the Corporazione Industrie Estrattive (mining industry corporation) and national director of the Associazione dei Combattenti. He later taught constitutional law at the University of Rome.

For further information see: *Chi è?* (1936); NO (1928; 1937).

MSF

PERRONE, MARIO (b. Alessandria, January 1, 1878) and **PIO** (b. Castellazzo Bormida, October 30, 1876; d. Rome, 1952). Major Italian industrial leaders, the Perrone brothers had inherited a series of important factories from their father, including the Ansaldo firm. They increased the Ansaldo holdings greatly, turning it into an immensely powerful cartel that manufactured munitions, automobiles, engines, steel, and machinery. Like most of the other key industrial complexes, the Ansaldo company made huge profits during World War I and worked closely with the government. As early as 1914 they contributed to Mussolini's funds for *Il Popolo d'Italia*, and in 1917 urged General Luigi Cadorna (q.v.) to stage a military coup d'état. In 1918, however, they came to terms with Mussolini and provided him with ever-increasing funds. After the Fascist seizure of power the Perrone brothers supported the regime and, against the free enterprise policies of Finance Minister Alberto De Stefani (q.v.), pushed for a government-regulated and protected economy.

For further information see: DSPI; NO (1937); Adrian Lyttelton, *The Seizure of Power* (London: Weidenfeld & Nicolson, 1973).

PVC

PERRONE COMPAGNI, MARCHESE DINO (b. Florence, October 22, 1879). A Blackshirt (*see* SQUADRISTI) and prefect, Perrone Compagni came from an old and distinguished Florentine noble family. A "Fascist of the first hour," he organized and led Blackshirt expeditions in Tuscany in 1919-20 and presided over the provincial *fasci giovanili*. In 1920 Mussolini appointed him political secretary for Tuscany, and he became a leading exponent of reactionary agrarian Fascism. Late in 1921 he was made, along with A. Gandolfo (q.v.) and Italo Balbo (q.v.), one of the commanding generals of the Fasci di Combattimento (q.v.), and during the March on Rome (q.v.) he commanded a Blackshirt column.

In 1924 Perrone Compagni became *federale* of Florence and a consul in the Militia (q.v.), but Mussolini's efforts to consolidate his power over both the government and the party brought Perrone Compagni into the state administration.

In December 1926 Mussolini appointed him one of eight new Fascist prefects, specifically prefect of Reggio Emilia. During his three years in that office (until January 1930) he worked successfully to break the authority of the regional Fascist *ras* (q.v.) over the province and waged a vigorous campaign against the local leader, Giovanni Fabbrici. He was rewarded by Mussolini in August 1932 with appointment as minister of state and in April 1934 was made a senator.

For further information see: *Chi è?* (1936); NO (1937); Adrian Lyttelton, *The Seizure of Power* (London: Weidenfeld & Nicolson, 1973).

PVC

PERSICO, EDOARDO (b. Naples, February 8, 1900; d. Milan, January 11, 1936). A writer, critic, painter, and decorator, Persico joined the Group of Six established in Turin in 1928, which opposed the Novecento Movement (q.v.) and favored modern architecture and Impressionist painting. Members of the group included Enrico Paulucci, Carlo Levi (q.v.), Francesco Mesuno, Giorgio Chessa, Nicola Galante, and Jessie Boswell. The group represented the rationalists' style of architecture and supported the international style in the spirit of Walter Gropius, Le Corbusier, Frank Lloyd Wright, and Mies Van Der Rohe. Persico participated in one of the great feats of Italian architecture guided by the Group of Six, the Sixth Milan Triennale (1936), where he designed the Great Hall.

After his early training in Naples, Persico moved to Paris in 1920. In 1927 he settled in Turin, where he was impoverished and politically harassed. In Milan in 1929 he wrote for the architecture journal *Casabella* directed by Giuseppe Pagano (q.v.).

For further information see: Giulia Veronese, *Edoardo Persico, Tutte le opere (1923-35)*, 2 vols. (Milan: Edizioni di Communità Milano, 1964); Bruno Zevi, *Storia dell'architettura moderna* (Turin: Einaudi, 1955).

JH

PETACCI, CLARA (b. Rome, February 28, 1912; d. Giulino di Mezzegra, Dongo, April 28, 1945). Mussolini's famed mistress for almost a decade, Petacci came from a well-to-do family that moved in high social circles (her father, Dr. Francesco Petacci, was senior physician to the Vatican). An attractive but rather vaporous young woman with a superficial acquaintance with poetry and music, she first met Mussolini at Ostia in the spring of 1932, but she had had a school-girl crush on the dictator for years. She visited with Mussolini at Palazzo Venezia on a number of occasions thereafter but married a young army officer and did not see Mussolini again until 1936, following a separation from her husband. From then on she was his devoted companion and mistress, spending her time either in a small apartment in Palazzo Venezia or at her family home, waiting to see Mussolini at night or during the Duce's moments of leisure. Over the years she remained blindly in love with Mussolini (although he frequently maintained brief liaisons with other women). Their relationship soon became the subject of common gossip that later grew into bitter criticism, especially because her brother Marcello was thought to have been involved in illicit gold trading. In 1940 she underwent surgery for an extrauterine pregnancy, during which she lost her expected child.

Despite the growing criticism of his increasingly open association with Petacci, Mussolini remained attached to her. After the 1943 coup that unseated the dictator, Petacci followed him north to Salò (*see* ITALIAN SOCIAL REPUBLIC) and was installed in a villa on Lake Garda. Captured and held by partisans in April 1945 at Dongo, she asked to be executed with Mussolini. She was shot by Walter Audisio (q.v.) outside the gates of Villa Belmonte a few moments before Mussolini.

For further information see: Richard Collier, *Duce* (New York: Viking, 1971); Clara Petacci, *Il mio diario* (Milan: Associati, 1946); Myriam Petacci, "Dopo sedici anni," *Oggi* (March-May, 1961).

PVC

PIACENTINI, MARCELLO (b. Rome, December 8, 1881; d. Rome, May 18, 1960). An architect and university professor, Piacentini led the return to Imperial Roman architecture—a style favored in the 1930s by the Fascist regime. Piacentini authored *Architettura d'Oggi* (1930), the first Italian work on modern architecture, and in 1931 designed a new city plan for Rome. Along with Giuseppe Pagano (q.v.), Piacentini designed the Institute of Physics at the University of Rome in 1937. In 1938 Piacentini proclaimed that "modern architecture continues in the Italian spirit: it is monumental," and he eventually replaced Pagano as Mussolini's leading architect. Along with Pagano and others, he drew up the plans for the projected 1942 Esposizione Universale di Roma in the "Imperial Roman" style.

A member of the prestigious Accademia San Lucca and the Royal Academy of Italy (q.v.), Piacentini contributed to city planning and building in many Italian cities (including Brescia, Bergamo, and Genoa) and was on numerous government commissions. He directed the journal *Architettura*, organ of the Fascist Union of Architects. He was also responsible for the Triumphal Arch of War Heroes in Genoa (1923) and the Court of Justice in Milan (1933-40).

For further information see: Antonio Munoz, "Marcello Piacentini," *Architettura e arti decorativi* (September, 1925); Luciano Patetta, *L'architettura in Italia. 1919-1943. Le polemiche* (Milan: Cooperativa libreria universitaria del politecnico, 1972).

JH

PICCIO, PIER RUGGERO (b. Rome, September 27, 1880; d. Rome, 1965). An Air Force general, Piccio was Italy's third-ranking World War I ace (twenty-four victories) and became the new Air Force's Commandant General in January 1923 and then first Chief of Staff in May 1925. Piccio resisted subordination to Aldo Finzi (q.v.), Alberto Bonzani (q.v.), and Italo Balbo (q.v.), considering them incompetent. Piccio's prestige and Fascist sentiments protected him until opposition to Balbo's propaganda flights forced his dismissal in February 1927. As air attaché in Paris (1927-39), delegate to the Geneva Disarmament Conference (1932), and Italian Commissioner for the Paris International Exposition (1935), Piccio advocated Franco-Italian understanding. An honorary aide to the king and senator from November 1933, Piccio broke with Fascism in 1943, serving the OSS (Office of Strategic Services) in France and Switzerland.

For further information see: Giuseppe D'Avanzo, *Ali e poltrone* (Rome: Ciarrapico, 1976); I. Mencarelli, *Cenno biografico su Pier Ruggero Piccio* (Rome: Ufficio storico dell' Aeronautica militare italiana, 1971).

BRS

PINI, GIORGIO (b. Bologna, February 1, 1899). A Fascist journalist, Pini took a law degree, was an interventionist (*see* INTERVENTIONIST CRISIS, 1914-1915), and fought in World War I. In 1920 he joined the *fascio* of Bologna and participated in numerous *squadristi* (q.v.) actions. He directed *L'Assalto*, *Il Resto del Carlino* (1928-30), *Il Giornale di Genova*, *Corriere Mercantile*, and *Il Gazzettino* of Venice. In December 1936 Pini became editor in chief of *Il Popolo d'Italia* (q.v.) and as such was in almost daily contact with Mussolini, who telephoned Pini regularly.

Following the July 1943 coup, Pini adhered to the Salò Republic (*see* ITALIAN SOCIAL REPUBLIC). After directing *Il Resto del Carlino* again, in October 1944 he was made undersecretary of interior. Pini was the titular head of a group of "moderate-liberal" Fascists composed mainly of journalists and intellectuals. His appointment was therefore intended as a moderating influence on the excessively brutal policies of Interior Minister Guido Buffarini-Guidi (q.v.).

For further information see: Giorgio Pini, *Itinerario tragico, 1943-1945* (Milan: Omnia, 1950); Giorgio Pini, *Filo diretto con Palazzo Venezia* (Milan: FPE, 1967).

PVC

PINTOR, GIAIME (b. Rome, October 30, 1919; d. Castelnuovo al Volturno, December 1, 1943). A young hero of the anti-Fascist resistance (*see* RESIS-TANCE, ARMED), Pintor's life and his tragic death symbolized the drama of Italy's finest young people in the face of Fascism and war. A poet and critic, Pintor was a first-rate student of German literature and translated the poetry of such major writers as Rainer Maria Rilke, Hugo von Hoffmansthal, and Ernst Junger. After an initial period in which he supported the ideals of the regime—typical of many young students who had grown up under Fascism—he turned against Fascism and joined the Communist underground.

In 1943 Pintor fought in the defense of Rome against the Nazis and then went south to Naples to organize volunteer resistance groups. He was greatly disillu-sioned by the degree to which the Allies controlled liberated Italy and the resist-ance forces, and in November he decided to make his way across enemy lines to Lazio, where he hoped to join the partisans. He was killed en route by a German mine, having left behind an eloquent letter to his brother explaining his motives and hopes that the Armed Resistance would "reopen the possibilities of the Risorgimento."

For further information see: DSPI; Bianca Ceva, "A proposito di Giaime Pintor e la letteratura della resistenza," *Movimento di Liberazione in Italia* 58 (1960); Charles F. Delzell, *Mussolini's Enemies* (Princeton: Princeton University Press, 1961); G. Pintor, *Il sangue d'Europa* (Turin: Einaudi, 1950); A. William Salomone, *Italy from the Risorgimento to Fascism* (Garden City: Doubleday, 1970).

PVC

PIRANDELLO, LUIGI (b. Girgenti d'Agrigento, June 28, 1867; d. Rome, December 10, 1936). One of the most important playwrights of the twentieth century, Pirandello studied at the University of Rome and took a degree from the University of Bonn in 1891. He returned to Italy and for many years taught at a teachers' training college in Rome.

Already at the turn of the century he had produced a number of fictional works, such as *Amori senza amore* (1894), *L'esclusa* (1901), *Beffe della morte e della vita* (1902-03), and *Quando ero matto* (1902), that reflected his life-long encounter with illusion and reality. In the years up to the end of World War I he produced a prodigious body of novels, short stories, and plays that brought him international fame as a writer of rich narrative and incisive social-psychological penetration.

During the 1920s he devoted all his energies to writing for the theater and authored a number of plays that remain as major examples of that art form: *Sei personaggi in cerca d'autore* (*Six Characters in Search of an Author*, 1921), *Enrico IV* (Henry IV, 1922), *Vestire gli ignudi* (*To Clothe the Naked*, 1922), *La Vita che ti diedi* (*The Life I Gave You*, 1923), *Ciascuno a suo modo* (*Each in His Own Way*, 1928), *Come tu mi Vuoi* (*As You Desire Me*, 1930), *Questa sera si recita a soggetto* (*Tonight We Improvise*, 1930), *Quando si è qualcuno* (*When One is Somebody*, 1933), and *Non si sa come* (*No One Knows How*, 1935). In all these works Pirandello explored the malaise of his age and the disorientation and crumbling of values. He directly confronted the crisis of consciousness of the middle classes, whose faith and understanding of the exterior world had been shaken, themes expressed not only in his language but in the revolutionary new form that he pioneered. He won the Nobel Prize in 1934.

Pirandello's attitudes toward Fascism were difficult to define: he signed Giovanni Gentile's (q.v.) "Manifesto of Fascist Intellectuals" (*see* "MANIFESTO OF ANTI-FASCIST INTELLECTUALS") in 1925 and accepted membership in the Royal Academy of Italy (q.v.). Moreover, when he assumed the directorship of the Art Theater in Rome in 1925, the regime began subsidizing him. Like many intellectual and cultural figures of great stature, Mussolini demanded only the use of his prestige and passive compliance with the regime. This Pirandello gave him. Yet, the larger import of his work may well be interpreted as the expression of the defeat of an entire generation before the political and social triumph of Fascism.

For further information see: L. Lugnani, *Pirandello: Letteratura e teatro* (Florence: Nuova Italia, 1970); A. Navarria, *Pirandello prima e dopo* (Milan: Osservatore, 1971); G. F. Vene, *Pirandello fascista* (Milan: Sugar, 1971).

WEL

PIRELLI, ALBERTO (b. Milan, April 28, 1882; d. October 19, 1971) and **PIRELLI, PIERO** (b. Milan, January 27, 1881; d. Milan, 1956). Important Italian industrial leaders, the Pirelli brothers inherited a vast network of rubber and cable factories (including the Società Pirelli & Co.) and financial concerns from their father, Giovanni Battista Pirelli. During the years after 1902 they greatly expanded their holdings into other areas of the Italian economy. Both brothers took degrees in law and held numerous public and private posts. In World War I Alberto served as head of the foreign division of the Ministry of Munitions, while Piero was attached to the Comando Supremo. Alberto served at the Paris Peace Conference and on many postwar international debt conferences; he was acting president of the Confindustria (*see* INDUSTRY) in the 1930s and a minister of state; like his brother, he was also a member of the National Council of Corporations. Piero also functioned as vice-president of the Fascist Confederation of Industrialists. Immediately before the March on Rome (q.v.), the Pirellis supported Mussolini's entrance into a coalition government, and they openly endorsed his premiership after having received guarantees of industrial tranquility. The Pirellis, like other industrial leaders, shared considerable responsibility for the seizure and maintenance of power by Mussolini.

For further information see: *Chi è?* (1936); NO (1937); Roland Sarti, *Fascism and the Industrial Leadership in Italy* (Berkeley: University of California Press, 1971).

PVC

PIRZIO BIROLI, ALESSANDRO (b. Campobasso, Molise, July 23, 1877; d. Rome, May 20, 1962). A general and military governor and a hero of the battle of the Piave (June 1918), Pirzio Biroli was afterwards head of a military training mission to Ecuador, first inspector of Celeri (cavalry and the sharp-shooter *bersaglieri*) and commander of the Udine Division and of the Trieste Corps.

He commanded the Eritrean Corps in Ethiopia and then became Governor of Amhara in June 1936. Rodolfo Graziani (q.v.) blamed him for the August 1937 revolt, which Pirzio Biroli attempted to smother in mustard gas. After scheming with his cousin, Alessandro Lessona (q.v.), to replace Graziani with the duke of Aosta (*see* SAVOIA, AMEDEO DI, DUKE OF AOSTA), Pirzio Biroli was dismissed in December 1937. Pirzio Biroli remained unemployed until Ugo Cavallero (q.v.) made him commander of the Ninth Army in Albania in February 1941. Pirzio Biroli failed against the Greeks, though defeating the Yugoslavs in Macedonia.

As commander in Albania and Montenegro and then governor of Montenegro in October 1941, Pirzio Biroli's pitiless reprisals failed to crush widespread insurrection. Despite German protests, he formed an alliance with the Chetniks and protected many Yugoslav and Greek Jews. Pirzio Biroli escaped to southern Italy in December 1943. Ethiopia and Yugoslavia later accused him of war crimes.

BRS

PIUS XI, POPE (b. Desio, Milan, May 31, 1857; d. Vatican City, February 10, 1939). Pope from 1922 to 1939, Pius XI, formerly known as Achille Ratti, served as archbishop of Milan before his election as pope. Mussolini considered Pius XI sympathetic to Fascism because he had permitted the Fascist flag to fly in the Duomo of Milan in November 1921. To confront the Fascist regime, the pope envisioned creating a solid Catholic bloc unified under the leadership of conservative Catholics handpicked by himself. He indirectly aided in the destruction of Luigi Sturzo's (q.v.) Popular party (*see* PARTITO POPOLARE ITALIANO). In 1924 he forbade the Popolari from forming an alliance or cooperating with other opposition parties and helped force Sturzo to relinquish his leadership role. While the Popular party collapsed, Pius XI encouraged and strengthened Catholic Action (*see* AZIONE CATTOLICA ITALIANA), an organization which continued to operate throughout the Fascist period. It was during Pius's term that the Lateran Pacts (q.v.) were signed which settled the long-standing dispute between the Italian State and the Church. Although he received some unfavorable publicity for his tacit support of Mussolini's Ethiopian invasion (*see* ETHIOPIAN WAR), in 1938 he openly disagreed with Mussolini over the implementation of Fascist racial policies.

For further information see: DSPI; D. A. Binchy, *Church and State in Fascist Italy* (Oxford: Oxford University Press, 1941); Guido Gonella, *Il pontificato di Pio XI* (Rome: n.p. 1939); Luigi Salvatorelli, *Pio XI e la sua eredità pontificale* (Turin: Einaudi, 1939); Richard Webster, *Christian Democracy in Italy, 1860-1960* (London: Hollis & Carter, 1961).

MSF

PIUS XII, POPE (b. Rome, March 2, 1876; d. Castelgandolfo, Rome, October 9, 1958). From a family of petty aristocrats (his father, Filippo Pacelli, was a lawyer in the papal consistory), Eugenio Pacelli began his education at the school of the Divina Provvidenza. At the age of nine he entered the state-run Visconti *liceo*, graduating in 1894. That same year he entered the Collegio Capranica for training as an ecclesiastical diplomat and the next year enrolled in the Ateneo Pontificio Sant-Apollinare as well as in the University of Rome.

Ordained a priest in April 1899, two years later he joined the office of the papal secretary of state as a trainee under Monsignor Pietro Gasparri (q.v.), then secretary of the Holy Congregation for Extraordinary Ecclesiastical Affairs. From 1902 to 1914 Pacelli laid the basis for a brilliant academic and ecclesiastical career. A professor of canon law at the state university, in 1903 he was made an administrative assistant for the Congregation, in 1911 appointed undersecretary, and in 1914 secretary. In 1908 he made his first visit to the United States as a lecturer at the Catholic University in Washington, D.C.

In 1915 Pacelli went on his first diplomatic mission as envoy to the Austrian Emperor Franz Josef in an effort to prevent the spread of war; in the spring of 1917 he became papal nunzio in Munich and was made a bishop. In June 1917 he met with Kaiser Wilhelm II in order to persuade the Germans to agree to a separate peace. In 1920 he was transferred to Berlin, where he remained through 1929. During this period he negotiated concordats with Bavaria (1924) and Prussia (1929), the first of which was considered a model for the series of concordats that marked the policies of Cardinal Gasparri.

In December 1929 Pacelli was made a cardinal and on February 10, 1930, became papal secretary of state. He signed the concordat with Nazi Germany in 1933 and frequently went abroad on diplomatic and religious missions. His visit to the United States enabled him to meet President Franklin D. Roosevelt, with whom he was in frequent contact during World War II. In 1937, while at the inauguration of the Basilica of Lisieux, he made political contacts in Paris and reaffirmed the Catholic mission of France at a time when the popular front was in power. This struggle against "atheism" in the guise of materialism and communism was to form the basis of his pontificate.

Pacelli was elected pope on March 2, 1939, at the age of sixty-four. Fascist leaders saw in Pius XII a pope who was well-disposed toward the regime and able to overcome the crisis over Catholic Action (*see* AZIONE CATTOLICA ITALIANA) that had broken out in 1938. In reality, Pius adopted a rigidly diplomatic policy toward the great powers that was devoid of strong condemnations of political systems and ideologies (at least with regard to Fascism and Nazism), but also without overt political compromises. He was therefore accused of not having denounced the mass genocide of the Jews in Nazi Germany and Hitler's aggression against neutral countries. His position has been explained as resulting from the fear that explicit acts of condemnation would have resulted in Nazi retribution against millions of Catholics. He did, however, create the Ufficio Vaticano d'Informazioni and gave help and refuge to political and racial refugees. During the Nazi occupation of Rome he was dubbed "Defender of Rome" ("Defensor Urbis").

In a famous radio talk of August 24, 1939, Pius attempted to avert the outbreak of World War II. Similarly, he also worked with Roosevelt to keep Italy from entering the conflict.

With the liberation of Rome, Pius XII's major preoccupation became the Communist peril in Italy and in Europe, a subject on which he frequently lectured Western leaders. The anti-Communist struggle became the constant theme of his papacy in the postwar period, and he ordered the Church hierarchy to do everything possible to secure the electoral victory of the Christian Democrats (*see*

CHRISTIAN DEMOCRACY) in April 1948. This intervention in domestic Italian politics constituted a difficult political burden for the Christian Democrats. His strong conservatism also found expression in doctrinal matters (for example, the condemnation of the new theology in his encyclical *Humani generis*), although he endorsed giving wider national representation in the College of Cardinals.

For further information see: Ennio Di Nolfo, *Vaticano e Stati Uniti, 1939-1952* (Milan: Angeli, 1978); Carlo Falconi, *I Papi del ventesimo secolo* (Milan: Feltrinelli, 1967); Igino Giordani, *Pio XII* (Turin: SEI, 1961); Arturo Carlo Jemolo, *Chiesa e stato in Italia negli ultimi cento anni* (Turin: Einaudi, 1973); Giovanni Spadolini, *Le due Rome* (Florence: Le Monnier, 1973).

SR

PODESTÀ. Initially the Fascist government merely tinkered with communal and provincial institutions, reflecting the tensions between its revolutionary aspirations and accommodation with existing elites and systems of government. But from 1925 to 1926, following Mussolini's extremist resolution of the Matteotti Crisis (q.v.), there was a conscious attempt to break with the liberal parliamentary system and give government and society a distinctly Fascist mold. Changes in local government therefore formed part of a wider program aimed at creating the centralized, unitary, and hierarchically structured Fascist state.

The first Podestà law of February 1926 applied to communes of not more than 5,000 inhabitants, affecting 7,337 of 9,148 communes in all and about 14 million of a total population of nearly 40 million. The Podestà replaced and exercised the powers previously held by the elected mayor (*sindaco*), communal council (*consiglio communale*), and executive committee (*giunta*). He was appointed by royal decree for a renewable period of five years, and his deliberations were subject to the approval of the prefect and the provincial administrative committee (*giunta provinciale amministrativa*).

The one concession to popular control was the optional establishment of a purely consultative municipal council (*consulta municipale*) of at least six members, set up at the discretion of the prefect who had wide powers over the choice of members.

In September 1926 the Podestà was extended to the remaining larger and more populous communes. The *consulta* was obligatory for communes of above twenty thousand members, and its membership was meant to harmonize with the recent corporative reforms.

The new institution was justified in Fascism's familiar antidemocratic rhetoric and was also viewed as a civilizing, deprovincializing agent of change in backward, rural areas. But it did not as yet represent complete centralization: the commune retained its independent judicial status, and certain powers were still exercised autonomously by the Podestà, who was an unpaid honorary office holder, not a career functionary.

Central government controls existed, however, through the prefect, and these were progressively intensified, culminating in the new provincial and communal law of March 1934 which, subject to minor modifications, completed the Fascist local government edifice. Also, in practice the *consulta*, although usually established in larger centers, lapsed in small and medium communes.

In the immediate postwar period, elected local councils dominated by Socialists or Catholics were a vital prop to the powerful union organizations of peasants and rural workers. The Podestà institution sealed the often forcible Fascist takeover of communal administrations between 1921 and 1925 and, with the labor force now regimented in Fascist syndicates, signified the consolidation of the political and economic restoration achieved by squadrist (*see* SQUADRISTI) Fascism. The official 1926 norms for the appointment of Podestà certainly aimed to encourage the entry of a new Fascist ruling class. But the unpaid nature of the office, the insistence on the possession of certain educational qualifications, and above all, the sheer inadequacy of local Fascist cadres facilitated the return of traditional elites to positions of local power.

For further information see: A. Aquarone, *L'Organizzazione dello Stato totalitario* (Turin: Einaudi, 1965); U. Marchetti, *Mussolini, i prefetti e i podestà*, 2d ed. (Mantua: Mussolinia, 1929); P. Morgan, "I primi podestà fascisti: 1926-32," *Storia Contemporanea* 9, 3, 1978; E. Rotelli, "Le trasformazioni dell' ordinamento communale e provinciale durante il regime fascista," in *Il fascismo e le autonomie locali*, ed. S. Fontana (Bologna: Mulino, 1973).

PM

POLICE AND INTERNAL SECURITY. The advent of Fascism changed very little in the complex structure or basic ideological persuasion of the Italian police, who were fervent anti-Marxists prior to 1922, became Mussolinians rather than true Fascists during the dictatorship, and emerged after 1945 without significant alterations in either personnel or political outlook.

Italy's Napoleonic heritage conferred upon the country an awkward dualism in her law-enforcement structure, fostering a tradition of rivalry and mistrust between the two principal corps of police. Much of the behavior of police officials prior to and during Fascism is more easily understandable in terms of institutional competition than political conflict. Founded by a restored Savoyard monarchy in 1814, the Arma dei Carabinieri Reali continued under Fascism as the senior branch of the Italian Army, responsible to the Defense Ministry for a wide variety of military duties, including important activities in the field of intelligence, but also responsible to the Interior Ministry for normal civilian police duties. This dual command structure gave the Arma a substantial autonomy that was only limited by very strong prime ministers like Giovanni Giolitti (q.v.) and Mussolini.

Since 1848 the law enforcement apparatus of the Interior Ministry had been located within the Direzione Generale della Pubblica Sicurezza, headed by a senior police official usually called Capo della Polizia under Fascism. Law enforcement leadership in each province was provided by the prefect through a corps of executive civilian personnel, who directed the activities of a group of uniformed enlisted policemen, called Guardie di Città until 1919; Guardie Regie until 1922; and Agenti di Pubblica Sicurezza after the re-creation of the service in 1925.

In addition, each major municipal government maintained its own *vigili urbani* before, during, and after the Fascist period, while the Ministry of Finance commanded a Guardia di Finanza; none of these groups ever achieved political significance.

Historically the Italian police have always conceived their mission as the defense of the Italian State against subversion and insurrection, and the principal threat has always been perceived as coming from the left. Giolitti's energetic organization of the bureaucracy and his temporary honeymoon with reformist socialism provided the police with a transitory sense of self-confidence, a feeling shattered by the widespread strikes that erupted during the "Red Week" of June 1914, the strength of popular antimilitarism during World War I, and the "Red Years" (*biennio rosso*) of 1919-1920. By the time of the F. S. Nitti (q.v.) administration, both Carabinieri and Public Security forces were massively demoralized, stricken by bitter feuding between the Army and the Interior Ministry, and so unpopular that neither corps could fill thousands of vacant positions. The leadership of both groups faced the postwar Socialist challenge with real fear, knowing that police resources were inadequate to deal with any serious revolutionary threat from the left.

Shaken by evidence of disloyalty in the armed forces and what seemed to be a clear insurrectionary intent on the left, Nitti moved vigorously to reestablish police morale and prestige, reforming Interior Ministry forces into the Guardia Regia and recruiting many new Carabinieri. With the fall of Nitti's government and the subsequent rise in strength of Fascist Blackshirt squads (*see* SQUADRISTI), both Public Security forces and Carabiniere units felt sufficiently exposed and endangered to begin accepting support from the Blackshirts against what was seen as a common Bolshevik enemy. Both the Giolitti and Ivanoe Bonomi (q.v.) governments produced confused attitudes towards Fascism, ordering the police not to cooperate with the Blackshirts but usually turning a blind eye to the fact that these orders were generally disobeyed. While the police were occasionally capable of turning their guns on *squadristi* (for example, in the cities of Sarzana in July 1921 and Modena in September 1921), they more frequently regarded the Fascists as essential to the struggle against Marxism.

By the beginning of 1922 Carabiniere partisanship for Mussolini's movement had become very marked, while the Guardia Regia had fallen into the same paralysis that was steadily overtaking the rest of the government. Neither force offered more than sporadic opposition to the March on Rome (q.v.), and in most areas collaboration with the Blackshirts was undisguised. As prime minister one of Mussolini's first acts was to appease the monarchy, the Army, his own conservative allies, and the Carabinieri by abolishing the Guardia Regia (condemned principally because of its Nittian associations) and by transferring most of its personnel to the Arma. This constituted a massive blow to the Interior Ministry's

Direzione Generale, which was now forced to depend upon uncooperative Carabinieri for routine policing, but the remaining public security organization swallowed the affront, putting its intelligence-gathering machinery at Mussolini's disposal for operations against both dissident Fascists and Communists.

Initial Carabiniere enthusiasm for Mussolini cooled rapidly with the creation of the Milizia Volontaria per la Sicurezza Nazionale or MVSN (*see* MILITIA), which the status-conscious Carabinieri saw as a threat to their recently-won supremacy in the internal security field. Mussolini had created the MVSN to bring the riotous Blackshirt squads under central control, and the new organization was assigned important law-enforcement functions that initially brought it into conflict with the jealous Carabinieri. While Blackshirt specialty units did emerge and survive (forestry guards, railway police, and custodial officers), the MVSN actually played no significant role in law enforcement, although relations with both police forces were poor throughout the entire Fascist period.

The Matteotti Crisis (q.v.), however, proved to be the watershed for a major redirection of Mussolini's police policy. Few policemen believed that Mussolini was personally responsible for the murder, but the political consequences of the affair worried the Carabinieri, who began distancing themselves from the regime. More astute police leaders in the Interior Ministry, however, felt that only Mussolini could guarantee them the strong, anti-Marxist, law-and-order administration they wanted, and they worked to avoid either a return to a weak liberal government or the threatened "second wave" of extremist Fascists.

While the Rome *questura* (police headquarters) arrested Matteotti's murderers with embarrassing speed and Chief of Police Emilio De Bono (q.v.) mismanaged matters from the top, the police hierarchy generally closed ranks and worked to contain the scandal, keeping Mussolini minutely informed of both the Aventine (*see* AVENTINE SECESSION) resistance and the activities of Roberto Farinacci (q.v.)-style dissidents (*see* DISSIDENTISM). Public Security efforts were further strengthened by the appointment of Luigi Federzoni (q.v.) as interior minister and of Francesco Crispo-Moncada (q.v.), a professional policeman, as chief of police. With Mussolini's bold January 3, 1925, speech, even the hesitant Carabinieri moved back into line, but the Direzione Generale emerged as the net victor: professional police officers who had trained under Giolitti were henceforth freed from PNF (Partito Nazionale Fascista) (q.v.) interference, and Mussolini ordered the restoration of the Direzione's own uniformed police, who reemerged as the Corpo degli Agenti di Pubblica Sicurezza. Realizing that the primary focus of Carabiniere loyalty would always be the monarchy, the regime relegated the Arma to the countryside as rural police, permitting only a token presence in the cities.

A series of attempts on Mussolini's life in 1925-26 occasioned the emergence of Arturo Bocchini (q.v.) as chief of police. Bocchini was to dominate law enforcement in Italy until his death in 1940. Personally corrupt and never more than opportunistically loyal to the regime, Bocchini used his police to provide Mussolini with a valuable counterweight to the PNF, successfully resisting party efforts to dominate the field of law enforcement. Police action against opponents of the regime was more intelligent than might have been expected, relatively moderate, and largely successful. Bourgeois liberal opponents were kept under surveillance and treated with friendly persuasion rather than brutality. Communist party activists were regarded as a more serious threat, and by 1927 Bocchini had enlarged and strengthened the Direzione's Special Inspectorate (subsequently given the meaningless title of OVRA) to act against the clandestine enemies of the government.

Penal legislation of 1926 and 1931 stiffened the range of existing police powers, allowing the authorities to deter political criminality by acting against dissidents with three disciplinary procedures. The *ammonizione* included a verbal warning by a senior police officer, followed by a series of restrictions on the admonished person's liberty: a personal curfew, prohibitions against carrying arms, engaging in political activity, and associating with other suspected persons. *Vigilanza speciale* included all of the above together with the obligation to report periodically to the police. More serious was the *domicilio coatto*, or *confino*, which confined a politically dangerous individual (or a common criminal) in an isolated village or on an island. All of these measures could be accomplished without normal recourse to the courts.

On the eve of World War II, both Public Security and Carabinieri leaders reported to Mussolini that the German alliance was unpopular, and when the disasters of the war began to weaken confidence in Mussolini's personal rule, both corps of police began to make very tentative plans for an eventual transfer of power. By 1943 there were moderate anti-Fascists in charge of both police forces, including Carmine Senise (q.v.), Bocchini's successor as chief of police, and Azolino Hazon (q.v.), commanding general of the Carabinieri, to whom the king turned when the time came to place Mussolini in custody.

With the continuation of royal government in liberated southern Italy, both the Public Security forces and the Carabinieri enjoyed institutional survival after September 8, working under the supervision of the Allied Military Government (q.v.) as Anglo-American forces reconquered the peninsula. Under the Republic of Salò (*see* ITALIAN SOCIAL REPUBLIC), however, the Guardie of Public Security were reorganized into a Guardia Repubblicana, into which the few remaining Carabinieri were also forced after March 1944. Many Carabinieri were arrested by the German occupying forces and shipped off to concentration camps, while others took an active and often heroic part in the Resistance movement (*see* RESISTANCE, ARMED).

Just as Public Security guards and Carabinieri had maintained a substantial degree of independence under Fascism, albeit while enforcing Fascist laws, neither force changed enormously in the immediate postwar period, although the greater discipline and organizational unity of the Carabinieri, plus their contributions to the Resistance, helped them to emerge from the war with somewhat greater prestige. Those senior officials in both organizations who had been too closely identified with Fascism were quietly retired, but at the working level, policemen who had been anti-Marxists under Giolitti and Mussolini survived to be anti-Marxists under Alcide De Gasperi (q.v.).

For further information see: Guido Corso, *L'Ordine pubblico* (Bologna: Il Mulino, 1979); Angelo D'Orsi, *La Polizia* (Milano: Feltrinelli, 1972); Guido Leto, *OVRA, fascismo e antifascismo* (Bologna: Cappelli, 1951); Carmine Senise, *Quando ero capo della polizia* (Rome: Ruffolo, 1946).

ROC

POLVERELLI, GAETANO (b. Visso, November 17, 1886; d. Anzio, September 19, 1960). A journalist and Fascist minister, Polverelli first joined with Mussolini in 1914 and became an editor for *Il Popolo d'Italia*, writing on foreign and military affairs. In 1919 he moved to Rome, where he headed the Rome office of the paper and was among the founders of the capital's *fascio* (Polverelli was also present at the first meeting between Mussolini and Gabriele D'Annunzio [q.v.], which took place in Rome in June 1919). He participated in the March on Rome (q.v.) and in meetings of the Fascist national committee.

In 1923 Polverelli became political secretary of the Rome *fascio* and from 1928 to 1932 was head of the local journalists' union. The next year he was elected to Parliament. Personally ambitious, several times he tried to use his friendship with Arnaldo Mussolini (q.v.) to obtain a post in the government, and in December 1931 Mussolini made him head of his Press Office, where he remained until August 1933. As Capo dell'Ufficio Stampa, Polverelli proved to be a man of rigid severity and imposed harsh regimentation on journalists.

Between 1933 and 1941 his career paled into relative obscurity. He was a delegate to the League of Nations, president of the journalists' insurance fund, and a deputy. Then in January 1941 Mussolini appointed him undersecretary in the Ministry of Popular Culture (q.v.), where he attempted to mobilize newspapermen behind the war effort. In the last "changing of the guard" in February 1943, Polverelli replaced Alessandro Pavolini (q.v.) as minister. In that capacity he attended the final session of the Fascist Grand Council (q.v.) on July 24-25. Although he did not take an active role in the meeting and voted against the Dino Grandi (q.v.) motion, after Mussolini's fall he indicated his loyalty to the king.

For further information see: *Chi è?* (1936); NO (1928; 1937); Philip V. Cannistraro, *La fabbrica del consenso* (Rome-Bari: Laterza, 1975); G. Polverelli, "Dalla campagna d'Etiopia al colpo di stato," *Tempo* (September-November 1952).

PVC

POPOLO D'ITALIA, IL. This was the daily newspaper founded by Mussolini in Milan on November 15, 1914. He directed it personally until becoming prime minister in 1922. The paper was then directed by Arnaldo Mussolini (q.v.) until 1931 and by Arnaldo's son Vito from 1931.

Il Popolo d'Italia was first established as an interventionist (*see* INTERVEN-TIONIST CRISIS, 1914-1915) journal with money from Italian industrialists and the French and was an important element in bringing together left-wing and democratic interventionists and intellectuals. After World War I it grew increasingly nationalistic and supportive of the war veterans that Mussolini was courting and in March 1919 became the organ of the new Fascist movement.

Il Popolo d'Italia was the 'official' newspaper of the regime after 1922, and its editorial positions were necessary points of reference for the entire Italian press (q.v.). Mussolini continued to have direct influence on its content, often writing articles himself and keeping in almost daily contact by telephone with its director and editors. During the late 1930s the paper had a daily circulation of less than one hundred thousand, in addition to its special color-illustrated supplement *Rivista illustrata*, which sold more than sixty thousand copies. *Il Popolo d'Italia* also published a monthly journal of political commentary, *Gerarchia*, edited by Margherita Sarfatti (q.v.).

Il Popolo d'Italia ceased publication after the July 1943 coup that unseated Mussolini. The dictator, recognizing that his authority was severely limited by Hitler in the Italian Social Republic (q.v.), refused to reestablish the paper after 1943.

For further information see: DSPI; Philip V. Cannistraro, *La fabbrica del consenso* (Rome-Bari: Laterza, 1975); Valerio Castronovo, *La stampa italiana dall'unità al fascismo* (Rome-Bari: Laterza, 1970).

PVC

POPULAR CULTURE, MINISTRY OF. See **MINISTRY OF POPULAR CULTURE.**

POPULAR PARTY. See **PARTITO POPOLARE ITALIANO (PPI).**

PRAMPOLINI, ENRICO (b. Modena, April 20, 1894; d. Rome, June 18, 1956). A Futurist architect, sculptor, and painter from 1912 and later a member of the Neo-Futurists, Prampolini was editor of *Noi* and in 1918 wrote "Futurist Atmosphere Structure—Basis for an Architecture," which appeared in that journal. Prampolini designed the backdrop for a Futurist play by Anton G. Bragaglia (q.v.) called *Thais* (1916), which utilized geometric forms, colors, and effects in experimental forms. He also designed the Futurist Pavilion for the Esposizione di Torino in 1928 and did much of the decoration for the Exhibit of the Fascist Revolution (*see* MOSTRA DELLA RIVOLUZIONE FASCISTA) in 1932. During the Fascist period Prampolini received numerous prizes and awards from the government, including membership in the Royal Academy of Italy (q.v.).

For further information see: *Chi è?* (1948); Caroline Tisdall and Angelo Bozzolla, *Futurism* (London: Thames and Hudson, Ltd., 1977).

JH

PRATOLINI, VASCO (b. Florence, October 19, 1913). A major Italian novelist, Pratolini came from a working-class background and was self-educated. As a young, idealistic intellectual in the 1920s he began to contribute to liberal Fascist journals and believed that the regime was capable of stimulating a genuine transformation of Italian culture. His own populist views especially coincided with the antibourgeois thrust of the Strapaese (*see* STRACITTÀ/STRAPAESE) movement. He contributed to *Il Bargello* (Florence), the student journal that was increasingly critical of official policy, and in 1938 cofounded *Campo di Marte*, which the government closed down a year later for its "subversive" ideas.

Pratolini's break with Fascism did not formally come until 1943, when he joined the Communist underground. By then he had already begun the transition to neorealism that many other young Italian writers and intellectuals were making. His major works of the period were *Via de'Magazzini* (1942), *Il Quartiere* (1945), and *Cronache di poveri amanti* (1947).

For further information see: *Chi è?* (1948); Giorgio Luti, *Cronache letterarie tra le due guerre* (Bari: Laterza, 1966); Edward R. Tannenbaum, *The Fascist Experience* (New York: Basic Books, 1972).

PVC

PREFECTS. Under the liberal state, the prefect was the central government's direct agent and representative in the province. His responsibilities as electoral manager and executor of government policy often confused political and administrative functions. Such an effective instrument of control naturally figured in Mussolini's plans for the restructuring of the state, which initially promised little more than a strengthened central power but by 1925 were expressed in totalitarian (q.v.) terms of a supreme and indivisible state authority.

Up to 1925-26, however, the prefect's position was determined by the circumstances of Fascism's emergence as a mass movement in northern and central Italy between late 1920 and 1922. In this period the Fascist movement-party achieved control in the provinces, subordinating and even superseding prefectural authority in the process. Some prefects openly connived with Fascism's violent anti-Socialist offensive. More often, they were unable to maintain public order because of their local subordinates' complicity in squadrist (*see* SQUADRISTI) violence. Further undermined by contradictory or nonexistent guidance from central government, the prefects were abandoned to establish, as best they could, working relations with the local Fascist movement. By summer 1922 in many areas the party, buttressed by the squads, had usurped the prefects' functions and replaced them as the arbiter of provincial affairs.

This informal party-state dualism was left unresolved in the Fascist government's early years. Whatever Mussolini's basic wishes for "normalization," he recognized that the party was his major lever of power while Fascist control of the country was still incomplete and the loyalty of existing government organs untried. So despite central directives like Mussolini's circular to the prefects of

June 1923, which reiterated the principle of state supremacy and demarcation of party and state spheres of competence, party hegemony over the prefects remained unchallenged in the provinces. Local party pressures often secured the transfer of recalcitrant prefects or conversely, the retention of subservient officials.

Luigi Federzoni's (q.v.) appointment as interior minister in 1924 indicated a willingness to dispute party control. But his efforts foundered on the prefects' continued inferiority to the provincial squads, revived in response to the Matteotti Crisis (q.v.) and actively encouraged by party secretary Roberto Farinacci (q.v.). After Mussolini's apparent capitulation to extremist Fascism in January 1925, the central government ministries, particularly the interior, were exposed to the full force of the party's campaign for "Fascistization." Reflecting extremist pressures, legislation of November-December 1925 attacked freemasonry, strong among central and local bureaucrats, and gave the government powers to remove civil servants considered politically unacceptable to the regime.

Further legislation establishing the institutional framework of dictatorship restored and enhanced the prefects' powers. The law of April 1926 required the prefect to supervise and coordinate the various state, provincial, and communal services so as to ensure "unity of political orientation." Laws of April and July gave the prefect supervisory powers over syndical bodies; and the new Public Security law of November allowed him wide discretion in measures of public order (see POLICE AND INTERNAL SECURITY).

As Mussolini well realized, these measures allowed him to dispense with the irregular party methods of control that increasingly threatened the consensus he intended to make the foundation of the regime. The laws affecting public officials provided adequate formal guarantees of political reliability and made counterproductive the party's spectacular witch-hunt. Farinacci's disgrace early in 1926 and the braking of the party offensive against the bureaucracy were indications of Mussolini's strategy of conciliating important interests. Another was his much-publicized circular to the prefects in January 1927, which popularized the advances in prefectural powers embodied in recent legislation and clarified their implications for the party. The circular denounced "anachronistic" squadrism, now that the state had armed itself with the machinery of repression, and asserted that the prefect was "the highest authority of the state in the province," to which the party owed subordinate collaboration. By elevating the prefect as the active agent of the Fascist state, the focus and animator of provincial activity, the circular implied that the party no longer enjoyed an independent political role. It was to become a functionary of the prefecture.

So by 1927, institutionally at least, the prefect was restored to the key position in the state's structure. What made the prefect's revamped authority a reality in the provinces was the impact of Augusto Turati's (q.v.) 1926-29 purge, which by disciplining thousands of exsquadrists and their local bosses finally broke the power of the squads that had imprisoned many prefects since 1921.

Conflicts between prefects and the party would continue to occur in the late 1920s and 1930s, but eventually the primacy of the state's indivisible authority was respected in practice as well as in legislation. In 1937, for instance, a decade of rivalry between the party's Provincial Intersyndical Committees and the prefect-run Provincial Economic Councils was resolved in favor of the latter, which assumed the former's role in price control, resolution of labor disputes, and negotiation of labor contracts.

The prefect's provincial hegemony was not without limits. The provincial offices of the state agencies, steadily proliferating in the 1930s in response to depression, autarchy, and war, remained functionally responsible to their respective central ministries. But the prefect generally provided the political impetus and coordination to their various activities.

Once the 1927 circular had proclaimed state supremacy over the party and confirmed the prefect as the most important agency of the Fascist state in the province, the question of the "Fascistization" of the Interior Ministry's personnel and mentality became a critical issue. The first batch of "Fascist prefects" nominated in 1923 were retired military men, hardly the party militants who would expect elevation in 1926 to sensitive positions in the fully-fledged Fascist state.

The number of Fascist prefects certainly increased at a regular rate, representing about one-fifth of the total in 1928, a quarter in 1934, and a third in 1937, partly in response to pressures from party men anxious, in light of the party's relative decline, to occupy posts of genuine authority and prestige. However, selection criteria for Interior appointments were apparently not significantly relaxed, and an insistence on technical as much as political suitability exposed the insufficiency of existing party cadres. Again, the number of career officials serving as prefects continued at a high level, confirmed in a 1937 decree establishing that at least 60 percent of all future prefects had to be drawn from the Interior's own ranks. The bulk of vacancies appeared to be filled by the promotion of younger career officials, and philofascist and non-Fascist officials were promoted alike, especially since evidence of resistance to the party was a positive attribute after 1936.

The relatively controlled degree of "Fascistization" of the prefects can be explained by the sheer inadequacy of the new Fascist ruling class; the bureaucratic assimilation of party candidates who adopted the attitudes of their career colleagues; and perhaps above all, Mussolini's reluctance to overhaul an existing service that combined proven competence and a broad political loyalty.

If such was the case, then the Fascist state was run in the provinces by officials who were by no means all convinced Fascists, which would have significant implications for the effectiveness of the "Fascistization" of provincial life.

For further information see: A. Aquarone, *L'Organizzazione dello Stato totalitario* (Turin: Einaudi, 1965); R. De Felice, *Mussolini il fascista* (Turin: Einaudi, 1966-68); R. De Felice, *Mussolini il duce* (Turin: Einaudi, 1974); R. C. Fried, *The Italian Prefects. A Study in Administrative Politics* (New Haven: Yale University Press, 1963); A. Lyttelton, *The Seizure of Power. Fascism in Italy 1919-1929*

(London: Weidenfeld & Nicolson, 1973); U. Marchetti, *Mussolini, i prefetti e i podestà*, 2d ed. (Mantua: Mussolinia, 1929).

PM

PRESS. Of all the mass media, the press was by far the most important information and propaganda vehicle in Fascist Italy. Indeed, it has been said that Mussolini's government was the "regime of journalism." Mussolini and an exceptional number of his closest associates had been newspapermen before the Fascist seizure of power, and for them journalism had been more than a professional apprenticeship. Numerous party officials, government ministers, and intellectuals continued to write for or publish newspapers throughout the Fascist period. They used the press both to maintain their personal influence and for the dissemination of their own ideas and ideological views. During the first decade in power, the regime's propaganda policies were focused almost exclusively on the press, while radio (q.v.) and film (*see* CINEMA) began to come into their own only in the 1930s.

Until 1934, when the first real propaganda ministry was formed (*see* MINISTRY OF POPULAR CULTURE), control of newspapers was exercised mainly through Mussolini's Press Office. As early as July 1923 the king had signed a measure giving the government wide powers to confiscate or suppress newspapers considered dangerous to national interests. This authority was not, however, implemented fully until the Matteotti Crisis (q.v.) in 1924. A further series of "Exceptional Decrees" (q.v.) in late 1926 provided for the suppression of all "antinationalist" parties and newspapers. In spite of these measures, however, Mussolini—unlike Hitler in Germany—moved with relative slowness in consolidating his power over the press. During the early 1920s the leading mass-circulation dailies were the *Corriere della Sera* (Milan), *La Stampa* (Turin), the *Giornale d'Italia* and the *Messaggero* (Rome), *Il Mattino* (Naples), and *Il Resto del Carlino* (Bologna). There were also party organs of which the Socialist *Avanti!* had by far the largest circulation. The major Fascist dailies were Mussolini's *Il Popolo d'Italia* (q.v.), Italo Balbo's (q.v.) *Corriere Padano*, Roberto Farinacci's (q.v.) *Cremona Nuova*, and the *Impero*, published by Mario Carli (q.v.) and Emilio Settimelli. The newspapers of the Communist and Socialist parties were not suppressed until four years after Mussolini became head of the government.

The PNF (Partito Nazionale Fascista) (q.v.) played a direct role in the "Fascistization" of *Il Mattino*. Founded in the 1890s by Edoardo Scarfoglio and published in the early 1920s by his sons Carlo and Paolo, the latter signed Benedetto Croce's (q.v.) "Manifesto of Anti-Fascist Intellectuals" (q.v.) in May 1925. Farinacci therefore supported Giovanni Preziosi (q.v.), director of a rival Neapolitan daily, *Il Mezzogiorno*, in his effort to put *Il Mattino* out of business. By December 15 *Il Mezzogiorno* was publishing party edicts telling Neapolitans to boycott *Il Mattino*. Three days later the Roman daily *Impero* announced that the Scarfoglio brothers had sold the paper, and in December 1931 Luigi Barzini Sr. (q.v.) took over the editorship of *Il Mattino*.

The *Giornale d'Italia*, whose national circulation of three hundred thousand was surpassed only by the *Corriere della Sera* and *La Stampa*, was the paper of conservative, nationalist Liberals like Sidney Sonnino (q.v.), the paper's founder, and Antonio Salandra (q.v.), a member of its board of directors for many years. Under the directorship of Alberto Bergamini (q.v.) until November 1923, and Vittorio Vettori thereafter, the *Giornale d'Italia* regarded the Fascists as defenders of the social order. It sought an alliance between Liberals and Fascists until Mussolini denounced the paper for its half-hearted support in the Matteotti Crisis. By early 1926 it gave in to Fascist party pressure to change its management and its policies. In March a board of directors took office under the presidency of Enrico Corradini (q.v.); in May the paper's new director, Virginio Gayda (q.v.) announced that the *Giornale d'Italia* had become Fascist.

Unlike the *Giornale d'Italia*, the *Corriere della Sera*, under the directorship of Luigi Albertini (q.v.) and his brother Alberto, was more or less anti-Fascist after the March on Rome (q.v.). Previously, however, its position had been ambivalent. Albertini condemned the Liberal government for not stemming the tide of red subversion (his coowners of the *Corriere* included leading Lombard industrialists like the Crespi brothers [q.v.], the Pirellis [q.v.], and the De Angelis). But he also abhorred Fascist violence. Hence, while the *Corriere* acknowledged Fascist successes in restoring civil order and improving the economic situation, it criticized Mussolini's government on ideological grounds. After the Matteotti murder the *Corriere* went into opposition and tried to use its influence to force Mussolini's resignation.

From January 1925 until the ouster of the Albertinis in November, the *Corriere* had to refrain from all political commentary in order to be allowed to publish. Even so, the campaign against them in the Fascist press became more and more acriminous in its demands that either they leave or the paper be suppressed. On November 29 a brief notice announced that the Albertinis had sold their shares.

After 1926 there was no longer an overt opposition press in Italy, and during the 1930s even the nonparty dailies became increasingly conformist. The largest dailies lived on their own resources; only the *Resto del Carlino* was taken over directly by the party. Efforts to boost the circulation of Mussolini's daily, *Il Popolo d'Italia*, failed to bring the figure even up to one hundred thousand in contrast to the six hundred thousand of the *Corriere della Sera*. By 1938 in Germany the Nazi party directly controlled daily newspapers where party papers accounted for one-third of the total circulation in the country; in Italy the Fascist party dailies never had more than one-tenth of the total circulation. It is important to note, however, that the nation's only wire service, the Agenzia Stefani (q.v.), was headed by one of Mussolini's most loyal followers, Manlio Morgagni (q.v.).

The press in Fascist Italy did succeed, however, in promoting conformity. Most journalists, including Mario Missiroli (q.v.), Guelfo Civinini, Renato Simoni, Paolo Monelli, and Giovanni Ansaldo (q.v.) continued in their jobs, and their familiar bylines reassured the public. Eminent scholars contributed articles regularly to important daily and weekly newspapers, and some, like Luigi Einaudi (q.v.) and Alberto De Stefani (q.v.), continued to write for the *Corriere della Sera* in the 1930s. Only outspoken anti-Fascists like Luigi Salvatorelli (q.v.) were barred from the press. (Some of the leading journalists of the opposition press went into exile, but they were a small minority compared to their counterparts in Nazi Germany.) While adulation of the Duce and the regime was required, it was also well rewarded by government and party subsidies to hundreds of journalists.

The most frustrating aspect of Italian journalism under Fascism was having to keep quiet about many kinds of real news. What was left out of newspapers often had a greater impact than overt propaganda. From 1926 on orders from Mussolini's Press Office told editors what they could and could not print. Regarding speeches of the Duce and his interviews with the foreign press, only the versions disseminated by the Stefani Agency could be printed. Provocative pictures of women— either nude or in short skirts—were prohibited, as were all references to lovers' disputes, broken homes, train wrecks, floods, and other public calamities. Most crime news was also to be strictly censored.

Beginning in 1930 Lando Ferretti (q.v.) and his successors sent out numerous written notices (*Note di Servizio*) on thin sheets of paper (*veline*).These orders to the press covered hundreds of subjects and, taken together over many years, projected through newspapers the official image of a stable, orderly, vigorous "New Italy" revitalized by Fascism.

The enforcement of censorship orders was usually left to the newspaper editors themselves, but the prefects (q.v.) were called in when these orders were disregarded. In some cases the prefects would censor items on their own. In other cases Mussolini's Press Office would wire the prefect of a particular province to take action concerning some local news item. Apparently news about sex and crime (*cronaca nera*) continued to tempt editors to print such items in the hope of increasing sales, despite repeated orders to eliminate such stories. In the year 1937-38 alone over four thousand censorship orders were issued, and over four hundred reprimands were imposed on papers violating them.

Italians were especially badly informed about foreign affairs by their daily newspapers. From the late 1920s through the mid-1930s the general tone of the orders regarding foreign powers was to take a reserved position, for Mussolini did not want to offend any foreign government irretrievably. Even toward the end of the Ethiopian War (q.v.) the press was ordered to maintain an "absolute reserve" toward the international crisis over the Rhineland.

The Spanish Civil War (q.v.) was handled very carefully during the six months after it began. Only when Italian "volunteers" fought in Spain was the war there given extensive coverage. By 1938 the press was instructed to speak often of the Rome-Berlin Axis (*see* AXIS, ROME-BERLIN) and of Hitler while playing down events in Britain and France. Censorship of foreign news became particularly strict once Italy entered World War II.

It was very difficult for most Italians to get any news from abroad except from the Fascist-controlled press, radio, and newsreels. Foreign newspapers were frequently smuggled into the country.

In the 1930s the most important uncontrolled source for foreign news was the Vatican's *Osservatore Romano* (q.v.). Ordinarily this semiofficial Vatican daily printed only twenty thousand copies a day, but in the late 1930s its circulation was two hundred and fifty thousand. In addition to foreign news not available in the Italian press, the *Osservatore* had a half column of extracts from papers like the *Times* and *Le Temps*, which were forbidden in Italy.

Censorship and propaganda made the Italian press provincial. Even nationally circulated dailies had to limit the news to what was officially approved. The small-town press concentrated on local events in addition to the press releases on the "benefits" of the regime. Most of the provincial capitals had newspapers that were directly controlled by the PNF (Partito Nazionale Fascista) (q.v.) or local party bosses. The typical large-city dailies had more foreign and national news of specific events, but no presentations that might prompt their readers to see the Italian scene in an unfavorable light—such as free elections or trade-union activities. Most of the copy in the larger dailies concerned the nonpolitical activities of "personalities," as well as want ads, sports, entertainment, and serial novels.

Mussolini's sustained personal interest in the press accounts in large part for its importance to the regime. He spent several hours each day reading newspapers and clipping articles, regularly telephoned instructions to the editors of his Milan paper, *Il Popolo d'Italia*, and frequently wrote articles for it. It is revealing that during the last days of April 1945, while partisan and Allied armies closed in on his Salò Republic (*see* ITALIAN SOCIAL REPUBLIC), Mussolini was obsessed with studying and notating newspaper articles. Yet it is not surprising that the press played so important a role in a regime sustained to a great degree by propaganda.

For further information see: Philip V. Cannistraro, *La fabbrica del consenso* (Rome-Bari: Laterza, 1975); Valerio Castronovo, *La stampa italiana dall' unità al fascismo* (Bari: Laterza, 1970); Edward R. Tannenbaum, *The Fascist Experience* (New York: Basic Books, 1972).

PVC

PREZIOSI, GIOVANNI (b. Torella dei Lombardi, October 24, 1881; d. Milan, April 25, 1945). The major Fascist theoretician of political anti-Semitism (q.v.), Preziosi entered the priesthood as a young man but later left it for a career in journalism. As early as 1904 he began writing on emigration and demography. An interventionist in 1914-15 (*see* INTERVENTIONIST CRISIS, 1914-1915), he joined the Italian Nationalist Association (q.v.) and collaborated with Maffeo Pantaleoni in both the interventionist *fasci* of 1915 and in the Fascio parlamentare di difesa nazionale (q.v.). In 1913 he founded the journal *La Vita Italiana*, which he continued to publish for more than thirty years.

Preziosi's sustained interest in anti-Semitism did not emerge until 1919-20, but thereafter he became the earliest, most consistent, and fanatical proponent of racism in Italian Fascism. Believing in the existence of an "international Jewish conspiracy," he published an Italian edition of the *Protocols of the Elders of Zion* in 1920. From 1923 to 1929 he directed *Il Mezzogiorno* (Naples). He became increasingly well known in the 1930s, especially after Hitler came to power in Germany, and Preziosi found in Roberto Farinacci (q.v.) a powerful ally within the regime. Preziosi's ideas received serious attention from Mussolini only in 1937-38 during the preparations for the passage of the first Fascist anti-Semitic legislation and, with Farinacci's influence. He was made a minister of state in 1938.

After the 1943 coup against Mussolini, Preziosi fled to Germany. Together with Farinacci and Alessandro Pavolini (q.v.), he began a series of hardline radio broadcasts to Italy from a Munich station, inveighing against the "traitors" within Fascism. Hitler and Nazi officials considered him one of the few trustworthy Fascist leaders, and Alfred Rosenberg even wanted him as the head of a reconstituted Fascist government. He returned to Italy in December, and in March 1944—with pressures from Berlin—Preziosi was made head of a new racial office attached to the presidency of the Council of Ministers in the Salò Republic (*see* ITALIAN SOCIAL REPUBLIC). In this capacity he advocated extremist measures for the "final solution" of the Jewish question in Italy. He and his wife committed suicide in Milan on the eve of the liberation of the city.

For further information see: *Chi è?* (1936); F. W. Deakin, *The Brutal Friendship* (New York: Harper & Row, 1962); Renzo De Felice, "Giovanni Preziosi e le origini del fascismo," *Rivista storica del socialismo* (September-December 1962); Renzo De Felice, *Mussolini il rivoluzionario* (Turin: Einaudi, 1965).

PVC

PREZZOLINI, GIUSEPPE (b. Perugia, January 27, 1882). Prezzolini was a leading figure in the intellectual transformation of Italy that occurred at the turn of the century and against which the intellectual origins of Fascism must be seen. In 1903 he cofounded (with Giovanni Papini [q.v.]) and directed the cultural review *Leonardo* (Florence, 1903-07) and then *La Voce* (Florence, 1908-16). A proponent of anti-rationalist philosophy in what has been termed the "revolt against positivism," between 1903 and 1905 he also collaborated with Enrico Corradini's (q.v.) Nationalist, anti-Socialist journal, *Il Regno* (Florence). After the outbreak of World War I Prezzolini helped turn *La Voce* into an interventionist journal, and in 1915 he was the Roman correspondent for Mussolini's *Il Popolo d'Italia*. In 1916-17 Prezzolini directed the historical division of the Mobilization Office and after the war worked in the League of Nations.

Prezzolini's early views on Fascism, especially after the March on Rome (q.v.), were not uniformly positive, and his book *Le Fascisme* (Paris, 1925) vacillated between admiration and criticism. In 1930 he became professor of Italian literature at Columbia University, where he directed its Casa Italiana until 1940, and then became a major Fascist propagandist in the United States. After World War II he returned to Europe and lives in Lugano, Switzerland.

For further information see: *Chi è?* (1936); Giuseppe Prezzolini, *L'italiano inutile* (Milan: 1953); Giuseppe Prezzolini and G. Papini, *Vecchio e nuovo nazionalismo* (Milan: 1914); Giuseppe Prezzolini, *Le fascisme* (Paris: 1925); Giuseppe Prezzolini, *The Legacy of Italy* (New York: 1948).

PVC

PRICOLO, FRANCESCO (b. Grumento Nova, Potenza, January 30, 1891). Chief of staff and undersecretary of the Air Force from October 31, 1939, to November 15, 1941, General Pricolo took over the chaos Giuseppe Valle (q.v.) left and succeeded by June 1940 in preparing the Air Force to face war with some modern equipment and prospect of success. However, Pricolo's jealous refusal to delegate operational control over units cooperating with other services and his insistence (in accordance with Regia Aeronautica tradition) on a strategic role the Air Force was not equipped to play limited its effectiveness. Pricolo also served as Mussolini's confidential informant in Albania during the 1940-41 winter campaign. He resigned under pressure in November 1941 after a clash with Ugo Cavallero (q.v.), whose orders to send to North Africa Italy's first batch of modern fighters Pricolo apparently disobeyed (the aircraft were allegedly still awaiting engine sand filters necessary for desert operation).

For further information see: Francesco Pricolo, *Ignavia contro eroismo* (Rome: Ruffolo, 1946); Francesco Pricolo, *La Regia Aeronautica nella seconda guerra mondiale* (Milan: Longanesi, 1971).

MK

PUBLIC WORKS. From the moment he came to power Mussolini demonstrated a remarkably consistent commitment to a large-scale program of public works projects for Italy. Whether funded and sponsored by the central government, local municipalities, or the PNF (Partito Nazionale Fascista) (q.v.), Mussolini considered public works initiatives for two basic reasons: as concrete proof— propaganda—of the regime's "revolutionary" transformation of the country and as a partial solution to the unemployment problem.

Public works programs covered a wide variety of undertakings, including railroad expansion and electrification, the construction of roads, highways, and tunnels, the building of schools, public edifices, and popular housing, and urban renewal projects. The rebuilding of large sections of Rome and the archaeological excavations that coincided with the Romanità (q.v.) campaign also fell within the public works category. (The regime's land reclamation program of Bonifica Integrale [q.v.] was actually but one aspect of the larger public works idea.)

In the first ten years of the regime, almost 25 billion lire were poured into public works projects, more than the central government had spent in the previous sixty years. Although expenditures for land reclamation experienced a sudden drop during the depression of the 1930s, other public works programs were increased in response to rising unemployment. It is difficult to estimate the real impact of public works on the unemployment problem, but it is clear that they were successful in building the kind of popular consensus that Mussolini desired.

For further information see: Shepard B. Clough, *The Economic History of Modern Italy* (New York: Columbia University Press, 1964); Renzo De Felice, *Mussolini il duce* (Turin: Einaudi, 1974); Ministero dei Lavori Pubblici, *Opere pubbliche, 1922-1932* (Rome: 1933).

PVC

PUGLIESE, UMBERTO (b. Alessandria, January 13, 1880; d. Sorrento, July 15, 1961). A naval designer, Pugliese devised an unusual underwater protection system (1916) used in large Italian warships built after 1925. He directed the shipyards at Castellamare and La Spezia (1921-30) and served as director general of construction at the Naval Ministry (1930-34) before becoming inspector general of naval engineers and president of the Naval Ministry's projects committee (1934). Pugliese helped redesign the *Cavour* and *Doria* class battleships, designed the *Littoria* class battleships, the *Montecucoli*, *Aosta*, and *Capitania Romani* class cruisers, and influenced all surface vessel designs. The 1938 anti-Semitic laws (*see* ANTI-SEMITISM) forced Pugliese to retire, but Mussolini recalled him in November 1940 to supervise salvage of ships sunk at Taranto (*see* TARANTO, ATTACK ON). Pugliese's designs were excellent, but his antitorpedo system, not fully watertight, failed at Taranto and Matapan.

For further information see: Siegfried Breyer, *Battleships and Battlecruisers 1905-1970* (Garden City: Doubleday, 1973); Aldo Fraccaroli, *Italian Warships of World War II* (London: Ian Allan, 1968); *Enciclopedia Italiana*, Appendix I.

BRS

Q

QUADRUMVIRS. The Quadrumvirs were the four men appointed by Mussolini on October 16, 1922, to control and direct the March on Rome (q.v.): Emilio De Bono (q.v.), Cesare Maria De Vecchi (q.v.), Italo Balbo (q.v.), and Michele Bianchi (q.v.). Mussolini proposed that after October 21 the Quadrumvirs would assume total power over the Fascist movement in preparation for the assault against Rome. In reality, none of them played a leading role in the actual seizure of power.

During the Fascist regime, the four men were heaped with honors and given various positions in the government, but their influence on Mussolini and official policies varied greatly according to their individual status. As Quadrumvirs, each held a seat on the Fascist Grand Council (q.v.).

For further information see: DSPI; Antonio Rapaci, *La Marcia su Roma*, 2 vols. (Rome: Caresi, 1963).

MSF

QUEBEC CONFERENCE (September 1944). The second Quebec Conference (September 13-17, 1944), and subsequent Roosevelt-Churchill discussions at Hyde Park (September 17-19, 1944), led to a significant innovation in Allied policies in Italy. Churchill arrived at Quebec after an inspection tour of the Italian front. The British prime minister was impressed by Italy's evident need for economic aid and was determined to strengthen Britain's control over Italian affairs. Roosevelt's stimulus to action was an approaching presidential election in which the Italian-American vote could play a significant role in his own fortunes and those of the Democratic party. In addition, important civilian agencies of the United States government were pressing for a more aggressive American role in Italy, as were a number of powerful domestic special-interest groups. Roosevelt proposed a number of reforms aimed at increasing the economic assistance Italy received and decreasing Allied control over Italian politics. Churchill countered with a proposal for a reorganization of the Allied Control Commission (q.v.). After a week of negotiations Britain's reorganization scheme was accepted in exchange for a broad policy statement of Allied intent to institute economic and political reforms in Italy. This policy initiative was subsequently known as the "New Deal for Italy." Although the "New Deal" did not lead to immediate substantive changes in Italy's position, it did mark the first step in a major United States involvement in Italy.

For further information see: David W. Ellwood, *L'alleato nemico* (Milan: Feltrinelli, 1977); *Foreign Relations of the United States. The Conference at Quebec, 1944* (Washington, D.C.: U.S. Government Printing Office, 1972).

JEM

QUOTA NOVANTA (QUOTA 90). Despite efforts by Mussolini in 1925 to defend the value of the Italian lira and offset the impact of inflation, by the end of July 1926 the lira continued to depreciate to a new low of 153 to the English pound sterling (the pound had just been revalued to an artificially high level). Mussolini announced his intention to stabilize the currency in the Pesaro speech of August 18, 1926. His motives were clearly political and propagandistic. Finance Minister Volpi (*see* VOLPI DI MISURATA, COUNT GIUSEPPE) and most banking leaders agreed on the need to establish a strong deflationary policy, but while Volpi favored a rate of 120 to the pound, Mussolini insisted on 90. Although the Confindustria (*see* INDUSTRY) also demanded stabilization, the industrialists believed that Mussolini's "quota 90" was too high.

While not totally oblivious to the protests and concerns of the industrial-banking world, Mussolini put his decision into effect on December 21, 1927, at 92.46 lire to the pound. The result of his "victory" was to create the so-called "stabilization crisis" that hurt workers and small industrialists most and the Italian economy in general. Tariffs were raised and wages reduced to satisfy the industrialists. The price of wheat fell, imports declined, and unemployment rose.

For further information see: Renzo De Felice, *Mussolini il fascista* (Turin: Einaudi, 1968); Roland Sarti, "Mussolini and the Industrial Leadership in the Battle of the Lira, 1925-27," *Past and Present* 47 (May 1970).

PVC

RACISM. See **ANTI-SEMITISM**.

RADIO. Although Guglielmo Marconi (q.v.) pioneered the development of the radio after World War I, Mussolini was relatively slow to see the potential for its propaganda uses and did not move to control it fully until the late 1920s.

In 1923 Marconi pointed out to Mussolini that there were important political advantages in having a modern radio network in Italy, and in August 1924 the Unione Radiofonica Italiana (URI) was established. Stations were set up in Rome, Milan, and Naples over the next several years, and URI was given a temporary monopoly over broadcasting. In November 1927 the Ente Italiano Audizioni Radiofoniche (EIAR) replaced URI and to this day it remains a state-directed public agency. The government's control over EIAR's actual program content was exercised through a "committee of vigilance" established that same year, and only ten years later was a specialized division for radio created within the Ministry of Popular Culture (q.v.). A persistent problem, however, remained the fact that Italians could freely listen to either Radio Vaticana or to foreign broadcasts to obtain unbiased or noncensored news.

By the end of the 1930s more than one million radio sets existed in Italy, and every major city had transmitters. In 1937 the regime created the Ente Radio Rurale to distribute radio sets to the farmers and peasants in the countryside, and an inexpensive "popular" radio called Radio Balilla was manufactured that same year.

News programs were broadcast daily through the "Giornale Radio" program, which received its items from the official news bureau, Agenzia Stefani (q.v.). Over the years the variety of political propaganda broadcasts multiplied, but the bulk of programming consisted of popular entertainment—music, plays, comedy, sports events, and children's programs. Specialized radio broadcasts for classroom listening, farmers, and factory workers were also developed in the late 1930s. The most successful program of political commentary was Roberto Forges Davanzati's (q.v.) "Cronache del Regime" that was started in the mid-1930s during the Ethiopian War (q.v.); during World War II a group of very effective announcers—especially Mario Appelius (q.v.)—delivered daily "Commenti ai Fatti del Giorno" about the war situation.

After Mussolini's fall in 1943, EIAR was reestablished in the Salò Republic (*see* ITALIAN SOCIAL REPUBLIC) but was largely under German control and not very efficient. Mussolini himself wrote many of the texts for the "Corrispondenza Repubblicana" program of the period, but effective competition was provided by the partisan clandestine radios in the north and the Pietro Badoglio (q.v.) government in the south.

For further information see: Philip V. Cannistraro, "The Radio in Fascist Italy," *Journal of European Studies* 2 (1972); Franco Monteleone, *La radio italiana nel periodo fascista* (Venice: Marsilio, 1976).

PVC

RAHN, RUDOLF (b. Ulm, Germany, March 16, 1900; d. Düsseldorf, Germany, 1975). German ambassador and plenipotentiary in Italy from 1943 to 1945, Rahn took his doctorate at the University of Heidelberg in 1923. He entered the diplomatic service in 1927, working in the Secretariat of the League of Nations. He served in Turkey (1931-34), in Portugal (1937-39), and in France (1940-43) before becoming ambassador to Italy in 1943.

By the time he came to Italy Rahn already had the reputation of being a person in the confidence of the Nazi hierarchy, particularly of Heinrich Himmler, the head of the SS. In Paris he had served as a collaborator of the German ambassador, Otto Abetz, thus gaining experience in dealing with Vichy France as a German satellite. With Italy moving in August 1943 into an increasingly subordinate position in respect to Germany, Rahn counted as a visible sign of the "German menace" in the eyes of independently-minded Italians.

His arrival in Italy was, of course, followed closely by the Italian surrender to the Allies and the exercise of German control over more than half of the peninsula. Within the German supervisory administration Rahn held a significant position. As German ambassador to Rome and later to Mussolini's Salò (*see* ITALIAN SOCIAL REPUBLIC) regime (Rahn's headquarters were at Fusano), Rahn served also as the plenipotentiary of the German Reich for Italian affairs. This gave Rahn a role in the affairs of Italy equivalent to a partnership with the Army and the SS. The limits of the jurisdiction of Rahn on one side and of General Rudolph Toussaint and of Karl Wolff (q.v.) on the other were defined in several conferences in 1943 and 1944. His most significant impact was in the field of economic affairs, where he sought to arrest runaway inflation and opposed Mussolini's program of socialization, but also sought to manage Italian industry and agriculture to provide the greatest possible support to the German war effort. To this end he sponsored harsh control measures involving the sending of Italian workers to Germany, severe action against strikers, and the threat to transfer Italian industries threatened by the Allies into German territory.

In 1945 he was interned and not released until 1951. Thereafter he engaged in business and publishing activities including the publication of his apologetic memoirs.

For further information see: Enzo Collotti, *L'amministrazione tedesca dell' Italia occupata, 1943-1945. Studio e documenti* (Milano: Lerici editori, 1963); Rudolf Rahn, *Ruheloses Leben; Aufzeichnungen und Erinnerungen* (Stuttgart: Europäischer Buchklub, 1952); Luigi Villari, *The Liberation of Italy, 1943-1947* (Appleton, Wisconsin: Nelson, 1959).

ERB

RAS. The paramilitary bosses of provincial Fascism, the *ras* rose to sudden prominence during the armed terrorist offensive against the Socialist movement in 1921. These local tyrants, who derived their name from the term for Ethiopian chieftains, represented the most extreme form of power taken by Fascism as a movement based on the use of organized violence. Most of the *ras* began their careers in the Fascist movement as organizers and commanders of the action squads. With the increasing militarization of Fascism in the second half of 1920, their personal power grew with the expanding range of activities of the squads. As punitive expeditions against working-class leaders and institutions became the chief function of the movement in the winter of 1920-21, the *ras* used their base in the squads to extend their control over strictly political offices in the Fasci di Combattimento (q.v.), the local organizational cells of Fascism. Combining violence and intimidation with an ideology that exalted discipline, charismatic leadership, and force, they gradually emerged as fairly self-sufficient dictators of Fascism in their respective provinces.

The rise of the *ras* depended, to a great extent, on the general breakdown of state authority and the rule of law in Italy after the war. The absence of clear directives and support from a succession of weak governments in Rome between 1919 and 1922 encouraged prefects and their subordinates to come to terms with the *ras* and to tolerate their extra-legal activities. After two years of strikes and labor disturbances, many police officials openly collaborated with the squads in their assaults on the Socialists. Thus buttressed by the tacit and open support of state officials, the *ras* were able to exert near total power within the borders of their provinces.

As a group, the *ras* came from a wide range of social classes. The sons of aristocrats, large landowners, and successful professionals as well as ambitious parvenue could be found in their ranks. Often the *ras* were recent immigrants to their provinces; virtually all of them were extremely young and lacking in technical skills and education for the responsibilities that they exercised. With few exceptions they ruled through fear and intimidation and had a vested interest in maintaining a climate of violence and illegality in order to legitimize their power.

The dominant position of the *ras* in the provinces assured them an influential and independent role in the Fascist movement in the period prior to the March on Rome (q.v.). As the warlords of Fascism, they strongly favored a violent seizure of state power; their own reliance on coercion made them intransigent foes of any policies on the national level that might stabilize the political and social situation in the country. In the summer of 1921 the *ras* demonstrated their independent strength by spearheading a revolt within the movement that forced Mussolini to drop his proposals for a Pacification Pact (q.v.) with the Socialists. Although the *ras* finally recognized Mussolini as the unquestioned leader of Fascism in the fall of 1921 when the movement was transformed into a party, they continued to keep a tight hold on positions of power in the provinces. Not surprisingly, the following year they were the chief proponents of the March on Rome that helped bring Mussolini to power.

After the March on Rome in October 1922, the *ras* continued to be both a source of strength and of weakness for Mussolini. The Duce still relied on their coercive might to impose order and to stifle political opposition in the provinces, and on their ability to mount impressive mass meetings and processions. The *ras* also proved to be an important source of strength for Mussolini during the elections of 1924 by controlling their districts and delivering votes by any and all means. On the other hand, the independence of the *ras* tended to limit Mussolini's own authority, while their brutality and coercive methods alienated respectable public opinion. Moreover, recurrent jealousies and rivalries among the *ras* provoked serious conflicts within the PNF (Partito Nazionale Fascista) (q.v.), a continuous source of instability and disorder that hampered Mussolini's restoration of state authority.

During the transitional years between 1922 and 1925, the *ras* were outspoken enthusiasts of a "second wave" of Fascist violence, and their pressures contributed to Mussolini's decision to set up a dictatorial regime in January 1925. Ironically, the very authoritarian state the *ras* had urged upon the Duce was the agent that finally broke their power as independent political actors. Centralizaton and bureaucratization of the party after 1926 undermined their local bases of power; the Fascist police took over the repressive functions previously performed by their squads. Some of the provincial bosses refused to accept the new regime and were violently purged, but most of the leading *ras* remained in public life, becoming high-level functionaries in the party and burgeoning Fascist state bureaucracy.

For further information see: Paul Corner, *Fascism in Ferrara, 1915-1925* (London: Oxford University Press, 1975); Renzo De Felice, *Mussolini il fascista* (Turin: Einaudi, 1966); Adrian Lyttelton, *The Seizure of Power: Fascism in Italy, 1919-1929* (London: Weidenfeld & Nicolson, 1973).

ALC

RAZZA, LUIGI (b. Monteleone di Calabria, December 12, 1892; d. Cairo, August 7, 1935). A Fascist journalist and minister, Razza came out of the revolutionary syndicalist tradition (he was a disciple of Filippo Corridoni [q.v.]). As a young man Razza organized peasants in Puglia, was an avid interventionist in World War I, and a member of the Fasci di Azione Rivoluzionaria (q.v.). He fought as a volunteer in the war, attended the Piazza San Sepolcro rally in March 1919 (*see* SANSEPOLCRISTI), organized the Fasci di Combattimento (q.v.) in the Trentino area, and served as an editor for *Il Popolo d'Italia*.

In 1923 Razza was secretary of the Fascist syndicates in Milan, was elected a deputy in 1924, and in 1927 became national secretary of the Federation of Agricultural Syndicates. The following year he was appointed president of the Confederation of Agricultural Syndicates and a member of the Fascist Grand Council (q.v.). He served also as the first president of the Commission for Internal Migration, and in January 1935 Mussolini made him minister of public works. He died in August of that year in an air accident over Egypt.

For further information see: DSPI; NO (1928; 1937); David D. Roberts, *The Syndicalist Tradition and Italian Fascism* (Chapel Hill: University of North Carolina Press, 1979).

PVC

REALE, EGIDIO (b. Lecce, April 24, 1888; d. November 1, 1958). A diplomat, lawyer, and Republican anti-Fascist, Reale spent a major part of the Fascist era in exile in Switzerland. A member of a Republican industrialist family in Rome, he took his degrees in law, economic and commercial science, and international law. His law practice in Rome (1912-19) was interrupted by voluntary service in World War I. In 1914 he was named to the directorate of the Republican party (*see* PARTITO REPUBBLICANO ITALIANO), a position that he held until 1926.

Because of his anti-Fascist views and his party activities, he was arrested and sentenced to confinement. He managed to take refuge with his family in the Swiss Ticino, where he resumed his professional career and his anti-Fascist activities in exile. He instituted an ambitious publishing program, "Nuove Edizioni di Capolago," the first product of which was Guglielmo Ferrero's (q.v.) *Liberazione*. Reale taught at a number of educational institutions, including the Academy of International Law (The Hague) and the Institute of International Studies (Geneva).

In 1945 he returned to Italy. He became minister plenipotentiary and envoy extraordinary (1946-53) and ambassador (1953-55) to Switzerland. In 1955 he served as president of the Italian Commission for UNESCO. He continued to contribute to a number of journals and was named to numerous European juridical and diplomatic academies.

For further information see: *Chi è?* (1948); Frances Keene, *Neither Liberty Nor Bread* (New York and London: Harper & Brothers, 1940); Egidio Reale, *La politique fasciste et la Société des nations* (Paris: A. Pedone, 1932); *Egidio Reale e il suo tempo* (Florence: La Nuova Italia, 1961).

CLK

REALE, EUGENIO (b. Naples, June 8, 1905). A legislator, cabinet member, and diplomat in post-World War II governments, Eugenio Reale devoted his efforts to organization and direction of the Italian Communist party (Partito Comunista Italiano—PCI) (q.v.) for a quarter century. Born into a prosperous family, he participated in youth organizations of the Socialist party. While completing his medical degree, he undertook many political activities, becoming secretary of the PCI in Naples. He joined other young southern intellectuals in supporting the PCI's new policy (the *svolta* of 1930) of revolutionary efforts inside Italy. Reale, Emilio Sereni (q.v.), Manlio Rossi-Doria, and Giorgio Amendola developed a network of industrial cells which printed and distributed clandestine periodicals.

In 1931 Reale was arrested for his sub-rosa activities. His 1932 prison sentence by the Special Tribunal for the Defense of the State (q.v.) began a decade of confinement and surveillance. After being conditionally pardoned, he began to reestablish the underground Neapolitan Communist organization. He was again arrested after May Day 1935 and again sentenced to "supervised liberty."

Reale left Italy in 1937 for the PCI Foreign Center in Paris. He assisted in editing *La Voce degli Italiani*, contributing articles under the pseudonym "Jorano." He was interned in France in 1940, then arrested, and ultimately extradited to Italy, where he was transferred to the workhouse at Imperia. Freed in July 1943, he returned to Naples to reorganize the PCI. Reale's efforts to regain the initiative from the Trotskyites in the rebuilding of the General Confederation of Labor (*see* CONFEDERAZIONE GENERALE DEL LAVORO) produced a violent confrontation. In the PCI's first National Council, he took a position in favor of unified Socialist-Communist unions. And in the *Giornale del Popolo* he continued to defend the Committee of National Liberation (q.v.) and the politics of unity in polemic with Trotskyites and Bordigists (*see* BORDIGA, AMADEO).

With the liberation of Italy Reale began an active career in public office. A deputy to the Constituent Assembly (*see* COSTITUENTE), he was appointed to the High Court of Justice (1944). He served as undersecretary of foreign affairs in the cabinets of Ivanoe Bonomi (q.v.), Ferruccio Parri (q.v.), and Alcide De Gasperi (q.v.) and then as ambassador to Poland (1947). A member of the PCI Central Committee, Reale participated in the founding of the Cominform. He remained active in PCI affairs until leaving the party in 1956 after the events in Hungary.

For further information see: DSPI; MOI (4); Eugenio Reale, *Nascita del Cominform* (Milan: Mondadori, 1958); Paolo Spriano, *Storia del PCI*, vols. 2-5 (Turin: Einaudi, 1969-75).

CLK

REFERENDUM OF 1946. The Referendum of 1946 was the outgrowth of a pledge made to the Italian people by the British and American governments on October 13, 1943, when Italy was recognized as a cobelligerent of the Allies. The pledge promised that at the end of the war the Italian people would be able to choose the form of government they desired. On October 21, 1943, King Victor Emmanuel III (q.v.) wrote to General Noel Mason MacFarlane, Chief of the Allied Military Mission in southern Italy, promising that a Parliament freely elected after the end of hostilities could act as a constituent assembly and reform all institutions completely. The king would respect the nation's will as manifested by its elected representatives.

After the end of the war a long struggle began over the implementation of the promises. Promonarchist forces sought to delay the day of reckoning. They also sought to remove the power of decision from an elected assembly to a popular referendum. After prolonged maneuvering, the postwar Italian government of Alcide De Gasperi (q.v.) set the date of June 2, 1946. On that date the Italian people, through universal adult suffrage, would choose between a monarchy or a republic. They would at the same time elect delegates to a constituent assembly from lists of nominees put forward by the political parties.

In the weeks preceding June 2 the monarchist forces enlisted the Vatican and the Roman Catholic Church in the effort to save the House of Savoy. They persuaded King Victor Emmanuel III to abdicate on May 10, 1946, in favor of his son Umberto II (q.v.). They bombarded the Allied Control Commission (q.v.) with unsuccessful pleas to postpone the date. They converted the campaign from a choice between monarchy or republic to a struggle between monarchy and communism.

On June 2, by a vote of 54 percent to 46 percent, the Italian people chose a republic. There was a clear monarchist majority in the south, especially in the zone of Naples, with republican majorities in the center and north. Enrico De Nicola (q.v.), a distinguished Neapolitan jurist and the last president of the pre-Fascist Chamber of Deputies (*see* PARLIAMENT), was picked by the cabinet to be the provisional president of the Republic. Thus the reign of the House of Savoy (1861-1946) came to an end. It had paid for Victor Emmanuel's twenty years of collusion with Fascism and for his escape from Rome on September 8, 1943, the day of the announcement of Italy's surrender to the Allies, leaving central and northern Italy defenseless and helpless against a Nazi occupation force.

For further information see: Fernando Etnasi, *2 Giugno 1946: Repubblica o monarchia?* (Rome: DIES, 1966)

NK

RENZETTI, GIUSEPPE. Mussolini's confidential agent in Berlin, Major Renzetti served on the Italian commission in Upper Silesia in 1920-21 and married the daughter of a prominent Jewish family of Gleiwitz. He first met Mussolini during the latter's German visit in 1922. Consul in Leipzig in 1925, president of the Italian Chamber of Commerce (1926), and subsequently Italian consul general in Berlin, Renzetti maintained close contacts with Hitler and the other top National Socialists (particularly Göring) from the end of 1930 on. Renzetti assisted in the formation and frequently attempted renewal of the "Harzburg Front" of the German right and in the negotiations that produced the Hitler cabinet in January 1933. A rival of Vittorio Cerruti (q.v.), Renzetti conveyed to Rome Hitler's June 1935 request for the ambassador's removal; shortly before, Cerruti had apparently succeeded in arranging Renzetti's transfer to San Francisco. By early 1937 Renzetti was back in Berlin, and he remained there despite friction with G. Ciano (q.v.). In April 1940 Renzetti transmitted a Göring offer of a free hand in Greece in return for Italian entry into the war and that summer emphasized to German ruling circles Mussolini's aversion to a compromise peace with Britain. He died shortly after the end of World War II.

For further information see: Renzo De Felice, *Mussolini e Hitler* (Florence: le Monnier, 1975).

MK

REPUBLICAN PARTY. See **PARTITO REPUBBLICANO ITALIANO**.

RESISTANCE, ARMED. The Armed Resistance was an anti-German, anti-Fascist struggle that took place in the northern half of Italy after the Pietro Badoglio (q.v.) government's announcement of the armistice with the Allies on September 8, 1943 (*see* ARMISTICE) and the German seizure of the north. In addition to guerrilla warfare, there was widespread passive resistance as well as generous acts of assistance given to former Allied prisoners of war and other refugees. The Armed Resistance was made up of remnants of the Italian armed forces that had been disarmed by the Germans, supplemented by large numbers of men anxious to escape military and labor conscription by the enemy, and by numerous anti-Fascists who had exposed themselves after the coup d'etat of July 25. Resisters came from all walks of life but were especially numerous among the peasantry, workers, professional and middle classes. A good many lower clergy and women were also involved.

The first episodes of combat occurred in Rome, Naples, and Piedmont in September 1943. Thereafter, fighting was concentrated in central Italy, in the mountainous arc surrounding the Po Valley, and in the industrial cities. The Kingdom of Italy's declaration of war on Germany (October 13, 1943) gave formal sanction to the legality of the popular struggle. Henceforth, efforts were made in the south to organize an Italian Corps of Liberation (CIL-Corpo Italiano di Liberazione) to fight alongside the Allies in their drive up the peninsula, while in the north large numbers of young men flocked to the mountains to organize guerrilla bands against the Germans and Mussolini's puppet Italian Social Republic (q.v.). Still others organized terrorist units (GAP-Gruppi di Azione Patriottica) in the cities. There was also a concerted effort to foment industrial strikes in the northern cities in March 1944. American Office of Strategic Services and British Special Operations Executive officials established contact with leaders of the Armed Resistance during the autumn of 1943, arranging for radio communication, liaison officers, and supply drops to the bands. Such aid became increasingly important after the spring of 1944.

In January 1944 the Committee of National Liberation for Upper Italy (CLNAI-Comitato di Liberazione Nazionale per l'Alta Italia) was established in Milan to serve as a five-party clandestine government and to coordinate the struggle. This was supplemented in June by the formation in Milan of the Comando Generale/Corpo Volontari della Libertà (CVL), as the military side of the Armed Resistance was officially labeled. In August the Rome government dispatched General Raffaele Cadorna (q.v.) to serve as adviser to the CVL.

Though Communists have propagandized the "unity" of the Resistance, there was actually much rivalry for control of territory and access to supply drops, to say nothing of maneuvering for future political advantage. From the outset the Resistance consisted of two wings: (1) the autonomous units, made up initially from disbanded elements of the Italian Army and tending to be cautious in their military strategy and supportive of the royal government in the south; and (2) the more politically activist wing, identified with the Communist, Action, and Socialist parties and the new Committees of National Liberation (CLNs). The latter wing was the stronger. It called for vigorous guerrilla warfare and radical reconstruction of Italy's political and economic structure. Most favored a republic based on the new CLNs and an economy that would be socialized to a considerable degree, but were willing to defer the thorny issue of Church-state relations until after the war. Communist forces made up the largest single group—their "Garibaldi" units, commanded by Luigi Longo (q.v.) and Pietro Secchia (q.v.), comprising perhaps 40 percent of the total number of partisans. The Action party (*see* PARTITO D'AZIONE) recruited the second largest group—its "Giellisti" (from the Giustizia e Libertà organization) forces, coordinated by Ferruccio Parri (q.v.), comprising about 25 percent of the total and being especially numerous in Piedmont. The remaining 35 percent of the partisans were divided among the Socialists, Christian Democrats, and Liberals. The Socialists tended to concentrate their activity among the city workers. Christian Democratic resisters were conspicuous in Venetia and Lombardy. They and the Liberals often worked closely with the autonomous units.

One of the issues that tended to split the left wing of the Resistance was the protracted struggle between the CLNs and the Royal-Badoglio government in 1943-44, which culminated in the surprising decision of Communist leader Palmiro Togliatti (q.v.) to enter Badoglio's government in April, to the dismay of the Actionists and Socialists. In June this government was replaced by that of Ivanoe Bonomi (q.v.), who had headed the underground Rome CLN. At the same time King Victor Emmanuel III (q.v.) stepped aside in favor of Prince Umberto (*see* UMBERTO II) as lieutenant-general of the realm. Premier Bonomi governed with the support of all the CLN parties until November 1944, at which time the Socialists and Actionists pulled out, charging that he had become too conservative.

Rome was liberated by the Allies on June 4 without an uprising by the Resistance. Florence's liberation in August was a different story. There, as in other parts of central Italy, the partisans played an important role in the fighting, and they tried to make clear to Rome their preference for a government resting on the local CLNs rather than on prefects sent in by the central government.

After August 1944 the Armed Resistance shifted to the Po Valley and its mountainous rim. The Germans quickly undertook ruthless comb-outs of partisan "republics" in such valleys as Ossola and elsewhere. Supply drops for the Resistance had to be sharply reduced in late summer when Allied aircraft were diverted to help the Polish Home Army in its Warsaw uprising. Later that autumn high British leaders began to fear that the Italian Resistance might replicate what was occurring in newly liberated Greece, where leftist guerrillas were fighting against British-backed monarchist forces. Finally, in mid-November Italian resisters received their cruelest blow when General Harold Alexander advised them to discontinue large-scale operations, as the Allies could not push out of the Apennines until spring.

The growing tension between the Armed Resistance and the Allies was reduced, however, on December 7 by the important agreements negotiated at Caserta by a CLNAI delegation headed by Parri. The Allies promised substantial arms and financial aid to the CLNAI-coordinated Resistance, provided the latter obeyed all Allied orders, including the turning in of arms at the war's end. At the same time the Bonomi government agreed to recognize the CLNAI as its "delegate" in the north. During the spring of 1945 the pace of Allied contacts with the Resistance increased and the number of resisters swelled rapidly.

Early in April 1945 the Allies pushed down into the Po Valley. Resistance fighters played a major role in the liberation of the Apennine-Liguria region, Genoa, Bologna, Milan, Turin, and Venice. In Genoa and Venice they safeguarded port facilities; throughout the north they helped prevent the enemy from engaging in "scorch" policies. On April 25 Mussolini belatedly sought to bargain with the CLNAI in Milan but soon fled instead to Lake Como, hoping to escape into Switzerland. Partisans captured him and other Fascist hierarchs on April 27; he was executed the next day. April 25 (the day of Milan's insurrection) is celebrated as the climax of the Armed Resistance, though fighting did not end in many places until May 2. In Trieste the Resistance was badly split between pro-Italian and pro-Yugoslav groups.

Some two hundred and fifty thousand Italians took part in the Armed Resistance at various stages. Total casualties were high, exceeding those of the Allied forces in Italy. To some thirty-six thousand partisans killed on Italian soil must be added ten thousand Italian civilians killed in reprisals, while some ten thousand Italian soldiers fighting alongside the Allied forces fell in combat. Another thirty-two thousand Italians died fighting in foreign Resistance movements, while a similar number were killed in German internment camps. Some eight thousand Jews were deported from Italy and killed by the Germans.

The political impact of the Armed Resistance reached its peak during the first month after the liberation. Thus, Ferruccio Parri was chosen to succeed Bonomi as premier (June-December 1945), but the role of the CLNs disappeared rapidly after Allied Military Government (q.v.) was temporarily established in the north and the traditional prefectural administrative structure was reinstated. The advent of the Christian Democratic leader, Alcide De Gasperi (q.v.), to the premiership in December 1945 marked the eclipse of the Resistance era in Italian politics. But its echoes were still to be felt in the national referendum of June 2, 1946, when all of Italy north of Rome voted solidly in favor of a new republican form of government.

For further information see: Roberto Battaglia, *Storia della Resistenza Italiana*, rev. ed. (Turin: Einaudi, 1964); Charles F. Delzell, *Mussolini's Enemies: The Italian Anti-Fascist Resistance*, rev. ed. (New York: Howard Fertig, 1974); Charles F. Delzell, "The Italian Anti-Fascist Resistance in Retrospect: Three Decades of Historiography," *Journal of Modern History* 47 (March 1975); Guido Quazza, *Resistenza e storia d'Italia: Problemi e ipotesi di ricerca* (Milan:

Feltrinelli, 1976); Massimo Salvadori, *Storia della Resistenza* (Venice: Neri Pozza, 1955).

CFD

REVISIONISM. In the years immediately following Mussolini's seizure of power (October 1922), the Fascist party experienced considerable internal division that assumed two different forms: dissidentism (q.v.) and revisionism.

Broadly speaking, revisionism represented the ideas of a small, relatively isolated group within Fascism led by men like Massimo Rocca (q.v.) and Giuseppe Bottai (q.v.). The revisionists were mainly intellectuals and ideologues, or conservative to moderate urban leaders. They wanted to temper the revolution and reconcile Fascism with Italy's political-historical traditions, an aim that meant compromise with other political forces.

The revisionists demanded constitutional reform, the creation of new institutions to fulfill their socioeconomic ideas, and the establishment of an efficient authoritarian regime. Most immediately, however, the revisionists were concerned over the future role of the PNF (Partito Nazionale Fascista) (q.v.), which they insisted had to be reformed before the state itself. Rocca, perhaps the most controversial of the revisionists, envisioned the party as the training ground for an elite vanguard of technocrats that would, through his *gruppi di competenza*, establish a managerial state apparatus. Like the other revisionists, Rocca believed the time for "normalization" had come and that the party of the *squadristi* (q.v.) had fulfilled its purpose and could be transformed to other, more genuinely revolutionary purposes.

But Rocca and the revisionists quickly found themselves engaged in a bitter struggle for power with the intransigent Fascists—men like Roberto Farinacci (q.v.) who generally represented the provincial, agrarian Fascism of the *squadristi* and the local party *ras* (q.v.). These hardliners opposed compromise with non-Fascist elements and saw the party as a mass-based instrument for the conquest and control of the state. The intransigents demanded discipline and absolute authority of the party over the nation.

Mussolini stood between and above the revisionist-intransigent struggle that unfolded in 1923-24. By disposition his sympathy lay essentially with the revisionists, who therefore wanted to strengthen his personal authority in order to protect their position. But in the various "revisionist crises" that followed, Mussolini fluctuated from one side to the other, assuming the role of mediator who wanted to both reconcile the intransigents to his totalitarian dictatorship and to allow the revisionists room to explore their ideas. When the intransigents expelled Rocca from the party in 1923, Mussolini reinstated him, but when they appeared to be in the ascendancy in May 1924 and Rocca was purged again, he tacitly endorsed that action.

The outbreak of the Matteotti Crisis (q.v.) in the summer of 1924 resulted in the unleashing of the intransigents for a "second wave" of *squadrista* violence, but after 1926 Mussolini imposed normalization on the party and the nation. In the end

Mussolini—not the revisionists and not the intransigents—had his way. Neither position was completely purged, but neither ever triumphed. Over the next twenty years Farinacci played the role of intransigent gadfly whose influence variously rose and fell according to Mussolini's needs, while Bottai converted revisionism into a loyal cultural-ideological opposition that was allowed a limited degree of expression.

For further information see: Renzo De Felice, *Mussolini il fascista* (Turin: Einaudi, 1966); Alexander J. De Grand, *Bottai e la cultura fascista* (Rome-Bari: Laterza, 1978); Adrian Lyttelton, *The Seizure of Power* (London: Weidenfeld & Nicolson, 1973).

PVC

RICCARDI, ARTURO (b. Pavia, October 30, 1878). Chief of Staff and under-secretary of the Navy from December 8, 1940 to July 25, 1943, Admiral Riccardi was initially far more willing than his predecessor, Domenico Cavagnari (q.v.), to take the offensive and take risks, but after Matapan (*see* MATAPAN, BATTLE OF) he reverted to merely guarding the North African supply lines.

For further information see: Romeo Bernotti, *Storia della guerra nel Mediterraneo (1940-43)* (Rome: Bianco, 1960); Michael Salewski, *Die deutsche Seekriegsleitung, 1935-1945* (Frankfurt am Main: Bernard und Graefe, 1970-73).

MK

RICCI, RENATO (b. Carrara, June 1, 1896; d. Rome, 1956). A Fascist organizer and minister, Ricci volunteered for World War I and was decorated twice for his actions. He participated in Gabriele D'Annunzio's (q.v.) Fiume (q.v.) expedition and headed the legionnaires who occupied Zara in 1921. After being forced out of the area he returned to his birthplace and in May 1921 organized the first Fasci di Combattimento (q.v.) in the town. Ricci soon acquired a reputation as a violent Fascist and led many destructive expeditions. He partici-pated in the March on Rome (q.v.) and was appointed a consul general in the Fascist Militia (q.v.). In 1924 he was elected to Parliament and became a vice-secretary in the Fascist party. In 1927 Ricci organized and led the Avanguardie Giovanile Fasciste and served as president of the Opera Nazionale Balilla (*see* YOUTH ORGANIZATIONS), a post he held for ten years. In September 1929 he became an undersecretary for physical and youth education and in 1939 was made minister of corporations. He held this latter post until the final "changing of the guard" in February 1943.

Prior to July 1943 Ricci made contacts with the Germans and had links with Himmler through the Militia. He was considered a friend by the Nazis and was given their aid during the Salò Republic (*see* ITALIAN SOCIAL REPUBLIC). From September 16, 1943, to November 20, 1943, he headed the Militia in the republic. Ricci opposed the Militia's dissolution and the creation of a nonpolitical Army led by Italian generals. With German support he created a Republican

National Guard composed of Fascist Militia members and Carabinieri, which was responsible only to the minister of the interior and acted as an armed police force.

For further information see: *Chi è?* (1936); DSPI; NO (1937); Giorgio Bocca, *La Repubblica di Mussolini* (Rome-Bari: Laterza, 1977). F. W. Deakin, *The Brutal Friendship* (New York: Harper & Row, 1962).

MSF

ROATTA, MARIO (b. Modena, January 2, 1887; d. Rome, January 7, 1968). Chief of military intelligence, commander at Guadalajara (*see* GUADALAJARA, BATTLE OF), and twice Chief of Staff of the Army, General Roatta impressed Hitler as "the Fouché of the Fascist Revolution"—a description that gives this elusive figure too much credit. Roatta served with distinction in World War I both in Italy and France and was attaché in Warsaw from 1926 to 1930. In 1934 Alberto Bonzani (q.v.) chose him to head the Servizio Informazioni Militari (SIM) (q.v.). Perhaps involved in the murder of King Alexander of Yugoslavia, he received promotion to brigadier "for exceptional merit" in January 1935. In December 1935—January 1936, at the low point of Italian fortunes in Ethiopia (*see* ETHIOPIAN WAR), he made contact with Haile Selassie (q.v.) to arrange a negotiated settlement; subsequently, he planned to kidnap or assassinate the Ethiopian leader, but Mussolini vetoed it. In August 1936 Roatta met his German counterpart, Admiral Wilhelm Canaris, to coordinate aid to Francisco Franco (*see* SPANISH CIVIL WAR). By December Roatta was commander of the rapidly increasing Italian expeditionary force in Spain (CTV-Corpo di Truppe Volontarie), which he led in the capture of Malaga (February 1937), then in the Guadalajara offensive, intended as the decisive blow against Madrid (March 1937). Roatta blamed the ensuing disaster, which was a consequence of his own leadership and of the inadequacy of Italian staff procedure, doctrine, organization, tactical training, and logistics, on the "fanaticism and hatred" with which the International Brigades had resisted. The excuse did not save him from replacement by Ettore Bastico (q.v.). Nevertheless, Roatta remained high in Mussolini's esteem and subsequently commanded a mixed Italo-Spanish division and acted as liaison officer to Franco.

Briefly attaché in Berlin (August-October 1939), Roatta became Deputy Chief of the Army Staff under Rodolfo Graziani (q.v.) on October 31, 1939. After Graziani's departure for North Africa at the end of June 1940, Roatta made preparations for attacks on Switzerland (Mussolini lost interest), Yugoslavia (cancelled due to German displeasure, an outcome that "disappointed everyone," as Roatta put it), and Greece. In the latter case Roatta (with Carlo Geloso's [q.v.] assistance) produced the "Contingency 'G'" plan for a limited attack on Epirus; with modifications by Sebastiano Visconti Prasca (q.v.), the local commander, this was the plan applied in October 1940.

Roatta survived the ensuing Guadalajara-like debacle; Pietro Badoglio (q.v.) was a sufficient scapegoat. With Graziani's nervous breakdown after the collapse in Cyrenaica (*see* LIBYA [TRIPOLITANIA AND CYRENAICA]) (February 1941), Roatta became Chief of the Army Staff until January 20, 1942, when he exchanged posts with Vittorio Ambrosio (q.v.) and took command of Italian occupation forces in Slovenia and Dalmatia. There Roatta rivaled the Germans in economic extortion and ruthless repression of the partisan movement. However, he also aroused German displeasure by supporting the Serb Chetniks against the German-dominated Croat Ustasha regime and refusing to cooperate with German and Croat anti-Jewish measures on the grounds that they were "irreconcilable with the honor of the Italian Army." He was, however, not averse to imprisoning Croatian Jews in *Italian* concentration camps.

Transferred to Sicily in February 1943, Roatta relinquished command to Alfredo Guzzoni (q.v.) on May 29, immediately before the Allied landing, and once more became Army Chief of Staff. He immediately appealed for additional German divisions, a request that proved an embarrassment after the July 25 coup removing Mussolini caused the Germans to send more troops than Roatta had bargained for. After the armistice he fled Rome on the orders of Ambrosio, Badoglio, and the king, leaving the Army to cope with the Germans as best it might. Badoglio dismissed Roatta as Chief of Staff of the Army on November 12, 1943.

Tried in 1945-46 for his activities as head of the SIM and alleged part in the Rosselli (*see* ROSSELLI, CARLO AND NELLO) murders in 1937 and threatened with extradition to Yugoslavia for war crimes, Roatta escaped from a prison hospital and took refuge in Spain. His sentence in absentia was overturned on appeal in 1948; he returned to Rome in 1965.

For further information see: Mario Roatta, *Otto milioni di baionette. L'Esercito italiano in guerra* (Milan: Mondadori, 1946); Giacomo Zanussi, *Guerra e catastrofe d'Italia*, 2 vols. (Rome: Corso, 1945).

MK

ROCCA, MASSIMO (b. 1884; d. 1974). An important early Fascist and central figure in the bitter "revisionist" dispute of 1923-24, Rocca began as an anarchist, then moved toward a kind of nationalism around 1910, partly because of his experience among Italian immigrant workers in New York. He wrote under the pseudonym Libero Tancredi. He was an active interventionist, helping to organize the Fascio Rivoluzionario d'Azione Internazionalista (*see* FASCI DI AZIONE RIVOLUZIONARIA) in October 1914. As an early Fascist he was especially concerned with matters of foreign policy, but he played his most important role in Fascism in 1923-24, when his proposals sparked a bitter polemic with Roberto Farinacci (q.v.) and other extremists associated with violent *squadrismo* (*see* SQUADRISTI) and more particularly, with the Fascist party. Rocca is often portrayed as the moderate "normalizer" in this dispute, since he called for an end to Fascist disorder and even hinted that the Fascist party might have outlived its usefulness. He was not suggesting, however, that the Fascist revolution had gone far enough, but sought to develop new technical councils—the *gruppi di competenza* —as the foundation for a corporativist transformation of the Italian state. Rocca had won the task of developing such institutions in September 1922, but the organs that emerged were subject to party interference and rarely functioned effectively. Still, Rocca's revisionism seemed to be winning out by the late summer of 1923, so his opponents mounted a concerted effort against him. When the party executive voted his expulsion, Mussolini felt that the balance was tipping too far toward the intransigents and had the sentence changed to a temporary suspension from political activity. Rocca's attempt to revive his campaign led to another expulsion in May 1924, and this time Mussolini found it expedient to go along.

After the Matteotti (*see* MATTEOTTI CRISIS) murder, Rocca became ever more explicitly anti-Fascist, finally going into exile in France early in 1926. He returned to Italy after World War II, still publicizing a variety of corporativism, and contributing one of the most useful accounts of Fascism by a major participant, *Come il Fascismo Divenne una Dittatura* (Milan: Edizioni Librarie Italiane, 1952).

For further information see: Massimo Rocca [Libero Tancredi], *Dieci anni di nazionalismo fra i sovversivi d'Italia, 1905-1915* (Milan: Rinascimento, 1918); Massimo Rocca, *Il primo fascismo* (Rome: Giovanni Volpe, 1964).

DDR

ROCCO, ALFREDO (b. Naples, September 9, 1875; d. Rome, August 28, 1935). The most substantial Nationalist and right Fascist theorist, Rocco was also a major architect of the Fascist state in his position as minister of justice from January 1925 to July 1932. He had already embarked on a successful academic career in law when he emerged as the most forceful spokesman of the Italian Nationalist Association at its third national congress in May 1914. But Rocco developed his mature political conception only after the war, responding both to the trade union challenge of the *biennio rosso* ("red years") and to the difficulties that Italy faced in international economic competition. Since the liberal state seemed too weak to respond to either challenge, he proposed to transform the Italian state, using socioeconomic groupings to enable a revitalized political elite both to control the threatening mass society and to galvanize the nation's energies for production, international economic competition, and imperialist war. The trade union phenomenon, which in a liberal context threatened the state's sovereignty, could become a useful instrument of the state's purposes within a more coercive and hierarchical framework.

Rocco's thinking was bluntly elitist: only a select few could transcend their immediate personal concerns and grasp the nation's long-term interests. And the nation was an historical, almost biological organism with long-term interests distinguishable from those of the contingent individuals who happened to be alive at any one time. However, liberalism had enervated Italy's political elite, so Rocco proposed to restructure it by combining traditional bureaucratic and newer industrial circles in a statist-productivist order.

Rocco felt that the challenges of the industrial age could be surmounted only if the Italian state moved toward totalitarianism (q.v.), extending its sovereignty and mobilizing people more fully. As a totalitarian, however, he remained a juridical rationalist; his conception required codified law and had no place for charisma, intuition, or terror.

With Francesco Coppola (q.v.), Rocco began to publish *Politica*, the major organ of nationalism and right Fascism, in December 1918. He moved formally to Fascism in February 1923, when the Nationalist Association merged with the Fascist party, but he was already active in Mussolini's government, serving first as undersecretary of the treasury, then as undersecretary of war pensions. After several months as president of the Chamber of Deputies (*see* PARLIAMENT), he was made minister of justice in January 1925, as Mussolini was beginning to develop a specifically Fascist order. Rocco quickly achieved considerable power, since he impressed Mussolini with his energy and technical competence, and over the next several years he drafted a series of laws that fundamentally transformed the Italian state. These included laws enhancing the power of the executive vis-à-vis the legislature, laws restricting secret societies and disciplining professional activities, and the syndical law of April 3, 1926, which established juridical recognition of trade unions and their collective contracts, outlawed strikes and lockouts, and instituted a labor magistracy to deal with labor conflicts. He also had a major hand in the reform of the Chamber of Deputies of 1928, in the law on the Fascist Grand Council (q.v.) of 1928, and in drawing up the penal codes of 1931.

Rocco left office as part of the shake-up of the Fascist hierarchy in 1932. He was made a senator in 1934 and served as rector of the University of Rome until his death in 1935.

For further information see: Franco Gaeta, *Nazionalismo italiano* (Naples: Edizioni Scientifiche Italiane, 1965); David D. Roberts, *The Syndicalist Tradition and Italian Fascism* (Chapel Hill: University of North Carolina Press, 1979); Alfredo Rocco, *Scritti e discorsi politici*, 3 vols. (Milan: A. Giuffre, 1938); Paolo Ungari, *Alfredo Rocco e l'ideologia giuridica del fascismo* (Brescia: Morcelliana, 1963).

DDR

ROMANITÀ. The word "Romanità" (the essence of the ancient Roman tradition) was a key element in the official vocabulary of Italian Fascism and during the 1930s became something of an obsession in the regime's cultural rhetoric. Fascism, like similar movements elsewhere in Europe, sought to give its ideology legitimacy by claiming that its origins lay in an ancient and more glorious national past. The ethos of the Italic race and the traditions of ancient Rome, evoked in the mysticism and ritual surrounding much of Fascist public display, provided the regime with the national roots of official culture. It never claimed that history began with Fascism, but that Fascism was the fulfillment and rebirth of the true spirit and soul of the Italic race, which had found its first and greatest expression in Imperial Rome. It was no accident that the Fascists had established an Institute for Roman Studies in 1925, that the symbol of the regime was the Fascio Littorio (q.v.), or that Mussolini was referred to as Dux. In 1926 Gaetano Polverelli (q.v.), head of Mussolini's Press Office, suggested that the Augusteo, tomb of the first Roman emperor, be made into a "temple of fascism" and that the regime should display the most important artifacts of ancient Rome together with momentos of the Fascist movement in one large exhibit. Caesar and Mussolini were both presented as heroes of the same great national tradition, with Caesar as predecessor of Fascism.

These themes formed the basis for much of the cultural propaganda of the 1930s. Newspaper editors were instructed to devote considerable space to the idea of Romanità, while the release of Carmine Gallone's celebrated film *Scipione l'Africano* (1937) after the Ethiopian War (q.v.) was a clear indication that Mussolini's new empire was the re-creation of the Roman Empire. The adoption by the Fascist party of the Roman salute, the *passo romano*, and similar forms of public behavior were efforts to imbue Italians outwardly with the spirit and discipline of Roman life. Latin dramas and modern opera were performed at night in illuminated ancient amphitheaters to revive an appreciation for Roman culture.

One of the most important and vivid expressions of the Fascist commitment to Romanità was in architecture (q.v.). Although architectural styles varied greatly during the Fascist period, almost all the groups, from the rationalists to the academics, tended to look at buildings of the past for inspiration and to capture the "spirit" if not the form of Roman style—and this was because official policy dictated a strong preference in that direction. Hence, in one way or another the favored building style of the regime was a "modified" classical Roman architecture, sometimes with columns and arches and sometimes without, but almost always with a severe and streamlined monumentalism. Railroad stations, government centers, and party headquarters constructed on classical lines were permanent and obvious reminders of the Fascist assimilation of Romanità. The style was used widely in the Foro Mussolini, decorated with statues of Roman athletes; in the Città Universitaria of Rome; in entirely new cities like Latina; and in the ambitious but unrealized plans for the 1942 Esposizione Universale di Roma.

Given the emphasis on Romanità, it was natural that the regime would undertake a major commitment to archaeological excavations, especially in the city of Rome itself. Mussolini was determined to make his capital a "new Rome," one in which the imperial glory of the ancient world would stand alongside the equally impressive achievements of Fascism. Hence, he undertook the isolation and refurbishing of ancient monuments (which resulted in the demolition of many residential quarters in order to make the ancient monuments stand out) and the outlining of a major thoroughfare (the Via dei Fori Imperiali) that would connect the Colosseum and the heart of ancient Rome with the Victor Emmanuel II monument and Mussolini's office at Piazza Venezia.

The glorification of the Roman past and its identification with Fascism was publicly illustrated in a monumental propaganda exhibition called the Mostra Augustea della Romanità. Planned as early as 1932 under the direction of Professor Giulio Giglioli of the University of Rome to celebrate the two thousandth anniversary of the birth of the emperor Augustus, the huge exhibition opened in 1937 with sections on the early origins of Rome, its imperial conquests, the life of Augustus, the Roman army, law, and institutions, and, significantly, a section entitled Fascismo e Romanità. A concerted publicity campaign in the cities and countryside was aimed at drawing as many Italians as possible from all walks of life to the exhibition. Organized tours of schoolchildren and university students, Dopolavoro (q.v.) members, Fascist party youth organizations (q.v.), and the Militia (q.v.) were arranged with reduced railway fares so that "the masses can take a bath in Romanità." While careful attention was given to the presentation of historical and archaeological evidence of Rome's greatness, the real meaning of the entire show was made clear to visitors. Over the entrance were inscribed Mussolini's words: "Italians, you must ensure that the glories of the past are surpassed by the glories of the future," while symbolic impact was added during the closing ceremonies by the presentation of a live eagle to the Duce as a sign that the imperial tradition had passed to Fascism.

While it would be difficult to establish any real connection between the theme of Romanità and Fascist foreign policy, it is true that the Roman idea played a central role in Mussolini's public rhetoric and that the imperial myth was used to explain both the aims and the accomplishments of his foreign policy. Roman imperialism, and its association with *Pax Romana*, the Mediterranean as a "Roman Lake," expansionism, and Italy's "civilizing mission," all found expression in Mussolini's desire to build a new Roman Empire. It was for this reason that in the reconstruction of Rome Mussolini had a series of large marble maps erected on the wall of the basilica of Maxentius showing the stages in the ancient Roman conquests, followed by a map of Fascist conquests.

For further information see: Giuseppe Bottai, *L'Italia di Augusto e l'Italia d'oggi* (Rome: Istituto di Sturomani, 1937); Philip V. Cannistraro, "Mussolini's Cultural Revolution," *Journal of Contemporary History* (July-October 1972); Dino Cofrancesco, "Appunti per un'analisi del mito romano nell'ideologia fascista," *Storia Contemporanea* (June 1980).

PVC

ROMANO AVEZZANO, BARON CAMILLO (b. Naples, October 4, 1867). A career diplomat, Romano Avezzano received his law degree and joined the diplomatic corps in 1889. He was assigned to numerous posts including Cairo, Tunis, Paris, Washington, Peking, Belgrade, and Tokyo. From 1919 to 1921 he served as ambassador to the United States and in 1922 he became ambassador to

France, a position he held until February 1927. Although Mussolini took charge of the Foreign Ministry in 1922, he did not attempt to Fascisticize the diplomatic corps and continued to rely on men like Romano Avezzano to carry out his policies.

During his tenure in Paris, Romano Avezzano played a key role in attempting to establish a Franco-Italian alliance. He was also one of Italy's chief negotiators in the Corfu Crisis (q.v.) of 1923, the Ruhr crisis, and in discussions concerning French and Italian colonial questions. Romano Avezzano firmly believed that an alliance with France would greatly benefit Italy, and he intensely distrusted the British. In 1927, as a result of Mussolini's growing anti-French stance, Romano Avezzano resigned his post and retired from public life.

For further information see: *Chi è?* (1936); *NO* (1936); Alan Cassels, *Mussolini's Early Diplomacy* (Princeton: Princeton University Press, 1970).

MSF

ROME AGREEMENTS. The agreements of January 7, 1935, between Mussolini and French Foreign Minister Pierre Laval were the decisive step in Italian diplomatic preparation for the attack on Ethiopia (*see* ETHIOPIAN WAR). After preliminary negotiations in November and December, Laval arrived in Rome on January 4 in search of an alliance against Germany. A series of meetings with Mussolini, Fulvio Suvich (q.v.), Pompeo Aloisi (q.v.), and the French ambassador led to seven agreements, some public, some secret.

In Europe, Italy and France pledged consultation in the event of German violation of Versailles disarmament obligations or threats to Austrian independence and promised cooperation in retaining their military edge over Germany. In Africa, Italy partially or completely relinquished previous safeguards for the nationality rights of Italians in Tunisia and received in return strips of desert on the borders of Libya and Eritrea. From the Italian point of view the central agreement was that over Ethiopia, which was partly verbal and gave Mussolini a "free hand." Laval later denied any such bargain; the portion of the arrangement in writing merely conceded Italy economic primacy in Ethiopia. However, an earlier Italian draft discussed in negotiations on January 4 mentioned the intriguing possibility of "modifications of the status quo in the region in question." The French were thus aware of Mussolini's territorial aims, although they probably underestimated their extent.

The agreements led to a brief and informal Franco-Italian military alliance in defense of Austria—the Pietro Badoglio [q.v.]-Maurice Gamelin agreements of June 1935 (Gamelin was inspector general of the French Army). However, British opposition to Italy's attack on Ethiopia compelled Laval to straddle the fence between Rome and London and earned him Mussolini's undying enmity. Diplomatic isolation and League of Nations sanctions drew Italy away from France toward Germany in the winter and spring of 1935-36; G. Ciano (q.v.) repudiated what was left of the agreements in December 1938, during Mussolini's post-Munich campaign against France.

For further information see: Renzo De Felice, *Mussolini il Duce* (Turin: Einaudi, 1974); D. C. Watt, "The Secret Mussolini-Laval Agreement of 1935 on Ethiopia," *Middle East Journal* (Winter 1961).

MK

ROME PROTOCOLS. The Rome Protocols of March 17, 1934, between Italy, Austria, and Hungary were Mussolini's second line of defense (after the failed Four Power Pact [q.v.]) against National Socialist expansion on the Danube. Fulvio Suvich (q.v.) conducted the negotiations that led up to them during visits to Vienna and Budapest in January and late February 1934. The protocols were three: an agreement by which the powers undertook to consult together at the request of one of them, a general economic agreement providing for increased trade, and a bilateral Italo-Austrian tariff reduction agreement. Further accords implementing the trade agreements followed on May 14; all parties, but particularly the Hungarians, gained economic advantages, but the consultative agreement was the most important. Italy, as the great power involved, achieved with it a permanent treaty-sanctioned right of supervision of the foreign policies of the two smaller powers and replaced France as protector of Austria. Mussolini emphasized this development with a public declaration of support for Austrian independence, an independence that he had in the long run destroyed with his insistence that Austrian chancellor Engelbert Dollfuss out-Nazi the Nazis by bloodily suppressing the Vienna Social Democrats—the only reliably anti-Anschluss (*see* ANSCHLUSS) force in Austria (Dollfuss had finally taken Mussolini's advice in mid-February, immediately before Suvich's second visit).

Subsequently the three powers extended and revised the protocols (March 23, 1936) to require consultation before initiating negotiations with third parties. However, continued German pressure and Mussolini's post-Abyssinian isolation resulted in Italian acquiescence to the Austro-German agreement of July 11, 1936, which affirmed Austria's status as a "German state." Although Italy remained Austria's protector in theory and the Ciano-Hitler agreements of October 1936 reaffirmed the validity of the Rome Protocols, Germany was increasingly in command. After November 1936 no meeting of the Rome Protocol states took place until January 1938, when the Hungarians insisted on one. The Anschluss which followed (March 12, 1938) made the protocols meaningless.

For further information see: C. A. Macartney, *October Fifteenth* (Edinburgh: Edinburgh University Press, 1961); Jens Petersen, *Hitler-Mussolini* (Tübingen: Niemayer, 1973).

MK

ROSA, ENRICO (b. Selva Marcone, Biella, November 17, 1870; d. Rome, November 26, 1938). Rosa studied in Turin and then at a Jesuit school in Monaco. In 1901 he obtained a doctorate in theology and philosophy and three years later was appointed spiritual head of the clerics at the Istituto Sociale di Torino.

In 1905 Rosa went to Rome as a writer for *La Civiltà Cattolica*; from 1915 to 1931 he was both director for that journal and religious head of the Jesuit college there. Through the pages of *Civiltà* Rosa closely followed—and frequently denounced—the ideological and political actions of the Fascist regime, not as a democratic opponent but only where he saw potential conflict with the doctrines and interests of the Catholic Church. Following the Fascist attack against the offices of *Civiltà* on the night of May 27, 1931, he stepped down as director of the journal—the event having taken place in the midst of the conflict between the regime and Catholic Action (*see* AZIONE CATTOLICA ITALIANA). Because of his hostility to Fascism, Rosa was suspected of supporting the Alleanza Nazionale, a clandestine movement that sought an anti-Fascist alliance of the king, the pope, and Catholic Action.

He continued working for *Civiltà* in its offices at Via Ripetta until his death.

For further information see: Ambroggio M. Fiocchi, *Enrico Rosa, Scrittore della "Civiltà Cattolica," 1870-1938* (Rome: La Civiltà Cattolica, 1957); Sandro Rogari, *Santa Sede e fascismo: Dall'Aventino ai Patti Lateranensi* (Bologna: Forni, 1977); Richard A. Webster, *The Cross and the Fasces. Christian Democracy and Fascism in Italy* (Stanford, Calif.: Stanford University Press, 1960).

SR

ROSAI, OTTONE (b. Florence, April 28, 1895; d. Ivrea, 1957). Rosai was an Italian painter and a leading member of the Strapaese (*see* STRACITTÀ/ STRAPAESE) group, who were antibourgeois, anticosmopolitan, and stressed provincial values. As a cultural movement Strapaese represented a Fascist schism led by provincial *squadristi* (q.v.) such as Rosai in opposition to conformist dictates from Rome. Both the literary and artistic elements of the Strapaese movement were primarily Tuscan. Curzio Malaparte (q.v.) was Rosai's literary counterpart.

The official publication of the movement was *Il Selvaggio*, and members of the movement were sometimes referred to as "primitives." Mino Maccari (q.v.) and Ardengo Soffici (q.v.) edited the journal, while Ottone Rosai was a contributor.

Rosai was an authentic member of the working class, son of a cabinetmaker, and trained in that occupation by his father, a veteran of World War I. He attended the Florence Fine Arts Academy and was influenced by Cézanne, Daumier, Courbet, and Corot. He showed with the Futurists (*see* FUTURISM) in 1914, placing collages with those of the avant-garde such as Carlo Carrà (q.v.) and Ardengo Soffici. By 1919 his mature style was formed: in the confines of a limited perspective with a few strongly lit elements derived from the Tuscan tradition of Masaccio (Tommaso Guidi), the personages of a lower-working-class neighborhood conduct their affairs and are portrayed very simply. His works are clear and narrative, with the flavor of the Florentine trecento.

Rosai had a one-man show in Florence in 1921 and in Rome in 1922. His paintings were widely admired throughout his career and eventually brought him economic independence as well as widespread recognition.

Rosai was a literary figure as well. He edited not only for *Il Selvaggio* (Florentine Edition) but also *Il Bargello* and the Fascist review *L'Universale*.

For further information see: Ottone Rosai, *Dentro la guerra* (Rome: Novissima, 1934); Ottone Rosai, *Il libro di un teppista* (Florence: Vallecchi, 1920); Ottone Rosai, *Via Toscanella* (Florence: Vallecchi, 1928); Mario Tinti, "Ottone Rosai o della tradizione Toscana," *Emporium* (March 1935); S. Volta, *Ottone Rosai* (Milan: Hoepli, 1932).

MCG

ROSSELLI, CARLO (b. Rome, November 16, 1899; d. Bagnoles de l'Orne, France, June 9, 1937), and **ROSSELLI NELLO** (b. Florence, November 29, 1900; d. Bagnoles de l'Orne, France, June 9, 1937). Carlo and Nello Rosselli were born into a wealthy, professional Tuscan family and nurtured in the ninteenth-century democratic heritage of Giuseppe Mazzini, who had been an intimate of the family and had died in the family home in Pisa. They spent their formative years in Florence, where both were influenced by Gaetano Salvemini (q.v.). Nello, the pure scholar, chose the path of historical research and "quietist" resistance during the Fascist era; Carlo, the tireless activist, became progressively more radical in his politics and opposed Fascism through a series of political organizations, culminating in the influential Giustizia e Libertà (GL) movement (*see* ANTI-FASCISM). They maintained a close personal relationship until, in the prime of life, they were brutally murdered by French fascists.

World War I proved traumatic to the Rosselli family. The oldest brother, Aldo, was killed at the Austrian front in 1916. Both Carlo and Nello, who served in 1918 and 1919 respectively, were deeply affected by the conflict. They returned to Florence to continue formal education, having been particularly impressed with the valor and decency of the common men with whom they had fought.

While Carlo completed his degrees, he began to develop his fundamental political ideas of reformist socialism and to participate in anti-Fascist activities. In contributing to Piero Gobetti's (q.v.) *Rivoluzione Liberale*, he became acquainted with the work of Carlo Levi (q.v.), Luigi Einaudi (q.v.), and Gaetano Mosca. And he was horrified by the Blackshirt (*see* SQUADRISTI) violence that swept Tuscany in the years after the war. He joined the "apolitical" Circle of Culture in Florence in 1924 after taking degrees in social science (1921) and law (1922) with a dissertation on the economic influences of trade unionism. Nello finished his degree in history in 1924, writing his dissertation on Mazzini and the Russian anarchist Mikhail Bakunin.

As political conditions intensified in Italy, the Rosselli brothers became more overtly political. The Florence Circle was decisively anti-Fascist by 1924, when Giacomo Matteotti (*see* MATTEOTTI CRISIS) was murdered. Alarmed, Nello joined Giovanni Amendola's (q.v.) democratic group, and Carlo joined the reformist wing of the Socialist party (*see* PARTITO SOCIALISTA ITALIANO). While a lecturer at the School of Economics in Genoa, Carlo contributed to clandestine propaganda and anti-Fascist organizations. Then, after further Fascist repression in Tuscany, Carlo and Nello joined Salvemini and Ernesto Rossi (q.v.) in the creation of the sub-rosa newspaper, *Non Mollare!*, which daringly revealed the Fascist participation in Matteotti's murder.

In 1926 Carlo moved his anti-Fascist activities northward. With Pietro Nenni (q.v.) he founded *Il Quarto Stato*, a Socialist-Republican weekly that discussed abstract historical, social, and economic issues. Carlo's wife, Marion Cave, joined him in his opposition to the Fascist regime. They converted their Milan home to an underground halfway house for political exiles en route to refuge abroad. In December 1926, after assisting the escape of the old Socialist leader Filippo Turati (q.v.), Carlo was arrested with Ferruccio Parri (q.v.). It was the beginning of an open hostility with Fascist authorities that lasted throughout the final decade of his life.

Carlo eloquently defended his action in a notable public trial in Savona, but he was sentenced to five years' confinement on Lipari Island because of Mussolini's intervention. Nello had married Maria Tedesco and accepted a fellowship at the Royal Institute of Modern and Contemporary History. The Fascists simultaneously arrested Nello and Marion, who was ill and pregnant. Marion was later released, while Nello served four months on the island of Poriza. While at Lipari, Carlo wrote *Socialismo liberale* and further developed his political ideas in discussions with other anti-Fascists. Two of them, Emilio Lussu (q.v.) and F. S. Nitti (q.v.), joined Carlo in a daring escape on July 27, 1929.

Nello returned to his Tuscan villa where—under the surveillance of Fascist police—he wrote a history of the Risorgimento. By the fall of 1929 Carlo had taken up residence in Paris and launched the most significant phase of his political career. By temperament a man of constant renewal, Carlo rejected the passivity of the Anti-Fascist Concentration (*see* ANTI-FASCISM), as well as its commitment to the politics of the Liberal state, in favor of a program of concrete action. He began to organize a small group of intransigent anti-Fascist radicals, the embryonic Giustizia e Libertà.

Carlo insisted that GL become an autonomous supraparty movement with a basic program of reform acceptable to a broad spectrum of anti-Fascists. He sought to mold them into an articulate, militant vanguard of a Mazzinian revolution, independent of Marxists and Liberals. He expressed his evolving political thought in the GL publications which he edited, *Quaderni di Giustizia e Libertà* and the weekly *Giustizia e Libertà*. Similar principles comprised the GL revolutionary program of 1932: creation of a democratic republic based on universal suffrage, political liberties, separation of Church and state, a constituent assembly, and a "people's militia"; agrarian and industrial reform to produce a mixed economy, including nationalization of large-scale capital, "factory democracy," and widespread development of cooperatives; defascistization, including trials and confiscation of property; peace, disarmament, and a European federation.

The GL strategy focused on publicizing the deteriorating conditions in Italy, encouraging communication among anti-Fascists, and supporting and subsidizing the clandestine opposition within Italy. Thus GL utilized a range of propaganda methods including the smuggling into Italy of anti-Fascist tracts, the publication outside Italy of Mussolini's secret orders, and such dramatic gestures as the dropping of leaflets from the air over crowded cities. It was on such a mission that the poet Lauro de Bosis (q.v.) was killed.

Carlo Rosselli implemented the goals and strategy of GL within a setting of mounting international political tension that characterized the 1930s. The collapse of the Anti-Fascist Concentration and the advent of the popular front strategy threatened to isolate GL. Carlo searched unsuccessfully for a common basis of tentative agreement with the PCI (Partito Comunista Italiana) (q.v.) and PSI (Partito Socialista Italiano) (q.v.), particularly during the crises in Ethiopia and Spain.

Mussolini's intervention in the Spanish Civil War (q.v.) challenged the Giellisti to strike a blow for their cause. Carlo quickly organized a volunteer legion of GL members, anarchists, and Republicans, many of whom were veterans of World War I. He succeeded Mario Angeloni as commander of the Italian GL (Rosselli) Column, which fought with the anarcho-syndicalists of Catalonia against General Franco's Falangists in August 1936. Other Italians joined the Communist Garibaldi Battalion of the Comintern's international brigades. In defense of the Republican government of Madrid, the Garibaldi Battalion defeated Mussolini's troops at Guadalajara (*see* GUADALAJARA, BATTLE OF) in March 1937. Supporting the more extreme group, GL had reaffirmed its commitment to revolutionary action, but had further isolated itself from the popular front and the Western powers.

The Spanish Civil War had forced Carlo to reassess his plans for GL and had moved his political ideas leftward. His experience strengthened his conviction that Fascism must be met with force, and it also reaffirmed his political independence. But at the same time, the isolation of GL in Spain had made him more aware of the need to solicit support from the European democracies and to collaborate with the Socialists and Communists. In his first direct contact with Communists, he had been impressed with their organizational abilities and their military success. His 1937 writings focused more resolutely on the "political unification of the Italian proletariat" in an anti-Fascist revolution that would produce a decentralized republic. Clearly his political ideas were once again in the process of renewal, which has led his critics to accuse him of engaging in rhetorical posturing and opportunism.

It has also been suggested that Carlo "sealed his fate"—and, coincidentally that of his brother—by publicizing in *Giustizia e Libertà* the names and photographs of the many Italians taken prisoner by the Garibaldi Brigade at Guadalajara, thus humiliating Mussolini. On June 9, 1937, Nello and Marion visited Carlo at a health resort outside Paris where he was convalescing. After Marion's departure the Rosselli brothers were ambushed and killed on a lonely road by French fascist Cagoulards.

For further information see: Aldo Garosci, *Vita di Carlo Rosselli*, 2 vols. (Florence: Vallecchi, 1973); Carlo Rosselli, *Scritti politici e autobiografici* (Naples: Polis, 1944); Carlo Rosselli, *Opere scelte* (Turin: Einaudi, 1973); Nello Rosselli, *Mazzini e Bakounine: 12 anni di movimento operaio in Italia, 1860-1872* (Turin: Bocca, 1927); Nello Rosselli, *Carlo Pisacane nel Risorgimento Italiano* (Turin: Bocca, 1932); *Epistolario familiare: Carlo, Nello Rosselli e la madre, 1914-1937* (Turin: Einaudi, 1979); *Giustizia e Libertà nella lotta antifascista e nella storia d'Italia* (Florence: La Nuova Italia, 1978); Elena Aga Rossi, ed., *Il Movimento repubblicano, Giustizia e Libertà, e il Partito d'Azione* (Bologna: Cappelli, 1969); Gaetano Salvemini, *Carlo and Nello Rosselli* (London: For Intellectual Liberty, 1937); Nicola Tranfaglia, *Carlo Rosselli dall'interventismo a Giustizia e Libertà* (Bari: Laterza, 1968).

CLK

ROSSELLINI, ROBERTO (b. Rome, May 8, 1906; d. Rome, June 3, 1977). One of Italy's most famous film directors, Rossellini studied philosophy and the arts in a *liceo* and had been a member of the Fascist student film clubs, Cineguf. His first important professional work was as scene designer and assistant director for Goffredo Alessandrini's (q.v.) *Luciano Serra Pilota* (1937-38). During World War II Rossellini was assigned to the film division of the Ministry of Marine under Francesco De Robertis, making newsreels and documentaries. It was here that he began his experimental work that ultimately made him a pioneer and major artist in the neorealist genre. In 1941 he directed *La Nave Bianca*, followed by *Un Pilota Ritorna* (1941-42), and *L'Uomo della Croce* (1942). While all three films were officially considered Fascist propaganda works, they contained the technical and artistic seeds of his future films. The true birth of neorealism in film came in 1945-46 with Rossellini's *Roma, Città Aperta* and *Paisà*.

For further information see: Philip V. Cannistraro, *La fabbrica del consenso* (Rome-Bari: Laterza, 1975); Claudio Carabba, *Il cinema del ventennio nero* (Florence: Vallecchi, 1974).

PVC

ROSSI, AMILCARE (b. Lanuvio, Rome, January 1, 1895). A Fascist bureaucrat and publicist, Rossi was trained as a lawyer. A Nationalist interventionist in 1914-15 (*see* INTERVENTIONIST CRISIS, 1914-1915), he fought and was decorated in World War I. He joined the Fascist movement in 1919 and became a staunch Mussolini supporter. In 1924 Rossi was appointed to the new national directorate of the PNF (Partito Nazionale Fascista) (q.v.). He was later president of the Associazione dei Combattenti, a deputy from 1929 on, and a member of the

National Council of Corporations. Rossi served as a volunteer in the Italo-Ethiopian War (1935-36), and in February 1943 Mussolini made him undersecretary for the Presidency of the Council of Ministers.

For further information see: *Chi è?* (1936; 1948); DSPI; NO (1928; 1937).

PVC

ROSSI, CESARE (b. Pescia, Pistoia, September 21, 1887; d. Rome, August 9, 1967). A former revolutionary syndicalist and a founder of the Fascist movement, Rossi was one of Mussolini's closest collaborators until 1924. In his early days he stood in the left wing of the Socialist party and gravitated toward the syndicalists. He moved to Rome after his father's death in 1902 and wrote for a large number of journals and newspapers. His rabid antimilitarist articles frequently resulted in his arrest. In 1907 he and Michele Bianchi (q.v.) left the Socialist party and established a syndicalist organization in Rome, he was arrested for organizing demonstrations, and he then joined the armed forces.

In 1911 Rossi became an administrator in the Chamber of Labor in Parma and the next year was secretary of the syndicalist Chamber of Labor in Piacenza. He was simultaneously director of *Voce Proletaria* and became an officer in the Unione Sindacale Italiana (USI) in charge of propaganda.

He was an interventionist in 1914 and was among the signers of the manifesto of the Fascio Rivoluzionario d'Azione Internazionalista in October and helped promote the Fasci di Azione Rivoluzionaria (q.v.). He became a correspondent for *Il Popolo d'Italia* in 1915 and in 1919 was at Piazza San Sepolcro (*see* SANSEPOLCRISTI) for the founding of the Fasci di Combattimento (q.v.). He was one of Mussolini's most trusted followers and was a moderate who wanted to provide Fascism with a constitutional framework. He opposed the excessive violence of the *squadristi* (q.v.). As a member of the national council of the movement and vice-secretary, he played a leading role in the formulation of the Pact of Pacification (*see* PACIFICATION PACT) in August 1921.

Forced out of his positions by the intransigents before the March on Rome (q.v.), Mussolini made him head of his Press Office after becoming prime minister in October 1922, a post he held until June 1924. At that time Rossi was accused of complicity in the Matteotti Crisis (q.v.) murder because of his association with Amerigo Dumini (q.v.) and Aldo Finzi (q.v.), as well as because of his public threats against Matteotti, made in the Fascist press. Fearing that Mussolini would make him a scapegoat, he wrote his famous "Memoriale" that was published by Giovanni Amendola (q.v.) on December 27, 1924. In it Rossi accused Mussolini of responsibility for the Matteotti murder as well as for all the earlier Fascist violence. Rossi was arrested but released and fled to France, where he joined a group of ex-Fascists in exile. In August 1928 he was arrested again in Switzerland by Italian police and sentenced to thirty years imprisonment. At the end of World War II he was condemned by an Italian Republican court for Fascist crimes but not sentenced. He continued his journalistic career.

For further information see: DSPI; MOI (4); Renzo De Felice, *Mussolini il rivoluzionario* (Turin: Einaudi, 1965); Renzo De Felice, *Mussolini il fascista* (Turin: Einaudi, 1966); Cesare Rossi, *Mussolini com'era* (Rome: Ruffolo, 1947); Cesare Rossi, *Trentatre vicende mussoliniane* (Milan: Varese, 1958).

MSF

ROSSI, ERNESTO (b. Caserta, August 25, 1897; d. Rome, February 9, 1967). An economist and democratic radical of the Salveminian (*see* SALVEMINI, GAETANO) mold, Ernesto Rossi spent thirteen years in prison and confinement as a result of his anti-Fascist activities.

Son of an army officer, he advocated Italian intervention on the Allied side in World War I. He studied in the liberal-democratic setting of Florence, took a law degree, and taught economics. In 1923 he began to participate in the nascent Tuscan anti-Fascist movement. He joined Salvemini, Carlo and Nello Rosselli (q.v.), and others in the Florence Circle of Culture. During the Matteotti Crisis (q.v.), he participated in Giovanni Amendola's (q.v.) National Democratic Union. In 1925 he helped to produce the first clandestine anti-Fascist journal, *Non Mollare!*. When it collapsed under police pressure, he fled briefly to France to evade Fascist retaliation. Impatient, he returned four months later.

By late 1926 Rossi and Riccardo Bauer (q.v.) began to resume the development of a clandestine opposition movement within Italy. He produced and distributed underground propaganda, established contacts, and contributed to Luigi Einaudi's (q.v.) *Riforma Sociale*. Independent of party ties, Rossi was successful in winning the trust and cooperation of Milanese republicans and radicals.

In 1929 he joined Bauer, Carlo Rosselli, and others in the founding of Giustizia e Libertà (GL) and began to establish a network within Italy. In the summer of 1930 he contributed to the development of a militant GL campaign against government authorities in northern cities, including plans to use incendiary bombs. The campaign provoked a counterattack in which a police agent infiltrated the Milan GL unit and engineered the arrest and conviction of Rossi and Bauer who were sentenced to twenty years by the Special Tribunal for the Defense of the State (q.v.) in Rome. After nine years Rossi was transferred to confinement at Ventotene. But he remained a prisoner until Mussolini's fall. He maintained contact with family and anti-Fascist friends, and the clarity of his political observations made him an inspirational figure during his lengthy detention.

After July 1943 Rossi regained his liberty and resumed his political activities. He became an ardent advocate of a European federation, helping to found the European Federalist Movement in 1944, and working toward a United States of Europe.

He served as undersecretary for reconstruction in the Ferruccio Parri (q.v.) government (1945). In the postwar period he contributed regularly to the radical journal *Il Mondo* and conducted a series of journalistic campaigns in numerous books and journals against administrative corruption, the remnants of Fascism, and the financial elite.

For further information see: Aldo Garosci, *Vita di Carlo Rosselli* (Florence: Vallecchi, 1973); Elide Rossi, *Lettere ad Ernesto* (Florence: La Nuova Italia, 1958); Ernesto Rossi, *I padroni del vapore* (Bari: Laterza, 1955); Ernesto Rossi, *Il manganello e l'aspersorio* (Florence: Parenti, 1958); Ernesto Rossi, *Elogio della galera: Lettere, 1930-1943* (Bari: Laterza, 1968).

CLK

ROSSONI, EDMONDO (b. Tresigallo, Ferrara, October 6, 1884; d. Rome, June 8, 1965). The leading exponent of Fascist syndicalism, Rossoni's early career was spent in the revolutionary syndicalist movement. After private secondary education, he joined the Italian Socialist party (*see* PARTITO SOCIALISTA ITALIANO) at the beginning of the century. He participated in agrarian strikes and in the general strike of 1904. In Milan he moved toward the syndicalists, was a union delegate in 1907, and collaborated with the antimilitarist *La Gioventù socialista*. He quit the Socialist federation in 1907 and worked closely with the Chamber of Labor.

In 1908 Rossoni began a long period of exile in order to avoid arrest, going from Nice to Brazil, and in 1910, to the United States. In New York he wrote for *Il Proletario* and was a member of the IWW. Returning to Italy in January 1913, he was again active in syndicalist politics and strikes. In August, after having been arrested and released, he went back to New York. He adhered to the newly formed Unione Italiana del Lavoro (UIL) (q.v.) in 1914 and began publishing the interventionist paper *L'Italia Nostra*. Finally, in May 1916 he left for Italy for the last time, volunteering for combat in World War I and joining the Fasci di Azione Rivoluzionaria (q.v.). He became secretary general of the UIL in June 1918.

In 1919 Mussolini and his newly created *fasci* supported the UIL position for a time but then turned against it by 1920. In October the Fascists began establishing their own syndicates, creating in November 1920 the Confederazione Italiana dei Sindacati Economici (CISE). In the meantime, in May 1921 Rossoni went to Ferrara on the invitation of Italo Balbo (q.v.) to direct the local Fascist syndicalist movement (he was also head of the Chamber of Labor there). In the early discussions concerning the nature of Fascist syndicalism, Rossoni argued for apolitical unions. At the Bologna congress in January 1922 the CISE was dissolved and replaced by the Confederazione dei Sindacati Nazionali (CSN), of which Rossoni became secretary general.

As head of the Fascist unions, Rossoni fought a vigorous campaign against the Socialist unions and sought to make his own theories of corporativism (*see* CORPORATIVISM AND THE CORPORATIVE STATE) the basis of the regime. In the years that followed, however, Rossoni found serious problems facing him, including growing discontent among workers under his direction, the hostility of the landowners and industrialists, and the unwillingness of Mussolini to give his unions any real power. In this circumstance, Rossoni developed his idea of "integral syndicalism" in which workers and owners would join in mixed corporations under his control. The Palazzo Chigi Pact (q.v.) of December 1923 and the subsequent Palazzo Vidoni Pact (q.v.) of October 1925 spelled the end of this concept.

The final stages in the emasculation of Rossoni's syndicates took place between 1926 and 1928. The so-called *legge sindacale* of April 3, 1926, (n. 563) (officially known as the "Legal Discipline of Collective Labor Relations") legally recognized the Fascist unions and confederations and their collective contracts. Moreover, it also created special labor courts empowered to impose compulsory decisions and prohibited all strikes and lockouts. The bill expressly prevented the formation of "mixed" unions. In November 1928 there occurred the "*sbloccamento*" or "breaking up" of Rossoni's Confederazione Nazionale dei Sindacati Fascisti (which had replaced the earlier CSN) into a number of separate associations (confederations) corresponding to various productive sectors of the economy (industry, agriculture, transport, and others). This last great concession to the industrialists signaled the defeat of the syndicalist movement.

The remainder of Rossoni's political career was played out in a number of prestigious but not very powerful positions. He was undersecretary for the Presidency of the Council of Ministers from 1932 to 1935, minister of agriculture from 1935 to 1939, and then minister of state and a member of the Fascist Grand Council (q.v.). In this last capacity Rossoni was able to strike back at Mussolini during the July 24-25, 1943 session, when he voted in favor of the Dino Grandi (q.v.) motion that unseated Mussolini. After the German occupation of Rome in September, Rossoni took refuge in the Vatican. He was condemned to death in absentia at the Verona Trials (q.v.) in 1944; in May 1945 a postwar tribunal sentenced him to life imprisonment for having conspired in the suppression of liberty, but he fled to Canada. After the sentence was revoked in 1947, he returned to Italy and lived in retirement.

For further information see: DSPI; MOI (4); Ferdinando Cordova, "Edmondo Rossoni," in *Uomini e volti del fascismo*, ed. F. Cordova (Rome: Bulzoni, 1980).

PVC

ROYAL ACADEMY OF ITALY. In 1925, with the establishment of the dictatorship, Fascism began not only to alter Italy's political structure but also to regiment all segments of Italian society into what was to be labeled the corporate state. On January 7, 1926, a royal decree established the Reale Accademia d'Italia. Its purpose was "to promote and coordinate Italian intellectual activity in the sciences, the humanities, and the arts, to preserve the integrity of the national spirit, according to the genius and tradition of the race, and to encourage their diffusion" abroad. After a three-year delay, on January 17, 1929, the Council of Ministers approved its statute, and on October 28, 1929, Mussolini himself inaugurated the Accademia.

Modeled on the prestigious French Academy, the Italian counterpart numbered sixty members, chosen for their scientific, literary, and artistic achievements;

fifteen from each of four categories: physical sciences, moral (including history) sciences, arts, and letters. In recognition of their privileged position, academicians received a monthly stipend of 3,000 lire (it is interesting to note that in 1929 the yearly per capita income in Italy was 3,079 lire), enjoyed free first-class travel on the national railroads, and were entitled to wear an elaborate dress uniform and to be addressed as "Your Excellency." In addition, they were eligible to compete for the four annual Mussolini prizes awarded to members of the Accademia for outstanding work in their respective fields. In return academicians swore loyalty to Italy and Fascism.

The Accademia not only represented Fascist Italy's recognition of intellectual achievement but also functioned as one of the regime's propaganda conduits and followed its dicta. It sponsored lectures, meetings, research, and publications and in 1934 appointed a commission to compile a dictionary of the Italian language from which all Italianized foreign words were to be excised. By the end of the 1930s the Accademia had succeeded in coopting and bringing under the Fascist umbrella the leading exponents of Italy's cultural life.

The list of academicians included Italy's most eminent names in the arts, humanities, and sciences whose reputation owed little to Fascist support. Among them were Giovanni Gentile (q.v.), Luigi Pirandello (q.v.), Guglielmo Marconi (q.v.), Enrico Fermi (q.v.), Francesco Cilea, Umberto Giordani, Ottorino Respighi, Ildebrando Pizzetti, Salvatore Di Giacomo, Ada Negri, and Gioacchino Volpe (q.v.). In 1939 the fellows of the renown Accademia dei Lincei, which the government abolished in that year, were integrated into the Reale Accademia. This action ended what little unregimented intellectual activity had survived in Italy and turned covert anti-Fascists, like Luigi Einaudi (q.v.), Francesco Carlo Jemolo, and Concetto Marchesi, into "associates of the Fascist cultural apparatus."

Although it was reopened in the Salò Republic (*see* ITALIAN SOCIAL RE-PUBLIC), with the final collapse of Fascism at the end of the war in 1945, the Accademia, like other Fascist institutions, ceased to exist. During its active years, however, it had served a useful purpose. It had rallied to the regime many of Italy's intellectual elite, since a genuine attempt was made to reward talent rather than political loyalty in appointing members to the Accademia. As state functionaries, academicians participated in the national life and lent the luster and prestige of their reputations to Fascism.

For further information see: Philip V. Cannistraro, *La fabbrica del consenso* (Rome-Bari: Laterza, 1975).

EPN

RUFFINI, FRANCESCO (b. Lessolo, Ivrea, April 10, 1863; d. Turin, March 29, 1934). Ruffini was a leading professor of Ecclesiastical and Canon law and taught at Pavia, Geneva, and Turin. A liberal politician, Ruffini became a senator in 1914 and served as minister of public instruction in the Paolo Boselli government (1916-17). Ruffini's teaching career ended in 1931 when he refused to take the university oath (q.v.) to the Fascist regime along with eleven or twelve other professors. He was subsequently retired by the regime.

For further information see: DSPI; Renzo De Felice, *Mussolini il Duce* (Turin: Einaudi, 1974).

MSF

RUSSIA, ITALIAN FORCES IN. Mussolini sent Italian forces to Russia in 1941 by depriving other fronts, ultimately creating a disaster. Joachim von Ribbentrop first hinted of Hitler's plans for the invasion of Russia to Mussolini on September 20, 1940, and Hitler made stronger allusions to Galeazzo Ciano (q.v.) on March 25, 1941. Alerted by the SIM (*see* SERVIZIO INFORMAZIONI MILITARI) and Ribbentrop's other remarks, Mussolini ordered Ugo Cavallero (q.v.) to prepare a corps to invade Russia on May 30. Hitler told Mussolini his intentions on June 2 but revealed his schedule just hours before invasion. He already had accepted Mussolini's preferred corps. Mussolini considered Italian participation essential, telling Filippo Anfuso (q.v.), "if we are absent even the fact that I have been the first to fight communism will count nothing in face of the reality that the Italians were not there."

Discounting SIM reports from Moscow of Soviet strength, Mussolini anticipated a rapid German victory. He expected communism's downfall, gaining Russian resources, enhanced Balkan security, and a possible Turkish alliance against Britain. The sixty-one-thousand-man Corpo di Spedizione in Russia (CSIR, consisting of the Pasubio and Torino Infantry Divisions, Principe Amedeo duca d'Aosta Third Celere Division, *Tagliamento* Sixty-third Blackshirt Legion, and the Thirtieth Artillery Ragruppamento, supported by 5,500 vehicles and 89 aircraft) began departing July 10. Giovanni Messe (q.v.) became commander on July 17.

Untrained and unequipped for mechanized warfare, the CSIR trailed behind lightning German advances. Ignoring promises to Mussolini, the German High Command employed the Italians piecemeal, in rearguard operations between the Bug and Dneister rivers, refused to supply food, fuel, or transport, and confiscated all CSIR booty and prisoners. Constantly strung out for lack of trucks, the reunited CSIR first entered combat in late September, capturing 10,000 Russians in the encirclement of Kiev. The CSIR advanced through the Donetz Basin in October-November, encountering light resistance but serious transport problems. Messe halted near Gorlovka in early December. Warned by enemy probes, he rejected German orders to advance, dug in, and repelled fierce Russian assaults in the "Christmas Battle." Thereafter, despite Messe's precautions, frostbite rivaled combat casualties. Attacks and counterattacks followed until late March, when the CSIR reorganized for the 1942 offensive.

Mussolini had visited the Ukraine in August 1941. Messe failed to stress his inadequate transport, armor, and antitank guns. Mussolini already had offered Hitler nine more divisions, repeating offers that fall. Hitler advised their employment in Africa but reconsidered after the Battle of Moscow. While Mussolini acknowledged the Black Sea as Germany's sphere, the oil-rich Caucasus, Hitler's 1942 target, had attracted Italian attention since 1919 and provided access to the Middle East. Despite Japanese warnings of future American landings in North Africa and Cavallero's reluctance to starve Ettore Bastico's (q.v.) forces, Mussolini satisfied Hitler's request for six more divisions for Russia in February. Messe only learned of the creation of the Armata Italiana in Russia (ARMIR) and the selection of incompetent Italo Gariboldi (q.v.) as commander in late April. Messe met Mussolini on June 2, warning him that the ARMIR was underequipped and the Germans treacherous. Mussolini replied, "At the peace table the army's 200,000 would weigh even more than the CSIR's 60,000."

The ARMIR (Italian Eighth Army) left Italy between early June and late July 1942. Officially assuming command on July 9, Gariboldi dissolved the CSIR to weaken Messe's autonomy. The Eighth Army (227,000 men with 22,300 vehicles, 588 cannons, 380 antitank guns, and 74 armored vehicles) had three corps: the Second Corps (Cosseria, Ravenna, and Torino Infantry Divisions, and the Tre Gennaio Militia Ragruppamento); the Thirty-Fifth Corps (Pasubio and Sforzesca Infantry Divisions, Third Celere Division, and the Ventitre Marzo Militia Ragruppamento); and the Alpine Corps (Cunense, Julia, and Tridentina Alpine Divisions); the Vicenza Infantry Division served to guard lines of communication.

The CSIR struggled to the Don, while the ARMIR slowly arrived; the Second Corps in early August, the Alpini (originally destined for the Caucasus) in late September. The Second and Thirty-Fifth Corps withstood Russian counterattacks between August 20 and September 1 with heavy losses. The ARMIR, reinforced with German units and expanded to a Fourth Corps (the Twenty-ninth), held the Don northwest of Stalingrad between the Hungarian Second and Romanian Third Armies for ten weeks. Gariboldi rejected Messe's pleas to plan a mobile defense and prepare for retreat, prompting Messe's repatriation on November 1. The Russians launched their Stalingrad offensive on November 19-20, smashing the Romanians north and south of the city. They struck the Second Corps on December 11, forcing its retreat on December 17. Exposed, the Thirty-fifth and Twenty-ninth Corps fell back. The withdrawal became a calvary of fire and ice. The Alpini had been temporarily spared and held until January 17. Then, when ordered to retreat they were ferociously assaulted by the enemy and the weather. Superior Alpini leadership and training saved their corps from completely sharing the others' fate. By early February seventy-seven thousand Italians reached safety, leaving ninety thousand dead and sixty thousand prisoners. The survivors returned to Italy under official silence in March 1943.

Unjustly blamed by Hitler for Field Marshal Friedrich von Paulus's encirclement at Stalingrad by the Russians, the Eighth Army achieved little in Russia but heroism and death. Its vehicles, artillery, and infantry might have meant Axis victory in Egypt or Sicily. Ten thousand ARMIR prisoners returned from Russia in 1954.

For further information see: Lucio Ceva, *La condotta italiana della guerra* (Milan: Feltrinelli, 1975); Emilio Faldella, ed., *Storia delle truppe alpine* 3 (Milan: Cavallotti, 1972); Antonio Ricchezza, *Storia illustrata di tutta la campagna di Russia*, 4 vols. (Milan: Longanesi, 1971-72); Francesco Valori, *Gli italiani in Russia* (Milan: Bietti, 1967).

BRS

RUSSO, LUIGI (b. Verona, September 28, 1882). A Militia (q.v.) Chief of Staff, veteran of the March on Rome (q.v.), an original member of the MVSN (*see* MILITIA), and a Fascist deputy in 1924, Russo became a director of the National Veterans Association in 1925. Appointed Podestà (q.v.) of Udine in 1926, Russo served subsequently as prefect of Chieti, La Spezia, and Forlì. He became head of the Militia in October 1935. While Russo's Militia served adequately in Ethiopia (*see* ETHIOPIAN WAR), the three divisions he created for Spain collapsed at Guadalajara (*see* GUADALAJARA, BATTLE OF). Despite Russo's earlier insistence on these units' quality, he survived Mussolini's wrath, continuing his incompetent direction of the MVSN until November 1939. Russo then became undersecretary to the Presidency of the Ministerial Council until February 1943. As a PNF (Partito Nazionale Fascista) (q.v.) Directory member, Russo was also a deputy in the Chamber of Fasces and Corporations (*see* PARLIAMENT).

For further information see: NO (1937).

BRS

S

SALANDRA, ANTONIO (b. Troia, Foggia, August 13, 1853; d. Rome, December 9, 1931). Prime Minister from March 1914 to June 1916, Salandra was the chief mover in committing Italy to war on the side of the Entente in 1915.

Lawyer, expert author in economics and administration, and professor at the University of Rome (1879), Salandra entered the Chamber of Deputies (*see* PARLIAMENT) as a Liberal of the right in 1886, where he served until 1928. His career progressed rapidly at first. He served as undersecretary of finance from 1891 to 1892. From 1893 to 1896 he served in the same post and later at the Treasury. In 1899-1900 he was minister of agriculture. But the rise of the Liberal left and Giovanni Giolitti (q.v.) to prominence after 1900 limited Salandra's subsequent ministerial activity to participation in two brief governments led by his lifelong friend, Sidney Sonnino (q.v.). Under Sonnino, Salandra was finance minister in 1906 and treasury minister in 1909-10. Following Giolitti's resignation as prime minister in March 1914, Salandra replaced him with the prospect of a short tenure. The outbreak of war gave Salandra's government an unexpected extension of its political life, especially after the proclamation of Italy's neutrality (August 3, 1914) received the almost unanimous approval of the country. But, toward the end of 1914, after Sonnino joined Salandra's government as foreign minister, the two became convinced that Italy could not remain neutral for long. Under pressure from Giolitti, Sonnino negotiated with Austria for territorial concessions as the price of Italy's continued neutrality. By March 1915, when Sonnino concluded that Austria would never make the desired concessions, he opened negotiations with the Triple Entente (England, France, and Russia), leading to the Pact of London (April 26, 1915), which committed Italy to intervention in the war. Early in May Giolitti attempted to void the pact; but massive interventionist demonstrations (*see* INTERVENTIONIST CRISIS, 1914-1915) and, above all, the king's decision to honor the London agreement overrode the wishes of Giolitti and Parliament's majority. Salandra's expectation that Italy's intervention in the war on May 24, 1915, would lead to a rapid victory proved unwarranted. His refusal to admit large numbers of democratic interventionists into the government and a defeat in the Trentino led to Salandra's fall in June 1916 and to his political decline during the rest of the war years.

The paralysis of parliamentary government in the immediate postwar period and the specter of a Socialist revolution led Salandra to view the growing Fascist movement as a force to be harnessed in the restoration of the authority of the state. Prior to the collapse of Luigi Facta's (q.v.) government in October 1922, Salandra attempted to create a conservative Liberal-Nationalist coalition to provide "a legal form to Fascism's inevitable advent to power." Hence, when on October 28-29

Salandra failed to form a new government with Fascist participation, he recommended to the king that the mandate be offered to Mussolini, who accepted.

For the next two years Salandra collaborated with Fascism in the hope that he could help channel it in a conservative but constitutional direction. In December 1922 he accepted the appointment as Italian delegate to the Council of the League of Nations. He agreed to participate in the governmental list of candidates in the April 1924 parliamentary elections; and when the crisis precipitated by Matteotti's (*see* MATTEOTTI CRISIS) murder in June 1924 obliged Mussolini to reconstruct his government, Salandra gave his consent to the admission of two conservative Liberal ministers. But he became thoroughly disillusioned after Mussolini's dictatorial speech of January 3, 1925, which prompted Salandra to resign as delegate to the League the next day. In mid-January he made formal his breach with the regime in a statement to the press, explaining that his "loyal and disinterested collaboration had been in vain . . . a bitter delusion." Abstaining from politics after 1925, although appointed to the Senate in 1928, Salandra devoted the last years of his life to the writing of his memoirs.

For further information see: Antonio Salandra, *L'intervento, 1915: Ricordi e pensieri* (Milan: Mondadori, 1930); Antonio Salandra, *Memorie politiche, 1916-1925* (Milan: Garzanti, 1951); Antonio Salandra, *La neutralità italiana, 1914* (Milan: Mondadori, 1928).

SS

SALERNO LANDING, SEPTEMBER 9, 1943. On September 9, 1943, an Allied force composed of the U.S. Fifth Army under the command of Lieutenant General Mark Clark, with two British divisions, one regiment of British Commandoes, and a battalion of U.S. Rangers lending additional support, landed on the Italian peninsula. Despite the relative ease of the Allied landing, the Germans were not surprised. Salerno is ringed by mountains on three sides, which afforded the Germans excellent positions from which to concentrate artillery fire and infantry counterattacks on the Allied beachhead.

British and American units could not link up as planned because of stiff German resistance, and for a short time no additional landings were possible in the British sector. The British Fifty-sixth Division was pushed back, and when Panzer units breached the line composed of the U.S. Thirty-sixth Division, they were repulsed just short of the beaches, only after concentrated artillery fire at extremely close range. Reinforcements were finally landed, and two British battleships with fifteen-inch guns were employed to bolster the firepower the Allies had to rely on to repulse the repeated German counterattacks. To further lessen the strain on the Allied forces, U.S. heavy bombers and the British Fifth Division, which was pushing up from the toe of the peninsula, were called in.

With these concentrated efforts, opposition in the Salerno sector began to decrease rapidly, and the German commander, Field Marshal Albert Kesselring (q.v.), had to make a quick decision. He could remain in the Salerno sector, where his forces faced certain defeat, or he could fall back to the main line of defense in the south, the Gustav Line (q.v.). During the German retreat most of the bridges were destroyed and the roads were mined in an effort to delay the Allied advance until the main body of the German forces were safely behind the Gustav Line. With the retreat of the German forces from the Salerno sector, which began on September 16, the Allies were able to continue their drive up the Italian peninsula with the ultimate goal of liberating Rome from German occupation.

For further information see: Mark Clark, *Calculated Risk* (New York: Harper & Row, 1950); W.G.F. Jackson, *The Battle for Italy* (New York: Harper & Row, 1967); Gordon A. Shepperd, *The Italian Campaign, 1943-1945* (New York: Praeger, 1968).

WAJ

SALÒ, REPUBLIC OF. See **ITALIAN SOCIAL REPUBLIC**.

SALVATORELLI, LUIGI (b. Marsciano, Perugia, March 11, 1886). An historian and anti-Fascist, Salvatorelli took a degree in letters in 1909 and became a bureaucrat in the Ministry of Public Instruction. He dedicated himself to the study of Christianity and as early as 1912 was contributing numerous articles to Italian journals. A supporter of Giovanni Giolitti (q.v.), he believed that Italy should have remained neutral in World War I and feared that the collapse of the Hapsburg monarchy would create a large Yugoslav state dangerous to Italian interests. He fought in the war, however, and in 1921 became editor of *La Stampa* (Turin), a post he held until 1925. He was deeply involved in the political and intellectual battles of postwar Italy and in 1923 wrote his classic study of the sociointellectual origins of Fascism, *Nazionalfascismo*.

His anti-Fascist stance cost him his position at *La Stampa*, but he continued to write on historical topics. In 1942-43 he and other anti-Fascists founded the Party of Action (*see* PARTITO D'AZIONE), and in the final days of the war he edited *La Nuova Europa*, the party's weekly. After the war he wrote widely on historical subjects, including an important *History of Italy in the Fascist Period* in collaboration with Giovanni Mira.

For further information see: DSPI; Luigi Salvatorelli, *Thought and Action in the Risorgimento*, ed. Charles F. Delzell (New York: Harper & Row, 1969); Luigi Salvatorelli and Giovanni Mira, *Storia dell'Italia nel periodo fascista* (Turin: Einaudi, 1964).

MSF

SALVEMINI, GAETANO (b. Molfetta, September 8, 1873; d. Sorrento, September 6, 1957). A respected historian and an impassioned anti-Fascist, Gaetano Salvemini committed himself for more than a half-century to the life of scholar-activist. Born to lower-middle-class parents in a small town near Bari, he became a strong advocate of social and economic reform in southern Italy. His early education in Catholic schools nurtured a stern moralism that pervaded his later political and scholarly efforts and contributed to his anticlerical views. After taking his degree at the University of Florence in 1894, Salvemini began a career of teaching and writing history that he would follow ardently on both sides of the Atlantic for the rest of his life. His early writings, in themselves major contributions to modern historical study, include *Magnati e Popolani a Firenze dal 1280 al 1295* (1899), *La Rivoluzione Francese* (1905), and *Giuseppe Mazzini* (1905).

In 1901 Salvemini became professor of medieval and modern history at the University of Messina. A devastating earthquake killed his wife and five children in 1908, a tragedy that some believe contributed to the intensity with which he pursued his dual career. In 1916 he remarried (Fernanda Dauriac of Brest, France) and was appointed professor of modern history at the University of Florence, where he remained until the Fascists forced him into exile in 1925.

Salvemini's early political thought evolved from a youthful revolutionary Marxism to his own unique form of democratic socialism. Throughout, he rejected abstractions and developed an inductive approach to politics based on practical change, the *concretismo* for which he was to be known. Drawn to an affiliation with the Socialist party (1893) by his protest against the protective tariff, Salvemini had by 1902 recommended a program of specific action, which he persistently advocated until his resignation from the party in 1911: defense of small property, limitation on the power of the prefects, and universal suffrage.

Already known as an independent spirit, Salvemini after 1910 increasingly rejected the structures of organized politics. He was an outspoken critic of the government of Giovanni Giolitti (q.v.)—whom he labelled "il ministro della malavita" (minister of the underworld)—when he quit the Socialist party over its reluctance to oppose the Libyan War and to pursue universal suffrage. In 1911 he founded the radical newspaper *Unità*, in which he further developed the style of concrete socioeconomic criticism that he would later employ against the Fascists.

With the advent of World War I Salvemini opposed both the Socialists and Giolitti, supporting Italian intervention against the authoritarianism of the Central Powers in order to save the democracies and encourage national self-determination in central Europe and the Balkans. He won election to the Chamber of Deputies (*see* PARLIAMENT) in 1919 as an independent candidate on the veterans' ticket, and for two years opposed the government, the political parties, the Treaty of London, Gabriele D'Annunzio's (q.v.) designs in Fiume (q.v.), and the alternatives of the extreme right and extreme left. At the war's end Salvemini organized support for the Wilsonian program, while mounting an intense campaign in *Unità* against the politics of V. E. Orlando (q.v.), Sidney Sonnino (q.v.), the Italian nationalists, Clemenceau, and Lloyd George.

Mussolini's March on Rome (q.v.) in October 1922 caught Salvemini by surprise in Paris. Although already an opponent of his former Socialist acquaintance, Salvemini did not launch his anti-Fascist campaign until the Fascists had fully revealed themselves as antiparliamentarian, antilibertarian, and in complicity with industrialists, generals, magistrates, and other forces of conservatism. The political crisis that erupted in 1924 following the murder of the Socialist deputy Giacomo Matteotti (*see* MATTEOTTI CRISIS) traumatized the life of Salvemini just as it did the anti-Fascist cause. With students and faculty at the University of Florence, Salvemini formed the Circolo di Cultura as the hub of the Florentine resistance movement. When the Fascist police raided the office of the Circolo, Salvemini, Piero Calamandrei (q.v.), Carlo and Nello Rosselli (q.v.), and Ernesto Rossi (q.v.) created the clandestine publication *Non Mollare!* In August 1925, after an arrest related to the publication, Salvemini fled to France, thus beginning over two decades of political resistance in exile.

While lecturing, writing, and organizing in London and Paris from 1926 to 1930, Salvemini traveled to the United States on three lecture tours. It was in this transitional period that he began to express the views that gave focus to his American anti-Fascism of the 1930s and 1940s. The great power of the United States, he believed, would have a distinct influence on postwar Italy. But Americans, to his disappointment, were mistakenly sympathetic to Mussolini and ignorant of Fascism. Equally important—and equally disillusioning—was the fact that many Italian Americans found Mussolini a source of pride. Salvemini therefore began a two-pronged campaign against the Fascists: first, to expose the deceit of Fascist propaganda claims in a flurry of polemics published in American periodicals; and later, to attempt to mobilize Italian-American opinion to influence the Roosevelt administration on issues affecting wartime and postwar Italy.

In the summer of 1930 Salvemini returned to Europe, joining fellow *fuorusciti* (q.v.) in the activities of Giustizia e Libertà. He had founded GL the previous year with the Rosselli brothers, Ferruccio Parri (q.v.), and Riccardo Bauer (q.v.), as a coalition of the democratic left committed to resistance and ultimately to the creation of a democratic-socialist republic in Italy. In this transatlantic period Salvemini produced numerous articles as well as two significant books, *The Fascist Dictatorship in Italy* (1927) and *Mussolini Diplomate* (1932). It was after settling in the United States that he published *Under the Axe of Fascism* (1936), his highly provocative exposé of Mussolini's Corporate State.

In 1934 Salvemini accepted the Harvard chair as Lauro de Bosis (q.v.) lecturer in the history of Italian civilization. This began a fourteen-year residency in the United States, which included American citizenship in 1940. The resources of the Widener Library and the steady (if modest) income enabled him to intensify his anti-Fascist campaign. In an attempt to consolidate the earlier Italian exiles with those who arrived after the outbreak of war, in 1939 Salvemini founded the Mazzini Society (q.v.), an anti-Fascist organization dedicated to perpetuating the principles of Giustizia e Libertà and to influencing the American government on the "Italian question." At the same time, his tireless effort to convince the U.S. authorities to investigate American Fascists had led him to contact congressional committees and the FBI and to write the pamphlet "Italian Fascist Activities in the United States" (1940). After the Mazzini Society had begun to achieve considerable success, particularly in its attempts to counteract Fascist propaganda through its weekly *Nazioni Unite*, Salvemini broke with the leadership over its cooperation with former philo-Fascists and its support of the policies of the U.S. Department of State. In 1943 he and Giorgio La Piana authored *What to Do With Italy*, their plan for a postwar Italian society free of the monarchy, Fascism, and the Church.

In 1949, at age seventy-six, sadly disappointed at the political success of Christian Democracy, but drawn to the land of his birth, Salvemini resumed his professorship at the University of Florence. He spent his last years receiving friends and admirers at a villa in Sorrento.

For further information see: Gaspare De Caro, *Gaetano Salvemini* (Turin: Utet, 1970); Massimo L. Salvadori, *Gaetano Salvemini* (Turin: Einaudi, 1963); Gaetano Salvemini, *Opere di Gaetano Salvemini* (Milan: Feltrinelli, 1961-); Gaetano Salvemini, *Italian Fascist Activities in the United States*, ed. Philip V. Cannistraro (New York: Center for Migration Studies, 1977); Ernesto Sestan et al., *Gaetano Salvemini* (Bari: Laterza, 1959); Enzo Tagliacozzo, *Gaetano Salvemini nel cinquantennio liberale* (Florence: La Nuova Italia, 1959).

CLK

SANNA, CARLO (b. Senorbi, Cagliari, January 3, 1859; d. Rome, July 17, 1928). First president of the Special Tribunal for the Defense of the State (q.v.), as local corps commander in October 1922 Sanna cooperated with the Fascist takeover of Trieste. In June 1923 Sanna became president of the Supreme Tribunal of the Army and Navy. Elected a Fascist deputy in April 1924, Sanna headed the military subcommittee until his appointment to head the Special Tribunal in December 1926.

For further information see: NO (1928).

BRS

SANSANELLI, NICOLA (b. S. Arcangelo, Potenza, March 5, 1891). A Fascist party secretary, Sansanelli took a law degree and worked as a journalist. He fought in the Italo-Turkish War of 1911-12, and then in World War I, in which he was wounded and decorated. He was among the founders of the *fascio* of Naples and edited its newspaper, *L'Azione fascista*. He was a member of the executive committee of the PNF (Partito Nazionale Fascista) (q.v.) from 1921, was one of the signers of the Pact of Pacification (*see* PACIFICATION PACT) in August 1921, and took an active role in the preparations for the March on Rome (q.v.) (Sansanelli proposed the formal declaration issued at the Naples congress of the PNF in October 1922, calling for a southern "revolt" against the Liberal system of political patronage and local interest groups). He led a column during the March itself.

Sansanelli served as national secretary of the PNF from January 1923 to October 1924 and was a member of the Fascist Grand Council (q.v.). As party secretary he was not in a very powerful position because of his weak personality and the fact that Mussolini had not empowered the post with sufficient authority. During the debate that led to the fusion of the PNF with the Italian Nationalist Association (q.v.) in 1923, Sansanelli insisted on the complete dissolution of the latter group. He served as a deputy from 1924 and from 1926 to 1929 was *federale* of Naples. In the 1930s he held a number of minor government and party posts and directed *Il Mattino* (Naples) and *Italiani pel mondo*.

For further information see: *Chi è?* (1936); NO (1937); Raffaele Colapietra, *Napoli tra dopoguerra e fascismo* (Milan: Feltrinelli, 1962); Renzo De Felice, *Mussolini il fascista* (Turin: Einaudi, 1966).

PVC

SANSEPOLCRISTI. The Fascists used this term to denote those who attended the Milan rally of March 23, 1919, for the founding of the Fasci di Combattimento (q.v.). Mussolini and his closest followers met at 10 A.M. in a conference hall in the Palazzo Escercenti, No. 9, Piazza San Sepolcro. He announced the founding of the Fascist movement and outlined a general program of goals (*see* FASCISM).

The exact number of Sansepolcristi has been disputed, especially because the regime altered its own list from time to time when particular individuals fell from official favor, but 118 appears to be a fairly accurate number (*see* Appendix B). As a result of notices and announcements issued before the meeting, about five hundred others eventually sent statements of support.

Among these Fascists of the very first hour were F. T. Marinetti (q.v.), Michele Bianchi (q.v.), Italo Bresciani (q.v.), Roberto Farinacci (q.v.), Giovanni Marinelli (q.v.), Luigi Razza (q.v.), and Cesare Rossi (q.v.). The Sansepolcristi represented a widely diverse group that included intellectuals, workers, war veterans, syndicalists, former Socialists, nationalists, middle-class professionals, at least five Jews, and two women. It is clear, however, that the real inner core came from the political left, especially from revolutionary syndicalism, and that these men were the "professionals" with political experience and firsthand knowledge of organizational techniques. All but a handful were from the northern provinces of Italy.

For further information see: DSPI; G. A. Chiurco, *Storia della rivoluzione fascista*, I (Florence: Vallecchi, 1929); Renzo De Felice, *Mussolini il rivoluzionario* (Turin: Einaudi, 1965); Adrian Lyttelton, *The Seizure of Power* (London: Weidenfeld & Nicolson, 1973).

PVC

SARAGAT, GIUSEPPE (b. Turin, September 19, 1898). A Socialist leader, Saragat completed his degree in economics in 1919, joined Filippo Turati's (q.v.) Partito Socialista Unitario in 1922, and was elected to its directorate in 1925. He fled Fascist Italy in 1926, going first to Austria and in 1930, to France. He was active in Italian anti-Fascist circles as a journalist and writer on the philosophical aspects of Marxism. He emphasized the role of freedom above that of social justice or working-class solidarity, an attitude that helps explain his intense anticommunism. He returned to Italy in 1943 to help reorganize the Socialist party. In 1944 he was arrested by the Fascists, who handed him over to the Germans. Saragat succeeded in escaping and later participated in the Ivanoe Bonomi (q.v.) government. From 1945 to 1946 he was ambassador to France and, until January 1947, president of the Constituent Assembly (*see* COSTITUENTE). In the same month he split with the Socialist party over Pietro Nenni's (q.v.) policy of collaboration with the Communists and founded the Partito Socialista dei Lavoratori Italiani (PSLI) which, with the addition of a new Socialist group in 1951, changed its name to the Partito Socialista Democratico Italiano (PSDI). The Social Democrats cooperated with the Christian Democrats in the election of 1948 and until 1953 participated in the "Quadripartito" that governed Italy. As leader of the PSDI Saragat pursued a middle road in domestic politics and was pro-American in foreign affairs. He held a number of cabinet positions during the period and, with the coming of the Center-Left (a coalition of the Christian Democrats, the Social Democrats, the Republicans, and the Socialists), which he supported, became foreign minister in the governments of Aldo Moro. He successfully ran for president of the republic in 1964 as the candidate of the three laic parties of the Center-Left (that is, the coalition minus the Christian Democrats). He worked for the reunification of the Socialist parties (PSDI and PSI), which took place in 1966 but which lasted only until 1971.

Saragat served as president from 1965 to 1971. He was later president and secretary of the PSDI and is a life senator.

For further information see: Ugo Indro, *La Presidenza Saragat* (Milan: Mondadori, 1971); Giuseppe Saragat, *Quarant' anni di lotta per la democrazia* (Milan: Mursia, 1966); Nino Valentino, *La battaglia per il Quirinale* (Milan: Rizzoli, 1965).

                                                                                          SD

SARFATTI-GRASSINI, MARGHERITA (b. Venice, April 8, 1883; d. Cavallasca, Como, October 30, 1961). A mistress, confidante, and biographer of Mussolini, Sarfatti was a highly influential figure in the cultural and artistic policies of the Fascist regime. She was from a comfortable Venetian Jewish family, and in her early days she was an avid student of art and literature. A woman of acute intelligence and sophistication, while still in her teens she became a militant activist in the Italian Socialist party (*see* PARTITO SOCIALISTA ITALIANO) and in the feminist movement. As early as 1902 she began writing for such papers as *Avanti!* (Milan), the feminist-oriented *Rassegna femminile* (Florence), and the literary Socialist review *Avanti della domenica* (Florence); in 1912 she helped to found and wrote for *Difesa delle Lavoratrici* (Milan) along with such major Socialist women as Angelica Balabanoff (q.v.), Anna Kuliscioff, and Clara Zetkin. She moved to Milan before World War I and married a Socialist lawyer, Cesare Sarfatti, and both became close friends and supporters of Mussolini during his years as editor of *Avanti!*

The Sarfattis followed Mussolini's interventionist ideas and broke with the Socialist party at the same time in 1914. Their son Roberto (1900-18), who was killed in the war, was later the object of Fascist veneration. In 1915, when Mussolini founded *Il Popolo d'Italia*, Sarfatti became art editor for the paper and in 1919 joined Mussolini's Fascist movement.

In the years during the struggle for power Sarfatti and Mussolini became intimate friends, and she exercised an increasing influence on him. In 1921 she was made director of his journal *Gerarchia*, and in 1926 she published the first biography of Mussolini, *Dux*, an immensely successful book (for which Mussolini wrote the preface) that is still of use to scholars and for which Mussolini gave her a series of unpublished letters and diaries.

During the 1920s her reputation in the world of Italian art was such that she was dubbed the "dictator of the figurative arts." Sarfatti was one of the most avid admirers of twentieth-century modernism in the arts, and her political influence enabled her to sponsor successfully painters, sculptors, and architects working in that genre. She urged Mussolini in the 1920s to start thinking in terms of a coherent cultural policy, and her views account in large measure for the fact that the modernist current found official favor in the regime. In 1924 she was appointed head of the Italian judging committee for the International Exposition of Decorative Arts in Paris, and she also served as vice-president of the exposition itself. In Italy she was a member of various government committees dealing with cultural matters.

In 1925-26 Sarfatti was instrumental in founding the Novecento (*see* NOVECENTO MOVEMENT) art group in Milan, and it was a clear sign of her authority in the field that the committee for its first public exhibit included such important figures as Giovanni Treccani, Ada Negri, Ugo Ojetti (q.v.), F. T. Marinetti (q.v.), and Education Minister Pietro Fedele (q.v.) More important was the fact that Mussolini himself gave a major address at the opening of the exhibit on February 14, 1926, in which he outlined his ideas on the relationship between politics and art. The Novecento group—of which Sarfatti was known as the "godmother"—included such prominent artists as Carlo Carrà (q.v.), Giorgio Morandi (q.v.), Mario Sironi (q.v.), Gino Severini, and C. E. Oppo (q.v.).

In the late 1920s Sarfatti promoted the work of rationalist architect Marcello Piacentini (q.v.) against the more conservative Armando Brasini (q.v.). Yet despite her commitment to modernism—and it should be noted that the Novecento group was in some ways a compromise with traditional, classical forms—it has been suggested that Sarfatti may have been a major influence in promoting the theme of Romanità (q.v.) in Fascist propaganda.

In the 1930s Sarfatti's ties with Mussolini (and hence her influence on him) began to weaken, and by 1934 their intimate relationship had ended. She traveled in Europe and the United States on various cultural missions and continued to write and move in artistic circles. The final break came in 1938 with the passage of the Fascist anti-Semitic laws (*see* ANTI-SEMITISM). Sarfatti's articles, like those of other Jewish writers, were suppressed, a fact that she protested bitterly. In 1939 she left Italy on a passport provided for her on Mussolini's instructions. She lived in Argentina, the United States, and in Paris, and returned to Italy after the war. A month before her death at her Villa il Soldo on Lake Como, she was seen at an art gallery in Rome.

For further information see: *Chi è?* (1936); *Il Corriere della Sera*, October 31, 1961; *Enciclopedia Italiana* 30 (Rome: Treccani, 1936); Margherita Sarfatti, *Dux* (Milan: Mondadori, 1926), trans. *The Life of Benito Mussolini* (London: Butterworth, 1925); Margherita Sarfatti, *Storia della pittura moderna* (Rome, 1930).

                                                                                           PVC

SAVOIA, AMEDEO DI, DUKE OF AOSTA (b. Turin, October 21, 1898; d. Nairobi, May 3, 1942). Amedeo was viceroy of Ethiopia and the duke of Puglia. He abandoned his Army post during the March on Rome (q.v.) to join his father, the duke of Aosta (*see* SAVOIA, EMANUELE FILIBERTO DI). Amedeo was arrested by King Victor Emmanuel's orders but was subsequently released. Amedeo took leave, lived incognito in the Congo, and then returned to duty. He served intermittently in Libya under Rodolfo Graziani (q.v.), between 1925 and 1931, distinguishing himself at Bir Tagriff (February 1928) and in the Cufra Expedition (December 1930-January 1931). Despite his friendship with Italo Balbo (q.v.) and his passion for aviation, his father and Pietro Gazzera (q.v.) prevented Amedeo's transfer to the Air Force. Following his father's death, Amedeo, who was now the duke of Aosta, joined the Regia Aeronautica, commanding fighter units in Gorizia.

Victor Emmanuel (q.v.) vetoed his service in the Ethiopian War (q.v.) but agreed to his appointment as viceroy in November 1937. Amedeo inherited a rebellious colony from Graziani and received an insufferable superior, Attilio Teruzzi (q.v.), and two disloyal subordinates, Ugo Cavallero (q.v.) and Enrico Cerulli, from Mussolini. Despite frequent illness, he overcame these rivals and nearly pacified the empire, assisted by Guglielmo Nasi (q.v.) after May 1939. After warning Mussolini of the empire's vulnerability, Amedeo prepared for war with apprehension. He conquered some British territory in July-August 1940 but then abandoned offensive plans against Egypt. Plagued by growing insurgency and materiel shortages, Amedeo decided in December 1940 to defend selected redoubts, should anticipated British offensives succeed. Keren's (*see* KEREN, BATTLE OF) fall forced him from Addis, and he withdrew to Amba Alagi in April 1941. After two weeks' siege, Amedeo surrendered on May 19, later receiving the gold medal. Exhausted, he died in Nairobi.

For further information see: Alfio Berretta, *Amedeo d'Aosta* (Milan: ELI, 1956); Alfredo Ferruzza, "Il diario del vicere dell'Impero," *Gente* (February-March 1969); Luigi Romersa, "La vita di Amedeo di Savoia," *Tempo* (November

1957-February 1958); Alberto Sbacchi, *Italian Colonialism in Ethiopia 1936-1940*
(Ph.D. diss., University of Illinois at Chicago Circle, 1975); *La guerra in Africa
Orientale* (Rome: Ufficio storico dell'esercito, 1952).

BRS

SAVOIA, EMANUELE FILIBERTO DI, DUKE OF AOSTA (b. Genoa,
January 13, 1869; d. Turin, July 4, 1931). A potential Fascist candidate for king
and commander of the "undefeated" Third Army in 1915-18, the duke was Victor
Emmanuel's (q.v.) heir until Prince Umberto's (q.v.) birth. Military prestige
gained in World War I and subsequent national turmoil whetted the duke's royal
aspirations. Emanuele Filiberto plotted military dictatorship with Gabriele D'Annunzio
(q.v.) and Gaetano Giardino (q.v.), but the collapse of D'Annunzio's plans
brought the duke to Fascism. The duke's proximity to Fascist headquarters in
Umbria during the March on Rome (q.v.) was crucial in gaining Victor Emmanuel's surrender. Emanuele Filiberto made himself available again during the Matteotti
Crisis (q.v.) but only became head of Dopolavoro from December 1925 to May
1927.

For further information see: Renzo De Felice, *Mussolini il fascista* (Turin:
Einaudi, 1966).

BRS

**SAVOIA-AOSTA, ADMIRAL LUIGI AMEDEO DI, DUKE OF THE
ABRUZZI** (b. Madrid, January 29, 1873; d. Somalia, March 18, 1933). He was
the third son of Amedeo, duke of Aosta (king of Spain from 1870 to 1873 and
brother of King Umberto I of Italy). He was originally given the title "Infante di
Spagna," but his father abdicated the Spanish throne two weeks after his birth, and
the family returned to Italy where he was subsequently granted the title duke of the
Abruzzi. He chose a naval career, eventually rising to command the Italian fleet at
the outbreak of World War I. His naval service was, however, periodically
interrupted by geographic and scientific expeditions that made him one of the best
known Italians of his time.

The duke of the Abruzzi reached flag rank with promotion to rear admiral at the
end of 1909. At the outbreak of the Libyan War he was named inspector of torpedo
craft and conducted operations along the Albanian coast. In May 1912 he was
promoted to vice-admiral and in 1913 commanded the naval base of La Spezia. In
1914 he assumed command of the battle squadron and at the outbreak of World
War I was named commander in chief of the Italian fleet. The duke of the Abruzzi
proved an energetic and popular commander with something of the manner of the
grand seigneur, who also got on well with his Allies. But he was considered by
some critics to be too bold, too wedded to large ships and traditional methods of
warfare, and not sufficiently attuned to the changes the submarine had brought
about. However, there were widely divergent opinions about Abruzzi in naval
circles, and as time went on he became the target for the various frustrations

created by the indecisive nature of the naval war. In February 1917 he was finally eased out of his position, resigning ostensibly for reasons of health, and was replaced by Paolo Thaon di Revel (q.v.). Although promoted to admiral, he was given no further employment in the war.

In 1919 the duke became interested in Italian Somaliland and in 1920 founded the SAIS (Società Agricola Italo-Somala) in which he served as president. The SAIS received the largest single concession in Somalia, twenty-five thousand hectares along the lower Shebelle River. An extensive irrigation program was undertaken for the production of bananas, sugar, and cotton, and an administrative center (named Villagio duca degli Abruzzi) was built near Jowhar. By the mid-1920s the SAIS was showing a profit, although much of it was the indirect result of government aid.

The duke of the Abruzzi remained for the most part out of the public eye during the 1920s, largely because he spent most of his time in Somalia. This created at least the impression that, unlike his brother the duke of Aosta (*see* SAVOIA, EMANUELE FILIBERTO DI), he was maintaining a certain distance from the regime. Nevertheless he did represent the king of Italy on a state visit to Ethiopia in 1927. In 1928-29 he undertook the last of his expeditions to explore the sources of the Shebelle River in the Ethiopian highlands. In 1930 he was made a member of the Royal Academy of Italy (q.v.) and in 1932 became president of the newly formed Italia Shipping Line (*see* "ITALIA"—FLOTTE RIUNITE). In poor health, he resigned the position in October, and a few months later, knowing himself mortally ill, he elected to return to Somalia, where he died.

For further information see: Giotto Dainelli, *Il Duca degli Abruzzi* (Turin: Unione Tipografico, 1967); Robert L. Hess, *Italian Colonialism in Somalia* (Chicago: University of Chicago Press, 1966); Ufficio Storico della R. Marina, *La Marina Italiana nella Grande Guerra*, 8 vols. (Florence: Vallecchi, 1935-42).

PGH

SCHIAVETTI, FERNANDO (b. Livorno, August 20, 1892). A prominent anti-Fascist and Italian Republican party (*see* PARTITO REPUBBLICANO ITALIANO) leader, Schiavetti took a law degree and worked as a journalist. Committed to the Republican tradition of Mazzini, he was an active organizer for the party. He served as its political secretary after World War I and directed its journal, *La Voce Repubblicana*, until the Fascists closed it down in 1926.

Schiavetti joined the other *fuorusciti* (q.v.) in Paris in the 1920s, where he helped reconstitute the Republican party, headed a leftist faction called Azione Repubblicana Socialista (ARS), and was a member of the Concentrazione Antifascista (*see* ANTI-FASCISM). In 1933 he fused the ARS with the newly created Giustizia e Libertà movement of Carlo Rosselli (*see* ROSSELLI, CARLO AND NELLO) and was a member of the executive committee.

After the fall of France in 1940, Schiavetti fled to Switzerland. In 1943-44 he adhered to the new Party of Action (*see* PARTITO D'AZIONE) and after the liberation of Milan in 1945 directed its paper, *L'Italia Libera*. He was elected to the Constituent Assembly (*see* COSTITUENTE) in 1946 and later joined the Italian Socialist party (*see* PARTITO SOCIALISTA ITALIANO).

For further information see: *Chi è?* (1948); Charles F. Delzell, *Mussolini's Enemies* (Princeton: Princeton University Press, 1961); Santi Fedele, *Storia della concentrazione antifascista* (Milan: Feltrinelli, 1976).

PVC

SCHOOL CHARTER. The Fascist School Charter was drafted under Giuseppe Bottai (q.v.), the minister of national education, and approved by the Fascist Grand Council (q.v.) in February 1939. The Carta represented an attempt to break with the conservative elitism of the 1923 Giovanni Gentile (q.v.) reforms, toward a system more in conformity with the rural, mass-based orientation of the regime. Thus, the twenty-nine articles of the Charter defined the schools as one instrument for the formation of the "new Fascist man" and of the new culture. Special schools were established for the children of peasants and craftsmen in order to increase their attachment to the land. The reform sought to ease pressure on the white-collar-employment market by shifting students out of programs leading to the university and into technical-training institutes with terminal programs. Although there was some effort to democratize the schools by extending the age for common schools, the point of division was set at eleven years, too low to really overcome the disadvantages of poorer family backgrounds.

The reform left the classical *ginnasio-liceo* program, the core of Gentile's system, largely untouched, but flanked it by a series of specialized institutes that led only to specific university faculties. In this way it was hoped that the preeminence of the classical program would be lessened. Rules governing the state examination after the *liceo* were eased in response to complaints from parents, who resented the demanding system created by Gentile.

Some efforts were made in the direction of coordinating the schools and Fascist youth organizations (q.v.). Finally, manual labor as an educational device was introduced on all levels of schools in an attempt to instill respect for the world of physical work.

In the end, the Carta was limited by the resistance of conservative bureaucratic structures, social pressures for mobility, and the onset of World War II, which nullified the innovations of the reform.

For further information see: Teresa Maria Mezzatosta, *Il regime fascista tra educazione e propaganda, 1935-1943* (Bologna: Cappelli, 1978); L. Minio Paluello, *Education in Fascist Italy* (London: Oxford University Press, 1946); Tina Tomasi, *Idealismo e fascismo nella scuola italiana* (Florence: La Nuova Italia, 1969).

AJD

SCHUSTER, ALFREDO ILDEFONSO (b. Rome, January 18, 1880; d. Venegono, August 30, 1954). Schuster's Bavarian father had been in the papal service for twenty-five years. Schuster entered the monastic school of San Paolo Fuori Le Mura at the age of eleven and became a monk on November 13, 1899. He graduated with a degree in philosophy from the Collegio Internazionale di S. Anselmo and was ordained a priest in 1904. From 1908 to 1916 he served as head of the novices at the monastery and became an expert on liturgy and in April 1918 was elected abbot of San Paolo. A frequent inspector for the various dioceses of Milan in his capacity of apostolic envoy, in 1928 Schuster spearheaded the construction of the seminary of Venegono (Varese). On June 26 he became Bishop of Milan and on July 15, 1929, was made a cardinal by Pius XII (q.v.).

At the time of his appointment as bishop, a Fascist police report judged him to have been "favorably disposed toward Fascism, although not obviously so." Schuster was the subject of conflicting opinions: on the one hand, in the summer of 1930 he was denounced as an anti-Fascist by a group of priests from the Milanese Curia; on the other, he also received the opposite judgment in a letter signed in March 1930 by three hundred diocesans, including Stefano Jacini (q.v.)—this document condemned the blessings Schuster bestowed on Fascism in a letter to the *federale* of Milan on the eleventh anniversary of the founding of the *fasci*. Schuster was a strong defender of the rights of Catholic Action (*see* AZIONE CATTOLICA ITALIANA) and in 1938 pronounced a homily against racism in the Cathedral of Milan.

During the last few months of World War II he served frequently and with great energy as mediator between the Germans, the Fascists, and the forces of the Resistance (*see* RESISTANCE, ARMED). His primary goal was to avoid the last, extreme defense of Fascism on the retreat taking place in Milan and to prevent the Germans from causing destruction and taking hostages. He was the protagonist of the famous meeting in the Curia of Milan between Mussolini and the representatives of the CLNAI (*see* COMMITTEE OF NATIONAL LIBERATION) on April 25, 1945. After the war he turned his attention chiefly to what he believed was the Communist danger and the materialism of contemporary society.

For further information see: Giovanni Cordiglia, *Il mio cardinale* (Milan: Istituto di Propaganda Libraria, 1955); Frederick W. Deakin, *The Brutal Friendship* (New York: Harper & Row, 1962); Ildefonso Cardinal Schuster, *Gli ultimi tempi di un regime* (Milan: La Via, 1946).

SR

SCIPIONE (GINO BONICHI) (b. Marcerata, February 25, 1904; d. Arco, November 9, 1933). An Italian painter whose mature works were considered anti-Fascist, with Mario Mafai (q.v.) and Antonietta Raphael, Scipione formed the nucleus of the Roman School and brought about a decisive change in Italian painting by developing expressionist representation.

Scipione enrolled at the Academy of Fine Art in Rome (1919). He carefully studied the painting of El Greco, Goya, Tintoretto, and the baroque churches of

Rome, as well as reproductions of works by contemporary expressionists such as Soutine, Ensor, Pascin, and Grosz.

His systematic work as a painter began around 1925. He exhibited at the Bargaglia Gallery (1927) and the Doria Gallery (1928) in Rome. Beginning around 1928 he revolted against the reactionary neoclassical emphasis of Fascist art, espousing instead a romantic style based on direct experience and emotion at times described as "Catholic Surrealism." His sumptuous color and vivid fantasy won him a leading place among younger Italian artists. The years between 1929 and 1930 were most intense in production. In 1931 Scipione, who had been ill for some time with tuberculosis, had to cease work.

His expressionist work achieves a unity of life and language, an awareness of life's decadence. The result is a romantic and desperate cry that represented a dissident voice in Fascist culture, an anguished revolt against the established order. Adopted by young painters as an example of moral rectitude, his influence has increased since his early death. He was given a special memorial show at the 1948 Venice Biennale.

For further information see: Francesco Arcangeli, "Notes on Contemporary Italian Painting," *Burlington Magazine* 97 (April 1955); Giuseppe Marchiori, "Disegni di Scipioni," *Emporium* 104 (September 1946).

MCG

SCOCCIMARRO, MAURO (b. Udine, October 30, 1895; d. Rome, January 2, 1972). An Italian Communist leader and political figure, Scoccimarro received a degree in economics and in 1917 joined the Italian Socialist party (PSI) (*see* PARTITO SOCIALISTA ITALIANO). Scoccimarro served in World War I and was highly decorated. After the war he resumed his political activity, first as the secretary of the Socialist section in Udine and then as secretary of the provincial federation in Friuli. In 1921 he joined the Communist party (*see* PARTITO COMUNISTA ITALIANO) and became part of the party's directory and a member of *Ordine Nuovo*'s editorial board. In 1923 he became part of the party's secretariat along with Antonio Gramsci (q.v.) and Palmiro Togliatti (q.v.).

Between 1922 and 1925 Scoccimarro undertook many foreign missions for the party and represented it on the executive committee of the Third International. Arrested in 1926, he was accused of being one of the most important members of the Communist party and was sentenced to a long term of imprisonment. He continued to organize Communist groups while in prison and enlarged his reputation. In 1937 he was sent to Ponza and two years later, along with many other Communist leaders, he was transferred to Ventotene from which he was released in August 1943.

After September 1943 Scoccimarro remained in Rome and helped organize the Resistance (*see* RESISTANCE, ARMED) and the Communist party. He became a member of the party's central committee and that of the Committee of National Liberation (q.v.). In June 1944 he was appointed vice-commissioner for expurgation and from December 1944 to June 1945 was minister for Occupied Italy in the second Ivanoe Bonomi (q.v.) government. Under the first two Alcide De Gasperi (q.v.) governments Scoccimarro was minister of finance and was elected to the Constituent Assembly (*see* COSTITUENTE). In 1948 he was made a senator and in 1953 was elected as a deputy. From 1958 until his death he was vice-president of the Senate, a member of the Communist party's secretariat, central committee, and president of the party's central control commission.

For further information see: *Chi è?* (1948); MOI (4); *I deputati e senatori del terzo parlamento repubblicano* (Rome: La Navicella, 1958).

MSF

SCORZA, CARLO (b. Paola, Cosenza, June 15, 1897). *Ras* (q.v.) of Lucca, the last PNF (Partito Nazionale Fascista) (q.v.) secretary, and a *bersaglieri* and Arditi (q.v.) officer from 1916 to 1918, Scorza founded the Lucca *fascio*, launching their newspaper, *Intrepido*, in 1920. After gaining a reputation for brutality, Scorza led the Lucca squads in the March on Rome (q.v.), occupying Civitavecchia. As *federale* and Militia (q.v.) commander of Lucca, Scorza renamed his newspaper *Il Popolo Toscano*. Elected to the Chamber of Deputies (*see* PARLIAMENT) in 1924, he organized Giovanni Amendola's (q.v.) fatal beating. Augusto Turati (q.v.) appointed Scorza to the PNF Directory in 1926, though Scorza sought to succeed him in 1928. Reelected a deputy in 1929, Scorza helped destroy Leandro Arpinati (q.v.). In 1930 Giovanni Giuriati (q.v.) made him commander of the new Young Fascists, editor of *Gioventù Fascista*, and inspector of University Militia. Scorza led the campaign against Catholic Action (*see* AZIONE CATTOLICA ITALIANA) and then competed with Renato Ricci (q.v.) for control of Fascist youth organizations in 1931. In December 1932 Achille Starace (q.v.) dismissed Scorza from his posts and shut *Il Popolo Toscano*. Scorza remained a deputy, however, and slowly regained power, helped by Roberto Farinacci (q.v.), G. Ciano (q.v.), and service in East Africa (1935-36) and Spain (1938-39). After Starace's dismissal Scorza became president of the *Ente Stampa*, directing party publications. He served in Libya in 1940, barely escaping capture, and then dealt with PNF-Militia relations. In December 1942 Scorza became a PNF vice-secretary. Mussolini assigned him to investigate the March 1943 strikes (q.v.) in Turin, then appointed him PNF secretary in April, counting on Scorza's rhetorical abilities and squadrist (*see* SQUADRISTI) fervor.

Scorza's subsequent activities remain mysterious. He inherited a decadent party and partially revived it. "If we must fall, let us swear to fall in beauty," he demanded, backing his words with assaults on "defeatists." Scorza sought national mobilization under total PNF control and a high command purge, but a suspicious Mussolini refused. Thereafter Scorza appears to have schemed to replace Mussolini's dictatorship by PNF leadership, then to use the king and Mussolini to gain, respectively, Allied and German agreements to Italian neutrality. Scorza called the Fascist Grand Council (q.v.) meeting of July 24-25 but lost control to Dino Grandi (q.v.). After Mussolini's arrest Scorza ordered PNF cooperation with Pietro Badoglio and then hid. Captured by the Germans, Scorza was tried by the Fascists for treason at Parma in April 1944, but Mussolini ordered his acquittal. Scorza fled to Argentina in 1945.

For further information see: F. W. Deakin, *The Brutal Friendship* (New York: Harper & Row, 1962); Carlo Scorza, *La notte del Gran Consiglio* (Milan: Palazzi, 1968); Carlo Scorza, *Brevi note sul fascismo—sui capi—sui gregari* (Florence: Bemporad, 1930).

                                                                                    BRS

SEBASTIANI, OSVALDO (b. Ceccano, Rome, August 23, 1888). Mussolini's private secretary, Sebastiani maintained a rather low profile throughout the history of the regime. He took a law degree from Pisa, was an avid interventionist, and fought and was decorated in World War I. He was a 1919 veteran of the Fascist movement and served on Mussolini's secretarial staff from 1922 until 1934, when he was made Segretario Particolare after the resignation of Alessandro Chiavolini (q.v.), a position he maintained until Mussolini's fall from power in 1943.

For further information see: *Chi è?* (1936); NO (1937).

                                                                                    PVC

SECCHIA, PIETRO (b. Occhieppo Superiore, Vercelli, December 19, 1903; d. Rome, July 7, 1973). A leading Communist organizer and writer, Secchia was a militant member of the Socialist youth federation in 1919, immediately assumed an anti-Fascist position, and joined the Communist party in 1921. He was arrested by the Fascists in 1922 after organizing Communist cells in his home region, was released, and arrested again the next year. In Milan he became secretary of the local section of the Communist youth organization.

In June 1924 Secchia fled to France, where he worked to politicize factory workers and attended the congress of Communist international youth. He returned to Italy in 1925, was made a member of the Communist party central committee, and was arrested in November. After his release ten months later, he resumed his underground work, editing many journals. He was instrumental in the reorganization of the party that took place in 1930-31 and that gave them the best underground structure in Italy. The Fascists arrested him still another time in April 1931, and he remained in prison until 1943, when he participated in the defense of Rome against the Nazis. He then helped to organize partisan groups (including the Brigate d'assalto Garibaldi) and was a member of the party's directorate for northern Italy.

After the war Secchia was elected to the Constituent Assembly (*see* COSTITUENTE) and in 1948 was made a senator.

For further information see: DSPI; MOI (4); Paolo Spriano, *Storia del partito comunista italiano* (Turin: Einaudi, 1967-75).

                                                                                    MSF

SEGRÈ, EMILIO (b. Tivoli, February 1, 1905). The son of an industrialist, Segrè entered the University of Rome as an engineering student but shifted to physics and received his Ph. D. degree under Enrico Fermi (q.v.) in 1928. After a year in the Italian Army he joined the Rome physics faculty, where he continued research with Fermi until 1935, when he became professor and chairman of the physics department at the University of Palermo. The following year he visited the University of California physics department, and, because he was an opponent of Fascism, migrated to Berkeley in 1938 to work as a research associate in the radiation laboratory. He became an American citizen in 1944.

Segrè worked with Fermi in bombarding various elements with neutrons and observed similar work at Berkeley. While at Palermo he discovered technetium, a new element produced by the bombardment of molybdenum, and after moving to Berkeley he was a codiscoverer (with Glen Seaborg and others) of plutonium, soon to be used in making one of the first atomic bombs. From 1943 to 1946 Segrè was a member of the Los Alamos research group that put together and tested the first fission bomb. After World War II he returned to the California physics department as a full professor. His greatest success came in 1955 when he and Owen Chamberlain discovered the antiproton, a particle with the mass of a proton but bearing a negative charge. This discovery helped validate the theory of antimatter, advanced several years earlier by Paul Dirac and others, and won the Nobel prize in physics for Segrè and Chamberlain in 1959. Since 1972 Segrè has been a professor emeritus.

For further information see: *Current Biography* (*1960*), ed. Charles Moritz (New York: Wilson, 1961).

MMV

SENISE, CARMINE (b. Naples, November 28, 1883; d. Rome, January 24, 1958). A Fascist police chief, Senise became an administrator in the Ministry of the Interior in 1908 and during the March on Rome (q.v.) was head of the ministry's Press Office. In 1932 he was promoted to prefect and in the 1930s served under Arturo Bocchini (q.v.) as vice-chief of police. In December 1940 he succeeded Bocchini and retained his position until Mussolini removed him in April 1943 for not having taken strong action against strikers (*see* MARCH 1943 STRIKES) in northern Italy. During his tenure as police chief Senise made many enemies and was disliked by both the Germans and his fellow Fascists.

Shortly after his appointment as police chief, Senise had begun to make plans to halt internal disorders, should the Fascist government collapse, and during 1942 he began to anticipate the formation of a non-Fascist government. Senise knew about and helped plan the technical details of the July 25, 1943, coup d'etat. He met with other conspirators and helped arrange strategy for Mussolini's arrest. Once the former Fascist leader had been arrested and sent to Gran Sasso, Senise ordered that he be shot if he tried to escape, an order he later rescinded in fear of angering the Germans.

Senise regained his post as chief of police in the first Pietro Badoglio (q.v.) government and served until September 23, 1943. He was then arrested by the Nazis and deported to Germany.

For further information see: *Chi è?* (1936; 1948); DSPI; F. W. Deakin, *The Brutal Friendship* (New York: Harper & Row, 1962); Carmine Senise, *Quando ero capo della polizia 1940-1943* (Rome: Ruffolo, 1946).

MSF

SERENA, ADELCHI (b. Aquila, December 27, 1895). PNF (Partito Nazionale Fascista) (q.v.) secretary Serena joined the Fascists in February 1921. Serena became Aquila's Blackshirt (*see* SQUADRISTI) commander, *federale*, deputy (1924), and, in 1926, Podestà (q.v.). Appointed a member of the PNF National Directory in 1932 and then a party vice-secretary in December 1933, Serena ran the PNF during Achille Starace's (q.v.) Ethiopian service in 1936. Appointed to the Chamber of Fasces and Corporations (*see* PARLIAMENT) in 1939, Serena became Public Works minister that October, concentrating on military construction. Named party secretary in October 1940, Serena attempted a national mobilization. His intellectual shortcomings, lack of leadership, and feuding with the police over responsibility for internal order, as well as the association of the PNF with Italy's crumbling economy brought his dismissal in December 1941.

For further information see: NO (1937); Galeazzo Ciano, *Diary 1939-43* (Garden City: Doubleday, 1945).

BRS

SERENI, EMILIO (b. Rome, August 13, 1907; d. Rome, March 20, 1977). A leading Communist organizer and historian, Sereni took a degree in agricultural science in 1927. A member of the Communist party from 1928 on, he helped organize its activities in Naples. He was arrested in 1930 and condemned to fifteen years imprisonment. Freed in 1936, however, he went to Paris and became a member of the party's central committee in exile. During World War II he undertook propaganda work among the occupation forces and directed the journal *Parola del Soldato*. He was arrested by the Nazis in June 1943 and condemned to eighteen years in prison but was freed in 1944. Sereni then played a leading role in organizing the Communist forces in the Resistance, becoming a member of the CLNAI (Comitato di Liberazione Nazionale per l'Alta Italia) (*see* COMMITTEE OF NATIONAL LIBERATION) and president of the anti-Fascist provisional government of Lombardy.

After the war Sereni was a deputy in the Constituent Assembly (*see* COSTITUENTE) and in 1946 was minister for postwar assistance in the Alcide De Gasperi (q.v.) government and then minister for public works. From 1945 on he was a member of the Communist party's central committee and was made a senator in 1948, becoming a deputy twenty years later.

For further information see: DSPI; MOI (4); *I deputati e senatori del terzo parlamento repubblicano* (Rome: La Navicella, 1958); Emilio Sereni, *Il capitalismo nelle campagne* (Turin: Einaudi, 1947).

MSF

SERPIERI, ARRIGO (b. Bologna, June 15, 1877; d. Florence, January 1959). A Fascist minister and agricultural expert, Serpieri took a degree in agricultural science in 1900 and from 1907 to 1913 was a professor at the Politecnic Institute in Milan, after which he taught at the Istituto Superiore Forestale. He later directed the Istituto and became a well-known expert in all questions relating to agrarian economy.

Before World War I he associated with the reformist wing of the Socialist party and volunteered for combat in 1915. By the end of the conflict he had already developed a plan for the revitalization of the Italian economy that included increased production, a cutback in consumption, treaties for obtaining raw materials, and the opening of new markets.

Only a lukewarm Fascist, in August 1923 Mussolini nevertheless appointed him undersecretary in the Ministry of Agriculture, despite the objections of intransigent leaders like Roberto Farinacci (q.v.). He was relieved from that post in July 1924, having made extensive reforms in agricultural legislation.

In April 1924 Serpieri was elected a deputy, a post he held until 1939. In December 1928 he wrote the law establishing the Bonifica Integrale (q.v.) program, for which he became undersecretary in September 1929. He resigned from that position in January 1935, after the regime had cut back on its funding. He continued to write widely on agricultural topics.

For further information see: DSPI; NO (1928; 1937); Stefano Lepre, "Arrigo Serpieri," in *Uomini e volti del fascismo*, ed. F. Cordova (Rome: Bulzoni, 1980).

MSF

SERRATI, GIACINTO MENOTTI (b. Oneglia, November 2, 1872; d. Lombardy, May 11, 1926). One of the most popular leaders of Socialist opposition to World War I, Serrati was torn between his loyalty to the traditions of Italian socialism and the Third International during the tumultuous postwar era. He was first forced into political exile at the age of twenty-two. For the next eighteen years he worked as a Socialist propagandist among Italian emigrants in France, the United States, and Switzerland. Upon returning to Italy in 1912, Serrati became an advocate for moderation within the PSI's (Partito Socialista Italiano) (q.v.) revolutionary intransigent faction. When Mussolini deserted the PSI for interventionism, Serrati was chosen to replace him as director of *Avanti!*—a position he maintained until 1923.

As director of *Avanti!* during the war, Serrati defended both party unity and its official policy of neither supporting nor sabotaging the war. His personal views, however, were considerably to the left of this elastic stance. At the Kienthal

Conference and in the pages of *Avanti!*, Serrati expressed a sentimental solidarity with Lenin. Unable to reconcile this solidarity with his deeply rooted unitarianism, Serrati came to personify the equivocations of postwar Maximalism. By refusing to expel the reformists in 1920 as demanded by Lenin's "Twenty-one Points," he helped provoke the left schism at Livorno. In 1922 Serrati finally agreed to expel the reformists; hesitantly he gravitated toward the Third International faction. At the Communist International's Fourth Congress Serrati signed a manifesto calling for fusion between the PSI and PCI (Partito Comunista Italiano) (q.v.). To discourage this united front, Fascist police arrested Serrati and other "fusionists." A few months later in August 1923, Serrati was expelled from the PSI for collaborating in the Communist journal *Pagine Rosse*. In 1924 he joined the PCI. As a Communist Serrati concentrated on reviving autonomous union activity, despite Fascist repression. Serrati died en route to a clandestine Communist meeting in Lombardy.

For further information see: Franco De Felice, *Serrati, Bordiga, Gramsci e il problema della rivoluzione in Italia, 1919-1920* (Bari: De Donato, 1971); Tommaso Detti, *Serrati e la formazione del Partito comunista italiano: Storia della frazione terzinternazionalista 1921-1924* (Rome: Riuniti, 1972); Anna Rosada, *Giacinto Menotti Serrati nell'emigrazione (1899-1911)* (Rome: Riuniti, 1972).

NGE

SFORZA, CARLO (b. Montignoso, September 25, 1873; d. Rome, September 4, 1952). An Italian diplomat and anti-Fascist exile, Sforza played a significant role in the evolution of American policy in Italy between 1940 and 1952. After receiving a law degree in 1896, Sforza entered the Italian diplomatic service. He served as secretary to Italian Foreign Minister Visconti Venosta at the Algeciras Conference (1906), as Italian minister in China (1911-15), and as Italian representative to the Serbian Government-in-exile (1915-18). After World War I Sforza was Italian high commissioner in Turkey. In 1921 he became minister of foreign affairs in the last government of Giovanni Giolitti (q.v.). In this capacity Sforza negotiated the Treaty of Rapallo with Yugoslavia and aided Giolitti in settling the Fiume (q.v.) issue. These actions left a legacy of mistrust among Balkan states and aroused the ire of extreme nationalists in Italy.

After the fall of Giolitti's government in 1922, Sforza accepted the post of ambassador to France. He resigned this office in October 1922 as a protest against Mussolini's appointment as prime minister. From 1922 to 1926 Sforza remained in Italy where, as a member of the royal senate, he maintained his opposition to the Fascist regime. In 1926 he emigrated to France, where he played a minor role in exile politics. Sforza's talents as a diplomat were not particularly suited to the highly charged atmosphere of political maneuvers and ideological conflicts that dominated the Italian exiled community.

When France was invaded in May 1940, Sforza fled to Great Britain. In July 1940 he sailed to the United States where he remained until October 1943. Sforza quickly established himself as the spokesman and leader of a broad anti-Fascist coalition. He tirelessly pressed American politicians and diplomats to provide a mechanism through which anti-Fascist exiles could play a role in the democratic reconstruction of Italy. Sforza proposed the creation of an Italian national committee to serve as a government in exile and as a rallying point for all Italians outside occupied Europe. In addition, Sforza wished to form a volunteer military force of anti-Fascists, the Italian Legion, to make an Italian contribution to the liberation of Italy.

American policymakers were unwilling to create either a government in exile or a volunteer legion. Nevertheless, Sforza enjoyed a position of special influence with U.S. leaders. He personified a moderate approach to the reconstruction and democratic modernization of the Italian state. The United States also utilized Sforza in its efforts to assure the loyalty of Italians in South America. In August 1942 an American-backed congress of Italian anti-Fascist organizations met at Montevideo (*see* MONTEVIDEO CONGRESS) and chose Sforza as its leader.

After the Italian surrender the United States assured that Sforza was quickly returned to Italy in order to provide a democratic and moderate alternative to the Pietro Badoglio (q.v.) regime. During the next eighteen months Sforza played major roles in the Italian government and in the struggle over Italian policy between the United States and United Kingdom. He was a minister without portfolio in the second Badoglio government, high commissioner for defascistization, and presiding officer of the Consultive Assembly during the Ferruccio Parri (q.v.) ministry. The British government twice blocked Sforza's selection as foreign minister. The second British veto (December 1944) provoked the most serious public clash between the two Allied governments over occupation policies in Italy.

After the war Sforza finally returned to the Ministry of Foreign Affairs in the fourth Alcide De Gasperi (q.v.) government. From this position he led Italy into a close alliance with the United States. Sforza was a leading proponent of both the European Recovery Plan and the North Atlantic Treaty Organization (NATO). He was especially active in the affairs of NATO until ill health forced him to resign the post of foreign minister in 1951.

For further information see: James E. Miller, "Carlo Sforza e l'evoluzione della politica americana verso l'italia, 1940-1943," *Storia Contemporanea* 7 (1976); Carlo Sforza, *Contemporary Italy* (N.Y.: E. P. Dutton, 1944); Carlo Sforza, *Cinque Anni a Palazzo Chigi* (Rome: Atlante, 1952); Antonio Vasori, "La politica inglese e il conte Sforza, 1941-1943," *Rivista di Studi Politici Internazionali* 43 (1976); Livio Zeno, *Ritratto di Carlo Sforza* (Firenze: Le Monnier, 1975).

JEM

SICILIAN SEPARATIST MOVEMENT. One of the most important post-World War II Italian political phenomena, the Sicilian Separatist Movement arose from Sicily's continuing disillusionment with the Italian state and the excesses of Fascism. Organized prior to the Allied invasion of Sicily in July 1943, the movement appeared publicly as the Allies crossed the island. Led by the exdeputy and minister of state, Andrea Finocchiaro-Aprile (q.v.), along with some of the leading political figures of the island, the movement was labeled a reactionary effort to preserve the privileges and powers of Sicily's great landowners and the Mafia, but it had a large degree of popular support that cut across all socioeconomic lines.

The movement thrived on the disastrous economic conditions in Sicily, as well as on the Allied failure to rule the island effectively. With the reemergence of political parties, the appointment of Salvatore Aldisio (a leading Christian Democrat) as Sicilian high commissioner in August 1944, and deep internal divisions of their own, the separatists became increasingly more radical. Plans for a seizure of power were made in October 1944, and the next year the movement established the Esercito Volontario per l'Indipendenza della Sicilia (EVIS) under the leadership of Antonio Canepa, who was killed by Carabinieri in June 1945. In October, on the pretext of having committed treason by his appeal to the San Francisco and London conferences, Finocchiaro-Aprile was arrested. The movement was badly defeated in the elections for the Constituent Assembly (*see* COSTITUENTE) in 1946, and the granting of autonomy to the island effectively destroyed separatism.

For further information see: Giuseppe Carlo Marino, *Storia del separatismo siciliano* (Rome: Riuniti, 1979).

MSF

SIDI EL BARRANI, BATTLES OF (1940). The scene of an empty victory and a crushing Italian defeat, the unpromising desert around the town of Sidi el Barrani (sixty miles inside Egypt) fell to Rodolfo Graziani's (q.v.) forces on September 16, 1940, after Mussolini had spent the summer prodding the reluctant marshal to take the offensive. Beyond Sidi el Barrani Graziani refused to go, offering a variety of excuses. His forces were still there, deployed for the next bound into Egypt, when the small but well-trained armored and motorized forces of General Sir Richard O'Connor attacked without warning on December 9. Graziani's forward divisions disintegrated within three days, and the British proceeded into Libya, took Bardia and Tobruk, and enveloped what remained of Graziani's forces in Cyrenaica at Beda Fomm (February 5-7, 1941). The British offensive followed Taranto (*see* TARANTO, ATTACK ON) and the disasters in Albania and converted the Italian "parallel war" into an irremediable catastrophe that only Luftwaffe and Afrika Korps could retrieve. German intervention in turn reduced Italy to satellite status.

MK

SILONE, IGNAZIO (b. Pescina dei Marsi, L'Aquila, May 1, 1900; d. Geneva, August 22, 1978). A journalist and political activist, Silone made his greatest reputation as a novelist and was generally recognized as one of the major writers of his time. A participant in the creation of the Italian Communist party

(PCI-Partito Comunista Italiano) (q.v.), he converted in 1930 to socialism, which he supported until his retirement from politics twenty years later.

Born Secundo Tranquilli, son of a small landowner and a weaver of the Abruzzi, he was orphaned at fourteen when an earthquake killed his mother. He attended a Jesuit school in Rome until a doctor told him he was the victim of an incurable lung disease. His studies thus interrupted, he returned to his village where he joined the Peasant League of Pescina, the Federation of Land Workers of the Abruzzi, and the Socialist party (PSI-Partito Socialista Italiano) (q.v.).

In January 1921 he represented the Socialist Youth Federation at the Livorno Congress that established the PCI. He was elected to the central committee of the Communist Youth Federation and in the next decade assumed an active role in party leadership. He edited several newspapers, including *Avanguardia* and *Il Lavoratore*, contributed to numerous anti-Fascist journals, and took responsibility for the PCI underground. Elected to the PCI central committee, he traveled extensively—to Moscow, Germany, France, and Spain. In 1924, while organizing Communist youth groups in Madrid and Barcelona, he was arrested and ultimately expelled. In a Spanish prison he took the pseudonym Ignazio Silone.

In 1930 Silone's career changed directions abruptly. Upon returning to Italy, he found that the Special Tribunal for the Defense of the State (q.v.) had issued a warrant for his arrest and had already incarcerated his younger brother. He fled to Switzerland where he was to spend fifteen years in exile in the Ticino and in Zurich. He also became rapidly disillusioned with communism in this period. When he made his views public, he was expelled by the Swiss Communist party with the support of the PCI and the Communist International.

Nineteen thirty was also the year of Silone's first major literary success, *Fontamara*. Setting his novel among the peasants, landowners, and officials of a poor Abruzzi village, Silone conveyed a social message in the dignity and simple humanity of the struggles of his characters. *Fontamara* created considerable controversy and ultimately became a best-seller in fourteen countries. He produced his best works within the next eight years while in exile: *Der Faschismus* (1934); the peasant tragedy *Bread and Wine* (1936), which reasserted the basic themes of *Fontamara* and became his best-known work; and *School for Dictators* (1938), a political analysis in the style of Plato's *Republic*, characterized by *The Nation* as the most convincing attack on dictatorship in modern literature.

With the support of Olindo Gorni, in 1941 Silone established in Zurich the PSI Foreign Center. He coordinated communications among the various European Resistance movements (*see* RESISTANCE, ARMED), smuggled pamphlets into Italy encouraging "civil disobedience" among Italians, and published the clandestine journal, *Terzo fronte*. In December 1942 he was arrested and briefly confined by Swiss authorities. He joined the PSIUP (Partito Socialista Italiano di Unità Proletaria) in 1942 and remained adamantly opposed to unity with the PCI throughout the war.

His return to Italy in October 1945 bolstered the Socialist resistance and initiated the final phase of his political career. He joined the newly reestablished PSI, assumed editorship of *Avanti!*, and served in the Constituent Assembly (*see* COSTITUENTE) as a left-wing Socialist. When the Socialists split in 1947, he followed Giuseppe Saragat (q.v.) into the new Social Democratic party. In late 1949 he helped to found the Socialist Unified party, a rallying ground for dissident socialists.

Tiring of his many political campaigns, Silone retired from active politics in 1950 to return to his literary endeavors. He had been founder and president of the Teatro del Popolo, managing editor of *Europa Socialista*, and chairman of the Association for the Freedom of Italian Culture. In the 1950s he contributed an autobiographical segment to the anti-Communist anthology, *The God That Failed*, and served as coeditor of the anti-Communist review, *Tempo Presente*. His growing anti-communism at the height of the cold war was well-received in Western Europe and the United States, where he always had been more widely acclaimed than in Italy.

For further information see: DSPI; MOI (4); Aldo Garosci, *Storia dei fuorusciti* (Bari: Laterza, 1953); Paolo Spriano, *Storia del PCI*, 1-2 (Turin: Einaudi, 1967-69); Ferdinando Virdia, *Silone* (Florence: La Nuova Italia, 1967).

CLK

(SIM) SERVIZIO INFORMAZIONI MILITARI. The Servizio Informazioni Militari (SIM) was the regime's principal foreign intelligence service. Subordinate administratively to the War Ministry and operationally to the Army staff, its interests were broader and its resources greater than those of its naval and Air Force counterparts, the Servizio Informazioni Segreto (SIS) and Servizio Informazioni dell'Aeronautica (SIA).

SIM took shape as a modern intelligence service in World War I, but demobilization led to a drastic reduction in size and scope. Colonel Attilio Vigevano, chief from 1921 to 1926, nevertheless preserved the basic structure of the organization. His four immediate successors concentrated with some success on the military plans and internal politics of Italy's immediate potential enemies and victims, Yugoslavia and Ethiopia. SIM also coordinated Italy's support of Croat and Macedonian terrorism against Yugoslavia from 1928-29 on and helped with the subversion of Haile Selassie's (q.v.) chiefs.

In February 1934 Colonel Mario Roatta (q.v.) took over SIM. Roatta, a man of cynicism and drive, presided over a further politicization and considerable expansion of the service, which may have played a role in the assassination of King Alexander of Yugoslavia in October 1934. In September 1935 SIM supplied Mussolini with decrypts of messages between the Admiralty and British fleet in the Mediterranean which suggested that the fleet was short of antiaircraft ammunition and the British show of force a bluff. This evidence, along with Dino Grandi's (q.v.) reports from London and British assurances of goodwill, freed Mussolini to attack Ethiopia (*see* ETHIOPIAN WAR), despite the fear of many of his military subordinates that war with Britain would reduce Italy "to a Balkan level." In addition, SIM provided the Duce and his commanders with virtually complete knowledge of Ethiopian diplomatic moves in Europe and practically all Ethiopian tactical traffic. The service also cut off much of Ethiopia's arms supply by bribery, assassination, and sabotage. Finally, Roatta negotiated secretly with Haile Selassie in December 1935-January 1936 and subsequently planned to murder the monarch, a step Mussolini vetoed.

Having proved their usefulness, Roatta and SIM were charged under G. Ciano's (q.v.) direction, to aid the Spanish rebels (see SPANISH CIVIL WAR) in August 1936; Roatta coordinated Italian and German activities in discussions with his German counterpart, Admiral Wilhelm Canaris. But Roatta's duties in Spain took him away from day-to-day direction of SIM which fell to his deputy, Colonel Paolo Angioy, and to the head of the counterespionage section, Santo Emanuele. The latter, apparently at the orders of Mussolini, Ciano, and Filippo Anfuso (q.v.), arranged a sabotage campaign against the Spanish Republic and the June 1937 assassination of the Rosselli brothers (see ROSSELLI, CARLO AND NELLO). In postwar testimony Emanuele implicated both Angioy and Roatta in the latter affair. Besides operating in Spain, SIM also expanded into the Middle East from 1936 on by helping finance and arm the Palestinian Arabs.

Subversion, sabotage, and assassinations perhaps distracted SIM from its main task, the providing of timely and accurate military and political intelligence. The small size of its central staff of analysts and its narrow military viewpoint made farsighted and consistent assessment difficult, despite SIM's spectacular successes in purloining secret material from foreign embassies in Rome and in decrypting the diplomatic traffic of most of Italy's smaller neighbors. Lack of funds, which restricted its network of stations abroad to a mere five until Italy entered the war in 1940, also inhibited performance. Even in the purely military domain SIM had difficulty. It seriously exaggerated French strength in the Alps and Tunisia in 1939-40 (although the exaggeration may have been at least partly deliberate: General Giacomo Carboni [q.v.], protege of Ciano and head of SIM after the October 1939 change of guard, appears to have done his best to dissuade Mussolini tactfully from entering the war). Carboni's position inevitably suffered. His immediate superior, Ubaldo Soddu (q.v.), deprived SIM of Emanuele's counterespionage and "special services" section in April 1940, then procured Carboni's dismissal in September; the latter's sudden enthusiasm for the prospects of Italy's march on Alexandria did not save him.

As Carboni's successor Soddu chose the deputy chief of SIM, Colonel Cesare Ame, a dour professional who led the service until August 1943. Under Ame SIM expanded its foreign operations rapidly from eleven stations abroad in September 1940 to fifty-three in May 1941, with emphasis on North Africa, the Middle East, and the Balkans. By his own account Ame saved Italy's front in Albania in April 1941 by breaking into the Yugoslav command net with impeccably drafted and enciphered messages ordering the Yugoslav divisions attacking from the north to retreat. He also recaptured counterespionage after Soddu's forced retirement in January 1941 and subsequently acquired a supervisory role in coordinating all service intelligence activities under the aegis of Ugo Cavallero's (q.v.) newly authoritative Comando Supremo (q.v.). But Ame failed to achieve full control of Navy and Air Force intelligence, and the reorganization of November 1941, which hived off SIM's army sections to form an independent Servizio Informazioni dell'Esercito, left SIM as a mere department of the Comando Supremo with only a very small central staff in charge of assessment and dissemination of intelligence.

SIM played no part in Mussolini's overthrow in 1943. After July 25 Ame did help convince Berlin through his cooperative counterpart, Canaris, that Italy would remain loyal. SIM also monitored the arrival and deployment of German troops in Italy, although with indifferent accuracy and timeliness. In addition, the service served as a police arm of the Pietro Badoglio (q.v.) regime. Carboni, whom Badoglio reappointed chief of SIM on August 18, had Soddu arrested for alleged complicity in nonexistent Fascist plots, interrogated Cavallero, and organized the arrest that led to Ettore Muti's (q.v.) demise while attempting to escape. When the Germans moved on September 8-9, Carboni gave a few incoherent orders, emptied SIM's safe of hard currency and valuables, and disappeared. SIM fell apart along with the rest of the armed forces.

For further information see: Cesare Ame, *Guerra segreta in Italia (1940-1943)* (Rome: Casini, 1954); Giacomo Carboni, *Memorie segrete* (Florence: Parenti, 1955); Clara Conti, *Servizio segreto* (Rome: Donatello De Luigi, 1946); Carlo De Risio, *Generali, servizi segreti e fascismo* (Milan: Mondadori, 1978); Giorgio Pillon, *Spie per l'Italia* (Rome: Trevi, 1968).

MK/BRS

SIRIANNI, GIUSEPPE (b. Genoa, April 18, 1874; d. Pieve Ligure, August 13, 1955). Appointed undersecretary of the Navy on May 14, 1925 (under Mussolini), and then minister from September 12, 1929, to November 6, 1933, Admiral Sirianni subsequently joined the Cogne steelworks as president and director. He pressed for the construction of cruisers, destroyers, and submarines. Not until 1933-34 did the Navy turn to modernizing and increasing its battleships.

For further information see: Romeo Bernotti, *Cinquant'anni nella Marina militare* (Milan: Mursia, 1971); *Corriere della sera*, August 17, 1955.

MK

SIRONI, MARIO (b. Sassari, March 12, 1885; d. Milan, August 14, 1961). An Italian realist painter who was one of the founders of the Novecento Movement (q.v.), Sironi was a major protagonist in the attempt to formulate an aesthetic for the Fascist regime. He advocated a reevaluation of the plastic values that had been destroyed by impressionism.

He withdrew from the School of Engineering at the University of Rome in order to dedicate himself to painting. Study with Giacomo Balla (q.v.) brought him in contact with Umberto Boccioni and Gino Severini, with whom he became friends. Following a move to Milan, he briefly joined the Futurist (*see* FUTURISM) and Metaphysical movements, but his sympathies were with the study of form and value as advocated by the Valori Plastici philosophy.

These leanings flowered in his leadership role in the Novecento Movement. Sironi was among the original group of artists meeting in the Pesaro Gallery (Milan) in 1922 that called for a "return to order" and a nationalist orientation in which the Italian aesthetic tradition would be transmuted in the future. As art critic for *Il Popolo d'Italia*, he continued to shape the development of the movement.

In addition to the recovery of the roots of Italian aesthetics, Sironi supported the recovery of the technical traditions of such media as mosaics, fresco, and monumental relief. Projects reflecting these interests and Fascist ideology include the Milan Triennale Mural (Sironi was a board member), Chancellor's Palazzo Allegory (University of Rome), Palazzo del Ministero delle Corporazioni Window (Rome, "I Pescatori" awarded second prize by the Carnegie Institution, Pittsburgh, 1931), and Fiat Pavilion Decorations (Fiera di Milano).

For further information see: "Dix compositions de Sironi," *Cahiers d'art* 25 (1950); Ugo Nebbia, "Artisti d'oggi: Mario Sironi," *Emporium* 79 (January, 1934); Giovanni Scheiwiller, *Mario Sironi* (Milan: Hoepli, 1930).

MCG

SKORZENY, OTTO (b. Vienna, 1908; d. Madrid, July 7, 1975). Skorzeny was the SS lieutenant colonel made famous by his rescue of Mussolini in 1943. On September 12, 1943, Skorzeny and his small band of commandos staged a daring assault on Gran Sasso where Mussolini was being held and flew him to freedom in Germany.

In October 1944 Skorzeny was ordered to Budapest in an effort to prevent the Hungarian government from signing an armistice with the rapidly advancing Russian Army. The son of the Hungarian leader was held as a hostage while a regime more in line with the German position could be installed.

During the Battle of the Bulge in 1944 Skorzeny commanded a unit disguised as Americans to create confusion and disrupt Allied countermeasures to the German offensive. On May 17, 1945, he surrendered to American forces near Salzburg and was imprisoned at Dachau. On September 8, 1947, he was acquitted of torturing U.S. prisoners by an Allied tribunal and was transferred to Darmstadt to await his denazification trial. On July 25, 1948, Skorzeny escaped and made his way to Spain.

While living in Spain Skorzeny ran an import-export business and wrote his memoirs. In 1958 a Vienna court acquitted him of murder and robbery in Czechoslovakia during World War II.

For further information see: Otto Skorzeny, *Secret Missions* (New York: Dutton, 1950).

WAJ

SOCIALIST PARTY. See **PARTITO SOCIALISTA ITALIANO**.

SODDU, UBALDO (b. Salerno, July 22, 1889; d. 1949). The most political of the regime's political generals, Soddu dominated relations between Mussolini and the military establishment in the year Italy entered World War II. After service in Libya and in World War I, he was Capo di Gabinetto of the War Ministry under Federico Baistrocchi (q.v.), commander of the crack "Granatieri di Sardegna" Division, and Deputy Chief of Staff for operations under Alberto Pariani (q.v.), whom he succeeded as undersecretary of war on October 31, 1939. In the winter of 1939-40 he judged French defenses "indestructible." Politically he was more prescient, justifying to Victor Emmanuel III's (q.v.) entourage Mussolini's plan to usurp the monarch's prerogatives as supreme commander with the suggestion that it would be convenient for the king to avoid responsibility and remain in reserve "in case the regime were to become shaky or actually threaten to crumble." Whether this argument or the veiled threats from Mussolini that Soddu conveyed proved most persuasive is unclear; Soddu in any case secured the monarch's acquiescence and (presumably as his reward) became deputy chief of the new Comando Supremo (q.v.) under Pietro Badoglio (q.v.) on June 13, 1940. Retaining his old post, Soddu sought with success to undermine both Badoglio and Rodolfo Graziani (q.v.) and was instrumental in fending off Badoglio's feeble objections to the Greek enterprise (*see* GREECE, INVASION OF). After the attack lost momentum, Soddu engineered his own dispatch to Albania and his appointment (November 9) to replace Visconti Prasca (q.v.). On December 4, shortly after his replacement as undersecretary by Alfredo Guzzoni (q.v.) and promotion (contrary to all rules of seniority) to full general, Soddu panicked and telephoned Rome asking for a "political intervention" to stop the seemingly irresistible Greek advance. The suggestion apparently originated with General Mario Vercellino, one of his subordinates. Mussolini momentarily despaired, then dispatched Ugo Cavallero (q.v.) to Albania, where that inveterate optimist remained to supervise Soddu, whom Mussolini finally dismissed on December 29. Soddu retired from active service in mid-January.

For further information see: NO (1937).

MK

SOFFICI, ARDENGO (b. Rignano sull'Arno, April 7, 1879; d. Poggio a Caiano, August 19, 1964). A painter and literary figure, Soffici lived in Paris from 1899 to 1907 and was a follower of Cézanne. Upon his return to Florence he collaborated with the review *Leonardo* and cofounded *La Voce* with Giovanni Papini (q.v.) and Giuseppe Prezzolini (q.v.). After having bitterly attacked Futurism (q.v.), by 1914 he had himself become a member of the movement. He fought in World War I.

In 1919 Soffici joined a broad cultural movement that proclaimed a "return to order." Growing increasingly conservative, he ultimately became an extreme cultural chauvinist and relied heavily on tradition for inspiration. This evolution brought him to the Fascist movement and to Mussolini, an attachment that remained inflexible thereafter. Throughout the Fascist regime he consistently proclaimed that Fascism would produce a "cultural revolution" and urged Mussolini to adopt the Novecento Movement (q.v.) style as the official artistic and literary movement of the state. He was also involved for a time in the so-called Strapaese (*see* STRACITTÀ/STRAPAESE) movement that favored the traditional values of rural life, and he helped edit its journal, *Il Selvaggio*. He was appointed to the Royal Academy of Italy (q.v.) in 1939.

Soffici followed Mussolini north to Salò (*see* ITALIAN SOCIAL REPUBLIC) after 1943, writing frequently for *Il Corriere della Sera* (Milan).

For further information see: *Chi è?* (1936; 1948); Philip V. Cannistraro, *La fabbrica del consenso* (Rome-Bari: Laterza, 1975); *Enciclopedia Garzanti dell' arte* (Milan: Garzanti, 1973); Edward R. Tannenbaum, *The Fascist Experience* (New York: Basic Books, 1972).

PVC

SOLDINO MOVEMENT. An obscure anti-Fascist manifestation of 1923, the Soldino Movement demonstrated the continuing loyalty of many southern Italians to the monarchy. A spontaneous and confusing phenomenon, the Soldini displayed their monarchist sentiments by wearing small medallions that contained the king's picture in their lapels. Demonstrations of this sort were common in Calabria, Basilicata, and Sicily and were joined by Orlando liberals, Masons, and a few Socialists.

For further information see: Renzo De Felice, *Mussolini il fascista* (Turin: Einaudi, 1966).

MSF

SOLERI, MARCELLO (b. Cuneo, May 28, 1882; d. Rome, July 23, 1945). A parliamentary deputy and anti-Fascist, the Liberal Soleri was elected mayor of Cuneo in 1912. He was first elected to Parliament the next year and was reelected for the last time in 1924, after which the Fascists removed him. He was not in favor of Italy's entrance into World War I, but in 1917 he volunteered for combat and was wounded. He held many cabinet posts in the years immediately before the Fascist seizure of power, including undersecretary of the navy in the F S. Nitti (q.v.) government, minister of finance under Ivanoe Bonomi (q.v.) in 1920, and minister of war in the second Luigi Facta (q.v.) cabinet in 1922.

After his parliamentary seat was taken away from him, Soleri retired from public life until 1942, when he made contacts with the anti-Fascists. In May and June he was consulted by the duke d'Acquarone (*see* ACQUARONE, PIETRO, DUCA d') and others who were plotting to overthrow Mussolini. After September 8, 1943, Soleri was forced to go underground to hide from the Nazis. Following the liberation of Rome he was minister of the treasury in the Bonomi governments and served in the Ferruccio Parri (q.v.) cabinet in 1945.

For further information see: *Chi è?* (1936); DSPI.

MSF

SOLMI, ARRIGO (b. Finale Emilia, January 27, 1873; d. Rome, 1944). A Fascist minister, parliamentary deputy, and member of the Fascist Grand Council (q.v.), Solmi studied law in Modena and Rome and in 1898 published his famous work, *Associazioni in Italia avanti le origini del commune*. He became a professor of law at a number of universities including those at Camerino, Cagliari, Siena, and Parma, and in 1912 he went to Pavia where he continued to teach for more than twenty years.

Solmi supported Italy's entrance into World War I and during the conflict directed the Comitato Lombardo Unione Insegnanti, the purpose of which was to propagandize for the war both in Italy and abroad. To further carry out his prowar sentiments, Solmi directed *Azione*, the journal of the national Liberals.

After the war Solmi resumed his teaching career as professor of political science at Milan and professor of common law in Rome. In 1924 he was elected a deputy from Lombardy on a national-Fascist list. Solmi was a deputy until 1939, played a role on many legislative committees, and was a spokesman for several important pieces of Fascist legislation including the Lateran Pacts (q.v.) and the Carta del Lavoro (q.v.). In July 1932 he became an undersecretary in the Ministry of National Education and in January 1935 was appointed minister of grace and justice, a post he held until July 1939. In November 1935 he became a member of the Fascist Grand Council (q.v.).

After the war Solmi continued to write extensively.

For further information see: *Chi è?* (1936); NO (1928; 1937); Arrigo Solmi, *Italia e Francia nei problemi attuali della politica europea* (Milan: Treves, 1930).

MSF

SONNINO, SIDNEY (b. Pisa, March 11, 1847; d. Rome, November 24, 1922). Known primarily for his conduct of foreign policy during World War I, Sonnino's fifty years of public life as publicist, student of socioeconomic and political institutions, member of the Chamber of Deputies (*see* PARLIAMENT) from 1880 to 1919, and twice prime minister (1906, 1909-10) made him one of the major figures in pre-Fascist Liberal Italy.

After a brief career in law and diplomacy, he turned to studies on political representation, the condition of the peasantry (his writings include "La mezzeria in Toscana," 1874; *I contadini in Sicilia*, 1877), and other public questions developed in many articles in the *Rassegna Settimanale* (1878-82), which he founded with Leopoldo Franchetti. After his election to the Chamber, where he sat at center-right but remaining always an independent Liberal, he championed universal suffrage, equitable taxation, labor legislation, administrative reforms, and rectitude in government. His unquestioned competence secured him posts in Francesco Crispi's government of the left (undersecretary of the treasury, 1889; minister of the treasury, 1893-96). An article ("Torniamo allo Statuto," 1897) calling for the restoration of the monarchy's constitutional prerogatives and his support of Luigi Pelloux's governments (1898-1900) against parliamentary obstructionism earned Sonnino the undeserved reputation of reactionary.

Giovanni Giolitti's (q.v.) growing mastery of Parliament after 1900 permitted Sonnino only two brief periods as prime minister (February-May 1906, December 1909-March 1910), when his attempts at instituting a program of grand reforms were thwarted by the lack of a solid parliamentary base. Sonnino nevertheless supported Giolitti's Libyan venture (1911-12) and the introduction of universal manhood suffrage (1913). Upon Giolitti's resignation in March 1914 and Sonnino's refusal to chance a third brief tenure of office, the mandate went to Antonio Salandra (q.v.), Sonnino's collaborator for thirty years. With the outbreak of war, Sonnino at first felt that Italy should remain loyal to the Triple Alliance. He soon changed his views, and when he entered Salandra's government as foreign minister in November 1914, he began negotiations for territorial compensations from Austria as the price of Italy's continued neutrality. When, in March 1915, he became convinced of the futility of these negotiations, he turned to the Triple Entente (England, France, and Russia) and concluded the Pact of London (April 26, 1915) committing Italy to intervention in the war within a month in return for the Trentino, the Alto-Adige, Istria, and a portion of Dalmatia.

The course of the war and its results disappointed many of Sonnino's expectations. Victory did not come as quickly as expected, further exacerbating the hostility between neutralists (Giolittians, Socialists, and most Catholics) and interventionists of various political persuasions. When Salandra's government was replaced by Paolo Boselli's national coalition in June 1916, Sonnino remained at the Foreign Ministry, defending with vigor Italy's interests in the eventual partition of the Ottoman Empire (April 1917), proclaiming a protectorate over Albania (June 1917), and frustrating Entente efforts toward a separate peace with Austria at the expense of Italian territorial claims (August 1917). The Italian defeat at Caporetto (see CAPORETTO, BATTLE OF) (October-November 1917) shook Sonnino's position at home; he was nevertheless retained at the Foreign Ministry in V. E. Orlando's (q.v.) government but was further weakened because of the division between democratic interventionists favoring modifications of the Pact of London to satisfy Yugoslav aspirations and Sonnino's supporters insisting on total fulfillment of the pact. When this division surfaced at the Paris Peace Conference, with President Wilson as the defender of Yugoslav claims most signally but not exclusively over Fiume (q.v.), Sonnino had to defend his position there as well as at home. Unable to compromise its often bitter differences with Wilson and the Yugoslavs, Orlando's government was overturned in June 1919, after which Sonnino abandoned politics. In October 1920 he accepted an appointment to the Senate from his old political enemy, Giolitti, but never participated in its sessions.

For further information see: Sidney Sonnino, *Opera omnia di Sidney Sonnino*, 7 vols., Benjamin F. Brown and Pietro Pastorelli, eds. (Rome-Bari: Laterza, 1972-75); Sidney Sonnino, *Discorsi parlamentari*, 3 vols. (Rome: Tipografia della Camera dei deputati, 1925).

SS

SORICE, ANTONIO (b. Nola, November 3, 1897). Capo di Gabinetto of the War Ministry from 1936 to 1941, Colonel Sorice acted as Ubaldo Soddu's (q.v.) and Mussolini's agent in circumventing Army staff and Comando Supremo during the Albanian campaign. Dismissed in Ugo Cavallero's (q.v.) purge (May 1941), Sorice returned to power as undersecretary in February 1943, after Cavallero's dismissal. With Vittorio Ambrosio (q.v.) and Pietro Badoglio (q.v.) he took part in the plotting that preceded the king's removal of Mussolini and then served until September 1943 as Badoglio's war minister.

MK

SPANISH CIVIL WAR. Italy intervened in the Spanish Civil War (1936-39) principally to encourage the establishment of a conservative, authoritarian regime in southern Europe. Supporting General Francisco Franco's Nationalist cause against the Second Republic in July 1936 would keep French forces away from the Italian border and help block the expansion into the Mediterranean of democratic governments—an area into which Mussolini wished to extend Italian influence. Further, supporting Franco would force Hitler's Germany to become an ally of Italy, since the Germans also were committed to supporting the Spanish Nationalists.

By the end of the first month of fighting, Italy had agreed to extend credit, arms, and aircraft to Franco. Mussolini sent troops and advisors to reinforce Italy's commitment to Spain. By mid-January 1937 seventeen thousand Italians were in Spain. Italian air and ground forces soon participated in combat. Regular army units from Italy took part in most of the major battles of 1937 and 1938. The first and most famous open use of Italian troops came in March 1937 at the Battle of Guadalajara (*see* GUADALAJARA, BATTLE OF). The purpose of the campaign was to surround Madrid and capture it from the Republicans. Italian units numbering tens of thousands acted together under Italian and Spanish Nationalist command but were defeated, suffering losses of three thousand dead, four thousand wounded, and about eight hundred captured. The attempt to encircle Madrid failed, the British and French protested the Italian intervention, while Mussolini committed himself publicly to stay involved until his men won a victory and until it was certain Franco's fascist government would win the war.

Off the northeast coast of Spain (Republican territory) on Palma de Majorca, the Italians established a naval and air base that they used to hammer at northern military points and at the Mediterranean city of Barcelona. Moreover, from this important base naval units could be used to block the transit of Russian aid to the Spanish Republic. Throughout 1937 and most of 1938 ships sailing to Republican zones were attacked by Italian submarines, including uninvolved vessels from Britain and France in the Mediterranean. At Nyon, Switzerland, Mussolini finally agreed to stop the attacks on neutral shipping, although his forces continued their work sporadically until the end of the civil war.

By mid-1938 Mussolini had decided to reduce Italy's intervention in Spain. By this point it appeared only a question of time before Franco would win the war. Franco's forces already occupied the majority of Spain, leaving only Madrid and the northeast corner of the country to be seized. Ten thousand Italian troops withdrew, along with numbers of Fascist party military units, leaving twelve thousand under the command of General Gastone Gambara (q.v.) with the Littorio Division. Remaining forces also included some artillery and air units of a token nature.

All total, Italian intervention on behalf of Franco far exceeded that of Hitler's Germany. Approximately fifty thousand to seventy-five thousand Italians went to Spain where four thousand died. Over 660 airplanes, 150 tanks, and 800 artillery pieces, along with other equipment, found its way into Spain. Available statistics suggest that 1,672 tons of bombs were sent to Spain in addition to 9 million rounds of ammunition, 240,000 rifles, and 7,660 military vehicles. Italians took part in over 5,300 air raids and attacked 224 ships. Italy committed 91 warships and submarines, sinking over 72,800 tons of shipping. Count G. Ciano (q.v.) agreed that Italian aid cost his government 7,500 million lire ($410 million). Italy provided substantial ground combat support but proved even more useful with its air cover. Relations between the Italian and Spanish military units were not always harmonious due to language and command problems, but they functioned as productive fighting elements.

The Italian forces in Spain came from two sources. First, the Italian Army provided the Littorio Division made up of career personnel and recruits under the command of General Annibale Bergonzoli (q.v.). The Fascist Blackshirts (see SQUADRISTI) recruited three divisions: The Dio lo Vuole commanded by General Silvio Rossi, the Black Flames led by General Giovanni Coppi, and General N. Nuvoloni's Black Arrows. There were other Italians mixed in Spanish units and in other international brigades. The most important Italian in Spain was General Mario Roatta (q.v.), who commanded Italians at Guadalajara and later served as Mussolini's chief of staff before being disgraced. With their return to Italy in May 1938 came a hero's welcome for all the Italians serving Franco's cause. Victory parades in Naples and in Rome were reviewed by King Victor Emmanuel III (q.v.) and Mussolini, a reminder of the importance that the Italian government placed on its Spanish adventure.

Italy's involvement in Spain served several significant purposes to the Duce. First, following the conquest of Ethiopia he looked for an opportunity to flex Italy's military muscle while using the momentum of recent success to its maximum advantage at home. Second, he wanted to expand Italy's influence in the Mediterranean and at the same time help give birth to another fascist government.

Third, it would block French expansion into southern Europe while simultaneously drawing Hitler closer to him.

The results of Italian intervention were mixed. The Battle of Guadalajara made public what everyone knew—that the Fascists were actively internationalizing Spain's civil war. It also led the French to conclude that mechanized troops were not as effective as once believed; a belief that would cost France its independence in June 1940. Italy's aid helped Franco establish his long rule in Spain, although the Spanish hardly assisted Rome during World War II. Yet the intervention contributed to closer bonds between Italy and Germany. The civil strife in Spain led both Rome and Berlin to point at another instance of weakness on the part of the democracies, illustrating how appeasement played its insidious role.

For further information see: Galeazzo Ciano, *Diaries, 1937-1938* (London: Methuen, 1952); John Coverdale, *Mussolini and Franco: Italian Intervention in the Spanish Civil War* (Princeton: Princeton University Press, 1974).

JWC

SPECIAL TRIBUNAL FOR THE DEFENSE OF THE STATE. On November 9, 1925, Mussolini presented to the Chamber of Deputies (*see* PARLIAMENT) "measures for the defense of the state," the text of an unconstitutional law that was part of the so-called "Exceptional Decrees" (q.v.). The law created the Tribunale Speciale per la Difesa dello Stato and established severe penalties for anti-Fascist activity and crimes against the state. The Chamber passed the law (officially dated November 15, 1926, [n. 2008]) that same day, and the Senate approved it on November 20.

Article 7 of the law provided for the creation of the military tribunal and the selection of its officers: a president chosen from the generals of the various armed services (the presidents were: Carlo Sanna [q.v.] to July 1928, G. Cristini to November 1932, and A. Tringali Casanova [q.v.] to July 1943), five judges from the officers of the Fascist Militia (q.v.), and a *relatore* or prosecutor from the military judiciary. Crimes were made retroactive, and its sentences were not subject to appeal.

Although the tribunal was supposed to cease functioning after five years, it was periodically extended and continued until the fall of Fascism in 1943. It actually began to operate on February 1, 1927, and from then to 1943 a total of 720 sessions were held: of 5,319 people tried, 5,155 were sentenced, of which 29 were given death penalties and 7, life imprisonment. A large number of the victims were Communists (including Antonio Gramsci [q.v.]), and all were anti-Fascists. The tribunal was suppressed officially by the king on July 29, 1943, by royal decree.

For further information see: EAR (3); *Aula IV: Tutti i processi del Tribunale speciale* (Milan: La Pietra, 1976); Renzo De Felice, *Mussolini il fascista* (Turin: Einaudi, 1968); Cesare Rossi, *Tribunale speciale* (Milan: Ceschina, 1952).

RAM

SPIRITO, UGO (b. Arezzo, September 9, 1896). A philosopher and university professor, Spirito studied at the University of Rome under Giovanni Gentile (q.v.) and took degrees in law and philosophy. He taught at a number of universities, including Messina, Pisa, and Genoa, before moving to Rome in the mid-1930s. Spirito had wide-ranging interests in law, economics, the corporative system, and abstract philosophy and published widely over a long career.

He edited the *Giornale Critico della Filosofia Italiana* in 1920, *Educazione Nazionale* from 1923 to 1924, and cofounded *Nuovi Studi di Diritto, Economia e Politica* in 1927-35. In addition, he was editor of philosophy, economics, and law for the *Enciclopedia Italiana* (q.v.) under Gentile's general direction.

Spirito, once a loyal follower of Gentile's theories of actualism, turned against his former mentor's philosophical system in the 1930s and developed his own theory of "problematicism." Ultimately he came to reject the possibility of self-knowledge and agreed that science, although all-encompassing, was a hypothetical form of knowledge at best.

During the debate over corporativism (*see* CORPORATIVISM AND THE CORPORATIVE STATE) that marked the late 1920s and early 1930s, Spirito emerged as the proponent of "integral corporativism." At the Ferrara congress on corporative studies (May 1932), he provoked considerable polemic by the argument that under the corporativist system the concept of property assumed new meaning because capital and labor would merge in all large enterprises. Ownership would eventually pass from stockholders to producers, who would operate enterprises on the basis of technical expertise. The class struggle would therefore be eliminated, and this would be the essential meaning of Fascism. PNF (Partito Nazionale Fascista) (q.v.) leaders and conservatives attacked Spirito's idea as "Bolshevik" (he himself later called it "Communist"), and he developed a following among university students who wanted a return to the 1919 Fascist program.

Spirito was later the president of the Fondazione Giovanni Gentile and continued to publish into the 1970s.

For further information see: *Chi è?* (1936); *Dizionario enciclopedico italiano* 11; Ugo Spirito, *Capitalismo e corporativismo* (Florence: Sansoni, 1933); Ugo Spirito, *Dall'economia liberale al corporativismo* (Messina: Principato, 1939); Ugo Spirito, *Il corporativismo* (Florence: Sansoni, 1970); G. Santomassimo, "Il dibattito sul corporativismo e l'economia politica," *Italia Contemporanea* (October-December 1975); Edward R. Tannenbaum, *The Fascist Experience* (New York: Basic Books, 1972).

PVC

SPORT. The totalitarian ambitions of Fascism aimed at the creation of a highly regimented mass society in which all groups were socialized into a single national experience. Mussolini's Italy, like Nazi Germany and Soviet Russia, used sports as one means to that end. The Fascists recognized that active and spectator sports could effectively generate collective mass enthusiasm as well as produce a sense of community marked by an aggressive spirit vis-à-vis other countries. Moreover, sports also fulfilled the attitudinal thrust of early Fascist *squadrismo* (*see* SQUADRISTI), with its rhetoric of activism, violence, physical strength, and virility.

As early as 1923 Mussolini sought to bring sports under his control by appointing Aldo Finzi (q.v.) the president of the Italian National Olympic Committee (CONI-Comitato Olimpico Nazionale Italiano) and creating in the same year the Ente Nazionale per l'Educazione Fisica (ENEF) under General Francesco S. Grazioli (q.v.) to coordinate physical education in secondary schools. Perhaps the most enthusiastic Fascist sports theorist, however, was Lando Ferretti (q.v.), former editor of *La Gazzetta dello Sport* and writer of numerous articles and books on the subject. In 1925 he took over control of CONI (which became a PNF [Partito Nazionale Fascista] [q.v.] agency in 1926) and began to coordinate all sports activity on a national basis. As head of Mussolini's Press Office, Ferretti was able to create wider sports coverage in the Italian press.

In 1927 the party's youth organizations (q.v.) took over the functions of the ENEF, and on December 10, 1928, the PNF issued the Sports Charter (Carta dello Sport), which outlined the physical education responsibilities of the youth groups, the Militia (q.v.), and the Dopolavoro (q.v.). Thousands of provincial towns throughout Italy constructed sports fields and training camps with subsidies from the central government and the party. Physical training and individual and team competitive sports were increasingly emphasized in school curricula, especially after Achille Starace (q.v.) became party secretary in 1931. Thereafter mass collective sports, field calisthenics, marching exercises, and all manner of exercise became the order of the day. Starace himself often led other party *gerarchi* (leaders) in swimming and running meets, and a photograph of him leaping through a ring of fire appeared in the national press. The fact that mass spectator sports, especially soccer, became a national mania in Italy in the 1930s was due largely to Fascist sports policies and systematic mass media manipulation.

For further information see: Felice Fabrizio, *Sport e fascismo* (Rimini-Florence: Guaraldi, 1976).

PVC

SQUADRISTI. The armed fighting force of Fascism, the *squadristi* represented the most distinctive and innovative feature of Mussolini's movement and played a decisive role in the emergence of Fascism as a major political force between 1920 and 1922. The Fascist movement stressed military organization from its inception in March 1919. The first nucleus of this military force was provided by the demobilized elite shock troops of the Italian Army, the Arditi (q.v.), who served as Mussolini's personal bodyguard and spearheaded a much-publicized assault on the headquarters of the Socialist daily paper *Avanti!* in April 1919. Initially the *squadristi* were to prepare for an eventual national-revolutionary coup d'etat, coordinated with various Nationalist plots and Gabriele D'Annunzio's (q.v.)

expedition to Fiume (q.v.). When Fascism evolved into an armed terrorist reaction against the Socialist party and trade unions during the winter of 1920-21, the tasks and social makeup of the *squadristi* changed drastically. Resistance to "bolshevism" replaced preparation for a putsch as the exclusive function of the *squadristi*. In the wake of strikes and labor disturbances in 1920, Fascism strongly appealed to the youth of the lower middle class and lumpen-proletariat as well as to students and the sons of professional people, who rushed to join the squads.

Theoretically, the squads were organized along strict military lines with a rigid chain of command and clearly defined territorial responsibilities. In practice, however, the squads tended to develop along the lines of youth gangs, with highly informal organizations linked to local conditions and direct personal ties of camaraderie and loyalty. Usually they comprised bands of adolescents and young men who gravitated around specific bars, cafes, or brothels and who found their sense of group solidarity in shared bonds of kinship and friendship. Each squad reinforced this solidarity by adopting its own distinctive name, banner, membership card, and allegiance to a particular leader.

The informal organization of the *squadristi* did not prevent them from being a highly effective fighting force under the exceptional social and political conditions that prevailed in 1921 and 1922. Financed by local propertied interests and aided by the police and Army, they made use of a wide range of military tactics and principles to destroy the Socialist movement throughout much of northern and central Italy. The successful violence of the squads rapidly increased both the popularity and prestige of the entire movement. Indeed, the terrorist offensive of the squads coincided with a massive influx of new recruits into Fascism and its sudden elevation to political prominence on the national level.

The *squadristi*, however, proved to be a mixed blessing for Mussolini and the propertied classes. Living and operating in the relative isolation of the provinces, they developed a special mentality and system of values that were quite distinct from both the reactionary objectives of the old elites and the Duce's national political aspirations. Believers in their own myth of *squadrismo*, they claimed to be the true Fascists, and as men of action they strongly distrusted politics and politicians in general. Despite the connivance of their leaders with police officials, landowners, and industrialists, many of the rank and file in the squads saw Fascism as an anarchic and populist rebellion of "youth" against the established order and the older generation in all the other parties. The battle cry, *Me ne frego* ("I don't give a damn"), best expressed their contempt for all forms of authority and their vision of themselves as insolent and lawless musketeers. In contrast to Mussolini, the *squadristi* saw violence not as a limited instrument to achieve precise political objectives, but as an end in itself, the defining feature of their way of life. Punitive expeditions and random assaults on enemies were not only individual outlets for aggression and heroic fantasies but also provided their sense of group purpose and unity. Prior to the March on Rome (q.v.), potential conflicts of interest between Mussolini and the squads were more than offset by the advantages that the Duce derived from the squads. To a great extent, Mussolini could manipulate and guide the squads through their politically ambitious bosses, while the explosive violence of the *squadristi* provided a powerful weapon in the negotiations with other political forces that culminated in the Fascist leader's accession to power in October 1922.

After the March on Rome, the *squadristi* became more a liability than an asset for the Fascist hierarchy. Once the need to combat the Socialists became less pressing, the uncontrolled violence and lack of discipline of the *squadristi* tended to alienate influential conservative backers and to limit Mussolini's personal authority and his margins for political maneuvering in Rome. While as prime minister Mussolini viewed the restoration of state authority as the chief task of Fascism, the *squadristi* had a contrasting interest in maintaining a climate of tension and fear to justify their continued violent exploits. With the police under Mussolini's direction absorbing the repressive functions of the squads, they evolved into personal instruments of local Fascist bosses, who used them to intimidate notables and party rivals. At the same time many *squadristi* began to compensate for their diminished political role by indulging in various forms of corruption from blackmail to protection rackets and theft.

Mussolini's efforts to bring the squads under his control met with limited success in the years between 1923 and 1925. The discipline and regimentation of the Fascist Militia (q.v.), which had been created after the March on Rome to give them an occupation and a legal status, was tenaciously resisted by the *squadristi*, whose enduring camaraderie and personal loyalties proved to be fairly impervious to administrative measures from above. With the coming of the Matteotti Crisis (q.v.) in the summer of 1924, the *squadristi* once again began to usurp the functions of the police. Implacably hostile to any compromise with the anti-Fascist opposition, they provided some of the pressure that led Mussolini to set up a dictatorship in January 1925. The continued violent activities of the *squadristi*, however, forced the Duce to take more drastic action against them. Concerned with foreign opinion and the approval of industry, the Army, and the monarchy, Mussolini had the squads officially disbanded and the *squadristi* disarmed in October 1925.

For further information see: Renzo De Felice, *Mussolini il fascista* (Turin: Einaudi, 1966); Adrian Lyttelton, *The Seizure of Power: Fascism in Italy, 1919-1929* (London: Weidenfeld & Nicolson, 1973); Edward R. Tannenbaum, "The Goals of Italian Fascism," *American Historical Review* 74 (April 1969).

ALC

STARACE, ACHILLE (b. Gallipoli, Lecce, August 18, 1889; d. Milan, April 29, 1945). An important Fascist leader and long-time secretary of the PNF (Partito Nazionale Fascista) (q.v.), Starace came from a middle-class family and was trained as an accountant. He served at the front in World War I and was highly decorated. In 1919 he organized Fascist squads in the Trento and Alto Adige regions and in April participated in the Blackshirt (*see* SQUADRISTI) assault against the Milan headquarters of the Socialist daily, *Avanti!* The next year he represented the Alto Adige in the central committee of the *fasci*.

Starace rose rapidly in the Fascist hierarchy, not because of any exceptional intelligence but because from the outset he demonstrated his complete loyalty to Mussolini. In 1921 he was named vice-secretary of the PNF at the Rome congress. During the last months before the seizure of power, he occupied the cities of Trento and Bolzano with his squads, and he then commanded a column of Venetian Fascists during the March on Rome (q.v.). In November 1922 he was sent to Sicily to settle internal disputes within the Fascist movement and consolidated control over the eastern portion of the island. He was elected to Parliament on the *listone* (Fascist list of candidates) in 1924 and was named an officer in the Militia (q.v.) in 1926.

Newly appointed vice-secretary of the PNF in 1927, the next year he was sent to Milan to settle dissident quarrels in that city. As always, he demonstrated absolute obedience to Mussolini's wishes and imposed inflexible authority on the local party *gerarchi*.

In December 1931 Starace's loyalty was rewarded by his appointment as national secretary of the party, a position he held until 1939. The period in which he ruled the party has often been called the "Starace era," for he left his imprint on much of the public ritual and "choreography" of Fascism and set the tone for the life of the party. Although he lacked real substance as a political leader, Starace was intent on creating an atmosphere and a façade of Fascist vitality in the country he continually referred to as the "new Italy." Contrary to some of the other Fascist leaders who worked to maintain an elite party, he advocated the opening of the PNF rolls to millions of Italians and sought to regiment them in a military fashion through an increasingly elaborate bureaucratic structure. He sought to realize this goal by the use of carefully orchestrated mass demonstrations and rallies and the incorporation of military symbolism into daily life—for example, he ordered all party members to use the salute rather than shaking hands and instituted the *passo romano* (goose step) for party marches. He personally took the lead in trying to infuse the party with an enthusiasm for physical prowess through sports (q.v.) and gymnastics and in the mid-1930s led an assault on "bourgeois" mannerisms. Taken together, these and similar policies represented what Starace termed "lo stile fascista" ("the Fascist style"). True to his own inclination for military heroics, he volunteered for service in the Ethiopian War (q.v.) in 1935 and won further medals.

Starace's public posturing and his almost daily injunctions to party members (issued through his famous *fogli d'ordine* [order sheets]) made him the object of public ridicule and satire, so that by 1939 he was being openly criticized by other *gerarchi*. But while millions of Italians felt oppressed by his mania for regimentation, discipline, and display, his policies also contributed to the development of the image of Mussolini as the infallible and virile Duce (q.v.) of a reinvigorated nation.

The mounting criticism of Starace finally resulted in his dismissal as party secretary in October 1939 (he was replaced by E. Muti [q.v.]). Between 1939 and 1941 he served as chief of the general staff of the Militia, and from 1941 to 1943 he was at the front in Greece and Albania.

He never recovered from his fall from grace, but after Mussolini was ousted in July 1943 Starace, ever the faithful follower, went north to Milan. He wrote frequent and pathetic letters to Mussolini and implored him to lift the aura of disgrace that had befallen him. He was in and out of concentration camps because of several letters he had written to Pietro Badoglio (q.v.) after the 1943 coup and lived on the edge of poverty during the last year of the war. On April 28, 1945, partisans captured him in Milan (wearing slippers and a sweat suit) and the following day executed him. His body hung in Piazzale Loreto along with Mussolini's.

For further information see: NO (1928; 1937); Libero Montesi, "L'inventore dello stile fascista," in *I gerarchi di Mussolini*, A. & A. Boroli, eds. (Novara: De Agostinim, 1973); Guido Nozzoli, *I ras del regime* (Milan: Bompiani, 1972); Sandro Setta, "Achille Starace," in *Uomini e volti del fascismo*, ed. Ferdinando Cordova (Rome: Bulzoni, 1980).

MSF/PVC

STRACITTÀ/STRAPAESE. When Fascism came to power, it found itself heir to a variety of cultural movements and dispositions, from Nationalism to Futurism (q.v.), from populism to modernism. While all of them had pressed for cultural innovation, often since the turn of the century, and expected Fascism to be the political spearhead of this renewal, they were divided—sometimes bitterly—over the fundamental character of the hoped-for "cultural revolution." In the period between 1922 and 1939 a major, recurrent manifestation of this dilemma was the polemic between modernism and tradition that was embodied in the two movements, Stracittà and Strapaese.

A cultural movement that developed in the 1920s out of Massimo Bontempelli's (q.v.) *Novecento* review, Stracittà stressed a cosmopolitan, antiprovincial modernism in literature and the arts. Bontempelli argued that this "superurban" movement had an ideological content that made it attractive to the regime in ways that Futurism could not be. Essentially, Stracittà writers sought a convenient compromise between the Futurist rejection of all conventional rules and themes and the regime's desire to establish continuity with tradition. Yet despite its modernistic thrust, Stracittà was a confused and ill-defined movement that wanted to create an intellectualized aesthetic suitable to the political needs of Fascism— indeed, Bontempelli had openly admitted, in imitation of Mussolini, the dependency between art and politics. He rejected decadent romanticism and elitist avant-gardism as currents removed from popular concerns, and here too he understood the regime's interest in moving toward the people. With the demise of his *Novecento* journal in 1929, the themes of Stracittà were taken up by Telesio Interlandi's (q.v.) *Quadrivio* (1933-1943).

In contrast to the urban-oriented modernism of Stracittà was the rural, provincial, "populist" position of Strapaese. Its major exponent was Curzio Malaparte (q.v.), and the movement was centered largely in the Florentine review *Il Selvaggio*—the "wild one." Edited principally by Mino Maccari (q.v.) and Ardengo Soffici (q.v.), *Il Selvaggio* rejected the corruptions of urban life in favor of the "sober" traditions of the countryside.

In a sense Strapaese intellectualized the attitudes of the old Blackshirt *squadristi* (q.v.) of the provinces, who felt betrayed by the regime's compromises and disliked the conformism dictated from Rome. While Maccari, like Bontempelli, accused Futurism of having outlived its usefulness and suggested that its anarchy was dangerous to the regime, he also bitterly denounced the Novecento and Stracittà movements. He attacked modernity as "bastardly, international, superficial, mechanical—a concoction manipulated by Jewish bankers, pederasts, war profiteers, and bordello owners." In the late 1930s many of the proponents of its nationalist provincialism supported the regime's anti-Semitic policies. But if Maccari's populist, peasant stance and his brutal polemics combined into a call for the "continuing revolution," Soffici's position was more conservative and respectably bourgeois, so that Strapaese too had its internal contradictions.

For further information see: Massimo Bontempelli, *L'avventura novecentista* (Rome: Vallecchi, 1939); Giorgio Luti, *Cronache letterarie tra le due guerre* (Bari: Laterza, 1966); Mino Maccari, *Trastullo di Strapaese* (Florence: Vallecchi, 1927).

PVC

STURZO, LUIGI (b. Caltagirone, November 26, 1871; d. Rome, August 8, 1959). Founder of the Italian Popular party (*see* PARTITO POPOLARE ITALIANO) and a leading anti-Fascist, Sturzo was educated at the seminaries of Acireale and Noto and completed his studies in Caltagirone, where he was ordained a priest in 1894. Four years later he took a degree in theology from the Gregoriana in Rome and became interested in social and political issues.

In the 1890s he was involved in the Democrazia Cristiana movement, the forerunner of the Popular party. He was intensely committed to the economic and political reform of the Italian south. In 1897 he founded a *cassa rurale* (peasant credit fund) and an agricultural cooperative in Caltagirone and established the paper *La Croce di Costantino*. He was an advocate of local autonomy. In 1905 Sturzo became mayor of Caltagirone, a position he held until 1920.

Sturzo supported the Italo-Libyan War of 1912 as a means of opening markets for the south. Although convinced that Catholics should actively participate in politics, he opposed the 1913 Gentiloni Pact, which bound Catholics to vote for Liberal candidates who supported the Church. In 1914 he became a member of the executive committee of the Unione Popolare (*see* AZIONE CATTOLICA ITALIANA), a group of Catholic leaders working closely with the Vatican.

Sturzo saw World War I as part of a vast German plan for hegemony and welcomed Italy's intervention in the conflict. He hoped the war would destroy the Italian liberal system and bring about vast social reform. In August 1916 he became a member of a government supply commission. In 1919 he began working to organize a secular, mass-based political party dedicated to social reform. On January 18 in Rome, he founded the Partito Popolare Italiano (PPI). Its program called for the defense of the family, the right to work, local autonomy, freedom and independence for the Church, proportional representation, and the franchise for women. In June he became party secretary, after defeating those who wanted to make the party an instrument of the Church.

Sturzo envisioned the PPI as having an influence on legislation without assuming control of the government, but the November elections forced the PPI into a leadership position when it won one hundred seats in Parliament (q.v.) (second only to the Socialist party). In the May 1921 elections the PPI gained even more seats, but there were elements in the party who wanted collaboration with Mussolini. Sturzo adamantly rejected Fascist-Popular cooperation. In mid-1923 the Fascists declared him an enemy of the state and launched a concerted campaign against him.

When the Acerbo law (*see* ACERBO, GIACOMO) came before Parliament in 1923, the Fascists threatened the Vatican if the Popolari opposed the measure. On July 10 Sturzo, under pressure from the Vatican, resigned as secretary of the PPI. He continued his anti-Fascist propaganda, founding the *Bolletino Bibliografico* for that purpose. Fascist threats against him increased in 1924 during the Matteotti Crisis (q.v.), and in September *squadristi* (q.v.) invaded his home. On October 25 he left Italy for London, thus beginning two decades of political exile.

Sturzo remained in London until September 1940, constantly involved in anti-Fascist propaganda. He condemned the Lateran Pacts (q.v.) as a Fascist ploy to subordinate the Church to the government. As early as 1935 he was criticizing the Western powers for not taking action against the growing Fascist-Nazi threat. After Italy's entrance into World War II in June 1940, Sturzo's position as an "enemy alien" in London became difficult, and he barely escaped internment by the British. Narrowly escaping death in a German air raid, he left London on September 22 for New York City.

He arrived in the United States destitute and sick and went to a hospital run by the Church in Jacksonville, Florida. Although he did not maintain a high profile in the anti-Fascist activities in America, he was in contact with exiles and with the Mazzini Society (q.v.). He wrote widely on the Italian question, defending the Italian people as victims of Fascism and seeking a just peace for Italy. After the Allied invasion of Italy in 1943 he reopened contacts with anti-Fascist politicians. He returned to Italy in September 1946 but did not become active in postwar Italian politics beyond contributing to newspapers and journals. In 1952

Sturzo was made a senator and, although very ill, participated in parliamentary debates.

For further information see: F. Malgeri, ed., *Profilo biografico di Luigi Sturzo* (Rome: Cinque Lune, 1975); F. Piva and F. Malgeri, *Vita di Luigi Sturzo* (Rome: Cinque Lune, 1972); F. Piva and G. De Rosa, eds., *Scritti inediti di Luigi Sturzo*, 3 vols. (Rome: Cinque Lune, 1974).

MSF

SUARDO, COUNT GIACOMO (b. Bergamo, August 25, 1883; d. Bergamo, May 18, 1947). A Fascist minister and president of the Italian Senate, Suardo came from an old noble family. He took a law degree, was an avid interventionist, and fought in World War I. Soon after the war he joined the Fascist movement and thereafter served in numerous capacities as "Mussolini's faithful henchman." He was *federale* of Bergamo for a time, a deputy from 1924 to 1929, and first entered the cabinet as undersecretary for the Presidency of the Council of Ministers (July 1924 to December 1927). It was in this latter position that on January 2, 1925, he went to the king on Mussolini's behalf to request the dissolution of the Chamber of Deputies (*see* PARLIAMENT).

In July 1926 Mussolini appointed him undersecretary in the newly created Ministry of Corporations, a post Edmondo Rossoni (q.v.) had hoped to obtain. In November he was transferred to the Ministry of Interior as undersecretary, a post he held until March 1928. In January 1929 he was appointed to the Senate, in 1932 was made president of the Istituto per Infortuni sul Lavoro, and in 1935 volunteered for service in the Italo-Ethiopian War (*see* ETHIOPIAN WAR).

Suardo was chosen president of the Senate in 1939, and because that position automatically made him a member of the Fascist Grand Council (q.v.), it also made him a participant in the 1943 coup against Mussolini. Dino Grandi (q.v.) had obtained his signature on the motion against Mussolini, but during the Grand Council session of July 24-25, Suardo broke down and withdrew his support; instead, he proposed the fusion of Grandi's motion with those of Carlo Scorza (q.v.) and Roberto Farinacci (q.v.) and ultimately abstained from voting. Afterward he went north with Mussolini's followers to the Salò Republic (*see* ITALIAN SOCIAL REPUBLIC) and testified at the Verona Trials (q.v.).

For further information see: *Chi è?* (1936); NO (1928; 1937); Giordano Guerri, *Galeazzo Ciano* (Milan: Bompiani, 1979).

PVC

SUVICH, FULVIO (b. Trieste, January 23, 1887). Mussolini's chief diplomatic assistant in the preparation of the Ethiopian War (q.v.) left Austria-Hungary and volunteered for the Italian Army in 1914-15, helped found the Trieste Nationalist group, and became a deputy in 1921. He served as undersecretary at the Ministry of Finance (November 1926-July 1928), then as Italian financial representative to the League of Nations (1931-32). In July 1932 Mussolini appointed him undersecretary for foreign affairs after relegating Dino Grandi (q.v.) to London. Like his colleague Pompeo Aloisi (q.v.), Suvich was an exponent of Italian expansion in the Balkan and Danubian areas. He was the principal architect of the Rome Protocols (q.v.) of March 1934 designed to block German penetration into southeastern Europe. Following the temporary abandonment of Italian designs on Yugoslavia when King Alexander's murder (October 9, 1934) failed to bring collapse, Suvich helped negotiate the Franco-Italian Rome Agreements (q.v.) of January 1935, which permitted Mussolini to go ahead in Ethiopia. Pro-French and well-connected at Geneva, Suvich provided a respectable facade for Mussolini's war. But his firm opposition to an Anschluss (q.v.) and Italo-German rapprochement soon made him an embarrassment; he departed for Washington as ambassador in June 1936, shortly after the elevation to foreign minister of Galeazzo Ciano (q.v.), leader (at that point) of the pro-German faction. Suvich retired in 1938; he stood trial in 1945-46 for "acts of foreign policy and criminal actions intended to strengthen Fascism" but was acquitted.

For further information see: Pompeo Aloisi, *Journal (25 juillet 1932-14 juin 1936)* (Paris: Plon, 1957); Fulvia D'Amoja, *Declino e prima crisi dell'Europa di Versailles* (Milan: Giuffrè, 1967).

MK

SYNDICALISM. Emerging first in France during the 1890s, syndicalism began as a Socialist current emphasizing the role of the trade union (French *syndicat*; Italian *sindacato*), as opposed to a political party, in creating socialism. Despite promising beginnings during the first years of the twentieth century, the current was never more than a secondary force on the Italian left; however, it gave Italian Fascism a number of its most influential ideas, as well as such ideologues as Sergio Panunzio (q.v.), Agostino Lanzillo (q.v.), and Paolo Orano (q.v.) and such functionaries and labor leaders as Michele Bianchi (q.v.), Edmondo Rossoni (q.v.), Luigi Razza (q.v.), Livio Ciardi, and Mario Racheli. Although the transition from socialism to Fascism involved a good deal of doctrinal revision, syndicalism conveyed directly to Fascist corporativism (*see* CORPORATIVISM AND THE CORPORATIVE STATE) its antipolitical vision of a society of producers participating in public life in a direct and continuous way through organizations based on economic function. While Mussolini was influenced by syndicalism at various points in his career, he was not part of the prewar syndicalist current, nor did he, in any significant way, carry syndicalist ideas into Fascism.

The current was generally characterized as *revolutionary* syndicalism at first because of its militant, anticollaborationist, and antireformist stance. While syndicalism emerged in France from within the working-class Fédération des Bourses du Travail, it developed in Italy from within the Italian Socialist party (*see* PARTITO SOCIALISTA ITALIANO) as the strategic alternative of Socialist intellectuals dissatisfied with the reformism of Filippo Turati (q.v.). The first major spokesmen for Italian syndicalism, Arturo Labriola (q.v.) and Enrico

Leone, were Neapolitans, and Italian syndicalism developed partly as a southern reaction against the system being engineered by Prime Minister Giovanni Giolitti (q.v.), a system relatively favorable to northern industrial workers but offering little to the south. The syndicalist alternative began to emerge in 1902, especially in the pages of Labriola's newspaper *Avanguardia Socialista*, but it was the general strike of September 1904, given a syndicalist tone by Labriola and his colleagues, which publicized the syndicalist conception within the working class. Although the syndicalists remained active in the Socialist party until 1907, when most of them broke away, their major focus of activity was necessarily the labor movement. But while syndicalism appeared to have a promising future on this level early in 1905, it quickly began to encounter defeat in practice, largely because its major tactical weapon—the militant strike—seemed counterproductive to most workers. Thus reformists dominated the General Confederation of Labor (*see* CONFEDERAZIONE GENERALE DEL LAVORO), founded in 1906, and syndicalism remained influential only in a few organizations, especially in Parma, Ferrara, Piacenza, and Milan under such labor organizers as Alceste De Ambris (q.v.), Michele Bianchi, and Filippo Corridoni (q.v.).

During 1912-14 revolutionary syndicalism seemed briefly to be making a comeback in the labor movement, especially from within the new antireformist confederation, the Unione Sindacale Italiana, founded in 1912. But support among workers remained volatile, and in any case, the intervention crisis (q.v.) soon fragmented the organization, with most of the syndicalists abandoning it to the anarchists. The syndicalists tried again to develop a more substantial working-class base with the founding of another national confederation, the Unione Italiana del Lavoro (q.v.), in June 1918, but by 1921 many of its leading organizers and intellectuals had begun to opt for Fascism, which was beginning to develop labor organizations of its own.

Italian syndicalist doctrine developed in three stages: revolutionary syndicalism proper took shape from 1902 to 1910; a period of crisis and reconsideration followed from 1910 to 1917; the crystallization of neosyndicalism, which was carried in toto into Fascism, took place from 1917 to 1924. The ideas of Georges Sorel, the leading interpreter and theorist of revolutionary syndicalism in France, had some influence during the first phase; however, it was the earlier Sorel of *Avenir Socialiste des Syndicats*, emphasizing the moralizing force of trade union activity, rather than the mature Sorel of *Reflections on Violence* emphasizing violence and myth, who appealed to the Italians. Nor should Italian syndicalism be lumped with anarchism; despite some common enemies, the syndicalists always placed greater emphasis on structured organization and formal discipline than did the anarchists, and they had no faith in the revolutionary potential of spontaneous popular insurrection. The syndicalists focused instead on the process of psychological and moral development through trade union activity, a process, they argued, that would gradually make the industrial workers fit not only to revolt but also to offer society new and superior forms of social life.

It was disillusionment with the proletariat, which in practice seemed unable to see beyond its immediate material interests, that led the syndicalists to reexamine their concepts beginning in about 1910. Almost all of them supported Italian intervention in World War I and came to argue that socialism had to be a national proposition. But the decisive point in their gradual doctrinal revision was only reached when they decided that the revolution they wanted was necessary to replace political liberalism, not economic capitalism, and that social organization based on economic function could provide the basis for a postliberal form of politics. The ideas of Vilfredo Pareto (q.v.) and Giuseppe Mazzini were especially influential as the syndicalists revised their concept of the purpose of revolution. After World War I their neosyndicalist blueprint attracted a new constituency among the politically alienated young veterans—whose vague hopes for renewal eventually led many of them to Fascism. The syndicalists had a major influence on such young Fascist spokesmen as Dino Grandi (q.v.), Curzio Suckert Malaparte (q.v.), Augusto Turati (q.v.), Giuseppe Bottai (q.v.), and Italo Balbo (q.v.), and they helped to give Fascism the element of purpose and direction it needed to justify its position of power in the aftermath of the Matteotti Crisis (q.v.) of 1924.

Long-time syndicalists were heavily involved with the Fascist trade union movement from its inception in 1921, but the syndicalist contribution to Fascism was much broader—and certainly was not limited to the defense of working-class interests. Rather, the syndicalists offered a concept of the overall purpose of Fascism: the Fascist revolution was to replace parliamentary liberalism with a kind of totalitarian corporativism. This was to be a way simultaneously to foster a more intense kind of popular participation in public life, to expand the sovereignty of the state over aspects of socioeconomic life that had remained "anarchical" under liberalism, and to enhance production and a commitment to productivist values. Although this neosyndicalist corporativism had something in common with the blueprint that Alfredo Rocco (q.v.) and the Nationalists offered Fascism, its ultimate intention was more populist and less coercive. In fact, the underlying differences between the syndicalist and Nationalist currents in Fascism contributed to tensions that helped, in practice, to paralyze the regime.

The wider corporativist current into which syndicalism developed continued to push throughout the history of the regime, and, partly as a result, there continued to be institutional changes in a corporativist direction. But performance remained disappointing. The old syndicalists criticized, often remarkably explicitly, but their ongoing support gave the regime a veneer of revolutionary purpose and legitimacy that it merited less and less.

For further information see: Ferdinando Cordova, *Le origini dei sindacati fascisti, 1918-1926* (Bari: Laterza, 1974); A. James Gregor, *Italian Fascism and Developmental Dictatorship* (Princeton: Princeton University Press, 1979); Alceo Riosa, *Il sindacalismo rivoluzionario in Italia* (Bari: De Donato, 1976); David D. Roberts, *The Syndicalist Tradition and Italian Fascism* (Chapel Hill: University of North Carolina Press, 1979).

DDR

T

TACCHI VENTURI, PIETRO (b. S. Severino, Marche, August 12, 1861; d. Rome, March 18, 1956). A prominent Jesuit figure and clerico-Fascist, Tacchi Venturi took a degree in philosophy and theology from the Gregorian University in Rome and entered the Jesuit order in 1878. In the 1890s he worked on the staff of *Civiltà Cattolica* and became official historian for the Jesuits in Italy. From 1914 to 1921 he served as the secretary general of the order.

When Mussolini took power Tacchi Venturi displayed open enthusiasm for the new regime and played a major role in the secret contacts between Mussolini and the Vatican that ultimately resulted in the Concordat and Lateran Pacts (q.v.) of 1929. His pro-Fascist attitudes represented a widespread sentiment among the Italian Jesuits, but his decided sympathies for the regime earned him the dislike of Vatican elements during the tense period between 1930 and 1931, when the Church clashed with the Fascists over the fate of Azione Cattolica Italiana (q.v.). During the later years of the regime, Tacchi Venturi often appeared in public with Mussolini and other Fascist leaders.

For further information see: DSPI; *Chi è?* (1936; 1948); Renzo De Felice, *Mussolini il fascista* (Turin: Einaudi, 1969); Pietro Tacchi Venturi, *Storia della Compagnia di Gesù in Italia* (Rome: 1950-51).

MSF

TAMBURINI, TULLIO. Fascist intransigent, Tamburini served in World War I and became one of the first supporters of Fascism in Florence. After the seizure of power he became a consul in the Militia (q.v.) and gained a reputation as one of the most violent Fascist leaders. He became famous for his brutal raids against the opposition and in December 1924, during the Matteotti Crisis (q.v.), was among the Militia consuls who threatened to act against Mussolini unless he gave permission for a "second wave" of Fascist violence. In October 1925, as a result of his continued attacks and unlawful activities, Tamburini was dismissed as a consul and exiled to Libya.

Rehabilitated in 1936, Tamburini was promoted to the rank of prefect and in August was sent to Avellino. Three years later he became prefect of Ancona and in June 1941 was transferred to Trieste where he held the same position until August 1943. On October 1, 1943, he became chief of police in the Salò Republic (*see* ITALIAN SOCIAL REPUBLIC). Tamburini was arrested by the Germans in February 1945 for supposedly having secret links to the Allies and for being anti-German.

For further information see: NO (1937); Giorgio Bocca, *La repubblica di Mussolini* (Rome-Bari: Laterza, 1977); F. W. Deakin, *The Brutal Friendship*

(New York: Harper & Row, 1962); Adrian Lyttelton, *The Seizure of Power* (London: Weidenfeld & Nicolson, 1973).

MSF

TARANTO, ATTACK ON. The regime's greatest naval defeat took place on the night and morning of November 11-12, 1940, when British torpedo bombers attacked the Italian battle fleet at anchor in Taranto harbor, sinking the battleships *Littorio, Duilio*, and *Cavour* (the first two eventually reentered service). The consequence of poorly coordinated defenses and the naval staff's policy of fighting the war from land, the attack on Taranto gave the British temporarily control of the central Mediterranean and was one of the series of Italian defeats that produced German intervention and Italy's reduction to satellite status. A serious blow to the regime's prestige, it led to the dismissal of the chief of the Navy, Admiral Domenico Cavagnari (q.v.).

For further information see: Ian Playfair, G. M. Stitt, C. J. Molony, and S. E. Toomer, *The Early Success Against Italy* (London: Her Majesty's Stationery Office, 1954).

MK

TARCHIANI, ALBERTO (b. Rome, November 12, 1885; d. Rome, November 30, 1964). A respected journalist and moderate democrat and internationalist in the pre-Fascist period, Tarchiani was forced into exile by the press laws of 1925. He became an ardent anti-Fascist activist during his eighteen-year exile before returning to Italy during the Allied invasion. He played an important diplomatic role in the immediate postwar governments.

Born of staunch Mazzinian parents, he took a law degree after studying at the universities of Rome, Genoa, and Florence. In 1903 he began a long career in journalism as a reporter for *Nuovo Giornale* (Florence) and then moved to *La Tribuna* (Rome).

In 1907 he moved to New York as American correspondent for an Italian newspaper. While in the U.S., he developed an appreciation for American liberalism, particularly because of its commitment to individual freedom. At the outbreak of World War I, he returned to Italy to enlist as a volunteer. He saw duty on the German and Austrian fronts before returning to Rome to serve as chief of the News Bureau of War Propaganda.

After the war he joined the staff of the Milanese liberal daily, *Il Corriere della Sera*, where he quickly moved up the ranks. As editor in chief he became a major spokesman among the liberal critics of Mussolini. His provocations have led some to observe that Tarchiani was the major target of the Fascist press laws of 1925.

He then fled to Paris, where he associated with a number of anti-Fascist *fuorusciti* (q.v.). In 1929 he organized the daring rescue of Carlo Rosselli (*see* ROSSELLI, CARLO AND NELLO), Emilio Lussu (q.v.), and F. S. Nitti from Lipari Island. Mussolini's complaint led to the first of several arrests of Tarchiani by foreign authorities. Upon his release he joined Rosselli and others in the creation of Giustizia e Libertà (GL) (*see* ANTI-FASCISM) and served on the three-man executive committee with Rosselli and Lussu. GL became the main vehicle of his anti-Fascist activities until after the assassination of the Rosselli brothers.

He adhered to his moderate democratic philosophy while engaging in a myriad of activities in the 1930s. Often using the pseudonym "Atar," he contributed to many journals, including *Giovane Italia*, the GL periodicals, and *La jeune Italie*, which he founded with Randolfo Pacciardi (q.v.) in 1937. He also produced propaganda that was smuggled into Italy. One such effort, the daring daylight flight over Milan by Giovanni Bassanesi in July 1930, led to his brief imprisonment by the Swiss government. In addition, he represented GL on the executive committee of the Anti-Fascist Concentration (*see* ANTI-FASCISM). When Rosselli revised the GL political program leftward in 1935, he resigned his administrative duties and began to withdraw. Two years later, after Rosselli's death, he left the movement.

Before the fall of France he helped form an Italian National Committee in Paris as a source of volunteers for an anti-Fascist fighting force. In the spring of 1940, ahead of the Nazi invaders, he fled Paris with British assistance. After a brief stay in London he moved to New York, where he continued his political activities as a member of the newly formed Mazzini Society (q.v.). Selected as secretary of the organization in November 1940, he edited its newspaper (*Nazioni Unite*) and took primary responsibility for day-to-day coordination of its activities and development of a nationwide structure. He took a strong position against the admission of Communists into the Mazzini Society based on their "anti-democratic credo." At the June 1942 convention Tarchiani's liberal democratic forces prevailed, and he was reelected secretary.

Transported to Italy in September 1943 by the Allies, he landed at Salerno with the first liberation forces and proceeded to Anzio. He was attached to the U.S. Fifth Army to assist in the liaison activities with the Resistance. He engineered the rescue of Benedetto Croce (q.v.) and in September 1944 helped establish the National Liberation Front.

In 1944 Tarchiani became minister of public works in one of the Pietro Badoglio (q.v.) cabinets and then accepted a position as supervisor of national reconstruction under Ivanoe Bonomi (q.v.). In January 1945 he became the first post-Fascist Italian ambassador to Washington and served from 1945 to 1955.

For further information see: DSPI; Aldo Garosci, *Vita di Carlo Rosselli*, 2 vols. (Florence: Vallecchi, 1973); *Giustizia e Libertà nella lotta antifascista e nella storia d'Italia* (Florence: La Nuova Italia, 1978); Alberto Tarchiani, *Dieci anni tra Roma e Washington* (Milan: Mondadori, 1955); Maddalena Tirabassi, "La Mazzini Society," in Giorgio Spini, Gian Giacomo Migone, and Massimo Theodori, eds., *Italia e America dalla Grande Guerra a Oggi* (Venice: Marsilio, 1976).

CLK

TASCA, ANGELO (b. Moretta, Cuneo, November 19, 1892; d. Paris, March 3, 1960). An Italian Socialist leader, Tasca came from a working-class family. He studied at the University of Turin and in 1907 he cofounded the Fascio Giovanile Socialista, in which Antonio Gramsci (q.v.), Palmiro Togliatti (q.v.), and Umberto Terracini (q.v.) later collaborated. Tasca believed in the central importance of the trade unions as the vehicle for working-class advancement and worked closely with Bruno Buozzi (q.v.).

In 1919 he and Gramsci founded the Ordine Nuovo movement, but they quickly fell into disagreement over Gramsci's factory council concept—Tasca continued to rely on the unions. Tasca moved to the Italian Communist party (PCI-Partito Comunista Italiano) (q.v.) in 1921 but by the next year had become the center of a right-wing internal opposition to the ideas of Amadeo Bordiga (q.v.) and in favor of the *"fronte unico"* (single front). In 1922-23 he was secretary of the Turin branch of the Alleanza del Lavoro (q.v.); in December he went to Paris to organize anti-Fascist exiles, returning to Italy in 1924. With Togliatti he became a member of the executive committee of the PCI and while in Moscow came into conflict with the position of the International over the function of the party. When Gramsci became secretary of the PCI, Tasca found himself isolated from most of the party's leadership. In 1928, while in Moscow again, Tasca assumed an openly hostile attitude toward Stalinist policies and to the "social-fascist" position of the International. As a result, in September 1929 he was expelled from the party and became increasingly anti-Communist.

In 1933 he settled in France and collaborated closely with French Socialists and the next year became a French citizen. During World War II he collaborated with the Vichy government as a journalist and radio commentator. His study of the rise of Fascism is an important contribution to the subject.

For further information see: DSPI; MOI (5); Pietro Secchia, "L'archivio Tasca sul PCI," *Critica Marxista* (1967); Paolo Spriano, *Storia del Partito comunista italiano*, 5 vols. (Turin: Einaudi, 1967-75); Angelo Tasca, *I primi dieci anni del PCI* (1953); *Nascita e avvento del fascismo*, 2 vols. (Bari: Laterza, 1965).

MSF/PVC

TASSINARI, GIUSEPPE (b. Perugia, December 16, 1891). A Fascist minister and agricultural expert, Tassinari taught at the Reale Istituto Superiore Agraria in Perugia and fought in World War I. Tassinari joined the Fascist movement prior to the March on Rome (q.v.) and became one of its most dedicated followers. Throughout the 1920s, Tassinari wrote many books on Italian agriculture, directed *L'Italia Agricola* and *Giornale di Agricoltura*, and sat on many committees dealing with Italian agricultural problems. All these activities gained Tassinari a reputation as an expert in his field.

From 1929 to 1939 Tassinari was a parliamentary deputy and from May 1931 to January 1934 was a member of the Fascist Grand Council (q.v.). As an agricultural expert Tassinari was made an undersecretary in the Ministry of Agriculture and Forests in January 1935 and upon the death of Gabriele Conelli he became undersecretary for Bonifica Integrale (q.v.). On October 31, 1939, Tassinari was appointed the minister of agriculture and forests and continued to hold that position until removed in December 1941.

Tassinari fled to Germany after Mussolini's fall, and for a time the Germans considered him a possible successor to the Duce. Tassinari had Himmler's support and seemed to fit the German's qualifications. Mussolini's rescue from Gran Sasso ended Tassinari's aspirations.

For further information see: *Chi è?* (1936); NO (1937); Giorgio Bocca, *La Repubblica di Mussolini* (Bari: Laterza, 1977); Giuseppe Tassinari, *La bonifica integrale nel decennale della legge Mussolini* (Rome, 1939).

MSF

TERRACINI, UMBERTO (b. Genoa, July 27, 1895). An important Socialist and then Communist leader, Terracini took a law degree from the University of Turin. He joined the Socialist Youth Federation of Piedmont in 1911 (becoming its secretary in 1914) and the Partito Socialista Italiano (q.v.) in 1916. That same year he was arrested for antiwar propaganda and then drafted into the Army.

After World War I Terracini became secretary of the Socialist party for Turin and collaborated with the revolutionary Socialist leaders Antonio Gramsci (q.v.) and Palmiro Togliatti (q.v.) in the founding of the journal *Ordine Nuovo*. In 1920 he was responsible for directing the "Occupation of the Factories" (q.v.) in northern Italy, during which he ran the factory councils. He was elected to the Socialist party directorate in 1920.

Terracini attended the Livorno congress of the party in 1921 and was among the founders of the Partito Comunista Italiano (q.v.). He served as a member of the new party's executive committee until 1926 and directed its newspaper *Unità* in Milan. In July 1921 he led the Italian delegation of Communists to Moscow for the Third Congress of the Communist International and was elected to the International's presidium.

In 1926 the Fascists arrested Terracini, and he was condemned by the Special Tribunal for the Defense of the State (q.v.) to twenty-three years in prison. Liberated in August 1943, he made his way to Switzerland, where he remained until 1944. During the last year of the Resistance (*see* RESISTANCE, ARMED), he was secretary general of the provisional partisan government in the Val d'Ossola in Piedmont.

After the war Terracini was a member of the Consulta Nazionale (q.v.) and of the Costituente (q.v.), serving as president of the latter. As a member of the Communist party's directorate from 1945, he was influential in Italian politics and has served in the Senate since 1948.

For further information see: MOI (5); Guido Quazza, "Omaggio a Terracini," *Italia Contemporanea* 124 (July-September 1976); Paolo Spriano, *Storia del*

Partito comunista italiano, 5 vols. (Turin: Einaudi, 1967-75); Umberto Terracini, "Con Gramsci e Togliatti all'Ordine Nuovo," *Unità*, August 22, 1965.

PVC

TERRAGNI, GIUSEPPE (b. Milan, 1904; d. Como, 1943). One of the most prominent architects of the Fascist era, Terragni helped found the Group of Seven in 1926, which developed the Italian rationalist architectural style, an internationally derived style in the fashion of Mies van der Rohe, Le Corbusier, and Walter Gropius (*see* ARCHITECTURE). In their declaration the group claimed no break with tradition, only a transformation, and although declaring themselves anti-Futurists, they drew inspiration from the Futurists (*see* FUTURISM). While seemingly a paradox, the Group of Seven position attempted to synthesize Futurist and International visions of architecture into the service of the modern Italian state. The Group of Seven showed in the Fascist Union of Architects show in 1928, which was the first exhibit of the MIAR or Italian Movement for Rationalist Architecture.

Terragni's major works include Officina del Gas, 1927; Novocomum, Como, 1929; Casa del Fascio, Como, 1932-36; Mostra della Rivoluzione Fascista a Roma, Sala del '22, 1932; Sant'Elia Kindergarten, Como, 1936-37; he was a member of a team of architects competing for the Palazzo dei Ricevimenti e dei Congressi in the 1942 EUR (Esposizione Universale di Roma) complex intended as the site of a 1942 world's fair.

For further information see: Vittorio Gregotti, *New Directions in Italian Architecture* (New York: George Braziller, 1968); Bruno Zevi, *Storia dell'architettura moderna*, 3d ed. (Turin: Einaudi, 1955).

JH

TERUZZI, ATTILIO (b. Milan, May 5, 1882; d. Procida, April 26, 1950). A Fascist leader, Teruzzi abandoned an Army career in 1920 to train and direct Fascist squads in Lombardy. Mussolini, trusting him for his stupidity and lack of an independent power base, made him a party vice-secretary in November 1921. Teruzzi crushed the Milan general strike in August 1922, helped plan the March on Rome (q.v.), and directed the Emilia-Romagna column of Fascist squads. Appointed a PNF (Partito Nazionale Fascista) (q.v.) high commissioner in January-April 1923 despite his opposition to legalizing the squads as Militia (q.v.), Teruzzi helped orchestrate Fascist-Nationalist amalgamation. Rewarded by reappointment as a PNF vice-secretary in October 1923 and election as a deputy in April 1924, Teruzzi retained his seat until 1943. Roberto Farinacci (q.v.) obtained Teruzzi as interior undersecretary in May 1925 to be party watchdog over Luigi Federzoni (q.v.), but Teruzzi failed miserably. He became governor of Cyrenaica (*see* LIBYA [TRIPOLITANIA AND CYRENAICA]) in November 1926. After initial setbacks Teruzzi's forces, under Ottorino Mezzetti (q.v.), inflicted heavy Senussi casualties, clearing the area to the Tripolitanian border by May 1928 despite shortage of funds. Teruzzi became Militia chief of staff and a member of the Grand Council (q.v.) in January 1929. Under Teruzzi the MVSN (*see* MILITIA) expanded as a depository for the unemployed and undesirable. Friction with the military increased, though the few combat-efficient Militia units passed under Army control. Teruzzi organized six Blackshirt (*see* SQUADRISTI) divisions for the Ethiopian campaign (*see* ETHIOPIAN WAR), assuming the command of one himself in November 1935. Promoted to Army major general, he remained in Africa until late 1936. After Guadalajara (*see* GUADALAJARA, BATTLE OF), Mussolini sent Teruzzi to Spain as inspector general and commander of Blackshirts. Teruzzi helped reorganize Italian forces, though Ettore Bastico (q.v.) deprived him of command functions. After victory at Santander Teruzzi quarreled with Bastico and was repatriated in September 1937. In November Teruzzi became undersecretary of Italian Africa, devoting most attention to Ethiopia. His rapaciousness, arrogance, and disregard for the duke of Aosta's (*see* SAVOIA, AMEDEO DI) authority retarded efforts at pacification. Despite Mussolini's instructions, Teruzzi prepared the colonies for war poorly, even after becoming minister in October 1939. After June 1940 Teruzzi's ministerial functions virtually ceased, with East Africa isolated and Libya under Army control. Teruzzi's loyalty preserved his post in February 1943, and he supported the final efforts to revive Fascism. Arrested by Pietro Badoglio (q.v.) in August and freed by the Germans in September, Teruzzi rallied to the Italian Social Republic (q.v.) but received no further employment.

For further information see: Renzo De Felice, *Mussolini il fascista* (Turin: Einaudi, 1966); Alberto Sbacchi, *Italian Colonialism in Ethiopia 1936-1940* (University of Illinois at Chicago Circle: unpublished dissertation, 1975); Attilio Teruzzi, *Cirenaica verde* (Milan: Mondadori, 1931).

BRS

THAON DI REVEL, PAOLO (b. Turin, June 10, 1859; d. Rome, March 24, 1948). From a distinguished Piedmontese family with a long tradition of service to the House of Savoy, Thaon di Revel's father, Count Ottavio (1803-1868), had been King Carlo Alberto's minister of finance. He entered naval school in 1873, was commissioned a midshipman in 1877, and embarked on a highly successful naval career. From 1896 to 1900 he was an aide-de-camp to King Umberto, served as commandant of the Royal Naval Academy of Livorno from the end of 1905 to the end of 1907, and from November 1907 to November 1909 commanded the new battleship *Vittorio Emanuele*. He reached flag rank with promotion to rear admiral in April 1910 and in February 1911 became aide-de-camp to King Victor Emmanuel III (q.v.). On the outbreak of the Libyan War in September 1911 he assumed command of the Second Naval Division and took part in operations off Tripoli, Beirut, and the Dardanelles. At the end of the war in October 1912 he became inspector of torpedo craft. In March 1913 Revel became chief of the naval general staff and in June was promoted to vice-admiral.

From October 1915 to February 1917 Revel was Commander in Chief of Italian naval forces in the upper Adriatic. In February 1917 he was named a senator and returned as chief of the naval general staff and commander in chief of mobilized naval forces. With these enhanced powers he had surpassed all rivals and was clearly *the* man in charge of the Italian Navy. Allied officers found him, as one of them remarked succinctly, "a tough nut" and commented on his authoritarian ways and strict subjugation of his subordinates. He adapted realistically to the changed conditions of naval warfare created by the development of the torpedo, submarine, and aircraft, and followed a cautious policy which, while logical from the Italian point of view, often seemed to his British and French allies to be motivated by Machiavellian cunning in seeking to preserve Italian naval strength as much as possible for use as a diplomatic factor after the war. While Italy's weaknesses, particularly in antisubmarine craft, led Revel to frequently request assistance from the Allies, he jealously guarded the Adriatic as an Italian preserve. It was to a large extent due to Revel that the unity of command, represented by Marshal Foch on land, was never achieved at sea in the Mediterranean. The result was wasteful duplication of effort with the maintenance of a large French fleet at Corfu, in addition to the Italian fleet at Taranto, to contain much smaller Austrian surface forces. Revel's motives were indeed political as well as military, and with the collapse of Austria he moved quickly to establish Italian dominance in the Adriatic. By late 1918 there were nasty incidents with his erstwhile Allies, the French, whom he now regarded as supporters of that new threat to Italian dominance, the newly created Yugoslav state.

With the Allied victory Revel was heaped with honors and in November 1918 was promoted to admiral. As a technical advisor at the Paris Peace Conference he was a strong supporter of Sidney Sonnino (q.v.) and insisted on an integral application of the Treaty of London, which seemed to go far beyond his earlier ideas as to what territory was necessary to assure Italian domination of the Adriatic. Revel, in fact, split from his military colleague General Armando Diaz (q.v.), as well as Prime Minister V. E. Orlando (q.v.), who was inclined to yield on Dalmatia in order to claim Fiume (q.v.).

In November 1919 Revel became inspector-general of the Navy and in May 1920, president of the committee of admirals. Ultra nationalistic, anti-French, anti-Yugoslav (he would vote against the Rapallo Treaty), and authoritarian by reputation, Revel's name was sometimes mentioned along with that of the Duke of Aosta and other naval and military figures in terms of vague plots against the state. His exact role in the Fascist seizure of power is unclear and perhaps will remain so, although he was apparently one of those consulted by the king at the time of the March on Rome (q.v.). But if actions speak louder than words, it is significant that he promptly accepted the position of minister of marine from Mussolini, and his appearance in the cabinet along with General Diaz as minister of war—both representative of the victorious armed forces—brought considerable prestige and glamour to the new Fascist regime.

At the time of the Corfu Crisis (q.v.) in the summer of 1923 the Italian Navy was in a position to act rapidly in the seizure of Corfu. This was because Revel had issued secret orders to be ready for coercive measures against Greece well before the actual murder of General Telleni had given Mussolini his pretext. Revel had anticipated trouble with Greece once the ratification of the Treaty of Lausanne with Turkey confirmed Italy's possession of the Dodecanese Islands, and annoyed by what he considered the abandonment of Dalmatia and the recent evacuation of Albania, he felt the need to be ready to restore Italian prestige. He was, however, extremely critical from the technical point of view of the clumsy manner in which Admiral Marcello Soleri (q.v.) executed his orders in seizing the island. The Corfu incident did raise the possibility of complications involving Great Britain, and here Revel had to recognize Italy's weakness. He recommended the possible evacuation of major west coast ports such as Livorno and Genoa. He hoped, however, to partially offset British superiority at sea by concentrating Italian aircraft in the south with the idea of making Malta unusable as a base—a scheme that might well have been overly optimistic.

Revel's resignation as minister of marine in May 1925 was not over any question of political principle such as the Matteotti (*see* MATTEOTTI CRISIS) affair, which some had hoped might have opened his eyes to the real character of the regime. Revel's clash with Mussolini came over a technical question, the creation of a supreme chief of staff for the forces of Italy to be held by General Pietro Badoglio (q.v.), who would enjoy some degree of control over the Navy. Revel could not accept what was in his eyes a subordination of the Navy, nor did he agree with the creation of a separate Air Ministry, believing the Navy should have full control over aircraft designated for naval defense. Shortly after his resignation Revel openly debated the question with Mussolini in the Senate, but of course the measure was voted by a lopsided majority.

Revel held no further public offices beyond those that might be described as honorary in the numerous societies of which he was a member. In May of 1924, in recognition of his wartime services, the king bestowed on him the title "Duke of the Sea" (Duca del Mare), and in November 1924 he was promoted to the rank of grand admiral. In 1932 he became first secretary to the king for the Order of Saints Maurice and Lazarus and chancellor of the Order of the Crown of Italy. Revel, however, authoritarian in temperament, was obviously far more of a traditional monarchist than supporter of the regime, although he might have hoped, unrealistically, to use the Fascists and had in turn allowed the regime to use him. Revel's membership in the different orders of knighthood and family background gave him entree to the court and permitted him to mingle with the king and his circle with a certain ease that Mussolini and most of the Fascist hierarchy could never hope to achieve. In many ways the old admiral symbolized the situation in Italy where, unlike Germany, the crown served as an alternative focus of loyalty for the armed forces. Moreover the Navy was generally considered the least Fascist and most traditional of the services.

By 1943 the disastrous results of Mussolini's policy were evident, and various men sought to take advantage of Revel's access to the king to try and induce the sovereign to dismiss Mussolini. In April 1943 Revel was approached by the former Prime Minister, Ivanoe Bonomi (q.v.), and agreed to make the attempt. He reported that Victor Emmanuel had remained noncommittal. Nevertheless, according to General Cerica, in July 1943 the king did consider Revel for the role Badoglio was to play but quickly dismissed the idea since the admiral, then well into his eighties, was too old. Immediately after Mussolini's dismissal Revel was named president of the Senate. He appears to have exerted little influence and like his sovereign was tainted by his prior association with the regime. He was one of the senators purged (along with Badoglio) from the Consulta (q.v.) in 1945. In 1946 he was a candidate for the Constituent Assembly (*see* COSTITUENTE) on the list of the monarchist "National Liberty Bloc."

For further information see: F. W. Deakin, *The Brutal Friendship* (London: Pelican, 1966); Renzo De Felice, *Mussolini il Fascista* (Turin: Einaudi, 1966); Olindo Malagodi, *Conversazione della Guerra*, 2 vols. (Milan: Ricciardi, 1960); Guido Po, *Il Grande Ammiraglio Paolo Thaon di Revel* (Turin: S. Lattes, 1936); Ufficio Storico della R. Marina, *La Marina Italiana nella Grande Guerra*, 8 vols. (Florence: Vallecchi, 1935-1942); Roberto Vivarelli, *Il Dopoguerra in Italia e l'Avvento del Fascismo* (Naples: Istituto per gli studi storici, 1967).

PGH

TITTONI, TOMMASO (b. Rome, November 16, 1855; d. Manziana, Bracciano, February 7, 1931). A prominent pre-Fascist political figure, Tittoni held numerous important government positions. After taking a degree in law, he became a deputy in 1886, was prefect of Perugia (1898) and Naples (1900), and was made a senator in 1902. From 1903 to 1905 he served as minister of foreign affairs under Giovanni Giolitti (q.v.), and then as ambassador in London (1906), followed by a return to the Foreign Ministry from 1906 to 1909. In 1911 he was ambassador in Paris, where he worked to secure Italian intervention in World War I.

After the war he was again foreign minister under F. S. Nitti (q.v.) and headed the Italian delegation to the Paris Peace Conference. From 1920 to 1929 he was president of the Senate and in 1929 was appointed by Mussolini to the presidency of the Royal Academy of Italy (q.v.). In the latter two posts he exercised his great influence and personal prestige indirectly in favor of the Fascist regime. Tittoni was a major example of a leader of the old Liberal ruling elite whose passive support of the regime provided a degree of legitimacy to Fascism.

For further information see: DSPI; NO (1928).

PVC

TOGLIATTI, PALMIRO (b. Genoa, March 26, 1893; d. Yalta, August 21, 1964). One of the principal founders of the Italian Communist party (*see* PARTITO COMUNISTA ITALIANO), Togliatti attended law school in Turin, where he joined in local Socialist politics, met Antonio Gramsci (q.v.), and became an important collaborator of *L'Ordine Nuovo*. After he participated in the foundation of the Italian Communist party in 1921, he became a member of the central committee the next year. He supported Gramsci in the struggle against the positions of Amadeo Bordiga (q.v.), who was defeated at the 1926 Lyons Congress.

After the rise of Fascism Togliatti took refuge in Russia, where he became an important member of the Third International. Togliatti advocated a major underground effort in Italy to combat Fascism and in 1935 strongly supported a united front of all the popular parties opposed to Fascism, a policy later adopted by the international Communist organizations. Togliatti then served as secretary of the Commitern.

Togliatti participated in the Spanish Civil War (q.v.) as a major Communist leader from 1937 to 1939. In 1940 he returned to Russia, where he narrowly escaped execution during the Stalinist purges. In 1944 he returned to Italy and led the Communist party to a collaborationist attitude ("Svolta" or "about face" of Salerno). This policy aided in the formation of the Pietro Badoglio (q.v.) government immediately following the fall of Fascism. During the next several years Togliatti served in a number of cabinets and ministries without portfolio with Badoglio and Ivanoe Bonomi (q.v.), as vice-president of the Council of Ministers with Bonomi, and as minister of justice with Ferruccio Parri (q.v.) and Alcide De Gasperi (q.v.). This collaborationist policy, aimed at defusing the opposition of conservative elements in Italian society, failed when the Communist-Socialist bloc suffered defeat in 1948. The elections led to the political isolation of the Communist party. In the same year an attempt on Togliatti's life scandalized the nation.

During the 1950s Togliatti took positions favoring gradualism, independence for individual Communist parties, and Communist participation in power. International developments, especially the denunciation of Stalin and the invasion of Hungary, favored these policies. Togliatti favored the Russians against the Chinese in the ideological dispute that split the Communist world and just before his death argued that there were many roads to socialism and advocated greater independence for the Italian Communist party. These policies, summarized by the term "polycentrism," were adopted by his successors.

For further information see: Palmiro Togliatti, *La formazione del gruppo dirigente del partito comunista italiano nel 1923-24* (Rome: Riuniti, 1962); Palmiro Togliatti, *Lectures on Fascism* (New York: International Publishers, 1976); Palmiro Togliatti, *La politica di Salerno* (Rome: Riuniti, 1969).

SDS

TORRE, ANDREA (b. Torchiara, Salerno, April 5, 1866; d. Rome, 1940). A journalist and minister, Torre taught at the Liceo Vittorio Emanuele in Naples and during the reactionary period of Prime Minister Francesco Crispi directed the review *La Riforma*. A liberal politician, he collaborated with many newspapers and reviews and helped found *Il Giornale d'Italia*. He wrote for *Il Corriere della Sera* between 1906 and 1916 and urged Italian participation in both the Libyan War of 1911-12 and in World War I. He was elected to Parliament (q.v.) in 1909, and after World War I entered the government in 1920 as minister of public instruction in the F.S. Nitti (q.v.) cabinet.

In 1922 Torre founded *Il Mondo*, a newspaper of democratic orientation, and in 1927 was political editor for *La Stampa* of Turin. He was elected president of the Association of Italian Journalists four times and was active in Parliament. Although considered an anti-Fascist because of his liberal-democratic politics, Torre eventually became a Fascist supporter and was made a senator in 1929.

For further information see: *Chi è?* (1936); DSPI; NO (1937).

MSF

TOSCANINI, ARTURO (b. Parma, March 25, 1867; d. New York, January 16, 1957). Toscanini was one of the great conductors of the twentieth century, noted as much for his versatile performances combining elements of passion with intelligence and taste as for his fiery temperament. By the age of nine he was already making a name for himself at the conservatories at Parma and Milan, where his curriculum emphasized cello. Toscanini was noted for his phenomenal memory, which was made even more evident by his practice of never conducting with any score in front of him, regardless of the complexity of the work.

For most of his life Toscanini's center of creative endeavor oscillated between New York and Italy. By 1898 he was chief conductor at La Scala in Milan, a position that he had also attained at the Metropolitan Opera in New York by 1907. La Scala was extensively remodeled under his supervision, and upon its reopening in 1922 he served as its director.

In 1919, on the urging of the Futurist writer F. T. Marinetti (q.v.), Toscanini became involved with the nascent Fascist movement. He was attracted by the radical aspects of its early program (the abolition of both banks and the stock exchange, limitations to private capital, land for peasants, union participation in management, and other reforms). Toscanini was a candidate for the parliamentary elections of November 1919, and it would seem that Toscanini had allowed the inclusion of his name on the ticket because it would provide credibility and legitimacy to the movement. Toscanini, however, did no active campaigning, and none of the candidates on Mussolini's list were elected.

Following the March on Rome (q.v.), Toscanini began to distrust the Duce's intentions and was disgusted by his failure to live up to his antimonarchical statements of 1919. At a performance of *Falstaff* in December 1919 a group of Fascist hecklers demanded that the party hymn, "Giovinezza," be played, but Toscanini responded furiously by breaking his baton and storming from the orchestra pit.

During Toscanini's tenure at La Scala in the 1920s, he and Mussolini actually met probably two or three times. An opponent of totalitarianism and racism, by now Toscanini had grown alienated from the regime, but he feared that if he totally ignored Mussolini the consequences would be grave for La Scala, which existed by government charter. He did little, however, to heed what the Fascists ordered, and Mussolini was reluctant to attack so famous a personality.

Toscanini's relationship with Fascism worsened constantly. In December 1923 his old friend Giuseppe Gallignani, who had shown no particular sympathy toward the regime, threw himself from a window following a sudden "retirement" from his post as director of the Milan Conservatory. Toscanini, at Gallignani's funeral, is reported to have taken a wreath from the minister of public education, the very agency responsible for Gallignani's dismissal, and thrown it aside. Toscanini also, as a matter of course, refused to allow the obligatory portrait of the Duce to be displayed along side that of the king in La Scala.

One further confrontation occurred on the occasion of the premiere of Puccini's *Turandot* in 1926. Mussolini wished to attend this performance at La Scala, but "Giovinezza" would naturally be expected. Toscanini was firm in his resolve not to have it played, so the administrators of La Scala were in the odious position of having to choose between the Maestro and the Duce. To Mussolini's fury, they chose the Maestro. After this incident the management was presented with an opportunity to rid themselves of the controversial but popular Toscanini when he left before the conclusion of the season, and the Fascist press circulated rumors that he would not return. Toscanini, however, stayed on.

In 1928 Toscanini was invited to direct the New York Philharmonic. There followed a triumphant series of concerts and tours throughout the world, which permanently enshrined his name among the great conductors of American orchestras.

Toscanini had by no means severed his ties to Italy, however, and an incident in May 1931 further underscored the discomfort the regime was feeling over his continued presence and notoriety. Prior to a concert in Bologna, at which two high PNF (Partito Nazionale Fascista) (q.v.) officials were to be in attendance, the conductor was confronted by a band of Fascists who demanded to know whether or not "Giovinezza" could be expected. After Toscanini had informed them that he had no intention of playing the hymn, the gang beat the sixty-four-year-old Maestro, who was saved by his chauffeur. A riot then ensued outside his hotel, and the composer Respighi, who happened to be on hand for the concert, intervened on Toscanini's behalf. As a result, the Toscanini party was able to slip away in the middle of the night to Milan, where the Maestro's passport was seized and his house kept under surveillance. By early June his papers were finally restored, and he left at once for St. Moritz, to proceed after a period of rest to the Wagner Festival at Bayreuth.

Following the Bologna incident, but also as a result of a smear campaign against him waged by the Fascist press (he was lambasted in one newspaper article entitled "The Honorary Jew"), it was no longer safe for him or his family in Italy.

In New York once again he directed the newly formed National Broadcasting Company Symphony Orchestra, which he conducted for weekly radio broadcasts until he had reached the advanced age of eighty-seven. By the late 1930s he had ceased to appear at the Bayreuth and Salzburg festivals in protest of the Nazi treatment of Jewish musicians. In New York he became a member of the Mazzini Society (q.v.), a group of anti-Fascist Italian exiles who sought the establishment of an Italian republic after the fall of Mussolini. Toscanini was even offered the presidency of the society and signed a public manifesto in 1944 demanding the end of the Italian monarchy.

Following World War II Toscanini returned to Milan, where he gave concerts to fund the restoration effort of the war-damaged La Scala. The concerts were well attended, so the theater was soon repaired. Meanwhile in the United States his weekly broadcasts flourished, featuring mainly his favorite nineteenth-century composers, Beethoven, Brahms, Verdi, and Wagner. In 1950, at the age of eighty-three, he boldly ventured on his longest tour ever through the United States. He died in New York on the verge of his ninetieth birthday, not even three years after his retirement from public life.

For further information see: *Groves Dictionary of Music & Musicians*, ed. Eric Blom (New York: St. Martins Press, 1954); Harvey Sachs, *Toscanini* (New York: J. B. Lippincott, 1978).

MJF

TOTALITARIANISM. For all the methodological and ideological objections marshalled against it, the concept "totalitarianism" continues to enjoy wide circulation and remarkable acceptance among social scientists. Both Juan Linz and Leonard Schapiro have recently published works devoted to an analysis of the concept and its application in the comparative study of political systems. They insist that the concept serves both heuristic and empirical purpose in any such study.

The term "totalitarian" has had a relatively long history and initially was innocent of any specific negative connotation. It apparently first appeared in an account of a speech by Mussolini delivered on January 5, 1925, in which he announced that thereafter all of Italy was to be "Fascistized." In that speech Mussolini spoke of the "totalitarian" disposition that animated Fascism, a disposition that found its rationale, in all probability, in the social and political philosophy of Giovanni Gentile (q.v.) as early as the publication of his *I Fondamenti della Filosofia del Diritto (The Foundations of the Philosophy of Law)*, which appeared in 1916.

In the terms of Gentile's social philosophy, "totalitarianism" implied a seamless unity of inspiration, will, and opinion that would inform an entire population, a kind of effortless ideological consensus that would render homogeneous an entire community. That homogeneity and unity would be the overt expression of a more fundamental and organic reality, the reality of the historic and spiritual continuity of a people.

For Fascist intellectuals "totalitarianism" was the philosophic and political expression of a profound reality, the reality of historic continuity that distinguished their nation, through its language, culture, history, and customs, from that of any other nation. World history, for its part, was understood to be the arena in which such organic communities worked out their respective destinies, to give substance to the spiritual evolution of mankind. Each community, in discharging its historic task, takes on intellectual and emotional forms. These forms define the life space of individuals and provide its substance, without which the individual would never attain the fulfillment of self—without which the individual would forever remain nothing more than the promise of personality.

Given such conceptions, obedience to law, conformity to the rules of the language, recognition of the moral constraints of traditional practice, and respect for customary sanction were understood to provide the necessary spiritual or psychosocial conditions for individual maturation and development. Outside the rule-governed behavior of each man's historic community, with its law, science, art, religion, and political institutions, the individual would be shorn of all the essential attributes of humanity. In effect, philosophic totalitarianism accorded moral priority to the historic community vis-à-vis the individual. In fundamental contrast with liberal political thought, totalitarianism was irrepressibly collectivistic and organicistic in orientation.

All of this was demonstrably an intellectual inheritance from Hegelianism. Italian neoidealism, which was the immediate source of Fascism's totalitarianism, was its heir. When Gentile spoke of the totalitarian intentions of Fascism, he had just such Hegelian conceptions in mind.

Fascism attempted to translate these notions into political expression. Already opposed to the parliamentarianism of the pre-Fascist political system of Italy, Fascists very quickly put together a single-party alternative, suppressing opposition parties, the opposition press, and individual political dissidence in their effort to create and ensure consensus.

To further its purposes, the Fascist government passed legislation calculated to fashion a near-monopoly control over the information and educational media. They passed legislation that provided the government with monopoly rights over the organization of labor. After-work institutions (*see* DOPOLAVORO) made any escape from such tutelary control problematic at best. A number of state and para-state institutions were created that sought to influence the lives of citizens from the moment of conception (through agencies devoted to prenatal, postnatal, and perinatal care) through early adulthood (in youth organizations [q.v.] like the Children of the Wolf, the Balilla, the Fascist Vanguard, and the Young Fascists). Similar institutions were insinuated into economic life, and by the time the regime had reached maturity, wages, prices, the conditions of labor, the rate of profit, export and import opportunities, the availability of credit, and the allocation of capital resources were either fully controlled or significantly influenced by the Fascist government. By the commencement of World War II the Fascist government exercised more control over the lives and activities of its citizens than any other government save the Soviet Union.

All of this was laced together by a real or seeming commitment to a formal ideology (of variable content) identified with the "thought of Mussolini." Citizens were instructed in terms of the formal ideology through a variety of agencies. Intellectuals were confirmed in their positions by the party employing "moral" or "political" criteria. University professors were required to subscribe to an oath of loyalty to the regime. State subventions to students were conditional upon their good conduct. Journalists and artists were inscribed in Fascist syndicates, and businessmen were organized in Fascist confederations. Women were expected to become active members of appropriate formations of the party. Ultimately, through voluntary and compulsory membership requirements, all citizens were expected to take part in the functions of the party.

Activities designed to mobilize, integrate, and politically organize the masses attended all this. Public affairs took on many of the features of collective theater: marches, songs, national festivals, military displays, ritual observances, and the call to dramatic accomplishments (the "Battle for Grain" [q.v.], the "Battle for the Defense of the Lira" [see QUOTA NOVANTA], the "Battle for Autarchy" [see AUTARCHY], and so forth) kept collective life charged with emotion. Central to the dramaturgy was the cult of the leader (see DUCE), the source of collective inspiration and the embodiment of collective purpose.

All the features of compromise, tolerance, group competition, and differential representation characteristic of the old bourgeois system were expected to disappear in the face of all this. In its place the totalitarian system was to create a new man, collective in orientation, heterocentric in disposition, effortlessly committed to national purpose, and animated by a sacrifice and work ethic that would ensure the development of the "greater Italy" in the face of protracted multiple threats.

More than a little separated the social and political reality of Fascist Italy from the aspirations embodied in its doctrinal intentions. Throughout the Fascist period the military maintained considerable independence. With its millenarian roots, the Roman Catholic Church resisted the efforts to submerge it in the system with some success. Business organizations, so vital to Fascist developmental programs, continued to exercise considerable, if negative, control over various aspects of economic and political life. Finally, the traditional monarchy survived into the final phase of Fascism and was the immediate agency that brought down the regime in 1943.

The continued vitality of these extra-Fascist interest groups and the influence they continued to exercise over the regime provide the empirical grounds for identifying Italian Fascism as a "pre-" or "quasi-totalitarian," rather than a totalitarian political system. But for all that, the features of a distinctive and singularly modern political form clearly emerge. Fascist intentions, perhaps more so than in any similar system, were manifestly totalitarian. Fascism sought to create a consensus regime, informed by an official ideology, locked into bureaucratic controls over enterprise and information, institutionalized under the aegis of a unitary or single party and its capillary agencies, and obedient to a charismatic ruler who governed without effective opposition. It was a system explicitly opposed to the conception of the individual as the repository of natural rights forever insulated against the state. It abjured compromissary politics, the negotiated settlement of conflicting interests, and the tolerance of diversity. It rejected political agnosticism and identified all thought as necessarily committed, with its opponents either malefactors or fools to be either punished or reeducated. It wished to inspire an entire nation with a unity of revolutionary purpose fundamentally alien to liberalism and the multiparty and pluralistic political system in which liberalism had found historic expression.

Whatever more careful, substantive analysis might reveal, Fascist totalitarianism will remain prototypic of a modern political persuasion that has worked considerable influence in our century, a persuasion whose historic significance is by no means behind us.

For further information see: Domenico Fisichella, *Analisi del totalitarismo* (Florence: D'Anna, 1976); A. James Gregor, "Fascism as Totalitarianism," in *Interpretations of Fascism* (Morristown, N.J.: General Learning, 1974); Juan J. Linz, "Totalitarian and Authoritarian Regimes," in *Handbook of Political Science* 3, ed. Fred I. Greenstein and Nelson W. Polsby (Reading: Addison-Wesley, 1975); Leonard Shapiro, *Totalitarianism* (New York: Praeger, 1972).

AJG

TRENTIN, SILVIO (b. San Donà di Piave, Venice, November 11, 1885; d. Treviso, March 12, 1944). A Venetian professor and writer, Trentin spent most of the Fascist period in southern France ardently promoting a revolutionary Socialist position within the Giustizia e Libertà (GL) movement (*see* ANTI-FASCISM).

After completing his legal education, he taught public law in Venice and legal history at the University of Padua. He also served in the pre-Fascist Parliament (1919-21). During the Matteotti Crisis (q.v.) he supported Giovanni Amendola's (q.v.) National Democratic Union. In 1926 he fled to Toulouse, where he first worked as a manual laborer and then opened a bookshop that became a center of GL activities in southern France. He continued to write anti-Fascist tracts that were smuggled into Italy to keep domestic opposition alive and later gave refuge to the former premier F. S. Nitti (q.v.).

When Carlo Rosselli (q.v.) led GL in the direction of revolutionary socialism in 1931-32, Trentin moved into the avante garde of the organization. In 1934 he took greater internal responsibility and also represented GL in the central committee for the Anti-Fascist Concentration (*see* ANTI-FASCISM), which was consistent with his interest in cooperation among the exiles. But his support for anti-Fascist unity was inhibited by his growing opposition to social democratic reformism and to the specific grouping of parties in the Third International. Influenced by Trotsky's theory of "permanent revolution," he became convinced that basic constitutional and economic reform could come to Italy only through a process of revolution followed by an initial period of dictatorial force.

His relationship with Carlo Rosselli deepened in 1936. When the Rosselli brothers were assassinated shortly thereafter, Trentin joined Emilio Lussu (q.v.) and others in attempting to fill the void. He continued to find inspiration in the Russian experience, particularly in the idealism of the first year of the revolution and in the economic leadership of the state. But, disenchanted with Stalinism, he criticized the Russian "betrayal" of Marxist principles and of the revolution; and he condemned Western Communist parties for their blind adherence to the vicissitudes of Kremlin policy.

It was in the interwar period that Trentin developed his most original political ideas. He anticipated an Italian socialist-federalist state of administrative decentralization; autonomy of towns, factories, and unions; and worker self-management. He emphasized the need for an elite vanguard—rather than a political party—to provide leadership for the revolution in Italy.

In 1941, in spite of his opposition to the Communist and Socialist parties, he joined them in the Committee of Action for the Union of the Italian People. He represented GL on that committee, and he was committed to the overthrow of Mussolini, a separate peace, and the restoration of civil liberties. In 1942 he founded the partisan movement "Liberer-Federer," featuring a Rossellian federalist-revolutionary program.

In September 1943 he returned to Venice to assume a leadership role in the Resistance movement (*see* RESISTANCE, ARMED). He died of a heart attack as he was being chased by Fascist agents in 1944. In his memory the Party of Action (*see* PARTITO D'AZIONE) named the "Silvio Trentin Brigade" after him.

For further information see: Norberto Bobbio, *Ricordo di Silvio Trentin* (Venice: Marsilio, 1955); Frank Rosengarten, *Silvio Trentin* (Milan: Feltrinelli, 1980); Silvio Trentin, *Dix Ans de Fascisme Totalitaire en Italie* (Paris: Editions Sociales Internationales, 1937); Silvio Trentin, *Scritti inediti, testimonziane e studi* (Parma: Guanda, 1972).

                                                                              CLK

TRESCA, CARLO (b. Sulmona, March 9, 1879; d. New York, January 11, 1943). Tresca's earliest battles were fought in his native town in the Abruzzi, where as a rebellious youth he severed all ties with the propertied class of his birth and embraced socialism with the fiery militancy that characterized his entire career. A branch secretary of the Italian Railroad Worker's Union and editor of the newspaper *Il Germe* at the age of twenty-two, Tresca could have had a brilliant future in the Italian Socialist party (*see* PARTITO SOCIALISTA ITALIANO) if not for his one-man campaign against the local clergy and political clique. To avoid imprisonment for libel, Tresca departed for the United States in 1904, never again to see his homeland.

In Philadelphia Tresca assumed editorship of *Il Proletario*, the official organ of the Italian Socialist Federation of America. But Tresca soon wearied of the constraints placed upon him by the Federation, so he resigned as editor of *Il Proletario* and quit the Socialist party. This declaration of independence was indicative of the increasingly anarchistic bent of his ideas and personality. In 1908 Tresca set out alone for western Pennsylvania to inject revolutionary fervor into the struggles of the Italian coal miners and millworkers.

Tresca's reputation as a speaker and organizer had spread widely among labor circles, and in 1912 the Industrial Workers of the World (IWW) invited him to take charge of the Italian textile strikers at Lawrence, Massachusetts. The Lawrence strike propelled Tresca into national prominence and marked the beginning of his affiliation with the IWW, subsequent high points of which were the Paterson strike of 1913 and the Mesaba Range strike of 1916. During the strike of iron miners at the Mesaba Range in Minnesota, Tresca, Elizabeth Gurley Flynn (Tresca's lover since 1912), and Joe Errot alienated the IWW's chief "Big Bill" Haywood and ended Tresca's activities for the organization. After the United States entered World War I and several states passed "criminal syndicalist" laws for the specific purpose of destroying the IWW, Tresca would have been a sure candidate for conviction at the famous Chicago trial that condemned ninety-three members to lengthy terms of imprisonment in April 1918. However, since Tresca was no longer linked with the organization (he had never been a full-fledged member), the authorities were compelled to drop all charges against him. But Tresca did not emerge from the war years completely unscathed. His two newspapers, *L'Avvenire* (which he ultimately suppressed), and its successor *Il Martello*, were repeatedly confiscated.

That Carlo Tresca, a nationally renowned subversive and alien, managed to avoid arrest and deportation during the Palmer raids of 1919-20 is fitting testimony to his talent for survival. In the wake of the justice department's campaign to wipe out radicalism, Tresca became involved in what was to become one of America's most famous political trials—the Sacco-Vanzetti case. It was Tresca who brought the controversial IWW lawyer Fred Moore into the case as chief counsel and who helped generate nationwide publicity and financial support for the two men. Tresca stood in the forefront of the anti-Fascist movement in the United States militant minority. Long before the March on Rome (q. v.), Tresca had regarded Fascism as the White Guard of capitalism, and in the pages of *Il Martello* he excoriated Mussolini as the arch-traitor of the working class and attacked the monarchy for its cowardly complicity in the Fascist takeover. In 1923 the Italian embassy officially requested the state department to suppress *Il Martello*. The federal authorities hastened to comply with Fascist demands and prosecuted Tresca on charges of sending "obscene matter" through the mails. Sentenced to a year and a day, Tresca spent four months in a federal penitentiary in 1925 before public outcry over this transparent political frameup forced President Coolidge to issue an official commutation. After failing to rid themselves of Tresca by "legal" means, the Fascists resorted to violence. During a rally in Harlem's Little Italy in 1926, the Fascists attempted to bomb Tresca and other anti-Fascist leaders into the next world. To the tactics of *squadrismo* (*see* SQUADRISTI), the anti-Fascists sometimes responded with daggers and pistols.

By the 1930s he had become an implacable foe of the Communists. In contrast to anarchists like Kropotkin, Malatesta, and Goldman, who from the outset denounced the Bolsheviks as betrayers of the Russian revolution, Tresca initially gave grudging support to the Soviet regime, reckoning with very unlibertarian logic that a socialist state was preferable to a capitalist state. Throughout the 1920s, he regarded the Communists as necessary allies in the fight against Fascism and collaborated with them in such united front organizations as the Italian Anti-Fascist Alliance of North America. His attitude changed, however, as he observed the growing manifestations of Stalinism and what he regarded as the divisive conduct of the Communists in the American labor movement. Above all, it was the Communists' suppression of the anarchist revolution in Catalonia during the Spanish Civil War (q.v.) that turned Tresca irrevocably against the Communists.

After America's entry into World War II, Tresca's fight against Communists and Fascists was concentrated mainly on keeping them out of the Italian-American Victory Council (IAVC) and the Mazzini Society (q.v.). So long as Tresca was alive, Communists and Fascists (that is, those Fascists who became "ex-Fascists" after December 7, 1941) found their efforts to penetrate the Mazzini Society and the IAVC blocked. The obstacle was eliminated when an assassin fired a bullet into Tresca's brain.

Who killed Carlo Tresca? His associates generally believed that the murder was politically motivated. The two suspects most often accused were the "ex-Fascist" Generoso Pope and the Communist Vittorio Vidali. On the other hand, the possibility cannot be discounted that Tresca may have been the victim of an Italian underworld figure named Frank Garofalo whose motive was personal rather than political. Tresca's killers were never brought to justice, and the case remains unsolved.

For further information see: MOI (5); Nunzio Pernicone, "Carlo Tresca," *La Parola del popolo* (November-December 1979).

NP

TREVES, CLAUDIO (b. Turin, March 24, 1869; d. Paris, June 11, 1933). A journalist, lawyer, and legislator, Claudio Treves was a traditional reformist Socialist and—for the final seven years of his life—one of the major proponents of that position among the anti-Fascist exiles.

A member of an affluent family, he was nurtured in a setting of late-nineteenth-century Turinese democratic socialism. As a student he participated in radical politics and cultural life, joining the university radical *fasci* in 1888. He soon became disenchanted with Mazzinian radicalism.

He then affiliated with an independent union that brought him into contact with the Socialist League of Filippo Turati (q.v.), with whom he was to share an extended political alliance.

He was awarded a degree in jurisprudence and in the 1890s began his writing career and his association with European Socialists. He contributed articles to *Ventesimo Secolo* and *Avanti!* and in 1896 was named editor of *Grido del Popolo*. Two years later he moved to Milan, where his association with Turati grew closer. He contributed frequently to Turati's newly founded *Critica Sociale*.

At the start of the new century Treves began to participate more actively in the affairs of the Socialist party (PSI—Partito Socialista Italiano) (q.v.). He attended the conferences of the Second International and of the PSI, taking a leadership role when the Minimalists established dominance at the Florence Congress of 1908. He and Leonida Bissolati (q.v.) advocated socialism through gradual reform within the democratic process in *Avanti!*. He succeeded Bissolati as editor of *Avanti!* in 1910, continuing his intransigent reformism and opposing the Libyan War.

When Benito Mussolini and the Maximalists prevailed in 1912, Treves was relegated to the right-wing minority of the PSI, surrendering *Avanti!* to the Maximalist Giovanni Bacci. In the final decade of the Liberal state, Treves continued to support Turati's reformists. They advocated neutrality in World War I but supported the government after Caporetto (*see* CAPORETTO, BATTLE OF). They were outvoted by the Maximalists (revolutionaries) in 1919 and again in 1921, when the left-wing dissidents formed the Communist party.

Treves retained his alliance with Turati as the Socialists became more fragmented. He criticized the Communist International as a tool of the Russian state and in 1922 joined Turati, Giuseppe Modigliani (q.v.), and Giacomo Matteotti (*see* MATTEOTTI CRISIS) in creating a separate Labor party (PSU-Partito Socialista Unitaro). He edited *La Giustizia*, the PSU organ, and contributed to *Lavoro*, including the publication of the manifesto of the "gradualist" Socialists.

In November 1926, as Fascist repression mounted, he escaped to Paris with Giuseppe Saragat (q.v.) and Ferruccio Parri (q.v.), never to return to Italy. He resumed his journalistic activities, entering into polemic with Carlo Rosselli (q.v.) in the pages of *Il Quarto Stato*, under the pseudonym "Rabano Mauro." Taking an even more orthodox position of reformist socialism, Treves represented an older generation of Socialists, defending liberal democratic institutions under the increasingly radical criticism of the younger Rosselli. The naming of Treves as editor of *La Libertà* indicated the dominance of reformism in the Anti-Fascist Concentration (*see* ANTI-FASCISM). Again he engaged in polemic with Rosselli, while he continued to criticize the Fascist system.

While in exile in France he maintained his contacts with European Socialists. He remained an active leader in the concentration, attempting to forge a broad anti-Fascist alliance and to fuse the Socialist party of Italian Laborers (successor to the PSU) with Maximalist Socialists.

One of the last of the original generation of Italian Socialists, Treves died an hour after commemorating his former colleague Matteotti. His death, followed the next year by that of Turati, weakened the ranks of reformist leadership and brought the demise of the Anti-Fascist Concentration.

For further information see: DSPI; MOI; Gaetano Arfè, *Storia del socialismo italiano, 1892-1926* (Turin: Einaudi, 1965); Claudio Treves, *Polemica socialista* (Bologna: N. Zanichelli, 1921).

CLK

TREVES, PAOLO (b. Milan, July 27, 1908; d. Fregene, Rome, 1958). A writer, professor, and man of political affairs, Paolo Treves was a democratic Socialist and an opponent of Italian Fascism. Son of the reformist Socialist Claudio Treves (q.v.), he took his degree in law and political science and later worked as secretary to Filippo Turati (q.v.). He contributed to various journals and served in 1925 as an editor of *Giustizia*, journal of the Partito Socialista Unitaro (PSU) established by Turati, his father, and others three years before.

He remained in the Socialist underground movement from 1926 until forced into exile by the racial laws of 1938 (*see* ANTI-SEMITISM). He was Italian correspondent for *La Libertà* of Paris, the publication of the Anti-Fascist Concentration (*see* ANTI-FASCISM) edited by his father. Under police surveillance throughout the Fascist period, he was arrested in 1929 shortly after joining several Turinese professors in condemning the Lateran treaties (*see* LATERAN PACTS).

While in exile in England, he and his brother Piero participated actively in the Free Italy (q.v.) movement. Paolo was employed by British intelligence, and from 1940 to 1945 he directed a series of radio programs for the BBC aimed at encouraging resistance and support for Allied policy among the Italian audience.

In January 1945 he reentered Italy to begin an active political life in the postwar period. He again wrote for Socialist journals and founded, with Giuseppe Saragat (q.v.) and Matteo Matteotti, the Roman journal *L'Umanità*, of which he was named editor. In the realm of diplomacy he was attached to the Italian embassy in Paris (1945-46) and selected to the Consultative Assembly of the Council of Europe (1949).

A member of the Social Democratic party after it was founded in 1947, he was elected to the Constituent Assembly (*see* COSTITUENTE) and the first two Republican legislatures. He then served as undersecretary of foreign trade in the quadripartite governments of Mario Scelba (1954) and Antonio Segni (1955-57). He took a position as professor of the history of political doctrine at the University of Florence in 1950.

For further information see: *Chi è?* (1948); Paolo Treves, *Italy, Yesterday, Today, Tomorrow* (London: V. Gollancz, 1942); Paolo Treves, *Sul fronte e dietro il fronte italiano* (Rome: Sandon, 1945).

CLK

TRINGALI CASANOVA, ANTONINO (b. Cecina, April 11, 1888; d. Cremona, November 1, 1943). President of the Special Tribunal for the Defense of the State (q.v.) and a Militia (q.v.) officer, Tringali Casanova took a law degree and was an infantry captain in World War I. He joined the Fascist movement early in 1920 and organized *fasci* in Tuscany. He was a consul and lieutenant general in the Fascist Militia and served as the first mayor (and later Podestà) of Castagneto Carducci, Livorno. In January 1927 he was made a judge on the Special Tribunal, then vice-president in September 1928, and president in November 1932. It was in this latter capacity that, as a member of the Fascist Grand Council (q.v.), he took part in the fall of Mussolini, voting against the Dino Grandi (q.v.) motion. In September 1943 Mussolini made him minister of grace and justice in the Salò Republic (*see* ITALIAN SOCIAL REPUBLIC), but he died shortly thereafter.

For further information see: *Chi è?* (1936); NO (1928).

                                                                                              PVC

TURATI, AUGUSTO (b. Parma, August 25, 1888; d. Rome, August, 1955). Augusto Turati, *ras* (q.v.) of Brescia and PNF (Partito Nazionale Fascista) (q.v.) secretary from 1926 to 1930, became a journalist on a local Brescia liberal-democratic newspaper. He studied law at the university but did not graduate. An interventionist and volunteer, he was promoted to captain and decorated for bravery in World War I. Returning to journalism, he apparently had regular contacts with the Brescia *fascio* founded in April 1919 but did not play a prominent role in its organization until autumn 1920.

Under Turati, Brescian Fascism developed a distinctive character in some ways untypical of other rasdoms. Turati certainly shared the major preoccupation of Fascist bosses: he distrusted Mussolini's parliamentary maneuvers and "normalizing" tendencies, which threatened the provincial movement's "revolutionary" drive and its arbitrary and informal methods of control. This was made clear by his apparent involvement in a late 1921 pro-D'Annunzio (*see* D'ANNUNZIO, GABRIELE) conspiracy of dissident Fascists and by the staging of a march on the city of Brescia in December 1922 after conflicts between local Fascists and Catholics.

However, Turati appeared to distance himself from the major Fascist controversies of 1921-25 and from fellow *ras* whose exuberant demagogic style he despised. Also, he attempted to sustain an innovative concept of syndicalism (q.v.), which remained at the core of his Fascist beliefs. In Brescia, as elsewhere, Fascist unions were the appendages of squadrist (*see* SQUADRISTI) offensives against Socialist and Catholic bodies. But Turati resisted Fascism's exclusive identification with employers' interests and managed to create a relatively combative syndical organization by Fascist standards. This almost anomalous feature of Brescian Fascism emerged clearly during the 1925 metallurgical strikes, which made Turati a national figure.

The immediate background to the strikes was rising living costs in 1924-25 which, coinciding with the Matteotti Crisis (q.v.), made necessary some initiative from Fascist syndicates to deflect working-class discontent. The longer-term problem was how the syndicates, viewed suspiciously by workers and employers alike, were to gain recognition as exclusive representatives of the working class. Confident of his own union organization, Turati called a strike of Brescia's metallurgical workers on March 2, 1925. The FIOM's (Federazione Italiana Operai Metallurgici) extension of the strike to the whole industry only exposed Fascism's isolation among industrial workers, and hasty government mediation accelerated a wage agreement on March 16, which Turati only grudgingly accepted.

The strikes had important consequences for both Turati and the syndicates. Appointed party vice-secretary in June 1925 with responsibility for syndical affairs, he participated in negotiations culminating in the Palazzo Vidoni Pact (q.v.). This secured employers' recognition of Fascist syndicates, but through party-state mediation rather than direct action previously favored by Turati and at the cost of excluding syndicates from the factory floor.

Turati was nominated PNF general secretary in March 1926. His secretaryship marked a turning point in the regime's development. His mandate from Mussolini was to create a disciplined party, subordinate to the state, which would not, as under Roberto Farinacci (q.v.) in 1925-26, undermine with its "revolutionary" dynamism Mussolini's strategy of accommodation with the existing elites in Italian society.

In a dramatic restructuring of the party's membership and functions between 1926 and 1929, Turati expelled thousands of exsquadrists, suppressed newspapers representing their views, removed or neutralized provincial Fascist bosses, and recruited a more passive membership, particularly state employees. He subjected the party to centralized controls, replacing election of local party leaders with nomination from above and attempting to impose uniform bureaucratic procedures. Turati regarded the purge as a necessary preparation for the party's indispensable long term task: to create a Fascist Italy capable of surviving Mussolini. Hence, Turati emphasized party responsibility for the formation of a Fascist elite, and he gave impetus to capillary organs dependent on the party, aiming to "insert" into the regime wide areas of public and private activity, including sports, afterwork activities, social welfare, and "culture."

However, the effects of the purge itself destroyed the party's chances of exercising such an ambitious role. It would be difficult to activate an increasingly bureaucratized party deprived of its most energetic leaders and members and subordinated to an only partially "Fascistized" body of prefects.

The purge's impact also aborted Turati's hope of securing an influential party role in economic and syndical affairs. He promoted "provincial intersyndical committees" in 1927 during the reevaluation crisis as a concrete expression of the party's mediation of opposing class interests. They functioned intermittently, dependent on the will or otherwise of local party secretaries. Turati's campaign for party control of the syndicates achieved an alliance with Giuseppe Bottai (q.v.), minister of corporations, and the dismantling of Edmondo Rossoni's (q.v.) confederation of workers' syndicates in November 1928. But again, a devitalized party whose structure and composition mirrored the consensus at the basis of the regime was scarcely capable of imposing itself on employers as well as workers.

Disagreements between Mussolini and Turati became evident in 1929. By now a prestigious national figure, Turati expressed discordant views on various internal developments, criticizing overbureaucratic corporative reforms and government economic policies in face of the depression. Above all, Turati's exposures of corruption implicated Mussolini's own entourage and family, including his brother, Arnaldo (*see* MUSSOLINI, ARNALDO). Taking advantage of Turati's isolation among other Fascists, Mussolini accepted his third offer of resignation in September 1930.

Turati then worked for *Il Corriere della Sera* and in January 1931 was made editor of *La Stampa*. Still politically active, irregularities in his private life were ruthlessly inflated by Roberto Farinacci (q.v.) and other opponents in August 1932, and he was finally disgraced, expelled from the party, and forced into exile in Rhodes early in 1933.

Returning to Italy in 1937, he was readmitted to the party on the condition that he leave for Ethiopia to run an agricultural concern. Back in Italy in 1938, he eventually worked as a small-time consultant in Rome. After July 1943 Turati claimed to have resisted recruitment to the RSI (Repubblica Sociale Italiana) (*see* ITALIAN SOCIAL REPUBLIC) and aided the Resistance (*see* RESISTANCE, ARMED). With the liberation, he was tried and condemned for his Fascist activities but remained in open hiding until he received amnesty.

For further information see: Y de Begnac, *Palazzo Venezia: storia di un regime* (Rome: La Rocca, 1950); R. De Felice, *Mussolini il fascista* (Turin: Einaudi, 1966-68); R. De Felice, *Mussolini il Duce* (Turin: Einaudi, 1974); P. Morgan, "Augusto Turati," in *Uomini e volti del fascismo*, ed. F. Cordova (Rome: Bulzoni, 1980).

                                                                                         PM

TURATI, FILIPPO (b. Canzo, November 25, 1857; d. Paris, March 29, 1932). The principal founder of the Italian Socialist party (*see* PARTITO SOCIALISTA ITALIANO), Turati was trained as a lawyer at the University of Bologna. He participated in the Milanese Scapigliatura literary movement, publishing articles and poetry in the best-known journals of the period, such as *La Farfalla*. In the 1880s Turati became strongly attracted to politics, and he published the brilliant "Il delitto e la questione sociale" ("Crime and the Social Question") in 1883. Although he began as a Democrat, Turati soon supported the Partito Operaio Italiano (POI), a labor party founded by Milanese workers in 1882. Turati wrote the *Inno dei Lavoratori* for the POI, poetry later set to music, designed to explain Marxist principles in simple terms. He defended the POI leaders in court after the government dissolved the party in 1886.

In 1885 Turati met Anna Kuliscioff in Naples, and in collaboration with her, his Marxism became more orthodox. In 1889 he participated in the founding of the Lega Socialista Milanese, described as a "cell" for the future Socialist party, whose program was imbued with his ideas. In 1891 he established *Critica Sociale*, transforming a previous journal into the principal instrument for the diffusion of Marxism in Italy. He also worked prodigiously for the establishment of an Italian Socialist party against the strong resistance of anarchists, Operaisti (members of the POI), and the Marxist philosopher Antonio Labriola. He succeeded in August 1892.

Turati was the party's most influential early leader, working for a gradual, nonviolent course to socialism, which would be achieved by means of reform. At the end of 1894 he cooperated with the bourgeois Democrats in Milan in order to combat Prime Minister Francesco Crispi's repressive policies. He advocated similar cooperation for the Socialist party at the national level, but his ideas were not formally adopted. In 1898 he was charged with fomenting the disorders of that year and sentenced by a military tribunal to twelve years in prison. In the meantime, however, the Socialist party followed his policies, allying with other groups of the extreme Left and successfully obstructing the passage of restrictive legislation.

Released in 1900, Turati announced that cooperation with the "bourgeois" Left would be a standard feature of Socialist policy. In 1901 Turati advocated voting for the Liberal Giuseppe Zanardelli in order to keep in power a government sympathetic to the working classes and to prevent the installation of a conservative cabinet. Turati convinced his fellow Socialist deputies to violate the directorate's order and to support the cabinet, thus making Zanardelli the first person to receive Socialist votes. As a result, the government took a noninterventionist position in strikes and real wages increased dramatically. This laid the basis for future cooperation with Giovanni Giolitti (q.v.), Zanardelli's interior minister.

Turati triumphed at the Socialist congresses of 1900 and 1902, but changing economic and political conditions led to increased left-wing opposition, and in 1903 his faction lost control of *Avanti!* and much of the labor movement, forcing Turati to refuse a cabinet position. In 1904 the Left seemed dominant, but Turati's forces recovered in 1905 and 1906 and formally recaptured control at the 1908 congress. Turati was dominant until the Congress of Reggio Emilia (1912), when revulsion against the Libyan War, which Turati had denounced but which part of the reformist wing supported, favored the rise of the left wing.

Turati advocated Italian neutrality in World War I, sanctioning the war effort only after Caporetto (*see* CAPORETTO, BATTLE OF). From 1919 to 1921 he opposed the Maximalist (revolutionary) majority's desire for violent revolution on the Communist model, predicting that in Italy violence would provoke a reaction that would annihilate the workers' movement. As Fascist violence increased he participated in an effort to construct a government coalition that would act against the Fascists, and this resulted in his expulsion by the party in 1922. Turati then founded the Partito Socialista Unitario (PSU), which had Giacomo Matteotti as its secretary. After Matteotti's (*see* MATTEOTTI CRISIS) murder, Turati was a prime mover of the Aventine Secession (q.v.). Turati fled Italy in a daring motorboat escape organized by Carlo Rosselli (q.v.) and Ferruccio Parri (q.v.) in 1926 and went to Paris, where he became the chief inspiration of the anti-Fascist movement. He attempted to achieve international recognition for the Italian exiles, emphasizing that Fascism was a capitalist phenomenon that would spread to other countries. He was instrumental in establishing the "Concentrazione Antifascista" (*see* ANTI-FASCISM) in 1927, which coordinated the anti-Fascist activities of the disparate exile groups. He also promoted the reunification of the two Socialist parties, which took place in 1930. After the foundation of the more resistance-oriented Giustizia e Libertà (GL), Turati modified his pacifist ideas and advocated agreement between the GL and the "Concentrazione," a goal which he achieved in late 1931, shortly before his death.

For further information see: Franco Catalano, *Filippo Turati* (Milan-Rome: Avanti!, 1957); Alessandro Schiavi, *Discorsi parlamentari di Filippo Turati*, 3 vols. (Rome: Tipografia della Camera dei deputati, 1950); Alessandro Schiavi, *Esilio e morte di Filippo Turati (1926-1932)* (Rome: Ed. Opere Nuove, 1956); Filippo Turati--Anna Kuliscioff, *Carteggio*, Vol. 1, 5, 6 (Turin: Einaudi, 1949-59).

SD

U

UMBERTO II (b. Racconigi, September 15, 1904). King of Italy from May 9, 1946 to June 2, 1946, Umberto II was the third child and only son of King Victor Emmanuel III (q.v.) and held the title of Prince of Piedmont from birth. He received an essentially military education and in 1923 was made an army officer. He married Maria Jose, daughter of King Albert I of Belgium, in 1930, and they had four children: Maria Pia, Victor Emmanuel, Maria Gabriella, and Maria Beatrice.

As heir to the throne Umberto naturally rose rapidly in rank: brigade general in 1931, division general in 1934, corps general in 1936, army general in 1938, and marshal of Italy in 1942. After the September 1943 Armistice (q.v.), the Allies refused to permit him to assume front-line command of the Italian armies of liberation.

The "institutional crisis" opened in 1944 when anti-Fascist leaders of Republican persuasion demanded the end of the monarchy that had so thoroughly compromised itself with Fascism. On June 5, 1944, Victor Emmanuel withdrew from the active exercise of power by naming Umberto "Lieutenant General of the Realm"—an action the king hoped would enable the House of Savoy to survive the forthcoming national referendum (*see* REFERENDUM OF 1946). Umberto assumed the throne when Victor Emmanuel abdicated on May 9, 1946. He "campaigned" actively with promonarchists in the weeks that followed, but when on June 2 the referendum decided in favor of a republic, Umberto left (June 13) for exile in Portugal. He resides today in Cascais, near Lisbon, and has the title of count of Sarre.

For further information see: DSPI; Robert Katz, *The Fall of the House of Savoy* (New York: Macmillan, 1971).

PVC

UNGARETTI, GIUSEPPE (b. Alexandria, Egypt, February 10, 1888; d. Milan, June 1, 1970). A poet and father of "hermeticism," Ungaretti's parents were from Lucca. From 1912 to 1914 he studied at the Sorbonne in Paris. In 1915 he transferred to Milan and fought in World War I. After the war he went to Marino, near Rome, where he worked as a journalist. He was on the editorial staff of *Il Popolo d'Italia* and wrote in many other Italian and foreign journals and magazines.

In 1936 Ungaretti moved to San Paolo, Brazil, where he taught Italian language and literature at the university until 1942. From 1943 to 1958 he taught contemporary literature at the University of Rome. He was made a member of the Royal Academy of Italy (q.v.) in 1942.

In the 1930s young writers like Ungaretti, Alfonso Gatto, and Carlo Bò sought to isolate their poetry from politics and the baseness of life. In one sense, this "hermeticism" was a form of anti-Fascism (*see* LITERATURE).

Ungaretti's poetic evolution has three essential phases: attachment to life, lyricism, and phonic values. The first was the poet's actual concrete story: his life experiences in Egypt, France, and Italy. Each experience is a refuge, a sort of pilgrimage toward the final goal of finding himself and finding God within himself. The second phase, lyricism, represents the inner story of Ungaretti's poetry. He succeeded in reaching an ever-greater artistic conscience expressed through a continuous improvement of techniques, and especially through the creation of a new poetic form using metaphor and analogy. The works that are most directly related to this phase are *Il Dolore* (1947), *Sentimento del Tempo* (1950), *Un Grido e Paesaggi* (1952), *Taccuino del Vecchio* (1960), and his most recent poems. In the third and final phase, phonic value, his words seem to deny their own sounds by giving life to silence. They tend to deny tangible physical things by creating images of light.

For further information see: *I meridiani* (Milan: Mondadori, 1969); G. Cavalli, *Ungaretti* (Milan: Mondadori, 1958).

WEL

UNIONE ITALIANA DEL LAVORO (UIL). In November 1914 after the USI (Unione Sindacalti Italiana) had expelled the interventionists, Alceste De Ambris (q.v.) and Tullio Masotti established the UIL. During the war, however, the interventionists worked within the broader-based Comitato Sindacale Italiano and the UIL never functioned. In May 1918, at the urging of the secretary of the Unione Sindacale Milanese, Edmondo Rossoni (q.v.), members of the USM and the CSI decided to resurrect the UIL in order to provide a labor organization that would represent the workers who had supported the nation at war.

Hence on June 9 and 10 delegates representing some fifty organizations and one hundred and thirty-seven thousand members met in Milan. As the foundation of their program, the delegates posited a strong nationalism and accepted the slogan of Rossoni's paper, *L'Italia Nostra*, "Do not deny the nation, conquer it." The delegates adopted a program that pledged the UIL to continue the struggle against capitalism, to strive for worker control of production, distribution, and exchange, and to reject any relationships with political parties. But because they intended the UIL to be the organization through which workers would participate in the national renewal, they also urged workers to work hard, since the delegates believed that the working class would benefit from an increase in production and national wealth.

At its second congress, held in Rome in January 1919, the UIL added an important point to its program. At the urging of De Ambris, the delegates demanded the expropriation of all land not under direct cultivation by its owners. This demand appealed to the landless peasants and to the veterans, and they joined the UIL in increasing numbers, swelling its ranks to over two hundred thousand by the beginning of 1920.

In March 1919 the UIL led the first occupation strike in the postwar period. The UIL had demanded an eight-hour day and a half-day holiday on Saturday from the owners of the Franchi-Gregorini steel plant in Dalmine. When the owners refused to grant the demands and threatened a lockout, the UIL responded with an occupation. The workers raised the tricolor over the factory and announced that they would continue production. The following day soldiers forced the workers to leave the plant, but the UIL, as Mussolini pointed out, had set an important precedent because the occupation had been "productive." The strike was, according to the Fascist leader, the first evidence of the strength of a movement that combined nationalism and revolutionary syndicalism.

Throughout 1919, influenced by Mussolini and De Ambris, the UIL seemed to draw closer to the Fascists. Late in the year, however, at its third congress, held in Forlì on October 18 to 20, Rossoni challenged the delegates to uphold the principles of revolutionary syndicalism, to reject all political alliances, and to reaffirm the autonomy of the UIL. Although they supported De Ambris's motion to allow individuals to join a political movement, the delegates rejected any alliance between the UIL and a political party.

When De Ambris resigned as secretary-general and joined Gabriele D'Annunzio (q.v.) in Fiume (q.v.), Rossoni replaced him and early in 1920 led the UIL in its support of the railway and postal strikes. The Fascists, who continued to hope that they would forge an alliance with the UIL, opposed these strikes. Thus, by early 1920 the Fascists recognized that they could not work with the UIL, and they began to form their own unions. The UIL responded to this tactic by becoming more anti-Fascist although Rossoni, who took control of the powerful Ferrara Chamber of Labor in June 1921, continued to urge the UIL to cooperate with the Fascists.

At the UIL's fourth congress held in Rome in September 1921, A. O. Olivetti (q.v.), speaking for Rossoni and others, urged the delegates to join a united front with the Fascists and Nationalists. The secretary-general, Guido Galbiati, opposed the idea. He and De Ambris stressed their opposition to the Fascists. The Fascists, as Galbiati pointed out, had been attacking UIL organizations even though the members of the UIL were interventionists and veterans who had continued to fight against socialism. The delegates reaffirmed the UIL's opposition to Fascism. In reaction to the UIL decision, Rossoni withdrew the Ferrara Chamber of Labor from the UIL and in January 1922 joined it to the National Confederation of Syndicalist Corporations.

The loss of Rossoni's followers cut the UIL membership to about seventy thousand in 1922. Throughout the year it continued to lose members at an alarming rate, particularly after the collapse of the Alliance of Labor in August. Out of desperation, the UIL attempted to form an alliance with the CGL (Confederazione Generale del Lavoro) (q.v.) in 1923. It was, however, too weak to maintain a separate existence and it was forced to merge with the CGL in March 1924. But by then it was too late to prevent the Fascist destruction of the trade union movement.

For further information see: Ferdinando Cordova, *Le origini dei sindacati fascisti, 1918-1926* (Bari: Laterza, 1974); Alfredo Gradilone, *Storia del sindacalismo* 3, *Italia*, 2 vols. (Milan: Giuffrè, 1959); Daniel Horowitz, *The Italian Labor Movement* (Cambridge, Mass.: Harvard University Press, 1963.

CLB

UNIVERSAL FASCISM. From its earliest days much of the rhetoric of Italian Fascism had been centered on the cult and ideals of youth. Many Fascists, including Mussolini, proclaimed that the movement would bring about a revolution of the young against the old, decadent bourgeois order. But by the late 1920s many Fascist intellectuals (especially those raised under Fascism) had begun to question the apparent shortcomings of the regime and its failure to reform Italian society. These alienated young people were the main force behind the development of the idea of "Universal Fascism." They called for a reinvigoration of European society. Their criticism was aimed not only at reforming Fascist institutions in Italy, but they also wanted to extend Fascist ideas on a worldwide plane.

Among the leading internal critics of Fascism who argued for the cause of youth were Giuseppe Bottai (q.v.), whose review *Critica Fascista* was one of the most important journals in the regime; Gastone S. Spinetti, founder in 1932 of *La Sapienza*; Berto Ricci, editor of *L'Universale* (established in 1931); and Asvero Gravelli, director of *Antieuropa* (1928) and *Ottobre* (1932). Gravelli was by far the leading exponent of creating an international Fascist movement. Numerous Fascist international organizations began to appear in Europe by the late 1920s, and in 1933 Mussolini brought the rapidly expanding movement under his control: he established the Comitati d'Azione per l'Universalità di Roma (CAUR), under the direction of Eugenio Coselschi (q.v.). CAUR argued that although Fascism was unique, a common denominator existed among fascisms in all countries that allowed for the setting up of a "Fascist International." Coselschi maintained that such a movement, of course, would naturally receive its leadership from Rome. CAUR sponsored a series of international meetings to develop these ideas, the first of which was held in Montreux, Switzerland, in December 1934, but it rapidly became clear that there were deeply rooted doctrinal differences between Italian Fascism and other similar movements, particularly German Nazism, that would hamper the formation of a "Fascist International." (At the 1932 Volta Congress in Rome, these doctrinal differences, especially racism, had already emerged.) Ultimately, these problems combined with Mussolini's foreign policy shift toward Nazi Germany to bring about the end of attempts to create an international. Instead, the Rome-Berlin Axis (*see* AXIS, ROME-BERLIN) replaced these efforts.

For further information see: Michael A. Ledeen, *Universal Fascism: The Theory and Practice of the Fascist International* (New York: Fertig, 1972).

PVC

UNIVERSITY OATH. Loyalty oaths were frequently used in the Fascist regime in order to rid the administration of undesirables and to secure the adhesion of public figures to the government. In 1925 all state bureaucrats who could not be proven compatible with the political policies of Fascism were subject to dismissal. In 1927 a decree forced all state employees to swear an oath of allegiance to the king, to the constitution, and to the laws of the state.

Unlike public administrators, university professors were exempt from these earlier oaths, but in 1931 Giovanni Gentile (q.v.) proposed—and Mussolini approved—a decree coercing professors to pledge their faith in Fascism and to Fascisticize their students. The decree went into effect on November 1, 1931, and although there was widespread anti-Fascist sentiment among academics, most of them took the oath. The specific number of professors who refused to swear their allegiance to Fascism is not known, but about eleven or twelve out of one thousand two hundred did so (the difficulty of ascertaining the exact number is explained by the fact that a number of professors either resigned or were dismissed at the same time for varying reasons). Some or all of the following were included in the group who refused to take the oath: Ernesto Buonaiuti, Mario Carrara, Gaetano De Sanctis (q.v.), Antonio De Viti de Marco, F. Atzeri-Vacca, F. Luzzatto, A. Rossi, G. Vicentini, P. Sraffa, Giorgio Errera, Giorgio Levi della Vida, Piero Martinetti, Bortolo Negrisoli, Francesco Ruffini (q.v.), Edoardo Ruffini-Avondo, Lionello Venturi (q.v.), Vito Volterra, Giuseppe Antonio Borgese (q.v.), and Vittorio E. Orlando (q.v.).

For further information see: EAR (2); Renzo De Felice, *Mussolini il duce* (Turin: Einaudi, 1974); Charles F. Delzell, *Mussolini's Enemies* (Princeton: Princeton University Press, 1961).

MSF

VALLE, GIUSEPPE (b. Sassari, December 17, 1886). In effect successor to Italo Balbo (q.v.) as head of the Air Force, General Valle became deputy chief of the air staff in August 1929, chief of staff in February 1930, and undersecretary (under Mussolini) in November 1933. Valle continued, although with less emphasis, Balbo's tendency to prize propaganda flights and "firsts" over training and individual exploits (such as Valle's own bombardment of the defenseless city of Barcelona on New Year's Eve, 1937) over organized efficacy. Valle enthusiastically supported the Ethiopian War (q.v.) and proposed an apocalyptic Douhet-style (*see* DOUHET, GIULIO) offensive to raze the enemy's cities and burn off the Somali bush. The absurdity of this strategy and the requirements of the Army eventually compelled him to commit the Air Force to ground support (above all the spraying of mustard gas). When the war threatened to escalate into an Anglo-Italian duel, Valle proposed desperate measures: improvised "sacrifice squadrons" would crash obsolete aircraft packed with explosives into the British battleships (the aircraft in question lacked the speed or range necessary to do the job effectively). The Spanish war (*see* SPANISH CIVIL WAR), which Valle also enthusiastically supported, did not bear out his claims that air power alone would bring victory by smashing the Republic's cities. In 1939, Valle's equivocations about the Air Force's readiness (the service possessed roughly a third of the two thousand three hundred combat-effective aircraft he claimed) led to his dismissal along with Alberto Pariani (q.v.) in the October 31, 1939, "change of the guard." Mussolini refused to honor Valle's subsequent self-justificatory pleas for new employment.

For further information see: Giuseppe Valle, *Uomini nei Cieli* (Rome: C.E.N., 1958).

MK

VATICAN. See **AZIONE CATTOLICA ITALIANA; CHRISTIAN DEMOCRACY; PIUS XI, POPE; PIUS XII, POPE; LATERAN PACTS; PARTITO POPOLARE ITALIANO**

VENTURI, LIONELLO (b. Modena, April 25, 1885; d. Rome, August 14, 1961). Lionello Venturi was an eminent art historian and outspoken anti-Fascist. Son of renowned art historian Adolfo Venturi, he graduated from the University of Rome in literature. From 1909 to 1915 he served as a director of state galleries, including the Academy of Art in Venice, the Borghese Gallery in Rome, and the Gallery of Urbino. A volunteer in World War I, he was wounded and decorated. From 1915 to 1932 he occupied the chair of art history at the University of Turin, where he also contributed to a number of art journals.

In 1931 Venturi was one of the professors who refused to subscribe to the Fascist university oath (q.v.) of loyalty to the king and to Fascism. For this act of defiance he was dismissed from his teaching position. In 1932 he escaped a police dragnet with his son Franco and Mario Andreis. Father and son joined Carlo Rosselli (q.v.) in Paris until 1939.

Venturi joined the *fuorusciti* (q.v.) in New York in 1939, remaining in the United States until 1944. He assisted other Italian exiles as president of the Italian Emergency Rescue Committee. He taught at several universities, including Johns Hopkins. Active in anti-Fascist politics, he participated in the founding of the Mazzini Society (q.v.) in 1939 and was named to the executive board in June 1942. In 1943 he joined prominent American liberals in their campaign to influence American policy on the "Italian question." But he soon became disillusioned at the direction taken by the U.S. Department of State and the British Foreign Office. Along with Gaetano Salvemini (q.v.) he criticized the Roosevelt administration for soliciting the participation of "pre-Pearl Harbor Fascists" in the wartime and postwar planning apparatus.

After the liberation of Italy he returned to take a position as professor of art history at the University of Rome.

For further information see: DSPI; Aldo Garosci, *Vita di Carlo Rosselli* (Florence: Vallecchi, 1973); Frances Keene, *Neither Liberty Nor Bread* (New York and London: Harper & Brothers, 1940).

CLK

VERONA TRIALS. Following the creation of the Italian Social Republic (q.v.), Fascist militants and fanatics demanded punishment for the "traitors" responsible for the July 1943 coup and the fall of the regime. At the first meeting of the Council of Ministers (October 13), the new government declared its intention to punish "crimes against the state" under the military penal codes, as the former regime had done with the Special Tribunal for the Defense of the State (q.v.) in the 1920s. In November the Republican Fascist party congress met in Verona, and the manifesto issued by party secretary Alessandro Pavolini (q.v.) called for the creation of a special tribunal, which the Council of Ministers officially authorized on November 24.

The major targets of the cries for vengeance were those members of the Fascist Grand Council (q.v.) who had voted against Mussolini during the July 25, 1943 session, of whom only six had been taken into custody by the Fascists: Galeazzo Ciano (q.v.), Emilio De Bono (q.v.), Giovanni Marinelli (q.v.), Luciano Gottardi, Carlo Pareschi, and Tullio Cianetti (q.v.). The focus, however, was clearly on Ciano, Mussolini's son-in-law, who was held in the Scalzi prison with the others under close German surveillance. Despite the profound human drama that unfolded over the months preceding the trials between Mussolini and his daughter Edda (Ciano's wife), Mussolini made it clear that he had "disinterested himself" in

Ciano's fate, for the credibility of his leadership and of the new regime was at stake.

The trial opened on January 8, 1944, in the great hall of Castelvecchio, under the presidency of Aldo Vecchini and with Vincenzo Cersosimo as examining magistrate (there were nine members of the tribunal in all, two of whom were later shot by partisans). The prisoners each gave explanations of their actions and motivations, and the prosecution presented witnesses and dubious evidence of the complicity of the men in the conspiracy against Mussolini. On January 1, speeches were made on behalf of the defense, and the next day verdicts of guilty and the death penalty were announced against all but Cianetti, who was sentenced to thirty years in prison. The executions were carried out by a firing squad on January 11.

For further information see: Giorgio Bocca, *La repubblica di Mussolini* (Rome-Bari: Laterza, 1977); Vincenzo Cersosimo, *Dalla istruttoria alla fucilazione* (Milan: Garzanti, 1961); Frederick W. Deakin, *The Brutal Friendship* (New York: Harper & Row, 1962); Renzo Montagna, *Mussolini e il processo di Verona* (Rome: Omnia, 1949).

PVC

VICTOR EMMANUEL III (b. Naples, November 11, 1869; d. Alexandria, Egypt, December 28, 1947). King of Italy from July 29, 1900, until his abdication on May 9, 1946, Victor Emmanuel III was the only son of Umberto I and Margherita di Savoia and held the title of Prince of Naples from birth. In addition to studying history, politics, and law, he received military training and was entrusted with a number of commands after 1887. In October 1896 he married Elena, daughter of Prince Nicholas of Montenegro. She bore him five children: Jolanda, Mafalda, Umberto, Giovanna, and Maria.

He ascended the throne after the assassination of his father. Victor Emmanuel III helped bring to an end the reactionary period that had characterized the preceding four years. For the next two decades he followed the constitutional custom of choosing the premiers in accordance with the parliamentary majority. Though he felt no affection for Giovanni Giolitti (q.v.), prime minister most of the time between 1900 and 1914, the king gave his support to the economic development and social reforms that took place in those years.

In foreign policy Victor Emmanuel kept Italy in the Triple Alliance with Germany and Austria-Hungary but also promoted a rapprochement with the Triple Entente (France, Britain, and Russia) in such a way as to secure the Entente's consent to Italian occupation of Libya as a result of the war against Turkey (1911-12). In the interventionist crisis (q.v.) of May 1915, the king lent his support to the conservative government of Antonio Salandra (q.v.), which favored intervention in the Great War on the side of the Entente. The king departed for the front immediately after the start of hostilities (May 24, 1915). He remained there throughout the war, designating Tommaso, duke of Genoa, to serve as his lieutenant general in Rome. The king displayed strong leadership at the time of the

Caporetto (*see* CAPORETTO, BATTLE OF) disaster, when he appointed General Armando Diaz (q.v.) to replace Luigi Cadorna (q.v.) and convinced the Allies (at Peschiera on November 8, 1917) that Italy could successfully defend the Piave River line against Austria. Two days later he issued a firm proclamation to this effect.

During the postwar political strife, however, Victor Emmanuel did not behave so worthily. When the Fascists threatened to march on Rome in October 1922, the king refused to sign Premier Luigi Facta's (q.v.) proclamation of martial law. Instead, he listened to pro-Fascists in the Court and entrusted the premiership to Mussolini. Although not personally enthusiastic about Mussolini, he felt no confidence at all in Giolitti and other Liberal politicians. Thus, he made it clear that he was ready to sacrifice liberalism to the authoritarianism that Mussolini promised to give Italy. Two years later the king refused to dismiss the compromised Fascist premier when Giacomo Matteotti (*see* MATTEOTTI CRISIS), leader of the right-wing Socialists, was assassinated by Fascists. Victor Emmanuel acquiesced in Mussolini's establishment of the Fascist dictatorship after January 3, 1925.

Although he occasionally complained in private about certain actions by Mussolini that infringed on his sovereign prerogatives, the taciturn monarch gave his support to the 1935-36 war in Ethiopia (*see* ETHIOPIAN WAR) (which brought to him the title of "Emperor of Ethiopia"), to the 1936 intervention in Spain in favor of General Franco (*see* SPANISH CIVIL WAR), and to the 1939 invasion of Albania (*see* ALBANIA, INVASION OF) (which brought him the title of "King of Italy and of Albania"). He also approved the Pact of Steel (q.v.) (May 1939) between Fascist Italy and Nazi Germany, and he did not oppose the anti-Semitic measures that Mussolini introduced in the late 1930s. At the outbreak of World War II, when the only sensible political course was neutrality, Victor Emmanuel signed Italy's declaration of war against the Allies on June 10, 1940.

But when the war brought a series of Italian defeats, the king feared the loss of his throne. Confiding in no one except Duke Pietro d'Acquarone (q.v.), his minister of the royal household, he timidly began to consider ways of removing Mussolini. These maneuvers came to a head in the wake of the Allies' invasion of Sicily and heavy aerial bombardment of Rome in July 1943. As soon as the Fascist Grand Council (q.v.) voted against Mussolini, the king arranged for his arrest at the royal villa on July 25. Thereafter he appointed Marshal Pietro Badoglio (q.v.) to head a royal dictatorship composed only of technocrats. The king would have nothing to do with bona fide anti-Fascist politicians; his own preference was "a Fascism without Mussolini."

On September 8 the royal government announced the armistice with the Allies. Fearing a German seizure of the capital, the royal family and Badoglio fled that night from Rome to take refuge with the Allies in Brindisi (and after February 1944 in Ravello). Their flight from the undefended capital aroused intense criticism. On October 13, 1943, the king was compelled by the Allies and Badoglio to declare war on Nazi Germany. (His daughter Mafalda was to die in a German concentration camp in 1944.) Henceforth Victor Emmanuel's continuation on the throne depended chiefly on the Allies. While Churchill supported him strongly in order to ensure continuity of the government that had signed the armistice, Roosevelt was much less inclined to keep the aged monarch on the throne. When Soviet Russia seemed ready to collaborate with Victor Emmanuel for opportunistic reasons in April 1944, however, the Anglo-Americans decided to push him aside and make Crown Prince Umberto lieutenant general of the realm. The king persuaded the Allies to delay implementation of this decision until Rome was liberated (June 4), but they would not let him return to that city. He retired to Naples, withdrawing from political life.

Finally, on May 9, 1946, he reluctantly abdicated in favor of Umberto II (q.v.). Promonarchists hoped that this action would enable the House of Savoy to survive the forthcoming referendum on the monarchy (*see* REFERENDUM OF 1946). Victor Emmanuel III went into exile in Alexandria, Egypt, where he died the following year and was buried in the Cathedral of St. Catherine. When Italy voted for the republic on June 2, 1946, Umberto II also went into exile (Oporto, Portugal).

For further information see: Silvio Bertoldi, *Vittorio Emanuele III* (Turin: UTFT, 1971); Paolo Puntoni, *Parla Vittorio Emanuele III* (Milan: Aldo Palazzi, 1958).

CFD

VIDUSSONI, ALDO (b. Trieste, January 21, 1914). A living symbol of the inability of the regime's elite to renew itself, Vidussoni served as secretary of the PNF (Partito Nazionale Fascista) (q.v.) from December 26, 1941, to April 19, 1943. His only qualifications were his youth, a gold medal for valor, and a hand and eye lost in Spain. His elevation from chief of the GUF (Gruppi Universitari Fascisti) youth organization to party secretary met with universal disbelief and scorn. Anonymous letters described him as the perfect specimen of Fascist youth: "wounded, ignorant, and half-witted." Vidussoni survived because he shared Mussolini's hatreds: of the Slavs, incorporated in 1941; of the Church; and of the untrustworthy and effete bourgeoisie. Vidussoni tried to close down exclusive haunts of Roman high society such as the Golf Club ("Golf is the sport of the *signori*") but met G. Ciano's (q.v.) outraged opposition. He also attempted to rejuvenate the PNF, but pressure from his entourage reversed that policy in December 1942 with the reappointment to leadership positions of a number of old-guard Fascists, including Vidussoni's successor Carlo Scorza (q.v.). The great Turin and Milan strikes of March 1943 (*see* MARCH 1943 STRIKES) fully revealed Vidussoni's failure to dominate the party and the home front and led to his dismissal. He subsequently rallied to the Salò Republic (*see* ITALIAN SOCIAL REPUBLIC) and became a member of the directory of the Fascist Republican party.

For further information see: Giordano B. Guerri, *Rapporto al Duce* (Milan: Bompiani, 1978).

MK

VISCONTI PRASCA, SEBASTIANO (b. February 27, 1883). Probably the most incompetent of the regime's generals, Visconti Prasca served in World War I, attended the War College, and then was attaché in Belgrade from late 1924 until 1930, when repeated Yugoslav complaints of espionage led to his recall. In 1933 he became chief of Pietro Badoglio's (q.v.) Secretariat and in 1934-35 inspected the East African war preparations as Badoglio's agent in the struggle to discredit Emilio De Bono (q.v.). However, in the summer of 1935 Badoglio dismissed Visconti Prasca allegedly because the general's office had failed to keep secret the text of the Badoglio-Gamelin military agreements that provided for Italo-French support in case of German aggression (Visconti Prasca claimed that his rival Mario Roatta [q.v.] had framed him). By 1938 Visconti Prasca was back in favor as attaché in Paris and encouraged Mussolini to seek a compromise solution in the Czech crisis. In May 1940 Mussolini and G. Ciano (q.v.) sent him to Albania to replace Carlo Geloso (q.v.). Summoned to a council of war in Rome in mid-August, the general undertook to prepare a coup de main to seize Epirus. But the Germans objected, and Badoglio and Roatta reprimanded Visconti Prasca for jumping channels. He continued his preparations, but not until mid-October did Mussolini's definitive decision to attack Greece (*see* GREECE, INVASION OF) give him free rein; with megalomaniacal self-assurance the general promised a "shattering success." The plan that Visconti Prasca had prepared to implement the Army staff's "Contingency 'G'" directive deployed four exiguous attacking divisions on a frontage of over 100 kilometers and ignored the better weapons, better training, and (after mobilization) numerical superiority of the Greeks. The offensive, launched at Mussolini's insistence in a torrential downpour on October 28, collapsed by November 8; Mussolini replaced Visconti Prasca with Ubaldo Soddu (q.v.) and ignominiously retired Visconti.

For further information see: Visconti Prasca's unreliable *Io ho aggredito la Grecia* (Milan: Rizzoli, 1946).

MK

VITTORINI, ELIO (b. Syracuse, July 27, 1908; d. Milan, February 12, 1966). A major Italian literary figure and anti-Fascist, Vittorini came from a working-class Sicilian background. He left his native Sicily in 1927 and moved to Venezia Giulia, where he earned a living as a laborer. In 1930 he settled in Florence and did proofing for *La Nazione*. It was here that he encountered many of the modern literary movements and their leaders, who were beginning to move away from Fascism and eventually toward a more committed literature. He collaborated with the young writers of *Solaria* and *Il Bargello*, especially with Vasco Pratolini (q.v.). In 1933 he published his first major work, *Il Garofano Rosso*.

The turning point for Vittorini seems to have been the Spanish Civil War (q.v.), which convinced him of the evils of Fascism. In 1938 he began publishing segments of his major work, *Conversazione in Sicilia*, issued in complete form in 1941. More than any other literary work of the period, *Conversazione* made the break away from the abstract, hermetic literature of the 1920s and 1930s and toward realism.

In 1941 Vittorini joined the Communist underground in Milan, working on clandestine editions of *Unità*. He was arrested in 1943 and during the German occupation fought in the Resistance. In September 1945, following the liberation, he published the first issue of *Il Politecnico*, a cultural journal that posited a new relationship between politics and culture and that eventually prompted a polemic between its editor and Communist leader Palmiro Togliatti (q.v.). As a result, in 1947 Vittorini broke with the party.

For further information see: Edward R. Tannenbaum, *The Fascist Experience* (New York: Basic Books, 1972); Elio Vittorini, *Conversazione in Sicilia*, ed. E. Sanguinetti (Turin: Einaudi, 1970); Elio Vittorini, *Diario in pubblico* (Milan: Bompiani, 1957).

PVC

VOLPE, GIOACCHINO (b. Paganica, Aquila, February 16, 1876; d. Sant'Arcangelo, Forlì, October 1, 1971). Gioacchino Volpe, foremost Italian historian to embrace Fascism, studied at Pisa, Florence, and Berlin. He occupied several teaching posts, including professor of modern history at the Universities of Milan (1905-24) and at Rome (1924-40), where he also served as director of the Institute of Modern and Contemporary History and filled the chair in medieval history (1940-46).

Volpe began as a medievalist, writing on Italian communes and heresies. His innovative economic-juridical approach dominated Italian medieval historiography for several decades. Volpe ascribed institutional changes to the interactions between economic conditions and class relationships. Religious ferment was conceived as an expression of social unrest and economic distress. This framework was enlarged with his work entitled *Il Medioevo* (1927). Undertaken against the background of World War I and Fascism, it indicated Volpe's appreciation of the roles of personalities and politics in history.

Volpe was an ardent interventionist who participated in the war as an infantry officer. He was an early adherent to Fascism, believing the youthful enterprise had the vision and dynamism to realize Italy's aspirations. Between 1924 and 1929 Volpe sat in Parliament as a Fascist deputy. His *Storia del Movimento fascista* (1939) marked him as the official historian of the regime. It was the historian's companion piece to Mussolini's, the practitioner's, and Giovanni Gentile's (q.v.), the philosopher's, *Doctrine of Fascism* (1932).

Volpe's *L'Italia in Cammino* was the antithesis of Benedetto Croce's (q.v.) liberal and elitist *Storia d'Italia*, published in the autumn of 1927, six months after

Volpe's work. His major scholarly effort was *L'Italia Moderna* (2 vols., 1943-52). Disillusionment with World War II offered a clearer perspective. Risorgimento and post-Risorgimento statesmen, the Savoyard dynasty, and the parliamentary regime were endowed with genuine creativity in spite of fundamental deficiencies.

Volpe refused to support the Italian Social Republic (q.v.) or the Resistance (*see* RESISTANCE, ARMED), preferring the monarchy of Victor Emmanuel III (q.v.) and the Pietro Badoglio (q.v.) interim government. His library was burned, and he was deprived of his chair and pension. The changing political-ideological climate of the fifties and Volpe's acknowledged worth as an historian influenced his former colleagues and students to forgive his Fascist past.

For further information see: Innocenzo Cervelli, *Gioacchino Volpe* (Naples: Guida, 1977); Benedetto Croce, *Storia della storiografia italiana* (Bari: Laterza, 1921); Giorgio Di Giovanni, *Il realismo storico di Gioacchino Volpe* (Rome: Giovanni Volpe, 1977); Edward R. Tannenbaum, "Giacchino Volpe," *Historians of Modern Europe*, ed. Hans A. Schmitt (Baton Rouge, Louisiana: Louisiana State University Press, 1971).

RSC

VOLPI DI MISURATA, COUNT GIUSEPPE (b. Venice, November 19, 1877; d. Rome, November 16, 1947). An Italian industrial-financial entrepreneur and Fascist minister, Volpi came from a lower-middle-class family and abandoned legal studies at Padua for private business. He began his career by establishing an agricultural export concern in the Balkans. In 1905 he started the famous Società Adriatica di Elettricità (SADE) that eventually controlled the electrical industry in Venice, Emilia, and the Romagna, and later also the mechanical, iron, and navigation industries of Venice. Ultimately Volpi came to hold positions in more than forty companies. In 1906 he began Italian economic penetration into Montenegro.

His business ventures in the Balkans brought him to the attention of Premier Giovanni Giolitti (q.v.), and in 1912 he helped to negotiate the Peace of Ouchy with Turkey. During World War I he was president of the Committee for Industrial Mobilization and served as a delegate to the Paris Peace Conference. In July 1921 Volpi was appointed governor of Tripolitania (*see* LIBYA [TRIPOLITANIA AND CYRENAICA]) and while in that post did much to modernize the territory and increase Italy's hold over the region, all of which he accomplished with often excessively harsh methods. On October 16, 1922, he was made a senator.

When Mussolini came to power, Volpi immediately arranged a private meeting with him (it is possible that he had joined the PNF [Partito Nazionale Fascista] [q.v.] as early as January 1922). In July 1925 Mussolini made him minister of finance in place of the more conventional Alberto De Stefani (q.v.) and also secured for him the title of Count di Misurata. As minister Volpi was instrumental in settling Italy's war debts with the United States and England, and he negotiated a $100 million loan from the Morgan Bank. In accord with Italy's major industrial leaders, Volpi was intent on imposing a deflationary monetary policy but objected to Mussolini's stabilization of the lira at the artificially high rate of ninety to the British pound (*see* QUOTA NOVANTA). In July 1928, after Mussolini no longer felt a need for his services, Volpi resigned as minister. He returned to private business, was appointed head of the Venice Biennale, and in 1934 became president of the Confindustria (*see* INDUSTRY) on the suggestion of Alberto Pirelli (q.v.).

Volpi's closest associates in the regime had been moderate Fascists like Giuseppe Bottai (q.v.), Luigi Federzoni (q.v.), and Dino Grandi (q.v.), and his loyalty to the regime had been without suspicion until late 1942. At that point he began to realize that World War II was turning against the Axis (*see* AXIS, ROME-BERLIN). By the spring of 1943 there was widespread speculation that his support for Fascism was wavering, and in April he resigned as head of the Confindustria on the demand of minister of corporations Tullio Cianetti (q.v.). In September he was arrested by the Germans but managed to escape to Switzerland in July of the following year.

For further information see: *Chi è?* (1936); DSPI; NO (1928; 1937); Salvatore Romano, *Giuseppe Volpi* (Milan: Bompiani, 1979); Roland Sarti, "Giuseppe Volpi," in *Uomini e volti del fascismo*, ed. F. Cordova (Rome: Bulzoni, 1980).

MSF/PVC

WILDT, ADOLFO (b. Milan, March 1, 1868; d. Milan, March 11, 1931). A sculptor, draftsman, and printer who flourished under the Fascist regime, Wildt's mature style was a highly original form of naturalistic expressionism, which was both romantic and idealized.

His many works in marble are characterized by an exquisite carving technique, the theories of which were published in a small monograph. Wildt advocated direct carving in marble to ensure that the subtleties of form, undercutting, light, and shadow would be controlled by the artist. He opposed the then fashionable practice of making models in clay or plasticine from which the final sculpture was reproduced by mechanical methods in pointing workshops.

Wildt was widely shown and patronized during the Fascist regime. He was a major exhibitor at the Venice International Exhibition (1922), the second Novecento Exhibit (Milan, 1929), and the Prima Quadriennale of National Art (Rome, 1931). His marble portrait bust of Margherita Sarfatti (q.v.), patroness of the arts and mistress of Benito Mussolini, portrays her with a "modern" hair style, a noble, tender expression, delicate features, and a face of angelic purity.

Mussolini commissioned portraits of himself from many artists, including Adolfo Wildt. Wildt's bust of the Duce is a tour de force of creative marble carving. It shows Mussolini as handsome, virile, strong, stern, wise, compassionate, and invincible. A simple neoclassic band, alluding to imperial revival, encircles the noble brow. The smooth, ageless features and deep, hollow eyes create an aura of immortality. In his sculpture of Mussolini, Wildt skillfully summarizes the image of the flawless leader, the image projected in Fascist propaganda.

For further information see: Giorgio Nicodemi, *Adolfo Wildt* (Milan: Ulrico Hoepli, 1929); Kineton Parkes, "Adolfo Wildt and the Art of Marble," *Apollo* 2 (April 1930); Francesco Sapori, "Nel Primo decennale dell'era fascista: ritratti del Duce," *Emporium* 76 (November 1932); Adolfo Wildt, *L'arte del marmo* (Milan: Hoepli, 1922).

MCG

WOLFF, KARL (b. Darmstadt, May 13, 1900). Wolff was the German Waffen SS general who was primarily responsible for the surrender of German troops in northern Italy on May 2, 1945.

Wolff had been one of the closest associates of Heinrich Himmler, the chief of the SS, serving as his senior aide and then as head of his personal staff. He was aware of Himmler's abortive contacts with members of the German resistance movement during August 1943. Himmler reverted, however, to a pose of loyalty to Hitler and directed the arrest and punishment of those involved in the 1944 assassination plot. But with the approach of military defeat, Himmler again entertained contacts with resisters. He vacillated between loyalty to Hitler and inclinations to take over the leadership of the state and secure an armistice.

Wolff had become commander of SS troops in Italy, responsible for the security of areas behind the line of military operations. As the military situation deteriorated in northern Italy, Wolff engaged in secret negotiations with representatives of the American Office of Strategic Services. These began in March 1945, but the decisive time period ran from April 14 to May 2. By April 14 the German Armies faced ultimate catastrophe in the battles on the Po River. Wolff began to approach other army commanders in respect to surrender. At this point he was recalled to Berlin by Himmler, who had heard of Wolff's negotiations and opposed them, although he was himself in touch with the Allies. Wolff was able to convince Himmler and later Hitler that he was simply trying to arouse antagonism between the opposing Allies. But on his return to Italy he found the situation more desperate than ever. A plea for help in surrendering Italian forces was made by Marshal Rodolfo Graziani (q.v.). After the capture and execution of Mussolini and his mistress, Clara Petacci (q.v.), on April 28, Albert Kesselring's (q.v.) successor on the Italian front, General Heinrich von Vietinghoff-Scheel, gave his approval to Wolff's negotiations, and a surrender instrument was signed the following day. But Kesselring, now overall commander in the West, delayed his approval until after the death of Hitler. Fighting finally ceased on the afternoon of May 2, 1945.

An unpleasant aftermath of these negotiations was a controversy between Stalin on one side and Roosevelt and Churchill on the other. Stalin accused his Allies of attempting to negotiate a separate peace with the Germans. Wolff's close association with Himmler and Himmler's own approaches to the Western Allies seemed to support the accusation. Both Churchill and Roosevelt vehemently denied the justice of Stalin's suspicions, and bad feelings were healed before the death of Roosevelt on April 12, 1945. However, the incident is often regarded as the beginning of the postwar cold war.

Wolff was arrested after the war and tried for war crimes but released in August 1949. After a second arrest in July 1964 he received a sentence of ten years imprisonment.

For further information see: F. W. Deakin, *The Brutal Friendship. Mussolini, Hitler, and the Fall of Italian Fascism* (New York: Harper & Row, 1962); Heinz Hohne, *The Order of the Death's Head. The Story of Hitler's S.S.* (New York: Ballantine Books, 1971); Andrew Mollo, *A Pictorial History of the S.S.* (New York: Stein and Day, 1977); G. A. Sheppard, *The Italian Campaign, 1943-45. A Political and Military Re-assessment* (New York: Praeger, 1968).

ERB

WOMEN. See **FASCI FEMMINILI**.

YOUTH ORGANIZATIONS. The Fascist youth organizations were perhaps the single most powerful instrument of political persuasion available to Mussolini's dictatorship. Established by the regime to mobilize the support of young people of all ages and classes, they grew to embrace over five million children, adolescents, and young adults by 1940. The organization as a whole developed haphazardly under party auspices, at least until 1926, when the regime, true to its slogan "make way for youth," began a systematic attempt to reform Italian youth according to Fascist ideals, using both its party auxiliaries and the state school system. The earliest groups, growing up along side of the Fasci di Combattimento (q.v.) in 1920, were the Fascist University Groups (Gruppi Universitari Fascisti), more familiarly known as GUF; these included men and women students ages eighteen to twenty-eight. The most renowned formations were the Balilla for boys ages eight to fourteen, named after the legendary Genoese streetboy whose rock-throwing exploits against the city's Austrian occupiers in 1746 were cited as an exemplary display of heroic protonationalism. Other groups founded in the mid-1920s included the Avanguardisti for adolescent boys and two cohorts "to train the future mothers of new fascist generations": the Piccole Italiane (ages nine to fourteen) and the Giovani Italiane (ages fifteen to seventeen). The remaining gaps were filled in October 1930 with the institution of the Fasci Giovanili di Combattimento as a party recruiting ground for young men from eighteen to twenty-one who were no longer in school; and in November 1934, with the establishment of the wolf-cub groups or Figli della Lupa for children ages six to eight, the activities of which were to be "consonant with the very tender age of these new recruits to Fascism." In October 1937, with the foundation of the Gioventù Italiana del Littorio (GIL), all of these groups were finally unified under the jurisdiction of the PNF (Partito Nazionale Fascista) (q.v.).

Before 1937 the Opera Nazionale Balilla (ONB) had been mainly responsible for all of the children and adolescent groups, the sole exception being the girls' groups, which had been entrusted to the women's *fasci* at the end of 1929. When the ONB was first established on April 3, 1926, it took the already existing youth groups out of the hands of the PNF, whose still chaotic administrative structure and high degree of politicization hardly seemed appropriate for a social-educational institution that was to dominate the political instruction and physical education of Italian youth. For its entire first decade it was headed by Renato Ricci (q.v.), a Fascist die-hard from Carrara province, whose personal loyalty to Mussolini, as much as his pioneering work in the field of youth organizing, accounted for his remarkably long tenure in this powerful and much disputed position. During 1927-28, the ONB's monopoly over youth organization was sanctioned by law in spite of strong resistance from the Vatican; the "additional" clauses to the founding statutes, published on January 12, 1928, explicitly prohibited the creation of any new youth groups and dissolved all branches of the Catholic Boy Scouts except those in towns of more than twenty thousand inhabitants. Although enrollment was not made compulsory until 1937, already in December 1927 Minister of Education Pietro Fedele (q.v.) had strongly recommended that all children join; they were deprived of any alternative in April of the following year, when all potential competitors were suppressed with the sole exception of the youth circles of the Catholic Action (see AZIONE CATTOLICA ITALIANA) movement. This exemption was justified by the "prevalently religious ends" of these groups and was in fact forced on the regime to enable it to resume negotiations for the Concordat (see LATERAN PACTS) with the Church; it did not extend to the Catholic Boy Scouts, however, which remained outlawed for the duration of the regime.

The very rapid growth of the ONB's operations after 1926 was closely bound up with the Fascistization of the Italian school system after the mid-1920s. From September 1929 on, when the Ministry of the Interior relinquished its supervision over the agency and it became a branch of the Ministry of National Education, the national offices occupied the same building on Viale Trastevere in Rome. The ONB continued to have a separate budget, and Ricci stayed on as its head in the post of undersecretary of state for physical and youth education. Beginning in February 1928 the ONB also established a two-year training course at the Fascist Academy of Physical Training at the Farnesina Palace in order to graduate its own instructors. Nevertheless, the agency always relied heavily for its local staffing on elementary schoolteachers, especially in small towns and villages, where employees of the public school system, who received points of merit toward promotion for their service, were almost invariably in charge of the youth groups. During the 1930s the youth organizations impinged increasingly on public-school life, often demoralizing the regular teaching staff and disrupting the school curriculum with their incessant demands on student attention and energies.

The ONB's main original charge was to provide a semimilitary physical fitness training based on drill, gymnastics, and sport, thereby remedying an obvious deficiency in the regular school curriculum. But Ricci had apparently grasped the signal importance of the public-school plant and personnel in a still underdeveloped society, and he always interpreted very broadly the notion of developing a new "Fascist pedagogy." Accordingly, he built the ONB into an empire, taking charge of the operations of the National Agency for Physical Education, the National Institute to Combat Illiteracy, the Association for the Mezzogiorno, as well as the management of all rural schools with twenty or fewer pupils. By invading the fields of competence of many other state as well as party agencies, the ONB inevitably clashed fiercely with the PNF itself. In 1931 Ricci took issue with Carlo Scorza (q.v.), the head of the GUF and the newly founded Fasci Giovanili, who was directly responsible to the party secretary. The agency clashed again with the PNF in 1935 when the minister of national education, C. M. De Vecchi (q.v.), sought control of the recently established national Littoriali cultural competitions and the PNF courses of political preparation. These jurisdictional disputes were stilled only in 1937 when the ONB was incorporated into the GIL and the whole organization placed under party supervision.

In addition to exercising exclusive control over physical training, the youth organizations carried out premilitary reviews, organized sports and recreational facilities, and provided various forms of assistance. The Case Balilla, constructed in hundreds of towns, were centers for a vast range of extracurricular activities, from radio listening and amateur theatrical performances to sewing courses and propaganda lectures. Obligatory rallies—the most memorable and often the most distasteful aspect of belonging to the Balilla—were held Saturday afternoons ("Sabato fascista") in the school year and consisted of roll calls, marching drills, and calisthenics. The committees of notables and public officials supervising local operations sponsored prizes for worthy students and supplied grants of food, clothing, and books for needy scholars. The ONB also ran a nation-wide system of seaside and mountain summer camps where hundreds of thousands of children spent from one week to three months annually. Fascist propaganda inevitably permeated all of these activities; overtly, as in the swearing of oaths of loyalty to the Duce, or more insidiously, by means of the militaristic routines of the vacation camps. Those Balilla boys and Avanguardisti who demonstrated special promise of becoming future cadres of the regime were elected to spend a week in the "Dux" camps near Rome or to represent their districts in special national competitions, the Ludi Juvenilis, held annually in mid-May in Rome.

The two young adult organizations were more immediately concerned with forming and replenishing a new Fascist elite. The Young Fascist, founded by order of the Fascist Grand Council (q.v.) on October 8, 1930, was established at a time of intense competition with the Church and was intended to build "an ample reservoir" of working-class youth to fill the lower ranks of the party and Militia (q.v.). Consequently, its fortnightly bulletin, *Gioventù Fascista*, was more militantly Fascist and its premilitary training more intense than that in any other part of the Fascist youth movement. In fact, membership fluctuated wildly so long as there were other avenues of access to the party. Not until the mid-1930s, by which time the party card had become necessary for many menial jobs, and advancement through the youth groups was primary means of gaining entry into the PNF, did membership rise substantially, to about 1,175,000 in 1939.

Although numerically the much smaller organization, with one hundred thousand members in 1939, the GUF was by far the more important in terms of replenishing the Fascist elite. Socially, it reflected exactly the overwhelmingly bourgeois composition of Italy's university-student population, a sizable minority of which participated actively in its mainly cultural activities. GUF members could avail themselves of a whole range of extracurricular activities designed to prepare them for social promotion in the Fascist state. In addition to subscribing to the official weekly, *Libro e Moschetto*, many sections published their own journals, and in the late 1930s some had even set up their own experimental film groups. GUF members could also attend courses and lectures at the Istituto Nazionale di Cultura Fascista (q.v.) and in Milan at a special Scuola di Mistica Fascista (*see* MISTICA FASCISTA); if they were interested in a career in the Fascist bureaucracy, they might also graduate from a two-year Centro Nazionale di Formazione Politica in Rome. The Littorial Games were by far the most important of all the Fascist initiatives to form a new national cultural elite. Held annually from 1934 to 1940 in key Italian cities, the games combined competitive examinations with a national student convention. The highly coveted title of "Lictor" was awarded on the basis of examinations by committees of experts in subjects as varied as Fascist doctrine, colonial and corporative studies, creative writing, musical composition, and poster design. Winners and runners-up included many who later distinguished themselves as cultural and political leaders in postwar Italy. The regime also added a competition for "Lictor of Labor" in the late 1930s to display its increasingly populist political rhetoric; but this title never achieved the prestige of the academic disciplines and fine arts.

In their effort to form a politically engaged younger generation, the dictatorship had to tolerate some degree of political activism among students, much more than it ever tolerated among workers and peasants. In the late 1930s this took the form of a short-lived campaign to "reach out to the people" in the factories and farms, and as many memoirs of the "Generation of the Littorials" testify, the GUF's cultural forums occasionally were used to criticize specific policies of the regime. However, the political activism of a privileged student population was more usually channeled into an exacerbated nationalism, into political demonstrations protesting ostensible foreign slights of Fascist Italy, and into rallies celebrating its imperialist victories, or into calls for a renewal of the Fascist revolution according to the ideas of the "first hour".

The Fascist youth organizations had a powerful impact on youth growing up under the regime, although membership itself was by no means universal. An estimated 30 to 40 percent of the population between ages eight and eighteen never joined at all, the vast majority of whom were probably working-class youth and young women, especially those who left school before age fourteen. However, even before enrollment was made compulsory, the overwhelming majority of middle-class children joined either out of conviction or because of the material advantages offered, or as a result of teacher pressure, parental fears, or a simple desire not to be excluded from such a highly visible form of sociability. The generation born after World War I in Italy thus experienced Fascist regimentation as something entirely routine. Having had little or no contact with alternative organizations or cultural models, it was inevitably susceptible to propaganda that identified everything pre- or anti-Fascist as decrepit or inept and the regime itself with dynamism and energy of youth.

For further information see: Gino Germani, "The Political Socialization of Youth in Fascist Regimes: Italy and Spain," in *Authoritarian Politics in Modern*

Society: The Dynamics of Established One-Party Systems, eds. S. P. Huntington and C. W. Moore (New York: Basic Books, 1970); Michael Ledeen, "Italian Fascism and Youth," *Journal of Contemporary History* 3 (1969); Ruggiero Zangrandi, *Il lungo viaggio attraverso il fascismo* (Milan: Feltrinelli, 1962).

VDG

ZANIBONI, TITO (b. Monzambano, Mantua, February 1, 1883; d. Rome, December 27, 1960). A Socialist deputy and would-be assassin of Mussolini, Zaniboni studied at the agricultural school in Brescia and spent two years, from 1906 to 1908, in the United States. Prior to the Italian entry into World War I, Zaniboni, who had become a Socialist supporter before the Libyan War, held various positions in the provincial government of Volta Mantua and published numerous articles against Italian intervention. In 1915 Zaniboni was drafted into the military and was wounded and decorated for his actions during the conflict.

Zaniboni was elected a parliamentary deputy from the Udine in November 1919 on the Italian Socialist party's (*see* PARTITO SOCIALISTA ITALIANO) list, and although he supported a pacification pact with the Fascists, Zaniboni soon established himself as a leading anti-Fascist. In October 1922 Zaniboni helped found the Partito Socialista Unitario and continued to speak of cooperation with the Fascists as a means to pacify the countryside and weaken the Communists.

In 1924 Zaniboni lost his seat in Parliament but played a leading role in trying to depose Mussolini during the Matteotti Crisis (q.v.). Throughout 1924 Zaniboni made contact with many anti-Fascists and dissident Fascists and in the summer began to think in terms of Mussolini's assassination. Zaniboni decided to kill the Duce on November 4, 1925, but thanks to an informer, the police knew of his plan and arrested him minutes before the attempt. Although Zaniboni was probably acting alone, the regime claimed that there had been a widespread conspiracy and used the incident as an excuse to dissolve Zaniboni's party, to close down the anti-Fascist press, and to pass the Exceptional Decrees (q.v.).

Along with a group of suspected conspirators, Zaniboni was tried before the Special Tribunal for the Defense of the State (q.v.) in April 1927 and sentenced to thirty years' imprisonment. In March 1942 he was sent to Ponza and was freed after the fall of Fascism. Zaniboni presided over the Bari Congress of anti-Fascist parties in January 1944 and a month later became high commissioner for expurgation in the second Pietro Badoglio (q.v.) government. In July 1945 he helped found the Unione Socialdemocratica Italiana but in later years became less involved in political affairs.

For further information see: *Chi è?* (1948); MOI (5); Tito Zaniboni, *Testamento spirituale* (Milan: Baldini and Castoldi, 1949).

MSF

ZIMOLO, MICHELANGELO (b. Vicenza, February 13, 1885). An early irredentist, Zimolo was active between 1902 and 1910 in anti-Austrian and anti-Socialist propaganda. He joined the Nationalists before World War I, was an interventionist, and fought in the war. In May 1919 he was among the founders of the *fascio* of Florence and then in 1921 was founder and secretary of the *fascio* of Dalmatia. Zimolo was a member of the party's central committee in 1921-22 under Michele Bianchi (q.v.) and in the *giunta esecutiva* of April 1923. A Fascist provincial "chieftain," he was of an intransigent disposition, and Mussolini made him *alto commissario* in 1923. He also took a leading role in the expulsion of the revisionist Massimo Rocca (q.v.) from the party in 1924.

Between 1923 and 1924 Zimolo served as secretary of the Fascist university groups, GUF (Gruppi Universitari Fascisti) (*see* YOUTH ORGANIZATIONS) and was a deputy from 1924 to 1929. He became Fascist secretary for Friuli in 1926, after which he moved into the diplomatic service as consul general in various overseas posts.

For further information see: NO (1928; 1937); *Annuario diplomatico del regno d'Italia* (Rome: Ministry of Foreign Affairs, 1937); Adrian Lyttelton, *The Seizure of Power* (London: Weidenfeld & Nicolson, 1973).

PVC

ZOPPI, OTTAVIO (b. Novara, January 16, 1870; d. Milan, 1962). A Fascist general, military author, and general of Arditi in Italy and Libya (1918-19), Zoppi championed mobile warfare. As inspector of Alpini (1926-30), commander of the Bologna Corps (1930-33), and inspector of infantry (1933-35), he joined F. S. Grazioli (q.v.) and Federico Baistrocchi (q.v.) in seeking a highly trained and mechanized Army. Fascist connections saved Zoppi from Pietro Badoglio's (q.v.) and Pietro Gazzera's (q.v.) wrath, and he retired in December 1935. Zoppi, a senator after 1929, devoted himself to writing and senate military affairs, denouncing Alberto Pariani's (q.v.) policies. In May 1940 Mussolini placed Zoppi on the PNF (Partito Nazionale Fascista) (q.v.) Directory.

For further information see: John Sweet, *Iron Arm: The Mechanization of Mussolini's Army, 1920-1940* (Westport, Conn.: Greenwood, 1980); Ottavio Zoppi, *Il Senato e l'Esercito nel ventennio* (Milan: Zucchi, 1948).

BRS

ZURLO, LEOPOLDO (b. Campobasso, December 3, 1875). In charge of theater censorship during the Fascist regime, Zurlo took a degree in law and in 1900 entered the civil service in the Ministry of Interior. He was made a vice prefect in 1920 and had been a member of the Commission for Motion Picture Censorship attached to the ministry. In 1928 he worked with Dino Alfieri (q.v.), head of the Ente Nazionale della Cooperazione, and was promoted to prefect in 1932.

In 1931 Mussolini transferred theater censorship from the prefects to the office of police chief Arturo Bocchini (q.v.), and Zurlo was placed in charge of the operation. In 1935 the office was moved to the newly created Ministry for Press and Propaganda, and Zurlo continued his functions under the direction of Nicola De Pirro (q.v.).

Theater censorship was viewed mainly as a function of politics rather than culture. Plays were rejected largely because they contained overt anti-Fascist themes, although sometimes the regime's broader cultural policies were also monitored by Zurlo's office. Between 1931 and 1943 about 15,650 plays were reviewed but only 1,000 were actually prohibited.

For further information see: *Chi è?* (1936); Philip V. Cannistraro, *La fabbrica del consenso* (Rome-Bari: Laterza, 1975); L. Zurlo, *Memorie inutili* (Rome: Ateneo, 1952).

                                                                          PVC

APPENDICES* ───────────────

* Appendices A, B, E, and I were compiled by Philip V. Cannistraro; C and D by Mario Missori; F, G, and H were compiled by Brian R. Sullivan; J is taken from a report of the Intelligence Section of the Press Intelligence Division, April 12, 1944, National Archives, Washington, D.C., RG 208, Office of War Information, Entry 367.

Appendix A
Chronology of Important Events

January 1861	Kingdom of Italy proclaimed
July 29, 1883	Benito Mussolini born
March 1889-February 1891	Francesco Crispi prime minister
September 1893	Italian Socialist Party formed
December 1893-March 1896	Francesco Crispi prime minister
March 1896-June 1898	Antonio Di Rudinì prime minister
June 1898-June 1900	Luigi Pelloux prime minister
1903	Giovanni Giolitti becomes prime minister, remaining in office with brief interruptions until 1914
1904	General strike a failure
1906	Confederazione Generale del Lavoro founded
1910	Italian Nationalist Association founded
1911-12	Italo-Turkish War; Italy seizes Libya
July 1912	Reggio Emilia Congress of the Socialist party; Mussolini made a member of the party's executive committee and editor of *Avanti!*
March 1914-June 1914	Antonio Salandra prime minister
June 1914	"Red Week" strikes and agitation
August 1914	World War I breaks out; Italy remains neutral until May 1915; the Interventionist Crisis
October 1914	Mussolini advocates "active" neutrality: Fascio Rivoluzionario d'Azione Internazionalista formed
November 1914	Mussolini founded *Il Popolo d'Italia*; he is expelled from the Socialist party
December 1914	Fascio d'Azione Rivoluzionaria founded
May 1915	Italy enters the war on the side of the Triple Entente
September 1915	Mussolini drafted into army and sent to front
June 1916-October 1917	Paolo Boselli prime minister
October-November 1917	Battle of Caporetto
October 1917-June 1919	Vittorio E. Orlando prime minister
November 11, 1918	Armistice signed
January 1919	Partito Popolare Italiano formed
March 23, 1919	Mussolini creates the Fasci di Combattimento
June 1919-June 1920	Francesco S. Nitti prime minister
June 28, 1919	Treaty of Versailles signed
September 1919	Gabriele D'Annunzio occupied Fiume
November 1919	Parliamentary elections: Mussolini and Fascists defeated; Socialists and Popolari win major victories
June 1920-July 1921	Giolitti prime minister
1920	Confindustria formed by industrialists
August-September 1920	Occupation of the factories in the north

September 1920	D'Annunzio proclaims Regency of Carnaro in Fiume; Fascism spreads into countryside; Squadristi violence begins
January 1921	Italian Communist party founded
Spring 1921	Arditi del Popolo formed
May 1921	Mussolini and thirty-five Fascists elected to parliament
July 1921-February 1922	Ivanoe Bonomi prime minister
August 1921	Pact of Pacification between Fascists and Socialists
November 1921	PNF created: Michele Bianchi its secretary
February 1922	Luigi Facta prime minister; Pope Pius XI elected; Alleanza del Lavoro formed
August 1922	General strike a failure—broken by Fascists
October 27-28, 1922	March on Rome
October 31, 1922	Mussolini prime minister
November 1922	Mussolini given extraordinary powers by parliament
December 1922	MVSN created
January 1923	Fascist Grand Council created; Nicola Sansanelli PNF secretary
May 1923	Gentile educational reform program
August 1923	Corfu incident
October 1923	Francesco Giunta PNF secretary
November 1923	Acerbo election law approved
December 1923	Palazzo Chigi Pact; press laws enacted; Nationalists fuse with PNF
January 1924	Italy annexed Fiume
April 1924	Parliamentary elections under the Acerbo law: Fascist list wins 374 seats
June 1924	Socialist deputy Giacomo Matteotti murdered; Aventine Secession; Anti-Fascist opposition develops
January 3, 1925	Mussolini's speech to parliament: the dictatorship proclaimed; the "Second Wave" of Fascist violence begins
February 1925	Roberto Farinacci PNF secretary
April 1925	Congress of Fascist Intellectuals
May 1925	Manifesto of Anti-Fascist Intellectuals; the Dopolavoro established
October 1925	Palazzo Vidoni Pact; the "Battle for Grain" launched
March 1926	Augusto Turati PNF secretary
April 1926	Fascist syndical laws approved; The Opera Nazionale Balilla youth organization formed
July 1926	Ministry of Corporations created; several attempts on Mussolini's life
November 1926-January 1927	Exceptional Decrees are issued; Special Tribunal for the Defense of the State created
April 1927	Anti-Fascist Concentration organized in Paris; Charter of Labor issued
December 1927	Quota Novanta

December 1928	Bonifica Integrale program begun; Fascist Grand Council made a constitutional organ
February 1929	Lateran Pact signed
March 1929	Plebiscite; Giustizia e Libertà founded in Paris
October 1930	Giovanni Giuriati PNF secretary; conflict with Church over Catholic Action
August 1931	Loyalty oaths for university professors and teachers
December 1931	Achille Starace PNF secretary; anti-bourgeois and Romanità campaigns
November 1932	New PNF charter issued
July 1933	Four Power Pact signed
February 1934	Corporations established
June 1934	Mussolini and Hitler met in Venice
July 1934	Nazis assassinated Austrian chancellor Engelbert Dollfuss; Stresa Front
October 1935	Italy invaded Ethiopia; League of Nations sanctions imposed
May 1936	Mussolini proclaims victory in Ethiopia and creation of Italian Empire
June 1936	Galeazzo Ciano named foreign minister
October 1936	October Protocols signed in Berlin: the Rome-Berlin Axis formed
1936-1939	Mussolini and Hitler intervene in the Spanish Civil War
May 1937	Ministry of Popular Culture created
September 1937	Mussolini visited Hitler in Vienna
October 1937	Youth groups organized under the GIL
March 1938	Hitler annexed Austria with Mussolini's approval
May 1938	Hitler visited Mussolini in Italy
July 1938	Anti-Semitic legislation adopted in Italy
September 1938	Munich Conference
March 1939	Chamber of Fasci and Corporations replaced Chamber of Deputies
April 1939	Italy occupied Albania
May 22, 1939	Pact of Steel between Germany and Italy
August 23, 1939	Nazi-Soviet Non-Aggression Pact
September 1939	German invasion of Poland; Britain and France declare war on Germany; Italy declared its "non-belligerency"
October 1939	Ettore Muti PNF secretary
March 1940	Hitler and Mussolini meet at the Brenner Pass
June 10, 1940	Italy enters the war on Germany's side and invades France
June 18, 1940	Mussolini met Hitler in Munich
September 1940	Tripartite Pact between Italy, Germany, and Japan
October 1940	Italy attacked Greece; Mussolini and Ciano met Hitler at the Brenner Pass
October 28, 1940	Hitler met Mussolini in Florence
October 30, 1940	Adelchi Serena PNF secretary
January 1941	Mussolini summoned by Hitler to the Berghof

June 1941	Germany declares war on Russia; Mussolini sends Italian expeditionary force
December 1941	Aldo Vidussoni PNF secretary
1942	Allied victories and landing in North Africa; Party of Action organized
January 1943	Casablanca Conference of Allies
February 1943	Mussolini reshuffled Italian government
March 1943	Strikes in northern Italy
April 7, 1943	Mussolini met Hitler at Salzburg
April 19, 1943	Carlo Scorza PNF secretary
July 10, 1943	Allied landings in Sicily
July 19, 1943	Mussolini met Hitler at Feltre
July 24-25, 1943	Fascist Grand Council repudiates Mussolini's leadership; Marshal Pietro Badoglio named prime minister
July 25, 1943	Mussolini arrested
September 3, 1943	Allied troops land on mainland of Italy; Committee of National Liberation formed; Armed resistance begins
September 8, 1943	Italy announces armistice with Allies and declares war against Germany; King and Badoglio flee to Brindisi
September 12-13, 1943	Mussolini rescued from Gran Sasso by Germans
September 14-15, 1943	Alessandro Pavolini PFR secretary; Italian Social Republic proclaimed
October 1, 1943	Liberation of Naples
January 1944	Verona Trials: Ciano and other Fascist rebels executed; Allies land at Anzio
June 1944	Liberation of Rome; CGIL formed
June 1944-June 1945	Ivanoe Bonomi prime minister
July 20, 1944	Mussolini in Berlin for last meeting with Hitler
July-August 1944	Liberation of Florence
April 5, 1945	Consulta Nazionale created
April 25, 1945	Partisan victory in the north; Milan liberated
April 26, 1945	Mussolini arrested by partisans
April 28, 1945	Mussolini executed by partisans
June 1945-December 1945	Ferruccio Parri prime minister
December 1945	Alcide De Gasperi prime minister
May 9, 1946	Victor Emmanuel III abdicated; Umberto II king
June 1946	Referendum on the monarchy
February 1947	Peace Treaty with Italy
January 1, 1948	Italian Republic officially proclaimed

Appendix B
Sansepolcristi

Angiolini, Francesco
Attal, Salvatore
Aversa, Giuseppe
Barabandi, Renato
Bartolozzi, Ettore
Benvenuti, Ettore
Besana, Enrico
Besozzi
Bianchi, Camillo
Bianchi, Michele
Binda, Ambrogio
Boattini, Vittorio
Bonafini, Napoleone
Bonavita, Francesco
Boschi, Ettore
Bosi, Nereo
Bottini, Piero
Bozzolo, Natale
Brambillaschi, Giovanni
Brebbia, Giselda
Bresciani, Italo
Bruzzesi, Giunio
Capodivacca, Giovanni
Cappurro, Giuseppe
Carabellese
Carli, Mario
Catteneo, Luigi Natale
Cerasola, Federico
Chierini, Gino
Chiesa, Ernesto
Ciarrocca, Guido
Colombi, Giuseppe
Consonni, Ferruccio
Corra, Bruno
Costantino, Michele
Cottarelli, Leonardo
Dagnino, Ettore
De Angelis, Ernesto
Deffenu, Luigi
Del Latte, Guido
Dessy, Mario

Dondena, Giovanni
Ercolani, Luigi
Fabbianini, Nino
Facchini, Antonio
Falletti, Pietro
Falugi, Quintillio
Farinacci, Roberto
Fasciolo, Benedetto
Ferradini, Ferruccio
Ferrara, Gaetano
Ferrari, Enzo
Fiecchi, Arturo
Franceschelli, Aldo
Fraschini, Alcide
Franzi, Erminio
Frigerio, Armando
Funi, Achille
Galassi, Aurelio
Garibaldi, Decio Canzio
Ghetti, Domenico
Giampaoli, Mario
Gioda, Mario
Goldmann, Cesare
Greppi, Filippo
Jachetti, Francesco
Jeckling, Manlio
Longoni, Attilio
Luzzatto, Riccardo
Mainardi, Oreste
Malusardi, Edoardo
Mangiagalli, Luigi
Manteca, Luigi
Maraviglia, Carlo
Masnata, Giovanni
Marchi, Marco
Marinetti, F. T.
Marinelli, Giovanni
Martignoni, Rodolfo
Marzagalli, Giuseppe
Marzari, Quirino
Massaretti, Luigi

Mazzi, Tito
Mecheri, Eno
Melli, Gino
Moili, Mario
Momigliano, Eucardio
Morisi, Celso
Moroni, Paolo
Mussolini, Benito
Nascimbeni, Mario
Pasella, Umberto
Pesenti, Guido
Pianigiani, Guido
Podrecca, Guido
Pozzi, Alessandro
Pozzi, G. P.
Raimondi, Carlo
Ranzanici, Angiolo
Razza, Luigi

Riva, Celso
Riva, Ubaldo
Rocca, Giovanni
Rossi, Cesare
Rossi, Carlo
Rossi, Giuseppe
Scarani, Cleto
Scarzi-Ranieri, Angiolo
Semino, Virginio
Tacchini, Ezio
Tagliabue, Enrico
Teruzzi, Regina
Vajana, Alfonso
Vecchi, Ferruccio
Vezzani, Menotti
Zappi, Ferdinando
Zoppis
Zuliani, Mario

Appendix C
Ministers and Undersecretaries of the Mussolini Government

(OCTOBER 31, 1922—JULY 25, 1943)

President of the Council of Ministers[1]

Mussolini, Benito: October 31, 1922—July 25, 1943

Undersecretary:

Acerbo, Giacomo: to July 3, 1924
Suardo, Giacomo: July 3, 1924—December 21, 1927
Giunta, Francesco: December 21, 1927—July 20, 1932
Rossoni, Edmondo: July 20, 1932—January 24, 1935
Medici del Vascello, Giacomo: January 24, 1935—October 31, 1939
Russo, Luigi: October 31, 1939—February 6, 1943
Rossi, Amilcare: from February 6, 1943

Minister without Portfolio

Giuriati, Giovanni: March 11, 1923—January 24, 1924

Foreign Affairs
Minister:

Mussolini, Benito: to June 17, 1924 (Interim)
Mussolini, Benito: June 17, 1924—September 12, 1929
Grandi, Dino: September 12, 1929—July 20, 1932
Mussolini, Benito: July 20, 1932—June 11, 1936
Ciano, Galeazzo: June 11, 1936—February 6, 1943
Mussolini, Benito: from February 6, 1943

Undersecretary:

Vassallo, Ernesto: to April 26, 1923
Grandi, Dino: May 14, 1925—September 12, 1929
Fani, Amedeo: September 12, 1929—July 20, 1932
Suvich, Fulvio: July 20, 1932—June 11, 1936
Bastianini, Giuseppe: June 11, 1936—October 14, 1939
Benini, Zenone: April 18, 1939—July 31, 1941 (For Albanian Affairs)
Bastianini, Giuseppe: from February 6, 1943

---

[1]The official title, president of the Council of Ministers, was changed on December 24, 1925, Law 2263, to head of government, prime minister secretary of state. Mussolini assumed that title by royal decree on January 3, 1926.

Interior
Minister:

Mussolini, Benito: to June 17, 1924
Federzoni, Luigi: June 17, 1924—November 6, 1926
Mussolini, Benito: from November 6, 1926

Undersecretary:

Finzi, Aldo: to June 17, 1924
Grandi, Dino: July 3, 1924—May 14, 1925
Teruzzi, Attilio: May 14, 1925—November 6, 1926
Suardo, Giacomo: November 6, 1926—March 13, 1928
Bianchi, Michele: March 13, 1928—September 12, 1929
Arpinati, Leandro: September 12, 1929—May 8, 1933
Buffarini Guidi, Guido: May 8, 1933—February 6, 1943
Albini, Umberto: from February 6, 1943

Colonies (Italian Africa[2])
Minister:

Federzoni, Luigi: June 17, 1924
Mussolini, Benito: June 17—July 1, 1924 (Interim)
Lanza di Trabia, Pietro: July 1, 1924—November 6, 1926
Federzoni, Luigi: November 6, 1926—December 18, 1928
Mussolini, Benito: December 18, 1928—September 12, 1929
De Bono, Emilio: September 12, 1929—January 17, 1935
Mussolini, Benito: January 17, 1935—June 11, 1936
Lessona, Alessandro: June 11, 1936—November 20, 1937
Mussolini, Benito: November 20, 1937—October 31, 1939
Teruzzi, Attilio: from October 31, 1939

Undersecretary:

Marchi, Giovanni: to July 3, 1924
Cantalupo, Roberto: July 3, 1924—November 6, 1926
Bolzon, Pietro: November 6, 1926—December 18, 1928
De Bono, Emilio: December 18, 1928—September 12, 1929
Lessona, Alessandro: September 12, 1929—June 11, 1936
Teruzzi, Attilio: November 20, 1937—October 31, 1939

Justice (Grace and Justice[3])
Minister:

Oviglio, Aldo: to January 5, 1925
Rocco, Alfredo: January 5, 1925—July 20, 1932
De Francisci, Pietro: July 20, 1932—January 24, 1935

---

[2]The title was changed by royal decree (n. 431) on April 8, 1937.
[3]The title was changed by royal decree (n. 884) on July 20, 1932.

Solmi, Arrigo: January 24, 1935—July 12, 1939
Grandi, Dino: July 12, 1939—February 6, 1943
De Marsico, Alfredo: from February 6, 1943

Undersecretary:

Milani, Fulvio: to April 26, 1923
Mattei-Gentili, Paolo: July 3, 1924—September 12, 1929
Morelli, Giuseppe: September 12, 1929—July 20, 1932
Albertini, Antonio: July 20, 1932—January 24, 1935
Tumedei, Cesare: January 24, 1935—November 15, 1936
Putzolu, Antonio: from March 5, 1940

Finance
Minister:

De Stefani, Alberto: to July 10, 1925
Volpi di Misurata, Giuseppe: July 10, 1925—July 9, 1928
Mosconi, Antonio: July 9, 1928—July 20, 1932
Jung, Guido: July 20, 1932—January 24, 1935
Thaon Di Revel, Paolo: January 24, 1935—February 6, 1943
Acerbo, Giacomo: from February 6, 1943

Undersecretary:

Lissia, Pietro: to July 3, 1924
Rocco, Alfredo: January 1—March 8, 1923
De Vecchi, Cesare Maria: January 1—March 8, 1923 (War Pensions)
De Vecchi, Cesare Maria: March 8—May 3, 1923
Rocco, Alfredo: March 8—September 1, 1923 (War Pensions)
Spezzotti, Luigi: July 3, 1924—July 14, 1925
D'Alessio, Francesco: July 28, 1925—November 6, 1926
Frignani, Giuseppe: November 6, 1926—July 9, 1926
Suvich, Fulvio: November 6, 1926—July 9, 1928
Boncompagni-Ludovisi, Francesco: July 21, 1927—July 9, 1928
Casalini, Vincenzo: July 9, 1928—July 20, 1932
Rosboch, Ettore: July 9, 1928—July 20, 1932
Puppini, Umberto: July 20, 1932—April 30, 1934
Arcangeli, Ageo: April 30, 1934—January 24, 1935
Biachini, Giuseppe: January 24, 1935—July 15, 1937
Lissia, Pietro: February 18, 1941—February 13, 1943
Pellegrini, Giampietro Domenico: to February 13, 1943

Treasury[4]
Minister

Tangorra, Vincenzo: to December 21, 1922
De Stefani, Alberto: December 21—December 31, 1922 (Interim)

[4]The Ministry of the Treasury was suppressed by Royal Decree n. 1700 on December 31, 1922, and its functions were transferred to the Ministry of Finance.

Undersecretary:

Rocco, Alfredo
De Vecchi, Cesare Maria (War Pensions)

Public Instruction (National Education[5])
Minister:

Gentile, Giovanni: to July 1, 1924
Casati, Alessandro: July 1, 1924—January 5, 1925
Fedele, Pietro: January 5, 1925—July 9, 1928
Belluzzo, Giuseppe: July 9, 1928—September 12, 1929
Giuliano, Balbino: September 12, 1929—July 20, 1932
Ercole, Francesco: July 20, 1932—January 24, 1935
De Vecchi, Cesare Maria: January 24, 1935—November 15, 1936
Bottai, Giuseppe: November 15, 1936—February 6, 1943
Biggini, Carlo Alberto: from February 6, 1943

Undersecretary:

Lupi, Dario: to July 3, 1924
Siciliani, Luigi: to April 15, 1923 (Antiquities and Fine Arts)
Giuliano, Balbino: July 3, 1924—January 6, 1925
Romano, Michele: January 6, 1925—November 6, 1926
Bodrero, Emilio: November 6, 1926—July 9, 1928
Leicht, Pier Silverio: July 9, 1928—September 12, 1929
Di Marzo, Salvatore: September 12, 1929—July 20, 1932
Ricci, Renato: September 12, 1929—November 12, 1937 (Physical and Youth Education)
Solmi, Arrigo: July 20, 1932—January 24, 1935
Del Giudice, Riccardo: December 5, 1939—February 13, 1943
Bodrero, Emilio: February 18—May 15, 1941
Rispoli, Guido: from February 13, 1943

War
Minister:

Diaz, Armando: to April 20, 1924
Di Giorgio, Antonio: April 20, 1924—April 4, 1925
Mussolini, Benito: April 4, 1925—January 3, 1926 (Interim)
Mussolini, Benito: January 3, 1926—September 12, 1929
Gazzera, Pietro: September 12, 1929—July 22, 1933
Mussolini, Benito: from July 22, 1933

Undersecretary:

Bonardi, Carlo: to July 3, 1924
Clerici, Ambrogio: July 3, 1924—May 4, 1925

[5]The title was changed by Royal Decree n. 1661 on September 12, 1929.

Cavallero, Ugo: May 4, 1925—November 24, 1928
Gazzera, Pietro: November 24, 1928—September 12, 1929
Manaresi, Angelo: September 12, 1929—July 22, 1933
Baistrocchi, Federico: July 22, 1933—October 7, 1936
Pariani, Alberto: October 7, 1936—October 31, 1939
Soddu, Ubaldo: October 31, 1939—November 30, 1940
Guzzoni, Alfredo: November 30, 1940—May 24, 1941
Scuero, Antonio: May 24, 1941—February 13, 1943
Sorice, Antonio: from February 13, 1943

Navy
Minister:

Thaon di Revel, Paolo: to May 8, 1925
Mussolini, Benito: May 8, 1925—January 3, 1926 (Interim)
Mussolini, Benito: January 3, 1926—September 12, 1929
Sirianni, Giuseppe: September 12, 1929—November 6, 1933
Mussolini, Benito: from November 6, 1933

Undersecretary:

Ciano, Costanzo: to February 5, 1924
Sirianni, Giuseppe: May 14, 1925—September 12, 1929
Russo, Gioacchino: September 12, 1929—November 6, 1933
Cavagnari, Domenico: November 6, 1933—December 8, 1940
Riccardi, Arturo: from December 8, 1940

Air Force[6]
Minister:

Mussolini, Benito: August 30, 1925—January 3, 1926 (Interim)
Mussolini, Benito: January 3, 1926—September 12, 1929
Balbo, Italo: September 12, 1929—November 6, 1933
Mussolini, Benito: from November 6, 1933

Undersecretary:

Bonzani, Alberto: May 14, 1925—November 6, 1926
Balbo, Italo: November 6, 1926—September 12, 1929
Riccardi, Raffaello: September 12, 1929—November 6, 1933
Valle, Giuseppe: November 6, 1933—October 31, 1939
Pricolo, Francesco: October 31, 1939—November 15, 1941
Fougier, Rino: from November 15, 1941

[6]On January 24, 1923, with Royal Decree n. 62, a Commissariato per l'Aeronautica was created that supervised both military and civil air operations. The Ministry was created by Royal Decree n. 1513, August 30, 1925.

Public Works
Minister:

Carnazza, Gabriello: to July 1, 1924
Sarrocchi, Gino: July 1, 1924—January 5, 1925
Giuriati, Giovanni: January 5, 1925—April 30, 1929
Mussolini, Benito: April 30, 1929—September 12, 1929
Bianchi, Michele: September 12, 1929—February 3, 1930
Crollalanza, Araldo: February 13, 1930—January 24, 1935
Razza, Luigi: January 24, 1935—August 7, 1935
Cobolli Gigli, Giuseppe: September 5, 1935—October 31, 1939
Serena, Adelchi: October 31, 1939—October 30, 1940
Gorla, Giuseppe: October 30, 1940—February 6, 1943
Benini, Zenone: from February 6, 1943

Undersecretary:

Sardi, Alessandro: to July 3, 1924
Torre, Edoardo: January 4, 1923—April 30, 1924
Scialoja, Antonio: July 3, 1924—January 12, 1925
Petrillo, Alfredo: January 12, 1925—October 31, 1925
Bianchi, Michele: October 31, 1925—March 13, 1928
Crollalanza, Araldo: July 9, 1928—February 13, 1930
Leoni, Antonio: February 15, 1930—January 24, 1935
Coboli Gigli, Giuseppe: January 24, 1935—September 5, 1935
Calletti, Pio: from February 18, 1941

Industry and Commerce (Industry, Commerce, and Labor[7, 8])
Minister:

Rossi, Teofilo: to July 31, 1923

Undersecretary:

Gronchi, Giovanni: to April 26, 1923

Agriculture[8]
Minister:

De Capitani D'Arzago, Giuseppe: to July 31, 1923

Undersecretary:

Corgini, Ottavio: to June 7, 1923

[7]The title of the Ministry of Industry and Commerce was changed to the Ministry of Industry, Commerce, and Labor by Royal Decree n. 1560, June 14, 1923.
[8]On July 5, 1923 (Royal Decree n. 1439), the Ministry of Agriculture and the Ministry of Industry, Commerce, and Labor were united into a new Ministry of National Economy. On September 12, 1929 (Royal Decree n. 1661) the Ministry of National Economy was suppressed and its services divided as follows: agriculture and forests to a new Ministry of Agriculture and Forests, and commerce and industry to the Ministry of Corporations.

National Economy[8]
Minister:

Corbino, Mario Orso: August 1, 1923—July 1, 1924
Nava, Cesare: July 1, 1924—July 10, 1925
Belluzzo, Giuseppe: July 10, 1925—July 9, 1928
Martelli, Alessandro: July 9, 1928—September 12, 1929

Undersecretary:

Serpieri, Arrigo: August 1, 1923—July 3, 1924
Banelli, Giovanni: July 3, 1924—October 31, 1925
Larussa, Ignazio: July 3, 1924—July 14, 1925
Peglion, Vittorio: July 3, 1924—November 6, 1926
Balbo, Italo: October 31, 1925—November 6, 1926
Bastianini, Giuseppe: November 6, 1926—June 23, 1927
Bisi, Tommaso: November 6, 1926—July 9, 1928
Josa, Guglielmo: July 9, 1928—September 12, 1929
Lessona, Alessandro: July 9, 1928—September 12, 1929

Agriculture and Forests
Minister:

Acerbo, Giacomo: September 12, 1929—January 24, 1935
Rossoni, Edmondo: January 24, 1935—October 31, 1939
Tassinari, Giuseppe: October 31, 1939—December 26, 1941
Pareschi, Carlo: from December 26, 1941

Undersecretary:

Marescalchi, Arturo: September 12, 1929—January 24, 1935
Serpieri, Arrigo: September 12, 1929—January 24, 1935
Canelli, Gabriele: January 24, 1935—April 19, 1937
Tassinari, Giuseppe: January 24, 1935—October 31, 1939
Nannini, Sergio: October 31, 1939—February 13, 1943
Pascolato, Michele: October 5, 1941—February 13, 1943
Fabrizi, Carlo: from February 13, 1943
Spadafora, Gutierez: from February 13, 1943

Labor and Social Welfare[9]
Minister:

Cavazzoni, Stefano: to April 26, 1923

Undersecretary:

Gai, Silvio: to April 26, 1923

[9]On April 27, 1923 (Royal Decree n. 915), the Ministry of Labor and Social Welfare was suppressed; on June 14, 1923 (Royal Decree n. 1560) its services were transferred to the Ministry of Industry, Commerce, and Labor.

Corporations
Minister:

Mussolini, Benito: July 2, 1926—September 12, 1929
Bottai, Giuseppe: September 12, 1929—July 20, 1932
Mussolini, Benito: July 20, 1932—June 11, 1936
Lantini, Ferruccio: June 11, 1936—October 31, 1939
Ricci, Renato: October 31, 1939—February 6, 1943
Tiengo, Carlo: February 6, 1943—April 19, 1943
Cianetti, Tullio: from April 19, 1943

Undersecretary:

Suardo, Giacomo: July 2—November 6, 1926
Bottai, Giuseppe: November 6, 1926—September 12, 1929
Josa, Guglielmo: September 12—November 9, 1929
Trigona, Emanuele: September 12, 1929—July 20, 1932
Alfieri, Dino: November 9, 1929—July 20, 1932
Asquini, Alberto: July 20, 1932—January 24, 1935
Biagi, Bruno: July 20, 1932—January 24, 1935
Lantini, Ferruccio: January 24, 1935—June 11, 1936
Ricci, Renato: November 20, 1937—October 21, 1939
Cianetti, Tullio: July 22, 1939—April 19, 1943
Amicucci, Ermanno: from November 4, 1939
Lombrassa, Giuseppe: February 26, 1942—June 2, 1943
Baccarini, Giovanni: from April 30, 1943
Contu, Luigi: from June 2, 1943

Post and Telegraph[10]
Minister:

Colonna, Giovanni Antonio: to February 5, 1924
Ciano, Costanzo: February 5—May 3, 1924

Undersecretary:

Terzaghi, Michele: to November 10, 1922
Caradonna, Giuseppe: November 10, 1922—May 3, 1924

Communications
Minister:

Ciano, Costanzo: May 3, 1924—April 30, 1934
Puppini, Umberto: April 30, 1934—January 24, 1935
Benni, Antonio Stefano: January 24, 1935—October 31, 1939
Host Venturi, Giovanni: October 31, 1939—February 6, 1943

---

[10]Suppressed on April 30, 1924, Royal Decree n. 596, its services passed to the new Ministry of Communications, created by the same decree.

Cini, Vittorio: February 6, 1943—July 24, 1943
Peverelli, Giuseppe: from July 24, 1943

Undersecretary:

Caradonna, Giuseppe: May 3—July 3, 1924
Carusi, Mario: July 3, 1924—November 6, 1926
Celesia di Vegliaso, Giovanni: July 3, 1924—November 6, 1926
Panunzio, Sergio: July 3, 1924—November 6, 1926
Martelli, Alessandro: November 6, 1926—July 9, 1928
Pala, Giovanni: November 6, 1926—May 4, 1928
Pennavaria, Filippo: November 6, 1926—July 20, 1932
Cao, Giovanni: July 9, 1928—July 20, 1932
Riccardi, Raffaello: July 9, 1928—September 12, 1929
Pierazzi, Ferdinando: September 12, 1929—July 20, 1932
Lojacono, Luigi: July 20, 1932—January 24, 1935
Postiglione, Gaetano: July 20, 1932—January 24, 1935
Romano, Ruggero: July 20, 1932—January 24, 1935
De Marsanich, Augusto: January 24, 1935—February 13, 1943
Host Venturi, Giovanni: January 24, 1935—October 31, 1939
Jannelli, Mario: January 24, 1935—February 13, 1943
Marinelli, Giovanni: November 5, 1939—February 13, 1943
Arcidiacono, Domenico: from February 13, 1943
Peverelli, Giuseppe: February 13, 1943—July 24, 1943
Scarfiotti, Luigi: from February 13, 1943

Liberated Territories[11]
Minister:

Giuriati, Giovanni: to March 1, 1923

Undersecretary:

Merlin, Umberto: to March 1, 1923

Press and Propaganda (Popular Culture[12])
Minister:

Ciano, Galeazzo: June 26, 1935—June 11, 1936
Alfieri, Dino: June 11, 1936—October 31, 1939
Pavolini, Alessandro: October 31, 1939—February 6, 1943
Polverelli, Gaetano: from February 6, 1943

---

[11]The Ministry was suppressed by Royal Decree 291 on February 25, 1923 and its duties transferred to a variety of other ministries.
[12]The Ministry had been formerly an Undersecretariate of State, headed G. Ciano from its creation on September 6, 1934, by Royal Decree n. 1434, to June 26, 1935, when it became a Ministry by Royal Decree n. 1009. The title of the ministry was changed by Royal Decree n. 752 on May 27, 1937.

Undersecretary:

Alfieri, Dino: August 22, 1935—June 11, 1936
Polverelli, Gaetano: January 12, 1941—February 6, 1943
Rinaldi, Renato: from February 15, 1943

Exchange and Currency[13]

Minister:

Guarneri, Felice: November 20, 1937—October 31, 1939
Riccardi, Raffaello: October 31, 1939—February 6, 1943
Bonomi, Oreste: from February 6, 1943

Undersecretary

Gatti, Salvatore: February 18—May 8, 1941

War Production[14]
Minister:

Favagrossa, Carlo: from February 6, 1943

[13]The Ministry had been an undersecretariate since its creation by Royal Decree n. 2186 on December 29, 1935 and was headed by Guarneri, who became minister by Royal Decree n. 1928.
[14]On May 23, 1940 (Royal Decree n. 499), an Undersecretariate for War Manufacturing was created and was headed by Favagrossa. The Ministry was created by Royal Decree n. 24 on February 6, 1943.

Appendix D
Ministers and Undersecretaries of the Italian Social Republic
(SEPTEMBER 23, 1943—APRIL 28, 1945)

Head of Government

Mussolini, Benito

Undersecretary of State for the Presidency of the Council of Ministers

Barracu, Francesco Maria

Foreign Affairs
Minister:

Mussolini, Benito

Undersecretary:

Mazzolini, Serafino: March 8, 1944—February 23, 1945
Anfuso, Filippo: from March 19, 1945

Interior
Minister:

Buffarini-Guidi, Guido: to February 21, 1945
Zerbino, Valerio: from February 21, 1945

Undersecretary:

Zerbino, Valerio: May 6, 1944—February 21, 1945
Pini, Giorgio: from October 25, 1944

Grace and Justice (Justice[1])
Minister:

Tringali Casanova, Antonino: to November 1, 1943
Pisenti, Piero: from November 3, 1943

National Defense (Armed Forces[2])
Minister:

Graziani, Rodolfo

[1] The title was changed by decree of November 10, 1943.
[2] The title was changed by decree of January 6, 1944.

Army
Undersecretary:

Basile, Carlo Emanuele, from June 27, 1944

Navy
Undersecretary:

Legnani, Antonio: to October 21, 1943
Ferrini, Ferruccio: November 5, 1943—February 16, 1944
Sparzani, Giuseppe: February 16, 1944—February 21, 1945
Gemelli, Bruno: from February 21, 1945

Air Force
Undersecretary:

Botto, Ernesto: to March 8, 1944
Tessari, Arrigo: March 8—July 29, 1944
Molfese, Manlio: July 29—November 22, 1944
Bonomi, Ruggero: from November 22, 1944

Finance[3]
Minister:

Pellegrini, Giampietro

National Education
Minister:

Biggini, Carlo Alberto

Agriculture and Forests[4]
Minister:

Moroni, Edoardo

Communications
Minister:

Peverelli, Giuseppe;   to October 26, 1943[5]
Liverani, Augusto: from November 5, 1943

---

[3]Pellegrini was also named minister of exchange and currency, but on October 9, 1943 a decree suppressed that agency and transferred its functions to the Ministry of Finance.
[4]The title was changed by decree of January 19, 1945.
[5]Peverelli did not assume his position.

Undersecretary:

Liverani, Augusto: October 7—November 5, 1943

Corporative Economy (Industrial Production[6])
Minister:

Gai, Silvio: to December 31, 1943
Tarchi, Angelo: from December 31, 1943

Popular Culture
Minister:

Mezzasoma, Fernando

Undersecretary:

Cucco, Alfredo: from February 29, 1944

Public Works
Minister:

Romano, Ruggero: from October 3, 1943

Labor[7]
Minister:

Spinelli, Giuseppe: from January 22, 1945

Undersecretary:

Fabrizi, Carlo: from January 22, 1945

---

[6]The title was changed by decree of January 19, 1945.
[7]The ministry was created by decree of January 19, 1945.

Appendix E
PNF National Secretaries[1]

Bianchi, Michele: November 20, 1921—January 13, 1923
Sansanelli, Nicola: January 13, 1923—October 15, 1923[2]
Giunta, Francesco: October 15, 1923—April 23, 1924[3]
Direttorio Provvisorio: April 23, 1924—August 7, 1924[4]
Direttorio Nazionale: August 7, 1924—February 12, 1925[5]
Farinacci, Roberto: February 12, 1925—March 30, 1926
Turati, Augusto: March 30, 1926—October 8, 1930
Giuriati, Giovanni: October 7, 1930—December 7, 1931
Starace, Achille: December 7, 1931—October 31, 1939
Muti, Ettore: October 31, 1939—October 30, 1940
Serena, Adelchi: October 30, 1940—December 26, 1941
Vidussoni, Aldo: December 26, 1941—April 19, 1943
Scorza, Carlo: April 19, 1943—July 25, 1943
Pavolini, Alessandro: September 14, 1943—April 28, 1945 (*Partito Fascista Repubblicano*)

[1]Before the creation of the PNF in November 1921 the Fasci di Combattimento were administered through a frequently changing structure. On March 21, 1919, a seven-man *giunta esecutiva* had been appointed. On March 23 at the San Sepolcro rally, a larger *comitato centrale* had been selected. On May 6 a Segretaria Nazionale was chosen consisting of Attilio Longoni as political secretary and Enzo Ferrari, Celso Morisi, Alberto Bertoldi. Umberto Pasella replaced Longoni in the summer of 1919 as political secretary and was purged in November 1921.

[2]On January 13, 1923, the Fascist Grand Council created a *segretariato politico* consisting of Sansanelli, Bianchi, and G. Bastianini over which Sansanelli presided; a *segretariato amministrativo* of Marinelli and Dudan was also set up. On April 25, 1923, these were replaced by a *giunta esecutiva* that included Bastianini, P. Bolzon, A. Caprino, A. Dudan, Farinacci, F. Lantini, M. Maraviglia, Sansanelli, Starace, M. Zimolo, and G. Marinelli. Sansanelli and then Bianchi served as general secretaries of the *giunta*.

[3]Giunta served as political secretary of a provisional *direzione nazionale* of five members that also included Bolzon, Cesare Rossi, Teruzzi, and Marinelli. Bastianini, V. Buronzo, L. Freddi, A. Gravelli, Maraviglia, and Sollazzo also held specialized appointments in the *direzione*.

[4]The Direttorio consisted of Roberto Forges Davanzati, Cesare Rossi, Alessandro Melchiori, and Giovanni Marinelli. On June 16, 1924, another provisional Direttorio replaced this one: Forges Davanzati, P. Barnaba, A. Belloni, A. Cucco, Farinacci, I. Foschi, Grandi, Maraviglia, Melchiori, and Sergio Panunzio.

[5]The Direttorio Nazionale, elected by the Consiglio Nazionale of the PNF, included Arpinati, Barnaba, Bonelli, Caprino, Ciarlantini, Colisi-Rossi, Cucco, De Cicco, De Marsico, Farinacci, Felicioni, Forges Davanzati, Gray, Igliori, Maraviglia, Masi, S. Mazzolini, Melchiori, Menesini, Ricci, A. Rossi, and Sardi. Farinacci and Forges Davanzati comprised its executive committee.

Appendix F
Chiefs of Staff[1]

Chiefs of the Supreme General Staff

Badoglio,[2] Pietro	June 8, 1925—December 4, 1940
Cavallero, Ugo	December 4, 1940—February 1, 1943
Ambrosio, Vittorio	February 1, 1943—November 18, 1943

Chiefs of the Army General Staff

Vaccari, Giuseppe	February 3, 1921—April 11, 1923
Ferrari, Francesco Giuseppe	April 11, 1923—May 4, 1925
Badoglio,[3] Pietro	May 4, 1925—February 1, 1927
Ferrari, Francesco Giuseppe	February 1, 1927—February 23, 1928
Gualtieri,[4] Nicola	July 29, 1928—February 4, 1929
Bonzani, Alberto	February 4, 1929—October 1, 1934
Baistrocchi,[5] Federico	October 1, 1934—October 7, 1936
Pariani, Alberto	October 7, 1936—October 31, 1939
Graziani, Rodolfo	October 31, 1939—March 24, 1941
Roatta,[6] Mario	March 24, 1941—January 20, 1942
Ambrosio, Vittorio	January 20, 1942—February 1, 1943
Rosi, Ezio	February 1, 1943—May 19, 1943
De Stefanis,[7] Giuseppe	May 19, 1943—June 1, 1943
Roatta, Mario	June 1, 1943—November 18, 1943

Chiefs of the Naval General Staff

De Lorenzi, Giuseppe	February 11, 1921—May 9, 1923
Ducci, Gino	May 9, 1923—May 13, 1925
Acton,[8] Alfredo	May 13, 1925—December 15, 1927

[1]These tables refer only to the period October 1922-July 1943. For information on the armed forces command of the Italian Social Republic, see Giorgio Pisano, *Storia della guerra civile in Italia, 1943-1945*, Vol. 2 (Milan: FPE, 1966).

[2]Badoglio's position included the powers of Army Chief of Staff until February 1, 1927. Thereafter the title of the position was a misnomer, for there was no separate Supreme General Staff. Only after Cavallero returned from the Albanian Campaign in May 1941 was he able to create a staff organization to coordinate the Italian Armed Forces.

[3]On June 8, 1925, Badoglio became Chief of the Supreme General Staff, which position included the powers of Army Chief of Staff until February 1, 1927.

[4]There was no Army Chief of Staff between February 23 and July 29, 1928.

[5]Simultaneously undersecretary of war.

[6]Acting Chief of Staff since June 30, 1940 when Graziani became Governor of Libya.

[7]Ad interim; officially Deputy Chief of Staff.

Burzagli, Ernesto	December 15, 1927—August 16, 1931
Ducci, Gino	August 16, 1931—March 22, 1934
Cavagnari,[9] Domenico	March 22, 1934—December 8, 1940
Riccardi,[9] Arturo	December 8, 1940—July 26, 1943

Chiefs of the Air Force General Staff

Piccio,[10] Pier Ruggero	January 24, 1923—February 8, 1927
Armani, Armando	February 8, 1927—October 25, 1928
De Pinedo,[11] Francesco	October 25, 1928—August 28, 1929
Valle,[12] Giuseppe	August 28, 1929—November 11, 1933
Bosio, Antonio	November 11, 1933—March 22, 1934
Valle,[13] Giuseppe	March 22, 1934—October 31, 1939
Pricolo,[13] Francesco	October 31, 1939—November 15, 1941
Fougier, [13] Rino Corso	November 15, 1941—July 26, 1943

[8]Previously Chief of Staff, December 1, 1919—February 11, 1921.

[9]Simultaneously undersecretary of the Navy.

[10]Piccio was officially Commandant General until his appointment as Chief of Staff on May 13, 1925.

[11]De Pinedo was officially Deputy Chief of Staff. The Air Force had no Chief of Staff between October 25, 1928, and February 22, 1930.

[12]Valle was officially Deputy Chief of Staff until February 22, 1930.

[13]Simultaneously undersecretary of the Air Force.

Appendix G
Militia Commanders and Chiefs of Staff

Commanders

De Bono, Emilio	January 14, 1923—October 22, 1924
Balbo, Italo	October 22—December 1, 1924
Gandolfo Asclepio	December 1, 1924—August 31, 1925
Gonzaga, Maurizio	September 12, 1925—October 9, 1926
Mussolini,[1] Benito	October 9, 1926—July 26, 1943

Chiefs of Staff

Bazan, Enrico	December 1, 1924—December 18, 1928
Teruzzi, Attilio	December 18, 1928—October 31, 1935
Russo, Luigi	October 31, 1935—November 3, 1939
Starace, Achille	November 3, 1939—May 25, 1941
Galbiati,[2] Enzo	May 25, 1941—July 26, 1943

Republican National Guard Commanders

Ricci,[3] Renato	September 16, 1943—August 24, 1944
Mussolini,[4] Benito	August 24, 1944—April 25, 1945

Republican National Guard Chiefs of Staff

Chiappe, Umberto	November 28, 1943—April 2, 1944
Nicchiarelli, Niccolò	April 2, 1944—April 26, 1945

[1]With Mussolini's assumption of the Militia command, actual direction of the MVSN passed to the Chief of Staff.

[2]Galbiati was succeeded by Quirino Armellini, who supervised Militia dissolution. The MVSN was formally abolished on December 6, 1943.

[3]Until November 20, 1943, Ricci was officially commander of the Militia, revived under the Italian Social Republic. He then assumed command of the new Republican National Guard, which superseded the Militia.

[4]With Mussolini's assumption of the Republican National Guard command, actual direction passed to the Chief of Staff, Nicchiarelli.

Appendix H
Governors of Italian Colonies

Tripolitania

Volpi, Giuseppe	July 16, 1921—July 3, 1925
De Bono, Emilio	July 3, 1925—December 18, 1928[1]

Cyrenaica

Baccari, Edoardo	October 1, 1922—December 1, 1922
De Gasperi, Oreste	December 1, 1922—January 7, 1923
Bongiovanni, Luigi	January 7, 1923—May 24, 1924
Mombelli, Ernesto	May 24, 1924—November 22, 1926
Teruzzi, Attilio	November 23, 1926—December 18, 1928
Siciliani, Domenico	January 21, 1929—March 13, 1930
Graziani, Rodolfo	March 13, 1930—May 30, 1934
Nasi, Guglielmo	June 1, 1934—April 23, 1935

Libya

Badoglio, Pietro[2]	December 18, 1928—December 31, 1933
Balbo, Italo[3]	January 1, 1934—June 28, 1940
Bruni, Giuseppe	June 28, 1940—June 30, 1940
Graziani, Rodolfo	June 30, 1940—February 11, 1941
Gariboldi, Italo	February 11, 1941—July 19, 1941
Bastico, Ettore	July 19, 1941—February 5, 1943

Eritrea

Feroni, Giovanni Cerrina	April 14, 1921—June 1, 1923
Gasperini, Jacopo	June 1, 1923—June 1, 1928
Zoli, Corrado	June 1, 1928—July 16, 1930
Astuto, Riccardo	July 16, 1930—January 15, 1935
Gabelli, Ottone[4]	January 15, 1935—January 18, 1935
De Bono, Emilio[5]	January 18, 1935—November 27, 1935

[1]For governors of Tripolitania after this date, see Libya.
[2]Governor of Tripolitania and Cyrenaica until January 21, 1929, thereafter officially single governor of Tripolitania and Cyrenaica.
[3]Governor of Tripolitania and Cyrenaica until December 21, 1934, thereafter officially governor general of Libya. Tripolitania and Cyrenaica had been united in the Colony of Libya on December 3, 1934.
[4]Acting governor, thereafter vice-governor under DeBono and Badoglio. Gabelli administered Eritrea while his superiors were occupied with military affairs.
[5]In his capacity as high commissioner for the colonies of East Africa.

Badoglio, Pietro[5]	November 28, 1935—May 31, 1936[6]
Guzzoni, Alfredo	June 1, 1936[7]—April 1, 1937
De Feo, Vincenzo	April 1, 1937—December 15, 1937
Daodice, Giuseppe	December 15, 1937—June 2, 1940
Frusci, Luigi[8]	June 2, 1940—May 19, 1941[9]

Somalia

Ricci, Carlo	June 21, 1920—December 8, 1923
De Vecchi, Cesare Maria	December 8, 1923[10]—June 1, 1928
Corni, Guido	June 1, 1928—July 1, 1931
Rava, Maurizio	July 1, 1931—March 7, 1935
Graziani, Rodolfo	March 7, 1935—May 22, 1936
De Rubeis, Angelo[11]	May 22, 1936—May 24, 1936
Santini, Ruggero	May 24, 1936[12]—December 15, 1937
Caroselli, Francesco Savero	December 15, 1937—June 11, 1940
Pesenti, Gustavo[13]	June 11, 1940—December 31, 1940
De Simone, Carlo[13]	December 31, 1940—March 9, 1941

Oltre Giuba[14]

Zoli, Corrado	July 16, 1925—December 31, 1926

[6]Badoglio became viceroy of Ethiopia on May 9, 1936.

[7]As of this date Eritrea's boundaries were expanded and it became one of the five provinces of Italian East Africa.

[8]In his capacity as commander of the Northern Military Sector with powers as acting governor of Eritrea and Amhara.

[9]The date of Frusci's surrender. Commonwealth forces had captured Asmara on April 1, and Massawa on April 8, 1941.

[10]De Vecchi became governor on October 21 but did not arrive in Somalia until December 8, 1923.

[11]De Rubeis was named vice-governor December 19, 1935, and served as acting governor after January 7, 1936, while Graziani directed military operations.

[12]On June 1, 1936, Somalia's borders were expanded and it became one of the five provinces of Italian East Africa.

[13]In his capacity as commander of the Giuba Military Sector with powers as acting governor of Somalia.

[14]Britain ceded the territory of Oltre Giuba to Italy on July 15, 1924. Zoli was high commissioner, with the rank of governor, until July 1, 1926, when Oltre Giuba was joined to Somalia. Zoli continued to administer the territory until January 1, 1927.

Italian East Africa[15]

Badoglio, Pietro[16]	May 9, 1936—May 22, 1936
Graziani, Rodolfo[17]	May 22, 1936—December 21, 1937
Di Savoia, Amedeo	December 21, 1937—May 19, 1941
Gazzera, Pietro[18]	May 23, 1941—July 6, 1941
Nasi, Guglielmo[19]	July 6, 1941—November 27, 1941

Vice Governors General of Italian East Africa

Petretti, Arnaldo	July 7, 1936—December 15, 1937
Cerulli, Enrico	December 15, 1937—May 5, 1939
Nasi, Guglielmo[20]	May 5, 1939—November 27, 1941
Trezzani, Claudio[21]	May 15, 1940—June 2, 1940
Daodice, Giuseppe[22]	June 2, 1940—June 21, 1940

Amhara

Pirzio Biroli, Alessandro	June 1, 1936—December 15, 1937
Mezzetti, Ottorino	December 15, 1937—January 1, 1939
Frusci, Luigi[23]	January 1, 1939—May 19, 1941
Nasi, Guglielmo[24]	May 19, 1941—November 27, 1941

[15]Italian East Africa was formed on June 1, 1936, from the territory of the Ethiopian Empire and the colonies of Eritrea and Somalia. Italian East Africa consisted of five provinces: Eritrea, Somalia (both expanded from their 1935 boundaries), Amhara, Harar, and Galla and Sidama, and a separate district made up of Addis Ababa and its surrounding territory. Italian East Africa was administered by a governor general with the title of viceroy of Ethiopia.

[16]Badoglio was named governor general of Italian East Africa and viceroy of Ethiopia on May 19, 1936. He departed Addis Ababa on May 22, turning over his powers to Graziani, but did not officially leave office until June 11.

[17]Graziani became governor general of Italian East Africa and viceroy of Ethiopia on June 11, 1936.

[18]After the surrender of the duke of Aosta at Amba Alagi on May 19, 1941, Gazzera was appointed acting governor general of Italian East Africa.

[19]Vice-governor general of Italian East Africa.

[20]While holding a number of other positions after May, 1940, Nasi continued to hold the title of vice-governor general until his surrender at Gondar on November 21, 1941.

[21]Acting vice-governor general.

[22]While Daodice continued to hold the title of governor of Eritrea, he carried out the functions of vice-governor general until his surrender at Jimma, June 21, 1941.

[23]In his capacity as commander of the Northern Military Sector.

[24]In his capacity as commander of the Western Military Sector.

Harar

Nasi, Guglielmo	June 1, 1936—May 5, 1939
Cerulli, Enrico	May 5, 1939—June 11, 1940
Nasi, Guglielmo[25]	June 11, 1940—February 4, 1941
Gorini, Pompeo[26]	February 4, 1941—March 9, 1941
De Simone, Carlo[25]	March 10, 1941—April 24, 1941

Galla and Sidama

Geloso, Carlo	June 1, 1936—July 9, 1938
Felsani, Armando[27]	July 10, 1938—August 12, 1938
Gazzera, Pietro	August 12, 1938—July 6, 1941

Addis Ababa

Bottai, Giuseppe	May 5, 1936—May 27, 1936
Siniscalchi, Alfredo	June 1, 1936—September 23, 1938
Medici, Francesco Canero	September 23, 1938—January 1, 1938

Shoa[27]

Cerulli, Enrico	January 1, 1939—May 5, 1939
Nasi, Guglielmo	May 5, 1939—June 2, 1940
Daodice, Giuseppe	June 2, 1940—April 3, 1941
Frangipani, Agenore[28]	April 3, 1941—April 6, 1941

[25] In his capacity as commander of the Eastern Military Sector.

[26] Acting governor.

[27] On January 1, 1939, the territory of Addis Ababa was expanded by the annexation of territory from Amhara and Galla and Sidama, becoming a new province of Italian East Africa, named Shoa. The vice-governor general was simultaneously governor of Shoa.

[28] Acting governor, after Addis Ababa was declared an Open City on April 3, 1941, and the government of Italian East Africa transferred to Jimma. Commonwealth forces occupied Addis Ababa on April 6, 1941.

Appendix I
The Fascist Grand Council

(JULY 24-25, 1943)

Mussolini, Benito
*Albini, Umberto: Undersecretary, Ministry of Interior
*Acerbo, Giacomo: Member
*Alfieri, Dino: Member; Italian Ambassador in Berlin
*Balella, Giovanni: Secretary of Syndicalist Organizations
*Bastianini, Giuseppe: Undersecretary, Ministry of Foreign Affairs
  Biggini, Carlo Alberto: Minister of Education
*Bignardi, Annio: Secretary, Confederation of Agricultural Workers
*Bottai, Giuseppe: Member
  Buffarini Guidi, Guido: Member
*Cianetti, Tullio: Minister of Corporations
*Ciano, Galeazzo: Member
*De Bono, Emilio: Quadrumvir
*De Marsico, Alfredo: Minister of Justice
*De Stefani, Alberto: Member
*De Vecchi, Cesare Maria: Quadrumvir
  Farinacci, Roberto: Member
*Federzoni, Luigi: Member; President, Royal Academy
  Frattari, Ettore: President, Confederation of Agriculture
  Galbiati, Enzo: Commandant of the Fascist Militia
*Gottardi, Luciano: President, Confederation of Industrial Workers
*Grandi, Dino: Member; President of the Chamber of Deputies
*Marinelli, Giovanni: Member
*Pareschi, Carlo: Minister of Agriculture
  Polverelli, Gaetano: Minister of Popular Culture
*Rossoni, Edmondo: Member; Minister of State
  Scorza, Carlo: Secretary of the Fascist Party
  Suardo, Giacomo: President of the Senate
  Tringali-Casanova, Antonino: President, Special Tribunal

The asterisk (*) indicates those members who voted in favor of the Grandi motion.

Appendix J
Italian Place-Names Altered during the Fascist Regime

Between 1923 and 1941 the Fascist government changed the names of numerous towns, cities, communes, provinces, and regions in Italy. Generally, these alternatives were the result of cultural propaganda or administrative reorganization. The nationalist impulse of Fascist cultural policy was strongly anti-foreign, so that the regime Italianized many place-names of foreign origin (for example, Camosio instead of Chamois); moreover, during the 1930s the official emphasis on "Roman" themes was reflected in the frequent adoption of Latin names (Lucania, Nettunia, among others). From time to time the regime also made an effort to consolidate several communes into single, larger units under new designations (for example, Massa, Carrara, and Montignoso became Apuania). In these instances, the original place-names generally remained in common usage despite the official administrative change.

The word *Frazione* requires some explanation: certain communes were enlarged through the absorption of outlying localities known by this term; again, while they often retained their original names in practice, administratively they became integral parts of the commune. The word "province" in brackets after a name (such as, Carnaro) indicates that the entire province was officially renamed, while the provincial capital still retained its old form.

In the post-World War II period most of the place-names adopted by the Fascists (especially the Latin form) were officially abandoned and reverted to their original forms.

In order to facilitate the use of this information, the list is reproduced in two parts: Section 1 gives the old name first; Section 2, the "new" Fascist name first. The date of the change, along with the province and region in which the place is located, are also provided.

SECTION 1.

Old Name	New Name	Date	Province	Region
Anzio Nettuno	Nettunia	1939	Rome	Lazio
Arbatax di Tortoli	Tortoli	1940	Nuoro	Sardinia
Aspra (frazione of)	Roccantica	1939	Rieti	Lazio
Avelengo	Merano (frazione of)	1931	Bolzano	Venezia Tridentina
Ayas	Aias	1939	Aosta	Piedmont
Bagni della Porretta	Porretta Terme	1931	Bologna	Emilia
Bagni San Giuliano	San Giuliano Terme	1935	Pisa	Tuscany
Barano d'Ischia Casamicciola Forio Lacco Ameno Serrara Fontana	Ischia	1938	Naples	Campania
Basilicata (region)	Lucania	1932	-	Lucania
Bellizzi Irpino	Avellino (frazione of)	1938	Avellino	Campania

Bernate Rosales	Casnate con Bernate (frazione of)	1937	Como	Lombardy
Biscari	Acate	1938	Ragusa	Sicily
Borgo Panigale	Bologna (frazione of)	1937	Bologna	Emilia
Borgo San Donnino	Fidenza	1927	Parma	Emilia
Cabiaglio	Castello Cabiaglio	1939	Varese	Lombardy
Campovico	Morbegno (frazione of)	1938	Sondrio	Lombardy
Canevino	Pometo (frazione of)	1936	Pavia	Lombardy
Cantonale	Chignolo Po (frazione of)	before 1938	Pavia	Lombardy
Carrara Massa Montignoso	Apuania	1938	Apuania	Tuscany
Carroceto	Aprilia	1936–37	Littoria	Lazio
Casamicciola *vide* Barano d'Ischia	Ischia	1938	Naples	Campania

Old Name	New Name	Date	Province	Region
Casotto	Val d'Astico (frazione of)	1940	Vicenza	Veneto
Castelletto Monforte	Monforte d'Alba (frazione of)	1930	Cuneo	Piedmont
Castelponzone	Scandolara Ravara (frazione of)	1934	Cremona	Lombardy
Ceves	Vipiteno (frazione of)	1931	Bolzano	Venezia Tridentina
Challant	Villa Sant'Anselmo	1939	Aosta	Piedmont
Chambave	Ciambave	1939	Aosta	Piedmont
Chamois	Camosio	1939	Aosta	Piedmont
Champorcher	Campo Laris	1939	Aosta	Piedmont
Chatillon	Castiglion Dora	1939	Aosta	Piedmont
Chiavazza	Biella (frazione of)	1940	Vercelli	Piedmont
Chiavrie	Caprie	1937	Turin	Piedmont
Cossila	Biella (frazione of)	1940	Vercelli	Piedmont

Place		Year	Province	Region
Crosara	Marostica (frazione of)	1938	Vicenza	Veneto
Donnaz	Donas	1939	Aosta	Piedmont
Doues	Dovia d'Aosta	1939	Aosta	Piedmont
Figliaro	Mirabello Comasco (frazione of)	1931	Como	Lombardy
Fiume (province)	Carnaro	1936	-	Venezia Giulia
Forio *vide* Barano d'Ischia	Ischia	1938	Naples	Campania
Forni di Val d'Astico	Val d'Astico (frazione of)	1940	Vicenza	Veneto
Fossarmato	Pavia (frazione of)	1939	Pavia	Lombardy
Frassinere	Condove (frazione of)	1936	Turin	Piedmont
Friuli (province)	Udine	1936	-	Veneto
Gerace Marina	Locri	1934	Reggio Calabria	Calabria
Gerace Superiore	Gerace	1934	Reggio Calabria	Calabria
Giarre Riposto	Ionia	1939	Catania	Sicily

611

Old Name	New Name	Date	Province	Region
Girgenti	Agrigento	1927	Agrigento	Sicily
Gonnesa (part of) Portoscuso Serbariu	Carbonia	1937–40	Cagliari	Sardinia
Grinzane Cavour	Alba (frazione of)	1930	Cuneo	Piedmont
Intra Pallanza	Verbania	1939	Novara	Piedmont
Ioannis	Aiello (frazione of)	1931	Udine	Veneto
Lacco Ameno *vide* Barano d'Ischia	Ischia	1938	Naples	Campania
Ladinia	Corvara in Badia	1938	Bolzano	Venezia Tridentina
La Thuile	Porta Littoria	1939	Aosta	Piedmont
Linate al Lambro	Peschiera Borromeo (frazione of)	1933	Milan	Lombardy
Maiolati	Maiolati Spontini	1940	Ancona	Marche
Massa Carrara Montignoso	Apuania	1938	Apuania	Tuscany

Melma	Silea	1935	Treviso	Veneto
Mercatino Marecchia	Novafeltria	1941	Pesare e Urbino	Marche
Mercato San Severino	San Severino Rota	1934	Salerno	Campania
Metti	Bore (frazione of)	1932	Parma	Emilia
Mirabello	Pavia (frazione of)	1939	Pavia	Lombardy
Mizzole	Verona (frazione of)	1933	Verona	Veneto
Mogorella-Ruinas	Ruinas (frazione of)	1936	Cagliari	Sardinia
Montecatini in Val di Nievole	Montecatini Terme (frazione of)	1940	Pistoia	Tuscany
Montecelio	Guidonia-Montecelio (frazione of)	1937	Rome	Lazio
Monteleone	Vibo Valentia	c. 1924	Catanzaro	Calabria
Montignoso Massa Carrara	Apuania	1938	Apuania	Tuscany
Montu Berchielli	Montalto Pavese (frazione of)	1938	Pavia	Lombardy

Old Name	New Name	Date	Province	Region
Moschiena	Valsantamarina (frazione of)	1941	Fiume	Venezia Giulia
Mossano	Barbarano Vicentino (frazione of)	1939	Vicenza	Veneto
Nese	Alzano Lombardo (frazione of)	1939	Bergamo	Lombardy
Nettuno Anzio	Nettunia	1939	Rome	Lazio
Oneglia Porto Maurizio	Imperia	1923	Imperia	Liguria
Oulx	Ulzio	1937	Turin	Piedmont
Oyace	Oiasse	1939	Aosta	Piedmont
Paceco	Trapani (frazione of)	1938	Trapani	Sicily
Pallanza Intra	Verbania	1939	Novara	Piedmont
Perno	Monforte d'Alba (frazione of)	1930	Cuneo	Piedmont
Pian di Castello	Mercatino Conca	1940	Pesaro e Urbino	Marche

Platischis	Taipana	1931	Udine	Veneto
Pola (province)	Istria	1936		Venezia Giulia
Policastro del Golfo	Capitello	1938	Salerno	Campania
Pont Bozet	Pianboseto	1939	Aosta	Piedmont
Porto Civitanova	Civitanova Marche (frazione of)	1938	Macerata	Marche
Porto Maurizio Oneglia	Imperia	1923	Imperia	Liguria
Portoscuso *vide* Gonnesa	Carbonia	1937–40	Cagliari	Sardinia
Porto Viro	Contarina Donada	1937	Rovigo	Veneto
Pozzolo	Bore (frazione of)	1932	Parma	Emilia
Praduro e Sasso	Sasso Marconi	1935	Bologna	Emilia
Praly	Prali	1937	Turin	Piedmont
Prati	Val di Vizze (frazione of)	1931	Bolzano	Venezia Tridentina

Old Name	New Name	Date	Province	Region
Pre Saint-Didier	San Desiderio Terme	1939	Aosta	Piedmont
Quintano	Pieranica (frazione of)	1931	Cremona	Lombardy
Rebbio	Como (frazione of)	1937	Como	Lombardy
Rhemes	Val di Rema	1939	Aosta	Piedmont
Riposto Giarre	Ionia	1939	Catania	Sicily
Robbiate Paderno	Paderno Robbiate	1933	Como	Lombardy
Roure	Roreto Chisone	1937	Turin	Piedmont
Rovi Porro	Rovellasca	1939	Como	Lombardy
Ruino	Pometo (frazione of)	1936	Pavia	Lombardy
Rupin Grande	Monrupino (frazione of)	1932	Trieste	Venezia Giulia
Saint Oyen	Sant'Eugenio	1939	Aosta	Piedmont
Saint Rhemy-Gosses	San Remigio	1939	Aosta	Piedmont
Saint Vincent	San Vincenzo della Fonte	1939	Aosta	Piedmont

San Rufino	Leivi	1934	Genoa	Liguria
San Paolo Albanese	Casalnuovo Lucano	1936	Potenza	Lucania
Sant'Andrea in Monte	Bressanone (frazione of)	1940	Bolzano	Venezia Tridentina
Saponara di Grumento	Grumento Nova	1932	Potenza	Lucania
Scorticata	Torriana	1938	Forlì	Emilia
Serbariu *vide* Gonnesa	Carbonia	1937–40	Cagliari	Sardinia
Serrara Fontana *vide* Barano d'Ischia	Ischia	1938	Naples	Campania
Spadafora (frazione of)	Venetico	1940	Messina	Sicily
Taglio di Porto Viro	Porto Viro (q.v.)	1932	Rovigo	Veneto
Taranto (province)	Ionio	1938	-	Apulia
Taurano	Lauro (frazione of)	1939	Avellino	Campania
Terranova Pausania	Olbia	1939	Sassari	Sardinia
Tomba di Pesaro	Tavullia	1940	Pesaro e Urbino	Marche

Old Name	New Name	Date	Province	Region
Torre d'Arese	Magherno (frazione of)	1937	Pavia	Lombardy
Trevano Uggiate	Uggiate Trevano	1937	Como	Lombardy
Tunes	Vipiteno (frazione of)	1931	Bolzano	Venezia Tridentina
Valchiusa	Vico Canavese	1935	Aosta	Piedmont
Valle Superiore Mosso	Mosso Santa Maria (frazione of)	1938	Vercelli	Piedmont
Vallanara	Marostica (frazione of)	1938	Vicenza	Veneto
Valrovina	Bassano del Grappa (frazione of)	1938	Vicenza	Veneto
Vasto	Istonio	1938	Chieti	Abruzzi-Molise
Vayes	Vaie	1937	Turin	Piedmont
Venaus	Venalzio	1937	Turin	Piedmont
Verezzi	Borgio Verezzi (frazione of)	1933	Savona	Liguria
Verres	Castel Verres	1939	Aosta	Piedmont

Vidolasco	Casale Cremasco Vidolasco (frazione of)	1934	Cremona	Lombardy
Villabella	Valenza (frazione of)	1938	Alessandria	Piedmont
Villaga	Barbarano Vicentino (frazione of)	1939	Vicenza	Veneto
Villa Vergano	Galbiate (frazione of)	1937	Como	Lombardy
Zuglio	Arta (frazione of)	1932	Udine	Veneto

SECTION 2

New Name	Old Name	Date	Province	Region
Acate	Biscari	1938	Ragusa	Sicily
Agrigento	Girgenti	1927	Agrigento	Sicily
Aias	Ayas	1939	Aosta	Piedmont
Aiello (frazione of)	Ioannis	1931	Udine	Veneto
Alba (frazione of)	Grinzane Cavour	1930	Cuneo	Piedmont
Alzano Lombardo (frazione of)	Nese	1939	Bergamo	Lombardy
Apuania	Massa Carrara Montignoso	1938	Apuania	Tuscany
Aprilia	Carroceto	1936–37	Littoria	Lazio
Arta (frazione of)	Zuglio	1932	Udine	Veneto
Avellino (frazione of)	Bellizzi Irpino	1938	Avellino	Campania
Barbarano Vicentino (frazione of)	Mossano	1939	Vicenza	Veneto

Barbarano Vicentino (frazione of)	Villaga	1939	Vicenza	Veneto
Bassano del Grappa (frazione of)	Valrovina	1938	Vicenza	Veneto
Biella (frazione of)	Chiavazza	1940	Vercelli	Piedmont
Biella (frazione of)	Cossila	1940	Vercelli	Piedmont
Bologna (frazione of)	Borgo Panigale	1937	Bologna	Emilia
Bore (frazione of)	Metti	1932	Parma	Emilia
Bore (frazione of)	Pozzolo	1932	Parma	Emilia
Borgio Verezzi (frazione of)	Verezzi	1933	Savona	Liguria
Bressanone (frazione of)	Sant'Andrea in Monte	1940	Bolzano	Venezia Tridentina
Camosio	Chamois	1939	Aosta	Piedmont
Campo Laris	Champorcher	1939	Aosta	Piedmont
Capitello	Policastro del Golfo	1938	Salerno	Campania

New Name	Old Name	Date	Province	Region
Caprie	Chiavrie	1937	Turin	Piedmont
Carbonia	Gonnesa (part of) Portoscuso Serbariu	1937–40	Cagliari	Sardinia
Carnaro (province)	Fiume	1936		Venezia Giulia
Casale Cremasco Vidolasco (frazione of)	Vidolasco	1934	Cremona	Lombardy
Casalnuovo Lucano	San Paolo Albanese	1936	Potenza	Lucania
Casnate con Bernate (frazione of)	Bernate Rosales	1937	Como	Lombardy
Castello Cabiaglio	Cabiaglio	1939	Varese	Lombardy
Castel Verres	Verres	1939	Aosta	Piedmont
Castiglion Dora	Chatillon	1939	Aosta	Piedmont
Chignolo Po (frazione of)	Cantonale	before 1938	Pavia	Lombardy
Ciambave	Chambave	1939	Aosta	Piedmont

Civitanova Marche (frazione of)	Porto Civitanova	1938	Macerata	Marche
Como (frazione of)	Rebbio	1937	Como	Lombardy
Condove (frazione of)	Frassinere	1936	Turin	Piedmont
Contarina Donada	Porto Viro	1937	Rovigo	Veneto
Corvara in Badia	Ladinia	1938	Bolzano	Venezia Tridentina
Donas	Donnaz	1939	Aosta	Piedmont
Dovia d'Aosta	Doues	1939	Aosta	Piedmont
Fidenza	Borgo San Donnino	1927	Parma	Emilia
Galbiate (frazione of)	Villa Vergano	1937	Como	Lombardy
Gerace	Gerace Superiore	1934	Reggio Calabria	Calabria
Grumento Nova	Saponara di Grumento	1932	Potenza	Lucania
Guidonia-Montecelio (frazione of)	Montecelio	1937	Rome	Lazio

623

New Name	Old Name	Date	Province	Region
Imperia	Porto Maurizio Oneglia	1923	Imperia	Liguria
Ionia	Giarre Riposto	1939	Catania	Sicily
Ionio (province)	Taranto	1938	-	Apulia
Ischia	Barano d'Ischia Casamicciola Forio Lacco Ameno Serrara Fontana	1938	Naples	Campania
Istonio	Vasto	1938	Chieti	Abruzzi-Molise
Istria (province)	Pola	1936	-	Venezia Giulia
Lauro (frazione of)	Taurano	1939	Avellino	Campania
Leivi	San Rufino	1934	Genoa	Liguria
Locri	Gerace Marina	1934	Reggio Calabria	Calabria
Lucania (region)	Basilicata	1932	-	Lucania

Magherno (frazione of)	Torre d'Arese	1937	Pavia	Lombardy
Maiolati Spontini	Maiolati	1940	Ancona	Marche
Marostica (frazione of)	Crosara	1938	Vicenza	Veneto
Marostica (frazione of)	Vallonara	1938	Vicenza	Veneto
Merano (frazione of)	Avelengo	1931	Bolzano	Venezia Tridentina
Mercatino Conca	Pian di Castello	1940	Pesaro e Urbino	Marche
Mirabello Comasco (frazione of)	Figliaro	1931	Como	Lombardy
Monforte d'Alba (frazione of)	Castelletto Monforte	1930	Cuneo	Piedmont
Monforte d'Alba (frazione of)	Perno	1930	Cuneo	Piedmont
Monrupino (frazione of)	Rupin Grande	1932	Trieste	Venezia Giulia
Montalto Pavese (frazione of)	Montu Berchielli	1938	Pavia	Lombardy

New Name	Old Name	Date	Province	Region
Montecatini Terme (frazione of)	Montecatini in Val di Nievole	1940	Pistoia	Tuscany
Morbegno (frazione of)	Campovico	1938	Sondrio	Lombardy
Mosso Santa Maria (frazione of)	Valle Superiore Mosso	1938	Vercelli	Piedmont
Nettunia	Anzio Nettuno	1939	Rome	Lazio
Novafeltria	Mercatino Marecchia	1941	Pesaro e Urbino	Marche
Oiasse	Oyace	1939	Aosta	Piedmont
Olbia	Terranova Pausania	1939	Sassari	Sardinia
Paderno Robbiate	Robbiate Paderno	1933	Como	Lombardy
Pavia (frazione of)	Fossarmato	1939	Pavia	Lombardy
Pavia (frazione of)	Mirabello	1939	Pavia	Lombardy
Peschiera Borromeo (frazione of)	Linate al Lambro	1933	Milan	Lombardy

Pianboseto	Pont Bozet	1939	Aosta	Piedmont
Pieranica (frazione of)	Quintano	1931	Cremona	Lombardy
Pometo (frazione of)	Canevino	1936	Pavia	Lombardy
Pometo (frazione of)	Ruino	1936	Pavia	Lombardy
Porretta Terme	Bagni della Porretta	1931	Bologna	Emilia
Porta Littoria	La Thuile	1939	Aosta	Piedmont
Porto Viro *vide* also Contarina Donada	Taglio di Porto Viro	1932	Rovigo	Veneto
Prali	Praly	1937	Turin	Piedmont
Roccantica	Aspra (frazione of)	1939	Rieti	Lazio
Roreto Chisone	Roure	1937	Turin	Piedmont
Rovellasca	Rovi Porro	1939	Como	Lombardy
Ruinas (frazione of)	Mogorella-Ruinas	1936	Cagliari	Sardinia
San Desiderio Terme	Pre Saint-Didier	1939	Aosta	Piedmont
San Giuliano Terme	Bagni San Giuliano	1935	Pisa	Tuscany

New Name	Old Name	Date	Province	Region
San Remigio	Saint Rhemy-Bosses	1939	Aosta	Piedmont
San Severino Rota	Mercato San Severino	1934	Salerno	Campania
Sant'Eugenio	Saint Oyen	1939	Aosta	Piedmont
San Vincenzo della Fonte	Saint Vincent	1939	Aosta	Piedmont
Sasso Marconi	Praduro e Sasso	1935	Bologna	Emilia
Scandolara Ravara (frazione of)	Castelponzone	1934	Cremona	Lombardy
Silea	Melma	1935	Treviso	Veneto
Taipana (frazione of)	Platischis	1931	Udine	Veneto
Tavullia	Tomba di Pesaro	1940	Pesaro e Urbino	Marche
Torriana	Scorticata	1938	Forlì	Emilia
Tortoli	Arbatax di Tortoli	1940	Nuoro	Sardinia
Trapani (frazione of)	Paceco	1938	Trapani	Sicily
Udine (province)	Friuli	1936	-	Veneto

Uggiate Trevano	Uggiate Trevano	1937	Como	Lombardy
Ulzio	Oulx	1937	Turin	Piedmont
Vaie	Vayes	1937	Turin	Piedmont
Val d'Astico (frazione of)	Casetto	1940	Vicenza	Veneto
Val d'Astico (frazione of)	Forni di Val d'Astico	1940	Vicenza	Veneto
Val di Vizze (frazione of)	Prati	1931	Bolzano	Venezia Tridentina
Valenza (frazione of)	Villabella	1938	Alessandria	Piedmont
Valsantamarina (frazione of)	Moschiena	1941	Fiume	Venezia Giulia
Val di Rema	Rhemes	1939	Aosta	Piedmont
Venalzio	Venaus	1937	Turin	Piedmont
Venetico	Spadafora (frazione of)	1940	Messina	Sicily

629

New Name	Old Name	Date	Province	Region
Verbania	Intra Pallanza	1939	Novara	Piedmont
Verona (frazione of)	Mizzole	1933	Verona	Veneto
Vibo Valentia	Monteleone	c. 1924	Catanzaro	Calabria
Vico Canavese	Valchiusa	1935	Aosta	Piedmont
Villa Sant'Anselmo	Challant	1939	Aosta	Piedmont
Vipiteno (frazione of)	Ceves	1931	Bolzano	Venezia Tridentina
Vipiteno (frazione of)	Tunes	1931	Bolzano	Venezia Tridentina

INDEX

About the Editor-in-Chief

PHILIP V. CANNISTRARO is Professor of History and Politics, Drexel University, Philadelphia, Pa. His earlier books include *La Fabbrica del concenso: Fascism e mass media* and *Poland and the Coming of the Second World War*.